P9-AFY-882

PETER COFFEE

teaches

PCs

201 West 103rd Street,
Indianapolis, Indiana 46290

Peter Coffee

Peter Coffee Teaches PCs

Copyright © 1998 by Que Corporation

All rights reserved. No part of this book shall be reproduced, stored in a retrieval system, or transmitted by any means, electronic, mechanical, photocopying, recording, or otherwise, without written permission from the publisher. No patent liability is assumed with respect to the use of the information contained herein. Although every precaution has been taken in the preparation of this book, the publisher and author assume no responsibility for errors or omissions. Neither is any liability assumed for damages resulting from the use of the information contained herein.

International Standard Book Number: 0-7897-1703-4

Library of Congress Catalog Card Number: 98-85044

Printed in the United States of America

First Printing: September 1998

00   99   98   4   3   2   1

Trademarks

All terms mentioned in this book that are known to be trademarks or service marks have been appropriately capitalized. Que Corporation cannot attest to the accuracy of this information. Use of a term in this book should not be regarded as affecting the validity of any trademark or service mark.

Art Permissions: Logitech Inc. (Figure 5.13); A.T. Cross Co. (Figure 5.15); Microsoft Corp. (Figure 5.17); CH Products (Figure 5.18); Olympus America Inc. (Figure 8.12); Kinesis Corp. (Figures 5.7, 5.8, 5.10); Adesso Inc. (Figure 5.9); Sony Electronics Inc. (Figure 8.11, 9.4); SPSS Inc. (Figure 14.37).

Executive Editor
Angela Wethington

Acquisitions Editor
Stephanie J. McComb

Development Editor
John Gosney

Managing Editor
Thomas F. Hayes

Project Editor
Lori A. Lyons

Copy Editor
Malinda McCain

Indexer
Nadia Ibrahim

Technical Editor
Larry Seltzer

Production
John Etchison
Christy M. Lemasters

Contents at a Glance

Table of Contents

Preface

"Experience is the name everyone gives to their mistakes."

—Oscar Wilde, *Lady Windermere's Fan*, Act III

"People need to know that computers and programs are not perfect." That was the first advice I got on how to focus this book. That recommendation came from a reader of my column in the nation's information technology newsweekly, *PC Week*.

The weirdness of computers, especially their software, is surely the most important thing for users to understand. Most of the time, personal computers give their users new abilities to be productive at work and to be creative at play. It's vital, though, to appreciate the ways that PCs can surprise us.

A carpenter using a loose-headed hammer will think about where that hammer's head might fly if it comes off; a cook whose oven runs too hot will get in the habit of checking it against a reliable thermometer. When a PC fails, or appears to fail (for example, by appearing to lose your saved files), its behavior may seem much more mysterious; there may not seem to be simple preventive measures. I hope that this book will make the connections clear.

Why This Book?

I could take an issue of a popular periodical, such as *PC Magazine*, and go through its pages one by one while explaining the things that each page assumes you know. If I did that, I'd wind up with quite a substantial (but hard to follow) book.

When I look at the advertisements in a PC publication, or even in a mainstream magazine like *Family Fun*, I see a huge collection of assumptions:

- I see assumptions about people's understanding of abstract ideas like megabytes and megahertz.

- I see assumptions about people's awareness of the risks of relying on software, and the hazards of trusting sensitive information to digital storage devices and public data networks.

- I see assumptions about the ways that people deal with unfamiliar symbols and with specialized vocabularies.

This book makes no assumptions. We're going to begin at the beginning, and follow the implications until we get to the modern, incredibly capable PC. We'll also explore some of the most surprising things that these machines can do for our work and our recreation.

We'll begin with things that we can see, and drill down into things that we'll have to envision—but that we can still understand if we approach them in systematic ways. By the time we finish our exploration of PC technologies, you'll know *why* PCs can do such remarkable things; you'll also have my recommendations for a host of hardware and software products that I believe are best-of-breed examples.

We're Not Done Making Mistakes

In the course of working for 10 years in Big Oil and Big Defense, I wound up finding my way around the insides of five generations of PCs. I've made most of the mistakes that it was possible to make along that journey. This book gives you the benefit of my 10-year head start on those mistakes, compared to most PC users.

My head start came about because there were parts of my job, a decade ago, that required a then-advanced PC resembling today's typical home or desktop machine. I needed a 32-bit, graphical, multitasking networked workstation long before anyone would have called such a thing by its present-day label: "a Windows PC for office applications and high-end strategy games."

This book is meant to help you get productive on what's now a common machine, without the lengthy trial-and-error process that I went through as a 1980s early adopter.

I sometimes get a little evangelical about this stuff, but I'm not a PC zealot. I'd be the first to say that these machines were hard to use 10 years ago, and that many of their first-generation problems are far from solved.

I'm writing this book to make your first few days, and months, of using your PC a lot less frustrating than mine.

—*Peter Coffee*

About the Author

Peter Coffee is the Advanced Technologies Analyst for *PC Week* Labs. He reviews programming tools, decision support products, and engineering/scientific software in the national IT newsweekly with 400,000 subscribers and more than a million readers. He also contributes technical articles on topics that have included microprocessor design, spread-spectrum communications, electronic commerce standards, and the mathematics of modern cryptography.

In his weekly print column, "PC at Work," Peter addresses technical, managerial, and social issues related to the needs of personal and departmental computing. He is also a biweekly contributor to "Off the Cuff," *PC Week*'s new online column of breaking-news analysis.

Peter received his engineering degree from MIT in 1978, then worked with Exxon Corporation and The Aerospace Corporation in New Jersey, Florida, Louisiana, Alaska, and California before becoming a full-time writer in 1989. While at Aerospace, Peter created one of the country's first in-house corporate desktop computing newsletters, later serving as the company's first manager of PC planning. He subsequently worked in applications of artificial intelligence to spacecraft operations. Peter served as president of the Personal Computer Professionals Association, a regional management group; he is a frequent speaker and newsletter contributor for the Los Angeles Chapter of the Association for Computing Machinery, and is a frequent and highly rated speaker at professional conferences and trade shows throughout the U.S.

Following his first book, the unique four-color tutorial *How to Program Java* (published in 1996), Peter co-authored *How to Program JavaBeans* (one of the first tutorials on Java-based component development) in 1997 (both published by ZD Press).

Peter has been active in volunteer science teaching in Los Angeles area elementary and middle schools, developing and teaching classes whose topics have ranged from celestial mechanics and extraterrestrial intelligence to covert communication techniques. He has taught classes in data processing, management science, and artificial intelligence for Pepperdine University, Chapman College, and UCLA Extension. He earned an MBA from Pepperdine in 1985 and is active as a community Web site operator, radio ham, and amateur astronomer. Father of three sons, Peter sings and conducts in church and chamber vocal groups and is also a low-brass musician and occasional composer.

Dedication

To Carolyn, Harry, and Lucille—for getting things started

Tell Us What You Think!

As the reader of this book, *you* are our most important critic and commentator. We value your opinion and want to know what we're doing right, what we could do better, what areas you'd like to see us publish in, and any other words of wisdom you're willing to pass our way.

As the Executive Editor for the General Desktop Applications team at Macmillan Computer Publishing, I welcome your comments. You can fax, email, or write me directly to let me know what you did or didn't like about this book—as well as what we can do to make our books stronger.

Please note that I cannot help you with technical problems related to the topic of this book, and that due to the high volume of mail I receive, I might not be able to reply to every message.

When you write, please be sure to include this book's title and author as well as your name and phone or fax number. I will carefully review your comments and share them with the author and editors who worked on the book.

Fax: 317-581-4663

Email: `office@mcp.com`

Mail: Executive Editor

General Desktop Applications
Macmillan Computer Publishing
201 West 103rd Street
Indianapolis, IN 46290 USA

Introduction:
Welcome to Wonderland

"She had plenty of time as she went down to look about her, and to wonder what was going to happen next."

—*Lewis Carroll*, Alice in Wonderland

This book will help you make the most of convenience features like Windows, and new technologies like digital multimedia, on today's high-performance and remarkably affordable PCs.

A Windows PC makes it easy to get started, compared to the DOS machines that people bought (and even liked, most of the time) ten years ago. But the convenience, and apparent simplicity, of Windows come at a price.

The price of that convenience is that Windows tells lies.

Windows tells its lies with a perfectly straight face, and with only the best of intentions. The Windows "shell" tries to get you started more quickly, but it does that by making things seem simpler than they are.

Making things as simple as possible is good, but Windows goes too far: It hides information that you may actually need, and it doesn't provide much of a safety net for the times when its illusions break down.

I want to give you the knowledge you'll need to keep going when Windows can't keep up appearances—when Windows starts to let reality show in unexpected ways.

This isn't rocket science, or even computer science. It's just a matter of knowing a problem when you see it, and not being caught by surprise.

I want to help you avoid being misled by the simplifications, and even the little white lies, that your Windows PC tells you while it's trying to make things easy.

Reality Check

This book will show you how things really are, inside your PC's box and behind its pretty-face display. I don't want to teach you how to build a PC, or even repair a PC. I'll even leave it up to you to decide if you want to program your PC. I want to make your PC more understandable, but only to the point that this helps you use it to do what interests you.

A remarkable number of PC problems can be recognized, and solved, without any tools but your keyboard and mouse and display. All it takes is a good understanding of what's really happening behind the graphical façade. That understanding is what I want to share with you.

I also want to show you some of the things that PCs can do today, at professional levels of speed and capability, with only a hobbyist's budget and level of expertise.

Many of the things that you've probably heard about "what computers can't do" are wrong. I'll show you a variety of hardware and software options for greater productivity at work and a better life at home.

What You Need to Know

Very quickly, we'll see that none of your PC's façade is real. We'll see how easily your PC and its software can get confused by hidden programming errors or inconsistencies. We'll demonstrate that under the surface—just barely under the surface—is the radically different, but thoroughly consistent world of what a PC actually does and how a PC actually works.

A PC is a machine: Call it a data pump. The real machine works with raw data, no matter how much it tries to hide the details.

The little pictures (or icons) that you see on your screen are just groups of data. A part of the machine can display that data as colored dots on your display, and your eye puts those dots together (just as it does with a newspaper photograph or television picture). But the icon isn't real, and neither is that icon's connection to a file that you might want to use or a program that you might want to run.

It's easy for your machine to get confused and show you an icon that doesn't have anything to do with what it pretends to represent. We'll see how this happens, and how you can sometimes fix it with a few clicks of your mouse. (The rest of the time, the problem usually fixes itself.)

A file that you open by clicking on an icon doesn't exist, either—not as any kind of physical object. A file is just a name for another set of data, just as an icon is a picture that's supposed to tell you what kind of data you're seeing.

While one part of your machine paints pictures on the screen, another part of the machine uses the bytes in a filename to go find other bytes (the contents of that file). It's easy to get the machine confused here as well, and to get a complaint from your PC that data can't be found.

Losing your work, or saying that it has lost your work, are two of the three worst things that a PC can do to you. Giving you incorrect results is the third, and a much less common form of error.

We'll see, though, that things often aren't as bad as the computer seems to think they are—that data is harder to lose than you might think, even when you try to make it go away.

When your PC does find what you ask it for, the bytes that get loaded into memory from the disk will go through many different transformations before they seem to appear on your screen. They may appear as a document, or a picture, or a table of numbers that remember their relationships to each other and recalculate themselves with every change that you make.

Most of the time, the transformations take place so smoothly and quickly that you can forget they're even happening, in the same way that you turn the key and start your car's engine with no need to know the steps that happen along the way.

Beyond "Go Fast" and "Go Slow"

But you need to understand your PC's reality, for the same reason that you need to know that your automobile has a battery and a gas tank. Most of the time, when you want to drive somewhere, you turn the key, wait for the engine to start, and push the "go fast" and "go slow" pedals while turning the "go this way" wheel. Well and good.

There are mornings, however, when turning the key doesn't get the engine started. As a driver, you want to know the difference between an engine that won't turn over (probably a battery problem) and an engine that cranks but won't catch (probably an ignition or fuel problem). You'll follow different strategies, based on these different symptoms, to get yourself where you want to go with minimum wasted time or money.

We're going to build the same core understanding of what's going on inside your PC. We'll apply that understanding to see how a PC can take you to different places—beyond the office space of word processing, spreadsheets, and databases.

It's Not Your Fault

When I started this book, I invited the readers of my *PC Week* column to tell me what I should include. I expected lists of acronyms, notes on important concepts, and other concrete suggestions. The most important suggestions I got, though, involved attitudes rather than facts.

One reader said, "Tell people that computers are stupid as dirt. After all, that's what they're made of." (By "dirt," that reader meant the silicon and copper and other materials that we dig out of the earth to refine and assemble into a PC.)

In short words, when things get weird between you and a personal computer, it isn't you. It's the machine. We'll reinforce this idea throughout the chapters to come.

Plan of the Book

I'll begin with the PC as a self-contained box, looking at nothing but the things that you normally get as part of a new machine.

I'll show you some useful things about getting around in Windows: things that are, unaccountably, left out of the built-in animated help screens that are supposed to show you the lay of the land.

We'll quickly break through the Windows façade to see what's really happening inside our most basic applications—text editors and word processors—and to see what's really going on inside the file system that tries to organize our PC's long-term storage of our work.

When we get to the bottom of the file system, we'll see that it's really just a way of looking at a huge collection of bytes. I wish that I could say, "you don't need to know about bytes," but that would be a lie.

There are all sorts of ways that the byte foundation winds up showing through the cracks in the software that tries to hide them. We'll see why bits, bytes, and higher-level packages of bytes are the fundamental language of PCs.

We'll continue with an insider's tour of the processor and memory systems that are really the heart and mind of your PC. We'll demystify the buzzwords, like MMX and ROM and RAM, that constantly appear in PC advertising and technical literature.

After we understand the basic box, we'll build on your basic PC system by looking at your options for "peripheral" equipment such as displays, printers, scanners, digital cameras, and other devices that plug in to the system to make it more useful.

One of the things that you'll someday wonder is whether your PC is keeping up with the demands of new, continually improving software. I'll share what I've found out about various approaches to upgrading a PC. I'll show you some of the approaches to testing a PC and seeing how it compares to the ever-advancing state of the art.

We'll conclude by introducing the wide range of applications software for both basic tasks and exotic special interests. We'll look at things that your PC can do on its own, and at the broader world of the Internet that opens your PC to many new capabilities.

When you're ready, turn on your PC and turn to Chapter 1. We have some digging to do.

Bibliography

Several books often pop up in my chapter-opening quotations, or that I cite in the text. You might want to investigate these titles if you're interested in deeper knowledge, or a broader perspective, on why computers are interesting as well as useful.

Many of these titles are from MIT Press, and for these books I provide an URL that will take you directly to that book's page on the MIT Press Web site.

For other titles, I provide an URL that will take you to that book's page on the Amazon.com Web site. There are other online bookstores, but I've dealt with Amazon on many occasions and have always had good results.

The Computer Contradictionary
Stan Kelly-Bootle

http://mitpress.mit.edu/book-home.tcl?isbn=0262611120

Computer Ethics: Cautionary Tales and Ethical Dilemmas in Computing
Tom Forester and Perry Morrison

http://mitpress.mit.edu/book-home.tcl?isbn=0262560739

Computer Lib
Ted Nelson

Out of print

Computers Under Attack: Intruders, Worms, and Viruses
Peter J. Denning, Editor

http://www.amazon.com/exec/obidos/ASIN/0201530678/002-4518794-1833060

Cybernetics or Control and Communication in the Animal and the Machine
Norbert Wiener

http://mitpress.mit.edu/book-home.tcl?isbn=026273009X

Dream Machines
Ted Nelson

Out of print

Hackers: Heroes of the Computer Revolution
Steven Levy
	`http://www.amazon.com/exec/obid`
	`os/ASIN/0385312105/002-4518794-`
	`1833060`

Neuromancer
William Gibson
	`http://www.amazon.com/exec/obidos/`
	`ASIN/0441569595/qid=902411858/sr=`
	`1-2/002-4518794-1833060`

The New Hacker's Dictionary Eric S. Raymond, Editor	`http://mitpress.mit.edu/book-` `home.tcl?isbn=0262680920`
PC Magazine	`http://www.zdnet.com/pcmag/`

The Soul of a New Machine
Tracy Kidder
	`http://www.amazon.com/exec/obidos/`
	`ASIN/038071115X/qid=902386116/sr=`
	`1-1/002-4518794-1833060`

Systemantics
John Gall
	`http://www.amazon.com/exec/obidos/`
	`ASIN/0961825103/qid=902415669/sr=`
	`1-1/002-4518794-1833060`

The Trouble With Computers Thomas K. Landauer	`http://mitpress.mit.edu/book-` `home.tcl?isbn=0262621088`

Where Wizards Stay Up Late:
The Origins of the Internet
Katie Hafner and Matthew Lyon
	`http://www.amazon.com/exec/obidos/`
	`ASIN/0684832674/qid=902386332/sr=`
	`1-2/002-4518794-1833060`

*"The question
is," said
Humpty Dumpty,
"which is to be
master—that's all."*

—LEWIS CARROLL
*Alice's Adventures in
Wonderland*

Making the Box Answer Back

OMEDAY YOU'LL PROBABLY REENACT a scene from the *Star Trek* TV series: You'll say, to an apparently empty room, "Computer!" A voice will answer, "Working." And you'll tell it what you want.

While we enjoy that happy vision, let's get started down the road that leads to understanding your present-day PC. I assume that you've plugged in the system according to the directions supplied and that you've connected the keyboard and display, along with some kind of pointing device (probably a mouse). Now, turn on your PC and see what happens.

Booting Gets Your PC Ready to Begin

When you start your machine, it goes through a process called *booting*. This doesn't mean that you're kicking the machine to make it work, although it sometimes feels that way.

At times, booting is the only solution to a nasty problem—usually a software error that gets your system totally confused. When that happens, the image of giving it a good strong kick can be quite satisfying.

Booting is actually short for "bootstrapping," which comes from the old saying about "lifting yourself by your bootstraps." When you turn on your PC, it begins a process of making itself smarter—lifting itself up, in effect, one step at a time.

Your PC's most rudimentary smarts are literally built in. A microchip of permanent, unchangeable memory (*read-only memory*) called the "boot ROM" tells your PC where to look (usually on its hard disk) for the software (such as Windows) that gives your machine its full capability.

Memory Gives Your PC Room to Work

While your machine is booting, you'll probably see messages on the screen that show your PC counting up its available memory supply. My good friend Don (a loyal Macintosh user) likes to say that a computer's memory is like an office worker's desktop—the place where things have to be for you (or your PC) to see them and think about them.

A PC with too little memory is like an office worker with a tiny grade-school desk—time gets wasted putting one thing away to make room for taking out something else.

Swapping things from the desk drawer or file cabinet (a role played by your PC's hard disk) to the desktop (the PC's memory), and back again, is inefficient when you're trying to work on a complicated project. When your desk is too small, you have a hard time putting various items together into a comprehensive result.

A Windows PC with less than 16 megabytes of memory is not much fun to use. Twice that amount, or even four times that amount, is not excessive. A 64-megabyte machine is not an extravagance. Adding memory will speed your work, in most situations, to a greater extent than will a "faster" machine.

The Floppy Disk Drive: An Electronic Lifeboat

In addition to checking its available memory, your PC probably makes a sort of grunching noise as it checks the floppy disk drive to see if that device is connected.

Many PCs try to boot from whatever they find in the floppy disk drive, if a disk is in that drive when you start your PC. This gives you a means of providing "rescue" instructions to a PC. You might need to use the floppy disk drive when the normal startup process, using software stored on the hard disk, isn't working correctly.

An excellent idea is to prepare a floppy disk that will start your machine and make its attached accessories available by providing any special software they require. Such an *emergency boot disk* could make the difference between a minor inconvenience and a major disruption. The Norton Utilities package, from Symantec, automates the process of preparing such a rescue disk; I discuss this product in Chapter 2.

☞ *To learn more about Norton Utilities, see **pg 79**.*

You might accidentally leave a floppy disk in your PC's drive slot—a floppy disk that doesn't have startup software. This might happen if you copied a file to a floppy disk as a backup, or to take to another PC, and forgot to remove that disk from the drive when you finished.

If a *data disk* (a floppy without startup software) is in your drive at startup, you might get a message from your PC that a non-system disk is in the drive. This isn't a problem—just push the button to pop out the disk. You don't even need to take the disk all the way out of the drive.

After you've removed that foreign floppy, you can usually get your machine back on track by just pressing the Spacebar to say, in effect, "Let's try that again."

CAUTION

It's early to start sounding warnings, but I should use this opportunity to get you sensitized to some of the PC's vulnerabilities.

Attempting to boot from an unknown floppy disk can expose your PC to common forms of so-called *computer viruses*.

Virus and "Trojan Horse" programs are forms of malicious software, each with its own special characteristics. I'll discuss the entire subject in Chapter 17's section on "cybercrime."

NOTE
You've probably seen a floppy disk, even if you haven't had reason to use one yet yourself. It might seem odd that we call it a "floppy disk" when it is obviously neither floppy nor disk-shaped.

In Chapter 5, I'll open the plastic case of a floppy disk and we'll see why its name is actually correct—and also why a floppy is more delicate than it looks.

In addition to checking the floppy disk drive, your PC might send a signal to your printer (if you have one connected and turned on) that makes the printer go through a brief throat-clearing. This is called resetting the device, and it's normal.

A MOMENT OF RESPECT FOR THE HARDWARE
When your PC finishes checking the health of the floppy drive, the printer connection, and any other attached devices, it starts to chitter away as it reads its startup software from the hard disk.

At this point, you're probably hearing three different sounds: the whir of a cooling fan, the hum of a spinning hard disk, and the delicate clicking of the hard disk's *head* (its magnetic probe, used for reading and writing data) as it moves back and forth among many different locations.

Most of the time, we can ignore the fact that a PC is made up of real live electrical and mechanical hardware. Often we act as if we're just working with ideal data. These noises you're hearing are a reminder, however, that a PC is a machine and needs the same care and consideration as any other delicate piece of equipment.

While your PC completes its startup cycle, I'll ask you to take a look around and see if you're respecting the needs of the hardware. Is there room for air to flow around the back of the machine? Most PCs have a cooling fan that draws air through the cabinet, exhausting at the rear. If it's hard to push air out the back, the fan won't draw air smoothly through the enclosure.

Why is it so important to keep your PC cool? Well, think about it: The box is drawing something like 100 watts, perhaps even more than that if it's generously equipped with memory and disk storage units; it's not doing much in the way of mechanical work, not pumping water or chopping wood. All the energy that your PC consumes eventually turns into heat, either from mechanical friction (for example, in the bearings of the hard disk) or electrical friction (the power that gets lost to resistance in the PC's electronics).

Apart from giving your PC room to breathe, it's a good idea to place it on a table that's solid enough to prevent too much shaking. Vibration is not a friend to an operating hard disk.

You'll also be happier, in the long run, if you arrange a workspace that doesn't invite accidents, such as spilling of food or drink into a keyboard or other part of your PC.

In particular, if your printer is in a kitchen or family room or other high-activity space in your house, I recommend some kind of cover that will keep those Cheerios out of the paper path. I speak from experience.

Storage Is Where Things Stay When the Power Goes Off

Your PC is still starting up, and now it's putting up some kind of Windows opening screen. Behind the scenes, your PC is "reading in" the equivalent of thousands upon thousands of words of operating instructions.

Your PC's operating rules—and its other knowledge of tasks such as word processing or game-playing—are probably coming from a primary storage device: usually, a hard disk. Disks are *nonvolatile* storage; that is, the contents of the hard disk remain intact when the PC's power is turned off.

☞ *To see what a hard disk really looks like, from your PC's point of view, see **pg 74**.*

Your PC doesn't need any help from you to find the files it needs to get itself started. When these opening formalities are finally complete, most Windows systems show you a screen that resembles what you see in Figure 1.1. The names and locations of the symbols on the screen don't matter to what we're doing now: What matters is the general layout of a working area (or *desktop*) and a control area (or *taskbar*), usually at the bottom of the screen.

NOTE
If you're using some variation of the older Windows 3.0 or 3.1, the screen you see will look quite different from the one in Figure 1.1. You've probably been using that Windows 3.x machine long enough, however, that you can start up a DOS session without my specific instructions. The item named Main in the Windows 3.x Program Manager should serve as your point of entry.

Users of Windows 3.x don't need to do more than skim the next several paragraphs, up to the heading "According to Convention."

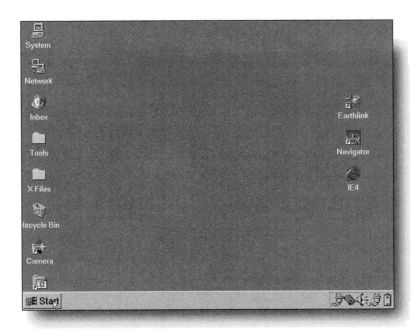

FIGURE 1.1
The opening screen on most Windows PCs has one crucial feature: the Start button, usually at lower left as shown here. Point at Start with your mouse or other device, and click (usually with the left button) to get your main menu or to find the command for shutting down your PC.

Your screen won't show exactly the same things as the one shown in the figure, but the only thing that really matters right now is the button at lower left, labeled "Start." (Someone might have placed your taskbar at another edge of your screen, but the Start button should still be in one of your corners—unless the taskbar is hidden.) If you have a Start button somewhere in view, your Windows PC is ready to do your bidding.

NOTE
Absurd as it might sound, you also click Start to get the menu command for shutting down your PC. Use the Shut Down command, rather than simply turning off the power, so that your PC can get itself sorted out before it tells you it's ready to power down. Some machines handle that power-off step by themselves; you should wait for an onscreen instruction to turn off the power before you reach for the Big Switch.

Putting You in Command

If this is the first time you've looked your PC in the face, please take some time to learn the basics of getting around in the Windows environment (or whatever you're using on your PC).

In Windows 95, you can quickly get to a good interactive tutorial on basic operations. Begin by pointing at the **Start** button (at lower left in Figure 1.1) with your pointing device. (Most of the time, I'll just say "your mouse" from now on even though you might be using something else, such as one of the alternative pointing devices we'll see in Chapter 5.)

Click on **Start**, usually with the left button of your mouse, to get the main menu. Then, point at **Help** on the menu that appears and click.

When you get the window of Help Topics, click on the item labeled **Introducing Windows**, and then click the button labeled **Open** at the bottom of the window. Click on the sub-item **Getting Your Work Done** and click **Open** again. Finally, click on **The Basics** and click on the button that has now changed its legend to **Display** (as shown in Figure 1.2).

Windows 3.x, and also the new Windows 98, use different steps to bring you to your basic information on how to perform the most common Windows operations. If you're on either a Windows 3.x PC or a leading-edge Windows 98 machine, you'll follow its version of the basic Help tutorial.

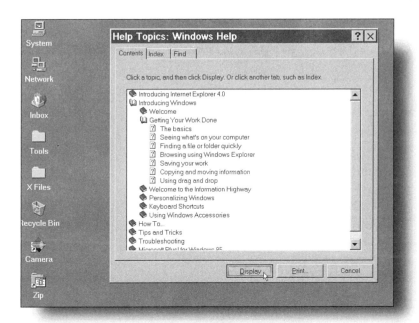

FIGURE 1.2
On Windows 95, you get to this Windows Help Topics list by choosing the Help command from the main Start menu. You need to "drill down" a bit to get to the display shown here, by opening the topic "Introducing Windows" and then opening the subtopic "Getting Your Work Done." You might have thought that getting your work done would be at the top of the list, but at least you now know where to find it.

What Windows Doesn't Say About Itself

Surprisingly, the Windows 95 built-in tutorial omits some basic and useful information. For example, the item titled "The Basics" includes instructions on *scrolling*. This item tells you how to move up or down through a long list of items, for example, that is too long to fit all at once on your display.

The animated lesson shows you how to use a *scrollbar*, which is the bar that usually appears at the right or bottom edge of a window on your screen. A scrollbar usually has a little arrow-shaped symbol at each end and a little gray box (the *scroll box*) positioned somewhere along the length of the bar. Some people call that little gray box a "thumb"; others call it a "slider," and still others call it the "elevator."

You can click on the arrow at either end of a scrollbar to shift your attention from one group of data to another. You can also click on the sliding box and drag the mouse (keeping its button depressed) to accomplish the same thing more quickly. Scrolling by dragging the thumb is useful when you know, for example, that you want to get to a position that's roughly halfway through the data you're examining.

The animated Windows tutorial doesn't mention, though, that you can click your mouse in an empty part of the scrollbar, between the thumb and either end-of-bar arrow. When you click in either space, you move the slider toward the point where you clicked, scrolling your data by screens instead of by lines (as shown in Figure 1.3).

FIGURE 1.3
The mouse doesn't appear to be pointing at anything useful in this screen photo, but those "empty" spaces on your scrollbars are actually handy places to click for page-by-page scrolling through a long collection of data.

Clicking in the empty part of the scrollbar isn't an obvious thing to do: The scrollbar looks as if it has definite places where you should click to make it do things. Nevertheless, the page-by-page scrolling you get by clicking in the empty region is perhaps the best way to go through a file—it's faster, clearly, than the line-by-line scrolling you get by clicking on the arrows, but it gives you more of a chance to browse your data than you get when you drag the box in large motions.

It's perplexing that something so useful is ignored by the orientation material that is part of Windows 95. It's not the only thing, though, that some people feel left to learn by experience on Windows machines or on any other kind of computer.

Drag Corners for Same-Shape Stretching

The Windows help files make a similar omission when they teach you how to change the size of a window onscreen. The animated demonstration shows that you can drag any edge of a window to stretch or shrink the window at that boundary. The demonstration also shows that you drag at any corner, with the onscreen pointer of your mouse changing shape to show where this can be done.

What the help files *don't* point out is that in some programs, a substantial benefit results from dragging at a corner, in one operation, instead of dragging a vertical and a horizontal edge in successive separate operations. When you drag a corner, many programs assume that you want to keep the proportions of an object the same (see Figure 1.4). When you drag at separate edges, the program assumes that you mean to change those proportions.

I have seen many documents produced on PCs with electronically "pasted" photographs that are too tall or too wide—the faces look as if they've been stretched in a fun-house mirror. I believe that these come from failed attempts to restore the original proportions after stretching or shrinking the width and the height in separate operations.

If you're resizing a photograph you're placing in one of your documents, dragging at corners to change the size can help you avoid distortion of the faces and other parts of the image. (I mention faces in particular because the eye and brain are especially sensitive to tiny changes in facial appearance.) Not all programs give you this assistance, but it's worth a try to see if this built-in aid is offered.

FIGURE 1.4

When you paste a piece of clip art or a photograph into a document, you'll probably want to adjust the size. If you start dragging the edges, you might have a hard time getting the proportions back as they were when you started. You'll do better to drag at the corner, where the mouse pointer usually turns into an angled and double-headed arrow. Dragging corners often lets you change an object's size without altering its shape, depending on the software you're using.

There's Almost Always a Way to Copy Data

The Windows help files also leave out some useful options for such basic tasks as copying information from one program to another or from one place to another in a document, spreadsheet, or other piece of work.

To begin with, the Windows help files show you an example of *cutting* and *pasting* a sentence from one place in a document to another. The demonstration never explains, though, what happened to the stuff that was cut before it was pasted to its new position.

Understanding where things go when they're cut, or where the duplicate is created when something is copied, is vital. A cut and a copy do exactly the same thing, except that a cut destroys the original and a copy leaves the original in place.

Both cut and copy operations put a copy of the original item in a data container, normally invisible, called the *Clipboard*.

You can see what's in your Clipboard by clicking your **Start** button to bring up your main menu, clicking on the **Programs** item of that menu, clicking on the **Accessories** item of the Programs submenu, and finally clicking on **Clipboard Viewer**. You get a new window on your screen, which shows whatever your Windows machine is currently prepared to paste.

If you press the Print Screen key on your keyboard, you suddenly see a copy of your computer's display appear in the Clipboard Viewer window, as shown in Figure 1.5.

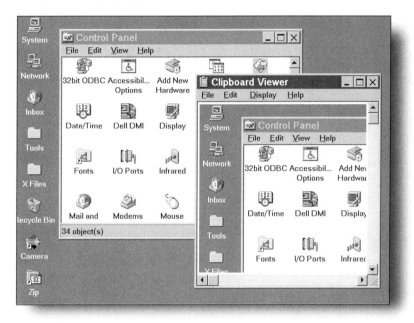

FIGURE 1.5
The Clipboard Viewer makes it easier to remember what you last cut or copied while you were editing a piece of work. It also lets you save a cut or copied item so that it won't be lost permanently the next time you do another cut or copy operation. The Print Screen key captures an image of your display to the Clipboard, as shown here.

This built-in screen capture facility is just one of the things you can do with the Clipboard. Screen-capture tools, including more advanced products such as Inner Media Inc.'s Collage (which I used in preparing this book), let you illustrate a tutorial, explain a problem you're having, or grab anything you see on your screen so that you can put it into a report or presentation.

Shortcuts That Build Themselves

You might find it tedious to go clicking your way through one menu after another when you want to run something as basic as the Clipboard Viewer. You can do this more directly by clicking on **Start**, then clicking the main menu's **Run** command, and then typing `clipbrd` (yes, spelled just like that) in the box that pops up (as shown in Figure 1.6).

FIGURE 1.6
If you know exactly what you want, the Run command (available from your Start menu) lets you
get it without pointing and clicking your way through multilevel menus. Past commands are automatically stored in a drop-down list, available by clicking the arrow at the right end of the command entry field.

The next time you want to run the Clipboard Viewer, you won't even have to type
the command. You can just click on the little arrow at the right-hand end of the
Run command field to see a drop-down list of the commands you've given before.
This self-building menu remembers the things you've done, making it easier to do
them again—but most people don't even realize that Windows is so helpful to
users who don't mind "old-fashioned" command-line interaction.

Knowing the Inner Windows

Now that you've seen where copied things go, I probably don't need to tell you
that copying a second item pushes your first copied item off the Clipboard. The first
item disappears, vanishing "into the great bit bucket in the sky," as PC people
often say. Unlike the Windows Recycle Bin, which gives you a chance to get a file
back (see Figure 1.7), the fictional pipeline to the mythical bit bucket is a one-way
connection!

With the Clipboard Viewer open, though, you can save the current contents of the
Clipboard to a file (by clicking on the Viewer's File menu). Then, you can retrieve
and paste that saved Clipboard file whenever you like.

You can generally paste something as many times as you like, in as many different
places as you want. Pasting just means copying *from* the Clipboard *to* the target
location.

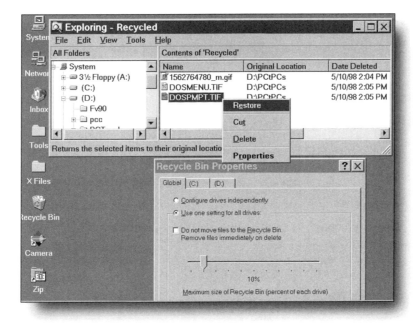

FIGURE 1.7
The Recycle Bin is an automatic feature that lets you review your recently deleted files and change your mind by restoring the file's information to the folder where that file used to be. You get to decide how much of your disk space you're willing to allow for this purpose, or you can disable this feature and have files be deleted immediately—which isn't as permanent as it sounds.

When "Standard Shortcuts" Don't Work

It's a drag, literally, to go mousing up to the menu bar whenever you want to copy, cut, or paste. You can use keyboard shortcuts for these common operations. The Windows help files tell you that the standard keyboard command for copying is Ctrl+C (hold down the Control key while pressing the letter C) and the standard command for pasting is Ctrl+V.

Sometimes, though, the "standard" keyboard commands for copying and pasting don't work at all or (worse still) do something completely different because a particular program took over those keyboard shortcuts for itself. When Ctrl+C doesn't copy, Ctrl+Insert almost always works; when Ctrl+V doesn't paste a duplicate of the last thing you copied, Shift+Insert can often be used instead.

Dig Deeper from the DOS Window

When you're comfortable with basic operations, such as opening and closing a window on the screen and copying information from one place to another, you're ready to do some digging. We'll begin at what's called the *command line*.

Console Windows Give You Direct Connections

The Run command we just saw, with its pop-up list of past commands, is a simple form of a command line. The things we want to do now, though, will be easier to follow if we use something more general. We'll use a facility called a *console window*.

On a Windows 95 or Windows NT machine, you get a console window by running the DOS prompt command. This command is usually available from the Start menu, under the Programs category, as shown in Figure 1.8.

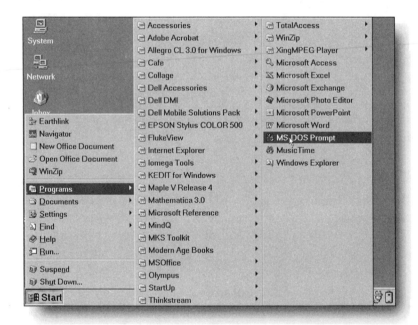

FIGURE 1.8

Your Start menu's Programs choice probably doesn't bring up a list as long as this one. In time, though, Start Programs can become an unwieldy way of getting to your commands, and you might decide to build a Tools window in the manner described in the text. For now, use Start Programs to get to the command for launching a DOS window you can use for some revealing experiments.

DESIGN YOUR OWN DESKTOP

Your screen most likely won't look exactly like the fragment shown. In the figures so far, I've shown the Windows taskbar at its usual location at the bottom of the screen so that you can easily match the figures against your display. Normally, though, I keep my Windows taskbar at the right edge of my screen (see Figure 1.9).

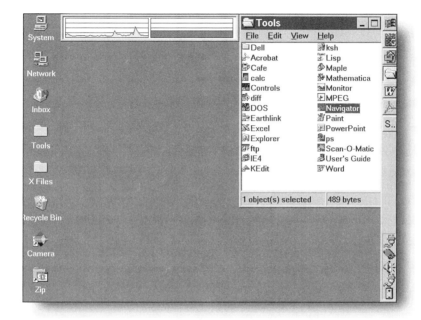

FIGURE 1.9

My personal preferences in arranging my Windows desktop include dragging the taskbar to the right edge of the screen, creating a Tools window of shortcuts to often-used programs, and displaying the System Monitor accessory to give me constant feedback on how hard my PC is working.

Perhaps you didn't realize that the taskbar could be moved. Move it by clicking your mouse on a blank portion of the taskbar and dragging it toward the edge of the screen that you prefer.

Also shown in Figure 1.9 are two other features of my normal Windows desktop. I've built a window called Tools that contains Windows shortcuts to my often-used programs. I find this more convenient than the normal Start menu.

You can make your own Tools window by clicking with the *right* button of your mouse on a blank space in the Windows desktop. Then, choose **New** and **Folder** from the options that appear in the shortcut menu.

continues

continued

The easiest way to open your new folder into a window is with a somewhat tricky maneuver called a "double-click." Pointing at the folder with your mouse, click the left button twice in close succession. If you take too long between clicks, nothing happens; try again with the clicks more rapidly paced.

Double-click operations are part of almost every Windows program. Double-clicking in text, for example, selects an entire word instead of just establishing the point where newly typed letters will be inserted. (We'll talk more about the implications of selecting words and larger units of text when we examine word processing tools and techniques in Chapter 13.)

If you find the double-click awkward to perform, click once on your new folder to select it for action. Then, pull down the **File** menu to reveal the available choice, **Open**. You can choose this action explicitly from this menu instead of choosing it implicitly with your double-click gesture.

When you have an open folder, you can use the menu that pops up when you click your right mouse button *inside* that window to create new Shortcuts to your favorite programs. If you don't have favorite programs yet, put off this piece of customization until it's useful.

My other personal desktop item, shown at top left in Figure 1.9, is the System Monitor desk accessory. The System Monitor gives you a graphical view of how busy you're keeping your PC in terms of both processor activity and memory usage.

You can display your system's activity, measured in many different ways, by choosing **Start**, **Programs**, **Accessories**, **System Tools**, and finally, **System Monitor**. Alternatively, you can just give the command sysmon from the Run box, as we did with the clipbrd command earlier. Convenient, eh?

According to Convention

From this point on, I'll assume that you are familiar with basic Windows conventions—such as the taskbar and the Start menu—and the display management options—such as moving and sizing the windows—used by different pieces of software. Such things are probably covered by a startup guide that came with your new machine, as well as by a built-in help system like the one I mentioned previously.

This book concentrates on things that most Windows users don't know and that don't call attention to themselves, but that you can use to get your work done more easily and with less wasted time.

Please Be Prompt

Now that you've opened a console window, you have a *command prompt* waiting for your instructions. That's what we call the odd-looking label that appears in the upper-left corner of the window, as shown in Figure 1.10.

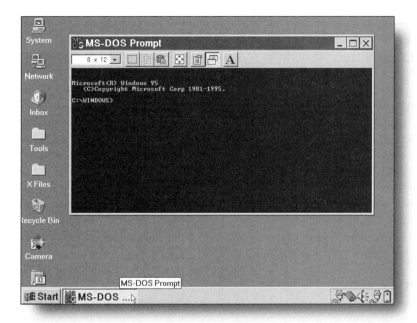

FIGURE 1.10
This command prompt used to be the first thing you saw when your PC completed its startup ceremonies. Windows makes it much easier to figure out your options, but we're going back to this
tried-and-true tool for giving specific commands and seeing their results.

The label at the head of the command line is called a prompt because it's
prompting you for input. It's not telling you what options you have, and most computer users consider a prompt a crude and unsatisfactory way of interacting.

We've already seen, though, that a command prompt like the one in the Run box
gives us efficient ways to ask for exactly what we want. This is just the beginning of
the process of taking charge of your PC.

Hey, PC, Talk to Me

The first thing that I want you to type at the command prompt is

```
echo Hello⏎
```

The ⏎ at the end of this command denotes the key on your PC's keyboard that
might be marked with that symbol, or that might be labeled Enter or Return.

Your keyboard might have two keys labeled Enter, with one of them at the far right
as part of a number-entry keypad. When I ask you to use the Enter key, please use

the one that is located in the normal typewriter carriage-return position (above the right-hand Shift key).

Most of the time, either Enter key will do the same thing, but some software uses the two different keys in different ways.

When you enter the `echo Hello`↵ command, you'll see that the system responds with the word, `Hello`, echoing back what you said. You gave the PC a command, ECHO, followed by a *parameter* to that command.

The combination of commands and parameters is one of the core ideas of interacting with a computer, whether you're using programs or writing programs. Commands are like verbs; parameters are like nouns and adjectives.

The incantations we use to control a PC are a specialized, but not mysterious, language. The PC's command language is much less irregular than many of the languages that small children learn without help. If anything, the languages of computers are easier to learn than "natural" language because they don't depend on attitude or tone of voice—at least, not yet.

Your Wish Is Its Command

To command a PC in useful ways, you have to know what things a PC can do (what commands it can follow); you also have to know what information it will accept, and use, in carrying out these commands (what parameters it permits or requires).

Does ECHO require parameters? Let's see what happens if we just type the command, by itself:

```
echo↵
```

You will probably get the reply

```
ECHO is on
```

This doesn't mean much right now, but it's useful to diagnostic programs, and we'll use this behavior of the "bare" ECHO command again in just a little while.

Right now, we're going to experiment with other parameters that you can use to make the ECHO command send its output to places other than our display screen. In the process, we'll start to explore the idea of a computer's file system, and we'll begin to appreciate why PC files are both flexible and fragile.

Hey, PC, Talk to Yourself

Issue the following commands. Be careful to use the \ key (backslash, usually on the same key as ¦) and not the / (the regular or forward slash, usually on the same key as ?).

```
mkdir \PCTeach↵
chdir \PCTeach↵
echo Hello > file1↵
```

I'll explain the first two commands in a moment, but right now you're probably wondering what happened to your `Hello`. The ECHO command doesn't seem to have worked.

Actually, though, ECHO worked exactly as it should. The difference is that this time it sent its output to a file called `file1` instead of using the screen.

The display screen is sometimes called the *standard output device*, and many commands use output to the screen as their *default* (what a computer does if you don't give it specific directions to do something different). When we used the > symbol, we *redirected* the ECHO command to send its output to another place.

The idea of default behaviors is important, because sometimes a system has been set up with unusual defaults; it's important to know how to get what you want, regardless.

If we said

```
echo Hello > con:↵
```

we would get the same thing we got before when we used the default output. The difference is that this time we say—specifically—that we want the output to go to the console, whose formal *device name* is con: (just as your PC's hard disk might have the device name c:). We'll talk more about device names in Chapters 2 and 5.

Single File, Please

So, what happened to `Hello` when we redirected ECHO to `file1`? You can find out by giving this command:

```
dir↵
```

You'll see something that looks very much like the following:

```
D:\PCTeach>dir

Volume in drive D has no label
Volume Serial Number is 3441-1201
Directory of D:\PCTeach

.               <DIR>        04-23-98  6:03a .
..              <DIR>        04-23-98  6:03a ..
FILE1                     8  04-23-98  6:09a file1
         1 file(s)                8 bytes
         2 dir(s)     438,542,336 bytes free

D:\PCTeach>
```

We'll understand all of this soon, but for now, just notice the line that begins with **FILE1**. That looks as if it might be the famous **file1** we used, following the > symbol, as a parameter to our earlier ECHO command.

Look at the date and time on that **FILE1** line as it appears on your screen: If your computer's clock is correctly set, it should indicate that the file was created just moments ago.

Let's see what **FILE1** contains. Give the command

```
    type file1↵
```

There's our mysteriously vanished greeting. It was echoed, not to the display, but to a newly created file named file1—where we can see it whenever we like.

We've crossed our second important threshold in making you the master of your machine. Your PC not only does what you tell it to do, it also remembers what you've said. It's beginning to have the makings of a useful and reliable assistant.

Fresh Raw Bytes

The first command in that group of three previously, beginning with `mkdir`, created something called a *directory* on your computer's storage device. Directories are also called *folders*, and they behave like the folders in an office filing cabinet. Folders make it easy to do things with related pieces of work.

The second command, beginning with `chdir`, told the computer to use the newly created PCTeach directory for any following commands involving writing or reading files. Notice that the command prompt changed from its previous appearance to a new look, something like the **D:\PCTeach** in the sample output previously.

NOTE

Don't worry if the first letter of your command prompt is C, or some other letter, instead of the D that you see here. Most PCs use the letter C as the name of their main hard disk, but many also have a D drive that is either a separate storage device or a separate *partition* on a single storage device. We'll talk more about partitions in Chapter 2.

It's somewhat safer to do experimental things on a D drive or D partition, if you have one, because the files that control your computer's overall behavior (its operating system) are generally on the C device or partition. But, you don't need to worry about this at the level where we're working in this chapter. Nothing that we do here will endanger your Windows installation or other critical files.

A moment ago, we looked at the contents of `file1` by giving the TYPE command. Strictly speaking, this didn't show us exactly what the file contained. Rather, it showed us the result of sending that content to the screen.

We can see that there's more to `file1` than meets the eye when "typed," because our TYPE command only produced five letters on our screen—but our DIR command told us that `file1` contains eight bytes of data.

What else is in that file? Let's look under the hood. We'll do this with a tool called DEBUG.

A Few Bytes More

Enter the command

    debug file1↵

DEBUG is a famously unhelpful program. When you start running it, its command prompt is just a simple dash. It's almost as if the program is saying, "You should not be doing this if you don't know what to do next."

NOTE

If you get the reply, Bad command or file name, try either

    c:\windows\command\debug file1↵

or

    c:\dos\debug file1↵

If neither of these works, you might not have the DEBUG utility program installed on your machine, but you can still read the following description of its behavior to learn more about the way a PC stores data.

You can enter a question mark as a command and get back the help screen shown in Figure 1.11. With help like this, who needs secret codes? I only mention this because computer commands sometimes include this rudimentary kind of built-in reminder of options available to make that command more useful.

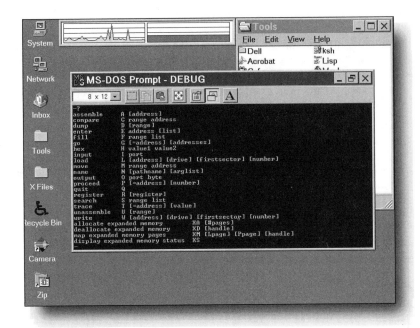

FIGURE 1.11
Even the crudest PC commands and tools sometimes have a limited form of built-in help. Most of the time, these bare-bones facilities are only enough to serve as reminders to an experienced user who needs help recalling a rarely used option. When all else fails, though, following a command with a ? or -? or /? might give you just the nudge you needed.

By the way, take a close look at the left edge of Figure 1.11. Do you notice anything odd? In Figure 1.11, the Recycle Bin's icon has changed from its normal "bin" appearance to an unrelated wheelchair symbol. I did not contrive this example of the random disconnection that sometimes takes place between Windows icons and the things those icons represent. This new look came about for no reason, and the icon returned to its usual appearance the next time I started this machine.

CAUTION
Treat DEBUG with caution and respect, because its careless use can confuse your PC in ways that will require a lot of low-level repair work (including, perhaps, reinstalling Windows or performing other drastic repairs to the software). Please don't try your own experiments with DEBUG unless you know exactly what you're doing. But don't worry about continuing with what we're about to do: The following experiments, working only on "junk" files, are perfectly safe.

From that cryptic **DEBUG** prompt, issue the command

```
D 100 107↵
```

where the **d** is for "dump." You're dumping a range of addresses, as we call the numbered locations in a computer's memory banks.

We'll talk about memory in much more detail later on, but for now, let's simplify by saying that memory is what goes away when the PC gets turned off; storage, or files, is the stuff that gets saved between sessions.

We're dumping memory locations 100 through 107 because that range contains eight values, and we want to see all eight bytes of `file1`. We're starting at address 100 because that's where DEBUG, by default, loads a file for inspection.

A Quick Brain Dump

The dump command produces output that looks something like this:

```
-d 100 107
0D74:0100   48 65 6C 6C 6F 20 0D 0A                        Hello ..
```

The output line begins by confirming the starting address of 100. The letters and numbers before the colon will probably be different on your machine, for reasons that we'll discuss later.

The eight two-character chunks of output that follow are the good stuff. This is why we're using this low-level tool. Each two-character item represents one byte of information. (We'll explore the origin of bytes, and their peculiar letter/number values, in Chapter 3.)

At the end of the line, DEBUG also tries to show what each byte will look like when a command such as TYPE sends that byte value out to your display. We can see that 48 appears to be a code for the capital letter *H*, that 65 is a lowercase *e*, 6C a lowercase letter *l*, and so on.

The letters that match up to byte codes are not arbitrary choices, and we'll explore their logic in Chapter 3.

Before we do that, however, note that the DEBUG output shows a space after the o in `Hello`, followed by two other values that DEBUG represented at the end of the line as periods. (Computer people usually call periods "dots.")

The space and the two extra "dot" bytes are the three mystery items we were looking for.

The space is there because we put a space between `Hello` and the `>` in the command that created this file. Computers have no imagination, and that's the way we want it.

The two remaining mystery bytes tell the computer to go back to the left edge of the screen (a *carriage return*, this code is called) and start a new line for subsequent output.

What will happen if we alter the file so that it doesn't do these housekeeping tasks, such as starting a new line, correctly?

This Is Brain Surgery

We can change the contents of our file with DEBUG's **e** (for Enter) command. We're going to replace the eight bytes of `file1` with the codes for `Hi<carriage return>Bye!<end of file>`. We enter a string of eight data bytes into memory, overwriting the values we loaded from `file1`, with these three commands (note that the **0** in **0D** is a numeral zero and not a letter O).

```
-e 100 48 69 0D 42 79 65 21 1A↵
-n file2↵
-w↵
```

The first command enters the new data into the range of addresses that DEBUG is using to hold the working copy of our current file.

The second command tells DEBUG that when we save the file, we want to use a different name (`FILE2`) so that we don't wipe out `file1` with the altered data.

The last command writes out the data to storage under the newly assigned name, returning the confirming message

```
Writing 00008 bytes
```

Then we quit the DEBUG program with the simple command:

```
-q↵
```

Did it work? Give the command

```
type file2↵
```

You should see something like

```
D:\PCTeach>type file2
Bye!
D:\PCTeach>
```

What happened to our friendly `Hi`? That part of our output from our TYPE command was covered up when the PC went back to the beginning of the line. The `0D` code produced a carriage return, but output continued without beginning a new line—because there was no `0A` code to give that new-line direction.

We didn't put either a carriage return or a new-line code at the end of the file, either. Notice that our next command prompt came on the line immediately after the final `Bye!`, without the blank line we got after `Hello` when we "typed" the contents of `FILE1`.

You can compare the results, if you like, because `file1` is still there.

Remember: Files Are Fragile

I said that we would see that files are both flexible and fragile. To see the flexibility, try this, being sure to repeat the redirection symbol:

```
echo Let's work together >> file1↵
```

You won't be surprised this time to get no immediate output because you now understand that our output is being sent to `file1`. Let's see what `file1` now holds:

```
D:\PCTeach>type file1
Hello
Let's work together


D:\PCTeach>
```

We see that when we used a double redirection symbol, we were giving a different command: not merely to write the output to the named file, but to check to see if that file already existed—and if so, to add the new output at the end. When we add data in this way, we say that we are *appending* data to a file.

To see how files can be fragile, suppose that you now want to add a blank line to the end of the file. You might try typing

```
echo >> file1↵
```

with the intention of adding a line that only holds one blank space.

If we do that and inspect the result, though, we see

```
D:\PCTeach>type file1
```

```
Hello
Let's work together
ECHO is on

D:\PCTeach>
```

What happened? Perhaps you'll recall that a few pages back, we investigated ECHO's response when we gave the command with no parameters. We got the response that we now see appended to `file1`, the message `ECHO is on`.

In other words, ECHO is too stupid to figure out from context that we wanted to ECHO a blank line instead of corrupting our log of ECHOed messages with a self-absorbed status report.

There's actually a good reason to give ECHO, or any other command, the option of writing its internal messages to a file: It lets us automate tasks and capture reports, instead of sitting with our noses glued to the screen for hours at a time.

What if we forgot to use a double redirection symbol and accidentally mistyped our last command the following way?

```
echo > file1↵
```

You can probably guess the answer: No matter how much data we had accumulated in `file1`, it would all be replaced with a new file containing only that useless status message.

If `file1` represented hours of accumulated data, perhaps from some costly lab experiment or some unique event, we might now be in despair. In Chapter 2, though, we'll see that this kind of accident might not be as devastating as it seems.

We'll also explore, in greater depth, the ways that a PC actually represents data in memory and in files.

What We've Learned

This is a good place to stop and assess what we've learned and to start accumulating a list of the questions that we still need to answer before we get to the end of this book.

We've seen that behind the pretty face of Windows (or any other graphical environment), computers are working with low-level representations of everyday concepts such as letters of the alphabet.

We've seen that we can issue commands interactively to make a PC respond to us immediately or to store its results in a form that we can look at whenever we want.

We've seen that we can bring data in from a storage device, inspect it, change it, and store the results, all with the simplest operations on individual memory addresses.

What's still not explained is the peculiar vocabulary of the PC, with its whimsical terms like byte and its cryptic notations like D:\PCTeach.

We have seen, though, that everything about a PC is there for a reason. PCs leave nothing to the imagination; even obvious behaviors, such as starting a new line for the next batch of output to the screen, have to be specified in detail. And any alteration of a command might change its meaning in annoying, or even destructive, ways.

"MS-DOS in a nutshell:
'COPY A+B A' will
combine A and B into a
file called A.
'COPY A+B B' will
destroy B, replacing it
with A."

—TED NELSON
Computer Lib

You and Your Faithful Files

HE STUFF IN A PC'S MEMORY goes away when you turn it off. A flaming squirrel's nest in your electric company's nearest transformer can cause a power hiccup that ruins your morning—unless, of course, you've been saving your work.

This chapter is about the stuff that happens behind the scenes of that simple word, *saving*.

Two Kinds of Bytes?

Saving is a transaction that takes place between your PC's memory and its storage. People often confuse the roles of memory and storage, perhaps because both are measured in bytes.

Floppy disks and performance-enhancing *cache* memories are usually sized in Kbytes, system memory is sized in megabytes, and today's hard disks are commonly sized in gigabytes.

Power Prefixes

We'll talk about the origin and the continuing need for *bytes* in Chapter 3. For now, you can think of bytes in a computer as being like the individual letters on a printed page.

We quickly get into thousands, millions, or billions of bytes on all but the tiniest computers: Most of the time, you'll hear about bytes in groups of *K* or *M*, with the even larger *G* and *T* becoming ever more common.

NOTE
We'll explore the crucial role of cache memories in Chapter 4.

The letters K, G, M, and T are borrowed from the international standards that give us such words as kilowatt and megahertz. Purists, this author among them, sometimes make a point of writing "kiloWatt" or "MegaHertz" because Watt and Hertz were names of scientists before they became units of measure, and because *Mega* (million, with a capital M) should be distinct from milli (one thousandth, with a lowercase m).

Context and custom are more important, though, than strict adherence to international standards. In everyday use, we know that a unit labeled MM is probably a millimeter (more properly written *mm*).

Most of the time, you'll be able to figure things out in the context of computers just as easily. If someone abbreviates "millions of bits per second" as mbps instead of Mb/s, you'll know that they probably don't mean to talk about thousandths of a bit per second.

Two Sizes of "K"

It is important to distinguish between the two different kinds of "thousand" that sometimes get confused in the context of PCs.

In the non-computer world, adding K or M or G or T on the front of a unit means that you're taking things in groups of a thousand, a million, a billion, or a trillion, respectively.

In the computer world, adding these letters in front of a unit means that you're multiplying by the tenth power of 2, or 1,024. This is easily remembered by saying "two to the ten is ten twenty-four."

Multiplication by 1,024 instead of 1,000 means that 64K does not mean 64,000 bytes but rather 2 to the 16th power bytes, or 64 times 1,024. Therefore, the actual value of 64K is 65,536.

NOTE
We'll see in Chapter 3, that this comes from adding ten bits to the end of a binary number.

A megabyte is not a thousand Kbytes but 1,024 Kbytes or 1,048,576 bytes. Each successive tier of what would normally be a factor of 1,000 is really—when we're talking about computers—a factor of 1,024. The difference accumulates as we climb the ladder past gigabytes (more or less billions) to terabytes (more or less trillions).

In the meantime, note that advertisers often find it advantageous to overlook these details. If you were selling a hard disk with a capacity of 2,100 megabytes, more or less, would you rather call it a 2.1 Gbyte drive or a 2.05 Gbyte drive? The former figure is 2,100 divided by 1,000, and the latter is 2,100 divided by 1,024.

NOTE
By the way, it's correct to say "giga" with a soft "j" sound, as if it were spelled "jiga-bytes." It is also quite common to pronounce the g as in "golf," so make your own choice: You can risk sounding affected to those who don't know better, or you can risk sounding ignorant to those who do.

Personally, I try to avoid using the giga- prefix in conversation, because I don't like either option. Within ten years, you will hear people speak mostly of terabytes of storage, and even petabytes (more or less quadrillions, or millions of billions). We can soon leave the jig/gig problem behind us, at least when we buy hard disks: Perhaps we'll just transfer the problem, though, to our future procurements of gigabyte-plus system memory.

Similarly, a 1.44MB floppy disk really has a capacity of 1,440 Kbytes and would more properly be called a 1.41MB disk (1,440 divided by 1,024). "This fine point," observes Eric Raymond in *The New Hacker's Dictionary*, "is probably lost on the world forever."

When in doubt, describe capacities in Kbytes. For that matter, if 2.4 percent makes a big difference, you're probably cutting things too close. Your PC runs better when Windows has room to breathe, because the system is constantly creating temporary files for various internal reasons.

Storage: For the Memories That Matter

There's a lot of overlap in the way we talk about memory and disk space, but these two PC subsystems have substantially different roles.

The biggest difference, perhaps, is that memory gets managed automatically and storage demands that you decide exactly how to use it. Your operating system (such as Windows) makes the important decisions about what to do with memory from one moment to the next, but you get to make the decisions—right or wrong—about the use of your storage.

There are many ways for you to hurt yourself while using your PC's disk space, which is also called the system's *nonvolatile storage*. "Nonvolatile" is a fancy word merely meaning that this kind of storage remains intact (we hope) when you shut down your machine (instead of vanishing like the contents of your PC's memory as soon as the power goes off).

Nonvolatile storage turns your PC into a tool for collecting, preserving, and analyzing records in addition to making computations with "live" data. But the data storage function brings out both the best and the worst characteristics of our PCs.

Today's Storage: Not Nearly Good Enough, But Getting Better

The distance between what we expect from data storage technology and what we actually have on our PCs today is enormous. The gap between what we expect and what we have becomes more dangerous, oddly enough, when PC designers try to hide the defects.

If we weren't encouraged to overlook the limits of PC storage, we wouldn't be so often surprised when those flaws corrupt or destroy our data.

What, Not *Where*

We really want a storage system that lets us *ask* for *what* we've saved, instead of *telling* the storage system *where* we saved it. Today, after you start up a program such as the Windows Notepad, how do you retrieve a piece of your earlier work? You have to meet the PC on its own ground by saying, via the program's menus, "File, Open" (as shown in Figure 2.1).

FIGURE 2.1

The File Open dialog box, used by most Windows applications, gives you a view of your file system, but rarely helps you find what you're looking for. It just lets you tell the PC where to let you look for yourself.

What do you get from the File Open dialog? You get, essentially, a window into the computer's file system. A PC behaves like an assistant who asks you what file drawer you want opened to get the work you've asked to see.

"Where do you want me to find that?" is not how we expect an assistant to answer our information requests. We expect to ask an assistant for the piece of work we want, without our needing to say where it's been stored.

You should be able to retrieve work by saying when you last used it or by describing key attributes such as the name of the person who received it. If I want to see last month's notes on my meeting with Roger and Mary, I should be able to say "Work Retrieve last month Roger Mary meeting."

Only in the latest generation of PC software, in products such as Microsoft Word 97, are mainstream software products beginning to offer file retrieval options that are based on *what* or *when* instead of merely *where* (see Figure 2.2).

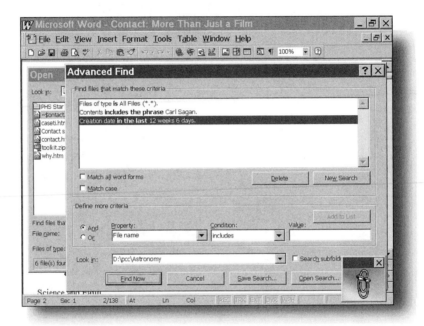

FIGURE 2.2
Some PC software, such as Microsoft Word, is beginning to offer more advanced ways of asking for what you want—instead of telling your PC where you think you left it. Word's Advanced Find dialog box lets you use date and time, contents, and other file characteristics to locate items of interest.

"File Save" Shouldn't Mean "File Destroy"

Your PC should be able to deal with the notion that you might have more than one version of a single piece of work. If you open a file, delete three paragraphs, and save the file, you should be able to start your day tomorrow by asking for last week's version.

What we have today, though, is all too often a gun that goes off while we're cleaning it. We're taught by experience to save whenever we have a moment to spare, thereby protecting ourselves from a hardware or software problem that might interrupt our session. Whenever we save our work, though, we wipe out the previously saved version, losing the option of changing our minds or responding to someone else's question about an earlier draft.

Version management doesn't require magic: Its core technology is used by programmers all the time for their own work. Some programs, such as Microsoft Word, make version-saving possible, if not especially convenient (as shown in Figure 2.3).

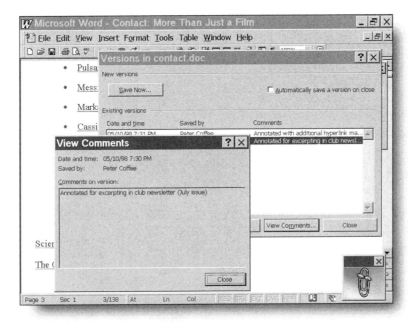

FIGURE 2.3
Versions of a file are easier to use than many similar files with slightly different names. With Word's versioning option, you save a version of a file, including some description of why that new version was created and the version's date and time.

You can arrange for Word to create a new, annotated version of a file every time you save it, or you can just choose the option of making a full backup of the previously saved version (the latter being the option I normally use). What's missing from our PCs, though, is a standard, obvious, reliable way of managing many versions of a file as the normal way of doing things.

As often happens, add-on software products are emerging to fill the gap: If they become popular enough, the function will eventually make its way into the basic capabilities of mainstream operating systems such as Windows.

If our storage systems can't actually be smart, it would be better if they didn't pretend to be less foolish than they are. If we saw our storage systems with their makeup off, so to speak, and worked with those systems at their own level, we wouldn't be surprised so often. There would be fewer ways for us to get trapped in apparent dead ends, such as the one in Figure 2.4, that are

NOTE
I'll explore file-version management in more detail when we talk about working with words in Chapter 13.

really just unexpected corners. In the case shown in Figure 2.4, spaces in a folder name have confused an old piece of software that was written before such naming was permitted. The file can still be opened by using File, Open from inside the program instead of opening the file directly from the Windows desktop.

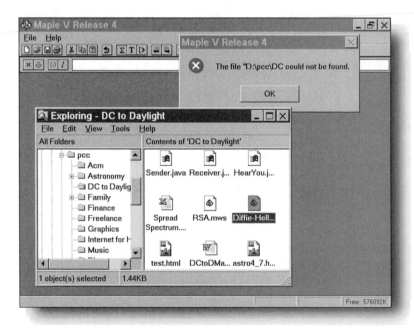

FIGURE 2.4
A user has tried to open a file that's stored in a folder whose name (DC to Daylight) has spaces in it. The program, an older version, has tried to read the full name of the file (including the name of its folder) and is confused by the spaces. The program is reporting that no such file exists. The solution is to open the file from inside the program rather than trying to open the file from the Windows desktop.

In the meantime, as I said earlier, data storage can be the worst as well as the best aspect of what our PCs do for us. It's annoying when we lose a few minutes' work to a software bug or a power hiccup that wipes out unsaved data in a PC's memory. It's tragic when we lose the work of days, weeks, or even years because of errors in our use of long-term storage.

Changing the Way We Think

A reliable, natural tool for storing and retrieving data makes our lives much more enjoyable. It greatly reduces the need to burden our minds with endless details.

We can explore new ideas with more courage when we know that we can easily return to any "place" we've visited before. The idea of a knowledge space, sometimes called *cyberspace*, isn't even all that new: Vannevar Bush spoke of tools for capturing and sharing knowledge in similar words back in 1945, in an essay titled "As We May Think."

Bush spoke of solutions based on microfilm, not the magnetic storage devices that our PCs and other computers use today. In other respects, however, Bush was remarkably farsighted.

Bushels of Bytes

For example, long before we had to organize our hard disks or search the Internet, Bush noted that "the difficulty seems to be not so much that we publish unduly. . . but rather that publication has been extended far beyond our present ability to make real use of the record." In short words, the problem is that we generate data far more efficiently than we search through prior work. This imbalance between creation and collaboration has existed for more than a century.

Bush pointed out in his 1945 essay that it took three decades for Gregor Mendel's experiments with pea plants to come to the attention of other scholars. Mendel's experiments became the foundation of modern genetics, but 34 years passed between his first published report in 1866 and the broader discussion of his results that began in 1900.

Bush had no idea, moreover, of how much worse our information balance would become. Our production of new data outpaces, by growing amounts, even the mere preservation (let alone the retrieval and the sharing) of literally priceless facts.

I hope that this chapter will give you a foundation for good decisions about how to capture and safely preserve your information assets.

Suppose We Pretend to Have Files

In Chapter 1, we used one of the outer layers of a PC's storage system. We did that when we gave the DIR command from a console window.

The DIR command is part of the vocabulary of DOS, Windows, and OS/2 PC users. Other types of computers, such as those running the UNIX operating system, have their own commands for viewing a directory of available data items. On UNIX, for example, you would usually type ls to see a storage list.

NOTE

Commands such as DIR and ls might seem quite oddly chosen, with excessive abbreviation. The custom of cryptic command names dates back to the use of mechanical teletype terminals, which needed a great deal of force to depress their keys.

To avoid fatigue, early systems programmers had good reason to devise the briefest possible command names. We'll live with that legacy as we continue to explore the internals of PC data storage.

And Its Name Shall Be Called. . .

In Chapter 1, when we redirected our ECHO command to send its output to the storage system, we gave that stored output a name. We were creating an illusion: an appearance of something called a *file*, which is just a way of naming and using a set of stored data.

Different types of computers put different restrictions on how we can name our files. For many years, most PC-type machines restricted the user's filenames to eight letters plus (if desired) an *extension* of up to three more characters—for example, filename.ext.

"Extension" sounds like something optional, but we'll soon see that filename extensions matter more than their name might suggest.

Making the Case for Clear Names

Some types of computers distinguish between capital letters and lowercase letters in filenames. On some types of computers, *File* and *file* would be different names and could be attached to different sets of data.

On most PCs today, you can use upper- and lowercase letters to make a filename easier to read, but these typographic choices affect only the displayed version of the filename. When searching for a file (either a program to run or a data file to open), Windows makes no distinction between (for example) a file named "Brian" and a file named "brian."

Internally, moreover, the computer still creates and uses an all-uppercase filename in the so-called 8.3 format. This behavior sometimes intrudes at inconvenient times.

For example, in Chapter 1, we saw a file system listing that included this line:

```
FILE1                        8   04-23-98   6:09a file1
```

The `FILE1` at the beginning of the line was the filename that the computer was actually using for low-level, internal operations involving that file. The `file1` at the end of the line was the name that we used when we created that file. A "cosmetic" operating system such as Windows uses the "print name" (`file1`) representation when it displays a file in a graphical view of a PC's data storage (such as the one in Figure 2.5); it also lets you use that name as a lookup tool for operations such as finding, copying, and opening a file.

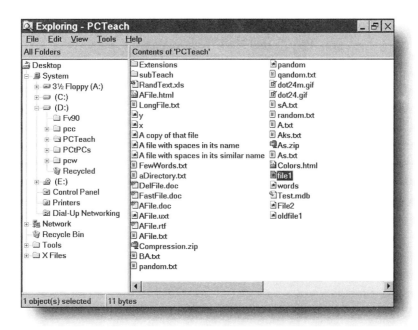

FIGURE 2.5
The Windows Explorer is a file-management tool that lets you see files in their nested folders and lets you move, copy, delete, rename, and perform other operations on files. Different icons indicate the types of files that Windows believes it's seeing, but Windows easily gets confused by badly chosen filename extensions (the part of the filename after the period).

Some Software Gets Lost in Spaces

One of the flakiest things about filenames is the inconsistent treatment of spaces. It would be nice if a file could have a name such as *April Invoice to Acme* instead of *APRINACM*. The Macintosh has always had this freedom, and other types of computers have tried to add a similar flexibility.

In Windows 95, for example, I can create a file called *A file with spaces in its name* by giving that name when I save a file from a word processor or other program. If I'm at the command line, though, and I want to make a copy of that file, how do I tell the computer to do that?

If I give a command such as *COPY A file with spaces in its name A copy of that file*, the spaces in that command mean two different things. The computer has no way to tell which spaces are parts of filenames and which are *delimiters* between different pieces of data (in this case, different filenames).

When we find ourselves in this or similar situations, we can often clear up the confusion by giving the computer a little extra information. In this case, I could type `COPY "A file with spaces in its name" "A copy of that file"` to get exactly what I want.

Because the computer is making up an eight-letter name for its own internal use, what does it do if I try to create files with different long names but the same beginning letters? What happens if I say, for example, `COPY "A file with spaces in its name" "A file with spaces in its similar name"`?

Recognizing this situation, Windows 95 gives the second file an internal name of AFILEW~2 to avoid a conflict with the first file, which it calls AFILEW~1. This means, though, that the internal name given to the file by Windows 95 doesn't just depend on the long name we gave it for our own convenience. The internal name also depends on the other names that happen to be around at the time.

It gets better. Suppose I make another directory of files that does not contain any AFILEW names. I copy AFILEW~2 into this directory and find that I have a new file named AFILEW~1!

The long name of the copy, like the long name of the original, is still *A file with spaces in its similar name*, but the files—identical in every other respect—have different internal names.

I'm going into all of this detail on this issue because there are still old-fashioned Windows programs (and, for that matter, programs that predate Windows entirely) that don't know how to see the long filenames of current Windows versions. Such programs only show their users the 8.3 internal names (as shown in Figure 2.6). If you ever find yourself in this situation, you're now prepared to recognize and work around the possible confusion.

If necessary, you can select a file in long-name view and use the right button of your mouse to pop up a menu that offers a **Properties** choice. One of the displayed properties is the file's **MS-DOS name**. This is a clumsy way of cross-referencing the two different names, but it's better than opening a DOS window and running a DIR command.

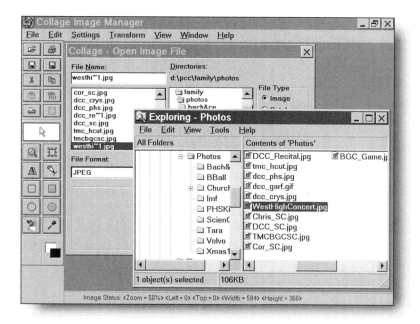

FIGURE 2.6
The file's long name (lower right) is WestHighConcert, without spaces that might confuse old software. An old graphics management program, however, only shows the user the internal 8.3 filenames. Figuring out which file you want could take a bit of creative interpretation.

What's in a Name

Ideally, a file's name would be purely descriptive, and you would be able to change the name of a file to anything you like without changing the way the data in that file could be used.

On the Macintosh, for example, there are two internal codes in every file—one to tell the computer what program was used to create the file and one to indicate what type of data is in that file. With creator and data-type signatures in every file, a Macintosh has no trouble filtering the user's view of the file system to show only the files that matter at any given time.

A Macintosh word processing program, for example, can offer to open only those files that contain words (instead of, for example, pictures). With PCs, things are more than a decade out of date as far as this sort of convenience is concerned.

On PCs, in general, the three-letter filename extension is the only clue a program can get as to what is inside that file. Some extensions are common, and sort of standard, but I say "sort of" because extensions' meanings can be ambiguous.

Graphics files, such as the ones that we used in our Chapter 2 tests of data-compression techniques, often use standard filename extensions. In Chapter 2, we used bitmap files and GIF files: These would usually have names such as dot.bmp or dot.gif, respectively.

Recognizable names are well and good, but this extension convention should be a convenience rather than a requirement. Let me give you an example of what's wrong with this way of doing things.

Useless Extensions: Zero Is No Hero

I was helping my wife prepare driving directions to her handbell choir's upcoming festival. I used MapQuest's interactive atlas, on the Internet, to create a map that showed both ends of the four-hour drive. (We'll see how to do things like this in Chapter 17.)

When I had the map the way I wanted it, I saved the image so that I could later insert it in a document along with other information. My Web-viewing software offered to save the picture under the MapQuest Web site's automatically generated name for that image, which was mqmapgen_v4.0, as shown in Figure 2.7. This name most likely indicates the version of MapQuest's software that created these interactive maps. It certainly doesn't tell us anything helpful about what is actually in the file.

FIGURE 2.7
This Web browser is trying to be helpful, offering an automatically chosen filename for a picture that we want to save. The automatic name, however, has an extension of ".0" that will not be recognized as an image file by most Windows graphics tools.

I wanted to be able to recognize the saved file when I next looked through my directory, so I typed in a different name. I was in a hurry and didn't think about including an extension. In fact, I had no idea what type of image this was. The PC was letting me ignore this question, even though it would later be quite important.

I typed the first thing that came into my head, the name of the destination city of Visalia. This gave me a file named Visalia, with no filename extension. I opened my graphics editor to enlarge the map, tried to open my new Visalia file, and I received a curt error message that this was not a supported file type.

Change Your File's Name and Change Its Life

Well. I went back to the Web site and viewed the image again. I noted that the title bar of my Web-viewing program said that this image was a GIF-type picture (see Figure 2.8). So, I renamed my already saved file with a .gif extension, making the name now Visalia.gif.

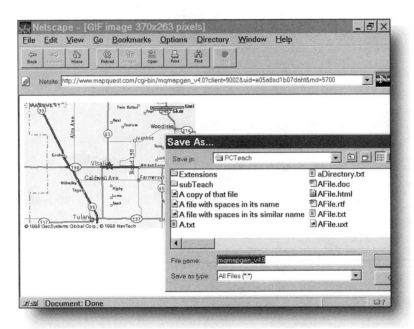

FIGURE 2.8
By viewing a Web-page image separately, we get the crucial information (in the title bar at the top of the screen) that this is a GIF-type file. Now, we can save the file with the right extension (.gif) so that it will be recognized by our graphics software.

Suddenly, all was well: My graphics editor now opened the file without complaint.

Users should not need to pay attention to this sort of thing. But PC users, unlike Macintosh users, do need to notice these details if they don't want to be derailed by trivial inconsistencies.

Not all PC software is this obstinate, by the way. Microsoft offers a free accessory program for Windows 95, a program called Paint, that doesn't care what name a file has. In my tests, Paint opened files and deduced their formats on its own, ignoring the filename extension.

On the other hand, one of Microsoft's flagship programs—the Internet Explorer 4.0 Web-viewing product—is readily confused about filenames versus file types. If I copy a GIF file and change the filename extension to anything other than GIF, Internet Explorer 4.0 will not open it correctly.

If I omit the filename extension or use an extension that is not one of the standard labels for common Internet data types, IE4 asks me to choose a different program for opening the file. Worse, if I use an incorrect but standard Internet-content extension, IE4 tries to open the file as if it were the indicated type. When it fails, it only displays the unhelpful symbol in Figure 2.9 to signal its confusion. The rest is up to the user to figure out.

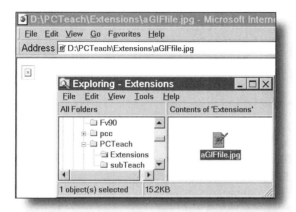

FIGURE 2.9
It's not just a matter of getting a program to consider opening a file by giving the file one of the "right" extensions. Some programs figure out the type of file for themselves, after they've agreed to open the file at all. Other programs (such as the one shown here) get cranky and uncooperative if they think a file is one sort when it's really another.

The Rumpelstiltskin Syndrome

It's up to you to name your file with the right kind of magic label to tell your PC what that file contains. I feel as if we're stuck in a digital parody of the legend of Rumpelstiltskin: "I'll give you your data, but first you have to tell me its secret name."

So it goes, however, and Appendix A will make the job easier with its description of common file types and their associated filename extensions.

It Knows, But It Won't Tell You

Before we leave this topic, I must warn you about another vexing problem that arises when a PC tries to hide its own limitations.

You see, Windows 95 *pretends* that file extensions don't matter: It normally *hides* the extensions in file system displays for files whose extensions are "registered."

For example, .doc is the extension for Microsoft Word files. A file whose name has a .doc extension appears with a Microsoft Word icon if you have Word on your PC, but the filename is shown without the extension unless you change that option in Windows.

It Thinks It Knows, and It Won't Listen to You

Suppose I have a file that contains a picture of the late famous pediatrician Dr. Benjamin Spock. Someone might have whimsically given this "baby doctor" photo a filename of baby.doc. In Windows Explorer, the file appears with a Word icon and with the truncated name, baby.

When I try to open this file as an image, I might get some kind of error message (depending on the limitations of the program that I'm using). Going to Windows Explorer and seeing the filename with (apparently) no extension, I might think I only need to rename the file to something like baby.gif, as shown in Figure 2.10.

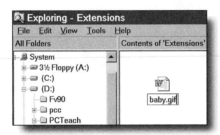

FIGURE 2.10
It looks as though I've succeeded in renaming this file to say that it's a GIF-type graphic. Note, however, that the icon is still the one you would usually see on a Word document. What's wrong?

Clicking on the file, with the *right* button of my mouse or other pointing device, I see the menu option **Rename**. I choose this option and add `.gif` at the end of the filename.

Perhaps I'll notice that the icon does not change. Windows still thinks this is a Word file. Why?

If I choose the **Options** item from the Explorer's **View** menu, I can disable the "helpful" feature labeled **Hide MS-DOS file extensions for file types that are registered** (see Figure 2.11). When the file display refreshes itself, I'll see what I did to myself: I named my file not baby.gif, but baby.gif.doc (as shown in Figure 2.12).

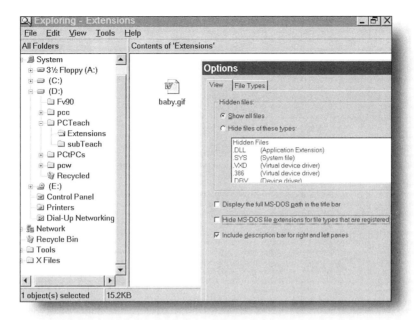

FIGURE 2.11
Uncheck the Windows Explorer option that hides registered filename extensions. Let's see if baby.gif has more to its name than Windows is showing.

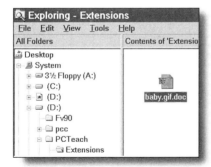

FIGURE 2.12
Indeed, there was more to baby.gif than met the eye. The file's original name was really "baby.doc," not just "baby." When I tried to rename the file baby.gif, I was really changing the name to baby.gif.doc. Windows still thinks this is a Word document file.

Windows hid the extension, not only when I was looking at the file, but even while I was trying to rename the file.

If I now choose the **Rename** command again, and this time strip off the final .doc from the name of this file, sanity returns. Both Windows and the programs that I use on Windows can now see what this file really is.

FEATURED PRODUCT: THINKSTREAM SCAN-O-MATIC

Our files increasingly tend to hold images and other "rich" data. Graphics content, presentations, and other highly visual data need something more than the Windows Explorer file-system viewer to help us see what we have and use it effectively.

For less than $80, Thinkstream Inc.'s Scan-O-Matic is a capable substitute for the file-viewing tool provided by Windows. The Scan-O-Matic window can display many different views.

In Scan-O-Matic's simple list view, the product adds useful data such as image sizes to the columns of file information you would normally expect. For many applications, though, I prefer the view that shows me reduced-size reproductions of file content, as shown in Figure 2.13. (Miniature views that suggest the appearance of a data object are often called *thumbnails*.)

Scan-O-Matic takes a little extra time to generate thumbnail views when it displays the contents of a directory, but overall, I find it faster than opening files to see what's inside.

Note in particular that the files in the Scan-O-Matic desktop view in Figure 2.13 are not image files, but are rather a document, a spreadsheet, and a presentation. For file types that Scan-O-Matic understands, even if they are not images, the program can still generate a handy thumbnail view.

The time savings yielded by Scan-O-Matic are especially nice when I'm dealing with files that have uninformative names, such as the automatically numbered files I get when I retrieve pictures from a digital camera. More than just a viewer, Scan-O-Matic also has built-in power tools for capturing, annotating, and electronically mailing files with mixed types of digital content.

Scan-O-Matic can also create its own *compound document* files that combine, for example, an image received by fax with your own graphics markups and text annotations. It's easy to assemble such combinations by dragging items together into a single *container*.

Built-in *wizards* step you through many tasks that are dauntingly complex for new users, including procedures such as assembling a Web page around an image you want to post to the Internet. We'll talk more about Internet content creation in Chapter 17.

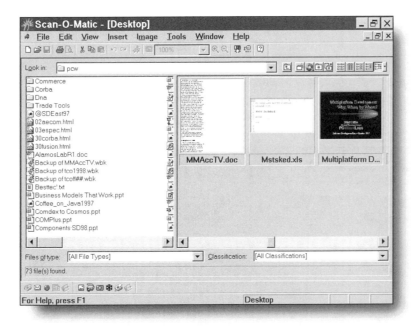

FIGURE 2.13
Reduced-size views, or thumbnails, make it easier to identify documents, spreadsheets, and pre-sentations as well as image files on the versatile electronic desktop of Thinkstream's Scan-O-Matic. The product also has options for manipulating images, combining them with notes, faxing and electronically mailing documents, and extending your file-handling power in other useful ways. Scan-O-Matic was one of *PC Week* Labs' finalists for Best Digital Media product introduction at the Comdex trade show in the spring of 1998.

Text File Formats: How Many Ways Can We Say It?

Graphics files aren't the only type of data that uses filename extensions to convey important information. Our files of words can also use a wide range of internal for-mats to store, essentially, the same document content. Extensions indicate the for-mat that's being used.

The distinctions between different types of document files are in the embellish-ments they can store along with the words.

For example, I might use the extension .txt (as in the filename aFile.txt) to say that the file contains unadorned text—that is, raw bytes of ASCII codes. A text file can be typed to the screen or edited by a wide range of editor and word processor pro-grams. Our Chapter 1 test file, FILE1, was a text file.

Nothing but the Bytes

When we used the DEBUG command to open FILE1 for the lowest-level view a PC provides, we saw the content of that file as a series of hexadecimal codes. If we open a simple text file (with a little more content than FILE1) by using a text editor (the next level up from DEBUG, as software tools go), we see its contents as words on the screen. Microsoft's Windows Notepad (see Figure 2.14) is a text editor.

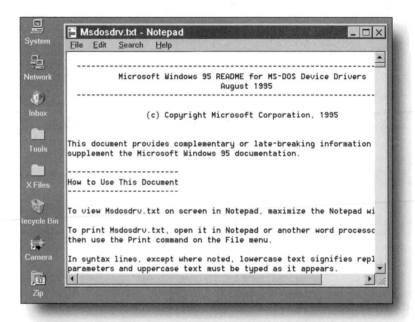

FIGURE 2.14
Microsoft's Windows Notepad is a simple text editor, which reads a stream of bytes and presents them as a document file without the formatting or other options that you'd get from a more full-featured word processor. Simple text files, such as Notepad reads and writes, are handy for electronic mail or supplementary software notes (often called Read Me files).

Notepad doesn't offer much in the way of options for how we look at words or how we print them or use them in other ways. Notepad lacks formatting options because it isn't meant to do anything more than edit a stream of bytes.

Notepad, like other programs of the text editor genre, displays a file in a font that's chosen by the program. A text editor has no provisions for styling text with special attributes, such as underlining or **boldfacing** the important words (which we would expect in a full-fledged word processor program).

May I CODE That for You, Sir?

If we open a raw text file with a more complex program such as the Windows WordPad accessory, we'll see the words in a *default font*. WordPad and other word processing programs let you change the style of lettering associated with text, on a letter-by-letter basis if desired, for special treatments such as *italicizing* a word or using a **distinctive font**.

WordPad and other word processing programs also let you save your elaborate formatting choices and use them when printing. To support such text-styling options, however, a WordPad file must store more than the text bytes alone.

A formatted text (or *rich text*) file must capture and store formatting codes over and above the byte codes for the letters and punctuation that make up the content of the file. *Formatting codes* represent characteristics such as choices of fonts and other attributes. The program must interpret these codes to figure out how the program should distinguish the data from other parts of the file.

When WordPad opens a raw text file containing no formatting codes, WordPad plugs in default formatting options. Opening a text file is a common operation, and many programs such as WordPad don't give you any message to call your attention to this operation of adding default format settings—which sets you up for a nasty potential problem.

Coded at No Extra Charge

If you open a raw text file with a program such as WordPad, make some changes (such as correcting the spelling of a word), and save the file to retain those changes—watch out! I give this warning because you might save the file accidentally in a WordPad format (*including* those special codes for choices of fonts and layout).

Figure 2.15 shows what happens when simple text gets all dressed up as a formatted "document" file. If this ornamented file gets opened and inspected by a program that's expecting to read a simple stream of bytes, your results might be quite unpredictable.

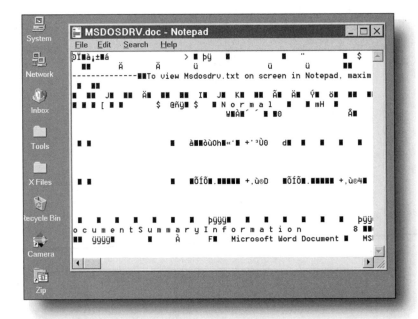

FIGURE 2.15
A simple editor such as Notepad doesn't know what to do with all the extra codes inserted into your text by programs such as Microsoft's Word or WordPad. If you try to open a word processing document with a program that doesn't recognize the document's format codes, you'll get an unreadable mess like this. Some electronic mail programs also get confused by these special codes.

A high-end word processing program such as Microsoft Word offers many different options for saving a file, accessible from the Save As menu. Word and similar programs generally read a file, without any help from you, in any of the formats the program can use when saving your work.

Let's see what happens to a small, simple text file when it gets saved in various ways.

Unicode Text: A Case of Overbyte

The first variation on a simple text file is a *Unicode* text file. We'll examine Unicode in Chapter 3; for now, we'll just say that it's a 16-bit standard that uses two bytes for every character instead of the single byte per character that we think of as a standard text file on a PC. Unicode can represent a larger set of possible characters and symbols, making it an important tool for extending PC use in non–English-speaking countries.

Figure 2.16 shows what a Unicode file looks like to a program that's reading each stored byte as a separate character of text. In this figure, I've switched from Notepad to an editor called KEDIT, which does a better job of displaying unusual content.

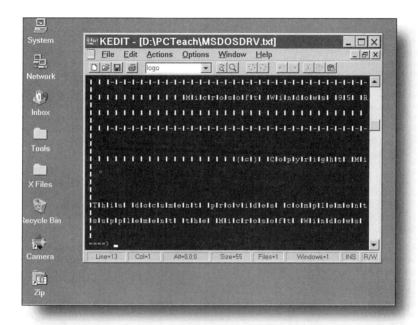

FIGURE 2.16
A Unicode file uses two bytes for each character in a file instead of the one byte per character that most file-editor programs expect. This gives Unicode more options for storing alphabets other than the one used for English and European languages. When ordinary text gets stored in a Unicode format and read by a standard text editor, the extra bytes show up as separators between the letters in the file.

An ordinary ASCII-type text editor such as Notepad or KEDIT interprets a Unicode stream as an interleaved sequence, separating our expected letters with ASCII 0 (null) characters. Those nulls are the "extra" bytes (from a U.S. point of view) in the two-byte Unicode values.

If someone happens to send you a Unicode text file, you'll probably be able to figure out what it says even if you don't have a word processor such as Microsoft Word that recognizes Unicode files and opens them correctly.

You Can't Be Too Rich

In Figure 2.17, we see our simple file as it would be saved in Rich Text Format. RTF, as it's also called, uses codes that can be transferred easily by electronic mail or other software.

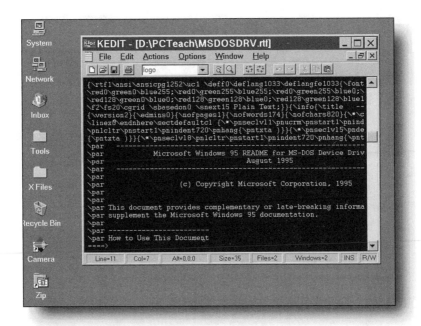

FIGURE 2.17
Rich Text Format uses only letters and symbols that can easily be processed by almost any file-management tool or electronic mail system. It lets simple text-handling software preserve the information on format and appearance that's been added to "raw" text by a full-featured word processing program.

RTF is "email friendly" because it uses only the characters known as the ASCII symbol set. ASCII characters are represented by only seven bits out of the eight bits in a standard byte.

The ASCII characters used by RTF leave a spare bit in each byte, and some communications software *assumes* that transmitted files follow the ASCII convention. Such software might use the remaining bit for error-checking, based on a technique called *parity*.

PARITY

Parity techniques detect, but do not prevent or correct simple errors in storing or transferring data. Here's how parity works.

We normally classify bits of data as having a value of 1 or 0. Parity uses a spare bit to signal corruption of the others by choosing either an odd or an even parity convention.

An *even parity* arrangement, for example, sets the eighth bit of a byte to make the total number of 1s in that byte an even number. If a byte comes through with an odd number of 1s, the computer knows that an error has occurred.

Some data communication tasks can't rely on a spare bit for quality assurance. We'll look at alternative methods for transferring all eight bits of each byte, with rigorous error-detection and even error-correction methods, in Chapter 7.

Let's Not Get Hyper About It

Another format that's growing in popularity is HTML, the Hypertext Markup Language of the World Wide Web. We will build an HTML file in Chapter 3 that will let us experiment with numeric coding of colors.

Figure 2.18 shows the internal content of an HTML version of our simple test-case file. Figure 2.19 compares the Notepad view of the simple text file against the view we get of the HTML version in a World Wide Web *browser*. Notice anything?

If you're looking closely, you'll see that the HTML view has inserted blank lines between the lines of text in our file. This was not done by our simple text editor and would not be done by WordPad or Word when opening a simple text file. Why was the HTML file treated differently?

Toe the Line on Paragraphs

We got a blank line that we didn't want in our HTML display. That's our cue to look at the difference, on a PC, between lines and paragraphs of text. When we store text material on a PC, this difference is important.

Many PC users have a well-trained habit of pressing the Enter key when they get to the end of a line of text. That's what they did on a typewriter, and that's what they do when they're typing on a PC.

If we use a PC only as an erasable typewriter, we might not realize how inefficient we're being when we break our lines by hand. If we do higher-level editing tasks, such as laying out multi-column reports or presenting the same information in different forms, we'll quickly earn a high return on the time we invest in learning a different way of doing things.

FIGURE 2.18

A page displayed on the Web uses special codes, called "tags," in much the same way that Rich Text Format (shown in Figure 2.17) uses its own special markup language. The Web's Hypertext Markup Language (HTML) is becoming even more common than RTF as a way of transferring documents between programs without losing format and appearance information.

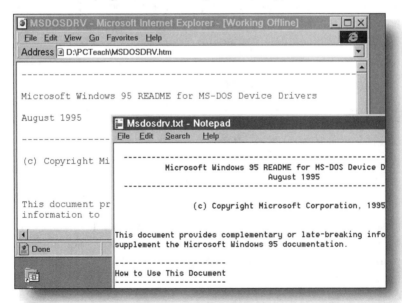

FIGURE 2.19

When we look at an HTML file in a Web browser, the HTML tags that separate paragraphs automatically generate blank lines as separators. If we just want to break a line, without adding a blank line, we need to do something different.

It's almost always preferred, when editing text on a PC, to make every paragraph a single long line as far as the file is concerned—that is, to press the Enter key only at the end of a paragraph, letting our editor or word processor worry about *wrapping* lines to fit the width of a page or a screen.

Even the simple Notepad editor can wrap long lines automatically. A full-fledged word processor can work much more naturally with text when it's broken into paragraphs rather than separated by a *hard return* at the end of every line.

For example, Microsoft Word lets us select an entire sentence by holding down the Ctrl key while clicking the mouse anywhere in that sentence's span. We can then copy or move the sentence as a single logical unit. The same is true for paragraphs, which we can select in Word by clicking the mouse to the left of the document's text area. We'll look at this sort of thing in more detail in Chapter 13.

If we enter lines with hard returns at their ends, each line becomes a paragraph as far as Word is concerned. As a result, we will wind up doing much more work if we have to move a sentence that spans several lines. We'll have to select lines and fractional lines by hand instead of letting Word figure out the boundaries of the sentence.

Our HTML file made this especially obvious. In HTML, a paragraph boundary implies that a line should be skipped—unlike the HTML line-break boundary, which merely begins a new line.

If we change HTML <P> (paragraph) tags to
 (line break) tags, we don't have the extra blank lines any more (see Figure 2.20). If the browser window is too narrow to hold our original lines, however, our lines will break in odd places.

If we remove the <BR> tags, a Web-viewing tool will fit the text to the width of the window even if we leave our text on separate lines (see Figure 2.21). This is the best of both worlds: The file can easily be viewed with a simple editor, or it can be delivered across the World Wide Web and viewed naturally by any connected device.

I'll revisit this topic in Chapter 13, which I'll devote to word processing tools and techniques for both basic and advanced applications. For now, I want to leave you with the idea that paragraphs—not lines—are the next unit of text above the character, the word, and the sentence.

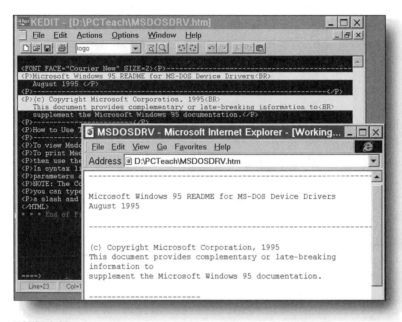

FIGURE 2.20

HTML break-line tags won't insert unwanted blank lines, but they do make it hard for the browser to flow text naturally when we view a Web page in windows of different sizes.

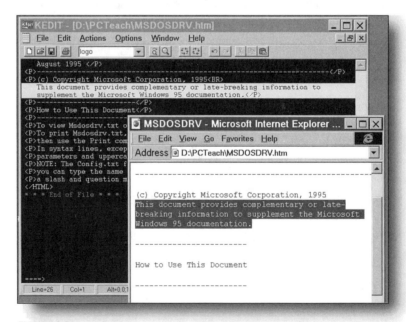

FIGURE 2.21

A Web browser actually ignores the line breaks in our HTML file unless we specifically mark them with line breaks or paragraph tags. This means that we can choose a convenient line length for viewing a file while we write it, and we can let the Web browser fit the text to the available window when someone else views it.

FEATURED PRODUCT: MANSFIELD KEDIT

You might wonder why anyone would spend $159 for what seems to be just a somewhat more capable version of the free Windows Notepad program. Be assured that KEDIT is well worth the price. I have used this tool for more tasks than I can remember.

Yes, KEDIT is primarily a text editor, meaning that it operates on a file as just a stream of bytes. It has no way of representing attributes such as font or size, though it will let you decide what font and size you want to use for displaying a file.

Unlike Notepad, KEDIT has virtually no limit on the size of the file it can load and view or revise. The program has exceptional facilities for finding the part of a file you need to see. My favorite feature is its capability to show only the lines that contain a certain pattern.

The upper portion of Figure 2.22, for example, shows KEDIT giving me only the lines in a file that contain the acronym DOS. The "shadow lines" tell me how many lines are hidden from view between each occurrence of my target phrase.

I sometimes use KEDIT'S selective-edit feature to see if I'm overusing a particular word or figure of speech when I'm writing. The program also lets me assemble a particular set of the lines of a file and save them to another file, so I can easily prepare a summary of a long collection of messages or researched articles.

In fact, I began the task of writing this book by collecting 400,000 words of my own past articles and going through them with KEDIT to pull out ideas or metaphors that I wanted to remember during this project.

The top-right portion of the figure shows how KEDIT lets you view a file in the hexadecimal codes of low-level byte values. We'll explore the use of these codes in Chapter 3.

We can look at side-by-side views of letters and codes, either seeing the same columns of a file in both formats (as I'm doing in Figure 2.22) or inspecting different sets of columns. We might be looking, for example, at some columns of descriptive text and other columns of machine-level data.

The lower half of Figure 2.22 shows KEDIT'S built-in scripting language, KEXX, which I've used over the years to customize the program until I'm not sure its own designer would recognize it.

The KEDIT program uses color for such purposes as showing you matching open and close parentheses or other paired markers in text. This is tremendously helpful in programming. We will see the importance of tracking nested parentheses in later examples, using Microsoft Excel formulas that have multiple nested expressions.

Along with its versatility and power, I use KEDIT year after year because of its exceptional reliability. It's nice to have at least *one* piece of software that always works.

FIGURE 2.22
KEDIT is one of the most reliable and versatile pieces of software I've ever used. It helps me find what I'm looking for in enormous files and lets me reformat text for different purposes with powerful and programmable editing functions. The upper window in this screen shows KEDIT filtering a file to show only certain lines, with the same data shown as both letters and hexadecimal codes; the lower window shows custom programming that I've done to make the PC keyboard handle various editing situations exactly as I prefer.

Are You *Sure* You Cleaned Up That Memo?

In a moment, we'll leave the subject of individual files to take on the topic of file systems. Before we do that, I want to show you one of the nastiest ways that a PC can surprise you.

In Figure 2.15, we saw that a word processing document quickly balloons to a surprisingly large file, thanks to all the additional codes it stores to represent such things as font information. To offset the growing bulk of their formatted document files, programs such as Microsoft Word sometimes offer Fast Save (or similarly named) options. A *fast save* stores a document in the form of a "base" version plus your recent changes.

A Fast Save operation is incremental. Because it only needs to update the changes to the file, the Fast Save is faster than rewriting the entire document out to the file storage system. Faster file saves encourage more frequent saving, which lessens the chance of losing unsaved work if the computer's operations are interrupted.

But here is the surprise. Look at Figure 2.23. It shows a document as it appears in Word, along with the raw content of that document's file. Now, look at Figure 2.24. The figure shows the result of deleting a portion of the original document and doing a Fast Save after that change.

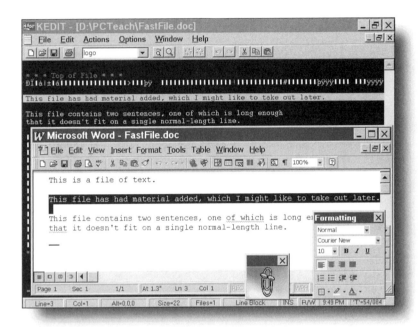

FIGURE 2.23
Text in a word processing file can also be viewed by a simple text editor if you know how to dig through the word processor's formatting codes. Sometimes, you can even see things that the word processor itself doesn't show.

In Word, the deleted material seems to be gone. In the raw file, however, the deleted passage is still there: The deleted passage can be viewed easily by anyone who cares to open the file with a text editor instead of a "sophisticated" word processor program.

The convenience of Fast Save could come at a very high price. You might draft a letter to each of three competitive bidders on a contract, for example, discussing each bidder's terms in detail. You might write one of these letters from scratch and then create the others by deleting and replacing certain paragraphs from the first letter that you wrote.

By the means that I've just shown you, a recipient of an emailed file might be able to open the file with the simplest of software to reveal confidential information you never meant to share with that person.

If you want to know *exactly* what you're giving someone, you can either give that person a printed version of the document or you can disable options such as Fast Save before saving a file to distribute in digital form. Inspecting the file with a simple editor program might be a wise precaution.

Personally, I favor sending simple text files whenever possible, and I always leave Fast Save disabled when using Word or other equivalent software.

FIGURE 2.24
Here's an example of using a simple text editor to see something in a word processing file that the word processor itself doesn't show. "Deleted" text is actually still there: The Fast Save option saved an instruction to treat the deleted passage as if it had been removed, but the data actually remains in the file. If you send a fast-saved file by electronic mail, the person who receives it might be able to read things that you thought you had removed from your final draft.

The Neighborhood Gets More Crowded

We saw some output from the DOS/Windows DIR command in Chapter 1, when we used the MKDIR command to start a new collection of files. We named that collection PCTeach.

When we last looked at the list of all the files in that collection, we had only one file, called FILE1—a rather brief list.

By the time I got to this point in writing this book, I had placed many more files in my PCTeach collection. A directory command in a more fully populated PCTeach neighborhood produces a longer list than the one we saw in Chapter 1.

At one point while writing this book, my PCTeach list looked like this:

```
Volume in drive D has no label
Volume Serial Number is 3441-1201
Directory of D:\PCTeach

.                  <DIR>         04-23-98  6:03a .
..                 <DIR>         04-23-98  6:03a ..
FILE1                     11     04-30-98 10:10a file1
FILE2                      8     04-23-98  9:19a FILE2
COLORS~1 HTM             313     04-30-98 12:08p Colors.html
TEST     MDB          67,584     04-27-98  3:13p Test.mdb
OLDFILE1                   8     04-23-98  9:04a oldfile1


WORDS                     12     04-30-98 10:00a words
AS       TXT             100     04-30-98  1:04p As.txt
AS       ZIP             116     04-30-98  1:04p As.zip
AKS      TXT           1,000     04-30-98  1:07p Aks.txt
SA       TXT             200     04-30-98  1:34p sA.txt
RANDOM   TXT           1,000     04-30-98  1:20p random.txt
A        TXT               1     04-30-98  1:14p A.txt
COMPRE~1 ZIP           4,076     04-30-98  2:32p Compression.zip
DOT24    BMP         360,054     04-30-98  1:36p dot24.bmp
DOT24M   BMP          15,662     04-30-98  1:36p dot24m.bmp
DOT24M   GIF           1,397     04-30-98  1:37p dot24m.gif
QANDOM   TXT           1,000     04-30-98  2:01p qandom.txt
PANDOM                 1,000     04-30-98  2:02p pandom
PANDOM   TXT           1,000     04-30-98  2:02p pandom.txt
BA       TXT             200     04-30-98  2:32p BA.txt
RANDTEXT XLS          75,776     04-30-98  3:59p RandText.xls
AFILE    TXT             143     05-02-98 10:21a AFile.txt
AFILE    RTF             406     05-02-98 10:22a AFile.rtf
FASTFILE DOC          19,456     05-02-98 12:41p FastFile.doc
AFILEU~1 TXT             292     05-02-98 10:23a AFile.uxt.txt
AFILE~1  HTM             424     05-02-98 10:24a AFile.html
```

```
AFILE     DOC          19,456   05-02-98 10:24a AFile.doc
DELFILE   DOC          28,672   05-02-98 12:43p DelFile.doc
ADIREC~1 TXT               0   05-02-98  1:15p aDirectory.txt
        29 file(s)         599,367 bytes
         2 dir(s)     434,364,416 bytes free
```

We need to be sure that we understand this output. Everything on this list has an important meaning for some operation or another.

Speaking Volumes

The first line of our DIR output says, `Volume in drive D has no label`. The third line says, `Directory of D:\PCTeach`. I got these outputs because, when I gave the command, my current drive was D and my current directory was PCTeach.

The current drive and current directory are important. When we're careless about controlling our drive and directory choices, we can wind up with programs that behave differently when we start them in different ways or at different times. We can wind up having trouble finding work that we were sure we had saved in a previous session.

What Makes a Directory "Current"?

When you start up your PC, a chip inside the machine has just enough built-in software to locate your data storage system (normally a hard disk) and to read from that storage unit the "real" software that your PC will use to run the machine and its programs. That "real" software is called the *operating system*, and in many ways, it is the personality of your PC.

The operating system makes the rules, for example, about how you can name your files and about what commands you can use to operate on those files. On a graphical machine such as a Windows PC, the operating system controls the basic appearance and behavior of menus and other forms of command. The operating system commonly also defines the file system.

Families of Files

The file system used by DOS/Windows, OS/2, UNIX, the Macintosh, and most other kinds of computers is *hierarchical*. There are family trees, so to speak, of files, with each storage device being a different family.

A storage device, such as a hard disk drive or a floppy disk drive, represents the root of a file family tree. The data collections closest to the root are listed in the root directory. Some of the data collections in a root directory are files; for example, each word processing document that you create is typically a separate file.

Files of Files

Many of the data collections in a typical root directory represent not individual files, but lists of files. A stored list of files, including their names and other information that lets the computer manage them, is called a *directory*.

Among the entries in a directory, there might be other directories. These "descendants" are called *subdirectories*.

There are excellent reasons to organize your files into a reasonable number of levels of directories and subdirectories.

To begin with, the root directory on a storage device is commonly fixed in size; that is, it can contain only a certain number of distinct items. (The most recent versions of Windows eliminate this problem.) If you populate the root directory entirely with subdirectories, however, each of these directories can grow to hold (in most cases) as many items as you want. You get better use of your storage capacity, as well as better organization of your files.

You can think of the root directory as being like a row of file cabinets. You can't put more file cabinets into a room after you've filled the space from one wall to another. You can, however, put additional folders into a drawer of a file cabinet much more easily than you can pack another file cabinet into a crowded room.

Another advantage of using subdirectories is that you can use the same filename more than once as long as you put the identically named files in different directories.

For example, you could put a file named "index" in every directory. Then, you could write a data management program that knows enough to look for an index file and have the program display that index whenever you open a directory without requesting a specific file. In fact, this is exactly what happens when you browse through different neighborhoods on the World Wide Web.

Paths to What We Want

Under DOS, it takes a degree of abstract thinking to keep straight the relationships among directories and subdirectories.

There are primitive commands for drawing graphical views of a file tree on a DOS text-only display, as shown in Figure 2.25. Much more intuitive, though, is to work with a graphical interactive display of the file system tree, using a tool such as the Windows Explorer shown in Figure 2.26.

When we have a root directory containing subdirectories, with additional levels of subdirectories below those, we are developing the notion of a *file pathname*. In Chapter 1, we created a file called FILE1. If we refer to the name of that file, we just mean FILE1. If we refer to the file path, sometimes called the *fully qualified path*, we mean (on my machine) D:\PCTeach\FILE1.

In short words, a path begins at a device name and follows what might be a chain of directory and subdirectory names all the way to the file.

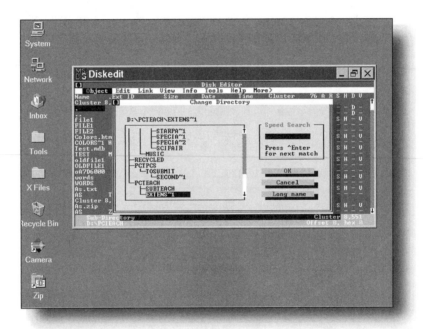

FIGURE 2.25
Older, DOS-type programs tried to give you a visual display of your files and their arrangement in directories (which Windows calls folders). The result, however, is not as easy to read as the more graphical view in Windows.

Where We Begin

Depending on how a PC is set up, the current drive and directory after startup varies from one machine to another. If you open a console window after starting up a Windows machine, you will probably be placed on the drive that holds the Windows software and in the directory that holds the Windows startup program—these are your current drive and directory.

Different operating systems have different commands for changing the current assignments. On DOS or Windows or OS/2, you type a drive's logical device name to make that drive current.

For example, if I open a DOS window and find my prompt reading `C:\Windows>`, I might want to be sure I do not start doing things to the directory that holds my Windows software. I can type `D:` and press Enter to make my logical D drive current.

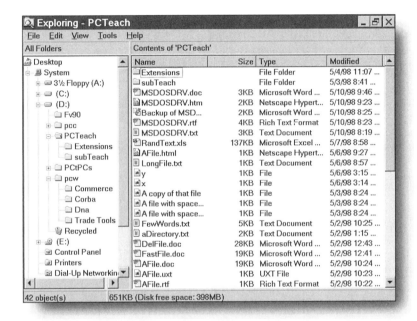

FIGURE 2.26
Windows Explorer gives a convenient, interactive view of your file system, but it only shows you what Windows thinks you want to know. It might hide file extensions, as we've seen before, and it certainly doesn't show such things as "erased" files—even if their data remains on your storage system.

Relatively Speaking

Because I've been keeping my text files for this book in a directory called PCTeach, I can type `cd PCTeach` and press Enter to make D:\PCTeach the default working area for any file-related commands I might subsequently give.

The command `cd PCTeach` looks for a directory called PCTeach that is itself located in my current directory. If I want to get myself to D:\PCTeach from any point in the D drive's file system, I need to type `cd \PCTeach`, where the \ character says "start your search at the root." This makes \PCTeach an absolute path name.

PCTeach (without the \) is a relative path name—relative, that is, to my current location in the file system.

If I know I want to reach a directory that is a "sibling" of my current directory, I can type `cd ..\OtherDirectory` and press Enter. That `..` is a special piece of path code: It means, "the parent directory of wherever I am right now." I can even go up two levels with a `cd ..\..` command.

This Also Works in Windows

You might wonder why I'm spending so much time on command-line stuff in an era when nearly everyone uses a graphical user interface. I have a good reason. When you are opening or saving files in Windows, you can still use expressions such as `..` to navigate easily around the file system, without mousing and clicking on little icons all day. Instead of pointing at the little icon that moves you up to the parent directory of the one that you're seeing in a File Save dialog, you can just type `..` and press Enter (which I find to be quicker).

It's useful to have a way of telling the PC to "do something in the directory above this one." Notations such as `..` let we give such directions, without having to find out where we are so that we can describe the parent location by name.

Near the head of the DIR output listing earlier in this chapter, you'll actually see the `..` entry listed and marked <DIR> to tell you that it represents a directory. It represents whatever directory is the parent to the directory that you're seeing in that listing. This means that every directory listing includes a `..` entry—unless it's a root directory, because a root directory, by definition, has no parent.

I'm Right Here

Before the `..`, though, there's another entry with just a single dot.

The directory that's labeled with a single `.` is the current directory itself. Why, you might wonder, do we need a name for the place where we already are?

Suppose I want to run a program named DATE that is located on my working machine at the fully qualified pathname of C:\mks\mksnt\date.exe. Note that date.exe is a filename with another "magic" extension: EXE is short for "executable," meaning a file that contains instructions for the PC to follow. In other words, an EXE file is a program.

If I open a console window, I can type the fully qualified pathname as a command:

```
C:\MKS\MKSNT\DATE.EXE↵
```

I'll get the output I expect—something like:

```
Mon May  4 13:41:43 PDT 1998
```

Suppose, though, that I'm sitting in the C:\MKS\MKSNT directory as my current drive and directory. Shouldn't I be able to type DATE↵ and then press Enter, without all of that path information on the front?

We can try it. I type DATE↵, press Enter, and I get quite a different response from what I expected, with the PC saying something like:

```
Current date is Mon 05-04-1998
Enter new date (mm-dd-yy):
```

Why is my PC not running my DATE.EXE command?

What's happened is that the command shell has recognized DATE as the name of its own built-in command for adjusting the PC's internal clock. The *command shell* is the piece of software that puts up a command prompt, waits for you to enter a command, and then tells the PC what to do with that command.

The command shell "feels" like part of the PC. It seems as much like part of the hardware as the "cook" button on your microwave oven. That appearance is deceiving: The shell is just another piece of software, and it can have quirks and foibles like any other.

In particular, if the command shell recognizes a command that I give as one of its built-in functions, the shell doesn't go looking for a program to carry out that command; it just uses the built-in behavior.

Perhaps you now see the value of having a name, . , for the current directory. If I type the command .\DATE↵ and press Enter, I am telling the PC, "I don't care if you think you know what to do when I say DATE. I want you to run the program called DATE that's sitting right here in this directory, thank you very much."

And sure enough, if we type .\DATE↵ and press Enter, we get this response:

```
Mon May  4 13:58:15 PDT 1998
```

By looking at the two different date/time responses, you can even figure out how long it took me to decide how I would explain this.

The schizophrenic behavior of the simple DATE command bears out a famous tongue-in-cheek warning in an essay by programmer Ed Post. He's widely known for his comment that "real programmers" like their tools to be "complicated, cryptic, powerful, unforgiving, and dangerous." The behavior that we've just seen in DATE meets several of his criteria.

The kinds of behavior that we have just explored are starting points for devious tricks to break computer security and can also lead to accidental destruction of data. Computers shouldn't be this subtle, but we just have to make the best of it.

Remembering Where You've Been

You can think it's either a quirk or a feature that the PC remembers the last current directory you used on each of your disk drives.

If I'm in the \PCTeach directory on drive D, for example, and I change my current drive to drive C, I might think that I can copy something to the root directory of drive D with a command such as `copy ThisFile D:`.

If I just copy to the drive, however, without saying specifically that I want to copy the file to the drive's root directory, I'll copy to the last current directory I used when I was on that drive. I need to say `copy ThisFile D:\` to be sure of getting what I want.

Alternatively, you can be glad that it's not necessary to state the target directory over and over again. For example, I can give a series of commands:

```
D:↵
cd \PCTeach\Extensions↵
C:↵
cd \OtherDirectory↵
copy FirstFile D:↵
copy SecondFile D:↵
copy ThirdFile D:↵
```

And so on. All the copies will go from my current directory on drive C to the chosen directory two levels down from the root directory of drive D. I don't need to repeat either the source or destination paths in these copy commands.

This memory of a current directory for each storage device is a trick that works in the graphical environment of Windows as well as it does from the command line of a console window. If I type `C:` or `D:` in the filename input area of a Windows File Save dialog box and press Enter, I can move back and forth between directories that are many levels down from the root of each drive.

I don't need to climb back up the tree to the highest level and then climb down again each time. When you have the underlying model of devices, paths, and current directories in your mind, these shortcuts seem quite obvious and are easy to remember.

It's Perfectly Logical

A *drive* may be either a physical or a logical device. A physical drive is a separate piece of hardware. Your floppy disk drive, for example, is a physical drive. On most machines, the floppy disk drive is normally called drive A, but that name isn't as permanent as it might seem.

Your Floppy Disk Has Two Names

If you open a console window under Windows, or if you're at a command line while running MS-DOS, you can change your current drive by entering a device name.

For example, if you type A: and press Enter, your command prompt changes to A:\. This means that your current drive is now your floppy disk drive, drive A; it also means that any operations you perform will affect the root directory of that drive.

Have you ever wished that you had a second floppy disk drive? If you're running DOS or Windows, your one floppy drive can actually pretend to be two different devices, A and B.

If you enter B: at your command prompt, making drive B your current drive, you'll get a message asking you to insert the disk for that drive. The machine is playing along with you, saying: "OK, you want to pretend that you have two drives, and now you want your one physical drive to act like drive B. Fine, put in the disk that you want to have in drive B."

We see that the floppy drive is a physical device but that its name can be either A or B—the name is a logical name, not a physical name.

Putting Up Partitions

Many machines also use two different logical names to refer to different parts of a single hard disk. Splitting a physical device into more than one logical device can let the computer make more efficient use of a single drive by carving each of the two *partitions* (as we call them) into smaller units.

Using two partitions, the computer can divide each partition into the maximum number of countable storage units that the computer can keep track of on a device. If I break a drive into two logical devices, I can carve the total space on each logical device into that maximum number of smaller units. I'll wind up with twice as many tiny units of storage, and I'll be able to use my total space more efficiently because I can allocate these smaller units with less waste.

We can see the minimum size of a unit of storage on a disk by creating a file that contains just one byte of data. We'll see what happens when we copy that file to each of three different storage devices on the PC that I'm using right now.

On the floppy disk drive, storing a file with one byte of data makes the reported available space go down by 512 bytes.

On logical drive D, which has a capacity of 499MBs, the available space drops by 8,192 (8K) bytes.

On logical drive C (another part of the same hard disk), which has a capacity of 1.52 Gbytes, the available space goes down by 32,768 (32K) bytes.

We see that larger devices can allocate space in larger chunks and that storing a large number of small files on a hard disk can waste a large amount of the space on that disk. It's as if you bought things with paper money and never spent your change: If you buy little things with $100 bills, you'll wind up with an awful lot of change that's not buying you anything. If you fill your wallet instead with $20 or $5 bills, analogous to smaller clusters, your unspent change represents much less waste.

More recent versions of Windows use a file system called FAT32 that can count a larger number of separate clusters and can therefore use smaller clusters on a disk of any given size. Smaller clusters reduce, but don't eliminate, the waste of disk capacity that comes from assigning each cluster to only one file (no matter how small the file might be).

I almost hate to point this out, but we've just spent many pages explaining just a few lines of that half-page of output from the DIR command I gave earlier. This demonstrates that there are, after all, a great many concepts that you're assumed to understand when working with a PC.

The rest of that DIR output, fortunately, is now familiar to us:

- We see internal names of files at the beginning of each line: We've talked about internal names and how these names can change without warning when we copy a file from one place to another.

- We see file sizes: We understand that these figures indicate the size of the content of the file, not the amount of space (generally larger) that's actually being used on the disk.

- We see the dates and times of most-recent file modification: We know that the date and time values that get "stamped" on a file depend on our setting the computer's clock correctly by using the command shell's DATE command (or the Windows Date/Time control, shown in Figure 2.27).

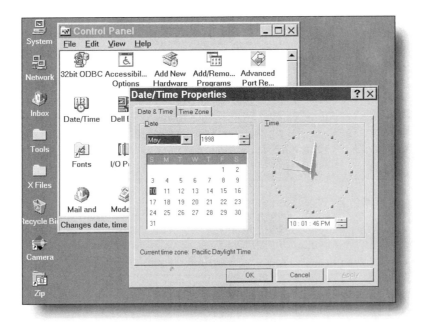

FIGURE 2.27
Many programs depend on knowing the dates and times of creating or modifying files. Your electronic mail, for example, might not be correctly displayed if your computer's clock isn't properly set. The Word Advanced Find option (shown in Figure 2.2) can't do its job if file dates and times aren't correct. The Windows Date/Time control panel lets you check your settings and even automates your twice-a-year changes between Standard and Daylight time.

- We see the *print name* of each file at the end of its line: We understand that the spaces in these readable print names can confuse some commands, and we know that we can use quotation marks around a long filename to prevent that confusion.

FEATURED PRODUCT: POWERQUEST PARTITIONMAGIC

We've just seen that a hard disk might have much more usable space if it's divided into partitions. Each partition can maintain its own list of separate units of storage, called clusters, that can be grouped into what we call files.

The latest versions of Windows aren't so affected by wasted space due to excessively large clusters, but there are other reasons why you might want to have separate partitions on a single hard disk. For example, you might want to run different operating systems if you become interested in the freeware Linux or the next-generation Windows NT.

Separate partitions can be set up with different software, and a utility program called a boot manager can tell the PC which partition to use when starting up the system.

You might also like the protection that you get by putting things in separate partitions. A physical problem, such as a failure of the hard disk itself, puts all the partitions on that disk at risk, but even a serious software failure might wipe out the file descriptions on only one partition.

For all of these reasons, it's useful to have a software tool that lets you move the boundaries between the partitioned areas on a disk—without clearing the disk and starting from scratch. Several products perform this function, but one of the best is PartitionMagic from PowerQuest Corp.

Operations that used to be tricky—and dangerous for anyone but an expert with perfect concentration—are automatic and well protected against user error when you use PartitionMagic. Some of its straightforward controls are shown in Figure 2.28. The product supports the latest version of the Windows file system, unlike some disk-management utilities that are confused by the new coding scheme that lets Windows use smaller clusters on even the largest hard disks.

And if you're using partitions as a safety measure, PartitionMagic makes it easy to copy an entire partition with one command.

Time to Stop Pretending

In the section "Putting Up Partitions" earlier in the chapter, I spoke of the unit of storage and of its different size on different storage devices. When we talk about units of storage, aren't we talking about files? No, we're talking about something closer to the physical reality of the actual storage medium.

Remember, near the beginning of the chapter I said that we would *pretend* to have files. It's time to shed that pretense and talk about what's actually happening in our PC's storage system.

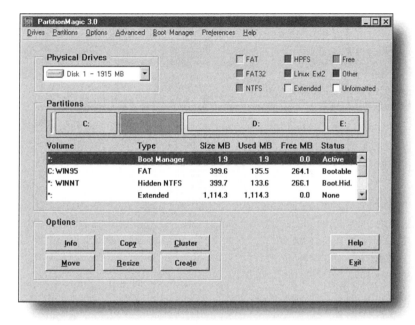

FIGURE 2.28
PartitionMagic almost makes you believe that disk partitions are real objects instead of made-up divisions between parts of a hard disk that you're using in different ways. This program lets you do things with simple point-and-click or click-and-drag operations much more easily and with much less chance of error than the tedious editing of cryptic tables required by earlier tools.

It's Got a Magnetic Appeal

A PC's storage device is typically a spinning disk, perhaps (in the case of a hard disk) in a vacuum-sealed container. The surface of the disk is coated with magnetic material. Different regions of that coating are magnetized in different ways to represent stored information. The magnetic information can be read by a tiny probe called a *head*.

We could work with a digital storage medium quite easily if we broke the medium into physical units, as we do with conventional media such as books. If we used a separate data cartridge for each of our documents, for example, we wouldn't need to deal with such complex ideas as the volumes and directories (or folders) that confront the new PC user.

Some low-cost word processors have used this approach of "one document per disk" to enhance their ease of use, but that just squeezes the balloon of confusion back out into the physical world. We would wind up needing a PC to hold the database that tells us which cartridge goes with which document.

We might as well just bite the bullet and do the whole job digitally.

We Know Our Data's Name—and Where It Lives

We saw before that a file storage device is broken up into fixed-size units. Even the smallest, one-byte data file ties up at least one of those units. When we pretend to create a file, we're really telling the PC to define a group of units and to give that group a name.

If you look at a randomly chosen location on a PC's data storage disk, you can't tell if the magnetic fields at that location are representing words or pictures or lists of files or any other possible type of data. All you can "see" (to use that verb loosely) is bytes.

When you use a tool such as the Windows Explorer to look at a disk, it's like looking at the card catalog in your local public library. You can see what collections of data (books/files) are supposed to be stored in that place (building/disk).

When you use a tool such as Microsoft's Access database manager to open a file, it's like opening a book and looking at the table of contents. You can see what data (chapters/tables) are supposed to be in that compilation (book/database).

I can take a book off the shelf without updating the library's catalog, and I can rip pages out of a book without changing the table of contents. In the same way, software can break the rules of the library (the file system) and change data in ways that the file system won't recognize.

If You Lie to Your PC, Your PC Will Lie to You

I can get down to the level of looking at the pages, so to speak, with a tool such as Norton DiskEdit from Symantec. In Figure 2.29, you can see DiskEdit's detailed view of the D drive's directory. Note the entry near the bottom-left corner of the figure, with the intriguing comment in the second column: `Erased`.

I hope this sends appropriate chills up your spine. Earlier we saw that the "convenience" of fast file saves in a tool such as Microsoft Word is a mixed blessing—we can think we've deleted material from a document when, in fact, the bytes are still in the file. It's as if we've crossed out something in the table of contents in a book without actually taking out the pages.

What we see in the DiskEdit display is like finding a book still on the shelves of the library even though its reference has been taken out of the central card catalog.

There's a special character, σ, at the beginning of the filename σORDS. That σ at the beginning of a filename is a signal to the file system that the bytes once used by that file are now available for other files, if needed.

I said in Chapter 1 that I would show you how a "destroyed" file might be resurrected. It's time for that demonstration.

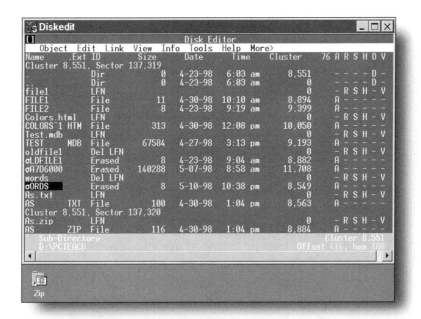

FIGURE 2.29
We can look at what's really on a disk instead of seeing what Windows Explorer thinks we want to see, with a tool such as Norton DiskEdit from Symantec. In particular, we can see that "erased" files are still very much present and that their data can still be examined.

We begin by copying a reference file of words, used by a spelling checker, into our PCTeach directory. We can confirm that we have a nice big collection of data there by giving a DIR WORDS command and getting back the following result:

```
WORDS                   999,922   10-10-96 12:18p words
```

This is almost a million bytes of data.

Now, we'll "accidentally" do something that a novice might think has destroyed this file. We'll echo the word Hello into this file, using the regular redirection symbol that starts the file over from scratch.

```
echo Hello > words
```

If we now repeat our DIR WORDS command, we get back the ominous reply,

```
WORDS                        8   05-10-98 10:49p words
```

This is terrible. Almost all of our data is gone. We might as well just erase this file with the **ERASE WORDS** command.

If we give the DIR WORDS command again, we'll now get the reply

```
File not found
```

If we go into the DISKEDIT display, however, we see that the WORDS file still has space assigned to it at cluster number 8,549. If we open that cluster, as shown in Figure 2.30, we don't just see the missing `Hello`; we also see a portion of the data that originally followed Hello in our initial file of reference spelling words!

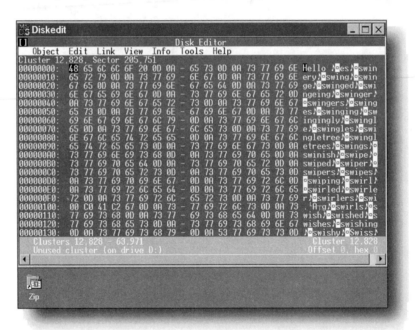

FIGURE 2.30
You might think you've destroyed a file by overwriting it with a mistaken command; you might think you've erased the file entirely. On the disk, however, much of the original data can survive an entire succession of accidental or intentional acts that you thought had removed that information. This might be good news, or it might be very bad news indeed, depending on the situation.

Additional searching on the disk finds more of the missing words. The content of that erased file has *not* been actually purged from the disk. If you act promptly, before other data gets written on top of the bytes that you really wanted to keep, you have an excellent chance of recovering erased data and putting it back into a normal file that's seen by DIR and other system functions.

Imagine, though, if the contents of an erased file were something that you really *wanted* to remove from a machine before someone else saw it. We see that we might have to use "brute force" techniques, such as storing sensitive material on removable media (floppy disks, for example), if we want convenient assurance that something has *really* been removed from a shared PC.

FEATURED PRODUCT: SYMANTEC NORTON UTILITIES

I still remember an early meeting of the Greater South Bay IBM PC Users Group in Redondo Beach, when Peter Norton (from nearby Santa Monica) was our guest speaker. His product, the Norton Utilities, was one of the first utility software products for the IBM PC; it made him an instant legend and soon brought him a well-earned fortune.

We used the Norton tools in our earliest IBM PC training classes, in much the same way that I used the current versions in this chapter to show you what's really happening on your disk. The notion of *unerasing* a file, for example, was popularized by the original Norton product.

The package has been steadily enriched over the years with more sophisticated functions as the Windows environment has created new ways for your PC to get confused—and as PC storage systems have become larger and more in need of regular complex maintenance. For example, the Norton product now lets you track the behavior of specific programs and store additional information (at the expense of additional disk space) that helps these programs load and be ready to go to work in much less time.

Your PC's performance can deteriorate over time as your disk becomes crowded with many small files, forcing Windows to split larger files into separate blocks of data on the disk and recombine them when you read them into memory. The Norton package includes programs to *defragment* your disk. This operation must be done with scrupulous correctness if you don't want to risk wholesale chaos, and the Norton tools have a deserved reputation for reliability.

The package includes a large collection of monitoring programs that are always running while you do other things. The Norton background tasks can recover normal operation after many types of software error, reducing your risk of losing unsaved work. These flexible capabilities are controlled from a somewhat complex but essentially friendly control panel (shown at lower right in Figure 2.31).

Most of Figure 2.31 is taken up by a view of the *disk map* produced by one of the Norton tools, Speed Disk, which relocates the pieces of files on a hard disk so that they are arranged for most efficient use. Rarely used files go to the edges, while often-used files are placed near each other in a portion of the disk that allows quick access. This reduces wear and tear on the disk and increases the speed of your PC's operations.

continued

Figure 2.32 shows the disk map following optimization. You can see that a much more uniform arrangement has been achieved, unlike the scattered pile of often discontiguous clusters that made up your files before this defragmentation process.

The Norton package includes a tremendous amount of multimedia training information to give you additional education in the "complicated, cryptic, powerful, unforgiving, and dangerous" (thanks again to Ed Post) world of the modern Windows PC.

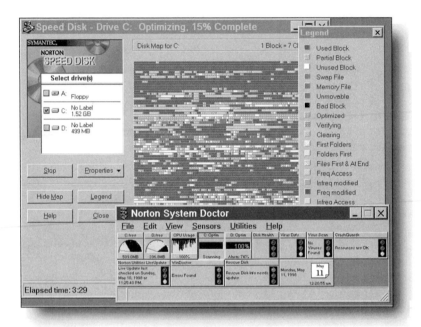

FIGURE 2.31
The main control panel (lower right) for Symantec's Norton Utilities combines continually updated measures of system activity with quick access to corrective tools for common PC problems. The common problem of disk fragmentation (pieces of files in different parts of the disk) is diagnosed by Speed Disk (background), one of the most-often used tools on a busy PC.

Opening the Nutshell

Perhaps you remember this chapter's opening quotation, sarcastically saying that MS-DOS (the foundation beneath Windows 95) could be summed up "in a nutshell" by one piece of dangerous behavior.

As Ted Nelson wryly noted in *Computer Lib*, his classic commentary on early computing technology, two apparently similar MS-DOS commands have wildly different results.

COPY A+B A will combine A and B into a file called A.

COPY A+B B will destroy B, replacing it with A.

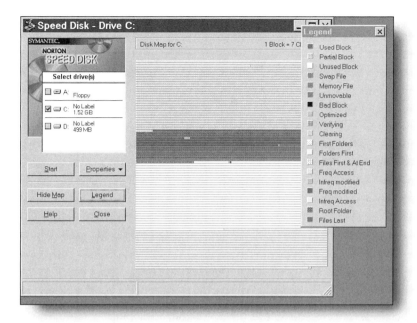

FIGURE 2.32
A hard disk works more quickly, with less wear on delicate parts, when files are grouped so that most of the activity on the disk is over a small portion of the storage area. Speed Disk moves rarely used files to the edges and leaves room for often-changed data to grow with minimal rearrangement.

By this point in this chapter, you can appreciate the reason why such similar COPY commands could have such different effects.

COPY A+B A means "Add to the end of file A the bytes that are labeled as File B." This is easy.

COPY A+B B means "Put the bytes that are labeled as File A at the place that's labeled File B and then add the bytes of File B at the end." By the time the command shell program gets to the second part of that operation, the File B data is gone.

Knowing that a file has no physical meaning, that it's just a label for a set of zones on a disk, makes it easier to "feel" this sort of thing and to keep from being surprised.

One-Way Data Doors

Throughout this chapter, we've seen that the illusion of neat, convenient files is an elaborate sham on several levels of deception. Behind the scenes is just a huge pile of bytes, with a bunch of scaffolding that makes the pile appear to have an orderly structure.

Our digital storage collections aren't like the files in "real world" file cabinets. We can easily examine old, yellowed paper files, even in academic collections that are hundreds of years old. Digital records don't have this kind of longevity, for many reasons.

Since Bush wrote his essay in the *Atlantic Monthly* magazine, we have introduced one generation after another of digital storage technology. Actually, this process began in the 1890s, even before Bush's essay, when punched cards were used to record U.S. census results.

With each subsequent upgrade in the speed, compactness, and cost-effectiveness of information storage, we have left another slice of modern history in what is—effectively—a locked box with lost keys.

The original punched-card format is one of the most enduring digital media: Punched cards remained in common use for almost a century, and if you came across an old card deck today, you could probably read it. The process would be slow, but you would not need to find or build a working model of an obsolete machine.

You probably could not readily use the data on an eight-inch floppy disk, or a 5 1/4-inch hard-sectored "Rainbow" floppy, or a magnetic card of the type used in 1970s IBM memory typewriters. It might take a visit to a swap meet to find a machine that could read the bits contained on such an obsolete magnetic record, and it might take months of detective work to figure out what those bits represented.

Tiptoe Through the Bit Field

From routine business records to irreplaceable space-probe measurements, there are uncountable cases of data that we might someday wish we could retrieve, but that will be lost, for all practical purposes, because no one has maintained the hardware needed to read an outdated form of storage.

Even worse, vast amounts of data disappear because early generations of digital media didn't have the storage life of paper. Magnetic media, such as tapes and disks, combine materials with very different behaviors, and we depend on razor-thin margins of error when we try to read their recorded information.

Microfilm, the medium that Vannevar Bush imagined we would use, is pretty tough stuff. You can heat it, cool it, spill coffee on it, and still figure out what it says by looking at it—at worst, with perhaps a magnifying glass or microscope.

Magnetic disks and tapes are much less rugged than microfilm. A disk or a backup tape consists of some mechanical foundation (substrate), typically some kind of plastic, that's been coated with a finely manufactured powder of material that can hold a magnetic field.

You could think of reading a disk or tape by moving a magnetic compass along its surface. At some points, the north end of the compass needle would point at the magnetic recording surface; at other points, the north end of the needle would swing away and the south end of the needle would be drawn toward your digital medium.

Different data codes would appear as different polarities of the stored magnetic field. We'll talk more about the technical problems of magnetic recording in Chapter 8, when we look at data backup alternatives such as tape drives and optical storage drives.

For now, it's enough to think of our digital storage systems as holding collections of tiny zones of captured magnetic fields, pointing in different directions and arranged in some way along the length of a piece of tape or across the plane of a spinning disk.

The magnetic zones of a digital storage medium aren't broken into physical units like the pages of a book. These magnetic zones are divided by special magnetic codes in the same way that the frames of a microfilm record are divided by dark stripes on the film. Microfilm and magnetic storage encode both their data, and the structure of that data, by similar means.

Digital records depend, therefore, on crisp magnetic pulses to tell a storage device how to decide even where to look on the magnetic medium, as well as what data is actually stored at any point, whether on disk or tape or any other type of magnetic record.

When you *format* a disk, you're laying down a fresh set of organizing codes. The extent of a formatting operation depends on the type of device and on other options, such as whether you want to make the operation reversible. Essentially, though, this is what formatting means, and like clearing the shelves of a library, it's a pretty drastic operation.

Believe It—Bits Are Breakable

If the magnetic codes that organize a storage medium grow weak or indistinct for whatever reason, the digital record is useless. Stretching of tapes, or storage of tapes or disks at excessive heat or humidity, can make a magnetic record unreadable.

I want to be sure that you appreciate the difference between magnetic and paper records. Paper records can be protected by a fire safe. As long as the paper doesn't reach a temperature at which it burns, the record remains.

Magnetic media can be damaged beyond recovery at temperatures much lower than those that make paper ignite. Leave an audio cassette on your car dashboard on a sunny day, and you won't get much music from the result, even in the length of time it takes a newspaper sitting right next to that tape to merely turn a little yellow. The film of magnetic particles can separate from the plastic layer that gives a disk or tape its structure.

In some cases, an aged magnetic tape might be playable one time, but the coating will flake off from the mechanical stress of being unwound and streamed past the sensor head. This fouls the mechanism, accelerating damage to the rest of the tape, and can leave the tape in a useless condition afterwards. Much of our archived space probe data is thought to be in this precarious condition today.

A media safe, with the insulation and humidity barriers required to protect magnetic media from the heat of a fire and the subsequent days of sitting in steaming debris, is different from the more common "fire safe." If you're relying on a floppy disk to store your financial records, with no paper backup, you should invest accordingly.

While you're at it, think about the other magnetic records—for example, irreplaceable videotapes—that you might also have in your office or home.

What We've Learned

We've drilled deep into the muscle and bone of Windows, getting past the cosmetic treatments of its graphical views to see what really makes it go.

We've seen that something as simple as a filename might be rendered in different ways by different programs. We've seen that parts of a filename might change the way a program tries to load a file—or might even lead the program to refuse your request to load that file at all.

We've gone beneath the file system and seen that filenames are just convenient ways of talking about clusters of bytes on a magnetic disk. We've seen some of the surprisingly simple ways to look at "deleted" passages of a document or read "erased" files.

Finally, I hope you've registered the fact that magnetic media is one of the least durable parts of PC technology, and you'll be wise to treat media failure like light bulb failure. It's not a question of whether it will happen, just a question of when.

"Without truth, the
computer won't
work...the bit is there
or the bit ain't there."

—LES SOLOMON
(quoted by Steven Levy), in
Hackers: Heroes of the
Computer Revolution

Representing Data:
Bits and Bytes, Words and Records, Colors and Codes

O MATTER HOW MUCH I'VE TRIED to avoid it, we've found ourselves constantly needing to talk about "bytes." If I could teach PCs without getting down to this level, I would.

We *could* talk about PCs without talking about bytes, but it's like trying to talk about life without talking about food. Bytes are what your PC eats, almost literally, and bytes are what your PC produces.

Your PC sends bytes, in one form or another, to everything but its display screen. Even the hardware that feeds the display uses bytes, in a special slice of memory, to represent colors and letters and more advanced multimedia before it sends its signals to your screen.

Whenever your PC has a hard time doing what you want, bytes are usually involved. The only alternative is broken hardware, which doesn't happen nearly as often as malfunctioning software.

Everyone's heard of bytes, but few people really grasp what they are—or why they're such a convenient, nearly universal unit of electronic information. In this chapter, you'll learn the whole truth about bytes, and at the same time, you'll master several other buzzwords of this information era.

We can't just jump into bytes, though, because bytes themselves are bundles of something else that's very, very simple—but also very important. Please don't groan or give up when I say this, but bytes are made of bits.

Why Bits?

Bit is a contraction of *binary digit*—which is worse than no explanation at all because now we need to define two words instead of one.

People are always talking about digital this and digital that, so we'll start with *digit*—the noun—and deal with the *binary* adjective after we understand what it's describing.

Digital Makes a Difference

If you look up "digit," you'll find that it comes from the Latin word *digitus*, which can mean either "finger" or "toe."

Depending on your experience with computers, you might therefore suspect that a digital computer is one that gives its users the finger while kicking them in the rear. I hope that by the end of this book you'll feel that you're the one who's in charge.

Putting bad karma aside, a digital computer is one that works with countable units of information—a computer that counts, so to speak, on its fingers.

Today, almost all computers are digital, based on counting, as opposed to the *analog* computers that did pioneering work in modern engineering and science.

To understand the strengths and the weaknesses of digital devices, we'll compare and contrast the digital and analog approaches to an everyday task: telling time.

Time After Time

The difference between analog and digital computers is much like the difference between analog and digital clocks. An analog clock is typically driven by an electric motor that's coupled to the local power frequency, and it moves its hands continuously; the rotation of the hands is *analog*ous to the rotation of the earth or the apparent motion of the sun across the sky.

You can measure the motion of the hands of an analog clock as accurately as you wish, reading the time to the tiniest fraction of a second—assuming, of course, that the mechanism is made to ensure smooth motion of the hands.

You could add new markings to an analog clock face, without changing the hardware behind it, to read the minute hand in units of minutes or half-minutes—even if you had originally marked the clock at only five-minute intervals (see Figure 3.1).

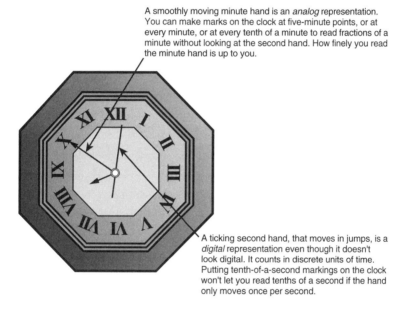

A smoothly moving minute hand is an *analog* representation. You can make marks on the clock at five-minute points, or at every minute, or at every tenth of a minute to read fractions of a minute without looking at the second hand. How finely you read the minute hand is up to you.

A ticking second hand, that moves in jumps, is a *digital* representation even though it doesn't look digital. It counts in discrete units of time. Putting tenth-of-a-second markings on the clock won't let you read tenths of a second if the hand only moves once per second.

FIGURE 3.1
This clock can be both analog and digital.

A clock with hands whose second hand only moves in discrete jumps, once per second, is a digital clock regardless of its appearance. A true analog representation is continuous and doesn't lock you into any of your early decisions about the desired precision of its measurements.

Analog Measurement: Accuracy Costs

The flexibility that you get from the analog approach has a cost attached. You have to construct an analog mechanism with exacting care, whether you want to read the time to the nearest minute or the nearest quarter hour. Any errors in the mechanism will accumulate over time until the clock is wrong by anyone's notion of acceptable accuracy.

We see the signs of accumulating error in other analog mechanisms, such as audio tape recorders. If you make a tape of a tape of a tape, the accumulated noise becomes so noticeable that the recording is almost useless. Before the advent of digital sound recording, professional audio equipment went to enormous lengths to minimize noise at each stage of the record-making process.

With analog hardware, proficiency counts, and there's almost always a process of things wearing out or getting a little bit out of adjustment.

Digital Devices: You Get What You Pay For

A digital clock is quite different. Instead of running some kind of continuous model of time, a digital timepiece is built around counting some kind of recurring event.

A traditional grandfather clock is actually a digital clock, even though its "readout" uses clock hands rather than numeric digits. The pendulum of a grandfather clock triggers a "chunky" movement of the mechanism each time it swings. If the pendulum swings once per second, there is no way that you can hook up an extra gear to give you a readout in (for example) tenths of a second.

An electronic digital clock usually counts the vibrations of a crystal. When a crystal is electrically tickled, so to speak, it quivers at a constant rate—like an ordinary tuning fork or pitch pipe, except that a crystal typically vibrates millions of times a second (compared to vibrations of only hundreds of times a second for common musical notes).

Vibrating crystals are important parts of personal computers: When you hear someone talk about the *clock rate* of a fast new PC, they're talking about an arrangement that includes just such a device.

A common digital clock (or wristwatch) uses a *divider circuit* to count a certain number of crystal vibrations before making its display "tick" upward. With millions of vibrations per second, an electronic digital timepiece can often give measurements in very small units. A common stopwatch usually reads out to the nearest hundredth of a second, but a different arrangement (using the same crystal) could read out in thousandths of a second—or less.

Point to Your Preference

We can't possibly, however, say anything about the time between a digital clock's smallest possible intervals. That's the essence of anything digital. A digital device, whether it's a watch or a cellular phone or a camera or a computer, works with specific units of information.

You can't change your mind later and start asking questions about anything more precise than the originally chosen unit of data. You pick your unit at the beginning, and you're stuck with it—speaking of fingers.

What do we get in return for this lack of flexibility? We stop being sensitive to the finicky adjustments that are always associated with analog operations. A conventional piano, for example, drifts a little bit out of tune whenever the temperature or humidity changes to any degree. Each of the piano's strings has its own, potentially independent errors.

A digital piano can stay exactly in tune because the pitch of every digital note can be tied to a single internal counter. We can even put that counter's vibrating crystal in a temperature-controlled chamber, as is done for exacting laboratory measurements, and get essentially perfect accuracy.

NOTE
We'll talk more about digital music in Chapter 8.

But Weren't We Talking About Computers?

We can build analog computers that use continuously changing signals in the same way that we can build analog clocks that use continuously moving hands. An analog computer can be an electrical model of a complicated system, such as water flowing through a pipe, faithfully imitating pressures and flows with electrical fluctuations.

But an analog computer, like an analog clock or a conventional piano, can easily be distorted by small imperfections in its parts. If an analog signal loses some of its strength while traveling over a long connection, the computer can't tell if the reduction is accidental or not. It might be an unintended loss of energy within the mechanism of the computer, or it might be a purposeful model of a physical process that makes some force get weaker.

A digital computer or other digital mechanism avoids many sources of error because it works with lists of counted events. A digital computer doesn't try to represent one continuous quantity, such as the flow of water through a pipe, with another continuous quantity, such as the flow of electrical current through a wire. Instead, a digital computer's programmer chooses some unit of water flow (perhaps milliliters per second) and writes a program to count (or simulate) the behavior of each unit, one at a time.

If you pick a unit of counting that's small enough to capture the details you want, you'll never need to worry about accumulation of errors as information gets passed along from one part of the system to the next. Whenever you pass information from one part of the system to another, you make a fresh start with a new and accurate list.

Compact discs, for example, don't have the background hiss that you might remember hearing on older analog records. A CD player reads lists of values from the disc and turns those values into something that sounds (to most ears) exactly like the original sound. You could "listen" with instruments that are more precise than your ears, however, and readily measure the differences (see Figure 3.2).

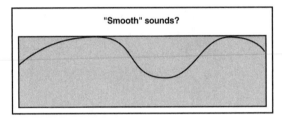

A piano's vibrating strings, and other natural instruments, make smoothly varying sounds that look like a curve (top) when measured with sensitive equipment.

Your CD player, and other digital instruments, settle for an approximation (bottom) that your ears hear as nearly perfect sounds—without the noticeable hiss that accumulates in analog recordings.

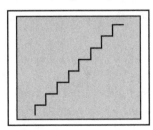

FIGURE 3.2
A CD player uses digital approximations of natural sounds. Duplicating digital sound just means copying a list of numbers, so digital copies are exact, without the accumulating noise that mars analog reproductions.

In the same way, you can look at a newspaper photograph with a magnifying glass and see that it's really made up of black dots rather than smoothly varying shades of gray (see Figure 3.3).

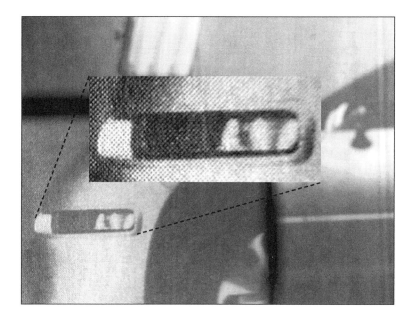

FIGURE 3.3
This magnified detail from a newspaper photo (lower left, further enlarged at center) reveals that the effect of smooth shading is created by dots of pure black of varying size and spacing. Below a certain size, details disappear in the space between the dots: a visual analog to the error in any digital approximation of the real world's continuous quantities.

Counting on electronic fingers is easier than measuring the length of electronic feet, so to speak. I hope this explains the importance of digits in computers and information systems.

We still need to put that "binary" word into some kind of real-world context.

All About Binary

A digital computer is based on principles of counting, rather than measuring, but we still need to decide exactly *how* we're going to count.

Perhaps it's been a long time since you thought about counting as a matter that required any decisions. Most people count from zero through nine, and then carry a one and start over with ten through nineteen. We repeat until we get to ninety-nine, and then carry twice into the hundreds column and just keep going.

Carrying the tens, or the tens of tens, is a natural way of doing things for people who come with ten handy digits as standard equipment (five of them on each hand). When we build an electronic computer, though, we have to ask ourselves if carrying tens still makes sense.

Ten is not an especially natural base for numbers being handled by electronic counting machines—and that's what a digital computer is: a collection of counters with other stuff wrapped around them.

Counting with Electricity

We could choose any number of voltage levels we like for representing different values of data, just as flashlights of different sizes use different numbers of 1.5 volt batteries, stacked end-to-end in their handles, to provide different levels of brightness.

Is there some number of electrical levels that makes, for some reason, more sense than any other? There is, and you might be surprised to learn that the ideal approach to electronic counting was determined half a century ago—when today's digital machines were barely envisioned by a handful of brilliant thinkers.

There Really Is One Best Way

One of the most original minds in the field of computational machines was that of Norbert Wiener, who wrote a book in 1948 titled *Cybernetics*. Wiener coined this often-misused word to mean a system that constantly compares its present state against its desired state, measuring the error and taking action to make that error smaller.

TWO CYBERNETIC SYSTEMS: YOUR THERMOSTAT AND YOU

The thermostat in a house measures the temperature of the room and compares it against the temperature that's been set. It turns on the heat or the air conditioning if the room is too cold or too hot. This is cybernetic behavior.

Older home thermostats are analog devices, with metal strips or springs that bend as the temperature changes. Many new thermostats are digital, using techniques once found only in research laboratories to measure temperature accurately without moving parts. Whether analog or digital, a thermostat senses when the room temperature wanders above or below the set point and "steers" the temperature back toward that target.

Cybernetic actually comes from a Greek word meaning "steersman." The word is often misused in such derivatives as *cyborg* (a popular term in fiction for a human-machine hybrid). The popular usage suggests that cybernetic means something synthetic or unnatural, but a human being is just as cybernetic—more so, in fact—than any computer ever built. Whenever you ride a bicycle, or even stand up and remain upright, you're engaged in a cybernetic process of sensing error and acting to reduce that error.

Complex manufactured cybernetic systems, such as the automatic pilot in an airplane, need to keep track of large amounts of information while making their decisions. Wiener wanted to figure out the most efficient possible method for representing information in an electronic device.

Suppose, said Wiener, that we want to record a number with some desired accuracy. We can understand Wiener's approach in terms of a children's guessing game. Imagine one player choosing a number, and the other being challenged to guess the chosen value.

If the players agree to use the range from one to one hundred, the guesser can begin by asking if the number is less than fifty. This immediately rules out half of the possible values. If the number is less than fifty, the guesser can then ask if the number is less than 25, and so on, until the exact value is known.

The Fastest Route to the Answer

At any point, if an exact result isn't needed, the guesser could stop, just as Wiener imagined choosing some acceptable error for representing the values of numbers in a computer. All digital systems have to accept some level of error, as we'll see later on.

In our guessing game, with each successive question, the player guessing the secret value is narrowing down the possible answer into one of several ranges. Here is the question: Is there some ideal number of ranges that we should use?

In the game we imagined above, a common strategy uses a numeric base of two; that is, each guess determines whether the answer is above or below some threshold, with only two possible answers at each stage.

You wouldn't start this game, with a span of possible values from one to a hundred, by asking, "Is the number less than ten?" Nine-tenths of the time, the answer would be "No," and you'd still have nine-tenths of the possible values left to consider.

Eliminating half of the possible answers with each successive question is a more efficient approach; in fact, it is the *most* efficient approach that can be used.

If It's Always True, It Isn't Information

We can prove that base two is the simplest and cheapest way to count when your "fingers" don't come for free but have to be constructed from electronic hardware. Start with the idea of an amount of information. How can information be measured?

We could start with what *isn't* informative. Imagine a statement that's always true: something like the prediction, "Tomorrow the sunrise will be in the east."

Would you pay for a prediction of eastern sunrise? Of course not, because it doesn't tell you anything you didn't already know. This isn't informative, even though it's true.

If we use the letter *I* to represent *information value*, the I of a known and unchanging fact is zero.

When You Only Know One Thing

What would be a "size 1" piece of information? A size 1 example could be the statement, "It's sunny outside." Knowing if this is true or false is useful.

We can represent true-or-false information with a simple light bulb that is either turned on or turned off.

We're accepting an error of plus-or-minus half of our unit of counting. We're accepting that *off* means "less than 1/2" (somewhere between dark and gloomy), and *on* means "more than 1/2" (somewhere between gloomy and blinding).

We can't be any more precise than half of our least significant bit. In this case, with only one bit, we can't get closer than half of the total possible range. That's the price of being digital.

Four for the Price of Three

If we want to cut our possible error in half (that is, be twice as precise), we're making I = 2. We're twice as well informed, so to speak.

We now need to represent four possible information states. If we still use a single light bulb, we need three different ways of turning on the bulb, because we need to be able to choose among three different levels of brightness.

Off now means "less than 1/4" and *full bright* means "more than 3/4." We'll use two in-between steps for the other possible ranges between "dark" and "blinding sun."

We would need three times as much hardware to control the bulb in this multi-level manner. Instead of just one sensor and switch, we now need a sensor and switch for each of the three steps of brightness.

Compared to the cost of turning the bulb on or off for I = 1, we'll have three times the cost when I = 2.

The Power of Two

Instead of controlling one bulb at different levels of brightness, though, we could use several bulbs and have each one be on or off.

If we used two bulbs, we could say that *both off* is "less than 1/4," *bulb A on* is "1/4 to 1/2," *bulb B on* is "1/2 to 3/4," and *both on* is "3/4 to 1." We get the same information as before, but with only two control decisions, one decision for each bulb.

Instead of three switches for a four-valued scale, we need only two switches for two two-valued scales. In general, Wiener showed that a group of two-valued scales would always be the least expensive arrangement.

We can record any amount of information by combining several scales, dividing each scale into only two possible values. We would represent four possible choices with the four possible combinations, 00, 01, 10, and 11. The first digit in each two-digit group is one scale, with two possible values 0 or 1; the second digit is a second two-valued scale.

We would represent eight possible choices with the eight combinations of only three digits 000, 001, 010, 011, 100, 101, 110, and 111. If we wanted to count from zero to ten, we wouldn't need ten different ways of controlling a single display. We'd just use four controllers to give us the sequence 0000, 0001, 0010, 0011, 0100, 0101, 0110, 0111, 1000, 1001, 1010.

You'll notice that these groups of digits look a lot like lists of numbers, except that we seem to be "carrying the one" whenever we get to two instead of counting up to ten before we carry.

Carrying at two is the cheapest way of counting when we're building a digital apparatus instead of using the double handful of digits most folks are born with. We get to the smallest possible error with the least costly hardware when we count, not in "base ten," but in "base two."

Don't be intimidated by the technical sound of *binary*. An airplane with two wings is a biplane, a meeting held every two months is bimonthly, and a base-2 number system is binary.

When we say binary numbers, we just mean numbers that are expressed with a base of two, in the same way that decimal numbers are numbers with a base of ten.

Digital computers work with bits (binary digits) not because computer engineers are pinheads, but because the engineers' bosses are bean counters. Computers count with ones and zeros (or Xs and Os, or highs and lows) because that's the cheapest way to do it.

Why Bytes?

If bits are the ideal way to count with electrical hardware, why are people constantly talking about bytes? The answer is remarkably simple, now that we've seen how we can represent a larger range of possible values with larger groups of bits.

We just observed, for example, that we could count to eight (all right, from 0 through 7, which is eight different values) by using a set of three bits. We can count from 0 through 15 (sixteen values) with four bits, from 0 through 31 (32 values) with five bits, and from 0 through 63 (64 values) with six bits.

Computer people almost always start counting things at zero, not at one, because so many computing tasks begin by deciding how many bits to use for representing a range of possible values. When you decide how many bits you're going to use, you've decided to work with a range of values that starts at zero and ends at 2^n-1 (where n is the chosen number of bits).

Take a Letter

A 6-bit field's vocabulary of 64 values is almost enough for everyday communication. For ordinary activities, though, we'd prefer to have the 26 uppercase letters of the alphabet, plus the 26 lowercase letters, plus the ten numeric digits and the arithmetic operators, plus an adequate set of punctuation symbols such as the period, the comma, the open and close parentheses, and so on. That's more than 64 symbols.

If we allow ourselves a seventh bit, we have 128 possible symbols whose codes can range from 0000000 to 1111111. This is ample for most needs, and a particular 7-bit code has become nearly universal among most information systems.

The widely used 7-bit code is called the American Standard Code for Information Interchange (ASCII). This acronym, pronounced "ask-key," is part of the language of the information age.

ASCII starts with an "A," but the actual list of ASCII codes does not begin with our alphabet. ASCII code 0 is a special character called *null*, which can be used when you want to leave room in a data structure. Think of it as a digital version of "This space intentionally left blank."

ASCII Antiquities

Codes 0 through 31 in the ASCII set are control codes, with special meanings such as "line feed" (code 10) and "carriage return" (code 13). We saw these particular codes and experimented with their effects in Chapter 1; we were looking at them with the DEBUG program, which showed us the codes in their hexadecimal form (where 10 was A, or 0A, and 13 was 0D).

Codes for controlling a typewriter aren't the only relics of ancient hardware that you'll find in the ASCII assignments. For example, code 7 is "bell" and was used to ring the alarm bell on a teletype terminal as a signal that a message was arriving.

We can enter the value of any ASCII code from 1 through 26 from a PC's command line. We do this by holding down the Control key (often labeled *Ctrl*) while typing a letter. Ctrl+A is an ASCII 1, and so on through Ctrl+Z for ASCII 26. By this convention, ASCII 7 (the bell code) is Ctrl+G.

If you open a console window, as we did in Chapter 1, you can type ECHO, followed by a space and the "keychord" Ctrl+G. On the screen, you will then see

```
echo ^G
```

You will see the symbol pair ^G, even though you did not enter a caret symbol (which is what we call the ^ that is usually on the same key as the 6). You will often see PC instruction manuals that use a caret in front of a letter as a way of saying, "Hold down the Ctrl key while typing this letter." This is *not* the same thing as typing a caret (Shift+6) followed by the letter.

When you press the Enter (↵) key, you will hear a beep—the PC's version of the bell.

Another ASCII anachronism is code 127, whose special value is "deleted." This is easy to explain. A binary 127 is the bit string 1111111. This value would punch out all seven holes across the width of a teletype terminal's paper tape—once the common recording medium for small volumes of data.

If an operator made a typing error, producing the wrong combination of holes, the tape punch device could back up one position and punch out all of the holes to signal a deleted character.

Put It on the Tab

Another low-order code that can affect our work is code 9, the tab character. Some programs store text with tab characters between columns of words or figures. This means that another program, when it reads that file, can place successive items into its own arrangement, such as a table in a document or a grid in a spreadsheet. A file that uses tabs to separate fields of information is called a *tab-delimited* file, and many PC programs give you the option of saving files in this format.

Tabs aren't handled in the same way by every program: Some programs expand tabs into spaces when they load a file, losing information about the desired column-by-column layout. Other programs collapse groups of spaces into tabs when writing a file out to the disk, thereby saving disk space (because each tab only takes up one byte of storage).

We can't make this annoying inconsistency go away, but we can learn to recognize the problem and correct it. For example, many word processors will let you search for tab characters with a special command to the search-and-replace tool.

Finally, for Humans

The "human-readable" ASCII codes begin with the space character. A space is *not* the same as a null, because spaces are data and nulls indicate an absence of any information.

The ASCII code for a space has the decimal value of 32. Because 32 in base ten is two 16s and zero 1s, a space appears in DEBUG (or in any other hexadecimal display) as a 20.

The space is followed by several punctuation characters before we get to the numeric digits (0 has the decimal code 48), and then more punctuation between 9 and A.

The letter *A* has the code value 65. You might see an expression such as `LetterPosition+64` in a program that converts alphabetic ordering into bytes for output to a printer or other device. That addition makes 1 into 65 (the code for A), 2 into 66 (B), and so on.

You'll see an ASCII conversion formula later in this chapter when we use a spreadsheet to build a file of randomly chosen letters to create a worst-case test for a data-compression program.

A Hex on Our Data

If we routinely try to use bit groups of seven or more at a time, we'll probably make many errors. It's just too easy for the eyes to glaze over when we're trying to decipher long strings of repeated symbols, and we'll get many runs of 1s that lend themselves to misreading.

Shall we group our bits into sets of four? We said earlier that with four bits, we can represent numeric values from 0 through 15. We can count 0, 1, 2, 3, 4, 5, 6, 7, 8, 9, A, B, C, D, E, F, and then carry the one and start over with 10.

We're counting in base 16, and such a numbering system is called *hexadecimal*.

After we learn to use "hex," working with pairs of 4-bit groups becomes natural. Instead of counting from 00000000 through 11111111, we can just count from 00 through FF to represent the values 0 through 255. Each digit in a hexadecimal number represents a 4-bit group that counts up some power of sixteen (1s, 16s, 256s…), just as each digit in an ordinary decimal number is counting up some power of ten (1s, 10s, hundreds…).

In base 16, the value FF means "15 sixteens plus 15 ones," or 240 plus 15, or 255—which is, of course, the highest value (2^8-1) we should be able to represent with a string of eight bits.

Digital Delicatessen

When programmers started working with groups of bits to represent common entities such as alphabet letters and numerals, they coined the term *byte* to mean "more than a bit." Byte began as an informal term, and it could mean anything from six to nine bits, depending on the machine that you were using.

Over time, byte has come to mean an 8-bit group on any hardware. This convention became uniform when many networks adopted 8-bit bytes as standard units for transferring data from one location to another, even between two different types of computers.

The whimsical spelling of byte was actually a safety feature, an effort to minimize the chance of confusion between bit and bite. Unfortunately, many common usages abbreviate both bit and byte to just the letter *b*.

You must rely on context to decide if people are talking, for example, about bits per second or bytes per second when they speak of *bps*. People who sell computer equipment like to brag about larger numbers, so it's common to rate the speed of modems (which send bytes over phone lines) in bits per second—which gives a number eight times as much as the same speed given in bytes per second.

As 8-bit bytes became the common parlance, groups of bits in other sizes took on y-based nicknames. Perhaps I should say "nycknames," because many of these playful terms follow the example of "byte" and replace an *i* with a *y*.

A 4-bit group, for example, which can be represented by one hexadecimal digit (0 through F), is sometimes called a *nybble*. A 16-bit string (two bytes) is sometimes called a *playte*, while 32 bits becomes a *dynner*.

Playte and dynner are rarely used and widely regarded as silly, but the more common terms for large bit groups are sadly ambiguous. On older machines, for example, with 286 or earlier versions of the basic PC processor design, a 16-bit string is called a *word*. On PCs with a 386 or more recent chip, the same size data unit is called a *half-word*. A 32-bit group might be called a *longword* on a 16-bit machine, or just a plain *word* if the machine stores 32-bit chunks in its working compartments and manipulates those units in its basic operations.

An approaching wave of 64-bit machines is led by the high-speed Alpha chips that processed the special effects in the movie *Titanic*. When 64-bit hardware takes over the high end of personal computing, it will make the meaning of "word" even more confusing: We'll have hardware and software coexisting at intrinsic word sizes from 16 to 64 bits.

NOTE
We'll talk about the ways that computers' central processors move "words" of data when we get to Chapter 4.

Back to the Byte

At least we have byte as a nearly universal term. That's one of the reasons you will usually hear memory capacity and disk storage volume described in aggregations of bytes.

The other reason bytes prevail as the unit of data volume is that, in most cases, each letter in a document is represented by one byte. Converting mentally between a 500-word memo (about 3,000 characters) and a 3 Kbyte file is easy.

As more of our data takes on rich formats, such as typographically styled text or photographs, the convenience of one byte per character becomes much less important.

The Address Space That Ate Cincinnati

Now that we understand bits, we can see why it's important to know when we're talking about 16-bit applications or 32-bit operating systems or other, similarly qualified terms.

A piece of software might have been written to work on a machine that handles only 16 bits at a time. Early IBM PCs had this limitation. With only 16 bits in a "word," a computer could only deal with a chunk of memory that was no larger than 65,536 bytes in size. That was the largest number of byte locations the computer could distinguish in a single memory bank. (At the time, 16-bit hardware was considered a major advance over 8-bit machines such as the Apple II.)

If a program needed to keep track of a large collection of things, such as a mailing list of a million magazine subscribers, the programmer needed to figure out some arbitrary way of representing that range of values. The program couldn't simply step its way through the list, counting as it went, because it would run out of fingers to count on before it got to the end of the job.

A 32-bit machine, beginning (on common PCs) with the 386 series of Intel chips, could address a single block of up to 4 gigabytes of memory. Almost no one actually had this much memory installed, but it was possible to make a machine pretend to have this much memory by using space on the disk to masquerade as a range of memory addresses.

> **NOTE**
> Disk space that imitates memory is called *virtual memory*, and we'll discuss it more fully in Chapter 4.

Now, people are already starting to talk about 64-bit systems. How large a value can you represent with a word of 64 bits?

It's meaningless to say that a 64-bit number can represent values slightly greater than 18 million trillion (18 quintillion). It's more useful to look at examples of numbers that large.

If you had started shooting movie film at 24 frames per second on the day that our universe began in the so-called Big Bang, you would not yet have exposed your 2^{64}th frame of film. You'd have shot roughly 11 quintillion frames, with plenty of film left for post-production editing.

If you went down to the beach and started filling barrels of water, you could drain the world's oceans before you filled your 2^{64}th urn. In fact, you could drain all of the oceans twice over and have many barrels to spare.

Does this mean that 64 bits will be overkill? Not at all—there are many useful tasks for a 64-bit information system.

For example, imagine a comprehensive, satellite-photo database that pictures every ten-meter square of the earth's surface in various spectral bands. This could be used for agricultural surveys, for example, or for locating chemical or biological hazards.

You would actually use up a 64-bit address space before you could accommodate all of the data involved in just one pass at a global surface photo gallery. You would quickly need much more capacity to do any kind of trend analysis, meaning that even 64-bit machines will still require skillful programming to work around address-space limitations.

Yes, the 64-bit machine will find plenty of work to do, as soon as software catches up with that hardware's potential.

Numeric Data Types

We talked about the emergence of bytes as convenient chunks of data for representing letters and numerals. In many cases, however, we build and buy and use computers to *compute*—that is, to count and to do more complex math operations.

The basic issues in computer-based math are the same, whether our numbers represent income taxes or the temperatures inside stars.

Integer and Fixed-Point Numbers

We've already seen how easy it is to use bits as electronic versions of our counting numbers, the non-negative integers from zero on up.

If we want to have numbers less than zero, we have to give up one of our bits for use as a "sign bit." We can use an 8-bit byte, for example, to cover the range from −128 to +127 instead of spanning the range from 0 through 255.

In "signed" integer formats, the value of the first bit tells us whether our value is in the lower half or the upper half of the represented range. Actually, this is true for unsigned numbers as well: When we count from 0 through 3, for example, the sequence 00, 01, 10, 11 has the first half of its values beginning with 0 and the second half beginning with 1.

Experienced programmers routinely think, and speak, in terms of using additional bits to divide things into binary (two-way) groups.

We can also use our electronic counting numbers (our integers) to represent fractional amounts, such as dollars and cents, by choosing an appropriate counting unit. If we want to be correct to the nearest penny, we can count in pennies and just put in the decimal point when we're done. If we want to be correct to a tenth of a cent, we can count in tenths of a cent and then round off to pennies and put in the decimal point when we put out a final result.

When the number of decimal places is fixed at the beginning of the job, we say it's a *fixed-point* numbering scheme. We can make fixed-point calculations, including integer calculations, as error free as we wish. All it takes is the right number of bits.

Fracturing Our Fractions

Things get tricky if we want to work with fractions in a general way instead of just pretending that the world comes in predefined chunks.

Almost everything about computers depends on pretending that the world comes in little pieces—sort of like Lego blocks.

Imagine sculptures that are made from Lego blocks instead of being carved and smoothed from stone. Imagine every painting being replaced by a mosaic, or a newspaper-photo style arrangement of different-colored dots.

The real world is smooth, unless you're a subatomic physicist; the digital world is chunky. Digital representation has its limits.

The biggest problem with digital fractions, using the binary system, is that there are many common fractions that cannot be exactly represented by any number of bits.

For example, consider the fraction 1/5. In our everyday decimal system, this is 0.2, or 20%. We have no problem representing this value exactly.

How do we write 1/5(base 10), or 0.2_{10}, in a system based on powers of 2? The value is less than one-half, so it is less than 0.1_2. (The first position to the right of a base-10 decimal point represents tenths; the first position to the right of a base-2 binary point represents halves.) The value of 0.2_{10} is less than 1/4, so it is less than 0.01_2. (We divide by two with each additional movement to the right, or *binary place*, just as we divide by ten with each additional decimal place.)

Our value of 0.2_{10} is more than 1/8, so it is something more than 0.001_2. It is more than 1/8 + 1/16 (0.125_{10} + 0.0625_{10}), so it is also more than 0.0011_2.

We can keep on going, homing in on the value of 0.2_{10} as closely as we wish, but we will never get there exactly. With four bits, the best we can do is 0.0011_2; with eight bits, the best we can do is 0.00110011_2; with sixteen bits, the best we can do is 0.0011001100110011_2 (see Figure 3.4).

Bit	0	•	0	0	1	1	0	0	1	1
Position value	1		$\frac{1}{2}$	$\frac{1}{4}$	$\frac{1}{8}$	$\frac{1}{16}$	$\frac{1}{32}$	$\frac{1}{64}$	$\frac{1}{128}$	$\frac{1}{256}$
Contribution	0		0	0	.125	.0625	0	0	.00078125	.00390625
Running total	0		0	0	0.125	0.1875	0.1875	0.1875	0.1953125	0.19921875

FIGURE 3.4
Our everyday base-10 numbers handle the fraction one-fifth (0.2) with ease, but a computer's binary numbers can't express this value exactly in any number of bits.

We see that our binary version of the everyday fraction $1/5_{10}$, gives us a repeating pattern—like the pattern that we get in our decimal system when we try to represent a fraction such as $1/7_{10}$ (0.142857142857142857...). Perhaps this demonstrates that we really don't have a problem. After all, we manage to divide things by seven to convert from weekly to daily figures, and we get along with the fact that this operation can never be exact in our everyday base-10 numbers.

Perhaps we can tolerate our 16-bit approximation to 0.2_{10}, which works out to the equivalent of 0.1999969482421875_{10}? This is only an error of 1.5 thousandths of a percent, and I'll cheerfully give that much of a margin to anyone who cares.

Floating-Point Physics

There are people who simply can't tolerate the tiny errors that most of us would never notice. An error of 0.0015% won't generally ruin my day, but I'm not an astronomer trying to put a solar probe into orbit around the sun.

On the scale of the distance from Earth to Sol, even so tiny an error multiplies up to more than 1,400 miles. That's serious if you're getting too close to the heat.

Scientific and engineering users demand less room for error, and that's why fractional math on PC-class machines is done with special mathematical hardware (built into 486 and Pentium chips, or plugged in as an add-on chip in earlier machines). The numeric *coprocessor*, as it is called, represents numbers internally with 80 bits of precision.

The numbers that are handled by the special math unit are called *floating-point* numbers, distinguishing them from the *fixed-point* numbers that we discussed previously. Floating-point numbers don't force you to choose a counting unit at the beginning of your work. Like the "scientific notation" that most of us learned (or will learn) in a high school science class, floating-point numbers combine a *significand* with an *exponent*.

When a scientist counts molecules in terms of Avogadro's number (about 6×10^{23}), the 6 is the significand and the 23 is the exponent. A floating-point math unit is usually processing 64-bit inputs and outputs that use one bit for the plus or minus sign, 52 bits for the significand, and 11 bits for the exponent.

A 64-bit floating-point number that uses this standard format can represent values as large as (roughly) 1.67×10^{308}, or as small as 4.19×10^{-307}, with the value being either positive or negative and having an accuracy of roughly 16 decimal places.

As noted before, the floating-point hardware actually stores and operates on these values with an internal 80-bit format that avoids almost all round-off errors.

Floating-point standards, including the proper methods for handling abnormal situations such as division by zero, are defined by ANSI/IEEE 754-1985 Standard for Binary Floating-Point Arithmetic. This is sometimes referred to more concisely as IEEE 754. A vendor of technical software might specify that its software performs its computations according to this standard.

Giving Bits the Business

A kind of math exists that needs to work with large numbers, larger than the value of 65,535 that we can represent with a 16-bit integer—larger, even, than the value of 4,294,967,295 (4.3 billion) that we can represent with a 32-bit integer.

I'm talking about the values in billions or trillions of dollars that we encounter in financial computations (especially those involving government operations or major investment markets). Not only can financial calculations involve large numbers, but these numbers often have to be handled with accuracy to the fraction of a penny: accuracy as defined by the rules of accounting, not programming.

We earlier saw, for example, that a simple fraction such as 1/5 cannot be represented correctly with any number of bits. Business operations cannot accept the errors that are unavoidable in base-2 calculations of base-10 dollars and cents.

Bits for Cents and Dollars

To perform accurate business math, a computer program can represent numbers in a format called Binary Coded Decimal, or BCD.

Binary Coded Decimal sounds intimidating; actually, though, it is easier to go back and forth between decimal numbers and BCD than it is to convert our base-10 numbers into "pure" base-2 equivalents.

Suppose we were working with the base-10 number 120, or 120_{10}. We could write this as the binary number 1111000_2; that is, $1 \times 64 + 1 \times 32 + 1 \times 16 + 1 \times 8 + 0 \times 4 + 0 \times 2 + 0 \times 1$. Note that this only requires seven bits.

Alternatively, we could convert the digits of our decimal number one at a time from decimal (0–9) to binary (0–1) notation. We would convert our value of 120, for example, to 0001 0010 0000.

I broke the 12-bit string into nybbles so that you could see, at least a *little* more easily, that the first group of four bits is a 1, the second group is a 2, the third group is a 0.

It's actually easier to convert 120_{10} to 000100100000_{BCD} than it was to convert it to 1111000_2. The BCD conversion just moves along the series of base-10 digits, converting them one at a time, while the base-2 conversion has to work with the entire value of the base-10 number and take it apart into its power-of-2 components.

When we work in BCD, we do base-10 math with base-2 representations of our digits. We don't have any of the errors that come from working in binary notation.

Why, then, isn't most computer math done in BCD? For one thing, as you see here, BCD uses more bits to represent a value—in this case, twelve bits instead of seven.

The other issue with BCD is that math operations on BCD numbers take more time than binary arithmetic. If we want to multiply 120 by 8, this is easy in binary. Each multiplication by two adds a zero to the end, just as multiplication by ten adds a zero to the end of a base-10 representation. So $120_{10} \times 8_{10}$ becomes $1111000_2 \times 1000_2$, or 1111000000_2.

If we're working in BCD, we have to do "long multiplication." We have to write software that keeps track of base-10–carrying operations. We wind up saying, internally, that $000100100000_{BCD} \times 1000_{BCD}$ is $0000_{BCD} + 000101100000_{BCD} + 100000000000_{BCD}$ ($0_{10} + 160_{10} + 800_{10}$).

BCD operation is much slower than doing simple base-2 math in the computer's native mode, even when a processor has

NOTE
We'll talk more about the idea of specialized instruction sets in Chapter 4.

special instructions built into it for efficient BCD operation. I mentioned previously that 64-bit hardware was on the way: We might well see BCD finally fade into the shadow of fast, precise, 64-bit systems for business applications.

We have already seen that we can make pure binary math as accurate as we wish by using a large enough bit string; we can also use IEEE 754 64-bit floating-point numbers, as we discussed earlier, to work with tens of trillions of dollars to the nearest penny. With these options available, the need for BCD isn't nearly as compelling today as it was when a processor's word was only 16 bits.

A World of Character Codes

One reason that bytes emerged as a standard unit of data was their close fit with the 7-bit chunks of ASCII character codes. The ASCII set is nowhere near large enough, however, to accommodate the needs of multinational computing.

In addition to the Roman alphabet used by English speakers and the extra characters used in European languages, we also want to represent the Japanese alphabets (both Katakana and Hiragana) and the Greek, Arabic, Cyrillic (Russian), and other sets of alphabetic or pictographic symbols.

E Pluribus Unicode

We can represent a much larger number of symbol sets if we use, not the 7-bit code of ASCII, but a 16-bit set (65,536 possible codes) called Unicode. The Unicode representation is built into current environments such as Microsoft's Windows NT operating system and into modern computing tools such as Sun's Java programming language, but Unicode is only slowly gaining support from devices such as displays and printers.

Fortunately, the 8-bit bottom range of Unicode's symbol space is identical to Latin-1, an 8-bit extension of ASCII. In addition to the 26 letters used in writing English, Latin-1 adds common characters with diacritical marks such as those in *façade* or *mañana*.

The numeric values of the 26 uppercase letters, the 26 lowercase letters, and the numeric digits 0 through 9 are the same in ASCII, Latin-1, and Unicode. You can do a lot of communication with computers and with other computer users by using nothing but the table of ASCII codes.

Character Counts

Certain features make character codes an efficient way of working with text. For example, ASCII uses consecutive numbers to represent consecutive letters. This means that operations such as alphabetic sorting become identical to numeric sorting.

You might think that any fool would think of assigning numeric codes in order to the letters of the alphabet, but some character codes actually don't follow this obvious principle. IBM's EBCDIC code (Extended Binary Coded Decimal Interchange Code) has all sorts of gaps and discontinuities in its assignments, with punctuation symbols and unassigned values interspersed among the letters of the alphabet.

Be glad that ASCII, not EBCDIC, was used in the original IBM PC and that it has become pervasive.

International Affairs

This is a good place to observe that there's a big difference between representing international alphabets (which Unicode does with ease) and representing multicultural habits and attitudes (which software developers often don't do at all).

For example, a European user of the WordPerfect word processing program once told a friend of mine about his first reaction to a so-called "localized" version of the program, one that was supposed to provide menus and built-in tools such as spell-check dictionaries in the user's own language.

When the European user pulled down a menu, he felt as if he were using a completely different program from the English-language version he had already learned. The menu commands, crudely translated from English into another language, were almost unrecognizable. "Imagine a menu command for 'spell check' being translated as 'verify letters,'" he said.

My friend's European associate adopted the "localized" version, anyway, because its dictionary was much better suited to his needs, but he used it by picking menu commands from memory. He knew, for example, from experience with the English-language version, that the fifth command in the first menu would let him save a file under a different name.

As the community of information becomes increasingly international, the members of that community need to deal with how much trouble it's worth to accommodate non-English-speaking users. It is a lot of trouble, as we saw when we waded into a Unicode file in Chapter 2.

Other Colorful Details

As long as we're talking about numeric codes, it's useful to note that numbers (expressed in bits and bytes) are a computer's only means of representing colors, as well as letters.

It's common to represent a color with three values, one each for the red, green, and blue components that we combine to make any other color. Look closely at the screen of a color TV or color computer display, and you'll see for yourself that every color on that screen is being constructed by different mixtures of red, green, and blue—RGB values, for short.

Sixteen Million Shades

We can describe a versatile palette of colors if we give ourselves eight bits for each component, or 24 bits in all. We can think of 24 bits as 4 + 10 + 10, which means that we can represent 16 times 1,024 times 1,024 values, or roughly 16 million different colors with this scheme.

We've already seen that an 8-bit byte is a two-digit number in base 16, or hexadecimal, with digits ranging from 0 through 9 and A through F for sixteen possible digit values.

If we use three bytes of zeros for black and three bytes of ones for white, our 24-bit color codes range from 000000 to FFFFFF.

Browsing Our Color Palette

We can see and experiment with these colors easily by using a text editor, such as the Notepad utility that comes on a Windows machine, along with a World Wide Web browser such as Netscape Navigator or Microsoft Internet Explorer.

In the code that's used to describe a page on the World Wide Web, a special notation called a *tag* can hold instructions for size and color and other characteristics of the text to be displayed.

NOTE
We'll learn more about HTML tags in Chapter 17.

One of the attributes that can be controlled with HTML markup tags is the color of the text. The format of the tag that's used to do this is `COLOR="RRGGBB"` (with two bytes of hexadecimal digit for each of the three color components).

We can build a file like this:

```
<HTML>
<BODY>
<B>
<FONT SIZE=30>
<FONT COLOR="000000">Hello</FONT>
<FONT COLOR="FF0000">Hello</FONT>
<FONT COLOR="00FF00">Hello</FONT>
<FONT COLOR="0000FF">Hello</FONT>
<FONT COLOR="444444">Hello</FONT>
<FONT COLOR="888888">Hello</FONT>
<FONT COLOR="CCCCCC">Hello</FONT>
</FONT>
</B>
</BODY>
</HTML>
```

and we can see the results on our screen, as shown in Figure 3.5.

A color of 000000, for example, appears as black; FF0000 (with all eight red bits and no others turned on) appears as red; 00FF00 (with all eight green bits on) appears as green; 444444 and 888888 are among the many possible shades of neutral gray.

Sometimes, Bits Are Just Bits

We often talk about bits and bytes as if they always had some kind of numeric value. It's true that a number corresponds to any combination of bits; for example, 10100100101010100101 (which I just made up by banging the 1 and 0 keys at random) can represent the decimal number 674,469.

Sometimes, though, it's more useful to think of a string of bits as a collection of separate "yes" and "no" items. We already saw, for example, that a 24-bit string can represent three separate color values, stuck together like cars on a freight train. We can let individual bits represent different pieces of data, individually or in groups of varying length, but all combined into a single binary word or other unit.

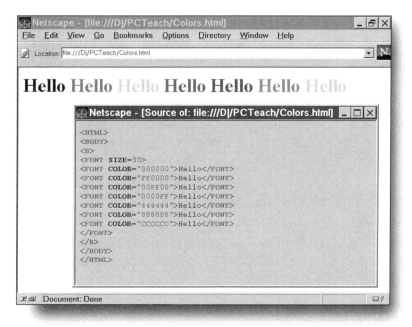

FIGURE 3.5
This Web-style page uses byte-sized codes (actually, six bytes apiece) to represent different colors or shades of gray.

Just the Facts, Please

Suppose that we wanted to describe the members of a club. Our members might be male or female (0 or 1, two possibilities), voting or nonvoting (0 or 1, two possibilities), senior or junior (0 or 1, two possibilities). A member might be in arrears on payment of dues, paid for the current year, or a lifetime member (00, 01, or 11, three possibilities, leaving the 10 code unused).

We could describe each member with a bit string: a gender bit, a voting bit, a seniority bit, and a 2-bit finance field. For example, a male, voting, senior member with lifetime status might have the code 00011, and a female, voting, junior member who has only paid for the current year might have the code 10101.

A bit-string representation lets us ask many questions about our members, with great efficiency, by using Boolean algebra: a kind of mathematics of truth and falsity named after mathematician George Boole (who developed his ideas in the 1800s, long before electronic computers were envisioned).

Let George (Boole) Do It

For example, we might want to find all of our male senior members who are not lifetime members. In Boolean terms, we are looking for all of the members whose bit strings have the pattern 0x00x—where I've used an x for "don't care."

Boolean algebra has its own ideas of adding and multiplying values. Boolean negation, or the NOT operator, just flips a value from true to false in the same way that a minus sign flips an ordinary number from positive to negative. In binary terms, NOT 0 is 1 and NOT 1 is 0.

Boolean addition behaves like the English word "or." If either A or B is true, then A OR B is true. In binary terms, we're saying that 0 OR 0 = 0, 0 OR 1 = 1, 1 OR 0 = 1, 1 OR 1 = 1.

The Boolean version of multiplication behaves like the English word "and." Only if A and B are both true will A AND B be true. In binary terms, 0 AND 0 = 0, 0 AND 1 = 0, 1 AND 0 = 0, 1 AND 1 = 1.

Picture-Perfect Bits

Another Boolean operation that's useful to computers is the "exclusive or," or XOR. The expression A XOR B only yields "true" if exactly one of the values A or B is true. If A and B are the same, regardless of whether they're true or false, then A XOR B is false. If A and B are different, regardless of which one is true, then A XOR B is true. The XOR operator is quite important in creating animated graphics.

We use XOR in animation because it lets us put a figure on a background and then remove the figure and restore the original background before we move the figure to its next position (creating an illusion of motion).

For example, suppose that our "moving" object is a white X-shaped figure, and suppose (for simplicity) that this is a black-and-white picture. We only need one bit of information to represent the choice between black and white at each tiny point in our image.

Our X-shaped moving object might look, as a pattern of bits in memory, like this:

```
0000000000
0000000000
0011001100
0011001100
0000110000
0000110000
```

```
0011001100
0011001100
0000000000
0000000000
```

Imagine that this figure moves across a background that is dark below and light above, such as a drawing with ground under sky. The background might look like this:

```
1111111111
1111111111
1111111111
1111111111
0000000000
0000000000
0000000000
0000000000
0000000000
0000000000
```

When the moving figure moves across the background, we XOR the figure with the background to produce a 1 wherever their bits are different, and a 0 wherever their bits are the same, like this:

0000000000	XOR	1111111111	=	1111111111
0000000000		1111111111		1111111111
0011001100		1111111111		1100110011
0011001100		1111111111		1100110011
0000110000		1111111111		1111001111
0000110000		0000000000		0000110000
0011001100		0000000000		0011001100
0011001100		0000000000		0011001100
0000000000		0000000000		0000000000
0000000000		0000000000		0000000000

If you look at the above result (the right-hand pattern) carefully, you'll see that our X is appearing in its original color of "white" (1s) against the "dark" (0s) ground. Its upper arms, though, are appearing in reverse as dark 0s against the white (1s) sky.

When our X moves to another part of the background, we XOR the moving X's bits against the first XOR's result. This gives us

0000000000	XOR	1111111111	=	1111111111
0000000000		1111111111		1111111111
0011001100		1100110011		1111111111
0011001100		1100110011		1111111111
0000110000		1111001111		1111111111
0000110000		0000110000		0000000000
0011001100		0011001100		0000000000
0011001100		0011001100		0000000000
0000000000		0000000000		0000000000
0000000000		0000000000		0000000000

We see that the original background is restored.

The XOR behavior of inverting colors shows up in a word processor when we select colored text by highlighting it with the mouse or other pointing device. For example, if we have red text, we saw earlier that each red dot on the screen might be represented by the bit pattern 111111110000000000000000—that is, by the maximum possible value for the red component and the smallest possible values of the blue and green components (giving eight bits to each component).

If we drag our mouse across that red text, the word processor can use an XOR operation to show that the text has been highlighted, changing the white background to black and changing the red foreground to its bit-by-bit opposite, 000000001111111111111111 (a bright blue-green). When we *deselect* the red text, another XOR flips the bits back to their original value; we restore the desired red-on-white appearance.

Filtering the Facts

Let's get back to the imaginary task that led me to bring up the subject of Boolean operations. We can use Boolean operators to look for our male, senior, non-lifetime members. As I said previously, this means that we want to find members whose records include the bit string 0x00x, where x means that we don't care.

We can find the pattern we're seeking with a succession of Boolean operations, as follows:

If a member's bit string is abcde, then

(abcde OR 01001)

will yield a1cd1.

That is to say, (a or 0) will have the same value as *a*, (b or 1) will always be *1*, and so on.

Continuing with the result of that initial *or* operation, we can perform a second operation:

(a1cd1 AND 10110)

This yields *a0cd0*, reasoning bit by bit as we did before.

The result of our successive Boolean operations has been to replace the "don't care" bits with 0s. We wanted the other three bits to be 0s, so a0cd0 will be 00000 if we have found a member who matches our search criterion. We can compare our final bit string against 00000 with an efficient hardware operation that is one of the fundamental instructions in any typical microprocessor.

The operations of OR, AND, and comparison against a field of zeros are all quite quick for computer hardware to perform. Building on the ideas we've developed here, we can operate on much longer bit strings for extremely complex pattern-matching tasks; for example, identifying patterns of behavior that indicate poor credit risks when approving or rejecting loan applications.

Bags, Lists, and Other Useful Collections

We've seen that strings of bits, often grouped into bytes and groups of bytes, can represent letters or numbers or colors—in fact, can represent anything if we're willing to accept some degree of chunkiness in the way we represent the world.

Error allowance, I can't say often enough, is the price we pay for representing things with any finite number of bits.

Useful applications of computers will almost always involve some group of information more complex than a simple bit string. Examples of so-called data structures include tables of numbers, lists of names, or paragraphs and pages of text.

When we devise the right approach to packaging information, our programs to manipulate that information almost seem to write themselves. A famous dictum states that data structures plus *algorithms* (procedures that operate on data) equal programs.

Everything begins with data. No information system can be any better than what it eats, so to speak.

Language Shapes Thought

In George Orwell's novel, *1984*, a thought-controlling government believes that people can't think about something if their language has no word to describe that idea.

Like Orwell's fictional "Newspeak," our choice of a programming language can affect our entire approach to a problem. Different programming languages have different "natural" ways of manipulating data.

Bags and Branches

The Smalltalk programming language lets us define bags and sets of data, where a *bag* might have duplicate members while a *set* does not. We can use bags and sets to imitate many real-world systems.

The REXX programming language lets us define many different data collections, including branching structures like the branches and leaves of a sort of data tree. REXX lets us make simple statements about groups of values and then override these general statements with details when we have them.

The Pascal programming language lets us define our own data types, such as days or colors or shapes, and automatically takes care of the gory details of making up underlying bit-codes for each of our invented values. Pascal is a good language for writing programs quickly and for making these programs easy to read and understand, but its convenience and clarity sometimes come at the expense of speed. The best Pascal-based tools, such as Borland Delphi from Inprise, are quite competitive in speed against most versions of performance-at-all-costs languages such as the tersely named C and C++.

Brawn and Brains

By contrast to Pascal, the FORTRAN language (whose name comes from "FORmula TRANslation") won't win any prizes for ease of understanding. FORTRAN is, however, well designed for maximum speed in working with groups of numbers (called *arrays*) that can represent many kinds of quantities; for example, the locations of orbiting satellites or the movements of oil in underground deposits.

The LISP programming language, whose name is a contraction of "LISt Processing," makes lists of values—including lists of lists—and can even build a list of commands that it then turns around and executes as a program. In this way, LISP programs can behave as if they are learning. The ability to "learn" makes LISP a widely favored tool for research into artificial intelligence.

Records: What Makes the World Go Around

Most of us don't need, or want, to write programs in the kind of programming languages I've been describing. Those languages are used, for the most part, by full-time *coders* (a slang term for *programmers*) or by people who write programs as a hobby.

Most PC users create their own solutions with spreadsheets when

NOTE
We'll talk about both spreadsheets and databases, in detail, when we get to Chapters 14 and 15.

they're working with numbers and arithmetic, or with database systems when they're working with lists of grouped information (such as name, address, telephone number, and other personal data).

Before we leave our current topic of data representation, I want to make one key point about databases and the records that they store.

Fixed-Format Fields

You can think of a database as a big table with columns, called *fields*, and rows, called *records*. In a database of club members, each person might be represented by one record. Each record would contain several fields, such as names and addresses and membership expiration dates.

Database tools can do their work more quickly if every record in a collection is laid out in the storage system as a uniform number of bytes. When all of the records in a group are the same length, the database "engine" can jump with great speed between different records, because it's easy to calculate the number of bytes to be skipped between any two records.

Uniform record size turns the record-skipping process into a simple multiplication, unaffected by the contents of individual records. Think of the convenience of flipping through a stack of index cards, some more filled with notes than others, compared to the greater difficulty of finding something in a single long list of entries that might have different lengths.

Please Fill In This Form

If every record is going to get the same amount of storage space, a database designer has to decide at the beginning how many letters to allow in a person's last name, for example. If a database designer allows for a 40-character last name when the average last name is perhaps only half that length, the average record will be wasting half of its allocated space.

If you have an unusually long last name, and you've often had occasion to curse the fill-in forms that don't leave adequate space, you now know why this happens. The paper form that you're filling in reflects the design of some database, somewhere, whose designer was trying to keep someone's storage costs under control.

Why There's a "Y2K" Problem

When the first generation of database systems was being designed, several decades ago, storage space was far more costly than it is today. Not only did designers try to avoid leaving more space than most people would need, as we discussed just above, but they also avoided recording information in individual records that was identical in all of their records.

For example, databases often did not bother recording all four digits of a year, because all of the years in the database began with the identical digits 19. Thereby hang too many tales.

It Made Sense at the Time

Old software, designed in the 1960s or even the 1950s, saved storage space by recording only the last two digits of a year. The leading "19" digits were assumed.

Incredibly, the U.S. government's Federal Information Processing Standards *specified* a date storage format of two digits each for year, month, and day. This decision wasn't made in 1950, when people might have been forgiven for assuming that technology would replace everything before the 21st century became a near-term problem. The two-digit year became a mandated format for federal government records, or for records involved in federal government transactions, beginning in 1970.

One would think that anyone who went to the trouble of writing a federal regulation on this subject would have thought a little farther ahead.

Sometimes, one can deal with two-digit years by applying a *sliding century window*. For example, one might assume that in the year 1998, any two-digit year less than 64 refers to the 21st century.

There are various conventions as to how a century window should choose its boundaries. Entering the numbers 12/31/29 into Microsoft Excel 97 on a day in April 1998, I found that it was interpreting this to mean a date in the year 2029. Entering the numbers 12/31/30 gave me a date in the year 1930.

If you don't specify a date display format that shows all four digits of the year, you might not realize that century window effects are taking place behind the scenes.

It's Much Worse Than You Think

Software does many other strange things with dates. In Sun's Java programming language, for example, there's a predefined Date data type. But, despite the promise that Java runs the same way everywhere, Date values behaved (when I last tested them) in different ways under different versions of Java.

For example, under Sun's version of Java, the date and time that came 128 seconds after midnight (in the release that I last tested) was 11:57:52 *p.m.* of the *date before*. In other words, after counting up to 127 seconds after midnight, the computer added one more second and wound up at *minus* 128 seconds relative to the midnight starting point.

As a newly minted expert in the behavior of binary numbers, you recognize this misbehavior. It's what happens when people aren't careful about carrying their ones. A one has been carried into the sign bit, turning a number negative instead of making it larger by one unit. The last two lines of the following table show what has happened.

Simple binary addition makes a "signed" number wrap around, turning into the most negative value possible for that many bits—making time, in this case, run backward.

Binary Code for "seconds after midnight"	Signed decimal value: "–" is past
1000 0000	−128
1000 0001	−127

continues

continued

Binary Code for "seconds after midnight"	Signed decimal value: "–" is past
1000 0010	–126
1111 1111	–1
0000 0000	0
0000 0001	1
0000 0010	2
0111 1111	127
1000 0000	–128

By contrast, Microsoft's version of Java's Date data type behaved in my tests as one would hope—it made time keep moving forward.

Other interesting quirks exist in computers' representations of dates. Some people have long used the year 99 as a special code. For example, an expiration date entered as 9/9/99 is a signal that a certain data record never expires."

People will pay dearly for programmers' convenience-driven decisions involving special codes that look like valid dates. Programmers would have saved us vast amounts of trouble if they had devised better ways to encode special situations without using values that would someday be legitimate and perfectly ordinary date or date/time entries.

It is impossible to anticipate all of the ways that computers in various tasks and situations will begin to act oddly, or fail to function at all, as arbitrary date conventions begin to break down near the end of the decade.

FEATURED PRODUCT: IST CENTURY PACKS

If you have a business that runs on PCs, you might just be starting to think about the number and variety of your PC-based work products—spreadsheets, databases, and so on—that might be contaminated with ambiguous dates or with formulas that won't work correctly in the year 2000 and thereafter.

A lucrative practice in "Y2K remediation" is growing and becoming more profitable as the urgency increases with the year 2000 getting ominously close. Rather than paying a consultant by the hour, some businesses are looking for automatic tools that can crunch their way through an office full of PC files and report potential problems.

Though expensive compared to most PC software, these Y2K tools can be cost effective. One set of tools that I've examined are the Year 2000 Packs from IST Development Inc.

Initially released in early 1998, the $6,000 package comes in different varieties for diagnosing problems in different families of PC software files. I looked at the version for Microsoft files, which automatically examines Excel spreadsheets, Access databases, and FoxPro databases. Figure 3.6 shows part of a report produced by the automated analysis.

The IST product looks at spreadsheet formulas, macros, procedure files, and other things that we won't discuss until much later in this book. It's not an electronic mind-reader; for example, it thinks that the word "know" might indicate a formula that's sensitive to date-handling rules, because "know" includes the trigger word "now."

The automatic report that IST's product creates can also suffer from tunnel vision. It shows you the tiny neighborhood around a potential problem, sometimes without enough context to decide if the problem is significant.

Products such as the IST Century Packs illuminate the difficulty of knowing a Y2K problem when you see one. On PCs, however, most Y2K problems will appear as obvious errors, not as sneaky little "gotchas" or total system breakdowns. In general, Y2K is much more a problem of massive corporate systems and industrial operations than of home or desktop PC applications.

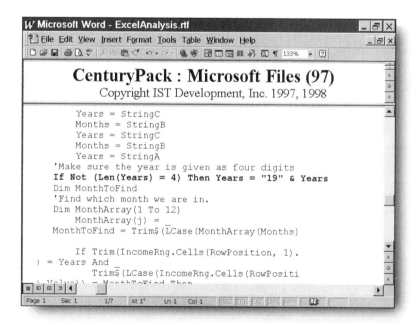

FIGURE 3.6
This automated report comes from IST Development's Year 2000 Pack for Microsoft files and shows potential Year 2000 (Y2K) problems in an Excel spreadsheet.

A Compressed Tour of Data Compression

Before we end our discussion of raw data, we're going to look at important techniques that we can use to package the stuff for convenient transportation.

It might seem that binary data, being made from the most efficient set of symbols we could devise, is always going to be in its most compact form.

We can quickly devise some examples, though, of data that wastes a lot of space—or time—if we're sending it across a communication link such as the Internet.

Large Economy Bytes

For example, suppose we have a file that contains the single letter *A*. There is no room to make this any more compact.

If we have another file, though, that contains a hundred repetitions of the letter A, there is obviously room for improvement. It would be much faster if we could say, "Take the next thing and make 99 copies before you come back for the item that follows."

If we have, not a hundred, but a thousand repetitions of the same letter A, we should be able to describe this collection with almost no further increase in the volume of the data we store or send. We just say 999 copies instead of 99 copies.

Can we get this kind of efficiency from a file compression program? This type of program is often used by people sending large files, such as (ahem!) chapters of a book, across the phone lines from one computer to another.

Zipping Right Along

One popular file compression program is WinZip, a $29 utility software product from Nico Mak Computing of Mansfield, Connecticut. I used WinZip version 6.3 to compress three files: one containing a single letter A, one containing a hundred of that letter, and one containing a thousand.

The one-letter file did not compress at all. The hundred-letter file compressed to only six bytes, compared to its original size of a hundred bytes. The thousand-letter file compressed to just eleven bytes, almost a 99% reduction in size.

You might wonder if it's all that useful to detect repetition in files—real documents don't contain long strings of repeated letters. Compression algorithms gain more power, though, by detecting more complex forms of wasted space, such as repeated groups.

For example, if we create a file that contains a hundred repetitions of *AB*, WinZip will squeeze this file down to seven bytes. That's just one more byte than the file that contained a hundred copies of A.

We can see that WinZip is simply encoding the same instruction, "Give me 99 more of these," with the original pattern now being AB instead of A.

A Spreadsheet Experiment

Even in completely random text, a compression program can find random chances to pack data into a smaller number of bytes.

I'm going to take this opportunity to show you how ordinary PC software—specifically, a spreadsheet—can be used as a tool to explore this sort of thing.

Most spreadsheets have some kind of random-number generator that we can use, for example, to simulate events that will fall into a predictable range.

NOTE
We'll see many applications of random-number generation in Chapter 14.

It's also common for spreadsheets to have some kind of function for displaying the letter of the alphabet that matches a number's value, using the ASCII code we discussed in Chapter 1.

In Microsoft's Excel spreadsheet, the formula `CHAR(INT(RAND()*26)+65)` means the same thing as the following list of instructions:

- Pick a random number between 0 and 1. A typical value of RAND() might be 0.769128, but a cell that contains this function takes on a different value whenever you recalculate the spreadsheet.

- Multiply the randomly chosen number by 26. This gives you a number that is not less than zero but is less than 26.

- Chop off the fractional part of the number that you've just produced and then add 65. This gives you a number that is the ASCII code for one of the uppercase letters, because A has an ASCII value of 65 and the other capital letters follow in sequence.

If we enter this formula in cell A1 of the spreadsheet and copy it to rows 2 through 1000, we will have 1000 randomly chosen letters. This random text does have some accidental patterns. There are letters in pairs and triplets, for example, and other accidental (but still compressible) arrangements.

If we copy this column into a text-editing program that can wrap these letters into a single long line of text, we will have a torture test for any file-compression program. When I use the approach that I've just described to build a file of 1000 random letters, and I feed the result to WinZip, it zips 1000 bytes of random-order letters into a little more than 620 bytes of compressed data. The number changes, up and down, for different random strings, but it's fairly consistent.

Reducing 1000 bytes to 620 is only a 38% reduction, but compressing a large file could make the difference between half an hour and less than twenty minutes of transfer time. And this is clearly a worst-case scenario for tasks that involve the compression of text. Normal words and sentences are much less random in composition.

If I change the preceding formula to `CHAR(INT(RAND()*13)+65)`, generating only letters from A through M instead of the entire alphabet, you might think I would wind up with more cases of coincidental repetition. You'd be right.

A file of 1000 random letters that only uses A through M shrinks by 47% when zipped, compared to the 38% reduction observed with files using all 26 letters. The more repetition a file contains, the easier it is to squeeze that file down to "give me some copies of this."

Pictures and Patterns

Unlike text, graphics files normally contain large amounts of repetition. This might be due, for example, to backgrounds of continuous uniform color.

To see what kind of compression we can get when working with graphics files, I used the Paint utility program that comes with Windows to put a single black dot in the middle of a white background measuring 400 × 300 dots.

When I saved this file as a 24-bit bitmap file, I was using 24 bits to store every single dot of color in this drawing as an independent piece of data. The principle is exactly the same as the 24-bit colors we used in our file of multicolored Hello's in the earlier section, "Browsing Our Color Palette."

My 24-bit graphic file was huge, amassing 360,000 bytes: 400 times 300 times 24, divided by 8 to convert to bytes from bits.

Actually, the size was 360,054 bytes, because the file also contained the information needed to arrange the dots into a 400 × 300 rectangle and to do other "housekeeping" tasks.

Looking at the enormous file with DEBUG, I confirmed that it contained almost nothing but strings of 1s, representing thousands of repetitions of 111111111111111111111111 (or FFFFFF, when viewed as hexadecimal numbers).

Buried in the middle of the file, like a tiny speck of pimento in an olive the size of a beach ball, were three bytes of 0s (see Figure 3.7). What a wasteful way to convey information.

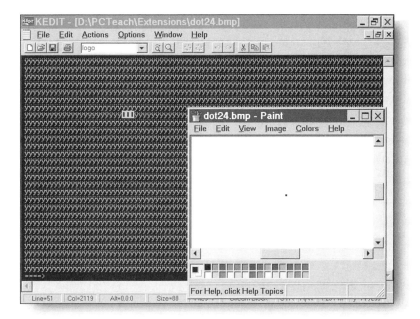

FIGURE 3.7
There it is: one little group of three null (ASCII 00) bytes (upper left), representing 24 bits of 0s embedded in 2,879,976 bits of 1s. This 24-bit chunk represents one black dot on a field of white (lower right) when we use 24 bits to represent each dot's color without using any kind of data-compression scheme.

Slimming the Bits

One way to reduce data volume is just to store fewer bits in the first place. This drawing contained just a black dot on a white background, so I didn't need 24 bits to represent the colors in the drawing. When I stored the same drawing as a mono-chrome bitmap (each point either black or white, a 1-bit decision), it took up less than 16,000 bytes: 1/24th the size, as you would expect.

It's still silly to store all those white background points individually, and you might well expect that zipping these files would produce dramatic results.

Zipping the 24-bit version squeezed it down to only 413 bytes; zipping the monochrome version yielded a compressed file of only 134 bytes. These are compressions of better than 99%, on the same order as those we obtained with our files of nothing but the letter A.

Squeezing the Bits

It would be nice if we could store pictures on a Web page, for example, with compressed efficiency but look at them without having to go through the steps to decompress a file. Several compressed-file formats have been devised for this purpose, including one called Graphics Interchange Format (GIF).

GIF, like the format used in zipping files, is a *loss-less* format. This means that a GIF file, when decompressed, restores all of the detail originally captured.

NOTE
There are many graphics compression formats that are more aggressive than GIF, tolerating some loss of fine detail to obtain more data compression. These work well for photographs, where minimal blurring of fine lines isn't readily noticed, but it doesn't work well for sharp-edged computer graphics or line art.

When we store our test image—black dot on white background—as a GIF file, it's less than 1,400 bytes in size. That's much better than even the monochrome bitmap, but it's ten times the size of the monochrome bitmap after zipping.

Tangling the Bits

Well, we can always zip the GIF file if we want to send it to someone… right? Surprise: The zipped version of the GIF file is *not* smaller than the zipped version of the monochrome bitmap!

The zipped GIF file is only 50% smaller than the unzipped version, compared to the 99% shrinkage we achieved when we zipped our bitmap files.

Why did our GIF file shrink so little? Because the GIF file had already been compressed, and it therefore contained decompression instructions as well as data.

A GIF file is designed to avoid wasting space with redundant information. The process of encoding a GIF file leaves WinZip with a much more difficult job than when it is compressing a nice, boring, highly repetitive bitmap.

What we've just seen is a common occurrence. Too many cooks spoil the broth, they say, and programs that try to do similar things can get in each other's way when they're used in combination.

Beginning with raw data and knowing exactly what you want to do with it gives you better results than piling one tool on top of another.

FEATURED PRODUCT: NICO MAK WINZIP

I've used Nico Mak Computing Inc.'s WinZip to illustrate the basic ideas of data compression, so let me tell you more about the product and why you might want to have it on your PC.

As we mentioned earlier in the book, PC files sometimes have problems traveling by electronic mail, because some email systems assume that they're only sending ASCII text information. ASCII, as we've noted in this chapter, needs only seven of the eight bits in a byte to represent letters and numerals and punctuation. Some systems assume that they can use the eighth bit for other purposes, such as detecting errors during data transmission.

Because some communication networks take liberties with what they think are "spare" bits, converting a file to a format that won't be harmed by eighth-bit alterations is sometimes useful. That conversion process is called *uuencoding*—pronounced "you-you-encoding"—and it's one of the facilities of WinZip (in addition to WinZip's main function of compressing files).

Since uuencode conversion adds *scratch* bits to a file, you might wonder if it makes files get bigger. In general, uuencoding enlarges a file by about one-third. Yes, Virginia, there are file *expansion* programs as well as file compression programs.

File compression makes it easier to make a backup copy of a large file (such as a detailed image) that will fit on a floppy disk. Your backup storage plan should give you backups that won't be destroyed by some event (such as a fire) that might destroy your computer. A floppy disk can easily go to some off-site location.

Even with compression, though, a zipped file might be larger than a single floppy disk's capacity. An especially helpful feature of WinZip is the way it automatically "spans" a single, compressed *archive* file onto more than one floppy disk. WinZip lets you see the entire archive you're building, or just consulting, in a convenient point-and-click control panel that's shown in Figure 3.8.

The zipped file format often shows up on electronic bulletin boards because compressed files can travel from one computer to another in much less time. WinZip has convenience features for working with your Web-viewing software, automatically unzipping a file while you're bringing it down to your machine.

WinZip also works with popular virus-scanning utilities, whose role we'll discuss in Chapter 17.

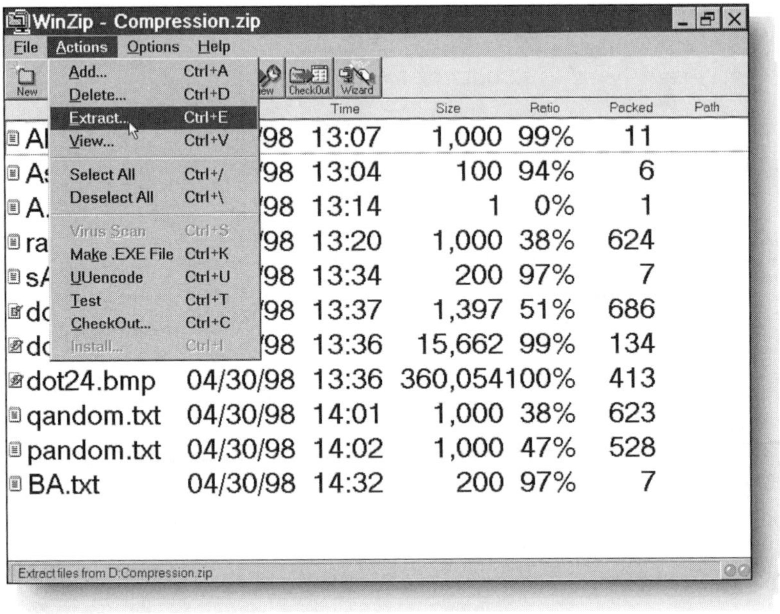

FIGURE 3.8

In this photo, WinZip is ready to rebuild a compressed file from its space-saving form to its full-length form, making the file ready to use with its original creating program. The window shows statistics on WinZip's success in compressing a collection of files into a single convenient archive file.

What We've Learned

The best and worst characteristics of computers are largely due to things we learned in this chapter.

We've seen why "digital is better," in that digital data representations are immune to the accumulation of noise and error that afflicts most other ways of representing information.

We've also seen that digital methods are compromised by their "chunking" of the real world's continuous behaviors. It takes more bits, meaning more computations and more storage space and more data-transfer time, to represent things like color in ways that our senses will find natural and convenient.

We can use the power of the PC itself, however, to analyze collections of data and look for opportunities to pack the same information into less space.

We've seen that the most common tools on PCs—spreadsheets, for example—can be used in uncommon ways to generate test data that lets us explore low-level behaviors. Finally, we've seen that PC utilities (file compression tools or graphical editing programs) behave in ways that make perfect sense when we understand the behavior of the bytes under the hood.

4

> *"I sit at one of
> these analyzers and
> nanoseconds [billionths
> of a second] are wide.
> I mean, you can see
> them go by. . . Time
> in a computer is an
> interesting concept."*
>
> —Ed Rasala,
> Computer Engineer
> (quoted by Tracy Kidder), in *The
> Soul of a New Machine*

The Heart of the Machine

THROUGHOUT THIS BOOK, we learn how a PC behaves by working with things that we can see (or pretend to see). The Windows user interface, the file system under that interface, and even the bits and bytes inside those files, all have behaviors that we can inspect (or feel as if we're inspecting) and that we can understand by that inspection.

The chips inside your PC might seem to defy our approach of hands-on learning. A microchip is a tiny, densely packed city of sub-microscopic devices, whose complex interactions can give any brain a strain.

When we finish this chapter, though, you will understand the essential workings of modern microprocessors and memories: the components whose speed and capacity determine most of what a PC can do.

A Quick Review: The Trail That Brought Us Here

In my sixteen-year process of learning how PCs function, I've found that nothing really sinks in until I need to know it. It's as if my brain needs to know that there's a hole to fill, needs to have a place that's ready to capture new information instead of letting it just run off.

In case your brain works like mine, I've tried to follow a consistent strategy in this book of showing you *why* you needed to know things before I've tried to explain their details. We began the book at the outermost layers of convenience provided by Microsoft Windows. We could have remained at that level and gone straight to the topics later in this book if Windows were always successful in its pretense of what a PC really does.

We Found the Cracks in Windows

We quickly established by our experiments in earlier chapters, though, that Windows is an incomplete false front. The fakeries of Windows are all too easy to expose.

To use our PCs effectively, and to get our jobs done when Windows can't hide the gaps in its design, we need to know more than Windows is willing or able to tell us.

We Found That Files Are Faulty

We moved down, therefore, to the next layer, where the "real" file system lives. We had to do this so that we could deal, for example, with the way Windows uses pieces of filenames (sometimes hidden pieces) to make important decisions about how it will use our information.

We found out that even the file system is a partial reality at best. We saw that different generations of software might see different names on a single file, or different names on identically copied files. We saw that a destroyed file, apparently overwritten with a smaller amount of new data, might actually have large portions that aren't disturbed. We also saw that an erased file doesn't actually disappear.

But We Can Believe in Bytes

It's important to see and understand the truth about what a PC does when it thinks we're not looking. To do this, we descended in Chapters 1 through 3 to the level where useful but make-believe objects (such as documents and databases) reveal themselves to be just different assemblies of bytes (at eight binary digits, or bits, to the byte).

For example,

- We found that a black dot on a screen of white is really just a clump of 00000000 bytes in the middle of a field of 11111111s.

- We found that different-colored text on a Web page is merely using a 3-byte (24-bit) code representing the red, green, and blue components of color for the PC to mix on its screen.

- We found that an erased file leaves its bytes right where they were before the erasure. The only change is a special byte at the head of the filename, signaling that these bytes of disk space are available for other use if needed.

Computing: It's Just Byte Processing

In short, we've seen that all of the words and pictures on our PC screens, and all of the contents of our various files, resolve into bytes: 8-bit bundles of binary data.

Now that we understand the byte-by-byte nature of the PC's raw material, we're ready to look at the processes that move the bytes around and put them where they can do useful things. We're ready to look at the piece of your PC that makes it a "computer": the tightly coupled system of processor, memory, and critical components in between.

Chips Don't Do Anything New

A processor's appearance (see Figures 4.1 and 4.2) isn't very informative, but software tools will let us expose its inner workings. We'll begin by comparing the processor's operations to familiar computational tools: paper, pencil, and a pocket calculator.

We'll see that what a processor does is nothing really new. A processor chip does things that we already understand; its importance comes from its capability to do these things in a fast, cheap, easily controllable form.

FIGURE 4.1
This is what a microprocessor looks like when it's installed in your PC. What you see here is a "packaged" chip: It doesn't tell you anything about the structure or function of the processor, any more than a picture of a person tells you anything about the design of a human brain.

FIGURE 4.2
This is a "bare" chip, or "die," outside its package. This isn't a Pentium; I used a much, much larger chip so that some of its structure would show without a microscope. An expert on microprocessor design could look at this picture and tell you, in general terms, which parts of this chip are performing what functions—simply from the appearance of certain areas, their texture, and their shape.

Big Chips Need Little Chips

<$`ICP Us;(Ce ntral pro- cessing Units)>

The central processor can't do a thing without a lot of help from other PC sub-systems. A central processor is like the hub of a wheel: its smooth operation at the center keeps the whole thing moving, but a wheel also needs a rim to roll on.

A PC's processor needs memory, a video display adapter, and other hardware at its "rim" to interact with the user and with other hardware devices. We'll look at some of the crucial connections between the hub and the rim before we get to the end of this chapter.

NOTE
The chip shown in Figure 4.2 is actually glued to the cover of a notebook, the 1997 edition of a portfolio produced each year by MicroDesign Resources for attendees at their annual conference. Many in the computer business consider this a must-attend event: it often includes the first public announcements of important new processor designs.

Your PC Is More Than Its CPU

It's common for people to talk about a PC as if its only important component were the single central chip. People sometimes say, "We bought a 233 MHz Pentium II," not even mentioning the amount or the type of their new PC's memory.

Up to a point, however, a given amount of extra money spent on additional memory will improve task performance more than spending the same money on the next faster model of microprocessor. We'll explore the reason for this behavior later in this chapter when we talk about *virtual memory*, a key ingredient in helping a PC handle worst-case workloads.

In this chapter, we'll give full credit to the vital role of the central processing unit, which from now on I'll just call the CPU. At the same time, we'll see how misleading it is to view a PC in narrowly focused, processor-centric terms.

Computer Architecture: Registers and Instructions

Unless you keep a scanning electron microscope in your kitchen, it's not convenient to look inside a PC's microchips. Instead, we'll start our exploration by working with models of chips.

Our models will have two advantages over the real thing. They'll be big enough to see without an electron microscope, and they'll be easy to handle—because you use them all the time. Our model of a PC CPU is just an ordinary pocket calculator; our model of its memory is just a sheet of stationery.

Meet the Pretendium Processor

Please get out a calculator, or imagine that you have one in front of you. (If nothing else is handy, you can use the Calculator accessory program that comes on a Windows PC.) The calculator will be our "processor" (you can think of it as a "Pretendium").

Put a sheet of paper next to the calculator and get out a pencil or pen. The paper will play the role of the PC's memory—that is, the kind of memory that people are talking about when they say their PC has "16 megabytes of RAM" (or more, or less).

On your sheet of paper, write down the following problem:

$$\begin{array}{r} 1 \\ +2 \\ \hline \end{array}$$

Even a simple arithmetic problem has all of the elements required to demonstrate what happens in your PC's CPU and memory subsystems.

Solve the preceding problem with your calculator. On most calculators, you'll press the keys 1 + 2 =; alternatively, you might have the type of calculator that uses the keystrokes 1 ENTER 2 + to get an identical answer.

Write down the answer, 3, on your sheet of paper, below the line under the 2. Now what, exactly, have we done here?

From the beginning:

- We used an external storage device (the paper) to record the values of the data on which we wanted to operate (our *operands*).

- We copied the values of our operands, 1 and 2, into "on-chip" storage compartments (by entering them into the calculator).

- We gave the "processor" an instruction to perform with our operands (by pressing the + key).

- We copied the result back to our external storage, leaving us free to solve other problems with the CPU while preserving an "off-chip" record of our answer.

We've just described all of the things that the central processor and memory do inside your PC. The differences between your PC and a paper-and-calculator combination are just matters of speed, complexity, and ease of doing the same thing many times.

A Real CPU at Work

In Figure 4.3, you see the screen of a PC running a program to do the same operation we just performed with paper and calculator. At lower right, you see the "human readable" version of the program, written in a programming language called C++.

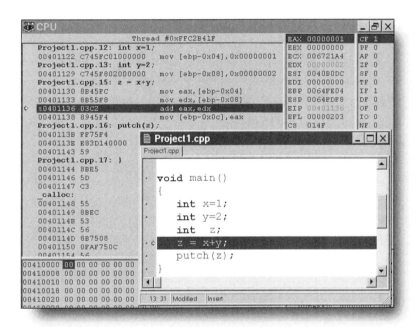

FIGURE 4.3
A program, as a programmer would write it (lower right) and as a machine would run it (upper left), can perform the same simple addition, 1 + 2 = 3, that we easily do with paper, pencil, and calculator—while showing us the fundamentals of far more complex operations.

It's easy to write C++ programs that look like an industrial accident in a punctuation factory, but I think you'll find this program understandable even if you've never programmed in this or any other language. In fact, this program is so simple that it looks almost the same in almost every common programming language.

Anatomy of a Program

Starting at the beginning of our program,

- We see that we have something named `main`, which must be the piece of the program that puts everything else in motion. Bigger programs are broken into several named sections to make their organization easier to understand, with `main` acting merely as master of ceremonies. The program here is so simple that the `main` section just does it all.

- We see that we have things we're calling `x`, `y`, and `z`. We're saying, up front, that `x` is 1 and `y` is 2. Because we don't change these values, we can say that `x` and `y` are *constants*.

- Our program also says that `x`, `y`, and `z` are all a type of thing that's called an `int` (for *integer*). From our discussion in Chapter 3, you'll understand that integers can be stored as simple binary numbers, without the complications of storing a number with decimal places.

- We see that `z` will get the value obtained by adding `x` to `y`. Because the value of `z` changes during the course of this program, we call `z` a *variable*.

- We see that we will send the value of `z` to the PC's display by performing a `putch` ("put character") operation. This program doesn't need any *input* statements, because it has all of its knowledge (the values of `x` and `y`) built in, but the program does perform *output* with `putch`.

- We see the word `void` at the very beginning of the program: this word means that this program will give no reply to any other program that asks this *adder* to run. You probably know some people who act that way.

Our adder has only two outcomes, both of the type called *side effects*, by which we mean that the state of the machine is changed when the program runs, in a way that persists even after the program ends. The first side effect is the storage of values in memory; the second side effect is the sending of the value of `z` to our PC's display.

Machine Instructions Control the CPU

The upper-left window in Figure 4.3 interleaves two types of instruction. The boldfaced lines are commands in the form that a programmer writes, repeating the program text at lower right; the commands between the boldfaced lines translate the program into the language of the machine.

The first boldfaced line ends with the command, `x=1`. Look at the machine instruction that follows this line. That machine instruction moves a value (hence the instruction's name, mov) into a location in the PC's off-chip memory. In this context, *off-chip* means anywhere that's not on the central processor chip, even though memory itself is also a kind of integrated circuit chip.

The mov instruction needs a memory address as its target. The instruction calculates the address of that target, a location in the PC's memory banks, by starting at a reference address. It finds the reference address in a special storage compartment on the CPU chip. The name of that compartment is EBP.

The instruction subtracts 4 from the value of EBP and stores the value 1 (which is what we assigned to x) in the memory location that has the calculated target address.

The expression that calculates the address reads [ebp-0x04], calculating the address that is four bytes below the reference location. The 0x prefix on the numeric value 4 tells us that we're seeing the displacement from our starting address in the hexadecimal form that we learned in Chapter 3.

At the moment, it doesn't matter that we're using hexadecimal, because 4 is 4 in either base ten or base 16. By the time we get farther down into the memory bank, this difference will be important.

It's Just Like Using Paper

The process that I've just described might seem very dense and complicated, but we can break things down into simple steps and compare the operations of the chip against what you did before with pencil, paper, and calculator.

When you got out a fresh sheet of paper, you could think of the top of that sheet as your starting point for recording information during the course of solving your problem. The top of the paper is your reference point, like the value in storage compartment EBP.

When you moved down from the top of the sheet to the first line on the paper, you were doing the same thing that our first machine instruction did when it subtracted 4 from the value in EBP. The machine instruction subtracted 4 because the normal "word" of data on a Pentium chip (which is what I'm using in this example) is 32 bits, or four bytes, in size. The machine is giving itself four bytes of room to store the value that we've named x.

The cryptic statement mov [ebp-0x04],0x00000001 is just the machine-language way of saying "Start at the top of your working memory area, go down four bytes to leave room for a 32-bit value, and store the value 1." As I said a moment ago, the 0x prefix in 0x04 and 0x00000001 just means that we're using the hexadecimal codes we learned to interpret in Chapter 3.

Our next machine-language statement goes down four more bytes to leave room for storing the value of **y**, just as you went down one more line on your sheet of paper to make room for writing the **2**.

Putting It All Together

Our next boldface line, **z = x+y**, indicates that we've gotten to the good part. After that boldface line come four machine instructions.

The first of these four instructions looks at the location of operand x, which you'll recall was four bytes below our reference address in compartment **EBP**. The instruction copies the 4-byte value it finds at the x location, using the processor's **mov** operation, into the 4-byte compartment (a 32-bit *register*) on the chip. The name of that destination register on our Pentium CPU is **EAX**.

Notice the display at upper right in Figure 4.3 (shown earlier), where we see eight digits (two hexadecimal digits per byte) to the right of the label **EAX**; these digits read **00000001**. We see that our first operand value is ready for addition to proceed.

The second machine instruction (in this group of four instructions) looks at the location of **y**, eight bytes below our reference address. It copies the 4-byte value at the y location (where we stored the value **2**) into another on-chip compartment called **EDX**.

Notice that the digits next to **EDX** at upper right have assumed the value **00000002**. In the binary hardware inside the actual chip, we're really storing a set of electrical states that we might write out as 00000000000000000000000000000010 (32 bits in all, with the binary value "one 2 plus zero 1s"). The hexadecimal version takes up less space on the screen and is easier to read.

In Figure 4.3, we've just gotten to the instruction that will perform the addition operation. That instruction is marked by an arrow and a fat dot at the beginning of the line at upper left, and by a little arrow in the "human-readable" instructions at lower right.

FEATURED PRODUCT: BORLAND C++ BUILDER 3

The dot and arrow symbols in Figure 4.3 are aids to tracing the operations of our program. These symbols appear by the grace of a debugger utility, a more advanced version of the DEBUG program that we used in Chapter 1.

The debugger that I used in Figure 4.3 is part of Borland C++ Builder 3, which is my personal recommendation for a C++ programming product if you're thinking of learning this widely used language.

I don't really like the C++ language as a tool for high-level problem solving, but C++ is popular both for intricate programming tasks and for introducing student programmers to fundamentals of this exacting craft.

C++ has this dual role for a single reason: it lets programmers say exactly what they want their hardware to do, in a way that's portable from one type of hardware to another. That is, I can easily translate a C++ program into the machine instruction formats that are used by a PC, a Macintosh, or almost any other type of computer.

I recommend Borland C++ Builder 3 because it does an unusually good job of letting you write a wide range of programs. C++ Builder has automatic aids for getting started on anything from the simplest program, such as the demonstration I'm conducting in this chapter, to a full-featured Windows application (as shown in Figure 4.4) or even an exotic Internet tool. Moreover, C++ Builder 3 is available in a basic package that sells for under $100.

The entry-level version of C++ Builder 3 is a good choice if all you want is a facility for exploring fundamental computing and programming concepts, much more easily than you can do that with DEBUG. If you later decide to take on more challenging projects, higher-level editions of the product will give you the additional tools to do just that.

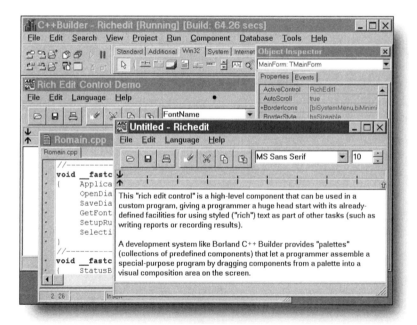

FIGURE 4.4
Borland C++ Builder does all that any product can to ease the task of writing simple and intermediate programs in C++. It's convenient for simple jobs, such as the console programs we use in this chapter to illustrate basic PC processor functions, and even for more complex projects such as writing your own word processor by assembling predefined modules (as shown here).

Programs Can Be Destructive

The machine instruction that actually performs our addition here reads add eax,edx. You can think of the instruction in English as saying "Add to EAX the value in EDX."

There's something important happening here: when we do this addition, *we are replacing the previous value* formerly stored in EAX. There will no longer be any copy of the value of x in any compartment on the chip. Anything that looks in EAX, expecting to find the value of x, will get the wrong number.

A *destructive assignment* operation, such as the one I've just described, is a crucial event in many common computer operations. Computers usually do not have enough on-chip storage compartments to give every constant and variable a dedicated location, so programs use the limited set of on-chip storage locations to hold different things at different times in the course of running a program.

It's easy for a complex program to make mistakes because a programmer didn't properly track the changing role of a single storage location.

On-Chip Registers: There Are Never Enough

A lengthy program benefits from having the values it uses right there in on-chip registers, right when it needs them, instead of constantly going off-chip to the PC's memory banks. Reading a value from memory takes much, much longer than using a value already on hand. Off-chip operations dramatically reduce the speed of running a program.

One of the most important decisions involved in designing a new CPU is the question of how many registers to provide. More registers require a larger chip that costs more to make, so we'll never have all of the registers we'd like.

Because registers will always be scarce, our automatic instruction translators (called *compilers*) must assign different registers to hold different combinations of program variables at different times during the run of a program. Efficient register allocation, sometimes guided by specific programmer instructions, is a challenge for both the human part and the software part of any programming system.

Because we have a limited number of registers, the final machine instruction (in the group of four that we've been examining) will "close the books" with one more mov command. The fourth and final instruction copies the value in EAX (which now holds our sum) to a third location in memory, twelve bytes down from our reference address (on the third "line," so to speak, of our electronic scratch paper). This is like writing the 3 at the bottom of the two-number setup shown earlier.

In the figure, we see the instruction calculating a target memory address of [ebp-0x0c]. Remember, 0x0c means the value of the letter C in a hexadecimal numbering system of 0, 1, 2, 3, 4, 5, 6, 7, 8, 9, A, B, C, making 0x0c the same thing as a decimal 12. The expression [ebp-0x0c] means "twelve bytes down from our reference address."

We wind up with our three values, x, y, and z (where z equals x+y), each stored in memory, just as we had them written down on our scratch paper. Figure 4.5 shows the bit-by-bit arrangement, indicating the relationship between byte addresses (relative to EBP), bit values, and variable names (which only exist in the mind of the programmer and in the human-readable version of the program).

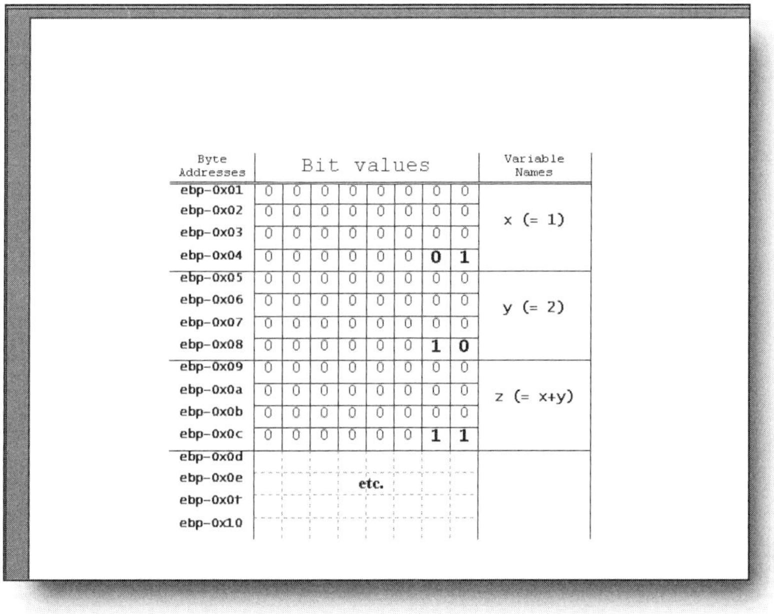

Byte Addresses	Bit values								Variable Names
ebp-0x01	0	0	0	0	0	0	0	0	
ebp-0x02	0	0	0	0	0	0	0	0	x (= 1)
ebp-0x03	0	0	0	0	0	0	0	0	
ebp-0x04	0	0	0	0	0	0	**0**	**1**	
ebp-0x05	0	0	0	0	0	0	0	0	
ebp-0x06	0	0	0	0	0	0	0	0	y (= 2)
ebp-0x07	0	0	0	0	0	0	0	0	
ebp-0x08	0	0	0	0	0	0	**1**	**0**	
ebp-0x09	0	0	0	0	0	0	0	0	
ebp-0x0a	0	0	0	0	0	0	0	0	z (= x+y)
ebp-0x0b	0	0	0	0	0	0	0	0	
ebp-0x0c	0	0	0	0	0	0	**1**	**1**	
ebp-0x0d									
ebp-0x0e			etc.						
ebp-0x0f									
ebp-0x10									

FIGURE 4.5
Easier to read than the C++ debugger's view, this figure shows the relationship between the addresses of bytes (left column), the names of variables (right column), and the actual bit-by-bit values that are all a CPU or memory can really "understand."

We leave behind the value of our sum in the EAX register on our processor chip, just as we left the value 3 displayed on our calculator and ready to use—should we so desire—in further calculations.

Output Tells Us When the Work is Done

When we use a PC to add numbers or to do other useful operations, we don't use a debugger to go inside and read the values stored in memory. We expect the PC to give us the answer on some kind of output device. That's why our simple program concludes with that final statement, `putch(z)`, to write the value of `z` to our output screen.

In Figure 4.6, I've opened a DOS console window (just as we did in Chapter 1) and I have run this program. I allowed the Project Manager in C++ Builder to give the program an automatically chosen name, Project1. The file that contains the readable version of the program is Project1.cpp, where CPP is the common filename extension for a file containing statements (*source code*) in the C++ language. The file that contains the machine instructions for the runnable version of the program is project1.exe, using the "executable" extension that we have seen before. We can run a program by typing the name of its EXE file as a command, as Figure 4.6 shows.

Well? Do we get the reply of 3 that we might hope to obtain by adding 1 and 2?

Ummm, apparently not. We don't get a **3** as our output. We get a ♥, as shown at upper right in Figure 4.6. What the heck is happening?

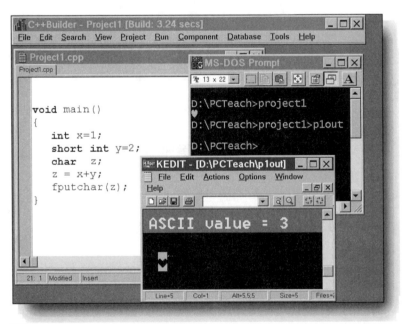

FIGURE 4.6
Our program does the same thing when we use other, shorter types of integer data (left), but it doesn't give us the answer we expect (upper right). We don't get the numeral 3, but rather the byte whose binary value is 3. If we want "human-readable output," we have to work for it.

A little valentine greeting might be a welcome gesture on February 14, but it's not a useful result from adding two numbers. As we usually do when the PC illusion breaks down, we're going to have to dig a little deeper to make sense of it all.

You guessed it, the answer involves bytes.

In Search of a Program's Output

When we wanted to examine the output from our ECHO command back in Chapter 1, we sent that output to a file. Let's do that output redirection trick once more.

Surprise. If we run the version of this program that we saw in Figure 4.3 and try to redirect its output to a file by using the > symbol that we learned in Chapter 1, we find that the program pays no attention. We get a ♥ on the screen, nonetheless.

Our output continues to go to the screen because this version of the program uses that bare-bones putch function, which talks directly to the display instead of routing its request through Windows. The Windows "traffic cop" never even knows, so to speak, that output is taking place. The putch command is simple, direct, and too rude to ask the PC if we had something special in mind.

If we change the last line of our program from putch(z) to fputchar(z), as I've shown in Figure 4.7, we get a somewhat more complex program that *will* pay attention if we redirect its output. This is typical of the tiny, technical decisions that a programmer makes before you ever get a chance to use a piece of software.

Before the widespread use of Windows, programs varied from each other in many crucial details, such as their ways of performing output. The use of Windows greatly reduces such software variability.

I have a reason for showing you these programmer tips, even though you might never write a program of your own. I want to reiterate, every time I get the chance, that there are more ways than you can imagine for a programmer to make a mistake (or even a legitimate design choice) that will make your PC do something completely useless.

Whenever your PC behaves in a convenient, apparently simple way, thank a programmer for properly dealing with almost uncountable details to yield that effect.

Programs Just Do What They're Told

In Figure 4.6, the window at left shows a modified version of our Figure 4.3 program. Besides changing putch to fputchar, I've made some other changes: specifically, I've used a variety of data types, employing the short int (16 bits) and the char (8 bits) as well as the 32-bit int to hold our three numeric values.

I'm bringing up these different data types to make another point about the choices that PC programmers have to make. None of the numbers in our arithmetic problem is larger than 255 (the maximum value that an 8-bit field can represent), so my use of these shorter data types doesn't change the behavior of the program.

Using short data types can reduce our use of memory, though, because we can allocate smaller slices of address space (instead of taking a 4-byte step down from the top of our memory area each time we allocate space for a constant or a variable).

Like the choice between doing our output with `putch` or `fputchar`, the choice of our program's data types is a programmer decision that has to be made up front. Should the programmer make a piece of software flexible, with data types that can hold extremely large values? Or should the programmer minimize future memory needs by using data types that are more compact (but also more restrictive)? Rest assured that at least some users will be angry, whatever the choice that gets made.

At upper right in Figure 4.6, we see the result of running our program in the normal fashion (producing that pesky valentine as its output), followed by a command to run the program and send its output to a file. This time, the output redirection seems to work as it should: we don't get a valentine, just a fresh command line.

At the bottom of Figure 4.6, we see the KEDIT editor opening the file that holds that diverted output. In the figure, I've just run a one-line program (which I wrote with KEDIT's built-in programming tools) to show the ASCII value of a chosen character.

Our mystery is solved: our program was, in fact, sending a **3** to the display. But that **3** was a binary code, a **00000011** bit group, *not* the ASCII code for the *numeral* 3.

It's as if we asked a child, "What's 1 plus 2?" We shouldn't be surprised if the child taps on the table three times, or makes three marks on a piece of paper, instead of drawing a perfectly formed numeral. Our PC has done the electronic version of tapping on the table instead of writing down the answer in a more presentable form. The little valentine we got from our program was the PC's display for the low-order ASCII 3 code.

Remember, the "readable" ASCII codes begin with the code for the symbol *0* at ASCII value 48. If we wanted to put out the numeral 3 on our screen, we would need to send an ASCII code with value 51. Even so simple a task as putting a human-readable number on the screen demands that some programmer should deal with this kind of detail.

A PC does exactly what we ask it to do, not what we "obviously" want it to do. As always, there's a reason for this annoyingly literal approach to following our instructions. At times, we might want to capture data in binary form from something like a camera or a temperature probe instead of as "formatted" numbers. A PC's central processor is just a fast and conscientious byte pump that does what it's told.

SPEED: MORE THAN DOING THE SAME THING FASTER

"Come on," you might be saying, "how can a PC be so fast if every little thing involves so many operations?" It might seem as if the adder program we've been studying in this chapter is a terribly roundabout way of adding numbers.

Yes, a PC does do things in a really indirect way. It breaks every problem into tiny little operations; it never sees obvious shortcuts that any elementary-school student would know. If you tell a PC to add zero to a number, it goes through the same rigmarole that it would use to do a problem worthy of its attention.

What makes computers fast is not any sort of "real" intelligence but rather their brute-force speed and their unthinking consistency. If you can execute an instruction every thousandth of a second, you can add up numbers pretty quickly—even if every addition that you perform uses six or seven separate instructions.

When you can do things that quickly, you wind up finding out you can actually do different things—not just the same things faster. Computers aren't our first discovery of this idea.

For example, imagine being alive in the 1800s when photography was just being invented. If someone had told you that someday you'd be able to take dozens of pictures in a second instead of needing several minutes just to expose one photograph, you might have laughed. You might have asked, "Why would I need three dozen pictures of the same thing?"

Would you have envisioned movies? Or slow-motion replays? Or any of the other applications of ultra-rapid imaging? It's the same way with computers: making them ten times faster gives us more than just the ability to do the same things ten times as quickly. More speed lets us do entirely new things, as we're still discovering.

The faster the chip, the easier it is to extend the PC's domain into new applications: for example, automated transcription of music from an electronic keyboard or digital capture of home videos for electronic editing and storage.

It's not just a matter of computer vendors trying to make you want the fastest thing (though that's certainly part of the picture). There are actually good reasons for owning a machine that's much, much faster than you ever thought you'd need.

How PCs Are Different from Macs. . .

You've seen that once you get below the cosmetic surface of a PC's windows, menus, icons, and files, the real tasks performed by a PC fall into four rather simple groups.

- The PC takes in data from the outside world, as when you gave it the input `Hello` back in Chapter 1.

- The PC stores data in files, as when you redirected the ECHO command to send its output to a file.

- The PC retrieves data from files, as when you loaded a file into memory with the DEBUG command.

- The PC moves data back and forth between memory and the storage compartments on the CPU chip, as we just saw in our adder program, and performs computations using on-chip data and the CPU's built-in instructions, such as **mov** and **add**.

Computer software is just lists of instructions for the chip to follow, with simple rules (but many of them) for when the chip should do one thing or another.

Different computers need different software because they use different chips that have different arrangements of registers and that understand different instructions. It's that simple. A Macintosh and a PC don't use the same kind of chip, so a Macintosh needs its own versions of software such as word processors or spreadsheets.

You might see the "same" program on a PC and a Macintosh, such as the Microsoft Word word processor or the Netscape Navigator Web browser. On each machine, however, you're seeing a different version of that program that has been *compiled* (translated into machine instructions) to give the right instructions to the type of chip that's in that machine.

But Data Can Go Anywhere

Moving software between different machines is hard, but moving data files between different machines is quite easy. And it's a good thing, too, or there would be no such thing as the World Wide Web.

The file that holds a document, such as a simple ASCII file, is not a list of active instructions. A document file is just a list of passive groups of bits, ready for a program to transform them into letters on the screen or some other kind of (hopefully) useful display.

The numbers in a document file might be ASCII codes, or Rich Text Format keywords (remember those from Chapter 2?), or Microsoft Word's hideously complex files, or any other format for representing information of any kind. Regardless, that file can be opened up and displayed and revised and stored by moving bytes back and forth between the file, the memory, and the chip.

Whether the chip is a PC chip, a Macintosh chip, or any other kind of processor doesn't matter. A document file doesn't care what kind of software or hardware reads and writes its bytes. The data just goes where it's told.

It's easy for programs on different kinds of computers to read and write the same kinds of data, but different kinds of computers need tricky helper programs (called *emulators*) to run each other's software. Emulators put a layer of software between a program's instructions and the hardware that's actually doing the job. Using an emulator is therefore much slower than running "native" code.

As a PC user, you won't generally need to worry about the performance or compatibility of emulation products, because the kind of native code that runs on PCs makes up the vast majority of the software sold today. Some Macintosh users and Unix workstation users use emulator programs such as SoftPC, a package for running PC and Windows software on other types of machines, but few commercial software buyers need to solve the opposite problem. There are few mass-market software products that are only sold for Unix or Macintosh with no Windows version available.

On the other hand, there are many Windows products that are not sold in versions for other platforms. Whatever the faults of Windows, and there are many, at least it's a case of misery having plenty of company.

IF YOU PAID A LOT FOR A PIECE OF UNIX SOFTWARE
In corporate settings, a product called Nutcracker from Data Focus, Inc. does some truly impressive tricks to make specialized UNIX software run on PCs using Microsoft Windows NT.

You're not likely to ever encounter a need to run UNIX software on your PC, but the option exists if you're willing to pay for the privilege. Nutcracker is an industrial-strength tool and can only be used in settings where skilled programmers are on hand and where those programmers have access to the underlying source code of the programs to be converted.

Special Jobs, Special Registers

When we explored the behavior of our simple addition program earlier in this chapter, we treated the registers on a Pentium chip as simple 32-bit storage compartments. We also noted the existence of other, special registers, such as the EBP register our program used as a reference point for choosing storage locations in memory. We ignored another important group of registers, however, that have a lot to do with the speed and capability of today's PCs.

This special group of registers that dramatically enhances a PC's capabilities is the *stack*, as it's called, of 80-bit registers that are used for two sets of operations.

Floating-Point Math on the 80-bit Stack

The PC's 80-bit registers used to be packaged in a separate chip called a math coprocessor. An early PC needed to have this extra chip installed, at extra cost, to run some kinds of software. This extra chip was an 8087 for a first-generation PC or an 80287 or 80387 for a second- or third-generation machine. Beginning with the 486 chips, however, PCs have had the math capabilities built in as standard equipment.

Whether built in or added on, the math coprocessor works with special instructions that use the 80-bit registers for highly accurate floating-point calculation. We discussed floating-point math, which lets a PC work with very large and very small numbers, in Chapter 3.

An extensive set of specialized floating-point instructions, including many for geometric calculations, makes the 80-bit registers extremely useful for such applications as computer-aided drafting.

Floating-point instructions, combined with today's high PC speeds, make PCs a viable option for all but the most exotic technical tasks. PCs are so cheap, compared to so-called "supercomputers," that even the most compute-intensive professionals might find using a battery of PCs (more than one per person) attractive, instead of sharing a single ultra-powerful machine.

Several years ago, for example, I had a conversation with a vice president at Intel named David House, who told me about his chance encounter with an oil company's engineering manager. The manager, learning that House was with the company that made his PC's processor chips, mentioned that he'd been buying many PCs to do seismographic analysis.

House, surprised, said that he thought this was the sort of task people did on supercomputers. The oil man said that they actually had several Cray "vector processor" supercomputers, but that his engineers found it much more predictable to do a job on a PC that they weren't sharing with other engineers.

Some of the engineers used two or three PCs at a time. The oil man concluded, "Before they go home at night, they have a night's work planned for their machines." The manager expected that by the end of the year, he'd be able to return one of his costly Crays—and these PCs were 386 machines, about a tenth as fast and twice as expensive as today's high-end Pentium systems.

The economic case for PCs in technical tasks just keeps getting stronger.

One Instruction, Eight Results: That's MMX

In homes and schools, the 80-bit registers on your PC's CPU will probably be more useful in their new role as multimedia specialists.

If you have a Pentium-family chip "with MMX," your chip has additional instructions built into its logic circuits that use the 80-bit registers for efficient graphics operations.

Suppose that your PC is set up to use 256 different colors on the screen at any time. This means that a single byte can represent the color of any single point on your display.

If we want to dissolve one picture into another, we need to make each byte gradually change from the value that it had in the first picture to the value it will have in the replacement picture. For every pair of bytes (one old, one new), we'd be doing the same calculation at the same time to make each dot on the screen show a gradual transition.

Because we're doing the same operation at every point on the screen, we say that we have a single stream of instructions. Because we have to apply that stream of instructions to many different pairs of bytes, we say that we have multiple streams of data. It would be nice if we could somehow bundle up the data and perform a common operation on several points at once, instead of going through the same routine of retrieving values and performing operations and storing results for every point individually.

The idea behind MMX is to use those wide, 80-bit registers to hold the data from several different locations on the screen at the same time, and to operate on that collection of bytes with a single instruction cycle instead of several repetitive cycles. When using its MMX instructions, the chip pretends that the 80-bit floating-point registers have turned into a different set of 64-bit MMX registers. The chip uses different names and different instruction codes to operate on the physical storage compartments that are already available on the chip and that often aren't being used by games or other media-intensive software.

I've used the simple example of dissolving one picture into another, but many other multimedia operations lend themselves to this MMX approach that's also called *SIMD* (single instruction, multiple data). SIMD is the simplest, most effective way to do *parallel processing*, where many cheap chips (or the big pieces of a single chip) get used in parallel to do more work in the same amount of time.

When you watch a TV weather report and see the weather commentator seem to float in front of a satellite photo, you're seeing this kind of processing at work.

When you use any piece of software that lets you seem to move through a three-dimensional maze or building, you're doing the kind of thing MMX can do with half as many operations as a conventional microprocessor. MMX is more than a buzzword: it's a real enhancement in making your PC faster.

Three Strategies for Speed

If you look at advertisements for the highest-performance PCs, you'll see them brag about three things: the clock rate, the memory capacity, and something that we haven't mentioned yet: the *cache*. Let's see how these three elements of a PC each make a significant contribution to the PC's performance.

The Clock Sets the Pace

PC ads talk about the processors' clock rates. Digital circuits use a clock that puts out a series of uniform pulses, just like the ticking of a grandfather clock (as we discussed in Chapter 3). To every device in the system, the clock pulse says, in effect, "Everybody take the next step."

Like an Assembly Line

With each clock pulse, the processor might put a memory address on the *address bus*; that is, the pathway to memory that tells the memory system which location it should read.

The processor might move its *instruction pointer* up by one position, telling it where to look for the code for the next instruction it should execute.

The processor might execute an instruction, in the manner that we observed in our adder example earlier in this chapter.

The clock makes the different parts of the system work in rhythm, all together, like the coxswain in the rowboat yelling, "Stroke! Stroke!"

More Speed Demands More Complexity

I'm giving a simplified description, because a modern microprocessor actually does many different parts of the process in an overlapping fashion on each clock cycle.

While one piece of the processor is figuring out where to get the next instruction, another part is translating the instruction that was previously retrieved, and another part of the processor is executing the instruction that was previously translated. The hardware design that makes this possible is called a *pipeline*, conveying the idea that it might take some time to empty out that pipe if we change our minds and decide to do something completely different. Heavily pipelined chip designs sometimes do a poor job of dealing with unexpected interruptions in their tasks.

A Pentium actually has two parallel pipelines that let the chip execute two operations at once. The chip can automatically detect situations in which this parallel approach might cause problems: for example, if two operations are both trying to change the same location in memory.

In general, today's different Intel-compatible chips compete at being clever about predicting the next thing a program will ask the chip to do. In the process, chips wind up having many more internal states, and the whole system winds up being extremely difficult to test. That's what it takes, however, to get the most possible computations out of every successive clock cycle.

The Clock Provides One Kind of Speed

For all of its importance, the clock rate only tells you how many times per second the processor takes its steps. There are other limiting factors on overall PC speed.

Higher clock rates boost the speed of *compute-bound* tasks, but many PC tasks are what we call *I/O-bound*; that is, their speed is limited by the PC's ability to get data in and out.

A faster clock rate makes the processor's operations proportionately faster, but that won't make your hard disk faster at moving its magnetic heads to a new location. A faster clock won't speed up your modem, and it certainly can't speed up another system at the other end of the Internet. Before you decide that your PC is too slow, make a careful assessment of which tasks are actually taking more time than you'd like. More MegaHertz might not matter.

Memory Lets Your PC Breathe

If the CPU is the heart of your PC, then the memory is its lungs. Like a person who's lost a lung, a PC that's short on memory just can't do as much without taking time to catch its breath.

When a PC has more memory, it can run more programs at the same time. If you want to write a complex document in a high-end word processing program, switching back and forth with an illustration tool and with a Web browser open at the same time for research, even 64 Mbytes of memory can start to be confining.

When a PC is short of memory, its operating system uses some space on the hard disk to masquerade as additional memory. Making disk space look like memory is called *virtual memory*, and it's an old technique on big computers but now quite feasible on PCs, as well.

Deficit Memory

Virtual memory uses a special section of the CPU, called the *memory management unit*, to create a fictional set of memory addresses. The memory management unit attaches some of these addresses to actual locations in the system's memory banks and attaches other addresses to storage locations in a swap file on the hard disk.

The *swap file* gets its name because the memory management unit swaps data back and forth between the hard disk and the physical memory, depending on which addresses are in demand at any time. Most of the time, this works fairly well because of something called *locality*: A running program tends to work with data and instructions from one range of address locations for a while before moving on to another set of locations.

A PC might be so short of memory that the "local" region (the *working set*) is too large to fit into physical memory's capacity. When the working set is large compared to the actual RAM on hand, the PC starts to swap stuff from memory to disk and back at a furious rate. This is called *thrashing*.

Thrashing is hard on the disk, and it does dreadful things to a PC's speed. If your PC's hard disk access light seems to be on almost all of the time, even when you're not doing hard disk operations such as loading programs or saving files, adding memory might greatly improve your system's performance.

Some Software Uses Memory More Efficiently

Getting the most from your memory also depends on your choice of appropriate software for the task you're trying to perform. If you want to manage a mailing list of a hundred people or so, you might find it easy to do that with the database features of a spreadsheet program. But a spreadsheet generally tries to load an entire *workbook* of data as a single block, and it could become sluggish if your list is in the tens of thousands of names.

A proper database program, which works with records one at a time or in small sets, is less likely to strain your PC's memory capacity. A database also runs less risk of losing valuable work with a poorly timed hardware or software glitch, whether on your power line or in your computer. When a database changes any record, it writes these changes to the disk, but a spreadsheet only saves changes when you save the entire spreadsheet file.

Even within a group of similar software products, memory management can have a huge effect on the time it takes to get a task over and done with. I once compared several statistics programs, and I was using test problems with several dozen data points and finding the different products to be comparatively fast.

When I made additional tests, with problems using several thousand data points, however, I was startled to find that the slower programs took two hundred times as long as their faster competitors to import data from a simple file. I don't mean a difference between half a second and over a minute—I mean a difference between just under a minute and well over an hour.

It's a nuisance, but you need to compare alternative software tools with problems of substantial size: their relative speed might become quite different as the size of the problem grows.

There Are Many Kinds of Memory

Memory is so important to a computer's performance that there are many different kinds, each with its own advantages and its own special name.

Many of the buzzwords surrounding PCs are the labels for different memory types. Whenever you hear a PC buzzword that ends with a letter M, there's an excellent chance that we're talking about some variety of memory.

At the beginning of Chapter 1, we said your PC has a tiny amount of built-in knowledge of how to get itself going. That "bootstrap" information, as we called it, lives in a chip called *Read-Only Memory*, or *ROM*.

ROM Is for Data That Doesn't Change

You could think of ROM as a sheet of paper like the one we used for our addition example at the beginning of this chapter, except that ROM's contents are "written in ink." We store information in a ROM chip by a process called "burning a ROM," which leaves a set of binary data permanently wired in place. A ROM chip, like a file stored on a hard disk, is nonvolatile memory: it doesn't go away when the power goes off.

You see ROM chips all the time in the form of game cartridges for Nintendo and other types of video games.

RAM Is a Misused Label

You also hear a lot about RAM, as when someone says that a PC "has 16 megabytes of RAM." Spelled out, RAM means Random Access Memory. This label applies to any data-storage device that lets you read any of its storage locations in more or less the same amount of time.

A video tape is not random access because it takes a long time to read information at the end of the tape if you start at the beginning. A video disk, however, is random access, because you can quickly position the reading hardware at any point. The same relationship holds between cassette tapes and CDs for music, for exactly the same reason.

Literally, the label RAM applies to a hard disk or a ROM chip, because both of these devices let us read the data at any location, in any sequence that we want.

Most of the time, though, a person who talks about the RAM in a PC is talking about the solid-state, no-moving-parts memory chips that are not ROM; that is, about the rewritable memory that can hold different data from one moment to another.

Two Common Kinds of (Misnamed) RAM

As if the misuse of RAM weren't enough, we also have to deal with two variations on that label that we find in a PC's ordinary memory system. The two common forms of rewritable memory hardware are *dynamic RAM* (DRAM) and *static RAM* (SRAM).

- Dynamic RAM (DRAM) is the most common form of memory chip in a PC because it offers a good tradeoff between performance and cost. You could think of DRAM as a set of microscopic buckets of electricity: a full bucket represents a 1 bit and an empty bucket represents a 0 bit.

  The problem with DRAM is that the buckets leak. A DRAM uses a tiny electrical device that can be charged up in the same way that you charge up a balloon by rubbing it against your hair so the balloon will stick to a wall. The charge doesn't persist, and the balloon soon falls.

  To keep DRAM's contents intact, a memory controller has to go through all of the DRAM addresses and *refresh* them often enough to make them stay clearly readable. DRAM is "dynamic" in the sense that it demands this constant attention, even when its contents are not changing.

  During the refresh cycle, DRAM's contents can't be read. If the processor tries to retrieve information from memory at that time, it has to endure *wait states* that the memory controller inserts to let the refresh process complete.

- Static RAM (SRAM) is the high-octane blend. Instead of little buckets of electricity, SRAM chips contain microscopic circuits that behave like switches. Because these switches can be "flipped" from one stable state to another, they're whimsically known as *flip-flops*. (There are no mechanical moving parts; this is all just a matter of changing the state of a circuit so that it does, or does not, conduct electricity.)

When an SRAM bit gets set to 1 or 0, it stays set (unlike a DRAM bit) until it's deliberately changed or until it's cleared by turning the power off.

An SRAM cell is more complicated than a DRAM cell, requiring about four times as many of the microscopic components that combine to create a memory chip. SRAM is faster because no refresh cycles are needed, but it costs more to build because it takes up a larger amount of space. Larger chips are more likely to have defects, meaning that more chips must be built to produce a given number of good ones. Larger chips mean that a factory can build and sell a smaller number of devices before its technology gets out of date, so the cost of the factory must be spread across that smaller number of units.

VRAM Clears Up the Picture

VRAM, or *video RAM*, is the third important variety of rewritable memory. We've talked about the fact that the tiny dots on your PC's display are just another way of looking at bytes of data. The display screen gets its good looks from a special bank of memory called the *video buffer*. You might think of the CPU as putting bytes into that video buffer whenever—and wherever—it wants to change the image on any part of the display; for example, when you're typing in your word processor and want to add a letter at the place where you just pressed a key.

Your display system doesn't need random access to the video buffer—the display controller scans the entire video buffer many times a second and constantly updates your screen's entire image.

A constant video update cycle has to be maintained if you're using the common, TV-type display. A picture-tube image starts to fade as quickly as it's drawn and must be refreshed constantly (not unlike the behavior of DRAM, come to think of it).

VRAM meets the need of the CPU (to change any point on the screen at any time) and the need of the display subsystem (to scan the entire video buffer repetitively). VRAM provides two sets of connections to the same memory cells. The CPU can update the video buffer, in a random-access fashion, from one side, while the display subsystem reads the result in a repetitive scanning process from the buffer's other side.

When the video subsystem needs to read a video buffer location in a PC that doesn't have a *dual-ported* video RAM, the video controller blocks the CPU from changing that buffer location until the video update is finished. This lockout behavior prevents annoying "snow" on the display, which was a problem on early PCs when they tried to do high-speed graphics. Though the results are better looking, this "collision prevention" slows down the CPU in much the same way as the DRAM refresh cycle. VRAM makes things run more smoothly.

Memory Versus Noise

We've talked about memory as big banks of bits, built from microscopic hardware that stores tiny amounts of electricity. You might wonder if real-world memory chips ever let a bit slip or get confused by electrical "noise" around or within your PC.

A radio transmitter (such as a cellular phone) creates an electrical field that a receiving antenna can sense as a voltage, even at quite some distance. If an antenna on the other side of town can feel that electric field, what does the signal do to electronic components that are just a few feet away? How would you feel if your PC rebooted whenever a neighbor used a cordless phone or whenever someone opened a nearby garage door with a remote control?

A device doesn't even need to be an "intentional radiator" (that is, something *designed* to transmit a radio signal) to create a serious problem for your PC. Electrical noise can afflict a PC from many different sources. Have you ever seen interference on your TV screen or heard a burst of static on a radio when you turned on a vacuum cleaner or a hair dryer? That interference can enter your equipment through the air as radio waves or through the power line as electrical voltages that sneak through the power supply.

Good electrical design helps a PC protect itself from noise through techniques that include filtering of incoming power and shielding against radio-type interference. All of these techniques add cost, and this is one of the things you pay for in a higher-priced PC.

Your PC also generates electrical noise, which can affect a nearby TV or other devices: there are legal restrictions on the amount of radio noise a PC can produce. A PC can't be sold without approval from the Federal Communications Commission (the FCC).

Low-cost PC producers have sometimes been found at the edge, or outside the edge, of compliance with FCC rules. This is sometimes a matter of inconsistent design and construction, and more rarely is a matter of deliberate fraud.

Even when a PC is fully compliant with FCC rules, that only means the PC will not cause interference to other devices. The FCC does not test a PC's ability to reject interference from outside signals such as those from a nearby radio transmitter.

The FCC's test procedures are also somewhat quirky; for example, the tests measure radiation all around a device but ignore radiation that goes straight up or down. Equipment items on stacked shelves might interfere with each other, even though each item is FCC compliant.

Changing equipment position or orientation might eliminate an interference problem, because many devices radiate in nonuniform patterns with pronounced "lobes."

Extra Bits Detect Errors

Instead of using higher-quality hardware to prevent bit errors, a PC can just use extra hardware to detect and correct bit errors when they occur.

For example, instead of using memory chips that merely store the eight bits of a byte, a PC could store nine bits for each byte. The first eight bits would hold the real data. The ninth bit would be a *parity bit*, which the memory controller would set to a value that depends on the eight "real" bits.

Out of the eight real bits in the stored byte of data, some will be 1s and some will be 0s. If there is an even number of 1s, an even parity rule would set the parity bit to 0. If there is an odd number of 1s, the parity bit would be set to 1, yielding an even number of 1s overall.

Now, if any single bit is corrupted by a memory hardware error, there will no longer be an even number of 1s, and the memory controller will detect that the stored byte value is no longer trustworthy.

Errors Can Be Corrected

Simple parity-bit arrangements can't tell us which bit is wrong. With a few more "spare" bits, though, we can give ourselves error correction, instead of merely error detection.

How do we teach a group of bits to correct its own errors? We can start with no protection at all and see how we build up from there.

Suppose we have four bits of data. With four bits, we can represent sixteen different values (0000 through 1111). Assume, for now, that we only need a sixteen-symbol vocabulary: we'll call these sixteen symbols our "words."

With no spare bits, there is no way to tell if any bit has been corrupted. Every possible four-bit pattern will match a valid word: we can't tell which patterns have been "munged" by faulty hardware or interfering signals. We would say that we have no *redundancy*.

Suppose that we add a fifth, spare bit to our original four-bit group. We then have 32 possible patterns (00000 through 11111). We could use a parity rule, as described above, to set the fifth bit so that we always have an even number of 1s.

If we use our fifth bit as a parity bit, there are only sixteen valid patterns (the ones with an even number of 1s). Each of these valid, even patterns matches one (and only one) of our sixteen words.

The other sixteen patterns out of the possible thirty-two will have an odd number of 1s. If we see an odd number of 1s, we know that an error occurred—but we don't know which of our five bits is wrong, so we don't have a full solution yet.

If we add two more bits, however, we have 7-bit sets that give us 128 possible patterns (0000000 through 1111111). That's eight times the number of words we set out to represent with our four bits of unprotected data.

Think about this. In our 7-bit word, we could have all seven bits correct. We could also have bit 1 wrong, or bit 2, or 3, or 4, or 5, or 6, or bit 7 wrong. That's eight possibilities in all that have a zero- or 1-bit error.

We previously noted, though, that we have eight times as many patterns available as we have words that we need to represent. Now we choose a set of eight patterns—a "correct" pattern, plus the seven patterns that differ in just one bit—and make all of these eight patterns acceptable ways of expressing one chosen word from our set of sixteen words.

We repeat this process across the board. We give each of our sixteen words its own unique collection of eight 7-bit patterns. We use some logical rules to set the extra three bits so that no 7-bit pattern matches more than one of our sixteen valid words.

Any 7-bit pattern that gets stored and retrieved with no more than one wrong bit will still match the proper data word.

Now, all we have to do is build a memory controller that's wired with the rules for setting the values of these error-correcting bits. This is hard to figure out the first time, but it's easy to do it once you know how—the perfect kind of task to wire into a computer.

Figure 4.7 shows a set of rules for single-bit error correction, devised in the form of an Excel spreadsheet and showing an example. You can apply these rules to pencil-and-paper examples and see that any wrong bit will produce the distinctive "signature" (also called a *syndrome*) that tells you which of your bits is incorrect.

This particular example is based on lecture notes by Dr. Bernd-Peter Paris, which he posted on the Web. You can skip these details without impairing your everyday use of your PC, but I feel an obligation to prove that this actually works. While researching this chapter, I found a surprising number of statements that error correction is possible, without demonstrations. I think you deserve better.

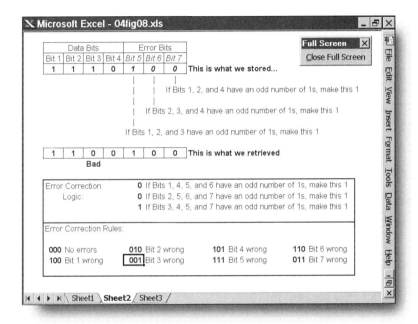

FIGURE 4.7
Error correction seems like magic. All it takes, however, is a few rules of logic to make every zero- or 1-bit error become just another way of saying what you meant to say. Three bits get computed and added to four bits of data: three "syndrome" bits get computed and used to diagnose any errors that later corrupt the 7-bit pattern.

Correction at No Extra Cost

Error correction might seem to require a lot of extra hardware. We need seven bits, in total, to correct one bit out of four. We need thirteen bits to correct one bit out of eight, which is clearly more costly than simply providing one parity bit for each group of eight.

We need twenty-two bits to correct one out of sixteen, compared to only eighteen bits to provide a parity bit for each 8-bit byte. We need thirty-nine bits to correct one bit out of thirty-two, compared to only 36 bits to do a simple parity check. But. . . we only need 72 bits to correct a one-bit error in a group of 64 bits.

We've reached a crossover point. With 72 bits, we can have a parity bit for each of eight bytes, or we can have single-bit error correction for the whole group of 64 bits.

We get a choice: we can narrow down an error to the nearest group of eight bits by using parity, or we can zero in on the error—and fix it—by using error correction.

Providing error correction instead of error detection is a simple design decision. This seems like a good thing to do, as PCs' memories get large enough (and the tasks that PCs do become important enough) to make higher reliability a worthwhile goal.

Cache Gets a Lot of the Credit

Finally, PC ads often mention the size of their *cache*. What is a cache, and what does it do for a PC? And is more cache always better?

Cache is a halfway solution to the problem of having too few storage registers on a CPU chip. In a way, cache is the opposite of virtual memory, because virtual memory uses slow disk space to make the PC's memory look larger; a cache uses limited CPU space to make the PC's memory look faster.

In our adder program, we saw the CPU computing addresses and exchanging data between those address locations and the on-chip storage registers. Suppose that we had a more complex, poorly written program that constantly exchanged data between memory and the CPU. Suppose that this program was always going to the same set of one or two memory locations instead of putting their values into registers and using those values without wasting time re-reading them.

Suppose we built an "assistant circuit," designed to keep track of the memory addresses where we'd been fetching data. Suppose we gave that circuit some simple rules for deciding when a value should be copied into a small but high-speed memory bank, along with a record of the address where that value can normally be found.

If the CPU tries to read a memory address that the "assistant" has stored in this fashion, the assistant will just hand over its copy of the corresponding value, without wasting time on a trip to the main system memory.

If a program is "local" in behavior, in the same way that we used this word when discussing virtual memory, many of our memory-access operations might turn out to be "cache hits." That is, we might be able to get much of our data from the stash in the cache of recently used addresses and their contents, much more quickly than we would get that data from the external memory system.

Perhaps you remember my saying, near the beginning of this chapter, that a calculator with one or more memories would be helpful in understanding how a processor functions. This is the time to make that connection. A memory in your calculator lets you put a value aside for future use without going out to the "memory" by writing it down on paper.

When you decide to store a value in one of your calculator's limited number of memories, you're acting as a *cache controller*.

I asked, near the beginning of this cache discussion, if more cache is always better. The answer to this question isn't simple. A cache is a chunk of very fast (and therefore expensive) memory, generally SRAM of the type that we discussed earlier, so it's good to have a clear idea of when the cost of getting more is worthwhile.

Obviously, cache speeds things up only if you look at the same set of memory addresses in a repetitive fashion and if that working set of addresses is not too large to fit in the cache.

If you cycle through a set of memory locations over and over again, and if that set is too large to fit in the cache all at once, you'll get the worst possible outcome. Your CPU will constantly be asking the cache controller, in effect, "Do you have this one?" And the cache controller will always be saying "No" and going out to memory to get the value—a value that it probably just threw out to make room for the one it used a moment earlier.

In this situation, even a large increase in cache size might still fall short of what's needed to make the working set smaller than the cache. You might feel that you wasted your money if you paid a dealer to add an optional extra-large cache, but you got no dramatic improvement in speed.

Another expansion, however, might make all the difference in the world if a repetitive process can suddenly run from the cache instead of requiring constant memory access. It will seem like the difference between cache and no cache, even if you added only a fraction of your starting cache capacity.

There are other tasks, though, in which cache does no good at all. If I'm generating mailing labels and moving in order through a list of a hundred thousand names, I never revisit the same data twice. My cache never gets a chance to prove its cleverness—at least, not with my data.

Printing labels does involve a kind of repetition, though: a repetition of one small set of instructions, reading a record and sending parts of it to the printer. If I could cache data in one place and instructions in another place, I would speed up repetitive operations even on data that I only touch once.

Today's fast CPUs make the most of every kind of operation by having, as I've just described, separate caches for instructions and data. Some people call this a "full Harvard" cache architecture. The other approach—a single high-speed memory bank storing both data and instructions—is just called a *unified cache*.

You can find both separate and unified cache designs at work in current-model CPUs. A Cyrix 6x86MX has a 64 Kbyte unified cache; an AMD K6 has two separate caches, each 32 Kbytes in size. An Intel P55C (Pentium with MMX) has separate caches, each holding only 16 Kbytes. Each of these chips does better at different tests of PC performance.

The CPU cache is only part of the story. The sizes that I've just given are for Level 1 cache hardware that's built right into the CPU, but most fast PCs also have a second layer of off-chip cache (typically 512 Kbytes).

The Level 2 cache can do sensible things, such as retrieving a sequential group of addresses (using a fast "burst" mode) instead of retrieving only the requested information. If the CPU then asks for a sequential group of bytes, the Level 2 cache already has the next several bytes on hand. In most cases, this practice saves more time by speeding data transfers than it wastes on retrieving unwanted data.

The choice of a cache design is one of those decisions that chip designers wrestle with before they produce a new CPU, and different tasks favor different choices. This is one of the many reasons why clock rate alone, as in "a 400 MHz PC," does not fully predict which machine will do your most important tasks most quickly.

Bits Are a Useful Myth

You've worked hard to get to this point. You've tunneled down through the pretty face of Windows. You've untangled the mislabeled maze of the file system. You've braved the cryptic commands of the microprocessor instruction set. You've opened the nested boxes of the registers that talk to the Level 1 cache that talks to the Level 2 cache that talks to the real memory that swaps bytes back and forth with the virtual memory.

In a substantial way, you now understand what happens inside a PC. For your graduation present, I'm going to peel off the last layers of illusion to talk about what really, really happens while we talk about mythical bits.

Life is Full of Formalities

This isn't the first time you've worked hard to master a formal system that's based on impossible perfections and idealized extremes. Think of geometry. There are no perfectly straight lines of infinite length. Think of economics. There are no perfectly rational decision-makers. Think of music. No one plays the notes exactly as written, in perfect tune and time.

We're used to the idea of learning a formal system that's based on impossible ideals. Such ways of thinking can be useful, but we have to accept the real world's limitations.

I want to explain, before we move on to Part II of this book, the things that keep a real PC from playing in perfect tune.

Real Electrons: Why Things Can't Just Get Faster

How fast can a PC run? We learned a few pages ago that the clock rate is the foundation of the PC's speed. Can we just keep turning up the tempo?

There are reasons why an ever-faster clock rate isn't something we should expect. As we start to think about wireless networks and portable digital communicators, we need to have our electrons under control if we don't want our devices to get themselves most seriously confused.

Fast, Faster, Ultrafast

Today, a fast PC clocks its processor at 400 to 500 million clock cycles per second, or 400 to 500 MegaHertz. If you hooked up a PC's clock to a well-designed antenna, a 233 MHz PC would do some nasty things to your local reception of TV Channel 13; a 560 MHz clock, which soon will be quite common, sits almost exactly on top of Channel 28.

Fundamentally, a PC is a box full of wires, coursing with signals that would love to turn into radio waves. It takes serious electrical engineering to maintain separate signals between each bit of a 32-bit word as it comes in from the PC's memory on 32 parallel wires.

A properly designed PC makes its connections look internally smooth to electrical signals, avoiding bumps in the pathways that cause signals to reflect (or to radiate). Undesired reflections and radiations confuse both the original signal and the signals on nearby wires. A properly constructed PC avoids opportunities for "crosstalk" between adjacent signal paths.

Lightspeed Is Too Slow

When one piece of your PC announces, in effect, that a certain bit is a 1 instead of a 0, how do other parts of the PC find out? An electrical voltage has to be created at one point in the system and has to become apparent at other points. This does not happen in zero time.

The time that it takes for a signal in one place to be felt at other points cannot be less than the time that it takes for light to go that distance. Light is fast, but we're talking about very short times: light travels only 12 inches in a billionth of a second. Billionths of a second (nanoseconds) are the most common unit for measuring time in today's high-speed digital circuits.

When you try to shove an electrical pulse through a real wire instead of just sending a beam of light through empty space, things get even more difficult. A real wire has a form of sluggishness, called *inductance*, that makes it fight back when you try to make a current start up quickly. Getting the current going takes a bit of time, and this process limits the speed with which a train of electrical pulses (such as a clock signal) can be sent.

Inductance differs from the more familiar phenomenon of *resistance*, which is what heats the wires in your toaster. Resistance opposes steady electrical flows, while inductance only opposes a change in electrical flow. Both are problems, but only inductance inhibits the continued growth of PC clock rates.

It would be easier, in some ways, if we didn't need to use a single clock signal to make all of the parts of a PC follow the same schedule. It might be attractive, in the future, to have a PC work like a factory, with packages of data moving around and carrying their own instructions for what should be done when they arrive at different locations. Engineers are exploring this and other options for breaking the built-in speed limits of current electrical designs for digital circuitry.

Already your PC is starting to look like a consortium of computers instead of just one, with such devices as your modem and your video display having their own memory and "intelligence" so that tasks are efficiently coordinated. This approach will be developed more deeply in future machines.

Building Better PCs: Only Real Engineers Need Apply

Today's high clock rates demand that a PC be designed and built with respect for electrical and radio principles and behaviors. It's no longer possible, as it was with 5 MHz PCs, to pretend that a bit in one part of a PC can be immediately seen by every other device inside the box.

In truth, there are no bits: there are just electrical signals. Most of the time we can get away with pretending, but someone has to deal with the reality if we want to keep on getting faster machines.

Real Atoms: Why Things Can't Just Get Smaller

Just as real electrons radiate energy in ways that we'd rather avoid, real atoms start to look kind of bumpy as we try to make more compact PC components.

For example, the latest generation of portable hard disks have some components that are only tens of atoms thick.

The connections between the parts of a microchip are so narrow that ordinary light waves can't be used to lay out their arrangements: it takes the tinier waves of x-rays to define these submicron features.

When we build circuits of submicron size and cool them close to absolute-zero temperatures to suppress the thermal noise of jostling electrons, new thresholds in computational power come within our reach. As early as 1988, researchers at Bell Laboratories were working with experimental transistors that were able to switch signals on and off in a trillionth of a second, requiring only a single electron to control them.

The next generation of memory might actually use a single electron to represent a bit, trapping that electron in something called a *quantum well*.

When we can build an entire CPU from components that manipulate individual electrons, we'll be able to fit a thousand processors in the space currently consumed by one chip. Each of these thousand processors would be a thousand times as fast as the chips we build today. Such a thousand-processor cluster would compare, scientists say, to the power of a human brain—if we can write software that uses those chips effectively.

When connections are smaller than light waves and signals consist of countable numbers of electrons, it might seem that we're getting close to natural limits on how small and how fast a computational device can be. Some leading figures predict continued advancement in gross computational speed: at Intel, for example, top officials have predicted the successful design of microprocessors with clock rates in GigaHertz (thousands of MegaHertz).

Other designers, however, assert that we will need to get most of our performance improvement over the next three decades by doing more things in parallel. I gave a simple example of parallelism in our earlier discussion of MMX technology. There's a great deal of research under way to develop methods for doing other, more complex things in parallel.

At some point, we'll have to make a choice between pushing the limits of logic by devising more parallel algorithms and pushing the limits of physics by trying to do sequential operations more quickly. Physics, in general, doesn't give in; eventually, we'll have to depend on programmers.

Real Science: Future Computing Solutions

There are two things that we'd most like to see from future computers. We'd like them to keep getting faster, and we'd like them to keep getting cheaper.

Nothing is faster, as a way of moving information from one place to another, than light. Electrical pulses inside a computer move at large fractions of lightspeed, but why don't we just build a computer that uses light instead of electrical voltage and current as its means of moving data from place to place?

Optical Computing: Work in Progress

When you think of beams of light, you might imagine miniature flashlights. A light-based computer won't use tiny light bulbs, though, any more than an electronic chip uses tiny light switches. Light-based computers would use small versions of the light-emitting diodes that you see on all kinds of equipment today, providing small and almost indestructible visual displays.

Light is already used to transfer digital information in situations where electricity is too dangerous. For example, I have a portable electronic measuring device that can transfer its results to a PC. Instead of an electrical connection, this device uses a cable that has tiny light detectors embedded in one end: these detectors work with equally small light sources embedded in the side of the measuring device.

For that matter, you use optical data transfer every time you operate a TV remote control. Remotes use light-emitting diodes that give off infrared light, with light waves that are longer than your eye can detect but that still cross the room quite nicely. An optical computer can use similar components, scaled down to microscopic size, and without some of the problems that afflict electrical connections (as we've discussed earlier).

On the Fringe: The Biochip

Even farther afield than optical computing is the idea of using biological techniques, such as pattern-matching with strings of DNA, to perform complex computations.

DNA-based computing is not science fiction. Some highly complex mathematical problems have yielded to the enormous amount of "calculation" that can be done with chemical selection processes on a container that holds billions of molecules. The chemical reactions all take place together, in massively parallel processing.

Both light-based computing and biochip computing might have important contributions to make, but they also present a common problem. We can barely understand the simple, step-by-step approach that's involved in programming the electronic computers we use now. We would need to develop entirely new ways of analyzing and solving problems to use all of the potential of parallel techniques, whether we use technologies based on electrons, photons, or virus-like "nanocomputers."

What We've Learned

This is a major breakpoint in our progress through this book. From this point on, we can treat the PC as a black box.

We can plug things into the box, such as printers and digital cameras; we can run things on the box, such as word processors and games; we can make the box do entirely new things by writing new programs or creating new digital content. These different ways of using a PC define the rest of this book.

The outside devices that plug into a PC will be passing bytes back and forth with the PC's processor, its memory, and its disks. We talk about bytes as if they were real, but we know that they're just a way of talking about electrical signals. Files are just a way of talking about bytes. Higher-level collections of data—documents and databases—are just a way of looking at a file or a group of files.

We've seen why a PC program and a Macintosh program can't run on each other's machines. Programs are tightly wedded to a particular set of registers on a chip and a particular set of instructions for working with those registers.

At the same time, we understand that a document or other data file can easily move from one kind of computer to another. Data can be manipulated in the same ways by different machines, as long as each machine has a set of instructions that matches its own CPU.

We've seen the interacting layers of hardware that determine how fast a PC can do its work, starting with the processor and its clock and working outward through the caches to the memory. We've also made the point, however, that software can use the hardware's speed efficiently or poorly: similar programs might yield quite different performance on the same machine. Performance tests need to use full-size problems to make good predictions of problem-solving speed.

From the Start button that we saw on the opening screen in Chapter 1, we've drilled down one layer at a time. In this chapter, we reached the point of looking at the individual instructions that a PC's CPU follows to do the most elementary things.

We've seen that at the foundation, a PC exposes uncountable ways for a program to do the wrong thing. We've seen that we can make wrong choices in the way that data is displayed, or that we can mistakenly store something in a place we thought we were using to hold something else.

Most software works most of the time, and most PC hardware works almost all of the time. As we finish this chapter, though, we understand how easy it is for computers (with help from people) to make ridiculous mistakes: mistakes like saying that 1 + 2 = ♥.

It will always be up to the user to recognize nonsense, even when the latest and greatest PC produces it.

*"Only connect...Live in
fragments no longer."*

—EDWARD FOSTER, 1910

The Practical PC

YOU SHOULD NOW HAVE A FIRM GRASP of the PC's core components and behaviors. Now, it's time to build a practical system around that core.

Chapters 1 and 2 showed us how to get around Windows without getting lost at its unmarked intersections. Chapters 3 and 4 showed us how a PC performs complex tasks in fractions of a second— tasks that required minutes or hours on the world's best available computers at the time of our first Moon landing.

In two respects, however, our tour of the PC's hardware is not yet complete. We've defined the heart (CPU) and lungs (memory), but we have not defined the bones (the mechanical components) or circulatory system (the power supply) a PC needs to make it a viable creature.

Nor have we defined the senses (the external data connections) this creature needs to perceive and communicate with the world around it.

The Plan for This Chapter

We begin with a look at the basic mechanical, electrical, and thermal support systems that keep a PC alive. We'll see how we can connect a PC to other devices, enabling a huge variety of useful and entertaining functions.

This chapter examines the essentials—and some of the luxuries—of PC input and output: the keyboard, the pointing device, and the growing variety of specialized controllers for realistic PC-based games.

We'll look at the types of connections that let us extend a PC with useful accessories such as printers, modems (which connect a PC to a phone line), scanners (which bring an image of a document or photograph into a PC), and the like. We'll look briefly at the popular Ethernet model for computer network connections, though we'll defer broader networking issues until our later chapters on modems and the Internet.

Finally, we'll look at a broad cross section of data storage devices, meeting every need from convenient removable storage of individual files to high-performance and high-reliability storage of vast amounts of data.

Look at the Back of the Box

Figure 5.1 shows the back of a typical PC system. We're going to work our way across the back panel, one connector and opening at a time.

The Fan: Low Tech, High Priority

When I was planning this book, I have to admit that the cooling fan was not on my first list of topics. When I looked at the photo I took for Figure 5.1, I realized what a mistake it would be to neglect this component and all of the issues that go with it.

FIGURE 5.1
This back-panel view of a Micron PC features the large fan exhaust and power connectors—which most PC users rarely worry about, but which deserve attention in proportion to their size.

Fans Break

The cooling fan is one of those unusual components of a PC that actually has moving parts. The keyboard, the hard disk, and the fan are the mechanical components that are almost always hard at work while a PC is doing its job.

It's no coincidence that in more than a decade of everyday PC use, I've had almost no hardware problems except with the mechanical subsystems.

Noise Has Its Costs...

I fondly remember one peaceful year when I did most of my work on a first-generation Macintosh, a machine with no hard disk and no cooling fan. Gosh, that was a quiet office.

When working late at night, I could have the radio turned down almost to the point of being inaudible, with no background whirring or blowing noise to cover up the music. It was great for the concentration.

I wonder if we realize the harm we've done by bathing ourselves in the white noise of hard disks and fans, as almost every desktop now includes a hot-running, fan-cooled PC.

...But the Heat Has to Go

However annoying the noise of that fan might be, getting the waste heat out of a PC's enclosure is essential. On more than one occasion, I've popped a CD-ROM out of a PC and found it quite hot to the touch: I've learned that this is a giveaway symptom of a sticking or stalled cooling fan. (On one exceptional occasion, the problem turned out to be something else: a service company's advertising sticker, neatly pasted over the PC's internal ventilation slots!)

When a PC seems suspiciously quiet, I've often found that a toothpick can be delicately poked into the exhaust vent and used to get the fan spinning. I've used this trick with at least three different PCs. I suspect that the typical problem is worn bearings that occasionally keep the fan from starting to move when the PC turns on.

How much heat does a PC produce? Measuring the temperature of the airflow leaving a medium-sized Pentium machine, I found it to be about 90°F, almost 20 degrees warmer than the temperature of the well-ventilated room. Inside the cabinet, in the CD-ROM slot (by no means the hottest point in the machine), the temperature was a feverish 102°F.

The air coming out of the top of the display was a torrid 113°F. On several occasions I've measured the chip-package temperatures of CPUs in up-and-running PCs, encountering on-chip temperatures exceeding 130°F.

Help Your PC Keep Its Cool

There are two reasons why a PC system's waste heat matters to you. First, your PC needs good ventilation if you don't want to cook its components into an early grave. The normal operating temperature of electronic components directly affects their lifetime.

Professional service technicians can look at a computer display, for example, and estimate whether key components will last for two years or more like five years, depending on the thermal conditions inside.

What's the second reason? In general, PCs either work or they don't work, but overheated chips can be an exception to this rule. Hot days, in poorly ventilated field sites, are the times that I've most often seen a PC give inaccurate results—while keeping a perfectly straight face. You might be better off with a PC that goes on strike than with one that only appears to be working correctly.

Your PC's performance might also suddenly drop for no obvious reason. This could be due to a safety feature in some systems, especially portable units with poor ventilation, whose processor clocks slow down if the system starts running too hot. Well-designed systems warn you when taking such measures.

Let's Not Waste Those Watts

The other heat-related issue is our computers' overall energy consumption. A PC at rest might directly consume a few tens of watts, which might not seem like a lot. A refrigerator's inside light bulb runs about the same.

A PC's display, however, consumes more like 100 to 200 watts. It's odd that people who would never leave one or two 100-watt light fixtures turned on when they leave a room routinely leave a PC's display turned on all day.

Power consumption is even worse than it seems, however, if you're working in an air-conditioned home or office. All of the power that gets used by a PC or its display turns, eventually, into heat. The air conditioning system needs more time to pump those thermal units out of the building.

An air conditioner, moreover, is not 100 percent efficient: It might require 150 to 250 watt-hours of energy to run during the time it takes to convey 100 watt-hours of heat to the great outdoors.

On average, then, a PC and its display that are left on all day increase an air-conditioned building's total power consumption by close to 500 watts. Office by office, desk by desk, this adds up quickly indeed: Most offices are air-conditioned year 'round, pumping excess heat out of the building even in winter months for just this reason (with lights, copiers, and laser printers adding to the heat load).

I once worked in an office in Louisiana that had no heating facilities at all because there were only a few days every several years when the office didn't have waste heat to spare.

Conversely, this is one good argument for leaving your home PC turned on all the time during the months when your heat is on. You'll use the energy, anyway, so you might as well enjoy the convenience of having your computer available on demand.

Is It Better for My PC to Run All Day?

You can find authoritative opinions on both sides of the question, "Should I leave my PC on all the time?" It's stressful for your PC to go through thermal cycles from cold to hot and back again, because this causes expansion and contraction of electrical components. This constant cycling can turn a microscopic flaw into an intermittent or broken connection. On the other hand, the bearings in a hard disk incur some wear while spinning.

Personally, I steer a middle ground. I generally leave my PC on all day, and often all night when I have many things open that would be a nuisance to close and reactivate. I turn off my monitor, though, whenever I leave my desk for more than ten minutes or so.

Laptop PC designs are more energy-aware than most desktop units, and a portable PC's cool-running flat-panel screen wastes much less power than a TV-style computer display. Most laptop systems can be "put to sleep" in a state that shuts down the hard disk as well as the display, without shutting down your software or closing your open files. I find this a much better way to work, because the noise of the hard disk goes away whenever I'm not using the PC.

As many users move toward a fully equipped laptop PC as their primary machine, the role of PCs in office power consumption might decline. There will rarely be reason to shut down your system completely, unless you're going to be away for days at a time.

The Power Connection

The watts that feed your PC generally come from commercial power sources, except of course for battery operation of portable systems.

It would be nice if I could say to the typical reader of this book, "If you don't live in a Third World country, you can assume that your power supply will be reliable and 'clean.'" It would be nice, but increasingly it isn't true.

For example, I live in a major suburb of Los Angeles, and I had at least four short power outages in the first five months of 1998. Other

NOTE
I'll talk about batteries for portable equipment in Chapter 9.

parts of the United States also suffer from outages and voltage reductions, especially in summer months during peak use of air conditioning systems.

If you live or work in an older home or office building, your electrical wiring might struggle to handle the simultaneous demands of computers, microwave ovens, space heaters, hair dryers, coffeemakers, and other intensive consumers of electrical power. None of this is good news for your PC.

Power to Your PC: It Is What It Eats

Figure 5.2 shows the kind of electrical power that a PC ought to see. This is an actual measurement of normal 120-volt alternating current from an outlet in my home.

In Figure 5.2, you see the continual changing of direction that gives commercial power its name of *alternating current* (AC). Unlike a battery's one-way flow, the back-and-forth flow of AC creates something like a very short-range radio signal in your PC's power supply.

One side of the PC's power transformer transmits energy to the other side, converting that power along the way into one or more different voltages of the kind that your PC's many components require.

The power supply also "rectifies" the AC into one-way, direct current (DC) power. Internally, your PC runs on the same kind of power that it could get from a battery.

A higher-quality power supply produces consistent output, even if it's fed by "dirty" power like the AC source I measured to produce Figure 5.3. Actually, the ugly curve in Figure 5.3 comes from the same outlet I measured to create Figure 5.2, but in Figure 5.3, an electric drill is plugged into another outlet on the same circuit and running at full speed.

You would see the kind of electrical noise that I show in Figure 5.3 as snow on a TV screen; you would hear it as static on your radio. A well-built power supply, however, can filter out these messy power spikes.

As I've said before in this book, you get what you pay for: Robust power management is one of the things that makes a top-tier PC worth the price.

Emergency Rations: A Backup Power Supply

You need to decide how much it's worth to have your PC be the last to know when the power goes sour, or even goes away.

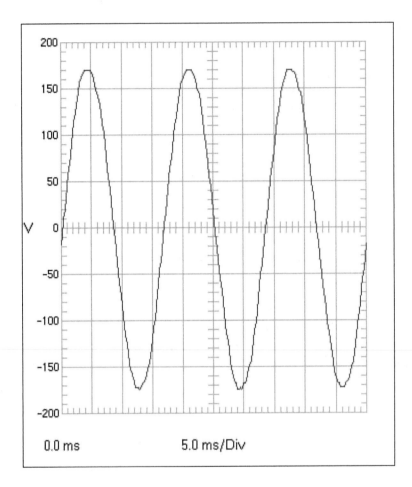

FIGURE 5.2

This figure shows the kind of clean, consistent commercial power that makes life easy for a PC's power supply. Unlike the simple one-way flow of electricity that comes from a battery, what you see here is an oscilloscope trace of *alternating current* (AC).

Sharp-eyed readers might notice that this home electrical power supply, usually called "120-volt" power, is actually peaking at ±170 volts. When we call this type of power a 120-volt (or, some-times, 110-volt or 115-volt or 117-volt) supply, we're talking about a form of average voltage rather than the "peak-to-peak" value that you can read from this display.

At a steady rate of 60 cycles per second, the AC voltage cycle pushes the flow of current in one direction and then the other. The oscillating signal creates an electromagnetic field in a power transformer. Electromagnetic coupling (like a very short-range radio signal) then produces the volt-ages required by a PC's various systems.

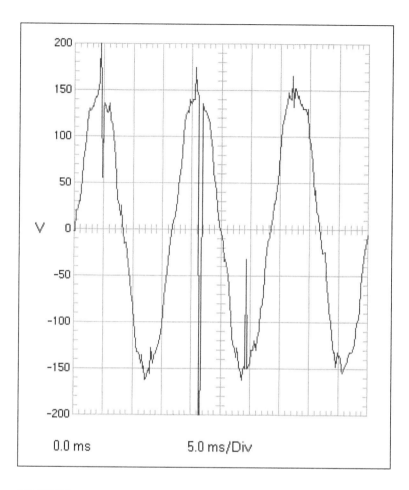

FIGURE 5.3
When other appliances are on the same power circuit as your PC, the PC's internal power supply might have a more difficult job due to electrical "spikes" like the ones you can see in this oscilloscope trace. These sudden voltage transients need to be smoothed out before they damage sensitive components.

Sometimes, a simple power failure would be a comparative blessing compared to the poltergeists that slither out of that AC outlet. Nearby lightning strikes can induce electrical surges that overwhelm even a well-built voltage regulator. Voltages can fluctuate wildly during the first few fractions of a second when power is restored following an outage. Your PC might easily suffer permanent damage during such electrical excursions. My first hard-disk PC lost its motherboard when this happened at a former employer's office.

You probably need a *power strip* just to give you enough outlets for your PC, monitor, modem, printer, answering machine, fax machine... you know what I mean. You might as well spend a few extra dollars for a power strip like the one in Figure 5.4, with built-in "surge suppressor" components that clamp down sudden electrical extremes before they can do costly damage. Every PC should have this basic protection unless your entire building has "conditioned power"—unlikely unless you work in a research facility.

FIGURE 5.4
A power strip comes in handy just for the extra outlets it provides for PC, modem, printer, and other appliances. A few dollars more will give you a surge-suppressor power strip like this one, with added components that block brief overvoltage spikes before they can damage your equipment.

A surge suppressor won't compensate, however, for dips in voltage due to other appliances on the same circuit or due to regional voltage reductions ("brownouts") at times of peak load. For sags as well as spikes, you need something with active components: a power conditioner or standby power supply like the Tripp Lite unit shown in Figure 5.5.

A basic battery-backup unit like the one in Figure 5.5 might have other useful features. For example, the one that I show (which nestles on the back-left corner of my desktop) has a surge suppressor for my phone line as well. I plug the Tripp Lite unit into the phone jack and plug my modem into the Tripp Lite. Induced power surges on the phone line, such as surges from nearby lightning strikes, won't make it into my modem (or go through my modem into my PC).

FIGURE 5.5
A standby power supply keeps a battery charged while powering equipment under normal conditions and switches from outside power to the internal battery quickly enough to keep your PC working without a twitch when the power goes out. The more you spend, the more reserve power you'll have and the more time you'll get to finish your work—and shut down when you're ready.

Like most small office units, however, my power backup doesn't have the fancy circuits needed to make commercial-quality AC like the pure "sine wave" power I showed you in Figure 5.2. Instead, my battery unit puts out the harsher, "square wave" power that you see in Figure 5.6.

A PC power supply doesn't care about the "unfinished" character of a battery backup's output, because the PC converts its incoming power into smoothed DC, regardless. There are other types of equipment, though, that are sensitive to the "edges" of a square-wave power signal.

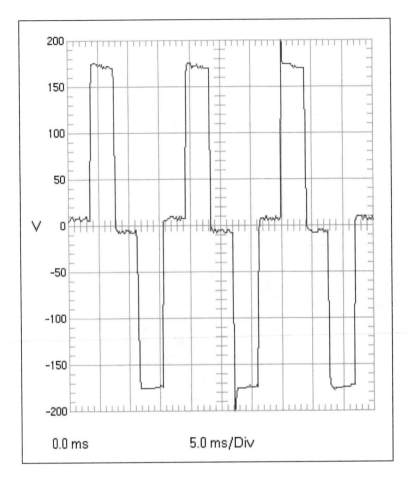

FIGURE 5.6
This oscilloscope trace shows the kind of power that comes from a basic battery-backup unit. This "square-wave" signal is fine for a PC, whose power supply turns it into smoothed "one-way" DC, but these abruptly rising and falling voltages are unkind to other types of equipment, such as hi-fi audio systems.

A perfectly adequate PC backup unit might not be suitable for other types of home or office appliances. Check the manufacturer's recommendations to see if they fit your intended use.

Keyboards, Pointers, and Pens

At lower right in Figure 5.1 is the keyboard connector. The keyboard connector in the photo is an older, large-style fixture. This PC connects its mouse to one of the two serial ports (at upper right in the photo) instead of having a dedicated mouse connection.

Most new PCs have identical, fairly small connectors for both the keyboard and the pointing device (usually a mouse, though some users prefer a trackball—we'll examine both of these options in a moment). Today's common connectors for these two devices are identical, so you need to check for identifying icons or labels.

The latest PCs avoid connector confusion by using a Universal Serial Bus (discussed later) and letting the USB controller figure out which device is which.

Keyboards: You Do Have a Choice

Most users accept the keyboard that comes with a new PC as if it were permanently wired to the machine instead of being a simple plug-in attachment.

Because the standard keyboard is already bought and paid for, I suspect most people feel (if only subconsciously) that they'd be wasting money if they bought a different keyboard for everyday use.

Many users, though, would get more work done with a keyboard of better quality or different design than the typical PC accessory. Two options, in particular, deserve your consideration.

Dvorak Keyboard Layout

It's never too late to think about moving from the traditional QWERTY keyboard (named for the first six letters at top left) to the so-called Dvorak arrangement (developed in 1936 by August Dvorak and William Dealey). The Dvorak setup places all five vowels on the "home row," all on the left hand, with other frequently used letters in the same row to the right. Many studies have found the result to be more productive, with less fatigue.

Unlike a mechanical keyboard, a PC's electronic keyboard can easily switch between QWERTY and Dvorak arrangements at the flip of a switch. Some keyboards have removable key caps that let the user move any letter to any position on the board.

Studies have found that it's possible to switch between QWERTY and Dvorak keyboards, as long as you don't go back and forth while you're learning a new arrangement.

Ergonomic Keyboard Design

With or without a Dvorak arrangement, an *ergonomic* keyboard tries to reduce the strain on a user's wrists and connective tissues. In 1989, the *Los Angeles Times* reported that of its 1,100 editorial employees, more than 200 were suffering from repetitive strain injuries (RSIs) due to constant use of keyboards. RSIs can lead to extended disability, with leaves sometimes lasting ten months.

Personally, I have no physical problems with extended typing as long as I use a desk that's deep enough for the full length of my forearm (elbow to wrist) to rest on the desktop. This is an old telegraph operator's rule, and it works for me. A 36-inch deep desktop is my most emphatic office furniture requirement.

Some people need a more complete solution, and for them I urge a tryout of at least one ergonomic keyboard. Some ergonomic designs look as if a traditional keyboard has been ripped in half or crushed by a pair of bowling balls. I've used one such keyboard, from Kinesis: It's pictured in Figure 5.7. A more adjustable Kinesis design appears in Figure 5.8, and a less radical arrangement from Adesso is shown in Figure 5.9.

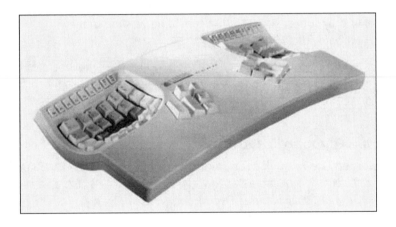

FIGURE 5.7
This Kinesis keyboard is undeniably strange in appearance, but it has loyal followers who prefer its shorter finger movements and unstrained wrist position.

A bird's-eye view of a combined design, with the Dvorak arrangement translated to the Kinesis ergonomic layout, appears in Figure 5.10.

Keyboard Choice: Comfort, Time, and Money

Ergonomic keyboards don't do a thing for me, perhaps because I like to use a keyboard while working in different positions.

FIGURE 5.8
This Kinesis design allows personal adjustment of relative hand positions. Many ergonomic keyboards take this approach.

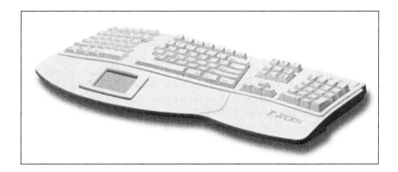

FIGURE 5.9
A less aggressive notion of ergonomic design appears in this board from Adesso.

Sometimes I'm typing, but at other times I'm on the phone and using the keyboard as a one-handed control panel rather than a two-handed text-entry device. When I use an ergonomic keyboard, I feel as if there's one and only one posture and hand placement that the keyboard's designers want me to use. I don't like that feeling.

To me, the most important ergonomic issue is the feel of individual keystrokes. I like a definite snap-through, rather than a keyboard whose keys just push back harder as they're depressed.

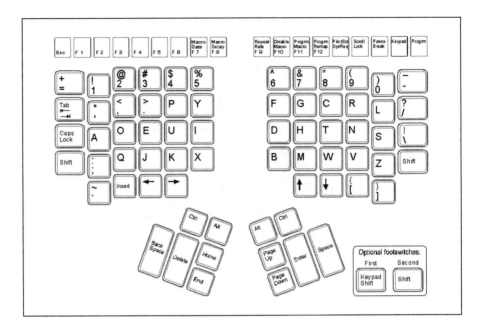

FIGURE 5.10
Two approaches to comfortable keyboarding join forces in this Dvorak version of the Kinesis ergonomic layout.

The snap-through key force behavior, preferred by many people who type for a living, requires expensive mechanical switches on each key that are rarely found on original equipment keyboards.

Because my job as a product reviewer requires me to use a wide variety of hardware, I've grown used to keyboards that I once would have said were unacceptable. I also rely on spelling checkers to catch my frequent accidental doubling of keystrokes on the lightly sprung, short-stroke keys of many laptop computers.

If you get to buy and use a PC that's actually "personal," I hope you'll think about the fact that a keyboard is a constant part of the connection between you and your computer. Taking time to find the one that suits you best is worth your while. And buying the right keyboard is worth the 5% or so that you'll add to the cost of your PC system, even if you already have a keyboard that's "good enough."

Pointing Devices: Tracking Your Options

I distinctly remember the conversation I had with a coworker in 1984, during which I asserted that the mouse was a fad. So much for my ability to forecast the future of technology.

In a way, though, I was right. As PC users become more experienced, they tend to find more ways to do things without taking their hands off their keyboards.

Menu shortcuts, such as Ctrl+C for Copy, and keyboard commands, such as Alt+Tab for switching through your open applications, are much less time-consuming and fatiguing than painstaking movements of the mouse. It's much quicker to select a sentence in your word processor by clicking once, anywhere in that sentence, with the Ctrl key held down, than by carefully dragging the mouse from the beginning of the sentence to its end.

Mechanical Mice Need Maintenance

There are times, I'll concede, when direct manipulation with a pointing device *is* the most efficient way to tell the machine what you want. Even in those situations, though, the device that comes with your PC might not be the best choice for you.

The mouse that typically comes with a new PC has mechanical rollers that translate the movements of a rubber-coated ball into vertical and horizontal components. Over time, it's common for the rollers to become fouled with dust, causing jerky and inconsistent response.

Most mice can easily be opened and cleaned with nothing more than a handkerchief. There is, however, another approach: the optical mouse or trackball.

Optical Devices: Clean and Simple

Instead of sensing movements with mechanical rollers, an optical mouse works in one of two ways. The mouse can bounce a beam of light off of a pad on the desk that's ruled with a grid of evenly spaced lines, detecting its movements across those lines by the reflections received by a sensor in the mouse. This approach has no moving parts at all.

Some people have found that the grid of fine white lines in faded denim jeans serves as an adequate tracking surface for one of these devices: The mouse can just be moved around on the user's thigh.

Personally, I don't like the approach of sensing motion over a fixed grid of reference lines, because the direction of movement is detected relative to the grid instead of relative to the body of the mouse. As I change position at my desk, I want the motion of my arm to translate into the same motion of the pointer on the screen, even if I'm sitting at an angle to the desk. With an optical pad, however, I have to sit squarely facing the PC or constantly adjust the position of the pad if I don't want to feel as if something's off kilter.

My desire to work in different positions, you'll recall, was also the reason that I don't like ergonomic keyboards. PC users who *do* sit up straight might find optical mice with grid-ruled pads to be quite satisfactory.

Another optical mouse design bounces a beam of light off the surface of a rotating ball that's made from a patterned reflective material. The mouse detects the movement of the ball by sensing the motion of the patterned markings.

Using a light beam to detect the ball's rotation has the advantage of eliminating dirt-collecting rollers, though it retains the ball as a moving part that might sometimes have to be cleaned or replaced.

Track Balls Turn the Mouse Upside Down

If your desk is small or messy, you might prefer a track ball instead of a mouse. You could think of a track ball as a mouse that lies on its back; instead of moving the body of the mouse to rotate a ball on the underside, you just move the ball directly with your fingers. Some arcade games use this type of control.

Track balls come in a wide variety of shapes and arrangements, including those shown in Figures 5.11, 5.12, 5.13, and 5.14. The choice of such a device is very much a matter of personal taste.

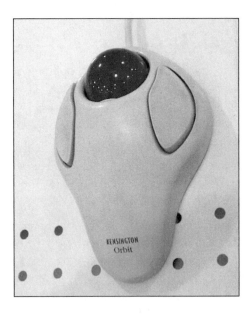

FIGURE 5.11
Kensington's Orbit trackball is equally suited to left- or right-handed users.

FIGURE 5.12
Despite its name, Kensington's ExpertMouse is a generously sized trackball with extra buttons that
can be programmed for special functions.

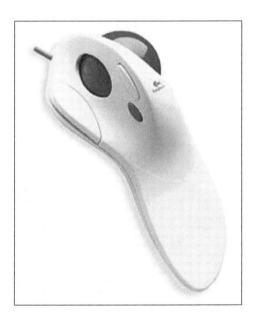

FIGURE 5.13
This MarbleFX model of Logitech's TrackMan Marble series allows fine manipulation, using fingers
and thumb from opposite sides of the optically sensed rotating ball.

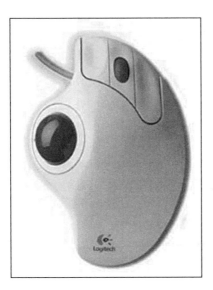

FIGURE 5.14
This elaborate Logitech TrackMan Marble+ combines three mouse buttons, an integral document scrolling roller, and an oversized optical trackball for flexible navigation and control.

A track ball, like a mouse, can use either mechanical or optical sensors to detect the movements of the ball. Many track balls, and some mice, have extra buttons or other added controls that work with accessory software to provide custom functions—for example, navigation shortcuts for moving more quickly through your documents.

Pen Devices: For Special Needs

The PC business has a recurring fantasy that someday people won't need to learn to type, that we will be able to work with a computer by writing with a pen-like stylus instead of pecking away at keys.

I've seen a great many attempts at pen-based machines. The novelty soon wears off. There's a fundamental problem with the idea of pen-based interaction.

When you think about it, most of us do most of our handwriting for ourselves to read. Few of us today make handwritten drafts of long documents that someone else will need to transcribe. Doctors use tape recorders; executives are increasingly unembarrassed about being seen using a keyboard.

When other people don't need to read what we write, we develop personal shorthands. This isn't like talking, when people can tell us if they can't understand what we say. We don't get that feedback on our handwriting when we're the only "audience."

It's tremendously difficult to develop software that can read a person's handwriting, because people so often develop personal styles (and might even have trouble themselves reading what they write). Pocket-sized devices are a natural milieu for pen-type input, and some people swear by these things (as we'll discuss in Chapter 9).

NOTE
I'm much more optimistic about computers transcribing speech, which they do today with surprising accuracy. If you're looking for a keyboard replacement, you might want to try a microphone (as we'll discuss in Chapters 8 and 9).

Another option is the CrossPad (see Figure 5.15), a full-sized clipboard with a radio-transmitter pen. The movements of the pen are sensed and recorded at the same time that the pen is writing on an ordinary sheet of paper. The recorded strokes are transferred to your PC as images. Software supplied with the CrossPad can optionally try to transcribe your notes as if you had typed them into a text editor.

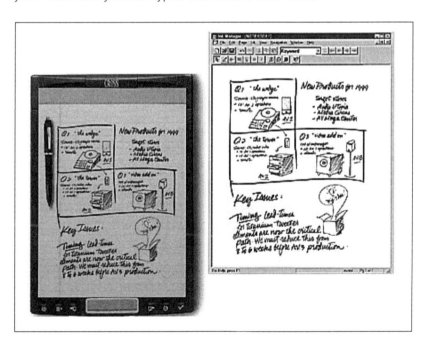

FIGURE 5.15
Using an ordinary paper pad with a radio-transmitting pen and a radio-tracking clipboard, the CrossPad lets you take notes or make sketches while it captures a digital record of your pen strokes. Sketches can go into your PC as images, and handwriting can be recognized (though not especially well) and stored as files of text.

A CrossPad is an expensive accessory, retail-priced at almost $400, but nothing less will give you much utility. At this point, I don't see pen-based input as a cost-effective part of the typical PC system.

Fun and Games

Before we move on to other forms of digital interaction, I have to pay my brief respects to the electromechanical wizardry that adds realism to advanced computer games.

You might have seen a *joystick* control on a first- or second-generation PC or game machine, but that won't prepare you for the sight (and the feel) of a high-end controller such as the Logitech Wingman Digital Extreme (see Figure 5.16). Like the cheap processors that make a Logitech Marble trackball work smoothly and reliably, a digital game controller uses cheap processing power to send clear digital signals (instead of easily degraded analog signals) to your PC. Most current-model PCs have the needed *game port* connection to use this kind of device.

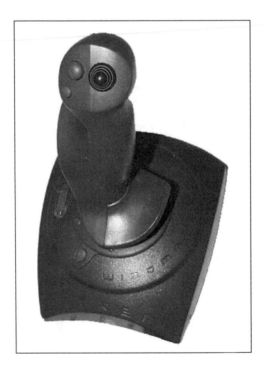

FIGURE 5.16
A high-end "joystick" such as Logitech's Wingman Digital Extreme is an entertaining add-on for PC users who want direct control of active games.

The most sophisticated game controllers have electronic actuators that can feed back pressures and movements to the user under the PC's control. Programmed force feedback, provided by controllers such as Microsoft's Sidewinder Force Feedback Pro (see Figure 5.17) and CH Products' Force FX (see Figure 5.18), creates a realistic feel for moving over simulated terrain or operating simulated aircraft controls.

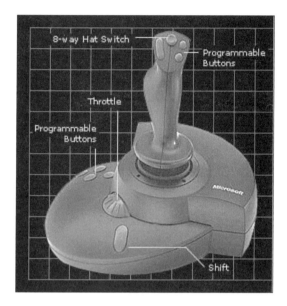

FIGURE 5.17
Microsoft's most advanced game controller, the Sidewinder Force Feedback Pro, is one of the few to offer built-in electronic actuators to create realistic forces that simulate interactive environments.

Accessory Connections: Ports of Call

When it's time to connect a modem, a printer, or many other types of external devices to your PC, there are two kinds of connections that you will probably need to make.

The basic, almost ancient connections between sources and destinations of digital signals are usually called by their common, if imprecise, names: the *serial* and *parallel* ports.

FIGURE 5.18
CH Products' Force FX is less elaborate than Microsoft's Sidewinder Pro, but shares its unusual capability of generating feedback forces that bring ordinary PC games somewhat closer to "virtual reality."

Ancient and Modern: The Serial Ports

Generically, a serial data interface is any connection that transfers bits in sequential streams. This contrasts with a parallel interface, which transfers a group of bits all at once.

A parallel interface must provide several signal paths that can be used at a single time, making parallel interface hardware more costly to build and a parallel interface cable more bulky and expensive. A serial interface is less expensive but considerably slower than parallel data transfer (all other things being equal).

The RS-232 (COM) Connection: Old Reliable

Almost any device that you can name has probably been connected, at some time and in some fashion, to a PC by means of the "old reliable" serial connection. On your PC, we're talking about the ports that go by the name *COM ports* (for "communications"): Most PCs have at least one, often two, known as COM1 and (if present) COM2. If your laptop PC has infrared connections for wireless printing and other tasks, the infrared link is probably a COM port as well.

The formal name of a standard serial connection is RS-232, but there's no useful meaning in this name. It's merely the label of a standard defined by the Electronics Industries Association. "RS-232" has no more intrinsic meaning than "Form 1040."

Like the CPU operations we studied in Chapter 4, the data transfer operations performed by a serial COM port seem incredibly clumsy when we break them down into their low-level steps. The saving grace is that the steps take place in a cycle that repeats many thousands of times a second, producing the smooth data transfers that we usually take for granted.

Nine Wires...or Maybe Not

A fully wired serial cable provides nine connections from one piece of equipment to another. Some equipment uses a nine-pin connector, like the two smaller connectors in Figure 5.19.

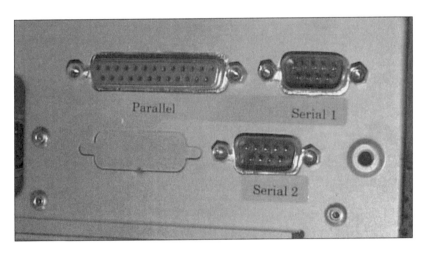

FIGURE 5.19
A typical PC has two 9-pin male connectors, providing two serial ports (also called COM or RS-232 connectors), and a 25-pin female connector for a parallel port (also called a printer port, an LPT port, or a Centronics interface).

The small trapezoidal sockets in Figure 5.19, helpfully labeled Serial 1 and Serial 2, are called DB-9 connectors. Connectors with pins, like the two DB-9s shown here, are called *male* connectors. The cable that plugs into this kind of port needs to have a *female* DB-9 plug, with a matching receptacle for each of the pins.

Some equipment still uses a larger, 25-pin connector (logically enough, it's called a DB-25) for each serial port connection. This is a waste of space: A DB-25 in serial-port service uses only ten of its 25 conductors (adding an extra electrical ground connection to the nine connections provided by a DB-9). Adapters are widely available, should you ever find yourself with a cable that has a DB-9 at the end and a PC that has a DB-25 on its backside.

Confusingly, most PCs also use a DB-25 connector for their parallel interface, as shown and labeled in Figure 5.19. Note, however, that the parallel DB-25 output connector is female (with receptacles), while a serial DB-25 output is typically male (with pins).

Even more confusing, there are two different ways to assign the nine different signals of a serial connection to the wires of the serial cable. A piece of equipment can be wired as Data *Terminal* Equipment (DTE) or Data *Communications* Equipment (DCE).

A PC is treated like an old-fashioned *dumb terminal* (a device that communicates with a computer at another location, with no local processing or storage) and is wired as DTE. Modems are DCE. A standard serial cable connects a DTE device such as a PC to a DCE device such as a modem without any problems.

Some printers, however, are also wired with serial connections. Remember that in the olden days, a printer was always connected to a distant computer, not to a nearby PC, so a serial printer is also considered a terminal device and wired as DTE.

When you connect a PC to a serial printer—or to another PC—you're wiring one DTE to another DTE. The wires in a standard cable aren't set up for this, so you need an inexpensive but vital adapter (called a *null modem*) to reroute the wires. With the null modem in place, each of your DTE devices "sees" the DCE connections it expects.

Be warned, though, that I had a reason for specifying a "fully wired" serial connection several paragraphs ago. Some low-priced cables only provide enough wires to connect the minimal pathways for sending and receiving data, ignoring the connections that let two devices exchange detailed information about their readiness to communicate.

In addition to the minimal data pathways, a complete serial interface includes paths for control information ("handshaking" circuits). When devices expect to see the *handshake* signals but a cable isn't wired to carry them, communication won't take place.

What's on the Serial Interface Wires?

With the proviso that a serial connection might not be using all of its specified connections, here is the layout of a serial interface. You might go for years without ever needing to know this; then again, you might soon find yourself the owner of a PC-controllable appliance (or even a children's toy) whose setup requires this knowledge.

I'll focus on the pin numbers that apply to the DB-9 connector that's usually installed on a PC. I'll also give the DB-25 pin numbers that apply to some PCs and to most modems.

To avoid confusion, I'll first give the name of the signal that's being sent on a particular pin—such as the Data Carrier Detected (DCD) signal or the Transmitted Data (TXD) signal—and then I'll tell you the direction in which that signal travels.

The metal shell of a DB-9 serial port connector on your PC is connected to the frame of the PC to serve as a safety ground. A DB-25 connector also uses pin 1 for this purpose. This is not, however, the ground reference level that's used for the sent and received signals.

Pin 1 of a PC's DB-9 (pin 8 of a DB-25) receives the Data Carrier Detected (DCD) signal that's raised by an external device when it detects a "live" communication line. If a modem loses its connection to the phone line, the modem disables DCD. Some equipment does not use this signal.

Pin 2 of a PC's DB-9 (pin 3 of a DB-25) receives data from the corresponding pin of a DCE device such as a modem. This signal is called RXD (*received* data), whether we're talking about the DTE device (the PC) or the DCE device—even though the DCE device is *sending* it to the PC.

Pin 3 of a PC's DB-9 (pin 2 of a DB-25) transmits data from the PC to the DCE device—to the DCE's pin 3 if the DCE has a DB-9, to the DCE's pin 2 if the DCE has a DB-25. This signal is called TXD (*transmitted* data), whether we're talking about the DTE or the DCE end of the connection, even though the DCE device is *receiving* it from the PC.

Pin 4 of a PC's DB-9 (pin 20 of a DB-25) sends the Data Terminal Ready (DTR) signal from the PC to the DCE device, indicating that the PC is ready to accept data. If the DTR signal disappears, a modem (for example) should hang up its phone-line connection.

Pin 5 of a PC's DB-9 (pin 7 of a DB-25) provides the "signal ground" reference connection. Transmitted and received signals are supposed to create a 12-volt difference against this reference level, with anything less than a 3-volt difference assumed to be electrical noise.

As connection length grows longer, desired signals get weaker and pickup of electrical noise gets stronger; the RS-232 standard is not suited to long-distance connections. A standard serial interface should not be used, in general, with cable lengths of more than 100 feet—less if you want to use high data rates in the tens of thousands of bits per second.

Pin 6 on either type of DB-series connector carries the Data Set Ready signal from the DCE device to the PC. DSR indicates that the DCE device is active. This is the counterpart to the DTR signal that's raised by the PC.

Pin 7 of a PC's DB-9, or pin 4 of a DB-25, carries the Request To Send (RTS) signal from the PC to the DCE device. This signal tells the DCE that data is ready to be sent by the PC.

Pin 8 of a PC's DB-9, or pin 5 of a DB-25, carries the Clear To Send (CTS) signal from the DCE to the PC, indicating that the DCE is ready to accept data. The RTS and CTS signals can be used to manage the flow of data between the two devices.

Finally, pin 9 of a PC's DB-9 (pin 22 of a DB-25) handles the Ring Indicator signal used by a modem to indicate that a call is coming in. It's often useful to have a modem-equipped PC that can answer incoming calls (for example, when the PC is serving as a paperless fax machine). We'll talk about modem technology and the uses of today's advanced modems in Chapter 7.

You can actually see the furious exchange of signals across the multiple wires, carrying both data and control information, while a serial port is active. If you have an external modem, there are usually visible indicators for each of the important signals.

If you have an internal modem, you don't have visible indicator lights to signal strange behavior on a connection, but some internal modems come with accessory software that displays similar indicators on your PC's screen.

A PC or data communications technician often has a small piece of equipment called a breakout box that can monitor the activity on the different wires of a serial connection. There are even "smart cables" with built-in processors that figure out which wire is which by looking at signal patterns. With such a cable, you can connect any two serial devices without concern for their DTE or DCE "gender."

USB: How We'll Connect Tomorrow

When I was talking about optical trackballs earlier in this chapter, I said that it is helpful to use cheap processing power to offset the limits of hardware. The same principle applies to serial data ports.

We often run out of serial ports on a well-equipped PC, especially when using a PC for innovative tasks such as home automation. It would be convenient if we could put more than one device on a single set of wires, wrapping the data for each device in a sort of electronic envelope.

The PC could use extra bits, wrapped around the data, to address each signal on a single pair of wires to be "read" by a particular piece of equipment. This "multi-plexing" of data requires processing power that would have run an entire PC at the beginning of the desktop computer revolution, but today this kind of capability costs less than $1 per device.

In general, a connection that's shared by several devices is called a *bus*, and the idea I've just described is called the Universal Serial Bus (USB). If you buy a new PC, you'll probably get one or two USB connections that can each communicate with up to 127 devices.

USB cables carry electrical power as well as data, meaning that USB accessories don't need their own power supplies. We can banish those little brick-like plug/transformers that take up so much space when we plug in a modem.

When you plug in a USB device, signals automatically go between the device and the USB controller in your PC to tell the PC that a new device is present and to register the device on one of three priority levels.

A USB device might be a *real-time* (no delay acceptable) device, such as a TV camera; it might be an intermittent but high-priority device, such as a game controller whose signals aren't continuous but are in need of immediate attention when they arrive; it might be a lower priority device that sends a lot of data but not on an urgent schedule (such as a scanner or still-image camera). All of these distinctions are handled automatically.

USB connections can handle high data rates, more than 100 times the speed of a conventional serial port. A fast USB device (such as a TV camera) expects to be serviced at 12 million bits per second, while a slow USB device (such as a keyboard) only expects a data rate of 1.5 million bits per second (still 15 times the top speed of a standard serial port).

Unlike the tedious process of configuring a serial port, following specific directions for installing a device such as a modem or printer, USB setup is automatic.

As I said, USB applies processing power instead of clumsy hardware: It only requires a four-wire connection, and two of those wires carry power. The confusing, inconsistent multiwire connections of DB-9 and DB-25 connectors will soon be mildly amusing lore of the crude early years of PCs.

Fast and Flexible: The Parallel Ports

Like the standardized, processor-driven connections of the Universal Serial Bus, the other two common connections on the back of a PC are fast, reliable, and fairly well standardized.

The connections that I'm talking about now are faster than standard serial ports, getting their higher speed from their large numbers of parallel pathways for data. It makes sense that these fast interface options are called, generically, parallel ports.

The Centronics (LPT) Interface: More Than a Printer Connection

When people speak of a PC's "parallel port" or "printer port" or "LPT port," they're usually talking about a female DB-25 connector (like the one labeled "Parallel" in Figure 5.19).

Like the RS-232 serial port, the common "Centronics interface" parallel port is a design that predates today's cheap processing power. The parallel port uses dumb wires, instead of smart logic, to send control information separate from data.

The parallel port can carry information in both directions, making it an option for high-speed data exchange with devices other than printers (for example, with external data storage devices such as the Iomega Zip drive covered later in this chapter).

Many PCs have only one parallel port and usually have that port connected to a printer; few users want to unplug and replug these inaccessible connections. It's common, therefore, for vendors to include a "pass-through" connector with any other PC accessory that wants a parallel-port connection.

A two-headed pass-through connector lets a single port on the PC serve more than one external device, but this is something of a kluge. Pass-through connectors are not as reliable as sharable USB ports.

Sharing is part of the design of USB ports (or SCSI ports, discussed below), but pass-through connectors for parallel ports are a "plug and pray" proposition. If you need reliable operation of more than one parallel-interface accessory to your PC, a second parallel port is a worthwhile option and can be added in several ways (though the details depend on your particular machine).

The SCSI Port: Seven at One Blow

Another type of parallel connection is the Small Computer System Interface (SCSI, pronounced "scuzzy") port. Some types of computers, such as the Macintosh, use SCSI as their primary means of adding devices such as extra hard disks. The SCSI port has also been a favorite for high-performance graphics equipment, such as scanners, though USB seems likely to take over this role.

Counting the Daisies

SCSI, like USB, is designed to handle more than one device on a single PC connection. Up to seven external devices can be connected, each to the next, in an arrangement that's called a "daisy chain."

Each of the devices that shares a single SCSI port must have an identifying number, 0 through 7 (yes, that's eight different numbers, but the SCSI controller in the PC needs one of those ID numbers for itself). Switches or electrical plugs or setup software can be used to assign these IDs.

The last device in the chain has to have a dummy connection to smooth the signals' path. This closure is provided by a terminator block, as shown in Figure 5.20.

Some low-cost SCSI devices have internal terminators, saving the cost of an external connector and block, but this design limits your flexibility: Only one such device can be used on any SCSI port, and it has to come at the end of the chain.

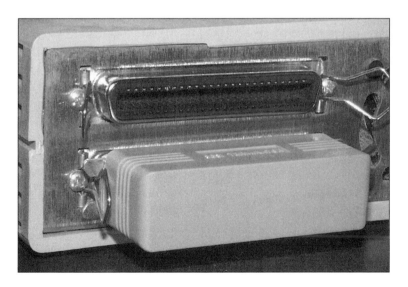

FIGURE 5.20
SCSI connectors typically come in pairs, as shown here, because SCSI devices are "daisy chained" by connecting each device to the next one that shares a single port on the PC. A single device, or the last device in a chain, needs a "terminator" like the one shown plugged into the lower connector in this photo. Some devices have a built-in termination block.

Many Kinds of SCSIs

Once a simple standard, SCSI has spawned enhanced versions driven by different vendors. Adaptec is a reliable source of devices (supporting both standard SCSI and its high-performance variants) that let you add a SCSI port to a PC that doesn't have one.

You should determine in advance the compatibility of a particular SCSI device with the SCSI controller you have or plan to purchase.

SCSI's Strengths Might Not Apply to You

In theory, SCSI is capable of very high performance in complex situations, such as streaming video from a CD-ROM drive while also retrieving data from a hard disk on the same controller.

A SCSI controller can send several different requests to a SCSI device such as a hard disk, perhaps retrieving data at the behest of multiple programs that are running at the same time.

A SCSI device can queue requests and handle them in the most efficient order instead of slavishly filling requests in the same order that they arrived. High-end SCSI variants can deliver 640 million bits per second (more than fifty times the speed of USB) across distances of almost 40 feet.

It's not likely, however, that your PC needs will call for industrial strength SCSI, and independent tests increasingly tend to show that simpler and cheaper solutions (such as EIDE, described later) are quite competitive with ordinary SCSI hardware.

Video Output: Looking Simply Radiant

The back of a PC typically includes other connectors that are ranked in columns as shown in Figure 5.21. Each column corresponds to an internal slot that can hold an electronic adapter, such as the one that generates video signals for your display.

I'll talk about video in detail in Chapter 6, but in this chapter I just want to talk about the video output signal as an electrical and radio-interference issue.

In Figure 5.21, you'll notice that some of the back-panel slots are open so that you can see into the PC's interior. Normally, any slot that doesn't hold an adapter should be covered by a plate like the ones that block slots 1, 4, and 8 (counting from left) in this machine. Uncovered slots, like slots 3 and 5 here, radiate energy that can interfere with TVs and other appliances.

FIGURE 5.21
Much of a PC's back panel consists of the "slots" that hold internal adapters. On this PC, left to right, are the video output, the sound card, and the network connections (along with some empty slots, two of them uncovered).

A quality PC takes pains to limit stray radiation. Figure 5.22 shows the interior of this PC's plastic cover, lined with a metal shield that has "fingers" around its edges to provide good electrical contact with the frame of the PC.

The video display, however, can't be covered with a metal shield, because you need to see it. Light waves and radio waves, unfortunately, are just different "colors" of the same kind of energy. This means that your bright, colorful display is also a major path for radio signal leakage.

Figure 5.23 shows a hand-held radio, tuned to the 150MHz clock rate of the PC in the background. Note the long black bar beneath the digits of the frequency display: That's a signal-strength indicator, showing that this PC's display is a veritable beacon of radio waves that can interfere with other activities.

You can't block all radio emissions from your display, but you can minimize the problem with a good-quality monitor, one that is well shielded, with a cable that has built-in traps to block most "parasite" signals.

FIGURE 5.22
The metal lining of this PC's top cover has springy "fingers" for best electrical contact with the frame, minimizing leakage of radio interference that could affect nearby devices.

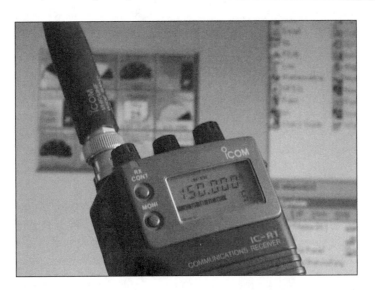

FIGURE 5.23
A hand-held VHF radio shows a strong signal (black bar under frequency readout) on the 150MHz clock frequency of the Pentium PC whose display is in the background. Different images on the screen produce different sounds on the radio; hard disk activity can also be "heard."

Ethernet: The Digital Cocktail Party

The rightmost column of connectors in Figure 5.21 are the ones on this PC's network card that can provide an Ethernet connection, using several types of wiring.

Surprisingly, many homes, and almost all offices and schools, are using some kind of network to let PCs communicate with each other and with shared devices such as central hard-disk storage systems and laser printers. Ethernet is a simple and popular choice for such connections.

Different types of wire or cable can readily be used for an Ethernet hookup. This card accepts more than one type of connector. The twist-on "bayonet" connector that's called a BNC (lower right in the photo) is rugged and convenient.

Ethernet lets many devices share a single pathway, but unlike a USB arrangement, there is no single "master" on an Ethernet. Any device can send to any other, and can try to send at any time.

An Ethernet device listens before it sends and will not send if the line is busy. This is called "carrier sensing."

If the line is quiet, any device can begin to send. This is called "multiple access."

When a device starts sending, it also listens. If two devices send at the same time, or close enough to cause a possible problem, both devices hear each other and stop sending. Each device waits for a small, variable delay time before it tries again; the odds are high that one device will get through before the other tries to send again. This is called "collision detection."

Carrier-sense multiple access with collision detection gives the Ethernet model its formal name of CSMA/CD. It's also called the "cocktail party" model because of its resemblance to people talking in a large, noisy group and backing off when they realize that someone else spoke first.

A malfunctioning Ethernet device can tie up the entire network by keeping the line continuously busy, so Ethernet isn't right for every situation. For home, school, and many office applications, the flexibility of adding new devices at any time often makes Ethernet appropriate.

Going Inside

The network connection is the last thing we can see from the outside of the PC. The cover is already off of the PC for its picture in Figure 5.22, so we might as well go in.

Meet the Big Chip

What everyone usually wants to see first is "the computer"; that is, the CPU chip whose behavior we explored in an abstract sense in Chapter 4.

Figure 5.24 shows the Pentium chip in this machine—or rather, shows the cooling fan on top of the chip, with the chip's ceramic package barely visible at the corners.

FIGURE 5.24
A Pentium chip can barely be seen underneath its attached cooling fan. Many PCs provide one of these chip coolers, and you can even buy a temperature probe that signals an alarm if your chip gets too hot—which can cause erratic results. I've measured chip temperatures during various operations, and some chips get substantially hotter when they're working hard (for example, the chips on a video display adapter).

BIOS: The Big Chip's Trusty Sidekick

No one ever asks to see it, and it's not nearly as interesting to look at, but the BIOS chip (the Basic Input/Output System) is a hugely important component of your PC.

The BIOS handles essential conversions between the high-level operations requested by your software and the low-level commands that a physical device can recognize. It's the BIOS, for example, that knows what to tell your floppy disk drive when a program asks to read a particular file.

Some things are wired into the BIOS, which is a form of read-only memory (ROM) of the kind that we discussed in Chapter 4. The BIOS, for example, tells your PC how to get itself going when you turn it on, so this information has to be stored in a form that doesn't go away when the power goes off.

Device Drivers: The BIOS Reading Room

The BIOS can also consult a library of software supplements, called device drivers, that give your PC the capability to use new accessories. When you install a new piece of equipment and you have to insert a floppy disk as part of the installation process, you're giving your PC a chance to add the needed device-driver files to its collection.

Device drivers are a demanding form of software because their speed affects basic operations such as putting things on the display. Because they emphasize performance, device-driver programs are especially likely to harbor tricky bugs that don't show up in early tests.

Of all the things that you might ever need to do to fix a PC, one of your most likely chores is obtaining an updated device driver from the company that made some accessory such as a fancy graphics card. Driver updates are often available by downloading them from a company's Web site, as we'll discuss in Chapters 10 and 17.

To be fair, though, device driver updates aren't always a matter of fixing a defect. Sometimes a driver update is merely an improvement in performance or capability that comes free—or at any rate, for no more than the cost of a local phone call and the value of half an hour of your time.

Some Settings Can Be Changed

When your PC boots up, it probably shows you the command that you can use to interrupt the normal startup process and take a side trip to examine the BIOS settings. Some of those settings can be changed, because they're not stored in ROM; they're in a special slice of memory that has its own little battery, keeping that memory intact when the PC shuts down.

When the battery for the configuration memory finally dies, the PC might get seriously confused. If you have a machine that's five to seven years old, you might want to get out its manuals and see if it's time for a bit of preventive maintenance such as a battery replacement. Most manuals will give you a recommended period, usually many years, after which the backup battery should be replaced. (Few people keep a PC long enough to encounter this problem.)

You might also have a BIOS that can be updated from a floppy disk or from an Internet download. Updatable BIOS chips use a type of memory that persists, like ROM, when the power is off, but that can be updated without special hardware. This is called a "flash" BIOS. You'll hear my saga of a BIOS update later, in Chapter 10.

It might seem that persistent but rewritable memory, like that of a flash BIOS chip, would be useful for all of our memory needs because it would keep us from losing our work when the power goes off. There is, of course, a catch: Such memory chips are only good for a limited number of rewrite operations.

The rewrite limitation of not-quite-read-only flash memory far exceeds the number of BIOS updates that anyone's likely to require before a PC becomes obsolete. The lifetime limit on rewrite operations is far too small, however, for typical PC tasks.

The Fastest Buses in Town

Looking through those uncovered gaps in Figure 5.21, you can dimly see the connectors of some empty slots inside that PC. Figure 5.25 shows a more direct, overhead view of a modern PCI slot and an older but still popular EISA/ISA slot.

FIGURE 5.25
A PCI slot (top) and an EISA/ISA slot (bottom) are the two most common types of connections for adding hardware inside an IBM-compatible PC.

ISA: Oldie But (Adequately) Goodie

A throwback to the first-generation PC, the 16-bit ISA card is still a solid platform for affordable expansion devices.

The ISA card's full name, Industry Standard Architecture, is a remnant of the "bus wars" of the late 1980s. People had previously been content with the unofficial label of "AT bus," referring to IBM's name for its 16-bit PC that used the Intel 286 processor. Things got ugly, however, when IBM introduced a high-performance bus called the Micro Channel Architecture. IBM announced that it intended to enforce its patent rights in connection with Micro Channel, as opposed to the somewhat relaxed attitude that the company had previously taken with regard to AT-related patents.

Competitors of IBM, who had copied the bus design of the 16-bit IBM PC-AT without paying IBM its patent royalties, promptly dropped the name AT bus to wrap themselves in the flag of industry standards.

From an engineer's point of view, the ISA (or AT) bus is a dreadful kluge. It demands the central processor to participate in virtually every operation involving any card in an ISA slot.

The ISA design made sense when a PC had only one microprocessor, but today's cheap processors make it more sensible—from a technical point of view—to let each card handle its own affairs. Still, today's PC often has much more CPU than it needs, and ISA cards are cheap to build. For commercial reasons, ISA slots persist, though Microsoft and others are trying to discourage the use of ISA slots in next-generation "PC 99" systems.

When a PC's internal management chips don't have to deal with the nuisance of ISA slots, the PC can be made "smarter" and easier to use.

EISA and Micro Channel: The Short-Lived Reign of the Masters

EISA, or Extended Industry Standard Architecture, had a well-defined "bus-mastering" capability. A *bus master adapter* could control its own interactions with other devices without involving the central processor. EISA also provided a wider data path, permitting 32-bit data transfers at high speeds.

Unlike Micro Channel slots, EISA slots can accommodate 16-bit ISA cards and can even accept a simple 8-bit card designed for a first-generation PC. This made EISA a marketing success, as far as suppressing buyers' interest in Micro Channel (which also had the initial stigma of higher cost and fewer available adapter cards).

Neither EISA nor Micro Channel ever became the mainstream desktop design, though EISA was an important enhancement for network server machines that interacted with many users at once. Servers use the distributed intelligence of EISA or Micro Channel bus-mastering disk controllers and network interface adapters to meet those manyfold requests without encountering data bottlenecks at the CPU.

Despite their value in servers, neither EISA nor Micro Channel was ready for the explosion of interest in multimedia PCs for entertainment and education.

VL Bus: A Chartered Express to the Display

What took the wind out of EISA's sails was the introduction of "local bus" designs. These provided a special set of signal paths for high-speed, high-priority tasks such as feeding the video display and the hard disk.

EISA was more than buyers needed for such jobs as connecting an internal modem, but it was slower and less cost-effective than the Video Local bus (VL bus) promoted by the Video Electronics Standards Association (VESA).

VL bus was not, however, a general-purpose design: It was costly to provide VL bus control circuits for only one or two slots in a system. The market was ready for a bus design that could handle a fairly large number of high-speed slots, holding cards that weren't expensive to build.

PCI Bus: What We Ride Today

Faster and more versatile than the VL bus, the Peripheral Component Interconnect (PCI) bus quickly became the popular choice for performance-critical expansion cards.

Transferring 132 Mbytes per second, PCI keeps up with almost everything. Its speed exceeds the 107 Mbytes/sec of VL bus and far outstrips the 8 Mbytes/sec of ISA bus connections.

The only thing that makes PCI look somewhat dated is the Accelerated Graphics Port connection that's appearing on new multimedia-oriented PC systems. Using special interconnecting logic, AGP devices can access the memory system at 528 Mbytes/sec.

AGP is in demand for game-playing machines, but PCI will remain the general-purpose workhorse for some time.

Interrupts and DMA: Conductors on the Bus

Earlier, I spoke of the need to avoid engaging the CPU in every operation of a PC accessory card. It would be utterly wasteful to have the CPU spend most of its time asking each card, in succession, "Do you need anything from me?" The latter approach, called *polling*, makes sense in some specialized situations, but in general, it's more efficient for a card to ask for help when it needs it.

A device on a bus can ask for attention by raising an *interrupt*. The device puts out a special signal that tells the CPU, "Pay attention." A CPU can define several levels of interrupt, reserving some levels for urgent tasks and *masking* others.

A CPU may ignore masked interrupts when it's involved in a high-priority task of its own. Other, *nonmaskable interrupts* (NMIs) are always noticed.

ISA cards only define a small number of interrupts, and no two cards can share a single *interrupt request line* (an *IRQ*, for short). Mixing ISA add-in units that come from different vendors is difficult, because there is no good way to coordinate IRQ assignments and no central authority to impose consistent choices. ISA cards remain in common use, so this problem persists.

Another means of reducing the burden on the CPU is *Direct Memory Access*. DMA is a limited form of bus-mastering that allows an accessory to communicate directly with memory. As with IRQs, the use of DMA requires coordinated assignment of a limited number of *DMA channels*.

Plug and Play: Almost As Good As It Should Be

In the mid-1990s, PC accessory vendors got high volumes of telephone calls from people who had just bought a PC add-on product—especially something like a sound card—but couldn't figure out how to install it. Some products had return rates of 90% or more, costing both retailers and manufacturers a huge amount of money.

This created the impetus for *Plug and Play*, an effort to define multi-vendor standards for asking a PC accessory what system resources it needs and coordinating its needs with those of other accessories in the system.

When Plug and Play works, it's wonderful. Cards carry "scratch pad" memories for their individual setup options. The PC can determine how a card is configured and can change configuration settings as needed (most of the time) to make different accessories work well together.

PC Cards (PCMCIA)

One of the ultimate forms of Plug and Play is the PC Card, formerly known by the unwieldy acronym PCMCIA (Personal Computer Memory Card Interface Association).

Not Just for Portable PCs

No longer used just for memory, PC Cards (as they're now called) are the preferred format for packaging portable computer accessories such as modems and add-on hard disks (like the one shown in Figure 5.26).

FIGURE 5.26
This removable hard disk, encapsulated in an almost indestructible PC Card, is practically an antique with its capacity of only 260 Mbytes. Hard disks, modems, network interface adapters, and many other devices are available in this convenient form.

All PC Cards use the same 68-pin connector and have the same shape (measuring 85.6 by 54.0 millimeters), but cards come in three types that differ in thickness. Type I cards are 3.3 millimeters thick, Type II are 5.0 millimeters, Type III are 10.5 millimeters.

Be sure that a system you're considering has adequate space to hold the number and type of cards you want. Some thin systems, for example, might provide two PC Card connectors but stack them so closely that you can only install a single card if it is of Type III thickness.

You should also check the thermal ratings of the cards you're thinking of buying and compare them to the total thermal rating of your portable system or other PC Card equipment. PC Cards do a lot of work within a small space, and they generate heat just like other parts of a PC. The "normal" operating temperature for a PC Card is a toasty 65°C or 149°F.

Since March 1997, new cards have been expected to come with a thermal rating to indicate the heat load that the card will impose on the PC's cooling system. A PC should be able to use any combination of cards that fit in the available PC Card slots if their thermal ratings do not add up to more than the total thermal rating of the system.

You can buy a PC Card socket that fits into the same type of "equipment bay" that would normally hold a floppy disk drive on a desktop PC. With this facility, you can move a PC Card hard disk between home and work, or between desktop and portable systems.

Hot Swaps and Portability: Theory and Practice

In theory, PC Cards can be "hot swapped"; that is, removed and installed in a running computer with no need to shut down the PC. This generally does work.

Also in theory, any PC Card will work in any device with a PC Card slot. This is less reliable, and should not be assumed.

If you plan to move a PC Card device among several different machines, don't make any purchase unless you can return it with no questions asked if you have compatibility problems.

System Memory: What You're Most Likely to Add

It's hopeful, and even likely, that the only reason you'll ever open your PC is to add more memory.

Unless you have a machine with at least 64 Mbytes of memory, I would say that a memory expansion is a likely event before you decide to donate your PC to a deserving charity and get a completely new machine.

Memory is a highly competitive market, and back pages of journals such as *PC Week* are filled with ads from vendors who can tell you, accurately, what type of memory module you need for your particular machine.

Figure 5.27 shows the banks of memory modules in one typical PC. These memory modules should be handled with care, but installing them requires no electronic skills. It's easier than adding oil to your car, and much easier than bathing your cat.

To expand your PC's memory, just follow the directions that came with your PC or your purchased memory units. Give particular attention to the matter of avoiding static electricity (like the sparks that jump from your fingertip to a doorknob in cold, dry weather).

You can damage memory chips with an electrical jolt that isn't big enough to make a visible spark. If you're careful to touch a grounded metal object (such as a metal faucet) before you handle the memory units, you'll probably have no problems with this process.

FIGURE 5.27
Memory units like these can easily be added, making your PC run memory-hungry Windows applications (especially those involving graphics) far more smoothly.

Mass Storage: Cherished Memories

Before we get into the really interesting stuff in the chapters still to come, we have one more category of boring "utility" hardware to cover.

People don't buy PCs to satisfy a personal interest in data storage hardware. We might buy a PC for its neat video capabilities, with the games and creative graphics that they enable; we might buy a PC for its exceptional sound system, with the realism that it adds to games. But no one buys a PC because they're blown away by its hard disk or because they sleep better at night just knowing that it has a tape backup drive.

On the other hand, nothing will make you lose more sleep than data storage that turns out not to have the bits you needed most, readily available when you need them. Nothing will keep you late at the office more often than projects that are too big to move with ease from work to home.

Mass storage has to be big enough, fast enough, portable enough, and reliable enough that you can get your work done, or nothing else that a PC can do will matter.

Floppy Disks

The floppy disk, like the ballpoint pen, is a miracle of modern manufacturing. Though made with incredible precision, it's still so cheap that these things flood our homes and offices in huge promotional mailings.

Figure 5.28 shows a typical 3.5 inch "floppy disk," which is obviously neither floppy nor disk-shaped. In the photo, I'm doing something that I urge you not to do: I'm sliding open the metal door that normally protects the magnetic recording medium from dust and other contaminants.

FIGURE 5.28
The floppy disk is the part *inside* the plastic shell, visible only when we unwisely open the shutter that protects the polished magnetic surface from dust and other contaminants.

Inside the Shell

Figure 5.29 shows a disassembled floppy, revealing the part that actually *is* a floppy disk. That flexible element is shown close up in Figure 5.30.

Lining the rigid plastic shell are cleaning pads, like the one shown at closer range in Figure 5.31. These pads trap small particles that manage to get past the metal shutter, preventing the particles from scratching the magnetic head as it writes and reads stored data in the form of magnetic codes.

I shouldn't say things that encourage you to think of a floppy disk as a rugged, well-protected repository for valuable data. You'd do better to imagine each of your floppy disks as a bare, fragile element like the one in Figure 5.30.

FIGURE 5.29
Taken to pieces, a floppy disk is revealed as an elaborate packaging system that protects (with rigid plastic) and cleans (with soft inner linings) the magnetic media element (front center).

FIGURE 5.30
The magnetic media element includes the hub that the drive engages, letting it rotate the disk for access by the floppy drive's magnetic heads.

I've had floppy disks in my shirt pocket, for example, when a sudden gust of wind has thrown bits of sand in my face—with some of those grains falling into my pocket and getting wedged in the metal shutter. It's a delicate operation to clean out the shutter without letting sand get inside the plastic shell.

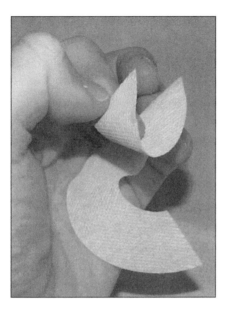

FIGURE 5.31
Looking rather like coffee filters, these liners can keep small particles out of the delicate area where the floppy disk drive's magnetic heads engage the recording surface.

Hard Disks

Much better protected than a floppy disk, a hard disk is encased in a sturdy metal enclosure (see Figure 5.32) and often protected from mechanical shock by vibration-damping mounts.

"Fast" Means Nothing

Hard disks compete on their *seek time* (how long they take to move to a new location), their *transfer rate* (how quickly they can move data on or off the drive), and their *capacity*. Saying that a drive is "fast" is meaningless without stating whether you're talking about seek time (important in database operations) or transfer rate (important in multimedia operations).

FIGURE 5.32
Tucked in a far corner of this PC's interior, the hard disk is the least replaceable part of the PC—and the part that's most likely to fail.

IBM drives are among the best, and their high-end Deskstar models suggest the standard of performance a drive should aspire to match. Deskstar drives provide typical seek times of under 10 milliseconds (thousandths of a second) and deliver sustained data rates of more than 12 Mbytes per second.

Handle Like Eggs

Inside the hard disk's metal housing, the "disk" is actually a stack of several metal platters on a common spindle. Both surfaces of each platter are coated with magnetic material, storing 2,000 to 3,000 million bits per square inch.

The stack of platters rotates at thousands of revolutions per minute, with rotation speeds nearing 10,000 rpm in better drives. Faster rotation means a shorter delay before a given section of the hard disk passes beneath a magnetic head (this time, lag is called the drive's "latency").

Unlike a floppy disk drive, a hard disk drive doesn't actually touch the magnetic recording surfaces with its heads. Any event that causes contact between a hard disk's heads and its fast-moving magnetic media surfaces will do the drive serious damage. In fact, such an event is called a "crash" (which is just as bad as it sounds).

Retrieving data from crashed hard drives is close to neurosurgery, involving delicate mechanical repairs in microscopically clean rooms. It's expensive. Making some effort to avoid putting yourself in a position to need quotations on such work is worthwhile.

For example, seriously shaking the table while a hard disk is running would not be a good idea, even though modern disks are far more rugged than early models.

In fact, if you promise not to treat hard disks like footballs, I'll admit that their shock resistance is especially high in the type of drive that's used in laptop computers. For example, an IBM TravelStar hard disk can handle a shock of 125 gravities while operating, or 400 gravities in its power-off state. (We explore the notion of "gravities" as a measure of equipment's toughness in Chapter 9.) Anything that can disable one of these disks will probably put the owner in the hospital as well.

IDE and EIDE

Many decisions are involved in writing and reading data with a sophisticated hard disk. Heads need to be moved to the right position; signals need to be read when the right part of the drive is passing by.

PC software products, such as word processors and spreadsheets, shouldn't be tied to a hard disk's mechanical details. The program should ask the operating system to save a *file*, and the operating system should ask a disk controller to write the data to a *logical unit* such as a particular cluster. A drive controller should then translate these requests into actual motions and operations of the hard disk's moving parts.

IDE (Integrated Drive Electronics) and EIDE (Enhanced IDE) combine the high-level controller circuits for the drive with the internal circuits that perform the lowest-level operations, such as regulating the rotation speed of the platters. This simplifies installation, compared to older arrangements in which the controller and the disk were purchased separately.

In what must seem a recurring theme of this chapter, the electronic parts of a hard disk controller have gotten dirt cheap. Controller components are so cheap that we don't worry about "wasting" an integrated controller by throwing it away when we discard a wornout drive.

No Hard Disk Lasts Forever

But speaking of hard disk drives that wear out, I have to emphasize that the operative word is "when" and not "if." Hard drives are like light bulbs: They're built to balance lifetime against cost, and the most likely time for a failure is when the drive first gets going.

More than half of the dozen or so hard-drive failures that I've seen occurred on startup, with no warning noises or other symptoms to say that it might be time to make a frantic last-minute backup of crucial files. Trust me, it will someday happen to you: You will either feel extremely smug that your backups were at hand, or you will feel terribly embarrassed that they weren't.

Backup and Distribution Media

The data storage media used for safety backups and for distribution of data have two characteristics in common. They have to be rugged, and they have to be cheap.

There are basically two approaches to backup storage. One approach, which I'll call "bulk backup," makes backups relatively quickly and stores them quite efficiently, but isn't convenient for routine data retrieval.

A bulk backup gives you the option of restoring data to your normal storage device if the usual working copy of your data is damaged (as by accidentally deleting a file). It lets you restore data to another storage device if your normal storage device becomes inoperative. These data restoration operations, however, can be tedious and time-consuming. Magnetic tape is the most common bulk backup medium.

Another backup approach, which I'll call "shadow" backup, behaves like an ordinary storage device: It lets you create and use files, just like a regular hard disk, though not with the same high speed.

A shadow backup has some important advantages, in my opinion, over a bulk backup. First, you make a shadow backup with the same operations you're used to performing every day—operations such as saving and copying files. You're not running some separate backup program that isn't part of your regular routine, with restrictions on what files you're allowed to use while the backup is in progress.

The other advantage of shadow backups is that you can easily verify that the backup is really getting made. This might sound silly, but I've lost count of the people who've told me about tape backup operations that only looked as if they were taking place.

All too many tapes have turned out to be unusable when they were needed. A software driver might have been out of date, for example, or there might have been some defect in the drive, but the tape went happily spinning from one reel to the other, so no one doubted that everything was working as it should.

By contrast, shadow backup devices look like hard disks as far as the PC is concerned, and it's easy to open a single backup file or to compare a group of files against their originals with common operating-system commands.

Removable Disks

My preferred backup device, for the reasons that I've just described, is the removable high-density disk. Some people sent me hate mail the last time I praised one particular type of disk in print, but that's life. I like the Iomega Zip drives, and I'm talking about the kind of preference that I express with pale green ballots bearing pictures of former U.S. presidents.

A Zip disk, shown in Figure 5.33, isn't much larger than a regular 3 1/2 inch floppy disk. A Zip disk spins faster, though, reducing latency and increasing the possible data transfer rate.

Further, the Zip disk packs data just as tightly on the outer tracks as it does on the inner tracks. A standard floppy disk, by contrast, puts the same number of sectors on each track, even though the outer tracks have a greater circumference. This means that floppy disks have much lower data density near their edges than near their centers.

Zip disks pack in more data yet by using small magnetic heads with a magnetic recording medium that isn't as easily remagnetized as the material on a standard floppy disk. The combined effect of the small heads and the reluctant medium is that data can be written and read in much smaller units of area.

All together, differences in media and drive technology let a Zip disk hold 100 Mbytes: about as much as 70 floppy disks.

It's true that a Zip disk's capacity isn't enough to back up an entire hard disk on any modern PC. It's true that there are other models of removable hard disk that store data at a lower cost per megabyte.

In my opinion, though, the vital question to ask about your backup data storage is this: "What will I do with this data when I need it?" If you have your backup data stored on a low-cost disk format that's not widely used, and your system is destroyed by fire, whose drive will you use to copy your data to another machine and get back to work?

Portable Zip drives like the one in Figure 5.34 are almost everywhere. The Zip disk format is so popular, with Zip drives even available as preinstalled options on new PCs, that I have high confidence that I will be able to get my Zip disk read by someone. I don't feel as confident about any other format—at least not yet.

Shedding Light on Denser Storage

I've explained the technical differences that let a Zip disk store much more data in about the same space as a standard floppy disk. A Zip disk, though, is still a strictly magnetic medium. Magnetic fields can't be focused as tightly as beams of light, so it stands to reason that light-based storage media can store bits with even greater density.

FIGURE 5.33
A Zip disk holds "only" 100 Mbytes, a small amount compared to some other removable media that have ten times this capacity, but Zip disks are widely supported by portable and built-in drives in new PCs—and the whole point of backup storage is being able to read it on something else when your own PC isn't working.

Hot Bits: Magneto-Optical Disks

Two common media use light and magnetism, in combination, to achieve high-density storage.

A magneto-optical disk applies a magnetic field to the storage material, but the combination of field strength and storage material characteristics normally wouldn't result in remagnetization. A laser beam, however, can be focused tightly on a small region within the area covered by the magnetic field, heating that small region and making just that tiny spot susceptible to magnetic change. This enables high data densities.

Tight Beams: Floptical (LS-120) Disks

A "floptical" disk uses light in a different way—not to make the recording, but to aid in determining the precise position where bits are being written or read.

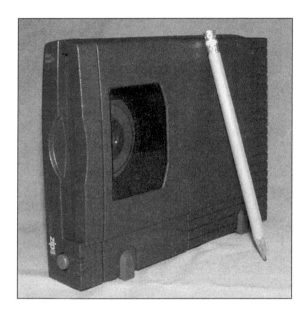

FIGURE 5.34
Portable Zip drives like this one can easily be moved from one machine to another. I put a pencil in the picture to show the drive's size: Without the pencil, in the first photo I took, the drive looked as tall as a refrigerator.

A standard floppy drive uses relatively imprecise magnetic markers to sense the position of the rotating medium, but a floptical drive uses a low-powered laser and carefully milled reflective grooves to provide more exact information.

With precise knowledge of magnetic track locations, bits can be packed more tightly. The density of the storage tracks can grow from 135 tracks per inch on a standard floppy disk to 2,490 tracks per inch on a 120 Mbyte floptical. Unlike Zip drives, however, a floptical drive can also read and write standard floppy disks at their usual density of 1.4 Mbytes.

Floptical drives are commonly marketed under the labels "LS-120" (the LS stands for Laser Servo) and "SuperDisk." These are clearly emerging competitors for the Zip format, though even the entry-level Zip drive (which uses the PC's parallel port) has roughly 1/3 the seek time and about 50% faster data-transfer rates than a comparable LS-120 device.

A high-end Zip drive (which uses a SCSI connection) has almost twice the data transfer rate of a high-end LS-120 drive (which uses IDE). There's room for both technologies in the marketplace.

Initially, LS-120 media are costing more than the easier-to-make Zip disks, which are themselves at the high end of the removable-media market. The media cost advantage might help Zip continue to spread.

Tape Backups

I've said some pretty negative things about tape. Personally, I've had bad experiences with the performance and reliability of tape, compared to other media. Still, it's one of my obligations in this book to give you the objective facts and let you draw your own conclusions.

Tape Storage Formats

Common tape formats for PC backup storage are Quarter-Inch Cartridge (QIC) and Digital Audio Tape (DAT). QIC is the mainstream format, but DAT is a standard that might plummet in price: DAT devices, like CD-ROMs, can spread their development cost across the entertainment sector as well as the computer market.

A QIC cartridge needs to balance the need for speed against the need for delicate management of the tension in the tape. Uneven handling leads to stretching and other forms of damage that harm tape's prospects for a long and reliable life. Scrimping on tape cartridges is a truly bad idea.

In situations in which tape's low cost is most important, a real slugfest is going on between new tape storage formats from Quantum (Digital Linear Tape), Sony (Advanced Intelligent Tape), and Tandberg (Multichannel Linear Recording).

Advanced tape technologies lend themselves to very high-volume situations, such as backing up large network servers with data transfer rates of several megabytes per second. A single tape cartridge holds tens of gigabytes (tens of thousands of megabytes) at a cost per tape of under $100. Tape drives in this class are costly, however, at prices comparable to what most people expect to spend on their entire PC.

Tape at a Home-PC Price

For under two hundred dollars, you can get a tape drive that's priced in line with a home-PC budget and sized for a personal workload. An Iomega Ditto unit, for example, uses QIC-style tapes with a capacity of several Gbytes apiece, providing data transfer rates (via parallel-port connection) of hundreds of Kbytes per second and retrieving any given file in under a minute.

Like the Zip drive, the Iomega Ditto is a good value and a popular format, with wide availability of competitively priced storage media.

Other consumer-priced tape drives, such as Hewlett-Packard's Colorado line, offer high performance but less storage capacity than the high-end Ditto units. There's a basic tradeoff here: Tape drives can take more time to perform more sophisticated data compression, or they can just get the data onto the tape as quickly as possible. There's plenty of room for choice and competition in this area. The Colorado drives are notable for exceptional ease of setup, guided by supplied advisor software.

Store Tape with Care

Generally, I find tape's performance underwhelming, but tape has low cost per unit of data stored. Be warned, however, that long-term archival of tapes is a delicate proposition.

Tapes should be kept at constant temperature and humidity if you don't want to retrieve old tapes from storage to find the magnetic coating flaking off the plastic backing that moves the material past the read/write heads. Yes, this warning applies to your home videotapes as well.

CD-ROMs

A Compact Disc Read-Only Memory (CD-ROM) uses the same technology as an audio CD, but in PC applications it typically carries data (up to 650 Mbytes) instead of digitized sound (which I showed you, briefly, in Figure 3.2).

Until very recently, any discussion of CD-ROM would have been filled with superlatives. A CD is virtually indestructible (unlike a floppy disk), it provides random access (unlike tape), and drive units are quite inexpensive (because the cost of research and development is shared across both music and computing markets).

Much new PC software is sold in CD format, with floppy disks available only with shipping delays and possibly an extra cost—a CD-ROM drive is more of a necessity than an option on any new PC.

A PC's CD drive also gives you the capability, in most cases, to play music CDs (controlled from the screen, keyboard, and mouse of your PC) when you're not using the CD drive to read software or data files.

CD-ROM is even getting ready to shed the "ROM" part of its name to become a recordable medium (CD-R, or CD-Recordable). A laser can bleach a layer of dye, sandwiched between protective layers of plastic in a Recordable CD. The bleached regions can then be detected by a standard CD-ROM player in the same manner as the tiny bubbles that mark data bits on a conventional CD-ROM.

Recordable CDs can only be "written" once, because the different methods of changing the CD's surface are irreversible. The CD-R's permanent state might be an asset, however, in archival storage of data that's meant to be a legal or historical record.

DVD

Have you ever used a microscope and adjusted the focus so that you could look at different layers of the same object? DVD (Digital Versatile Disk) uses a focus-change technique to record on two layers instead of the single layer used by a CD.

DVD can also record on both sides of the disk, giving a single disk four recordable tracks (really surfaces, but "tracks" is the common term). A drive can read two of these tracks without needing an extra set of heads (which no drive-maker has yet offered) and without disk-flipping.

A fully-loaded DVD can hold 17 gigabytes of data, as much as 25 CDs. Each of the four tracks (two on each side) can hold more than two hours of video with sound, at video quality better than standard television.

Just as CD-ROM gained leverage from audio CDs, DVD for computers gains leverage from DVD's role as a follow-on technology that could replace VHS for video rentals and sales. You should not, however, expect to record your own video on DVDs any time soon, because the compression techniques that are used to get all that video onto the disk are computationally intensive. We'll talk more about home digital video recording in Chapter 8.

Long-Distance Connections

This chapter has been about things that we connect to our PCs. A logical question is, how long can these connections be?

Cable Connections

In our earlier discussion of RS-232 serial connections, I noted the limitation on cable length to something on the order of tens of feet. Why do data connections have length limits when electricity travels hundreds or thousands of miles through wires to reach our homes?

Power lines have a much easier job than long-distance data connections. A power line carries an unvarying signal (as we saw in Figure 5.2), and the power line signal is at the low frequency of 60 cycles per second.

When a wire carries a rapidly changing signal like a train of data pulses that constantly switch between two different levels, there are "ringing" effects that act like electrical echoes. The longer the wire and the higher the rate at which the pulses are changing, the harder it is to cancel these echoes and discern the intended stream of bits.

Data wiring in buildings is rated on a scale from Category 1 to Category 5, with higher numbers indicating higher quality. Category 3 is barely adequate for Ethernet, so Category 5 should be seriously considered for any home network that might someday want to use that technology. The cost of the wire is tiny compared to the cost of installation, which takes the same effort and skill regardless of the grade of the cable.

Data cables must be installed with particular attention to the quality of their connections. Unlike power wiring, where all that's needed is electrical conduction, a data line needs connections that keep voltage and current in constant proportion along the entire route traveled by the data.

Sloppy connections create "impedance bumps" that cause electrical reflections and distort data. Poorly made connections can also act like crystal radios, pulling nearby radio signals into the data stream and blurring those crisp digital pulses.

When we talked about SCSI ports, I mentioned their need for a termination block at the last device on a SCSI "daisy chain." Network cables also need terminators, for the same reason: The cable needs something at the end to absorb any leftover energy, in the way that a beach absorbs the breaking ocean waves. A cable without termination behaves like the end of a swimming pool, reflecting leftover energy back toward the middle.

Data cables last, in most cases, much longer than the computers and other equipment that those cables are installed to serve. Cable should be selected and installed with care, because it's terribly expensive to do the job over again.

Can data be routed over normal house wiring, in the manner of low-cost intercoms or home-control systems? Well, you saw the electrical environment on a home power line in Figure 5.3. You can imagine how hard it would be to separate clean streams of bits from such chaos.

It is possible to use techniques developed by the military for jam-proof communications to send data across a "noisy" power line. This adds less than $10 to the cost of a device and might become common as the cost continues to drop.

Other solutions, however, need no wires at all and might overtake wired and cabled connections with their convenience of moving from room to room without the need to reconnect.

Wireless Connections

Two basic ways exist for carrying data between devices without wires. The first is infrared light, used by TV remote controls and increasingly by computer accessories such as digital cameras.

Many portable computers have infrared detectors for convenient walk-up access to printers, for example. Some handheld Personal Digital Assistants (which we'll examine in Chapter 9) rely on infrared signals to exchange electronic "business cards" and other forms of information.

Infrared has one characteristic that is both a major strength and a major weakness: infrared is light and therefore will not go around corners or through walls. This means that infrared needs a direct line of sight, which is a nuisance, but it also means that infrared doesn't radiate beyond the building for easy detection by snoops.

Radio technology is the other means of wireless connection, used by everything from the pen in a CrossPad (which we saw in Figure 5.15) to the satellites that handle your pay-at-the-pump gasoline purchases.

Radio, unlike infrared, goes everywhere (though microwaves are noticeably affected by heavy rain). Detection by unintended listeners can be blocked by two methods: highly directional antennas (resembling satellite dishes) and sophisticated encryption schemes.

I mentioned jam-proof communication techniques a few paragraphs ago when I was talking about putting data across home power lines. The same techniques, generically called "spread spectrum," give a radio connection greater reliability while using less power and making interception almost impossible.

Spread spectrum, as the name implies, spreads the energy of a radio signal across a wide span of frequencies, making it hard to zero in on the signal. Mathematical techniques let several signals occupy the same swath of frequencies while still being easily separated by their receivers.

The process of separating signals also squeezes them back down to their usual width, squeezing out radio noise in the process. Figure 5.35 shows two separate data signals, mixed with each other and with additional random noise, being reconstructed—error-free—by spread-spectrum methods.

It's the last time I'll say it in this chapter, but it really can't be said too often—spread spectrum, like USB and IDE, demonstrates the use of cheap processing power to replace expensive hardware. Feats of low-noise radio detection that used to require costly precision analog components can now be done, even better, with digital chips that become less expensive every year.

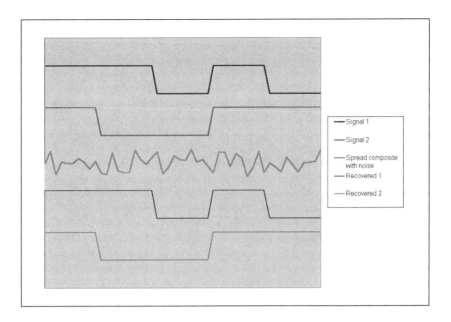

FIGURE 5.35
Spread-spectrum methods turn radio signals into something that looks like noise, making it extremely difficult to eavesdrop—and unlikely that a signal will even be noticed by anyone who's not looking for it. More than one signal can share a single channel while still being reliably separated into the original data streams.

What We've Learned

This will probably turn out to be the longest chapter in this book, because it embraces the many different technologies that wrap around the core of a PC to make it a useful appliance and a foundation for many different tasks.

We've gone from the most mundane piece of the PC, its cooling fan, to some of the most exotic PC technologies, such as SCSI and DVD. In all of these areas, I've tried to focus on common concerns: why you need to know something and what your options are.

I hope I've left you with a healthy respect for the importance of things that aren't very interesting compared to fast multimedia and games.

- Your PC will last longer if it's not overheating due to poor ventilation.

- Your life will be more pleasant if power interruptions or nearby thunderstorms don't destroy your work.

- You'll feel better about yourself if your work is backed up when your hard disk's hard life comes to its inevitable end.

- As long as you're spending thousands of dollars on a PC, you might as well think about another hundred or two for a keyboard and pointing device that let you do better work with less discomfort and fatigue.

With this chapter, you're past the hump of what makes PCs hard to understand. The stuff in this chapter is the stuff that really isn't like anything else. Very little in the world outside the computer resembles slots, or serial interfaces, or Ethernet connections.

For the rest of the book, we'll be able to make a chapter-by-chapter investigation of specific hardware accessories and software packages that add particular capabilities.

From here on, we'll be looking at ways of doing things on a computer that we already know how to do with other tools. This will be much easier to approach.

"If computers are the wave of the future, displays are the surfboards."

—TED NELSON,
in *Dream Machines*

Seeing Is PCing

A COMPUTER WITHOUT A DISPLAY or a printer might be doing a lot of work, but it would be hard to tell.

We value our computers in large measure for the help they give us in seeing things more clearly, understanding them more quickly, and sharing them more persuasively with others. That often involves our sense of vision, which means putting things into pictures or print, on screens or on paper.

It's ironic that people will earnestly debate the merits of the Pentium II in a PC versus the PowerPC in a Macintosh, while ignoring the gains in user speed and accuracy that can come from a better display or printer.

For example, research at MIT's Media Lab looked at different ways of displaying text on the screen. They found that the obvious way of drawing letters on a display made users 40 percent less efficient in proofreading text than they were with paper copies. A more sophisticated approach reduced this difference to only 2 percent.

Making a computer screen 98 percent as readable as paper, instead of only 60 percent, is a difference that's worth a lot. This isn't just a matter of what "looks nice." This chapter is about our choice of weapons in the battle to get more information out of our PCs.

Not Quite Immune to Progress

If displays and printers weren't so important, we'd find a way to get along without them, because they're among the least impressive examples of price/performance improvement in PCs and related technologies.

Monitors Are a Mess

The most complex, costly, and dangerous component of your PC system is that big, hot, radiating box full of high-voltage, short-lived TV-type components that we call a "monitor" or "display." The monitor is one of the only PC system components that's ever been accused of causing health hazards, and in Europe, the monitor is a heavily regulated product.

Alternatively, you could be using a flat-panel screen, like the one in almost every portable PC (and increasingly common on desktops as well). This type of display is actually a very large, elaborately packaged integrated circuit (a "macrochip"?), and it is one of the most demanding and costly types of chip ever built—its cost represents a large fraction of what you pay for a PC system.

Printers Are a Pain

Meanwhile, one of the most annoying, noisy, and high-maintenance components of your PC system is that clumsy mechanical contrivance called a printer. When your printer has a bad day, so do you.

Even on a good day, it could be hard to make things look as good on paper as they do on your screen. The physical materials and processes involved in printing are not nearly so consistent or well-behaved as are electrons and bits. Real-world phenomena such as humidity can make all the difference in whether a printer works well or poorly.

It's Hard to See Why They Don't Work

The cost and speed of most PC technologies move rapidly in desirable directions, but the PC's crucial input and output devices make much less rapid improvements. Displays and monitors share this trait with keyboards, whose selection we discussed in Chapter 5.

Displays and printers are far more complex than keyboards. We can literally put a finger on what makes one keyboard preferable to another. The inside story of a monitor or a printer involves much more exotic mechanisms, many of them microscopic or even invisible.

It takes solid technical information to choose the display and printer options that will boost your return on your PC investment. That's what this chapter provides.

Your PC's Fastest Interface

You might think that talking about connecting our computers to our brains is science fiction. Actually, we do it all the time. The PC's brain connector is its video screen; your brain's PC connectors are your eyes.

Faster Than a Speeding SCSI

The video connection from PC to brain, via the eyes, is an ultra-high-speed parallel interface. We talked about SCSI parallel interfaces, for example, in Chapter 5, with their latest versions reaching data rates as high as 640 million bits per second. Well, that's nothing compared to the data rates that flow across the screen-to-eye interface.

Worth *How* Many Words?

Consider one of today's better PC displays that divides the screen into 1,280 columns and 1,024 rows of dot-like "picture elements" (which PC people call *pixels* and TV people call *pels*). If we want near-photographic quality, we might give each pixel (each individual dot on the screen) a group of 24 bits to describe its color. (We looked under the hood of 24-bit color, using a Web browser, in Chapter 3.)

A single still picture on a display is often called a single "frame," using the terminology of moviemakers. On a display like the one we've just described, one frame comprises $1280 \times 1024 \times 24$ bits, or 31,457,280 bits of data.

We can compare such a frame's worth of data against the old saying, "A picture is worth a thousand words." An average word, using the first five chapters of this book as our sample, is five characters long. An 8-bit byte is more than sufficient to represent a letter, so an average English-language word represents no more than 40 bits of data.

At almost 32 million bits per frame, it looks as if a picture is worth more like 780,000 words.

Bringing Fast Computers to Their Knees

If we view "full-motion" video, at 30 frames per second, with each still image presenting more than 30 million bits of data, our video screen is transferring more than 940 million bits per second to our brains. This is almost half again the data rate that's achieved by high-end SCSI. I'll bet you didn't realize that your brain was so well connected to the world around you.

The bad news is that data rates like those of a video stream are a challenge for even the hottest PC hardware. For hardware makers, however, it's good news that this gap shows no signs of closing. I don't know that people will ever get a computer display that's *too* large, *too* sharp, or *too* colorful, and every improvement in any of these attributes creates more work for the byte pumps that feed the display.

More Than Multimedia

Visual displays with photo-realistic quality have applications other than literal imagery: They're important in visualizing technical data, simulation results, and even the most abstract mathematics. Everyone wants better computer graphics.

As Ted Nelson wrote in 1974, in his book *Dream Machines*, "Computer graphics is not a field. It is the frontier of every field. It is an ever-expanding pool of light, illuminating them all."

Rasters and Vectors

How should we best approach the task of turning the data inside a PC into an image, whether onscreen or on paper? There's not one obviously right or natural way—it's all a question of doing hard things with cheap hardware. What's cheap has changed a great deal as PCs have evolved.

Ever since Chapter 3, if not before, you've understood that everything in a computer is just some variation on a list of numbers. There are two ways to represent a drawing, a photograph, or any other visual object as a list of numbers: These two representations are the *raster* and the *vector*.

Vectors Are the Natural Way of Drawing

When you draw a picture with a pencil and a ruler, you're rendering vectors. A vector is just a technical name for a combination of a *magnitude* and a *direction*.

If I say, "I walked ten miles this morning," that's a *scalar* (a simple number). If I say, "I walked ten miles northwest," that's a *vector*.

The "CRT": An Electric Pencil

When people first started to use computers with visual displays, they devised electrical hookups that turned computer output into vectors; that is, into operations of drawing a line for a particular distance in a particular direction.

Turning electrical signals into visual displays is not a new idea. Engineers and technicians were doing this routinely, decades before the first computers were built, by using devices called oscilloscopes.

An oscilloscope shoots a beam of electrons at a screen whose back side is coated with a *phosphor*, a material that glows when struck by electrons.

The oscilloscope's electron beam passes between two facing pairs of metal plates. Applying a voltage to either set of plates applies a force to the passing beam, like a person twisting one of the knobs on an Etch A Sketch drawing toy (Etch A Sketch is a trademark of the Ohio Art Company).

One knob of an Etch A Sketch moves a pointer up and down, and the other knob moves the pointer from side to side. To get a diagonal line, you have to twist both knobs at once. In the same way, an oscilloscope applies combinations of voltages on its two sets of plates to deflect the beam at any angle, tracing any desired pattern on the screen.

Tubes? They Still Use *Tubes*?

The complete assembly of electron gun, deflection plates, and display screen is just a specialized type of electronic tube—perhaps the only kind of tube you use any more. Most electronic devices use transistors rather than bulky, fragile, and inefficient tubes (with their energy-consuming heaters that energize a stream of electrons enough to make them jump from one electrode to another).

The part of an electronic tube that radiates energy to other parts is the *cathode*, and people who first observed this effect called the invisible emissions *cathode rays*. We still call this display component a *cathode ray tube*, or "CRT."

TV Technology and Terms

A TV picture tube is a kind of CRT, but the picture-tube label implies a less precisely built unit that isn't suited to displaying fine details.

People often call a PC's display a *monitor*. This term once meant a high-end TV display used in the studio to check for defects in the broadcast; in other words, it was used to monitor (keep an eye on) the transmissions. That's why high-quality displays, capable of showing the crisp detail in computer graphics, are called monitors today.

Early Vector Text

The ray gun of a CRT can draw letters, as well as pictures, by manipulating the trace of the electron beam. Unlike an Etch A Sketch, a CRT doesn't have to draw with a continuous line. External circuits can turn the beam off to leave spaces in the traces.

Early displays used this letter-drawing, vector-based mode to produce letters about as good-looking as you'd get from an Etch A Sketch with a highly skilled user. As they say of a dancing bear, the impressive thing isn't the quality of the dancing but the fact that you can get the bear to do it. Early computer displays didn't begin to attempt the quality of text that we've come to take for granted on PCs.

The Moving-Pen Plotter (Visit Your Nearest Museum)

We also saw vector graphics in another form when computers drew color charts or large illustrations with slow, expensive moving-pen plotters. Almost a vanished technology today, the moving-pen plotter was a specialized robot that selected pens from a built-in rack or carousel. The plotter drew smooth lines by using motorized arms to move the pen across the surface of the paper or other media.

Plotters met the need for color output when we used a small number of colors— red and blue bars on a statistical chart, for example, or multicolored lines on a wiring diagram. Plotters weren't as successful in rendering shaded figures or photographs or other types of color output requiring hundreds or thousands of colors to do the job properly.

The moving parts of a plotter also represented a formidable problem of mechanical design and maintenance. Making plotters faster meant starting and stopping their pen movements more quickly while still positioning pens with accuracy measured in fractions of a millimeter. This required stiff, often massive structures, which means that fast plotters were expensive and affordable plotters were terribly slow. Color inkjet printers, for reasons discussed later, made plotters suddenly look like the hard way to do this job.`

When Memory Was Expensive

Vector graphics, whether onscreen or on paper, made sense when computer memory was an expensive (literally handmade) form of hardware. Vector devices can represent a line by storing just four numbers in a computer's memory: a starting point (vertical and horizontal position), and an ending point (ditto) or a horizontal and a vertical displacement from the starting point (either way, four numbers in all).

If you add another 4-bit number, using just a nybble of memory, you can specify any of 16 colors for your line. This is quite efficient.

Burning Bits, Burning Money

At any time before the 1980s, people would have been shocked at the alternative notion of mapping every point on the screen (or the page) to its own unique memory address. In the context of early computers, this would have seemed absurdly expensive.

For example, that 1280×1024 picture we discussed a few paragraphs ago (with its 24-bit color) consumes 3.75 megabytes of memory. This used to be the entire memory complement of a well-equipped technical workstation.

Rasters Are the Digital Way of Drawing

At today's lower memory prices, we can actually think about storing our graphical output, pixel by pixel, as a list of values in a memory bank—an electronic page, so to speak—before we deliver that output to the user.

There are advantages to building an image point by point in memory rather than building the image vector by vector on a screen or a hard-copy page.

Layers of Objects = Overlays of Bits

Suppose, for example, that we're displaying a drawing. If we want to put something "in front" of that drawing and we're generating that drawing as a series of vectors, we have a messy problem on our hands. We have to figure out where each vector crosses the edge of the foreground object and then generate two new vectors. We need one new vector for the part of the background object that's on one side of the new foreground object and another new vector for the part that's on the other side.

Things are much easier if we build up the image in memory as pixels rather than vectors. We can just take the memory addresses for the section of background that

we're going to cover with something new and write new values into those addresses to create the appearance of the object we're adding to the display. If we keep a
copy of what was originally there, we can easily restore the original values to make
the foreground object disappear again. By swapping and copying blocks of memory
around the machine, we can easily show temporary objects such as pop-up menus,
or to move an object across a background during an animated game.

When You Want to Show What You've Got

At any moment we can scan through the locations in our special slice of memory
(which is often called the "frame buffer"). We can send what we find in the frame
buffer out to a display screen by scanning the electron beam across the screen at
the same rate that we scan the frame buffer's addresses.

With fast, accurate devices such as today's inexpensive inkjets, we can apply the
same procedure to our printing tasks. We can print by scanning a set of four inkjets
(three colors plus black) across the width of a sheet of paper, blending colors on
the fly to give us the same effect as thousands of different-colored pens.

We don't need the elaborate positioning systems and sudden accelerations that we
needed for rapid, accurate plotting with moving pens. We just need smooth, predictable scanning by an inkjet print head (or by some other, even faster mechanism
such as the moving beam of light in a laser printer). We'll talk about these alternative printer technologies later in this chapter.

When we build an image by scanning and showing a collection of dots, letting the
user's eye turn those dots into the illusion of an image, we're doing *raster graphics*.
All it takes to make this approach quite practical, and even preferable, is cheap
computation and cheap memory. We have that, in abundance, in today's PCs.

Antialiasing Adds Apparent Accuracy

Like other aspects of computer design, raster graphics force us to decide how good
things have to be to be "good enough." A moving-pen plotter generated a perfect
line if you built a mechanical drive that could move the pen smoothly. That moving-
pen apparatus was an analog mechanism, of course, and therefore expensive.

A raster-graphics line is made up of separate dots. We have to decide how closely
we want to space the lines, and the dots on each line, to make patterns of dots
resemble continuous lines and solid figures.

We can be cheap and ineffective, drawing crude lines by using only one bit for
each point on the screen (as shown in Figure 6.1). Unless we only draw lines that
are vertical, horizontal, or at 45-degree angles, we wind up with "stairsteps" like
the ones in this figure.

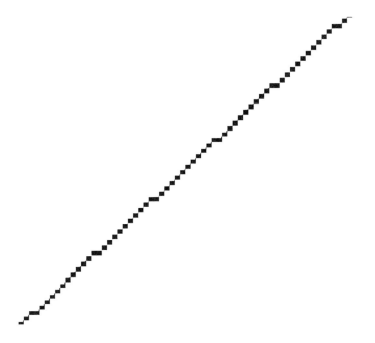

FIGURE 6.1
Drawing even a simple line gives unsatisfactory results with only one bit per pixel (each point either black or white). Diagonals are jagged, and anything but a 45-degree angle has distracting "stairstep" defects like the ones shown here.

Even if our lines are only on 45-degree diagonals, we'll still see so-called "jaggies" (slang for jagged lines). These come from trying to make a diagonal line out of dots placed corner-to-corner across the screen or the page.

What About a Few More Bits?

Suppose that we allow ourselves, not one bit, but two bits for each of the possible dot positions on the display. I'll use the common name, *pixels*, for these separately controllable points.

With two bits, we can represent four values (00, 01, 10, 11). This can give us black, white, and two intermediate shades of gray as possible pixel colors.

Figure 6.2 shows the result of using shades-of-gray flexibility when displaying letters of the alphabet on the screen. On the left is an enlarged letter *A* in the typewriter-like style called Courier that's included in Microsoft Windows.

On the right in Figure 6.2 is a modified Courier *A*, which I've doctored (purely by eye) with two shades of gray in some of the critical pixels.

FIGURE 6.2
When we use more bits per pixel, we can choose shades of gray to smooth angled lines like those in the letter on the right. Though blurry in this enlarged view, the result seems clearer when reduced to normal size for onscreen reading. This technique is called "antialiasing."

You might think that the version of *A* on the right would seem blurry and harder to read than the sharp, crisp version on the left. This is not what happens, however, when these letters are shrunk to normal reading size. (You can squint to see the effect.)

As I mentioned at the beginning of this chapter, MIT's Media Lab found that the "fuzzy" letters prove less fatiguing to read, and that users' task performance improves.

Picture This: More Bits Per Pixel

With content such as photographs, the effect of using more bits per pixel is even more dramatic.

Imagine a group of four pixels, in a 2 × 2 arrangement. If each pixel can be either black or white, these four pixels can give us five different levels of overall brightness: none white, one white, two white, three white, or all white. We'd need 4 bits of memory in our frame buffer to control these pixels' four independent states.

Alternatively, we could have just one big pixel, covering the same region of our display as the 2 × 2 block that we were just describing. We could use just 2 bits to set the brightness of one large pixel at any of four different levels.

Fat pixels with shades of gray would require half as many bits of frame buffer and one-fourth as many separately controllable points on the display as smaller pixels with separate black-and-white colors. Unless the picture is filled with fine details, we can get most of the benefit of four little pixels (with 4 bits of memory) from one big pixel (with 2 bits of memory). I'll show you how well this works.

Seeing Detail That Isn't There

Figure 5.23 shows a handheld radio in front of a computer screen, demonstrating the radio energy leakage from that display. The figure represents the detail that you can see with 8 bits per pixel, which gives almost as broad a range of brightness as your eye can detect in a single scene.

Figure 6.3 shows the same photograph of the radio in front of the screen, but rendered with only one bit per pixel—that is, in pure black and white. This is almost useless. You can't see the frequency display on the radio at all, nor can you see several labels, such as the one beneath the display or the one on the antenna.

Figure 6.4 increases the "color depth" to 2 bits per pixel, and the difference is huge. Figure 6.4 would look even better if it were as finely detailed as Figure 6.3, but Figure 6.4 uses "fat" pixels that are twice the size (each covering four times the area) of those in Figure 6.3.

FIGURE 6.3
With only one bit per pixel, each one either black or white, this photograph is almost unrecognizable except for a few detailed, high-contrast features.

FIGURE 6.4
This version of the same photograph has less detail, with only one pixel for every 4-pixel block in
Figure 6.3, but this photograph uses 2 bits per pixel; therefore, each pixel can have any of four different shades. Twice the bits, times one-fourth the pixels, means half the total memory requirement
for a picture that's actually more informative.

Take a Closer Look

We can see the difference in pixel size if we magnify the logo on the radio, which
is the most detailed object that's well focused in this picture. Compare Figure 6.5 (a
blowup of Figure 6.3) against Figure 6.6 (a blowup of Figure 6.4).

The logo in Figure 6.5 has 4 pixels for every pixel in Figure 6.6, but only in these
enlargements is that finer detail apparent. In fact, the letter *M* is at least as easy to
distinguish in Figure 6.4 as it is in Figure 6.3, even though the enlargement in
Figure 6.6 is not nearly as "M-like" as the enlargement in Figure 6.5.

Once More, the Powers of Two

What we see in Figures 6.3 through 6.6 is another demonstration of something
that I first introduced in Chapter 3: the remarkable information power of the powers of two.

When we go from one bit per pixel to two bits per pixel, we double the memory
cost per pixel. In the process, however, we can cut the number of pixels by 75%,
while actually getting *more* useful detail.

FIGURE 6.5
This enlargement from Figure 6.5 shows the close approximation to diagonal lines that comes from smaller pixels (known as higher resolution).

FIGURE 6.6
This enlargement from Figure 6.6 shows that this logo, so easily recognized in Figure 6.4, is much more coarsely drawn than the same part of Figure 6.3. Your eye uses shades-of-gray information to "see" fine detail that isn't actually present. Other information, such as the frequency display at lower left, is completely absent from Figure 6.3 but easy to read in Figure 6.4.

Overall, our memory requirements drop by half, and our display costs less to build. That's using our heads instead of our hardware.

How Many Bits Are Enough?

Your eye can handle a huge range of brightness, from starlight to sunlight, by opening and closing its pupils. At any given moment, however, the eye can't really deal with a range of brightness in a single scene that's greater than roughly 100 to 1. Within that range, your eye can detect the difference in brightness between adjacent areas that differ by more than about 1%.

Now, we want to represent a brightness ratio, from darkest to lightest, of 1 to 100. We want to multiply each level by 1.01 to get undetectable steps between adjacent levels of brightness, allowing smooth shadings in our image. Overall, therefore, we need about 460 steps: 1.01, multiplied by itself 460 times, gives an overall factor of roughly 97 to 1 (compared to our target range of 100 to 1).

To represent 460 different values, we need more than 8 bits (255 possible values) but not more than 9 bits (512 possible values). An 8-bit color depth, like the one in Figure 5.23 (which has served as our "reference photograph"), is not quite good enough. If you look closely at that figure, you might be able to see some contour-map effects in the brightness of the background near the upper-right corner.

A 9-bit gray scale, however, would fool most people, and 24-bit color probably deserves its "True Color" nickname. Few people will pay for more, because their eyes and brains won't be able to see the difference.

Colors: Making Them "Right"

Your eye and brain can identify colors more quickly and accurately than shapes. There's a reason why accountants use red ink for losses and black ink for gains: The eye can scan a ledger more quickly for numbers in red than it can scan for numbers with minus signs, or even for numbers in parentheses.

As we've just seen, adding color depth to a picture adds information—as far as our eyes are concerned—more quickly than adding more detailed renderings of shapes.

It's important, therefore, to understand the process of putting color into our PCs' output.

We Need Ways to Talk About Color

Inside a computer, colors are bits. In this chapter, we've seen 1-bit and 2-bit color, we've seen 8-bit quality in other illustrations, and we experimented with 24-bit color (8 bits each for the red, green, and blue components of a pixel) in Chapter 3.

Outside a computer, colors are more complex. More color is good, but correct color is sometimes even more important. If you want your output to look the same on paper as it does on the screen, consistency matters—but screens and printouts are made from different stuff with different characteristics.

You've surely seen a badly adjusted color TV, which shows how easy it is to upset the balance between different color components. If we didn't have a sense of what looks natural in the colors of grass or skin tones (for example), it would be hard to know when a color TV picture was even approximately right.

When it comes to color, professionals need more than "looks good." Graphics mavens have a lexicon of color that lets them discuss it precisely, and the terms that they use might come up when you're choosing a printer or a display.

Figure 6.7 shows a Windows color chooser—in this case, the one that lets you adjust the colors of your desktop elements to suit your personal preference. Many Windows programs offer similar choices, usually presented in similar ways.

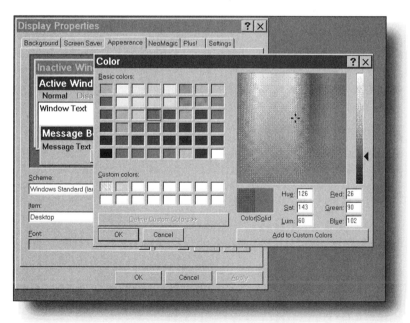

FIGURE 6.7
A color choice tool shows you different ways of describing the same color: as Red, Green, and Blue (RGB) components or as Hue, Saturation, and Luminance (commonly called Hue/Saturation/Brightness or HSB).

You can bring up a Windows 95 color chooser by clicking on the Start button and then choosing **Settings**, **Control Panel**, **Display**. When you get the Display Properties dialog box (left background in Figure 6.7), click on the **Appearance** tab near the top center of that box. Then, click the arrow next to the Color sample you see at lower right. Choose **Other**, and you'll be in the chooser shown in the figure.

A Different Set of "Primary" Colors

We've spoken of red/green/blue color and the use of one byte (8 bits) for each of these components (a possible numeric range of 0 through 255). But red, green, and blue are not the "primary colors" that your art teacher told you about. What gives?

Your art teacher was telling you about *subtractive* color. When you paint or draw, you put a chemical on your paper that only reflects a certain color, absorbing the other wavelengths of light—that is, subtracting those colors from the white light that's falling on the picture.

Red and blue paints, mixed together, yield dark purple because that's what's left when you subtract both non-red and non-blue from white.

In your color chooser, type 255 into the **Red** and **Blue** boxes and 0 into the **Green** box: You'll see, not dark purple, but bright pink. This is *additive* color, and it's different from mixing paints.

Pixels in Every Hue

When you enter red, green, and blue values, the color chooser computes and displays the corresponding values of hue, saturation, and luminance. For example, the bright pink color that we just constructed has Hue 200, Saturation 240, and Luminance 120.

Darker Shades

If we type the value 60 in the **Luminance** box, cutting it by half, we see that the red and blue values drop to half their previous values. The result is a darker shade of the same pink/purple hue.

Grayer Tones

If we return to the original **Luminance** of 120 and enter a value of 60 in the **Saturation** box, we get a color that's less colorful, more nearly gray. Looking at the RGB values, we see that we're now getting some green in the mix as well as reducing the strengths of the red and the blue.

If we drop the **Saturation** all the way to 0, we get a neutral gray with equal values of red, blue, and green. If we increase the **Luminance** to 240, we get the brightest white we can represent, with maximum values of all three RGB components.

Around the Color Wheel

Now, let's explore the meaning of *hue*. If we enter 255 for Red and 0 each for Green and Blue, we see that hue is 0. Pure green (0 Red, 255 Green, 0 Blue) has a hue of 80. Pure blue has a hue of 160.

Is this an arbitrary sequence? At a value of 0, hue is pure red. At 80, hue is pure green. At 160, hue is pure blue. This might remind you of your color spectrum from high school physics class. Do you remember "Roy G Biv," red/orange/yellow/green/blue/indigo/violet? That's what hue is giving us—a number for our progression along that spectrum.

What's beyond blue? If we try to enter a Hue of 240, we're automatically corrected to the maximum value of 239—which brings us back to red (with just a tiny trace of blue). We see that hue is a circle of values, mixing the different components of red, green, and blue in different proportions. Experiment on your own with intermediate values.

Hue gives us our position around the color wheel, so to speak; saturation gives us a measure of colorfulness versus grayness, and luminance gives us a measure of brightness versus darkness.

We don't have two different ways of quantifying color just to make life difficult. Red/Green/Blue is what we'll send to our display; Hue/Saturation/Luminance lets us make something "a little brighter" (for example) without needing to calculate Red/Green/Blue mixtures for ourselves.

Real-World Color Takes Hardware

Both Red/Green/Blue and Hue/Saturation/Luminance are just ways of describing the color we'd *like* to achieve. There's still the matter of making real hardware produce these colors, either by hitting phosphors with electron beams or by spraying inks on paper.

Color on the Screen

It would be nice if we could put red phosphors, blue phosphors, and green phosphors on the back of a CRT's screen. It would be wonderful if we could hit each type of phosphor with twice as many electrons to make it glow twice as brightly, getting the same brightness from the same electron jolt on any of our three colors.

Biased to Blue

If we had pure-color phosphors, with *linear* behavior (twice the jolt giving twice the brightness in a straight-line relationship), we could just turn our RGB numeric values into voltages and sweep our electron beams across the screen.

Real-world materials aren't so nicely behaved. We typically get more brightness for a given voltage from blue phosphors than from phosphors that are mostly red or mostly green.

Overall image brightness can be higher, for a given voltage level, if we accept a bluish bias in our colors. How can we characterize that bias?

How Blue Are You?

Have you ever discussed the colors of stars? Cooler stars are redder, hotter stars are bluer. You see the same effect in flames: A cooling charcoal fire is red, an intense welding flame burns blue.

We can speak of a *color temperature*: Redder shades of white are cooler, bluer shades of white are hotter.

A PC display also has a color temperature, commonly around 9,500° (measured on the Kelvin absolute temperature scale). This is substantially bluer than what most people think of as natural white (3,400–4,500°K), but our eye and brain quickly adapt to see backgrounds as "white" unless we compare them to some other reference color.

If you need to match onscreen colors against real-world colors, however, this difference becomes quite important, and the color temperature of your display (which is adjustable on high-end units) is something you'll care about.

Color on the Page

When we talk about printing, we're back to a more familiar world of subtractive color (even if you haven't previously thought of it in these terms).

Color inkjet printers are now, in my opinion, the obvious choice for most users who can only afford one printer. Not everyone agrees with this recommendation.

A color inkjet printer has a lower initial price than a laser printer, and inkjets can print on a wide range of media—on everything from normal paper to the plastic sheets you use with an overhead projector, or even on a transfer sheet for putting a design on a T-shirt.

On the other hand, laser printers deliver better-looking black-and-white text at a lower cost per page of output—especially on lower-cost papers that don't yield crisp results from an inkjet's spray.

Why Do We Need Black Ink?

Good color inkjet printers have three color cartridges, plus a black ink cartridge. You might think that the black is unnecessary—we can just combine the three colored inks to subtract every component of the incident light, leaving black.

A separate black cartridge is good for three reasons. First, black ink is cheaper than colored inks. Second, it's hard to make several passes with separate colors and have them all line up exactly (a problem called *registration error*); your eye is very good at detecting colored fringes around what are supposed to be black areas or letters. Third, spraying three colors of ink on the same region of the page gets the paper too wet, leading to a wrinkled appearance that printer designers call "cockle."

The Paper Is Part of the Process

Talking about inks is impossible without talking about the media that receive them. Paper is much more complex than it seems.

Inkjet printers work to extremely close tolerances, achieving remarkable accuracy in spraying their pinpoint dots. Being close to the paper makes it easier to aim the jets, but paper swells when it absorbs the ink; this can lead to dragging of the print head across the areas with high ink density.

Coated papers don't absorb as much ink, reducing the cockle problem. Coated papers also provide a clearer and sharper image, because they reflect light more consistently and because the edges of a figure are not blurred by absorption into the paper's fibers. Coated paper, however, adds a lot to your cost per page.

Fonts: Extended Families of Informative Design

When people speak of fonts, they're usually talking about the overall appearance of the letters they use in composing a document or a chart. Fonts are a complicated subject, and rendering readable text on PC displays and printers is a demanding technical challenge.

Technically, a *font* is different from a *typeface*. Times Roman is a common choice for PC-generated documents. Times Roman is a typeface, or *font family*.

When a font family is rendered in a particular size and style, such as Times Roman 12-point italic, the set of all possible symbols in that particular size and style is called a *font*. The difference between the font and the family is important.

Italic: More Than Just a Different Slant

For example, Figure 6.8 shows two styles of the letter *i* in the Windows Book Antiqua typeface. These are 72-point letters, meaning that they would normally appear 1 inch tall when printed, but the first letter is in the normal style while the second is italic.

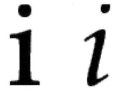

FIGURE 6.8
The italic *i* on the right is more than just a slanted version of the regular *i* on the left. The italic letter is a completely different design, though artistically crafted to produce a family resemblance when regular and italic letters are juxtaposed in text.

Perhaps you've never noticed this before, but the italic letter is not just a slanted version of the regular letter. It's a completely different design, even though regular and italic text in this typeface blends in an attractive way that merely makes the italic text seem more *emphatic* than the rest.

In the same way, the boldface font in a family is not just the regular font with thicker lines. A boldface font is a different design, artistically created to blend with the regular text while still adding useful **emphasis**.

A Story in Every Letter

Notice the smooth curves of that italic *i* in Figure 6.8. I've enlarged this letter in Figure 6.9, and you can see the extensive antialiasing that's creating this attractive appearance. Does a PC actually store this much information for every letter, in every possible size, in every style of every typeface available on the computer?

FIGURE 6.9
The graceful curves of an italic i are an elaborate effect that requires considerable antialiasing to achieve. Without this, text on the screen would be much harder to read.

Enormous amounts of storage space would be needed to maintain a pixel-by-pixel map, or "bitmap," of every symbol that we might ever want to use from many families of fonts. Hard disks eventually do get full, but CPUs these days often seem to have time on their hands. Can we save disk space by computing font appearance "on-the-fly"?

Vectors and Rasters Revisited

The choice between storing fonts or drawing them on-the-fly is a choice between raster and vector graphics, the fundamental choice that opened this chapter.

We can see the difference in Figure 6.10. On the left is a letter *k* in the typewriter-style Courier font, scaled up to an enlarged 72-point size. This font is stored in bitmap form as actual lists of which pixels to use for each letter in each size. This is a raster approach.

FIGURE 6.10
Bitmap fonts (like the plain Courier *k* on the left) are quickly drawn, but poorly scalable to other sizes. Vector fonts, like the TrueType Courier New *k* on the right, scale smoothly to any size.

The enlarged Courier *k* is unattractively chunky, because there's no information available on how to smooth the jaggies—even though this large rendering means there are plenty of pixels to spare for a more refined version.

TrueType Builds Fonts to Order

On the right in Figure 6.10, however, is a 72-point *k* in Courier New, a TrueType font. TrueType fonts are marked in Windows font lists with the TT symbol next to some of the font family names in the drop-down list I've enlarged in Figure 6.11.

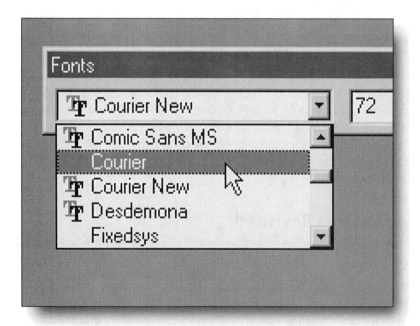

FIGURE 6.11
A drop-down font list marks the TrueType (vector) fonts with a distinctive TT symbol, showing you the fonts that will readily scale to any desired size.

TrueType fonts are stored as vectors, not as rasters. A TrueType font is actually a set of directions: "To make an A, go up to the right at an angle of 65 degrees from horizontal, then straight across to make the top before you swing down to the right. . ." and so on.

TrueType font design blends art and science to create efficient mathematical descriptions, not only for the letters themselves, but also for restyling those letters for effects such as boldfacing. The result gives us wonderful flexibility in composing documents, presentation charts, and the like.

Custom Sizes While You Wait

If you choose a non-TrueType font in a word processor, the drop-down list of available font sizes reflects the sizes that are stored and on hand in bitmap form. If you enter a different size in the font size field, one that's not on the list, you'll get a clumsily scaled version that probably won't look good.

If you choose a TrueType font, you'll get a drop-down list of available sizes that offers much more freedom. Furthermore, you should feel free to enter any other size, even a fractional size, if that's what you need to make something fit exactly right. It's just computation, and that's what your PC does.

Is there a speed penalty for using TrueType fonts instead of bitmaps? I'm sure that it's possible to devise a test that would show the difference, but I never notice any degradation in speed when I'm typing or printing or doing other font-intensive tasks.

You can waste much more time rewording things to fit a too-small space than you will ever spend waiting for a fast PC to redraw the letters to fit.

Energy Star: Look for the Logo

I'll conclude this chapter with some tips on choosing and using your display and your printer, but first I want to discuss a logo that you might see on these devices. I encourage you to look for the marking that appears in Figure 6.12, proclaiming that a piece of equipment meets Energy Star requirements.

Energy Star is a voluntary program of the U.S. Environmental Protection Agency, setting standards for efficient automatic management of power consumption by a wide range of equipment. To qualify for the Energy Star logo, office equipment must arrive from the maker with automatic power reduction behaviors set up and ready to take effect in normal use.

FIGURE 6.12
The Energy Star logo indicates voluntary compliance with standards of efficiency and automated power-reduction capability to cut the cost of operating electronic equipment.

The Display Properties dialog box in Figure 6.7 has a Screen Saver tab. Clicking this brings up a panel that includes the Energy Star settings for your PC's display.

An Energy Star monitor must automatically control its power consumption, after a selectable period of inactivity, with a two-step power reduction. After a short inactive period, the monitor must cut back to using no more than 15 watts (still enabling quick resumption of work). A longer idle period must trigger a deeper cut to 8 watts or less (which might require a noticeable warmup time for the CRT when work resumes).

Requirements for computer power reduction depend on the size of the computer's power supply. Printers must cut back to power demands between 15 and 45 watts, depending on the rated print speed.

Merely finding the Energy Star logo should not end your examination. You will get more benefit from energy-saving features if the controls for low-energy operation are easy to find and understand.

You might need to experiment to find the delay times that fit your style of work. You want power-down times that are long enough to keep you from being constantly distracted by a screen that goes black when you're reading it, but short enough to make a meaningful reduction in power use.

Buying Your Video Adapter and Display

Nothing would date this book faster than recommending particular models of PC displays or video adapters. Have you ever tried to buy a vacuum cleaner or a toaster that you saw highly rated in a consumer-products testing magazine? By the time the review is in print, the model has been discontinued. The monitor and video card market is just as volatile.

Short product cycles are a principal reason that I write most of my articles for a weekly industry newspaper, *PC Week*. I like to see my work in print before it becomes obsolete.

There are, however, some relatively timeless considerations to bear in mind as you go shopping. There are also a good many myths and misconceptions that it will be my duty, and my pleasure, to debunk before this chapter ends.

Safety, Health, and Ergonomics

Near the beginning of this chapter, I mentioned that CRT displays (commonly called "monitors") are actually accused of posing health hazards. If the screen weren't in the way, you'd be sitting square in the sights of a high-voltage electron gun, pointed straight at your face, and we've seen that we can detect the radio signals coming off that screen. Are these things dangerous?

Two Kinds of "Radiation"

There are two kinds of energy that people loosely call "radiation." *Ionizing radiation* can knock electrons loose from atoms—that's what "ionizing" means. X-rays and ultraviolet rays are examples of ionizing radiation, and this form of energy can be bad for living things.

High-energy particles emitted by radioactive materials are also a form of ionizing radiation, though they are not "rays" in the same sense as light rays or radio waves. Health effects of radioactive emissions can be fatal, and this association carries over in people's minds to less aggressive forms of radiation, as well; for example, when people talk about "nuking" food in a microwave oven.

Nonionizing radiation is energy such as ordinary light or radio waves (including microwaves) at wavelengths longer than those of ultraviolet light. Remember the color spectrum we talked about in our earlier discussion of hue? We're talking here about "hues" that are well below blue, down in the "colors" that we see as red and that we can measure as far below (or "infra") red.

Radiation in the infrared bands can cause heating of living tissue: In fact, a "heat lamp" is just a lamp that gives off most of its energy in this range. Longer waves, such as microwaves and radio waves, can also cause heating at high power levels because objects act like inefficient antennas and turn electromagnetic energy into heat.

A CRT's Real Problems Are Easy to Fix

CRT monitors don't give off significant amounts of ionizing radiation, which is the kind that's genuinely dangerous. Monitors' emissions of nonionizing radiation are limited by government regulations that are mainly designed to prevent undue interference with radio communications.

"Radiation filters" sold for use with computer displays are not especially effective, because radiation comes from other parts of the monitor as well. The significant emissions from a monitor are all, essentially, forms of light—if you shield the light it emits, a monitor doesn't function very well as a visual display.

One kind of light comes off of a monitor screen that serves no useful purpose. I'm talking about light that's reflected off of the screen from nearby windows or room lights. If you can see the reflection of a light in the screen of your monitor, you wind up squinting or straining muscles as you try to see around that reflection. You might not even realize that you're doing this, but arranging your workspace to minimize this problem is worth some effort.

A dirty screen also causes unconscious squinting and straining to see "around" the dirt. A clean screen increases your comfort level during extended work sessions.

Many of the problems that are laid at the door of computer displays are really problems due to spending long periods of time in a single position and in poorly ventilated or under-humidified rooms. Rest breaks, water breaks, stretching breaks, and other pauses in the routine will make you more productive overall.

See Better with Proper Adjustment

Many people don't adjust the controls on their displays to best advantage: The "brightness" control really sets the brightness of black areas and the "contrast" control sets the rate at which the brightness of non-black areas increases.

For best results, set the brightness control (when the monitor is fully warmed up) to the highest level that leaves black regions looking black, rather than gray. When this is done, leave that control alone and use the contrast control to adjust the screen's appearance to your preference.

Display Adapters: Feeding the Screen

Intense computer game players talk about display adapters the way stock car racers talk about tires and shock absorbers. The rest of us don't get nearly as excited, but we ought to have a few basic criteria in mind when comparing one PC's graphics capability to another's.

How Much Memory on the Graphics Card?

We've made some brief calculations of the large memory demands that come from lots of pixels with lots of bits per pixel. If graphics matter to you, 4 megabytes on the graphics card (preferably with an option to double that amount) would be a good level to seek.

How Much Resolution?

An 800 × 600 display, sometimes called "SVGA" quality, is the least that I would recommend. Having 1024 × 768 is substantially better, and 1280 × 1024 is not extravagant.

More pixels need more memory to hold the associated data, and all those bits put more strain on the PC to keep that picture up to date with what's going on inside the machine. This is very much a matter of deciding how much you want, versus how much you're willing to pay.

How High a Refresh Rate?

A CRT draws a picture by sweeping electron beams across the screen to give the phosphors a jolt that makes them glow. The phosphors start to fade, though, as soon as the beam goes on by. If the phosphors kept glowing for a long time thereafter, you wouldn't be able to see moving objects clearly—a moving object would be trailed by a visual echo of its previous positions on the screen.

Phosphor fading means that CRTs always have some degree of flicker. A CRT that updates more quickly flickers less. Typical update frequency is 60 times per second, or 60 Hertz (Hz), with higher frequencies of 75Hz or more in better quality equipment.

There's no point, though, in having a display adapter that can deliver 75Hz updates unless you're willing to pay for a monitor that can accept those speedy deliveries. There's certainly no point in paying for flicker reduction below the level where you stop noticing a problem. Buy with your eyes.

What Kind of Acceleration?

To speak of "acceleration" sounds as if I've gotten myself confused with those stock car racers I mentioned a few paragraphs back. In the context of computing, though, an *accelerator* is a companion processor that assists the CPU by taking on some share of the system's work.

An accelerator often uses specialized computing circuits; to continue the car-racing metaphor, the auxiliary graphics chip is sometimes called an *engine*.

An Outboard "Graphics Motor"

We can put a dedicated processor—a *graphics accelerator*—out on the video adapter. The CPU can send the accelerator a request, in effect, along the lines of "draw a circle" or "draw a line."

On receiving a high-level graphics request from the CPU, the accelerator does the pixel-by-pixel calculations and loads the needed pixel values into the *frame buffer* (which is sitting right there on the adapter, connected by a high-speed interface to the accelerator). The frame buffer then sends the result to the screen.

Hybrid Computing in Virtual Worlds

The CPU takes the computational shortcut of doing vector graphics, while the display adapter handles the grunt work of turning these vector statements into raster graphics (with all of the benefits we discussed earlier in this chapter). Menus appear more quickly, documents scroll more smoothly, and switching from one running program to another takes less time.

Mainstream video adapters have acceleration capability for two-dimensional operations, which are most of what you'll do on your screen unless you do advanced game-playing or technical computing. Better adapters also perform three-dimensional graphics calculations, aiding difficult tasks such as rotating a model of an apparently solid object on your display.

The two-dimensional view of data is giving way to the three-dimensional information visualization techniques that are sometimes called "virtual reality" or "cyberspace." Three-dimensional graphics acceleration will soon be more than a game-playing or science and engineering requirement, so you might want to anticipate this when choosing your graphics hardware.

Back to Those TV Roots

Other video adapter features, of varying interest to different users, include an output that can go to a standard TV (should you wish, for example, to use a projection

TV as a presentation or game-playing display) and an input that can accept television signals so that you can watch a video feed in a window on your PC's screen.

In Chapter 5, I mentioned AGP (Accelerated Graphics Port), a new high-performance connection from the graphics memory to the primary system memory. If your PC has all of the necessary internal plumbing for AGP, you should choose a display adapter that also supports it.

AGP will only work, however, as a full partnership between all of the involved subsystems.

CRT Monitors: Still Cost-Effective Champs

A CRT monitor is like an astronomical telescope. A major telescope, such as the one at Palomar Mountain, is just a thin film of aluminum (the face of the telescope's main mirror) with several tons of equipment to shape and aim that reflective surface. In a similar way, a CRT is a microscopically thin film of colored phosphors, with tens of pounds of metal and glass wrapped around it to keep that film in the right shape and to hit it with electrons in just the right places.

Size Does Matter

Size, almost always given as a diagonal measure, is the most obvious thing you get when you spend more for a monitor. Be warned that reputable monitor makers give the diagonal measure of the viewable area of the CRT, while others give the diagonal measure of the CRT including unusable area around the edges. Be sure that you're comparing equivalent numbers.

Sharpness Completes the Picture

Quality, however, has at least as much impact as size in determining your satisfaction with your display. It's quite a trick to line up several electron beams to accuracies measured in fractions of a millimeter while scanning these beams across the entire area of the display in 60 or more full-screen updates per second. Any lack of precision in manufacture or adjustment produces unsatisfactory images, with annoying color fringing or distortion.

Dot Pitch Blends the Colors

Brightness and sharpness duel with each other for priority in monitor design and calibration. More phosphor area means more brightness, but clear separation of the phosphors of different colors yields sharper display of fine details such as small text or intricate graphics.

If you look at the face of a display screen with a magnifying glass, you can see the adjacent elements of red, green, and blue phosphor whose light combines to make any desired color. These colored elements must be finely spaced to fool your eye into seeing white in the areas where the three color components are equally bright.

Because we want smooth color-blending, an important measure of a monitor's quality is the CRT's *dot pitch*; that is, the spacing (the smaller the better) between each pair of phosphor dots of a given color. For example, a monitor with a dot pitch of 0.25 millimeters has four red dots in every millimeter of width or height—likewise for green dots and blue dots.

Smaller spacings are good, but most users will see no improvement in dot-pitch reductions beyond 0.22 millimeters or so.

Dot Geometry: Striking a Balance

Alternatively, instead of dots, we could use stripes of differently colored phosphor. Dots on the screen, even in a tightly packed hexagonal arrangement, leave a lot of the screen's area unused. Stripes let us cover more of the screen with phosphor, giving us a brighter image, but one that is not as crisply detailed.

Some Tubes Are in Better Shape

A Sony Trinitron tube is the most common example of the striped phosphor arrangement, and this type of display is excellent for imagery and other graphics. The Trinitron is not as popular with those who work mostly with text, where fine detail matters more.

A particular advantage of the Trinitron tube is that it is vertically flat. The face of the tube curves outward like the side of a barrel, not like the side of a beach ball in the manner of a standard CRT. Because of this single-curved shape, a Trinitron tube does not reflect light from above and behind the user into the user's eyes. This reduces glare from ceiling lights and other room light sources.

Refreshing Resolution

As with display adapters, a monitor's crucial characteristics (apart from size) are its resolution (vertical and horizontal pixels) and its refresh rate. I described these attributes previously.

LCD Flat Panels: What We Really Want

New to our list of desktop PC options is the possible choice of a flat-panel display like the one in most portable computers.

Portable systems have used flat screens because the weight, bulk, and power requirements of a CRT are prohibitive for portable use. Desktop users have continued to buy CRTs for their brightness, their clarity (especially when viewed from off-center positions), and their lower cost for any given size.

As this book is being written, however, flat-panel desktop displays are not much more than twice the price of CRTs and falling quickly to prices that make them well worth considering. The shallow footprint of a flat-panel unit gives back a lot of desk space that seemed to be gone for good when PCs took over the prime real estate on most desks.

Flat-panel displays reflect even less room light than a Trinitron tube, they don't flicker, they don't have the distortion problems of CRTs, and they're ready for instant use with no need to warm up.

Liquid, Thin, and Active

The only flat-panel displays that are likely to attract the typical PC buyer are active-matrix, thin-film-transistor, liquid crystal displays (LCDs). That's a mouthful—let's break down those adjectives.

First, the liquid crystal part—how can a liquid be a crystal, or vice versa?

Discovered in 1888, liquid crystals were just a laboratory curiosity until a stable material with liquid-crystal behavior was developed in the 1970s. Behaving in some ways like solids, in other ways like liquids, the useful thing about liquid crystals is their response to small amounts of electrical current.

A layer of liquid crystal material can be packaged so that it switches between a reflective and a nonreflective state, depending on the applied electrical current. This creates a display that can easily be read in anything from ordinary room light to the brightest sunlight.

Alternatively, the liquid crystal material can be packaged so that each point on a screen acts like a tiny valve for a background light source. With colored filters arranged in a densely spaced pattern, a rectangular grid of light valves lets a display mix varying amounts of red, green, and blue light in each tiny region of the screen. This is the same principle as applying different-colored phosphors in a color CRT.

The least expensive variety of liquid crystal display puts the controlling electronics around the edge of the display screen. An addressing scheme controls a point in the middle of the screen by sending control signals for that point's entire row and that point's entire column. The result is a display that is easy to build, but not very responsive, because the control electronics have to distribute their attention among large groups of pixels.

A better flat-panel display puts the control electronics for each pixel right where they're needed. Each pixel has its own dedicated set of controlling transistors for each color. These transistors are actually embedded in the screen (hence the expression, "thin-film transistor").

Unlike a low-cost screen, whose matrix of liquid crystal elements just sits there and receives control signals from the outside, the better displays combine the display matrix and the active control electronics in a single assembly (hence the expression, "active matrix").

Costs Are High, but Falling

More things can go wrong in assembling an active-matrix display, compared to a simpler passive-matrix unit. This leads to high defect rates and high reject rates at the factory (where the material is recycled for another try) and keeps active-matrix costs relatively high. Increased use of automation and perfection of manufacturing processes moves those costs steadily downward.

When we use a flat-panel display with a desktop PC, we wind up doing something that seems rather silly. The video display adapter in a PC turns the digital contents of the frame buffer into analog electrical signals to feed a CRT monitor. When we use a flat-panel display, we have to turn that analog CRT input signal back into digital control codes for the liquid crystal panel's miniature light valves.

Can't we get rid of the middlemen and just control the digital flat-panel display with digital signals? In principle, we surely can, and this is the goal of the Digital Flat Panel Group.

As a cooperative effort of several video electronics makers, the Flat Panel Group has produced a specification for an all-digital interface (the Flat Panel Port). When available in future PCs, this output will support a display of up to 1024×768 resolution over a connection up to 5 meters long. Within a few years, the cost reductions achieved by Flat Panel Port electronics should make flat panels even more competitive with CRTs.

Buying Hard-Copy Equipment

Printers come in an enormous range of sizes and capacities, ranging from the kind that fit in a briefcase to the kind that would fill a small living room.

For the typical PC buyer, I expect the most likely choice to be a color inkjet unit, although this won't be as fast as a laser printer.

Lasers: Fast, But Expensive Up Front

A laser printer works just like a copier, except that a copier acquires the image it should put on paper by looking at an existing document through a lens. A laser printer draws the image from scratch, with a moving beam of light controlled by a PC or other device.

Both the laser printer and the copier use light to change the electrical characteristics of a printing element. The element attracts tiny particles, called *toner*, in an arrangement that matches the desired image. The toner then gets fused to the paper. The whole process takes place in just a few seconds, with a typical laser printer able to put out 6 to 12 pages per minute.

Ink Jets: Adequate Quality at Low Initial Cost

For less than half the price of a black-and-white laser printer, or one-tenth the price of a high-capacity color laser printer, a color inkjet printer that costs less than $300 will give you all of the color quality you're likely to need.

I'll break my rule against naming specific products in this section to tell you that I've had excellent experience with my Epson Stylus Color 500. I should also note that Epson's later-model Stylus Color 800 has won accolades from product reviewers, whether it's evaluated with or without regard to its cost. Put Epson on your list of printer candidates.

I will caution, however, that cost per page of printing ordinary black-and-white pages is higher for inkjet printers, due to the high cost of ink compared to a laser printer's dry toner. If documents are your main hard-copy product, a laser printer might pay back its higher initial cost with lower costs per page, and save you time, as well.

Multifunction Devices

If a laser copier and a laser printer are the same thing except for the source of their images, why buy two separate printing mechanisms? Why not just have a copier that can also plug into a printer port to download an image from your PC?

For that matter, why not make the same piece of machinery do added duty as a fax machine? Faxing is just printing, with a phone line in the middle. And a fax machine is a scanner that prints across a phone line, so why not set things up so that the fax machine's scanner can be tapped by your PC as a source of images you can store or use in other documents?

Sharing common hardware across related functions is the premise of multifunction devices made by several companies, including Sharp, Canon, Hewlett-Packard, and Brother.

Integrated units come in a wide range of prices, with and without color capability, and with varying degrees of independent operation. Some systems require that your PC be active to furnish memory and/or control, while other units can function on their own for many basic functions.

New multifunction devices appear quite often, and such periodicals as *PC Magazine* and *PC Computing* are the best source of up-to-date comparisons. At any time, reviews and other information on a broad cross section of current printers and related products can be found on the World Wide Web at `http://www.zdnet.com/products/printeruser/`.

You should be able to find a flexible color inkjet unit or a light-duty black-and-white laser unit for $600 or less.

What We've Learned

Originally, I expected this chapter to be only half this long. The more I thought about displays and printers, however, the more I realized how much there was to explain about the basic ideas and core technologies that make these things work so well, despite my critical remarks in the opening pages.

We've seen that when we devise a display or a printer, we have to deal with the user as a "signal-processing system." What looks good, is good. Nothing else matters, and it's not enough to know that one approach is theoretically better.

If the user can't tell the difference, we're wasting resources (including CPU capacity and memory), and therefore, wasting money.

We've seen that displaying and printing are basically the same, in that both involve judicious mixing of vector and raster graphics techniques. We've also seen that displaying and printing are basically different, because displays use additive color and printing uses subtractive color.

I often feel that people buy PCs from the inside out, picking a machine and then seeing how much printer and display they can afford, when they really ought to ask themselves what kind of output they need—what kind of page quality, what kind of display capability—and then buy a PC that can support output devices that meet those requirements. I hope you'll take this requirements-driven approach in assembling your PC system.

"Program a map to display frequency of data exchange, every thousand megabytes a single pixel on a very large screen. Manhattan and Atlanta burn solid white. . . your map is about to go nova."

—WILLIAM GIBSON, NEUROMANCER

Shake Hands with Your Modem

I'VE NEVER OWNED A COMPUTER that didn't have a modem; that is, a device for letting a computer communicate with other data sources across an ordinary telephone line.

To me, using a PC that can't connect to the rest of the world would feel like working in a kitchen without running water. I might have a whole kitchen's worth of the latest appliances, and I could probably cook some terrific meals, regardless, but many things that ought to be quick and easy would instead be slow and tiresome.

When PCs can communicate with each other and with shared collections of data and computational power on other, larger machines, we get the explosion of interactive energy that has made this an Information Age.

Consider two extremes. At one extreme, imagine a PC with practically no computational power of its own, but with high-speed connections to every other computer in the world. On the other extreme, imagine a PC with as much computational power as all of the world's other computers combined, but with much of that power wasted in reproducing others' work. Which of these information appliances would do more for you?

Fortunately, we don't have to choose either one of these unbalanced systems; they're just "thought experiments." I use them to make the point that a modem is a strategic component of your PC system and that proper choice and adjustment of this device can substantially enhance, or impair, your overall return on your PC investment.

What a Modem Does

The name "modem" is like other technical terms such as "radar": You can know what the named thing does without knowing what the name actually means. Radar lets us see things far away; modems let us share information with points even farther away.

To assemble your own best combination of PC capabilities, you need to know a little bit more than the label "modem." You need to understand the technology that makes one modem faster than another or—as I must warn you—the technical issues that can prevent the latest modems from delivering their promised performance on your particular telephone line.

To talk about what your modem can or can't do, we have to begin by examining what a modem is supposed to do.

All About Modulation

Most of what a modem does is covered in its name. "Modem" is a contraction of "modulator/demodulator."

Modulation is the process of putting information into some other carrier signal; *demodulation* is the process of recovering the information, possibly several kinds of information, from a modulated carrier.

It would be nice if we could just send bits across the wires from one PC to another, turning a voltage on and off with a switch. It would be a messy world, though, if we ran wires from your computer to every other location with which you'd like to connect.

If we gave every computer its own full set of point-to-point connections, things would quickly get out of hand in terms of both complexity and cost. What we need is a system that only needs one connection to your PC, using switching and sharing techniques to let any location talk with any other.

In fact, we have such a network already in place, connecting you to almost everywhere from almost anywhere. I'm talking about the telephone system. Telephones are optimized, however, for carrying the smooth analog signals of voices rather than the crisp on-off pulses of bits.

Modems serve as translators. A modem transforms the bits in your PC into electronic versions of precisely formed sounds. Signals with the character of sound are just what the phone system likes to pick up and deliver. The combination of modem and phone line lets you exchange information via signals to and from other modems around the world.

Begin with Nothing: The Carrier Wave

In Chapter 3, I began our study of bits by introducing a statement ("Tomorrow's sunrise will be in the east") that contained no information. We'll do the same thing now with the kind of signal that modems exchange with each other. Modems modulate, so we'll begin with a signal that has no modulation: a "carrier" signal, like the one I've shown in Figure 7.1.

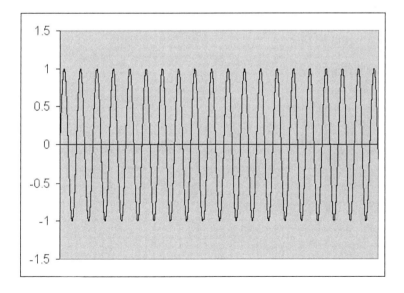

FIGURE 7.1
This periodic, repetitious signal has no modulation: At most, it conveys the information, "I'm here."

The signal in Figure 7.1 is an electronic version of the back-and-forth movements of a tuning fork. As the tines of a tuning fork vibrate, they put pressure waves into the air, making the air pressure go back and forth above and below its normal value.

Pressure waves in the air cause corresponding movements of your eardrum, which your ear then translates into electrical impulses that your brain interprets as sounds. Your ear demodulates the sound wave.

The steady hum of a tuning fork does not convey much information. At best, it says "I'm here," but you wouldn't be likely to interpret this signal as a sign of intelligent life. A signal like this could just as well come from many kinds of natural sources.

A periodic signal of constant strength and frequency, like the one in Figure 7.1, is called a carrier wave because it acts like a cargo carrier for information. Just as we put crates of goods in an empty railroad car, we add information to a carrier wave by modulating the carrier in any of several ways—or even in several ways at once.

Amplitude Modulation: Wiggling the Volume Control

We can add information to a carrier by adjusting the strength of the carrier signal, moving back and forth between loud and soft.

If you had a radio playing in one room of a building and you were listening from another room, you would probably notice if the radio's sound suddenly started to grow louder and softer in nonrepeating patterns of sudden change.

If you knew that your radio wasn't at fault, you would probably suspect that someone was playing with the volume control (or is it only parents of small children who think this way?). If done with intent and precision, the changing strength of the carrier signal can carry information.

For example, you could use the volume control to send the kind of pulses that a PC normally receives through a serial port such as an RS-232 interface (which we examined in Chapter 4). Figure 7.2 shows a simple data sequence, 1 0 1, being sent as the sequence "loud soft loud."

We are modulating the carrier wave of Figure 7.1 by changing its strength, also called its *amplitude*, and this method of communication is therefore called *amplitude modulation* (or "AM").

The nature of the carrier signal itself is almost irrelevant. In our imagined use of a radio and its volume control as a carrier wave and a modulator, it doesn't matter if the radio is tuned to All News or Top 40. The information we're talking about is in the changing loudness of the signal, not in the signal's other characteristics.

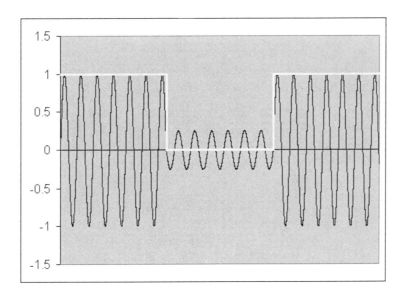

FIGURE 7.2
We can add information to the unmodulated carrier in Figure 7.1 by systematically changing the strength (technically called the amplitude) of the signal, creating what's known as amplitude modulation ("AM").

One Carrier, Many Messages

We can pay attention to the content of a radio program, or we can read a completely different message in the changes between loud and soft that we could overlay on that program. It's interesting to see that we can ignore one kind of information in a signal while easily detecting another. This means that one signal can actually carry more than one stream of information at once.

You could send Morse Code, for example, by turning up the volume of a radio in short and long bursts, representing the dits and dahs of the international standard for telegraphy. We might have two people listening to the result: one taking down the words of the radio announcer reading the news and the other transcribing the Morse Code message contained in the changing loudness of the announcer's voice.

The announcer might even be speaking a language that one of our imagined listeners doesn't understand: That listener would still be able to capture the Morse Code information embedded in the changing loudness of the speech.

Putting two kinds of information in one signal is just the beginning of *multiplexing*, the blending of many data streams into one signal, done in a way that lets those data streams be separated when the signal is detected.

Multiplexing is the mechanism, or family of mechanisms, that lets us put many telephone conversations (person-to-person or computer-to-computer) on a surprisingly small number of separate communication circuits. This is why our cities don't look like giant spider webs of wires, as people once predicted would happen if those newfangled telephones ever caught hold.

In our imagined use of the radio's volume control as a modulator, we're talking about *frequency division multiplexing*. The loud-soft pulses we create with the volume control would come fairly slowly. They couldn't come at rates of more than a few pulses per second, if even a skilled human listener is to read their pattern as a Morse Code sequence.

Meanwhile, the voice or music of the radio program would be in the audio-frequency range of roughly 100 to 3,000 cycles per second. It's the separation of frequencies, with the loud/soft pulses at tens per second and the voice or music at hundreds or thousands per second, that lets us separate frequency-multiplexed signals.

There are many ways of combining signals so that we can take them apart later on. For example, the spread-spectrum technique that we saw at the end of Chapter 5 performs *code division multiplexing*. By using a different coded pattern for each signal, we were able to separate two signals even after they'd been mixed with each other and with substantial amounts of interfering noise (as shown in Figure 5.35).

The simplest approach to multiplexing is so obvious that it scarcely seems to deserve its fancy label of *time division multiplexing*: We can just let different information streams take turns using a single channel. This is no more complex than the idea of having commercials use the same channel as a broadcast TV program—one kind of content simply alternates with the other.

Time division multiplexing lets us use simple hardware, but it requires careful coordination among the users of a channel. Frequency division multiplexing demands moderately complex hardware with less need for coordination among users. Code division multiplexing uses much more computational power than either of the other two methods, but computation gets cheaper all the time and coordination among the growing user community of communications networks becomes more costly.

You can figure out which kinds of multiplexing are becoming more important as the demand for public communications networks keeps growing, while cost of computing becomes almost vanishingly small.

Frequency Modulation: Always a Full-Strength Signal

When we devise a method of modulation, we want to think ahead to the problem of recovering the information at the other end of the communications link.

Amplitude modulation is easy to perform and easy to reverse at the other end to give us back our data, but how does AM perform on a less-than-perfect connection?

If our signal strength varies due to changing conditions on the line, there is no obvious difference between the intended modulation and the "accidental modulation" (another kind of AM?) that comes from imperfect connections. AM has poor immunity to noise.

Take another look, though, at the original unmodulated carrier in Figure 7.1. We see that it has another unchanging characteristic besides its amplitude—its frequency, shown in Figure 7.1 by the uniform spacing of the peaks and valleys in the curve.

Suppose that we vary, not the amplitude of the signal, but the frequency. We'll always hear the frequency we send, regardless of changes in the connection, just as a song on the radio sounds like the same tune whether the radio is playing in the same room or across the street.

If we only vary the frequency instead of deliberately turning down the volume to send the "soft" pulses of AM, our transmitted signal will always be at full power. Our listener can ignore any random changes in loudness, so we'll have high noise immunity with this approach that we call *frequency modulation* (or "FM"). Figure 7.3 shows our same sample sequence of data, a binary 1 0 1, being added to Figure 7.1's carrier by FM.

You've Known These Names All Along

In Figures 7.2 and 7.3, you can see the essential behaviors of both AM and FM radio, two "modulation" acronyms that you've probably been using almost all your life.

"Modem" will most likely join AM and FM to become your third everyday term that involves modulation, and now you know what all three of these terms mean.

A modem is a device that uses a combination of modulation techniques to convert, in both directions, between chains of bits and voice-like electronic signals. This conversion lets data travel across the established telephone network.

Just Another Phase: A Third Kind of Modulation

We can vary another signal property, in addition to amplitude and frequency, to add information to a signal.

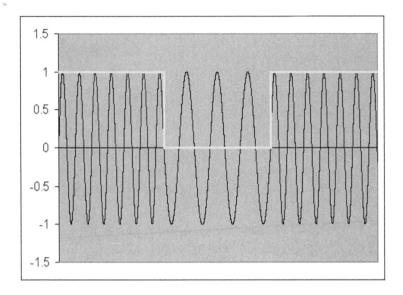

FIGURE 7.3
We can keep the strength of the signal constant but change the frequency (the number of repetitions per second) to convey information by frequency modulation ("FM").

Besides knowing how often a signal repeats (its frequency), we can also talk about when it begins each repetition. If we compare two signals of equal frequency and find that both signals start to rise toward their upward peaks at the same time, we can say that these signals are *in phase*.

Phase differences are excellent tools for detecting variations in signals. For example, have you ever noticed when one car's turn signal seems to be blinking in unison with another's, but after a few seconds you realize there's a drift?

You can't immediately see that one turn signal's frequency is different from the other's. You *can* tell the difference between both signals going on at the same time (in phase) and one signal going on when the other is going off (out of phase). The drift between in-phase and out-of-phase tells you that the frequencies must be different, even when the difference is quite small.

Detecting phase differences with electronic hardware is just as easy, and therefore inexpensive, but frequency measurement is more tricky. By various electronic techniques, moreover, we can deliberately change the phase of a signal to represent an information stream, retaining the advantage of the constant full-strength signal that made FM appealing.

Changes that carry information are modulation, so now we have a third option: *phase modulation*. Figure 7.4 shows our sample data, a 1 0 1 binary pulse train, being represented by phase modulation ("PM") of our Figure 7.1 carrier signal.

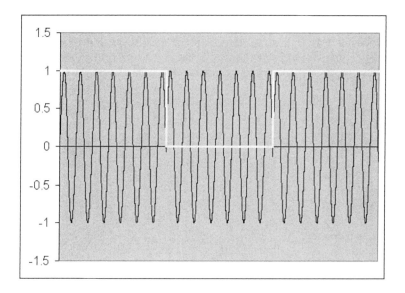

FIGURE 7.4
Changing the phase of a carrier by delaying it for some fraction of a cycle is another way to introduce information: by phase modulation ("PM"), which keeps the signal at full strength (like FM).

Notice in Figure 7.4 that when we shift from a data "high" to a data "low," the modulated signal has a sort of hiccup. The signal's positive peak is followed, not by a negative peak as usual, but immediately by another positive peak. The signal has been shifted by half a cycle.

We measure the progress of a repeating signal with the same 360 degrees that measure a circle. We would describe a half-cycle delay as a *phase shift* of 180 degrees.

How do we detect, or *demodulate*, a PM signal? Signal strength can be measured in absolute terms and so can signal frequency, but phase has meaning only when compared to the phase of some other signal.

Figure 7.5 shows one simple method of detecting phase changes. If we take the received signal and generate a second signal that is a delayed version of the one we received, we can subtract the delayed copy from the original.

If the delayed signal lags the original signal by exactly one cycle, the difference between the two signals will normally be zero (apart from small variations in signal strength). The delayed signal will go from negative to positive at the same time as the original, and its peaks and valleys will have equal strength and identical timing.

If the original signal goes through a phase change, however, we will see a sudden strong blip due to the momentary difference between the received signal and the delayed copy of that signal. The difference returns to zero when the delayed signal "sees" the new phase. The blips clearly mark our transitions from one phase to another.

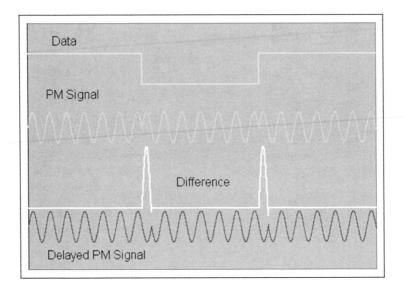

FIGURE 7.5
By delaying a received signal and subtracting the delayed copy from the as-received original, we cancel out parts of the signal that have a constant phase; we get pronounced blips at points of sudden "phase shift."

Modulation Versus Noise

Near the beginning of this discussion, we noted that interference with a signal can look just like deliberate modulation. Signal strength can change for various reasons. Unfortunately, so can a signal's phase.

If an outside electrical effect has a repeating behavior, causing phase to shift back and forth in a rapid and periodic way, the effect can even look like a changing frequency. For every form of modulation, therefore, some of what we see when we demodulate a signal might be accidental noise instead of actual information.

Speed Limits for Data Connections

Noise is one of two properties of a data connection that combine to determine a connection's maximum speed.

When I talk about the speed of a data connection, I'm *not* talking about the speed at which the signals move along the line. People are often confused about this.

For example, fiber-optic connections send signals as pulses of light through glass threads rather than pulses of electricity through metal wires. Fiber-optic connections are faster than wires in terms of their data rate, but this is not because light moves any faster than electricity. Actually, electrical pulses in wires move at speeds very close to the speed of light.

Fiber optics can carry more data than wires because fiber optics work with a carrier wave whose frequency is up in the range of light, around 500 million million cycles per second. That wasn't a stutter. I didn't say "million" twice by accident—I really do mean 500,000,000 MegaHertz (or 500,000 GigaHertz or 500 TeraHertz).

Bandwidth Lets More Data Flow

With a higher frequency, a carrier wave can carry more pieces of information. Think about an extreme case. With amplitude modulation, if we turn the signal's strength up and down at the same rate that the carrier signal is cycling, how can we tell the difference between the carrier and the data?

A fundamental rule of communication says that you can't usefully modulate a carrier at a frequency that's more than half of the carrier's frequency. If a channel can handle a higher-frequency carrier, though, we can modulate that carrier at a larger number of different frequencies (with frequency division multiplexing) or we can use a larger number of different coding patterns (with code division multiplexing).

Either way, raising the carrier frequency lets us put more information through a channel. This is what people mean when they talk about a channel having high *bandwidth*.

Low Noise Lets Us Pack In More Bits

It's well and good to have more bandwidth, but that bandwidth needs to be clean. Noise on a data channel is like trash on a multilane highway: You give up a lot of speed if you're constantly steering around random obstacles.

For example, suppose that we have a perfect connection, one that always gives us a perfect reproduction of our transmitted signal. If we send a signal of constant phase and amplitude, we'll get constant phase and amplitude at the other end of the line.

We could use amplitude modulation, not with just two levels of signal strength as I showed in Figure 7.2, but with any number of levels we wish. If we use two levels, each pulse can only represent one bit of data. If we use four different pulse strengths, however, each pulse is conveying two bits of data (because each pulse can represent one of the bit pairs 00, 01, 10, or 11). If we use eight different amplitudes, each pulse delivers a 3-bit package (000, 001, 010, 011, 100, 101, 110, or 111).

We could pack more bits into each change of state with phase modulation as well. In Figure 7.4, I showed two possible states: 0° shift and 180° shift. I could also use shifts of 90° and 270°, giving us four states, and therefore, two bits of data for each change of state. I could go to 45° intervals and have eight states at three bits per state.

On a perfect connection, there's no limit to the process of subdividing possible states. If I could detect 1,024 different signal strengths or phase shifts, I could send ten bits in every pulse. If I could detect 1,048,576 different states, I could send 20 bits in every pulse.

It doesn't take an electrical engineer, however, to figure out that we're starting to place a lot of trust in the perfection of our connection. If we use 5 volts as our full-strength amplitude, our scheme to pack 20 bits into one pulse demands that we tell the difference between signals whose voltage differs by less than 5 microvolts (millionths of a volt).

Noise Reduces the Number of Detectable Signal States

A cellular phone or walkie-talkie next to a communication line can introduce interfering voltages more than large enough to blur the dividing lines between finely spaced, multibit signal states. For example, I can measure about 12 millivolts (12,000 microvolts) in a one-foot piece of wire held about a foot away from an ordinary cordless phone when the phone is in use.

We have to separate the strengths of our signals enough to tell the difference between amplitude modulation and noise. We have to separate the phase shifts in our signals enough to tell the difference between phase modulation and "jitter" (the phase fluctuations in real-world circuits).

Whether noise affects the amplitude or the phase of our carrier signal, more noise makes it harder to tell the difference between similar signal states. Fewer identifiable states means fewer bits conveyed by each change in state, and a lower data rate overall.

If a telephone connection is designed to carry voices at up to 3,000 cycles per second, I should be able to change the signal state 1,500 times per second and clearly detect the changes.

I can separate my signal strengths by roughly 20 millivolts and have a separation larger than the interference that I measured in my cordless phone experiment. That was something of a worst-case experiment, with none of the protective measures that a real communications line would normally provide, so I'm being conservative here.

With slightly less than a 20mV separation, I can divide a 5-volt signal into 256 voltage levels, which means that I can convey eight bits with each change in state. Eight bits per state of change multiplied by 1,500 changes per second would give us a total data rate of 12,000 bits per second. A data rate of 12kbps isn't impressive today, but it's better than the 9,600bps that was considered a fairly fast data rate just a few years ago.

Calculations like the one I just made are the essence of answering the question, "How fast can a modem get?" More to the point, because signal-to-noise levels vary from one phone line to another (and even from one time of day to another), these principles determine how fast a modem it makes sense for you to buy.

Speaking of Speed: Baud Versus Bits per Second

People used to speak of 300-baud or 1200-baud modems, which delivered data rates of around 300 or 1200 bits per second. Because of this coincidence, some people still use "baud" as if it were a synonym for "bits per second."

Early modems used simple modulation techniques like the ones in the explanatory Figures 7.2 through 7.4 of this chapter; each change of signal state conveyed only one bit of data. *Baud* is the rate of change in signal state, so these modems had the same numeric rating for both baud and bits per second.

We've seen, however, that more refined methods pack several bits into each change of signal state. For example, we could modulate both amplitude and phase at the same time, defining a whole set of combinations of different amplitudes and different phase shifts.

Mapping the Combinations

We could create a map of sorts on which each point is a combination of amplitudes and phase shifts. We could have dozens of combinations, using states that are separated by comfortable margins compared to typical channel noise.

By these means, we could go well beyond the 12,000 bits per second that we estimated earlier, even while continuing to change the signal state at rates far below 12,000 times per second. Our baud would remain the same, even as our bit rate increased.

Bits, Not Baud, Are the Point

To the modem user, bit rate is what matters. Baud rate is only important to modem designers and other communication engineers. For this reason, you will rarely hear the word "baud" in modem discussions today.

If someone tells you that he just bought a "56,000 baud" modem, decide for yourself whether you want to think of that person as being pretentious, or merely ignorant.

Beyond POTS: 56K and ISDN

The kind of modem we've talked about so far is an ingenious device for turning the sow's ear of the analog telephone connection into a silk purse of high-speed data exchange.

In the not-too-distant future, though, analog modems will seem as anachronistic as the moving-pen plotters we discussed in Chapter 6 (whose design was once on the leading edge of color output technology).

The modems that we've talked about so far are built to work with Plain Old Telephone Service, as it's semi-officially called among the telecom *cognoscenti*: POTS, for short. Yes, people really use this term. There are better ways to connect.

More Bits, If You Can Handle Them: 56K Modems

The magical number of 56,000, more often spoken of as "56K," is much heard today when the subject of modems arises.

The demand for high-speed data connections is enough to get even the traditionally stodgy local phone companies running on Internet time, and so-called 56K modems are one of the happy results—at least, for some PC users.

A 56K modem is designed to bring information down to your PC at 56,000 bits per second, using ordinary telephone wires. In the United States, as of the time that this is written, you cannot receive data at rates of more than 53kbps, because the Federal Communications Commission restricts the power output of the modems used by service providers.

With or without such restrictions, however, a 56K modem depends on the same kind of process that can lead to inexpensive, digital, flat-panel display ports like the ones I described in Chapter 6. What's the connection between faster modem speeds and cheaper flat-panel connections? Both rely on getting rid of wasteful conversions back and forth between digital and analog signals.

Costs of Conversion

A regular modem converts digital information into analog signals for transmission to your local phone company switching center. Ironically, your phone company is most likely converting those signals back to digital form for transfer across the largely digital long-distance network.

When the switching center converts your analog signals to long-distance bits, it introduces—you guessed it—noise on the line. Figure 7.6 shows a digital approximation, based on 9-bit accuracy, overlaid on top of a pure analog signal; you can see a difference, as of course there would have to be.

We established in Chapter 3 that digital systems let you choose your tolerance for imperfection but force you to make that choice and accept some amount of detectable error.

We can think of the digitized signal in Figure 7.6 as a combination of the original analog signal plus a "quantization noise." I show these two components, the signal and the noise, in Figure 7.7. What we're seeing is that every time we go from digital to analog and back again, we lose signal quality, and therefore, reduce our maximum data rate.

Let's Get Rid of More Middlemen

When digital long-distance signals reach the local switching center that serves the other end of your connection, that center converts the signals back to analog mode for the so-called "last mile" (or "local loop") connection to the receiving modem. The receiving modem, with great ingenuity, turns them back into bits for the receiving computer.

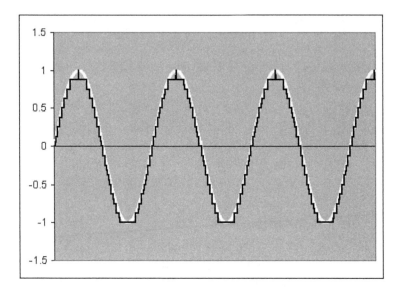

FIGURE 7.6
A digital approximation, no matter how many bits it uses, differs in measurable ways from an analog signal.

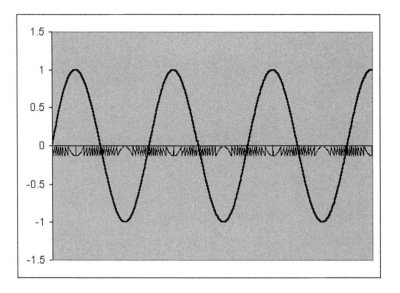

FIGURE 7.7
In this figure, we have plotted the digital approximation in Figure 7.6 as a combination of two signals: the original signal (large smooth curve) and a "quantization noise" (small jagged curve) that is the difference between the two curves in Figure 7.6. Every conversion from analog to digital modes introduces some noise of this kind.

In case you haven't been counting, I'll point out that we've made four conversions from one mode to another. We went from digital to analog in your modem, back to digital at the local switching center, back to analog at the other switching center, and finally back to digital in the receiving modem.

What a waste.

Traditional telephone connections are designed to deliver voices to analog telephone handsets, just as traditional display adapters are designed to deliver analog pictures to analog monitors. Digital data sources, like digital flat-panel displays, make it reasonable to keep our signals digital from end to end.

Minimizing analog/digital conversion is the goal of 56K modems, variously named with designations such as x2 from 3Com/U.S. Robotics or K56 Flex (incompatible with x2) from Lucent and Rockwell. These competing standards converge, as of the end of 1998, into a nonproprietary standard called V.90. The vital difference between V.90 and the previous incompatible approaches is in the agreement that's been reached to use the V.8 signaling standard (further discussed in the section "Modem Profiles," later in this chapter) to let 56K modems from different companies communicate their capabilities to each other.

If your local telephone line permits 56K service, your modem can communicate digitally with the telephone company's central switching installation. If the party with whom you're communicating also has 56K hardware and appropriate connections, your bits will stay bits the whole way.

Unfortunately, your phone company might already be squeezing more connections out of its existing lines by "concentrating" several last-mile connections on each pair of wires. If this is your situation, 56K service won't be available to you unless your phone company will move your service to a dedicated pair of wires. It doesn't hurt to ask.

V.90 modems automatically determine if a 56K connection is possible between any two points and fall back to the previous V.34 standard (see the section "Modem Profiles" later in this chapter) if a V.90 connection can't be made. This wastes, of course, the extra investment you made in V.90 equipment.

If you have a slower modem, or access to any modem at all, you can "try before you buy" with automatic line-test services offered by some modem manufacturers. Figure 7.8 shows the 56K information page on the Internet that's maintained by 3Com, whose U.S. Robotics brand is one of the premier names in modems and the one that often gets my Visa-bill votes.

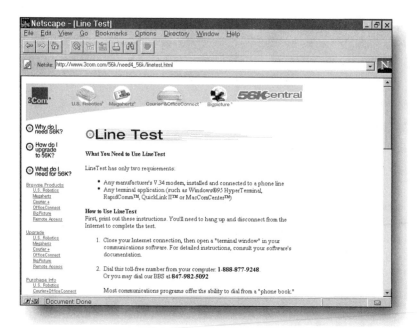

FIGURE 7.8
The Internet offers free access to testing instructions that will tell you if your local phone line can use a 56K modem.

From a site such as 3Com's, you can get instructions for connecting via toll-free telephone number with an automatic test facility (as shown in Figure 7.9) that will give you a diagnostic report like the one in Figure 7.10. As you see, my own local connection doesn't make the cut, so I know one extra-cost option not to choose the next time I buy a PC.

The Long "To Do" List for 56K

The 56K solution is by no means a full response to our growing demand for higher-speed digital connections.

Access to 56K service depends on particular characteristics of your local telephone line. In the words of the 3Com diagnostic report in Figure 7.10, ". . . line conditions can change from call to call." If you want a digital connection because you want more speed consistently, 56K might not meet your requirements.

The 56K service is also misleadingly named in that its top speed only applies to information coming down to your PC from the Internet or some other data source. Some people are content to "surf the Web," collecting information from others, and for them this asymmetry isn't a serious problem.

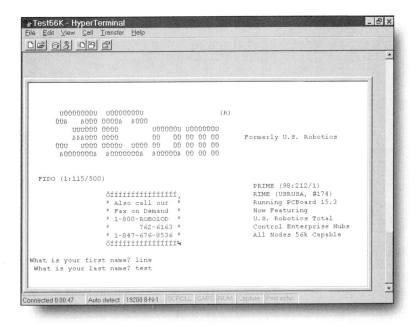

FIGURE 7.9
You need a modem to perform the test, but a friend with a PC and a modem can help you figure out if your local phone lines are good enough to merit a modem with 56K V.90 technology.

Some users, however, transmit large amounts of data; for example, when sending digital photographs to a family member or posting to a personal Internet page. Even with a "56K" modem, information goes up from your PC to the network at only 33.6kbps, even under ideal conditions.

On my own phone line, moreover, I would estimate that I can't connect any faster than 26.4kbps more than about half the time.

Incomplete and inconsistent: harsh words, but fair criticisms of the 56K (or V.90) connection.

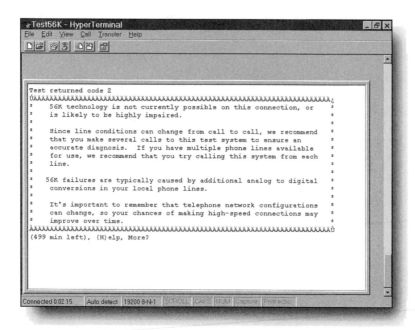

FIGURE 7.10

This diagnostic report from 3Com's automatic testing center tells the user of this phone connection that a 56K modem is unlikely to earn its keep unless the user can get a higher-quality line.

ISDN: "It's Simply Digital Now"

A more complete solution might be to change from POTS to ISDN service in your home or office if it's available in your area. Unlike 56K service, which depends on nonstandard approaches that aren't supported by all communication services, ISDN (integrated services digital network) is a well-defined standard: one that should give you higher speed than even an ideal 56K connection.

An ISDN connection typically combines two "B" channels for voice or data (each providing 64K bits per second of digital capacity) plus a D channel (of 16kbps capacity) that carries control information. Through the magic of multiplexing, these three channels get carried between your location and the nearest switching center on the same single pair of wires that's already in place to provide a single analog phone line.

The two B channels can serve two separate phone numbers, letting you have simultaneous voice and data communications. A suitable voice set, digitizing at the phone instead of at the central office, gives the same digital clarity to ISDN voice that you expect from Compact Disc audio and other digital sound sources.

Someday It Will Be Cheaper

In many areas, local phone companies find themselves pressed to provide an increasing number of residential phone lines (quickly nearing an average of two per home). In these regions, it benefits a telephone company to switch its customers to ISDN, which lets the company put two high-quality channels on one pair of wires.

The ISDN situation resembles the early years of tone dialing, which also reduced phone company costs by enabling the use of more reliable central-office equipment. As with tone dialing, we can expect phone companies to charge a premium for ISDN until they've recovered their initial investments. Then, it might suddenly become the norm—most likely, soon after the turn of the century.

An ISDN *What*?

You connect your PC to an ISDN line with an interface box that's often called an "ISDN modem." This is a silly name, because the whole point of ISDN is to get out of the business of modulating and demodulating by staying digital from one end of the circuit to another, but it's a common name, nonetheless.

Prices of ISDN adapters are falling quickly as ISDN becomes available in more areas. Pricing of ISDN service varies greatly with location.

Extreme Connectivity: Satellite and Cable

Even with both of a connection's B channels working together, ISDN only gives a user 128K bits per second. Unlike 56K service, ISDN's high speed goes in both directions, but you might want the fastest download speeds available for receiving such demanding content as video.

Slow Going Up, Fast Coming Down: DirecPC Satellite Service

Premium data access, at a price to match, is available via the DirecPC service that's offered by Hughes Network Systems (providers of the better-known DirecTV satellite TV service). DirecPC is an asymmetric link: You still use a modem and a phone line to send information up to the network, but your incoming data comes via satellite through a small dish antenna.

A DirecPC antenna connects to an ISA card (a type of plug-in PC enhancement that we discussed in Chapter 4) that goes in a slot in your PC. The DirecPC card feeds data to your PC at 400kbps, somewhat more than three times the speed of an all-data ISDN connection.

Pricing of DirecPC varies greatly with different pricing plans that offer different access options (including, for example, reduced rates for access at off-peak times). You can mix DirecPC with regular terrestrial service, paying for DirecPC time by the hour if you have an occasional but crucial need for its speed.

Going Fast in Both Directions: Call the Cable Guy

DirecPC can reach you almost anywhere, but most U.S. households are only tens of meters away from a cable TV "drop point." Perhaps you already have a cable connection in your home or office. If so, you might be able to jump to a data transfer rate in the millions of bits per second (in both directions) by means of a "cable modem."

Cable modems, so-called, give you a "Web tone"; that is, a connection that's always "live" without the delay of dialing up and shaking hands between your modem and the one at the other end of the line. Your data becomes just one more signal, along with the dozens of TV channels and other services that already multiplex their way along the cable.

Cable Modem

Also improperly called a modem, cable modems are a special kind of adapter that bridges a network card in your system to high-speed internet service running on the same wires as the cable TV network (more of the magic of multiplexing). Cable Modem service is only sparsely available, but if it's available to you, jump at the chance. Data rates are on the order of 1-2Mbps and connections are bidirectional. Best of all, unlike with real modems, you are always connected to the net; no more dialing up and waiting before you can start browsing.

Protocols: Party Manners for Our Modems and Connections

When you enter the world of data communications, you'll find the word "protocol" coming up in many contexts. As in the social world, a *protocol* in data communications is a set of rules for handling different situations.

You're likely to meet two families of protocols. One group is an alphabet soup of formal, international standards to let modems communicate with each other even when they're made by different companies.

The other protocols that commonly come up are the oddly named (and often quite informal) standards for packaging data so that we can detect any errors that might corrupt it during transmission.

Modem Protocols

You'll see the names of modem protocols, probably for the first and last times, when you buy and install your modem. This is definitely forgettable knowledge.

Modem protocol names often run around with tongue-twisting acronyms in front of them, such as CCITT and ITU or ITU-T. You might someday win Final Jeopardy by knowing that CCITT abbreviates the French name, Comité Consultatif International de Telegraphie et Telephonie; that is, the International Consultative Committee on Telegraphy and Telephony. This mouthful gave way to the current name of this body: the International Telecommunications Union—Telecommunication Standardization Sector, or ITU-T.

The standards issued by CCITT then, or ITU-T now, have names that begin with the letter V. A V.26 bis modem is a now-antique 1200/2400 bps modem for use on ordinary phone lines; V.26 bis gave way in the early 1990s to V.32 bis, the 14.4kbps modems that made many 9600bps modems obsolete before they were even out of warranty.

As this book is written, the prevailing standard—sort of—is V.34. The V.34 standard has fallen victim to the competitive pressure of huge consumer demand for the fastest modem in the West. Introduced in late 1996, V.34 was a standard for 28.8kbps modems, but vendors quickly pushed to extend this standard to support additional speeds of up to 33.6kbps.

At one time, there were modems that called themselves V.34+, V.34 bis, and V.34-1996. The last of these names was formally adopted to describe an enhanced V.34, often providing a speed increase of 2.4–4.8kbps on about 60% of typical phone lines.

While V.34 modems often connect at a speed of only 21.6 or 24.0kbps, a V.34-1996 modem more often achieves a connection at 26.4 or 28.8kbps.

Furthermore, though V.8 might sound like ancient history, V.8 bis is an important part of V.34-1996. V.8 is the protocol for starting up a connection, and a modem with V.8 bis (instead of the earlier V.8) will get connected more quickly after the modem at the other end of the line answers the phone.

V.34-1996 is better than V.34 at dealing with the hodgepodge of equipment that's still in use by commercial telephone companies and their switching centers. Special "echo canceling" circuits on telephone lines, for example, make voice calls easier to understand but limit the speed of data. V.8 bis can get around such obstacles to deliver a full-speed connection in situations where V.8 falls back to V.32 mode and delivers only 14.4kbps.

The heir apparent is V.90, which we discussed earlier in the section on 56K modems.

File Transfer Protocols

The other kind of protocol is something you probably see quite often if you use your modem to connect with computer bulletin boards or if you participate in other activities that involve exchanging files with remote locations.

When large files travel over imperfect phone lines, errors can arise. A corrupted byte in a long text file can cause an isolated typographical error, annoying but not fatal. A single erroneous byte in a program file, however, will most likely make the program work incorrectly. We wish to avoid the resulting waste of time.

File transfer protocols are rules for breaking files into pieces and wrapping those pieces in additional data that describes the content of each piece.

File transfer protocols can detect errors, and signal the sending location to re-send a piece of a file that doesn't come through correctly the first time. More elaborate protocols can even instruct the sending location to send smaller blocks (reducing the time spent re-sending) if the error rate is high, or to send larger blocks (streamlining operations) if the error rate is low.

Picking a Protocol

You decide which file transfer protocol to use, based on the list of protocols supported by the service to which you're connecting. If you're calling another PC user, the two of you agree on a protocol that both of you have available.

Your choice of a file transfer protocol is one of the options in communication software products, such as the HyperTerminal accessory program that comes with Windows 95. Figure 7.11 shows a communication service offering its list of transfer protocols in the background while HyperTerminal's options appear on the drop-down list.

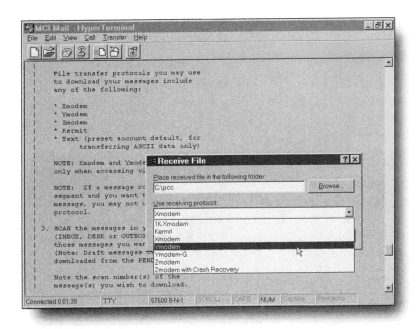

FIGURE 7.11
It's useful to know a thing or two about the fastest file transfer protocols so you can make a good choice from the list of options supported by your software and by the communications service you're using.

The Modern Protocols: Eternal Optimists

The list in Figure 7.11 is typical. XModem is popular, but not especially fast. YModem sends files in larger blocks than XModem, speeding operations and automatically falling back to a smaller block size (the same as XModem's) if a block contains more than five errors.

ZModem is faster still on good connections, because it doesn't wait for confirmation of each sent block. ZModem continues sending unless it's interrupted by a signal from the receiver, in which case it can still go back and retransmit the block that had problems.

If file transmission is interrupted by losing a connection, ZModem enables the sender to resume at the point of interruption instead of re-sending the entire file.

Kermit: Amphibians Can Go Anywhere

The Kermit protocol is old, and it's usually set up with options that make it slow, but it can get a file through to almost any kind of equipment under almost any conditions.

Newer protocols such as YModem make optimistic assumptions, usually justified by modern telephone company equipment, but Kermit can handle worst-case scenarios of noisy lines and other potential problems.

For small files, such as my non-Internet email, I routinely use Kermit to avoid the waste of time that results when a YModem transfer doesn't work and has to be repeated.

Squeezing, and Fixing, on the Fly

In Chapter 3, we looked at the idea of data compression with tools such as WinZip; in Chapter 4, we looked at the remarkable notion of data-encoding schemes that can detect (and even correct) memory errors. There are data compression and error-detection/correction schemes for data communications as well as for computer files and memory.

We can do data compression "offline" with a tool such as WinZip, before we send a file, or we can use a modem that has data-compression procedures built into the modem's own hardware. Note well that some modem-makers cite speeds based on compressed transmission, and we saw in Chapter 3 that some types of content are much more compressible than others. Your own effective speed might, therefore, be better or (more likely) worse than a vendor's claims. (For example, you won't get much additional compression from your modem when you transmit a WinZipped file.)

The standard approach to combined, on-the-fly error compression and correction is V.42 bis, another of our growing vocabulary of "V" names. V.42 bis includes the MNP compression/correction protocols, proprietary to certain brands of modems, so you need not be concerned about any MNP numbers that you sometimes hear in protocol discussions.

If your modem is going to compress data before it's sent, the modem needs to get data from your PC at a higher rate than the modem is using for its transmissions out to the network. You will want to set your PC to a Local Transmission Rate of 115,200 bits per second, which an older PC can't handle.

Newer PCs have a high-speed chip, a type 16550A Universal Asynchronous Receiver/Transmitter (UART), that can feed your modem at the speed it needs to make full use of all its capabilities. A 16550A is a debugged version of the earlier 16550, and it's worth checking the specifications of a new PC to make sure it uses the latest type of UART to control its serial ports.

A UART sounds like something you might ask your doctor to remove, but it's one of those key ingredients that make a PC much more than just its CPU. A faster CPU might save the typical user seconds or minutes over the course of a day, but a faster UART/modem combination can save tens of minutes several times a week.

Buying and Using Your Modem

Like other elements of your PC system, your modem's performance should be in balance with that of other components. In this case, the "other components" include things like your telephone line; PC-using neighbors might be able to tell you useful information about the performance they're achieving with various types of equipment.

An internal modem, plugging into one of your PC's slots, saves space. Personally, I prefer external modems like the unit shown in Figure 7.12.

I like the information I get from an external modem's indicator lights, which tell me clearly when the phone line is tied up (shown by the OH, or Off Hook, light) and when data is going back and forth (shown by blinking of the RD and SD, Receive and Send Data, lights).

I also prefer the ease of moving a modem to another machine by transferring a simple cable hookup instead of opening up the PC cabinet and going through a tedious process of handling small fasteners and possibly a time-consuming setup process. Few good things come free, of course, and an external modem typically costs more than an internal modem of comparable capability.

Hooking It Up

An external modem's connections, shown in Figure 7.13, are straightforward. One connector accepts the snap-in plug, commonly called an RJ-11 or "modular connector," for the cable that connects to your phone line. On the modem in Figure 7.13, this is the connector marked TELCO.

The other RJ-11 socket, marked PHONE, lets you plug a phone into the modem. The phone can use the line when the modem isn't active.

The 25-pin connector marked RS-232 is the serial interface to your PC, and we discussed its workings in Chapter 5. A USB modem will have a different connector.

The power connection speaks for itself. Unless you have a USB modem, whose power comes through the USB connection, your modem will probably come with a "brick" (an external power supply like the one at the right-hand end of the power strip in Figure 5.4).

FIGURE 7.12
Indicator lights, showing precisely what your modem is doing, are one of the benefits that come with an external modem.

FIGURE 7.13
External connectors and switches such as these typically let you connect your modem to a phone line, share the line with a regular telephone handset, control various modem options, connect the modem to your PC, and connect an external power supply (not needed by USB modems).

Making It March

Less obvious are the functions of the tiny switches, grouped together in the block between the PHONE and RS-232 connectors in Figure 7.13. These switches are called DIP switches, from "dual inline package." A DIP is just a type of module that mounts a block of these miniature switches directly on a circuit board.

DIP switches are becoming less common as more PC equipment takes on the built-in memory and local processing power to set and remember options through software instead of through manual settings.

On this modem, as on many others, the functions of option-setting switches are described by a placard—in this case, on the bottom of the unit (Figure 7.14). Various modem behaviors might need to be set in particular ways for use with particular communications software; the manuals that come with the modem and the software will give any needed details.

In Figure 7.14, below the section of the placard that describes the switch settings is a listing titled "Most-Used Commands." These open the door to a remarkable set of features built into most PC modems: the capability to accept commands from the PC, rather than merely relaying data.

We rely on a modem's built-in commands to perform tasks such as dialing telephone numbers under the PC's control. This is far more convenient than the former approach of dialing the number on a telephone and then pushing a button to switch the phone line over to the modem.

Most of the time, commands to your modem are handled automatically by communications software. Sometimes, though, your modem and a remote communications service might have trouble understanding each other. When that happens, you might be able to shift your modem out of its normal mode of passing data to the other system and into its mode of accepting local commands.

A common "escape sequence" for making your modem listen to you is the "+++" sequence shown in Figure 7.15. The modem usually replies, "OK." At that point, you can give commands with special codes from the modem manual, such as the one shown in Figure 7.15: AT H0, "Hang up the phone." Note the status message at bottom left in the figure; the communications software has detected the modem's resulting action of disconnecting the line.

Two modem behaviors are normally invisible, but you might someday need to adjust them. One is "echo" and the other is "flow control."

There's an Echo in Here

Echo is a familiar word: It's the first thing we told a PC to do.

When you're communicating with another computer, the other computer might confirm what you've typed by sending it back, or it might just accept it—leaving you to wonder if you hit the intended keys. Most of the time, a keystroke echo feature is a good thing.

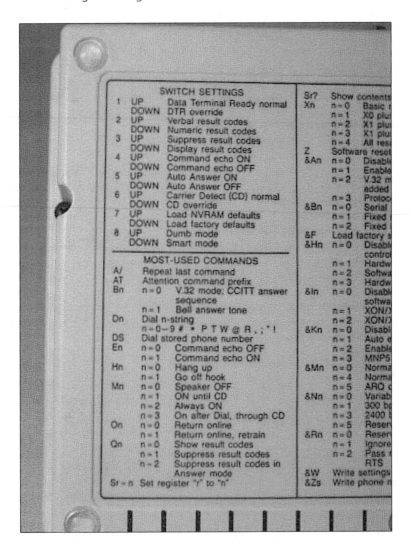

FIGURE 7.14

Switch settings and command codes won't be part of your everyday interaction with your modem, but knowing where to find them is like knowing where to look for the fuse box in your car: When you need to know, you *really* need to know.

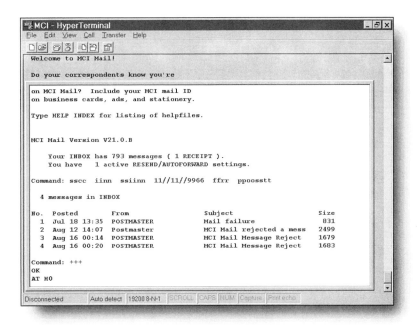

FIGURE 7.15
The escape command +++ tells the modem, "Stop passing data along; I'm talking to you now, not that other computer." The modem then acts on commands in its own little language, often summarized by a command list like the one in Figure 7.14 and almost always detailed in the modem's manual.

Remote computers turn off their echo at certain times, such as when you enter a password. This prevents passersby from looking over your shoulder and seeing your password sitting right there on the screen.

If a remote machine is not echoing your keystrokes when you want to see what you're typing, your communications software or your modem will do it for you. For example, in Figure 7.14, we see that Switch 4 determines whether the modem will echo back the keystrokes it sees when it's been placed in its command mode (as in Figure 7.15).

You could wind up, however, with a double echo—with two or more of your communications software, your modem, and your remote communication site all echoing back each keystroke that you type. This can lead to unhelpful results such as those in Figure 7.16.

Most communications software lets you fix the problem of overly enthusiastic echoing, as shown for the Windows HyperTerminal accessory program in Figure 7.17.

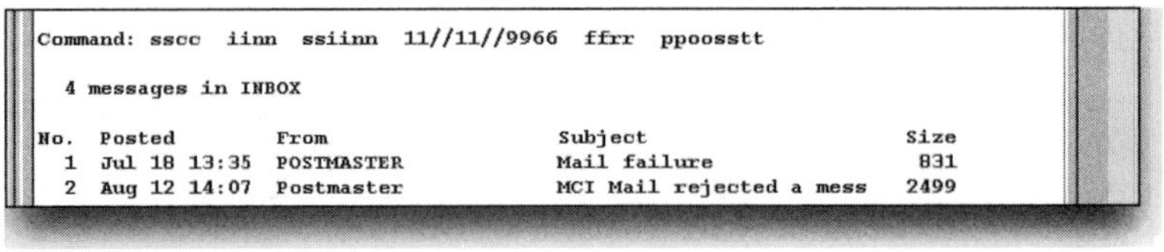

```
Command: sscc  iinn  ssiinn  11//11//9966  ffrr  ppoosstt

4 messages in INBOX

No.  Posted        From                 Subject                Size
  1  Jul 18 13:35  POSTMASTER           Mail failure            831
  2  Aug 12 14:07  Postmaster           MCI Mail rejected a mess 2499
```

FIGURE 7.16
The command was supposed to be "sc in sin 1/1/96 fr post" (Scan inbox since 1/1/96 for messages from addresses containing "post"), but the result on the screen looks like a serious keyboard problem. When too many echoes come back to the user, each typed letter appears twice on the screen—even though the remote computer is only seeing it once.

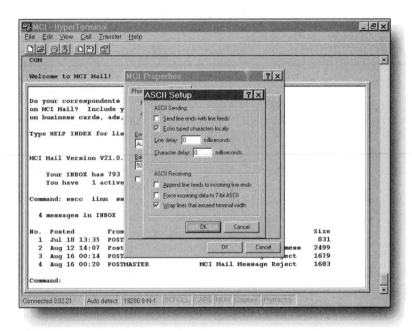

FIGURE 7.17
Communications programs such as Windows HyperTerminal have controls, somewhere in there, that let you adjust such behaviors as character echoing if you're not getting what you want.

For Best Performance, Go with the Flow

Another buried setting in most communications software is "flow control," the management of data flow between the PC and the modem.

Your PC will handle tasks more efficiently if it can hand the modem a large chunk of data and say "Call me when you're ready for more." Likewise, your PC will let you get more work done while you're downloading files if the modem only interrupts the PC when there's a nice large package of data to transfer to your hard disk.

In Chapter 5, we noted the presence of wires in the RS-232 interface that permit the exchange of flow-control signals between a PC and an external device. Now is the time when those signals become important. If you have the connections, settings like the ones shown in Figure 7.18 (combined with a high-performance UART) could enhance your communications performance.

Speaking of protocols, these exchanges of information between cooperating devices are commonly called "handshaking" operations—hence, the title of this chapter

The manuals for your particular communications software and modem must be jointly consulted. It's not a matter of right or wrong; it's a matter of getting the software and the modem (and the connecting cable) to agree on how things will work.

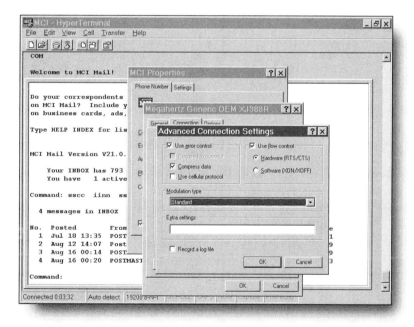

FIGURE 7.18
Hardware or software flow control? It's not a choice that you expected to face when you bought a PC, but hardware flow control lets your PC and your modem work together with peak efficiency, and software flow control lets them get the job done, though not as quickly, even if the connecting cable doesn't have all of the wires it should.

A Modem Is an Appliance

Most of this chapter has been about things you can't see. I want to close, however, by noting that a modem is an appliance, and an important one. I'd rather get through a week without a printer than a day without a modem.

If your modem is just plain hard to use, you might find yourself wishing you had bought with your eyes and fingers instead of buying what looked best on a specification sheet. The indicator lights should be clearly marked and easy to see in the lighting conditions at your workplace, the power switch should be easy to reach, and—my particular pet issue with modems—the built-in speaker should have an obvious and easily adjusted volume control like the one in Figure 7.19.

When you're dialing a new communications service and you're not getting connected, a modem's speaker gives you important clues.

For example, the modem speaker tells you if a voice is answering the phone when you dial a number at midnight; it tells you if the voice is saying angry things about baseball bats and Caller ID. This might help you realize that you've forgotten to enter an area code along with a long-distance number.

FIGURE 7.19
Modem performance is mostly a matter of invisible technology, but some things should be right there where you can see them; for example, the volume control for the modem's internal speaker that helps you figure out what's at the other end of that phone line.

What We've Learned

Like Chapter 6, this chapter was going to be half this long when I started writing it. I guess it could be double this length again and still not cover most of what there is to say about data communications—the hardware, the software, and the tips.

Some data communications issues fit better into Chapter 17, "Roses and Thorns: Imperfect Systems, the Internet and Cybercrime." In this chapter, I've tried to answer the basic questions of what a modem does, why it doesn't do it as well as we'd like, and what you should know to make modem use less mysterious and more productive.

I've tried to save you some money by pointing out that many things have to cooperate before a modem can be as fast in practice as its advertisements claim. You might get just as much real speed from a 28.8kbps modem (which you can probably find at a swap meet) as from the latest x2 or K56 Flex widget.

With satellite or cable service, you can get a lot of data delivered to your PC, at rates that would fill a floppy disk in seconds. We used to say that the world's fastest modem was a box of floppy disks and a Federal Express charge account; that's becoming less true as data rates increase and we come to expect same-day instead of next-day information.

Satellite service can cost you as much as buying several new modems a year. Alternatives, such as custom services that download requested data overnight, might meet your needs at much less cost.

Few things, though, will do more to make your PC useful than a modem that makes best use of available connections. A well-chosen modem will feed your PC a hearty and healthy diet of information and give you rapid, inexpensive communications with your office, your family, and much of the rest of the world.

*"Why should we limit
computers to the lies
people tell them
through keyboards?"*

—BILL GOSPER, QUOTED BY
STEVEN LEVY,
in *Hackers: Heroes of the
Computer Revolution*

Eyes, Ears, and
Voices

*I*N THIS CHAPTER, WE'LL LOOK AT THE huge range of options that a PC gives you for acquiring and using sound and image data, including everything from sound and images to music performance and composition. Sound and image hardware, with the added "intelligence" of easy-to-use software, can even let your PC read printed text and respond to spoken commands.

At the beginning of Chapter 7, I said that a PC without a modem was like a kitchen without running water. In the same spirit, I'll now assert that a PC without sound and image hardware is like a house without a radio or a TV.

A PC with only a keyboard and mouse, with no other input devices, is like a house that only receives newspapers—with the photographs trimmed out by censors. A house like that might be a good place for thinking, but someone who lives there would have a hard time keeping up with the rest of the world's current events and new ideas.

Your PC becomes a more interesting "place" and a better companion when it knows more about the world around it—when your time with your PC is entertaining, as well as informative. This chapter shows you how to make it happen.

Everybody's Doing It

After a display, a printer, and a modem, a digital sound recorder and digital camera (either still or video) are the next things you should think about plugging into your PC. Electronic instruments follow close behind, especially if you have a music student in your home.

Sound: It Works, and It Plays

It's lately become quite common for new PCs to come with microphones. These are built-in components of many portable systems and integrated into the displays of many desktop PCs.

Most PCs today have sound conversion hardware that transforms a microphone's signals into bit streams that your PC can save as files. The same hardware also turns special data files into rich stereo sound, enlivening games and educational software. We'll see how this is done and look at other options for using sound in the form of spoken commands to your PC.

Mainstream office software products now include the option of adding voice notes to your documents or including music or sound effects in your presentations. More elaborate software gives you the power of a broadcast studio, with extensive tools for enhancing and editing sound. These advanced techniques are beyond the scope of this book, but are covered by a growing number of books on multimedia production.

Without special assistance, however, and using nothing but standard hardware and readily available software, you and your PC can do (and undo) audio-editing operations that used to require painstaking, error-prone surgery on bulky magnetic tapes. I have to admit, there's a dark side to this flexibility: These undetectable editing features mean that you can't believe *anything* you hear.

You Ought To Be in Pictures

Digital still-image cameras have gone through an explosion of popularity, selling more than a million units every year in the United States alone. Digital video camcorder sales are coming up rapidly, also, as their prices (and the costs of storing their bulky video bit streams) rapidly fall.

In just a few years, digital imaging equipment has come down from the professional price range to fit within a home or small-business budget. Essentially all digital cameras include software for managing and editing images, so the warning that I just gave for sound recordings also applies to photographs—thanks to cheap computers, you can't believe anything you see.

There's still a big difference, though, between a basic digital camera ($300 or less) and an aficionado or professional unit ($1,300 and up and up and up). We'll see what makes that difference.

Let There Be Music

An electronic music keyboard—or other computer-controlled or computer-enhanced musical instrument—is also a likely candidate for inclusion in your PC system.

Electronic keyboards are surprisingly inexpensive and more compact than traditional pianos. Piano teachers report that electronic keyboards can actually be better than conventional pianos for developing certain aspects of a beginning student's technique.

An electronic instrument can imitate a wide range of conventional instruments, by means that we'll discuss in this chapter. An electronic wind instrument can sound like anything from a flute to a pipe organ; an electronic keyboard can sound like almost any instrument, or even like an orchestra. This variety can motivate students and provide new performance options for the accomplished amateur or professional musician.

Digital instruments encourage original composition: Simple software can produce a printable musical score from an improvised tune, without the labor of note-by-note transcription (as we'll see later in this chapter).

Another major benefit of electronic instruments, aided by your PC, is the convenience of practicing with headphones at any time (without disturbing others in a house or apartment). PCs have become so inexpensive that a family might well consider purchasing a system solely for music education, with the PC's other useful functions coming along as a bonus.

We'll Only Look at What Matters

We could spend many pages on the "front end" hardware of digital media tools. I don't plan to do that in this book, because we'd quickly wind up with a book-length tutorial on audio-video production. That's not what you paid for.

I will summarize the things that are the same in both traditional and digital media, so that you'll know what you *don't* need to learn anew if you're already knowledgeable in this area.

I'll provide more detail in areas where you'll need further information, regardless of your level of conventional audio-video knowledge, to make an informed choice of digital media equipment.

It All Begins with Transducing

Both sound and imagery need to be transformed into lists of values before your PC can accept or use them. We can make this conversion in several different ways.

Whether we're talking about sights or sounds, we have to begin by turning some kind of energy into electrical signals. In general, a device that turns one kind of energy into another is called a *transducer*.

Sound Is Simple

For sound, our transducer is a microphone. Microphones function by turning mechanical vibrations (caused by air pressure waves) into the electrical "vibrations" of an alternating-current signal.

In a former life, or so it seems now, I was active in radio and sound recording; I found microphones a fascinating subject. Some microphones pick up sound from only one direction, other microphones pick up sound from all around, and stereo microphones pick up separate signals from a single location.

Only the audio aficionado is likely to care, however, about these exotic options, and such people don't need me to tell them about such things. They already know, and a microphone's vital mechanisms are the same whether the recording gets made with analog or digital media.

If you already understood microphones before PCs came along, your knowledge remains current. If you didn't know anything about microphones before the moment that you read this paragraph, you probably don't need or want to know any more.

Eyeing the Details

Lenses, like microphones, use the same principles and designs in both conventional and digital devices. Whether you're taking snapshots or doing advanced amateur or professional photography, you don't need any extra knowledge of lenses to make the transition from film to digital technology.

Whatever you know about composing images, arranging light sources, and other basic elements of photography applies in equal measure to digital imaging. Some people might find this disappointing news, but people who wish they could take better pictures can't depend on a digital camera to elevate their skills.

It's true that digital photography lets you do many things on your PC that used to demand advanced skills and a personal photo darkroom. Digital tools can help you delete distracting items from a background or bring out detail by using mathematical noise reduction methods. You don't need to understand the math: These techniques are simple menu commands.

Even so, the foundation of good photographs is still an interesting subject, in a suitable setting, with appropriate lighting and focus. Good photographic technique is still the starting point of images that you'll share with pride.

Paying by the Bit

Digital media build a bridge between two technical domains. Digital cameras and sound recorders rely on the same principles as conventional media on their front end; they play by the same rules as digital data storage and digital data communications on their back end.

Good lenses and microphones are a necessary starting point, but you also need more bits (and higher rates of processing bits) to achieve high-quality results. As with hard disks and modems, there's a fairly direct connection between bit capacities (size), bit rates (speed), and costs—though prices are falling as quickly in digital media as in other digital technologies.

It Goes Beyond "Time Is Money"

How much speed, capacity, and quality do you need? And how much does it make sense for you to spend? The trade-off isn't as easy to make in this area as it is when you buy a modem, for example, because slow modems and fast modems deliver identical results when the job is done; the only difference is in how long they take to do it.

You wouldn't pay for a satellite link to the Internet if you only receive a large file once a month—you can always let that one big file come down to your PC while you're eating lunch. Buying digital sound or image hardware is a different kind of decision, because every recording or picture will reflect the capability of your gear.

If you want to produce a picture that looks good when blown up to poster size, you need a camera with high resolution. If you want to capture a family event to place in a personal archive, you need an audio or video recorder with high-fidelity sampling. We'll explore the meaning of these terms in depth before this chapter is done.

An Option for Every Budget

Regardless of technical details, it doesn't matter whether you plan to produce a certain kind of work once a day or once a year. You might have to confront the cost of a near-professional unit (what some video buffs call "prosumer" equipment, a hybrid of "professional" and "consumer") to get what you want. You *can* spend as much on a digital camera or sound recorder as you would spend for a not-so-basic PC.

The good news, though, is that you can make a nearly painless entry-level purchase and still enliven your PC experience. Just as any modem is better than none, any kind of digital camera or sound equipment will change your view of what a computer is good for.

But How Do Bits See or Hear?

You're probably not surprised when I say that more bits will cost you more money, but perhaps this raises a fundamental question: What does it mean, exactly, to have "more bits" of sound or "more bits" of picture?

It's easy to understand that more bits of text mean the ability to work with larger documents, and that more bits of numbers mean greater precision and more advanced forms of computation. It's harder to envision the connection between a PC's digital bits and a person's analog senses.

Almost every PC sold today includes a sound card, so let's begin with digital audio.

Digital Sound: It's Just a Hi-Fi Modem

Sound is inherently analog, and so is a sound transducer—that is, a microphone. Continuously varying air pressure goes in, and continuously varying voltage and current come out.

A speaker is also analog. Electrical signals make the speaker vibrate, producing pressure waves that our ears perceive as sound.

We have to go back and forth, therefore, between the continuous electrical signals that come out of a microphone or go into a speaker and the lists of values that go in and out of a digital computer. This is similar to the problem we faced in Chapter 7, when we had to go back and forth between the continuous tones of telephone signals and the bit streams of PC data.

A modem and a sound card have many functions and principles in common.

Unlike a modem, however, a sound card has to reproduce more than just amplitude, frequency, and phase. A sound card has to reproduce the character of a sound: It must capture, for example, the difference between a flute (see Figure 8.1) and a violin (see Figure 8.2) that are both playing the same musical pitch.

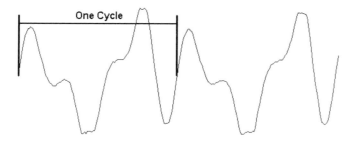

FIGURE 8.1
This is the sound of a flute, as it appears when converted to an electrical signal that mimics the sound's pressure waves. The shape of this wave is part of the flute's distinctive contribution to a musical composition.

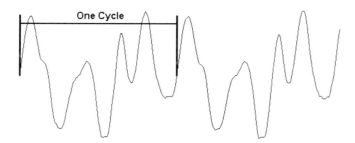

FIGURE 8.2
This is the sound of a violin, playing "the same" note as the flute in Figure 8.1, but clearly producing a different sound. Your ears can tell the difference, even though the frequency (the spacing between signal peaks) is the same.

Getting Our Sound in Shape

If we care about how something sounds, instead of just using frequency and phase to convey raw data, we have to make one of those pesky digital decisions. We have to decide up front how much data we want to capture, and pay for.

High-fidelity sound covers a wide range of frequencies. The low, "pedal" notes of a pipe organ extend down to tens of cycles per second (around 30Hz); the high end of normal hearing extends into the vicinity of 20,000 cycles per second (20KHz).

To turn continuous waves into lists of values, we can sample the wave at regular intervals. Figure 8.3 shows a continuous wave (the white line) being sampled at a constant rate (the black spikes).

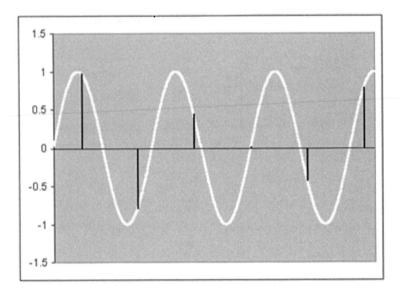

FIGURE 8.3
Periodic samples (black spikes) yield values that can be stored to represent a continuous waveform (white curve) for digital manipulation by your PC and its sound hardware.

We can measure the height of the wave, positive or negative, at each of the marks; the list of heights can be used to reconstruct the wave.

A Modem in Reverse

We have to decide how many bits we will use for each measurement. With more bits, we can represent a larger number of levels, more closely matching the actual height of the wave. This is just the reverse of what we discussed in Chapter 7, where we talked about using more signal levels to put more bits of information into each of the signals a modem sends.

Figures 7.6 and 7.7 show the result of approximating a signal with 3 bits of data per sample, envisioning the result as the original signal plus a "quantization noise." Figure 8.4 shows a lower-quality arrangement, with only 2 bits per sample; you can see that the quantization noise is greatly increased.

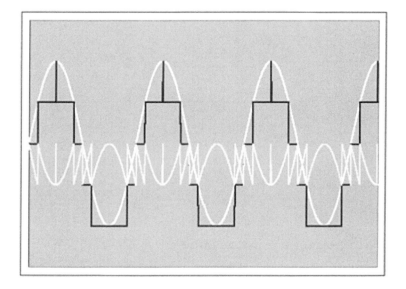

FIGURE 8.4
Coarse sampling, using only 2 bits to represent each sample, introduces severe quantization noise that corrupts audio quality.

Figure 8.5 shows a finer approximation, at 4 bits per sample: The quantization noise is greatly reduced. More bits per sample yield more accurate measurement but require more elaborate hardware.

NOTE
Your ear is a wonderfully sensitive detector, able to deal with everything from whispers to roars. Unfortunately, this means that audio quality is seriously degraded by any quantization noise big enough to see in a diagram such as Figure 8.4.

For good quality in a home audio system, the noise in Figure 8.4 should be no more than 0.1% as "tall" as the signal. You can see that this would require many more bits of accuracy.

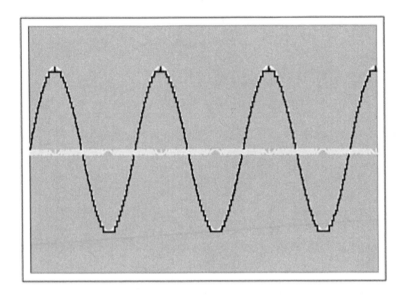

FIGURE 8.5
Using more bits per sample reduces the error of approximation, equivalent to reducing quantization noise and improving digital sound.

Knowing a Sound's True Name

We also have to decide how often we will measure the value of the waveform. The more often we measure, the closer we can come to matching a complicated shape.

To measure more often, however, requires faster hardware.

If our sample rate gets too low, we can get ourselves into real trouble. I constructed Figure 8.3 to demonstrate a fundamental problem: The samples in that figure (shown in black) are too far apart to reconstruct the sampled waveform (shown in white).

I don't just mean that we can't reconstruct the detailed shape of the wave. We can't even say, for certain, what frequency this wave has. That's because I've shown a sampling frequency that's low enough, compared to the sampled waveform, to exhibit a problem called *aliasing*.

The aliasing that happens in digital audio is different from the graphical aliasing we discussed in Chapter 6. When we talk about signals and samples, aliasing means that a given set of samples could come from any of several different signals.

For example, Figure 8.6 shows another possible signal that could produce the same samples we see in Figure 8.3. I've overlaid the two possible signals, along with the "aliased" samples: You can see that either signal matches the samples' description.

I could construct many other signals that would also match these samples.

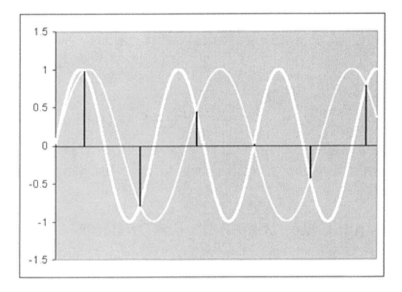

FIGURE 8.6
More than one signal could produce any given set of sample values. To avoid ambiguous results, samples must be taken at a frequency at least twice that of the highest frequency waveform to be sampled. High-fidelity audio extends to nearly 20KHz, so audio must be sampled at better than 40KHz (in the range used by audio CDs) for best results.

These Are Not Free Samples

From Figures 8.3 through 8.6, you can see that more samples per second and more bits per sample are both important to accurate digital recordings.

When we multiply more bits per measurement by more measurements per second, we wind up with the total number of bits we must store per second of recorded sound. The larger this number, the shorter the recording time per unit of storage.

If we want to put a recording on a floppy disk or send it across the Internet, we don't want to store any more bits than necessary. More sampling is better, but it increases every kind of cost (in terms of both money and time) that's associated with capturing and using digital sound.

Getting Back to Sound

Reversing the process and going from samples back to sound is a relatively simple task. A PC's sound system includes a digital-to-analog converter (DAC), which fits a smooth curve to a set of samples. The DAC then sends the result (as an electrical signal) to a conventional sound amplifier (like the one in any radio or stereo system).

Newer PCs can postpone the digital-to-analog conversion, sending the sound in digital form through a Universal Serial Bus of the type we discussed in Chapter 5. The DAC hardware can thus be decentralized, with the actual sound being generated "outboard" in USB-compatible speakers.

By putting all of the analog audio hardware out in the speaker, we avoid the need to send analog signals over long wires that run near a radio-noisy PC (which might put interfering static into the connection). We can match the power level and audio quality of the amplifier and the speaker in a single, unified design. USB speakers are a worthwhile innovation.

Advanced Sound: Conducting a Digital Orchestra

Instead of recording sounds bit by bit, cycle by cycle, we can capture the sounds of musical instruments in a compact and efficient form that lets us mimic any desired ensemble. In effect, we can store an entire orchestra and send each section of the orchestra its own separate part in an overall score.

There are two ways to represent an instrument. We can store a *wavetable* representation of each instrument, using the same kind of Read-Only-Memory (ROM) chip that holds a PC's startup instructions.

For example, we saw the "shape" of violin and flute tones in Figures 8.1 and 8.2. We can store these shapes, and those of many other instruments, as lists of values.

We can ask each stored "instrument" to play any pitch, at any loudness, by cycling through its wave shape at the desired number of cycles per second and by generating a signal at a strength that we control. For example, we would run through the wavetable at 440 Hertz for a concert A pitch.

Alternatively, we can store a mathematical formula that approximates the shape of an instrument's distinctive tone. When we want to hear that instrument's sound, we run that formula through a special chip called a Digital Signal Processor (DSP) to perform a *synthesis* operation. Synthesis is even more compact, in terms of the memory required, than wavetable sound, but synthesis is generally less realistic.

Creative Sound: Composing and Performing with MIDI

With an electronic "orchestra" stored inside a PC, ready to perform at our command, we don't need to limit ourselves to music written by others. We can send our PC orchestra the score of an original work, consisting of commands to play different pitches and volumes and note lengths on each of its built-in instruments.

We don't need to send very much information, because most of the bits are generated internally by the sound hardware, using either wavetable lookup or synthesis. All we need to send are messages, in effect, that say "Make this instrument start playing this note" and "Make that instrument be quiet."

We can use a standard vocabulary of commands to generate original music, either live from a keyboard (or other controller) or from a digital record of the desired commands. This standard vocabulary is the Musical Instrument Digital Interface, or MIDI.

Note the third word in the MIDI label: "Digital." MIDI signals are not music.

MIDI is a language of byte codes, just like the byte streams that go between a PC and a modem. Like the RS-232 protocol that links a modem and a PC, MIDI is a serial interface standard. MIDI cables only need a small number of wires, unlike a parallel interface with its many side-by-side connections.

A MIDI signal can carry 16 different channels of information, and we can even connect one MIDI instrument to another so that they play together or in harmony. A whole ensemble of MIDI devices can be connected in a "daisy chain" like the one we described for SCSI devices in Chapter 5.

The standard MIDI protocol transfers bytes at a rate of 31,250 bits per second (more than 3,900 bytes per second), and the typical MIDI command only requires two or three bytes. This makes MIDI commands so quick that no human ear can hear the time lags involved in sending them.

FEATURED PRODUCT: MIDISOFT MK-4902

Figure 8.7 shows a typical MIDI controller, resembling a small piano keyboard. This unit, an MK-4902 from Midisoft, is one that my oldest son often uses for original composition.

It's eerie to see my son playing on the keyboard and hear the music on the PC's speakers while a musical score appears on the screen to record his improvisations. He's able to edit, to combine multiple parts, to assign different parts to different instruments. He can save the result for electronic performance or print it out for performance on a conventional instrument.

FIGURE 8.7
This piano-like keyboard is actually a MIDI controller, a modem-like device that produces byte codes representing a vocabulary of concise but versatile musical commands.

FEATURED PRODUCT: MUSIC TIME DELUXE

Figure 8.8 shows a sample screen from Passport Designs Inc.'s Music Time Deluxe, a MIDI-compatible software package for composing and performing original music. My oldest son and I have both used it, finding it easy to learn and capable of creating fairly complex pieces.

I'm a brass player, so I don't get much benefit from our piano-style MIDI keyboard. I compose by using the mouse to drag notes and rests from an onscreen palette of objects onto the musical score I'm creating. I can quickly test and revise my compositions.

My son, a pianist, uses Music Time Deluxe with the MIDI keyboard pictured earlier. The keyboard came with its own composition software, but MIDI is MIDI and lets one vendor's products link easily with another's.

Passport's software "recognized" Midisoft's keyboard and worked with it perfectly. Unemcumbered by so-called "standards," our experience (and that of many professional musicians we know) has ratified MIDI's promise of vendor independence.

Music Time Deluxe comes with a library of demonstration files that are far more ambitious than anything that my son or I have yet written. It will be some time before we get beyond the program's capabilities, but MIDI has plenty of creative headroom for more advanced hardware and software to use when we need it someday.

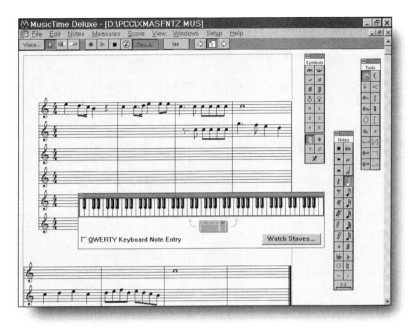

FIGURE 8.8
Music Time Deluxe works with MIDI hardware from any supplier conforming to this standard, allowing many instruments to share a single set of commands from a musical score that writes itself in response to keyboard input or electronic editing commands.

Intelligent Sound: Speech Recognition and Dictation

In addition to the entertainment of music and the utility of capturing spoken comments on a piece of work, sound can also be the entry point to the convenience of hands-off control by means of voice recognition.

There are three distinct grades of voice-input capability: navigation/control, dictation, and natural-language commands.

Navigation and Control: For Computer-Friendly Users

A set of formulas can easily be built that let a PC recognize a small set of simple words; for example, "File Open" or "Close Window." These formulas can work with the signals from a microphone after they've been turned into bit streams by the PC's sound card.

With simple command recognition software, you can keep your hands on the keyboard's "home row" instead of constantly reaching for the mouse or the keyboard's navigation keys. Touch typists find this a great benefit.

Because the command vocabulary is small, most command and navigation software is "speaker independent"; that is, it can be used by anyone, without training the PC to recognize your particular voice.

Products for voice-driven navigation and control do have one major drawback. These products, in general, do nothing to streamline the structure of program commands. The user must still navigate through menus and options, saying things like "Format Paragraph Left" in a product such as Microsoft Word. The difference with voice-based navigation and control is that the user can use spoken commands, instead of using movements and clicks of the mouse or the cursor keys that interfere with typing.

Experienced users won't mind "driving" through a product with their voices—they already think in terms of the menus of the programs that they know well. Users with physical limitations might much prefer this mode of interaction.

Our progress toward a computer that understands the user isn't significantly advanced, though, by basic voice-command technology.

Dictation: Some Training Required

The next step up from simple navigation and control is dictation software, which lets you dictate general-purpose text instead of typing it.

Dictation software needs to have a vocabulary of thousands of words, rather than the dozens of words of simpler command and navigation products. Dictation products gained early adherents among professional legal and medical transcribers, because special vocabularies of legal and medical terms could be learned once by the system and never be misspelled again.

Your PC Goes to Grammar School

It's not enough for a dictation product to turn sounds into words, one word at a time. Many words sound the same, and the software must have some kind of grammar model to decide which word to use at what times.

A good example is the sentence, "They're going to park their car over there." This is a true torture test for any dictation product, and some (such as IBM's ViaVoice) pass this test with ease.

In fact, the IBM dictation products that I've tested begin by interpreting that torture-test sentence as "They're going to park their car over their… "—waiting for you to provide a final noun to be modified by the possessive "their" at the end of that "incomplete sentence."

When you end the sentence by saying "Period," the software goes back and turns the final tentative "their" into a definite "there." The IBM dictation model is first-rate.

Hot Software Does It Continuously

Dictation products from Dragon Systems join IBM on the top tier, especially in the demanding area of recognizing continuous speech. Early dictation products required… painstaking… separation… of… spoken… words. This was not hard to learn, but it wasn't much fun.

Modern dictation products, notably Dragon's NaturallySpeaking Deluxe, do a pretty good job of letting you speak in a natural manner. With these "continuous speech" products, you can let your spoken words connect as they normally do, with the software separating your words automatically.

Taking Time To Enroll

Most dictation products require some time to "learn" your particular manner of speech. The installation and setup process might include a standard text, such as a short story, that you'll need to read aloud before you're "enrolled." More than one user can usually enroll on a single PC.

The enrollment process dramatically improves a dictation product's accuracy, and completing the one-time procedure takes only a few tens of minutes at most.

Natural Language

A third form of voice recognition software, in some ways more demanding than dictation products, is the natural language command tool.

Voice Xpress, from Lernout & Hauspie Speech Products, is the product I've tried that most fulfills the promise of a computer that understands the user.

I tested VoiceCommands with no individual training for my voice, but it was able to recognize a series of commands such as "Make this paragraph larger. Make it bold. Move it to the end of the document."

Note the substantial difference between natural commands and the formalized, menu-structured interaction of a navigation and control tool. There's a lot of practical research under the hood of a natural-language product.

Without something useful to do, your PC's CPU just sits around, waiting (at enormous speed) for you to press a key or click your mouse. Command recognition, based on natural language models, is a worthy application for all those processor cycles in today's fast PCs.

All About "Digital Film"

We can give a PC the sense of sight as well as hearing. Unlike microphones and lenses, though, digital light sensors are very different from their analog-media counterparts (namely, the various types of photographic film). These differences have a dramatic effect on digital camera performance and cost, whether we're talking about still or video images.

The technology in a digital camera is the same basic stuff that is transforming entire fields of study. Astronomy, for example, has been revolutionized by the speed and accuracy of collecting light electronically, instead of relying on the complex chemistry of film.

But even if your photo subjects are grandparents, rather than galaxies, you shouldn't buy a digital camera without a basic understanding of how this hardware works. In this respect, digital imagery and sound are much alike. No matter how good the recorder, you can't get concert-quality sound from a second-rate microphone, and imaging depends just as much on a quality transducer.

No Longer a "Kodak Moment"

The differences between conventional and digital photography begin when the image, collected and focused by the lens, is captured on some kind of recording medium. Quality and speed in digital photography all depend on the crucial piece of hardware that performs this capture and conversion.

In conventional and digital cameras alike, everything revolves around the moment of image formation. For example, no matter how good your lens, a conventional camera can't take good action photos with slow film.

Action photos demand a short exposure time so that the subject of the photo doesn't move very far while the picture is being formed. This means that the film must form an image as quickly as possible.

Fast film, however, isn't the ideal choice for portrait and other "posed" photography. With a stationary subject and controlled studio lighting, it makes sense to use one of the slower films that generally produce a clearer, less "grainy" image.

Digital photo media create a range of choices that are similar, but not exactly parallel, to the trade-offs of film-based photography. To understand our digital photography choices, we need to begin with the basics of how a digital camera turns light into electricity.

Photoelectric Sensors

When it comes to electronics, everything changes when people figure out how to do things with rugged, efficient, compact, solid-state devices rather than fragile, energy-wasting, bulky tubes.

The technology of cameras parallels the technology of displays. Modern digital cameras are replacing the old generation of "photomultiplier tubes" with new generations of transistor-based detectors, just as displays are replacing cathode-ray tubes with thin-film transistors and active-matrix liquid crystals.

Both old and new light-sensor technologies rely on a handy piece of modern physics: the discovery that light behaves in two quite different ways, depending on how you choose to look at it.

- Light behaves like waves, which means that we can focus light with lenses or take apart white light's colors with a prism.
- Light also behaves like particles, minuscule packets of energy; we call these particles *photons*.

When light strikes a layer of electronic material, the light of the image (focused in a wavelike manner with the camera's lens) knocks electrons loose (in particle-like collisions between the light's photons and the detector's atoms).

It's remarkably convenient that light displays this dual personality.

Yes, It's a Transducer

When photon collisions push electrons from one place to another, it's like pushing rocks up hill—we store energy in the pushed object.

By manipulating electrons, a digital camera's sensors transduce light energy into electrical energy. We can then amplify and process that electrical signal, just as we can amplify the tiny output of a microphone into anything from a telephone voice to an ear-splitting rock concert vocal solo.

A digital camera is built by assembling a grid of tiny photoelectric transducers. Each detects the light at a single point within a rectangular area, just as the atoms of conventional film detect the light at different points within a frame.

More precisely, each sensor detects a particular color of light at a single point. The better cameras sense red, green, and blue light with independent measurements, producing accurate color rendition. Less expensive cameras make a smaller number of separate measurements, using rules of thumb to estimate the colors that a less expensive sensor does not directly detect.

A digital camera is the flip side, so to speak, of a computer display. The camera turns an image into a rectangular array of electrical signals; the display turns those electrical signals back into an array of closely spaced lights that our eye and brain combine into an image.

Pixels, Money, and Time

As with chemical photographic film, we need to make choices among different digital camera technologies, based on the type of photography that we wish to do.

Some sensors need bright light to shoot a clear picture; other sensors function in far less light than we need to see ourselves. You can guess, I'm sure, which type is more expensive.

A digital sensor array with more units—which we call pixels, just as we do when speaking of computer displays—gives a more finely detailed picture, but we pay a price in money or time.

Real and Imaginary Pixels

A sensor with more pixels is more expensive to make. When you compare various models of digital cameras, it might seem that some are offering more pixels at a bargain price; take care that the quoted figures are genuine. Some cameras produce greater apparent resolution by mathematical operations on low-resolution sensors. A better camera's specifications state the actual physical resolution achieved by their sensors.

On a related subject, vendors quote different kinds of "zoom" ratios. Better cameras adjust the magnification of the camera's lens to achieve wide-angle and close-up effects—this is *optical zoom*. The lens projects its image onto the full area of the camera's sensor array, always yielding the camera's full resolution.

A lower-cost alternative to optical zoom is electronic enlargement of the image, spreading out the pixels near the center of the detected image to take up the entire frame. Enlargement based on pixel manipulation is *digital zoom*, and this is one case where digital does not mean "better." Digital zoom reduces resolution in close-up views.

Big Screen = Big Files

The data from a larger number of pixels demands more memory for the storage of each image. We can pay more for a camera with more memory, or we can live with storing fewer images.

We can also make a trade-off between the number of images we store and the quality of the images we'll be able to recall and reproduce.

For example, Figure 8.9 shows yet another version of the picture originally shown in Figure 5.23 and used in Chapter 6 to demonstrate the trade-offs between number and color depth of pixels.

In Figure 8.9, I've chosen a quality level of 30 (on a scale of 100) instead of the full-quality setting used in Figure 5.23. The JPEG-format, compressed-image file shrinks from 142Kbytes at quality 100 to only 23Kbytes at quality 30, but the appearance of the photo is almost unaffected.

NOTE
I wish that "JPEG" meant something useful, but it's just an abbreviation for the Joint Photographic Experts Group that developed this vendor-neutral standard for image compression. JPEG is a good standard for photographs, with better compression of highly variable colors than you'll get from popular PC image formats such as PCX. JPEG doesn't do as good a job, however, on images with regions of uniform color interspersed with fine details (such as captures of PC displays), a task that the PCX format handles well.

Figure 8.10 goes even lower on the scale, at a quality level of 5. The JPEG file shrinks by another factor of two, squeezing down to only 13Kbytes (less than a tenth of the full-quality file size), but only at this point is the image noticeably worse.

For ten times as many images, many people would accept the kind of image quality in Figure 8.10, especially in applications where artistic merit isn't an issue.

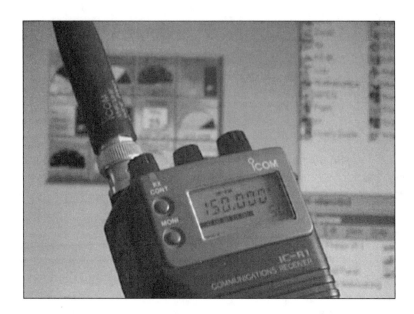

FIGURE 8.9

At a quality setting of 30 on a scale from 1 to 100, a JPEG image looks almost as good as the full-quality original in Figure 5.23—but the lower-quality image takes up 84% less storage space.

FIGURE 8.10

The picture is noticeably worse, but still adequate for many uses—and at this quality setting of 5 on a scale from 1 to 100, it takes up 91% less space than the full-quality original shown in Figure 5.23.

The Cost of Building Memories

When a camera's memory is full, we have to transfer the pictures to a PC's hard disk or to some other storage device.

The better digital cameras reduce the problem of image transfer speed by using removable storage media. Camera media range from tiny cards, little bigger than postage stamps, to full-size floppy disks (cheaper, but with less capacity and requiring a bulky floppy disk drive within the camera body).

With removable media, you can decide how many storage media units you need to buy and carry. With more media units, you can take more pictures before "downloading" to your PC.

You can send "exposed" media units to your office or to family members or friends, while continuing to use your camera. These media units can be read by various devices, or the other party can use a compatible camera as a media reader.

I use the word "exposed" in a figurative sense, because digital cameras use magnetic media that can be erased and reused just like a floppy disk. You only need to allocate permanent storage to pictures that you want to preserve, and you can do that with cost-effective media such as a Zip disk or magnetic tape (discussed in Chapter 5).

If you don't want to bother with the cost or the nuisance of a separate media reader, or if your digital camera doesn't have removable media at all, you'll just download your pictures to your PC through a serial interface. Most cameras use a cable; some have an infrared link that connects without wires to many laptop and some desktop machines.

Some cameras print their images without any help from your PC. Olympus, for example, makes a printer that produces snapshot-quality glossies. Epson's digital cameras include the necessary driver codes to communicate directly with Epson's color inkjet printers.

Where the Action Isn't

Apart from needing more storage capacity, a camera with more sensor pixels (more *resolution*) needs more time to read that data from its sensor and store that data in memory. This means that you will need to wait for a longer time between shooting pictures.

In some kinds of photography, the need to wait for several seconds between photographs is a serious limitation. Conventional cameras remain a better choice for fast-paced photography, because chemical photographic film does a form of "parallel processing"—the atoms in the film act independently to change their state as light falls on them.

The time it takes to produce an image on film is independent of the size of the negative (which determines film's usable resolution). With film, we can make an exposure and advance as quickly as we wish to the next frame, because film acts as its own removable storage medium as well as performing image detection.

In a digital camera, by contrast, image detection and image storage are handled by different subsystems, and the image has to be transferred from the detector to the storage unit.

We're used to taking pictures in action situations as quickly as we can press the shutter release and advance the film; professional photographers even use motor-driven cameras that shoot several pictures per second. A chemical camera can shoot pictures in rapid succession with anything from a pocket-sized "spy camera" to a studio camera with a large and finely detailed negative.

Unlike a film camera, a digital camera needs more time to read a higher-resolution image into the camera's memory (whether that memory is built in or removable) and to transfer the resulting bulky files from our camera to our PC. The most elaborate professional cameras speed the transfer process by using a direct, high-bandwidth cable connection from camera to computer, but this is not convenient for anything but studio or professional photo-shoot arrangements.

Personal digital cameras make different compromises in balancing capacity, convenience, and speed. These choices need to be considered in making your decision.

Established But Expensive: CCDs

The real breakthrough in solid-state imaging hardware came with the development of the *charge-coupled device* (CCD). In this context, "charge" refers to the electrical charge that's carried by individual electrons.

A charge-coupled device behaves like a tiny "light bucket": as light falls on a sensor, the sensor accumulates a packet of electrons.

The number of electrons produced by a sensor element goes up as the light gets brighter and as the recording time gets longer. In this respect, digital and chemical-film cameras are quite similar.

In astronomy and other low-light applications, very long exposures (several minutes or more) can be used to accumulate a detectable number of electrons. In ordinary daylight, CCDs can easily capture enough electrons to produce a first-rate image in only hundredths or thousandths of a second. This is quick enough for all but the most demanding action photography.

CCD cameras are costly, though, because they need several separate chips. One chip bears the specialized CCD sensors, which are expensive to build; one or more additional chips contain conventional transistors for tasks such as amplifying the signal and sending it to the memory unit. (It is possible, but not cost-effective, to perform these functions with the costly CCD transistors.)

FEATURED PRODUCT: SONY MAVICA

Many digital cameras look very much like their conventional counterparts, but one model is about as different as can be. Sony clearly designed the Digital Mavica as a computer peripheral that takes pictures, rather than adapting a conventional camera to use a sensor instead of film.

The Mavica starts with an ordinary floppy disk drive and wraps its other components around the shape (and bulk) imposed by this choice of a storage medium. The camera is boxy (as shown in Figure 8.11) and has no conventional viewfinder (the floppy disk would block any light path through the camera). You compose your picture by looking at the small preview/playback screen on the back of the unit. That screen might be hard to use in bright sunlight or in dim light when you're relying on the flash to illuminate the subject.

Limited to the floppy disk's 1,440Kbytes of storage, a Mavica isn't able to store very many images at any resolution higher than the 640 × 480 grid known as *VGA* resolution. With this relatively small pixel array, combined with built-in JPEG compression, a Mavica can store 15 to 40 images on one disk.

As with other cameras, the Mavica's actual storage performance depends on the complexity of the scenes and on the choice that the user makes between standard and fine image quality (as we discussed, and demonstrated, earlier).

FEATURED PRODUCT: OLYMPUS D-500L

Priced about 15% higher than Sony's Mavica, the Olympus D-500L (shown in Figure 8.12) is at the opposite extreme in design. The D-500L is a single-lens reflex camera, with true through-the-lens viewing and conventional controls.

The D-500L has 1.6 times the Sony's pixel count in both the vertical and horizontal directions (for a picture resolution of 1024 × 768 that meets all but the most demanding requirements). Professionals can add another 40% to the price and get a D-600L, with 1280 × 1024 resolution.

With more pixels, the Olympus cameras generate larger image files than the Mavica. These reside on a removable SmartMedia card, typically holding 20 images at the D-500L's full resolution and standard JPEG quality.

How good are the images from the D-500L, with its higher resolution and its ISO 180 sensitivity (compared to the Mavica's ISO 100)? If you would see its monuments, look about you: The photographs in this book were taken with my D-500L (which was, I should add, bought through ordinary channels and not furnished by Olympus).

FIGURE 8.11
Sony's Mavica cameras get their boxy shape—and their other distinctive features, good and bad—from the decision to build the camera around a floppy disk drive that provides inexpensive and convenient storage but limits data capacity.

Emerging and Affordable: CMOS Sensors

If you don't demand the high sensitivity of CCD detectors, you can fashion an array of light sensors from the same kind of CMOS transistors that perform other functions in a PC. For example, the memory that maintains your PC's date and time settings is normally CMOS RAM.

CMOS stands for "complementary metal oxide semiconductor." The "complementary" label means that two different types of material (positive and negative) are used, in a balanced arrangement that requires very little power.

A CMOS camera can use a single integrated chip, with transistors (all built with the same cost-effective process) to handle all of the camera's functions except the job of the lens. One CMOS chip can detect an image, amplify its signal, and transfer the signal to memory or to a PC or other device. The chip can even perform additional functions, such as maintaining the camera's date/time clock for logging of when your pictures were taken.

FIGURE 8.12
A true single-lens reflex camera that happens to use a digital sensor instead of film, the olympus D-500L gives the experienced photographer an easy transition to digital media while still meeting accustomed standards of quality.

With fewer chips, CMOS cameras are easier to build and will quickly become much less costly than CCD units. For "snapshot" applications, and even for imaging products in the price range of children's toys, CMOS sensors are an important development.

Hybrid Digital Photos: You Don't Need to Go All the Way

You can enjoy many of the benefits of digital photography without giving up the strengths of conventional film-based imaging.

Many photo laboratories now offer the option of receiving your pictures in electronic form. The lab develops your film in the usual way and then makes a digital image from your film negative. These digital images can be delivered to you via the Internet or by mail in the form of floppy disks or CDs.

You can also buy your own film scanner: a fixed-focus camera that can be simple and inexpensive because it only needs to take pictures of film negatives or slides. Some scanners also accept standard-sized photo prints. Scanners don't need to be especially sensitive, because they're only taking pictures of a stationary and well-lit subject.

Either negatives or slides can be imaged, because the color conversion required to go from a negative to a regular image is a very simple piece of computing. Color inversion uses bit-flipping techniques that we explored in Chapter 3.

Packaged "personal studio" setups, such as the Digital Photo Studio from Olympus, combine an Advanced Photo System (APS) camera with a film scanner. APS film comes in a convenient cartridge that lets you do such things as switch from one type of film to another without first having to finish a roll or waste its unused frames.

The developed APS cartridge drops into the scanner, whose resolution far exceeds what you could get in a general-purpose digital camera at any comparable price. You can then capture the image in digital form and perform "electronic darkroom" manipulations just as you can with an image that begins in digital hardware. I'll demonstrate some image manipulation capabilities in Chapter 16.

If you don't mind waiting for your film to be developed, or if you want the freedom to make large prints with fine details (which you can do from APS or 35mm negatives or slides), a film-based camera and a scanner could be your best entry point to digital photography.

Dynamic Imaging: Digital Video

For the most part, everything that I've said about digital still photography also applies to digital video. A digital video recorder needs to capture an image, turn it into a bit stream, record the bits by using efficient data compression, and transfer those compressed bits to your PC.

As with still photography, PC-compatible video offers a variety of approaches along a continuum from pure digital to hybrid digital and analog. The typical family is more likely to own a video camcorder than a digital camera before buying the family's first PC, so there's reason to investigate the options that begin with conventional analog formats such as VHS or Compact VHS.

Like the Olympus package described earlier, which starts with conventional APS film and scans it outside the camera, a video recording can start in analog form and get converted to bits on the way to your PC. A package such as Iomega Corporation's Buz Multimedia Producer costs less than $200 and combines all of the hardware needed to take VHS camcorder output and turn it into compressed digital video.

Unlike most forms of data compression, which your PC can do with its own CPU, the computations involved in video capture need a processor of their own (like the one on the PCI card that's part of the Buz package). You might not need specialized video compression hardware after the turn of the century, but it's a requirement for the systems available in 1998 or expected in 1999.

Everything involved in digital video pushes the high end of PC performance. The data-transfer rates involved, even with data compression, tax even high-throughput versions of SCSI interface design. The data volumes involved make a 20-Gbyte hard disk seem no more generous in 1999 than a 20-Mbyte drive (less than a thousandth as large) seemed in 1989.

As digital video becomes more common, more people will want the convenience of a single camera that records both video and still images in a form that their PC can use. Many video capture tools, including the Buz, can pull single frames out of a video sequence. The latest VHS camcorders capture and download digital still pictures on their own.

In general, though, the still photos offered by video cameras aren't in the same class as those from even a semiprofessional digital still camera such as a D-500L. The video cameras aren't optimized for clarity of single frames but for smoothness in continuous viewing.

Standing out from other hybrid video/still devices is Canon's Optura, which includes extensive custom processing hardware to generate clear still images (though with only moderate resolution) as well as high-quality TV sequences.

Notably, the Optura includes a "motor drive" mode that captures 30 clear still images per second, recording to its magnetic tape medium in digital form from the beginning. The Optura's still-image capture rate is faster than even the motor drives used with 35mm cameras, though it lacks the full sharpness of film images.

Intelligent Imaging: Scanners and OCR

Analogous to speech recognition with sound hardware is text recognition with imaging hardware. Optical character recognition (OCR) is a useful feature in a document scanner, a popular accessory in many offices that still receive documents on paper instead of via email.

Like a film scanner, a document scanner is a form of digital camera with relatively undemanding requirements for speed, sensitivity, focal range, size, or weight. For less than $500, you can get document scanning capability in a single unit that also includes facsimile and color printing capabilities. We discussed such multifunction units in Chapter 6.

One multifunction unit with scanning capability, coming out at about the same time as the first edition of this book, is Sharp's UX-2700CM (shown in Figure 8.13). Sharp's unit has the particular feature of infrared connection, avoiding the need to connect and disconnect a cable when using a portable computer with an infrared port at a shared fax/print station.

A scanned document can be analyzed by pattern-recognition software that picks out most letters based on matching their shapes against standard rules and then fills in many unknown letters by assuming the use of common words. Character-recognition programs use various methods to highlight questionable or indecipher-able text.

Software such as Thinkstream's Scan-O-matic (profiled in Chapter 2) can perform image enhancements to make life easier for character-recognition tools. For example, Scan-O-matic can detect any crookedness in an original fax and can rotate the image so that lines of text run straight across the image. Speckles due to dust or other sources can be removed by digital image-processing before character recognition is attempted.

When combined with facsimile hardware, character recognition can make almost all of your incoming data as easy to use, store, and search as your email messages.

When used for capturing images, a scanner requires a bit of care to produce excellent results. Media professionals scan a standard test pattern to detect any variations in color balance or image brightness areas and are able to correct these errors electronically before the scanned image is stored.

What We've Learned

One of the best reasons to own and use a PC is to share your ideas with others in a way that makes those ideas inspire action. Sound and imagery add to the persuasive power of the words and numbers that used to be a PC's only output.

Almost any audience is more fully engaged by richer media, and engaging your audience is more than half the battle.

I'm excited to see the sudden emergence of PC sound and image hardware that meets traditional tests of near-professional performance, while falling well within the price range of home or small-business buyers. The skill required to get sound and pictures into your PC, and to share them with other people, has plummeted almost as quickly as the cost—this equipment is becoming easy to use, as well as easy to buy.

FIGURE 8.13
Combining facsimile, printing, copying, and scanning with optical character recognition, Sharp's UX-2700CM connects via infrared link with nearby equipment (such as laptop computers with infrared data ports) to eliminate the need for cable hookups.

I've taken a somewhat unconventional approach in this chapter, treating digital sound and digital imagery in parallel and not as separate topics. I hope I've succeeded in bringing out the many concepts that apply to both types of media—their important similarities to conventional technology and the vital decisions about how many bits to use in the pursuit of acceptable quality.

Both sound and imagery can be treated as mere data, captured without analysis by the computer. The same data can also be the starting point for demanding computations, such as recognizing natural language commands or reading and storing text for efficient use by other software.

If your needs are at the "data" end of the continuum, your budget should go toward storage capacity and high-speed connections to other systems. If, on the other hand, your needs would be well served by intelligent processing of images and sounds, the fastest CPU available is your most cost-effective choice.

"Compaq's Portable
386-20 is a 20 pound
moveable computer…
for $7,995 with an
optional 100 Mbyte
drive for an additional
$2,000."

—COMPUTER & SOFTWARE NEWS,
DECEMBER 7, 1987

Portable
Possibilities

HE STUNNING RATE OF PC TECHNOLOGY improvement has been especially

obvious in the area of portable systems. Even when a "portable"

PC was as large and heavy as a "portable" sewing machine, I

encouraged people to think of buying a box that they could put

away when they weren't using it. The far greater speed, capacity,

compactness, and affordability of today's portable systems make

them even better candidates for the role of your primary PC.

Portables Keep Getting Better

In recommending a portable PC as your only PC, I'm not giving empty advice. This entire book, including both photos and technical art, originated on a portable PC— a system with 30 times the speed, 20 times the storage, and 40 times the memory of the system described in this chapter's opening quotation. All of this came at a price that was 40 percent less, *without* adjustment for nine years of inflation.

By the time I used it to write this book, my Dell Latitude XPi CD was already something of a "classic"—even at the age of only 18 months. Its CPU is a 150MHz Pentium, compared to the 233MHz Pentium II of a high-end laptop in 1998. My XPi's display resolution of 800 × 600 pixels is unimpressive, compared to the 1280 × 1024 resolution (or better) that users will probably expect in any portable system bought after 1999.

Imagery Demands Big Disks

My Latitude XPi CD's hard disk, 2Gbytes in size, predates my use of a digital camera. I have less than half the storage space that most camera users would probably prefer, now that bulky image files make up a growing fraction of online archives.

Hard disks of 4Gbytes or more are no longer rare in portable PCs, with 2Gbytes considered an entry-level configuration for any portable bought after 1997.

Surprisingly, Moore's Law Applies

Overall, the price/performance trend for portable PCs has proven almost as dramatic as that for microprocessor chips. Complex chips follow a growth curve known as "Moore's Law" with surprising consistency—they double their complexity, at more or less constant cost, every eighteen months.

At the Moore's Law rate, a technology improves by almost a factor of 130 in 10 1/2 years—in the time, that is, between this chapter's opening quotation and the time that I'm writing these words.

The latest available portable PCs (as I write this) are forty-fold faster and more capacious than 1987 machines, and cheaper by a factor of three. Their overall price/performance is up by a factor of 120, closely tracking Moore's Law.

Portable PC progress is all the more impressive because many key components of a portable PC are essentially mature technologies. Keyboards and displays, for example, can't get cheaper by making them smaller, as is the case for chips. People want *larger* displays and more desktop-like keyboards as portable machines become primary machines.

The pace of improvement in the portable PC is therefore even more astonishing, in its way, than the progress in microprocessors. It is due, I suspect, as much to more automated manufacture and larger production volume as to low-level technical advancement.

"Better?" Compared to What?

Even so, despite my personal reliance on portable PC systems, I have to put appropriate bounds on my praise of these products. For many people, a portable PC remains far too fragile, costly, and limited in what it can do under field conditions.

A Bow Toward Old-Fashioned Tools

Even the best portable PCs are bulky and delicate compared to an ordinary clipboard. Even the best portable PC batteries and power management systems can barely match the instant-on convenience, let alone the years of battery life, you expect from even the most elaborate business or scientific calculator.

Pen (or pencil) and paper lets you do anything from sketches to written notes and even budgets and schedules, in bright sunlight (which defeats many PC displays) and in poor weather (which discourages many users from taking their machines out of their cases). You never waste time booting a paper notebook for inspection by airport security, and even the fanciest leather-bound personal planner is unlikely to be stolen the moment you look the other way.

Do Portables Meet *Your* Needs?

With its two-handed keyboard, its fragile display, and its awkward shape for stand-up use, even the best available laptop or notebook PC is in many ways the last thing you'd design to go where the action is. Even for users who travel from one sit-down workplace to another, portable PCs can be a glaring example of the difference between what people want to buy and what hardware makers want to sell.

In my own case, what I really want from a portable PC is a fast modem (because I often need to transfer data while on the road), a large hard disk (to carry a full suite of software and reference data), and an excellent display (for work in the mediocre lighting of an airline seat or a hotel-room desk).

A fast CPU has little to do with my satisfaction with a portable machine. In fact, to achieve longer battery life, I normally enable the power-saving option of slowing down the CPU clock rate (see Figure 9.1). But portable PC makers generally push the latest, fastest chips because a premium-priced CPU helps vendors maintain overall profit margins. I'd have a hard time finding a portable PC whose resources match the profile of what I really want.

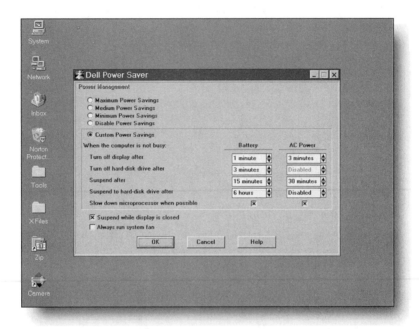

FIGURE 9.1
Power management options, such as these custom settings on a Dell XPi CD, let you choose your own compromise between convenience, performance, and battery life. Processor speed is rarely the most important thing in portable tasks, and slowing down the CPU is a good way to cut your power consumption.

Plan for This Chapter

If more people shared my views, vendors would have more reason to produce the kind of portable system that I'd like to see. This chapter will therefore try to bring you into my camp as a critical consumer of portable PC technology.

We'll examine the particular issues that challenge the designers of any portable PC, and we'll decide how to choose one compromise over another. The "least unacceptable system" is the best we'll be able to do, because all of the portable hardware options compromise on either technology or cost.

I hope to give you an engineer's appreciation of the stresses that we place on portable hardware—stresses that will probably continue to make a portable PC somewhat more costly than a desktop system of comparable power. You'll find it easier to anticipate, and avoid, the most likely hazards to your portable system's long happy life if you understand the impact—pun intended—that the real world can have on a hard-working information appliance.

Portable Power: The Care and Feeding of Batteries

Nothing does more to enhance, or impair, the value of a portable PC than the weight, cost, bulk, and lifetime of its batteries.

Power is a matter of supply and demand. Battery chemistry limits the supply; intelligent PC design determines the demand. Your knowledge of battery characteristics and of power management options will help you find the best possible balance.

Battery choices significantly affect the life-cycle cost of your PC. Rechargeable batteries only last for a certain number of recharge cycles before their capacity drops and shortens your PC's unplugged lifetime. Mismanaged batteries don't last as long, and the cost of replacing batteries can become a sizable fraction of your PC's total cost.

Proper choice and handling of batteries are also matters of personal safety and environmental protection. Carelessly handled, batteries can cause fires and other damage. Discarded batteries join the toxic waste stream, making a large contribution to some of our nastiest kinds of garbage.

A Pack for Every Portable?

Some portable PCs can use standard batteries, such as the common AA size. It's handy to have the option of picking up a batch of Duracells or Energizers when you're caught without a charged battery pack, but the cost of using non-rechargeable batteries adds up quickly.

Battery makers, particularly Duracell, made a brief attempt to create a standard for portable PC power packs, but Duracell left this market in the fall of 1997. Portable PC buyers wanted to get the maximum possible lifetime from their machines and proved willing to pay for rechargeable batteries that were designed for the best possible match with their PCs' charge-control and power-management circuits.

I'll assume that your primary mobile power source is some type of rechargeable cell, such as the lithium-ion unit in Figure 9.2. With its well-behaved charge cycle, fast recharge time, and built-in charge status display, the Dell power pack in the figure is one of Dell's differentiating features. Good battery technology gives Dell's machines long battery-life scores in magazine reviews, putting Dell consistently near the head of the pack on this high-priority measure of performance.

FIGURE 9.2
It doesn't look as high-tech as a chip, but this lithium-ion battery (with its built-in charge status monitor at upper right) is a vital part of a productive portable system. Note the battery ratings on the nameplate: voltage, capacity (milliamp hours), and current rating (amps).

The common rechargeable battery types are nickel-cadmium (abbreviated NiCd, or "NiCad"); nickel metal hydride (NiMH); lithium ion (Li-ion); and sealed lead-acid, sometimes called SLA but more commonly known as "gel cell."

All rechargeable batteries work by creating an electrical imbalance, in the same way that you might pump water uphill and let it run back down while driving a water wheel on the way. Recharging a battery is a more complex process than pumping water into an elevated tank, though, because the energy in a battery is stored in a reversible chemical reaction instead of in a simple mechanical form.

Most Batteries Get a "C"

A battery's capacity is measured in amp-hours at the battery's design voltage. A decent-sized battery might have an electrical capacity of about three amp-hours: enough "juice" to supply three amps of current for a period of one hour, or any other combination of amps and hours that multiplies out to three.

A typical battery might be designed to deliver one or two amps, on average, during one to three hours of work. An important number to know, when batteries are the subject, is the rating called the battery's "C" value. Measured in amps, C is the value of electrical current that would use up the battery's charge in one hour. Different batteries can handle peak currents that are differing multiples of "C."

NOTE
You can think of *voltage* as the pressure that makes electricity flow and *current* as the rate of that flow. More voltage produces more current, all other things being equal. Power (watts) equals voltage (volts) multiplied by current (amps). In a simple circuit, doubling the voltage doubles the current and therefore quadruples the power that's consumed.

NiCads: Too Hot to Handle?

Nickel-cadmium batteries are a proven technology, well suited to equipment that draws high peak electrical currents (such as a camera flash or a PC's hard disk during startup). NiCad batteries can deliver a current of 1 "C" or more; this means, for example, that a 3 amp-hour NiCad pack can deliver a current of three amps without undue strain.

It's useful to understand why some battery types, including NiCads, are preferred in "bursty" power applications with high peak currents, while other types of batteries are preferred for "slow and steady" power. To make the right choice, you need to think about the battery as a part of the circuit that it drives.

The Battery Joins the Party

When a battery powers a circuit, the battery is more than just a voltage source. The battery acts as part of the circuit—any current that flows through the circuit is flowing through the battery as well.

Any resistance in the battery becomes part of the resistance in the circuit. It takes energy to force current through a resistance; therefore, the battery consumes some of its own power. The higher the battery's resistance, the more of the battery's power is wasted in heating the battery—just as the resistance in a toaster or a hair dryer turns electrical power into heat.

Resistance: The Action Heats Up

You can calculate the power that's lost to electrical resistance by the formula I^2R, where I is current (in amps) and R is resistance (in ohms). A typical home circuit breaker can handle 15 amps; a standard 100-watt light bulb draws a little less than 1 amp, with that current passing through the bulb's resistance (when warmed up) of about 140 ohms.

Fifteen 100-watt fixtures, or three hair dryers, or any other 15-amp combination of loads is the most that a typical home electrical circuit will handle before its circuit breaker pops.

What would happen with no circuit breaker? Suppose we put 50 appliances on one circuit, each drawing about 1 amp. If we pull 50 amps through those wires inside your walls, the power loss in the wires will rise.

If R is the total resistance of the wires, switch connections, and other circuit elements, the power loss rises from 225 × R at 15 amps to 2,500 × R at 50 amps—an increase of more than 1,000%.

NOTE
At the same time that I^2R is turning power into heat, the wire is also suffering from voltage drop. Voltage loss in wires and other circuit components follows the simple formula IR (current times resistance). At 50 amps, voltage loss in the wire is more than three times as large as at 15 amps.

Lower voltage dims lights and can cause other problems; for example, one user reported that his PC would reboot every time he flushed his toilet. His home's electrical water pump would start, boosting the current and dropping the voltage in his old home's minimal wiring. The sudden voltage drop rebooted his PC.

The power lost in the wires doesn't just disappear; it turns into heat, and we're talking about more than ten times the heat that those wires were meant to handle. This might be enough to start a fire in the walls as the wires start to act like heating coils instead of providing efficient power connections.

Live Fast, Die Young

What does home wiring have to do with the little NiCad batteries in a PC or other portable appliance? NiCads are used in "bursty" applications because they have very little internal resistance. NiCads can deliver bursts of high current without turning much of their own energy into heat. This is the meaning of the NiCad's high "C" multiple: typically 1 or more, as previously noted.

The low resistance of NiCads is an asset when we're driving an electrical load, but there's a hazardous side to the NiCad cell's efficient design. Imagine a spare PC battery sitting at the bottom of your carry-on bag when a loose paper clip happens to lodge itself against the battery's contacts. The paper clip closes a circuit, with no resistance in that circuit except for the low resistance of the battery itself and the negligible resistance of the paper clip's metal wire.

The current in a circuit is the voltage in the circuit divided by the resistance. A 14.4 volt NiCad battery, with a low-resistance connection (such as a paper clip, a coin, or spilled liquid) directly across its terminals, might discharge tens or hundreds of amps through that connection—and, therefore, through the battery as well.

If you suddenly put, say, 30 amps through that battery, that's a current of 10 C or more. You're turning all of the battery's stored energy into heat, not in an hour but in just a few minutes.

Power loss goes up with the square of the current, so you're generating waste heat in the battery at roughly a hundred times the design rate. That battery is going to get very hot, very quickly—a fire, or even an explosion, can result. (Higher-quality batteries prevent this with internal safety devices.)

NOTE
The difference between a battery and a bomb is the rate of energy release. A battery in your carry-on bag is not as hazardous as a bottle of gasoline, but the principle is the same. Either one can be a convenient, compact energy source or a messy and hazardous nuisance. It's all a matter of taking sensible precautions.

Personally, I keep my spare batteries in zipped-up plastic bags to avoid accidental short circuits.

The NiCad Charge Account

Despite their hazard potential, NiCads' high-current performance and low cost make them the most popular type of rechargeable cell. In the long run, though, we pay in many ways for NiCad chemistry's performance; in particular, worn-out NiCads account for half of the toxic and carcinogenic cadmium that gets into U.S. garbage landfills.

Below C Level: NiMH Cells

NiCads are challenged by another battery chemistry, nickel metal hydride (NiMH), that doesn't use poisonous cadmium.

NiMH cells store about 50% more energy per pound of battery than NiCad cells. This doesn't mean that NiMH is a bargain—NiMH batteries also cost about 50% more, so the up-front cost per unit of energy capacity is about the same. NiMH merely opens the door to a longer time between charges, or lower battery weight.

NiMH has an advantage in battery size as well, storing 30% more energy per unit of volume than NiCads. On the down side, NiMH batteries can handle a current of only 0.2 C: This means, for example, that we need to carry a 5 amp-hour NiMH battery to yield the same healthy surge of 1-amp current we can get from a NiCad with only a 1 amp-hour rating.

A 1 amp-hour NiCad, good for a 1-amp peak current, weighs one-third as much and takes up one-fourth the space of a 5 amp-hour NiMH cell with comparable peak-current limits. For devices that draw high currents for brief periods, such as "wireless modem" radio transmitters, NiCads therefore retain an important edge.

Batteries on the Shelf

Another bonus for NiCads, as compared to NiMH cells, is that the NiCad holds its charge somewhat better when the battery is not in use. An NiMH battery loses about 30% of its charge per month of storage, while a NiCad loses roughly 20% of its charge for each month on the shelf.

For most portable PC users, though, a battery's shelf life is not a major issue; most of us can stay plugged in until just before we leave the office. Shelf life is more important if you want to charge several sets of batteries all at once and rely on them to get you through a long trip with no opportunities to recharge in the field. This pattern is not common among most PC users.

Batteries on the Road

NiMH batteries don't hold up as well as NiCads when the battery is almost fully discharged before recharging. In practice, therefore, the NiMH capacity advantage is reduced. The NiMH battery is better for frequent but short-duration duty, recharging the battery at every opportunity instead of using the deep-discharge cycle favored for NiCads.

Many portable PC users prefer the convenience of NiMH batteries, with their ideal pattern of "plug in whenever you can" and their readiness to go, fully charged, whenever desired. When properly used, however, a NiCad commonly lasts for three times as many charge/discharge cycles as an NiMH battery, reducing NiCads' overall cost as measured by dollars per total hour of operation.

Babysitting the Battery

In routine portable use, the benefit that we get from a NiCad's superior shelf life is outweighed by the finicky recharge cycle needed to maximize the NiCad's lifetime.

A NiCad cell works best with a predictable pattern of full charge, followed by nearly full discharge. If a NiCad cell is habitually used for only a fraction of its capacity, and if the battery is recharged with a charger that doesn't sense the battery's internal condition, a NiCad's usable life becomes much shorter.

At the start of a charge cycle, most of the energy that gets "pumped" into a NiCad gets stored in an efficiently reusable form. As the battery nears full charge, however, some of the charger's energy goes into producing waste oxygen. If the battery charger delivers too much current, excess oxygen builds up. This creates internal pressure that can damage the battery or even cause an explosion.

A low-cost, overnight-type NiCad charger delivers a steady, low-rate current that the battery can take without damage for days at a time—even indefinitely. This is called a "trickle charge" process, appropriate for equipment that's normally plugged into commercial power but designed to switch over to the NiCad cell if power fails.

Trickle charging is cheap and simple, but it doesn't match the profile of most portable PC operation (which often needs quick recharging). For portable PC operation, the ideal battery charger delivers high current, minimizing recharge time, for as long as the battery can turn that current into stored energy at an equal rate.

A "smart" battery charger measures battery temperature, recharge current, and voltage across the battery terminals to taper off the current at just the right time for best results.

What Is "Battery Conditioning"?

Early versions of "smart charge" devices used a cheap way of detecting the full-charge condition. When a NiCad gets past full charge into an overcharge state, its voltage (which has been rising throughout the charge cycle) starts to drop. It's easy to detect the voltage reduction that signals the overcharge state and to use that as a signal to switch into trickle-charge mode.

A small but significant overcharge leads to the so-called "memory effect" that used to plague NiCad batteries. If a NiCad is routinely overcharged, its voltage during use drops more quickly than it does in a cell that's in top condition.

If an appliance detects the voltage drop as a signal that it's time to recharge, we get a vicious cycle. Abusive recharging shortens the apparent battery life, leading to even earlier recharging, and the battery quickly deteriorates over just a few cycles of use.

Memory effect almost disappears when a battery charger uses a more sophisticated controller, sensing the rate of voltage increase during recharge and reducing the current as the voltage levels off—without waiting for the voltage reduction due to overcharge. Some battery chargers prolong the NiCad's useful life by a process called "battery conditioning," drawing down the battery (at its optimal rate) to about 10% of capacity before they begin recharging; this maximizes battery capacity, but lengthens recharge time.

A common myth says that NiCads should be fully discharged before recharging. In fact, full discharge can be quite damaging to most NiCad power packs. The problem is that a NiCad pack is actually a collection of several cells, each contributing 1.2 volts to the unit's total voltage. A 14.4 volt pack has 12 such cells, connected in series so that their voltages add, and possibly with several 12-cell chains connected in parallel so that their capacities combine.

Unless the cells in a power pack are carefully matched, as is done for critical applications such as batteries in space satellites, some of the cells in a pack discharge sooner than others. Attempting to fully discharge the pack can actually reverse the polarity (the "direction" of the charge) in the weakest cells. This change is not easy to undo. Unless corrected, polarity reversal in one or more cells will keep the power pack from returning to normal voltage even after a full charge cycle.

Other Battery Chemistries

Because NiCads are so touchy about the manner of their recharging and NiMH cells are so much less capable in high-current tasks, many portable devices use more exotic battery chemistries.

Lithium-ion batteries, found in newer and better portable PCs, have a "power density" (watt-hours per pound) even better than that of NiMH batteries, though they don't recharge as quickly.

Lithium-ion and lithium-polymer batteries combine high power density with the deep-discharge tolerance of NiCads and good shelf life characteristics. They should only be used, however, with properly designed charge controllers that avoid an overcharge state.

Lithium-based batteries minimize environmental damage and present few safety hazards when discarded at the end of their useful lives.

Lead-Acid: Tried and True

Lead-acid batteries, using the same basic chemistry as the battery in your car, are one of the most successful examples of product recycling, because 95% of the material in a worn-out lead-acid battery is reused. Two-thirds of the metal and plastic material in new lead-acid batteries comes from discarded units.

Automobile-type lead-acid batteries are impractical for portable use because of their liquid content, but modern Sealed Lead-Acid (SLA, or "gel cell") batteries use a gelled electrolyte in a leak-proof container.

Gel cells recharge slowly and operate best at low C factors. They hold their charge well in storage, though, and last for many cycles. Gel cells are often used in backup power supplies, for which their characteristics are ideal.

Some portable PCs have tried SLA chemistry, but users have not been impressed by its low energy density. Lead-acid cells burden the user with a third more pounds per watt-hour than NiCads.

Renewals Require Retraining

Rechargeable alkaline batteries, such as the Renewal batteries sold by Ray-O-Vac, have several advantages over regular alkaline batteries and NiCads.

Renewals share the good peak-current characteristics of nickel-cadmium and non-rechargeable alkalines, but they contain neither cadmium nor the toxic mercury found in many alkaline cells. This reduces toxic waste concerns when a Renewal cell loses capacity (typically after two dozen cycles or so) and has to be discarded.

Like standard alkalines, Renewals deliver 1.5 volts per cell rather than the 1.2 volts per cell of NiCads. This higher voltage (9 volts from a six-cell pack, instead of only

7.2) improves the performance of some portable equipment, though some devices have switches that must be flipped to correspond to the type of battery being used.

Like NiMH batteries, Renewals should be charged whenever it's convenient instead of being drawn down like NiCads. Many users have years of experience with NiCads and might need to be told several times that their well-developed deep-cycling habits are not merely unhelpful, but actually harmful to the lifetime of NiMH or Renewal batteries. Both of the latter battery types suffer reduced capacity and yield fewer charge/discharge cycles if they are fully discharged, even just a few times, before recharging.

What About Using Less Power?

We're not seeing Moore's Law rates of improvement in batteries. We've seen a threefold increase, from the 15 wh/kg of lead-acid cells to the 50 wh/kg of lithium-ion cells, but this climb has taken decades rather than years.

There are, however, two sides to the equation that determines the lifetime of our portable PCs. Increasing the supply of power is difficult, but reducing the demand might prove more feasible.

Chip designers have achieved 80% reductions in power consumption by adopting a circuit design technique that is called *asynchronous logic*.

Clocked Circuits: "Stroke! Stroke!"

In *synchronous* digital chips, a "clock" signal tells each part of the system when to move from one state to the next.

We discussed the importance of clocks in Chapter 4. We talked about the central processor chip retrieving instructions and executing commands to load values from memory, perform operations on those values, and store the results or send them out to the user or to other connected devices.

Clock signals resemble a children's game. Devices are free to do whatever they like between one clock pulse and another, but they must reach some specified state before the circuit "looks up" as the next clock cycle begins.

Designing and testing clocked circuits is relatively easy, because their state only needs to be known on clock-pulse boundaries. This reduces the number of test conditions.

In some ways, though, a clocked design seems ridiculous. Imagine that you work in an office building full of people, each with a telephone on his desk, with a building-wide public-address system that sends out a "beep" every minute. When you hear the "beep," you pick up the phone on your desk to see if anyone wants to say something to you.

You listen, or talk, and then you go back to work until the next "beep" from the speakers repeats the process. That's life inside a clocked circuit, and it wastes a lot of energy.

Asynchronous Circuits: "Any Calls for Me?"

Instead of picking up the phone at fixed time intervals, we think it's normal to work until the ring of the bell interrupts us. If we're making the call, we don't assume that the person at the other end is listening just because we punched that person's number; we wait, instead, for a confirming "Hello?"

Digital circuits can be designed so that any element "calls" another and waits for a reply, instead of demanding that every element "listen" at fixed time intervals. That's the essence of asynchronous logic, as opposed to the synchronous ("same time") logic that prevails today.

Asynchronous circuits use more transistors than simpler clocked circuits, because each subsystem needs additional hardware to exchange handshake signals with other parts of the system. (We've seen the term "handshake" before, in our discussion of modems in Chapter 7; a modem is also an asynchronous device.)

With more transistors, an asynchronous design can cost twice as much as a standard clock-driven chip. Overall, however, designers can offset higher chip cost with either smaller, lighter batteries or a longer battery life at a given size and weight.

Other Issues in Power Reduction

Asynchronous circuits are harder to test than clocked circuits, because many possible states can arise in the interactions between various handshaking subsystems.

Some devices get no benefit from a complex asynchronous design. For example, the transistors in a flat-panel display are active all the time, so there's nothing to be gained by adding more transistors that would merely confirm this fact.

Displays might slash their power consumption, however, through broader use of *cholesteric* liquid crystals that are stable in both of their states (both transparent and opaque). A cholesteric display retains its state, without a continuing power drain, instead of reverting to a blank display as soon as the power goes off.

In tasks that display rarely changing information, such as monitoring of production processes, cholesteric liquid crystals can dramatically reduce a system's power requirements.

Questions to Ask When You Buy

When you look at battery-powered devices, including portable PCs, every vendor will cheerfully quote you a figure for "battery life." The question is, does this life represent a reasonable expectation, given your own pattern of use?

It might be more useful to ask, "What's the amp-hour rating of the battery?" This is much less subject to interpretation. Different systems are more or less effective at reducing power consumption with intelligent power management, but heavy use (such as continuous writing or spreadsheet analysis) will not leave much room for power control. Amp-hours are an objective starting point for estimating how long a system will last when compared to other portable systems with similar hardware.

Also important is the time needed to replenish the battery, which in some cases is much longer if the system is in use while the battery is recharging. An external power unit can be designed for lower peak current, and thus for smaller size and weight and cost, if it charges the battery at a reduced rate when the system is turned on. Some adapter/chargers only perform a full-power recharge when the system is off or in standby mode. You should therefore determine a system's recharge time with the PC on and also with the PC off.

You might wish to find out if an external battery charger is included or is available as an option for your machine. Many people find it convenient to follow the rule of three batteries: one in the machine, a fully charged spare in your briefcase, and a battery in the charger in your hotel room or office.

The three-battery plan is especially suited to NiCads, because you'll want to use up most of a battery's energy before you recharge it. You might often find yourself with a half-charged power pack upon your return. With non-NiCad chemistries that encourage partial-cycle operation, you'll recharge whenever you get the chance, so a single spare is probably all you need or want to bother carrying.

Displays and Presentation Facilities

Displays used to be the worst parts of portable PCs, being monochromatic and dim long after most desktop systems had bright color CRT-type monitors. Today, however, the crisp bright color of an active-matrix liquid crystal is coveted even by desktop users, as well as being common in portable PCs. We discussed this trend in Chapter 6.

Also important in many portable applications is the video projector, commonly used in group presentations. Most portable PCs can easily drive a projector in the same way as an external monitor. Projectors are coming down quickly in size, weight, and cost, with useful projectors appearing late in 1998 that are almost as small and light as a laptop PC and that cost no more than $2,000.

Video projectors offer considerable advantages over plastic overhead transparencies or 35mm slides. You can edit your presentation only minutes before it begins and build up a library of digital "slides" you can quickly recombine to suit different situations.

Any professional organization with more than a dozen staff members should consider the purchase of a video projector. These projectors can often display TV signals from a videocassette player or other video source, as well as accept the output from a PC. Projectors are commonly available for rental, if your need is only occasional (for example, a quarterly meeting).

When using your portable PC with a projector, you can dim the PC's display or (in most cases) turn off that display entirely, using the projected image to guide your presentation. Dimming or disabling the PC's display greatly prolongs its battery life.

Dimming the display is a good battery-saving measure to employ on airplanes or in other dimly lit environments where the display's full brightness is not needed. Many portable PCs automatically go to a dimmer setting when operating on battery power.

Keyboards

Second only to displays as a weakness of portable PCs, the keyboard is a component that has seen considerable improvement—or perhaps we're just getting used to the compromises of portable keyboard design.

The issues in a keyboard are layout, key size, key spacing, stroke length, and mechanical feel. There is no substitute for trying out a keyboard and seeing for yourself if you can type quickly, with low error rates, on any given design.

Many portable keyboards lack the mechanical "snap" of a good desktop keyboard. This is especially true of the thinnest, flattest keyboards, which use "membrane" construction in which there is not a separate mechanical switch for each key.

On the plus side, membrane keyboards are very forgiving of liquid spills. Such keyboards do well in the coffee test (five ounces, with cream and sugar) used by my colleagues at *PC Computing* magazine in their annual torture tests of portable PCs.

Some people find it helpful to have an artificial "click" effect, provided by the PC's speaker, to augment the feel of a portable keyboard (see Figure 9.3). Sometimes, though, this cure is worse than the disease. For example, most PC keyboards have automatic repetition when a key is held down. On my Dell XPi CD, holding down the Shift or Control key triggers a chirping frenzy from the "key click" feature, even though nothing is happening.

Personally, I find it quite annoying to hear a furious sound that signifies nothing, as Shakespeare might have said. I do not use the key click on my Dell or on any other machine.

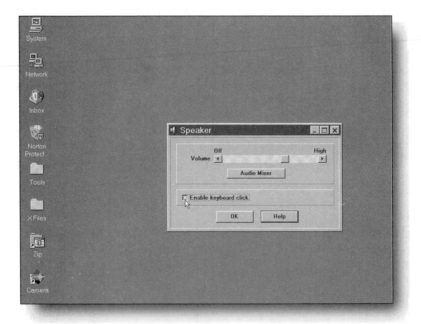

FIGURE 9.3
An electronic "key click" option can offset the poor force feedback of some portable keyboards, but can also be quite annoying if it repeats when you hold down the Shift or Control key.

You should check, in particular, the function of the Spacebar on a portable PC keyboard. Simpler keyboards sometimes use a linkage that is touchy about off-center strikes on the Spacebar. Depending on your personal typing technique, this might or might not be a problem for you.

Navigation keys, such as Page Up/Down and cursor movement keys, vary greatly in their placement from one portable keyboard to another. Again, I urge you to determine by hands-on trial whether you can live with any given arrangement.

Portable Pointing Devices

The Windows operating software that runs most PCs *can* be used without a pointing device.

I suggest, in fact, that every user spend at least a few hours pretending that her PC has no mouse or other pointing device. It doesn't take long to learn the keyboard conventions for selecting menu commands, selecting text in documents, selecting cells in spreadsheets, and performing file management tasks in the Windows Explorer or other file management tool.

The Keyboard Alternative

In dialog boxes, for example, the Tab key will usually move you from one field to another, the Spacebar will turn options on or off, and the up and down arrows will make choices in file lists or drop-down combo boxes.

Once learned, the keyboard shortcuts often prove quicker than using the pointing device, even on desktop machines. Keyboard operation saves even more time and aggravation on portable systems, with their often-substandard substitutes for a "real" external mouse.

Sad to say, particular Windows programs sometimes fail to follow design guidelines in areas such as using the Tab key to move through data-entry fields or providing Alt+<*letter*> shortcuts for program options and commands. Case-by-case experimentation is the only way to find out.

Trackballs and Touchpads

As I noted in Chapter 5, I personally favor trackballs, but these are becoming rare as built-in pointing devices. The touchpad (see Figure 9.4) seems to be today's pointing device of choice.

Most touchpads respond to fingertip movement for positioning the cursor, as with a mouse. Touchpad-equipped PCs usually have nearby pushbuttons and also respond to a tap or double-tap of the finger on the touchpad itself to perform the actions normally done with a click or double-click of the mouse.

FIGURE 9.4
Touchpads, like the one on this Sony laptop system, lack the precision of trackballs, but are lighter in weight and avoid any problems with dust or other contaminants.

Voice-Input Devices

If you plan to use your portable PC as a dictating machine, employing the voice annotation features of many modern office-type applications, you might want to consider a voice-oriented input device such as the Philips SpeechMike shown in Figure 9.5.

The SpeechMike, available in different versions with varying features, combines a microphone with a speaker that you can hold to your ear (for privacy or to minimize annoyance to others). A fingertip trackball is included in the same convenient unit.

FIGURE 9.5
The Philips SpeechMike gives your PC a single handheld control for voice input, personal audio output, and precise trackball pointer control.

No Moving Parts: The TrackPoint

Unique to portable systems, so far as I know, is the TrackPoint device originated by IBM. The TrackPoint is also known as the "eraser-head" because it looks rather like a pencil eraser embedded in the middle of your keyboard.

A TrackPoint is like a very small joystick, except that it uses rugged and sensitive transducers that detect pressure rather than the bulky movement sensors of the typical game-control device.

For best results, the TrackPoint's sensor readings need to be interpreted by rather sophisticated software. On IBM machines, for example, the TrackPoint responds to the difference between quick approximate motions (such as the ones you use to choose a window on the screen) and small precise motions (such as the ones involved in selecting text). The result, when you've invested about half an hour (or less) to learn the feel of the TrackPoint device, is an ease of operation that's popular with most users. Not all machines with TrackPoint-style hardware use it as effectively as IBM.

Handheld Machines

We don't *have* to find a way to put a desktop PC's display, keyboard, and pointing device into a portable form. We can reinvent the information appliance in a form that makes more sense for portable, even one-handed use, in a size and shape to fit into pockets rather than briefcases.

There have been many attempts to put the convenience and capability of an entire PC into a truly portable package, but these efforts always seem to trip over the gap that separates small keyboard size from practical typing speed.

The breakthrough seems to have been the idea that a portable system can be optimized for retrieving data and making simple choices, with minimal data entry. The portable unit then "docks" with a larger machine that does the user's heavy work and updates the portable unit's data. Small devices increasingly provide wireless connections, either radio or infrared, to keep their data up-to-date without the burden of cable or keyboard.

FEATURED PRODUCT: 3COM PALMPILOT
Far and away the leading choice in handheld, "personal digital assistant" designs is the 3Com PalmPilot shown in Figure 9.6. The PalmPilot, also sold by IBM under a different brand name, has become the hub of an entire sub-industry that sells everything from leather carrying cases to specialized time-management software.

PalmPilot users avoid the problem of keyboards by entering data with a pen-like stylus and a shorthand notation called Graffiti (see Figure 9.7). You can try Graffiti for yourself on an interactive Web page located at http://www.palm.com/products/input/index.html. (This is a worst-case trial, because you'll probably be trying to "write" with a mouse instead of using the PalmPilot's stylus.)

PalmPilots also let you pop up an onscreen keyboard (see Figure 9.8), which some users find more convenient. I still like the density, ruggedness, and "battery life" of a paper time-planning notebook, but I know many PalmPilot users who find them to be incredibly useful tools.

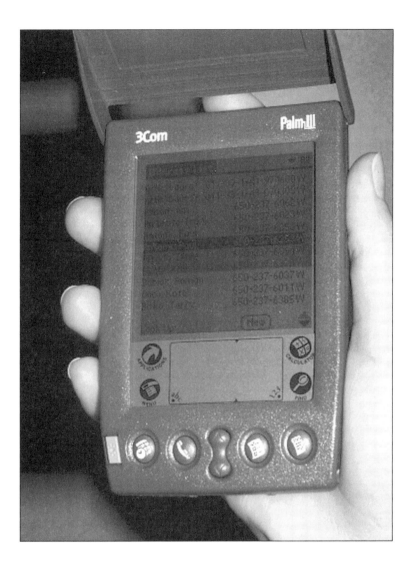

FIGURE 9.6
The 3Com PalmPilot finally got it right, judging from the huge popularity of this handheld adjunct to the standard PC. Handwriting recognition combines with convenient connection (wired or wireless) to a larger machine to keep a PalmPilot's data up-to-date.

FIGURE 9.7
Quickly learned, the Graffiti shorthand is far more readily recognized than free-form handwriting, giving handheld information appliances a convenient alternative to unsatisfactory portable keyboards.

FIGURE 9.8
If Graffiti isn't your style, an onscreen keyboard (used with a handheld stylus) offers another option for portable input without bulk or weight.

Staying Connected

Portable systems quickly lose their charm if they take away your vital connections to other information resources. Email, fax, and the Web are almost essential to productive work, and a portable system must meet these needs without cramping your mobile style.

Within an office, you can have wireless freedom by means of infrared or radio-frequency links. Infrared links, through transceivers mounted on ceilings or walls, are inexpensive and relatively free from concern about interception by eavesdroppers outside your building. On the other hand, infrared is a form of light and requires a line-of-sight arrangement, making an infrared setup tricky to install.

A high school freshman class in Redondo Beach, California, took part in an experimental program during 1998 that sought to replace their assignment books with rugged laptop computers using infrared networks to communicate (see Figure 9.9). The students found that they needed to locate the "sweet spots" in each classroom where the infrared link was reliable. Most found the program's first-year results unsatisfactory.

Radio links like those of a conventional cordless phone are more flexible than infrared links. IBM's Cordless Computer Connection uses 900MHz cordless-phone technology to give your computer a wireless modem attachment. Radio signals, unlike infrared, penetrate walls and go easily through windows (which block most infrared radiation, even though they pass visible light).

FIGURE 9.9
Redondo Beach high school student Katie Carlile was in the pilot freshman class that tested a specially designed, "ruggedized" laptop computer as a core educational tool. An infrared network was supposed to provide convenient exchange of data in the classroom, but initial results were disappointing: Only certain "sweet spots" in each room gave reliable connections.

Reviewers of IBM's product report a useful range of only 30 feet, with a disappointing battery life of only two hours between 15-hour recharge periods (the unit provides one of those low-cost NiCad trickle chargers that I described previously). These are implementation details; the basic idea is quite sensible.

For use farther afield, several standards exist, using radio signals at frequencies as high as 5,300MHz (5.3GHz). From our earlier discussion of bandwidth in Chapter 5, you'll appreciate that higher carrier frequencies permit higher data rates—the most aggressive wireless standard is the European HIPERLAN (HIgh PErformance Radio Local Area Networks), which delivers 23.5kbps.

At frequencies in the gigahertz range, however, even a heavy rain can weaken signals considerably. HIPERLAN has a design range of only 50 meters.

Another wireless standard is CDPD (Cellular Digital Packet Data), which uses the same radio frequencies as conventional cellular phones and achieves 19.2kbps from locations up to several kilometers away from the nearest relay site. Through the cellular telephone network, of course, a CDPD portable device can communicate with the entire world, though CDPD service isn't cheap at $30 to $100 per month (depending on your level of activity). Other Personal Communications Service (PCS) alternatives vie with CDPD in major metropolitan areas, with much contention for scarce radio spectrum space.

Getting connected becomes more useful if other devices know you're there. The question is, how can you move from place to place while keeping your usual address on the worldwide network?

The Internet works, in part, by assuming that addresses are grouped in geographic clusters like those of telephone area codes. If your normal Internet address (called an IP address, for "Internet Protocol") is in New York, the Internet's routing systems won't even look for you in Los Angeles.

Mobile Internet access can be achieved with Mobile IP, a well-thought-out extension to standard IP. Mobile IP lets you stay connected, no matter where you go—and even while you're going. Mobile IP sets up a "forwarding address," letting data sent to your normal address find your current physical connection to the network.

The hard part of Mobile IP is the problem of letting you change your forwarding address by remote control so you can move to a new location without returning to your base to change your settings. If this were too easy, others could do it without your knowledge, sending your data to another location for interception (or even alteration) on its way to you.

Cryptographic mechanisms, such as the ones used in electronic sales transactions, let your mobile device give notice of its new location.

NOTE
We'll talk more about network security and encryption techniques in Chapter 17's discussion of "cybercrime."

Mobile IP makes sure you receive information that was already on its way to your former connection.

Hard Knocks: The Hot (and Cold) Cruel World

A portable PC might have the world's most long-lived battery and a wireless modem that keeps it in touch from everywhere but the far side of the moon, combined with a desktop-class keyboard and pointing device and a beautiful display, all in a package that's as thin and light as an ordinary clipboard. None of this is useful if you have to treat the machine like a delicate laboratory instrument. A portable PC ought to survive any accident that doesn't put its owner into the hospital.

Shock and Vibration

Mechanical shock and vibration are measured in units of "g," where 1g is one earth gravity.

When a portable PC is sitting at rest, its internal components "feel" their normal weight. If you let your PC fall, ignoring air resistance, normal gravity will accelerate your PC to a speed of 9.8 meters per second (22 miles per hour) in the first second of falling, to twice that speed after two seconds—and so on.

Watch That Bottom Step

Falling is not a problem. Landing hard is a problem. When an object lands on a hard surface, it loses its downward speed in a very short time.

To a portable PC's components, losing downward speed feels just like gaining upward speed. Your PC feels like an astronaut on top of a rocket during the most stressful part of a launch. Your PC's components feel more than their usual weight, putting extra stress on their structural and electronic connections, just as a spacecraft's crew members feel five or six times as heavy during launch as when they're on the ground.

Suppose your portable PC falls off of a desk onto a carpeted floor. Falling three feet, on earth, takes about four-tenths of a second. When it hits the floor, your PC is moving at four-tenths of 9.8 meters per second, or almost 10 miles per hour.

Your PC has to go from 10 miles per hour to zero in the distance that the carpet can "squoosh" while absorbing the impact. Suppose that the carpet has 5mm of "give." Your PC is traveling at 4.2 meters per second when it hits, and it will travel that 5mm distance at an average speed half that fast (because its final speed is zero). Its average speed while slowing down will be about 2.1 meters (2,100mm) per second.

Five millimeters, at an average speed of 2,100 millimeters per second, is a trip that only lasts a few milliseconds. Your PC has to shed 4.2 meters per second of impact speed in 2.4 thousandths of a second; its deceleration is 4.2/0.0024 meters per second, per second, or almost 1,800 meters per second, per second.

One "g," as we said before, is only 9.8 meters per second, per second, so your PC is pulling over 180g during those 2.5 msec before it comes to rest. Your PC's parts suddenly feel as if they weigh 180 times their normal weight. This is what breaks your machine.

Landing on a sidewalk or some other unyielding surface reduces the deceleration distance from a feather-soft 5mm (relatively speaking) to a much smaller cushion—say, half a millimeter. The same impact speed must be shed in one-tenth the distance and ,therefore, in one-tenth the time. The shock to the system increases from 180g to more like 1,800g. Few PCs will survive this kind of treatment.

These Are Not "Good Vibrations"

If one-time mechanical shock doesn't get your PC, prolonged vibration might kill it the same way but in a less obvious fashion. If your PC gets shaken up and down, perhaps by riding on the floor of your car instead of on the seat, each up-and-down cycle involves an upward acceleration at the bottom of the motion and a downward acceleration at the top.

The faster the motion, or the bigger the bounces, the larger the accelerations and the more g's your PC will suffer. Vibrations don't involve g factors as high as a fall to the floor, but vibrations last for minutes or hours instead of milliseconds. Hardware doesn't do well in these conditions.

Too Hot or Too Cold

I don't think I need to go through calculations for heat and cold, because most of us know that a plastic tape cassette (for example) can melt if it's left on a dashboard during a hot summer day, and a flexible garden hose can crack if handled roughly when the temperature is twenty below. Extremes of heat and cold are also unkind to the plastics that keep your portable PC so lightweight.

"I left it in a cold car for three hours and then nudged it against the rubber bumper in the elevator on the way into the building—the screen completely shattered," said one of my colleagues in describing an early encounter with a "military grade" portable PC. "I guess it's only for armies that never have to move when it's cold."

Less obvious, but just as dangerous, is the way temperature changes cause stretching and contraction of different materials at different rates. This can loosen important connections.

What We've Learned

Most portable PCs flunk my criteria for both size and strength. When I think of how I use other portable hardware—my cellular phone, for example, or my electronic test and measurement equipment—I get annoyed with the current trend toward "desktop replacement" laptops.

Desktop replacements let me work on different desks, but I'd rather be able to work wherever the problem is. I'd like to see ruggedness and reliability get more attention than CPU speed and display size in laptop computer advertising and design.

Adequate power supplies and wireless connectivity are the technical characteristics that make the biggest difference between working all day without a desk and merely getting away for an hour or two.

The important thing is to think about *why* you want a portable information appliance, instead of buying something that's as much as possible like a desktop PC.

*"**upgrade** n. & v. trans. [from up + Latin gradus 'steep incline']...to replace obsolete stability with something less boring."*

—STAN KELLY-BOOTLE,
The Computer Contradictionary (2nd Ed.)

When the Honeymoon Is Over

F I WERE TRYING TO PRODUCE a PC version of the TV comedy series *Home Improvement*, I'd never come up with a better script than my diary of the day that I wrote this chapter.

Episode 1: An Ominous Silence

The day before, I had noticed that my Dell laptop system was running more quietly than usual. It was a sultry summer day, and I had gotten used to the whir of the cooling fan kicking in when things got hot.

Well, you know what we say about a suddenly quiet PC. As I noted in Chapter 5, this can be a warning sign that a low-tech (but high-impact) cooling fan has taken an early retirement.

A stalled cooling fan can be bad news, or even the first stage of terminal illness, for the rest of the machine.

Sure enough, I soon started getting temperature warnings from my laptop PC's internal battery charger. As I said in Chapter 9, a good battery charger keeps track of battery parameters such as temperature so that it can cut back, or halt, the flow of recharge current. This safety measure prevents the permanent damage that can come from pumping still more electrons into an overheated cell.

Me and My Fan Club

When I got battery temperature warnings twice in one day, I suspected that the cooling fan in my laptop system was not doing its usual conscientious job. The fan is supposed to come on automatically when temperatures at various points get into the danger zone, but I had not noticed its noisy whir at the times when the battery was overheating. I wondered if the fan, or its temperature sensor, might have failed.

I recalled that the power management screen on my laptop offered an option I had never used: "Always run system fan." I opened up my Power Saver window, clicked on the system fan option, and waited for that annoying but comforting sound… and waited… and waited.

In Search of a Solution

Well, I can't say that I was exactly surprised. I have a certain history with cooling fans. It was time to add a new chapter to that relationship.

I logged onto the Internet and went to Dell's support site on the World Wide Web. I hoped that this would be a problem a hundred other people had already solved.

We'll return to this dramatic tale after a brief public service message on the subject of technical support.

Technical Support: Someday, You're Going to Need It

For the second or third time in this book, I find myself using the same warning comment: "It's not a matter of 'if,' it's a matter of 'when.'"

I've already urged you to accept the eventual certainty of hard disk failures, power outages, and other potential disasters. I say "potential," because careful planning can limit the impact of these events. Any of these episodes can be either a nuisance or a catastrophe—the choice really is up to you.

Like the accidents listed here, a vendor support call is almost certainly in your future. As with any other traumatic event, planning can make the moment of truth much less painful.

What to Know Before You Need It

Most PCs come with software and documentation that can smooth your later encounters with the vendor's technical support staff. When you first receive your system, you should note the exact model number and serial number. These identifying numbers can someday tell a vendor important things about the hardware you're using, assuming that you're dealing with a reputable builder instead of just a "white box" assembler of generic PCs (no two exactly alike).

Take Help When Your PC Offers It

Many new PCs come with special software that generates—and optionally prints—a report on the system's configuration. It's common for a new PC to nag you, at the time that you start the machine, with a message to run such "get acquainted" software. A new PC, if equipped (as most are) with a modem, might even offer to call up its vendor and register your machine.

In the tech support saga that runs through this chapter, you'll note that I was always able to resume my problem-solving process where I'd left off, even when I found myself talking to different people over the course of the morning. I maintained my momentum because I was able to give each representative my system's identifying number, letting her pull up a log of all past support calls involving this unit.

Some vendors track their customer histories better than others. Dell wins awards for its technical support, and my experience says that they earn those honors. No tech support organization can do its job, however, without the vital statistics that tell the support technician your PC's life story.

Your PC might offer to produce a printed system description. It might offer to do other useful things, such as building a set of "rescue disks" that will boot the machine if the hard disk dies. Accept such offers today, because tomorrow your PC might not even be willing to say "good morning."

Buy a box of floppy disks at the time that you bring home your PC and plan to produce (and carefully store) that box of startup floppies. It will make you feel unbearably smart on the day that you finally need them—and trust me, you *will* need them.

Keep Details Where You Can Find Them

One of the nice things about a portable PC is that it usually has a carrying case. The pockets of a PC case are perfect places for copies of vital documents, such as the system setup report and the invoice that records the shipment date and other descriptive data.

Desktop machines might be harder to document, especially in active offices where systems move from user to user and from place to place.

Do not leave a system's "personal papers" in the shipment box, and try to avoid the bottom desk drawer. You'll never be able to find the papers in those obscure locations, let alone match them up with the PC that they describe.

It's better to get a flat plastic bag for the papers, taping it to the bottom of the PC (as long as this doesn't block any vents). If this doesn't work for you, I'm sure you can devise a solution that meets your needs—but you will do this only if you accept the fact that someday you *will* need those papers. Fate decrees that when you need them, you'll need them right away.

Better Than Built-in Obsolescence

When I say that a PC disaster is just a matter of time, it might sound pretty negative. After sixteen years, however, I've come to think of technical support as a feature rather than a bug.

Yes, it would be nice if a PC needed as little technical support as a microwave oven or a TV set, but I'm not prepared to define my PC as narrowly as I define those other appliances.

A PC is different from other consumer electronics in that most PC systems eventually combine an assortment of bleeding-edge technologies. If you buy a Sony videocassette recorder, you don't open it up a year later and add a JVC chip to expand the Sony's built-in functions. If you buy a Nikon camera, you don't buy a Canon auto-focus option two years later, plugging it in to replace the Nikon module. If you want a better camera or VCR, you buy one—you don't try to build it yourself.

Most electronic products are sold in their final form except for interchangeable parts such as camera lenses or tape cassettes. Because their basic configuration doesn't change, most electronic products work almost forever if they work for the first 30 days (often known as the "infant mortality" period). On the other hand, those products will never do anything new: They're born, they live, they die, but they don't evolve during their lifetime.

PCs, by contrast, are always being asked by their owners to do new things. When I installed a Pentium PC in our family room, I put it there to run strategy games, educational software, word processors, and spreadsheets. I didn't anticipate its use, two years later, for composing music with a MIDI controller keyboard. When I bought my current laptop system, I planned to use it for writing and communicating text and numbers. I didn't anticipate its use in processing digital photos and composing photo galleries for school and club Web pages.

On the Bleeding Edge

PCs can't just be designed, built, and sold as monolithic systems. People want to install new software, upgrade their operating systems, add new storage units and other accessories, and exercise advanced features that might not be mature at the time a PC leaves the factory.

A PC's Only Game Is "Tug of War"

Computer games, for example, represent a continuing tug of war between people who make video hardware and people who produce exciting software. To make the hardware follow complex software commands, you might need to install new video drivers. I warned you in Chapter 5 that these are high on the list of updates you'll likely have to make while you own a PC.

Installing new drivers, fortunately, is a lot less like brain surgery than it used to be. In general, no pulling or flipping or moving of chips or switches or jumper blocks is required. Most of the time, you'll get either a floppy disk in the mail or a file across the telephone lines via modem. Then you'll follow a few simple instructions, reboot your machine once or twice, and there you'll be.

Obtaining, installing, and setting up new drivers is not my idea of a good time, but at least it doesn't require taking the cover off of the machine and swapping an entire video card. I'll take new drivers over new boards any day.

USB: I Don't Want to Wait

The Universal Serial Bus, with its speed and its plug-in convenience, is a feature that most of us want to use as soon as it's out of the oven (even if it isn't fully cooked). Windows 98 will give many vendors their first experience with USB. I was there when Microsoft's Chairman, Bill Gates, crashed a late prerelease of Windows 98 in front of a huge trade show audience, merely by trying to plug in a USB scanner. Boy, did *that* moment make the evening news.

As I write this chapter, Windows 98 has just shipped, and Page 1 of *PC Week* is reporting that its early bugs (and the delays in version 5.0 of the high-end Windows NT) are encouraging many companies to look at non-Microsoft operating systems. This might be a futile exercise, given the massive inertia of companies' well-entrenched software selections, but these reports tend to dispel the hope that Windows 98 will be a debugged and enhanced version of Windows 95.

Even so, I want USB, and I want it soon—I don't want to wait for the year or two that vendors will need to be sure they're using it correctly. That's a choice I'm willing to make, though it's a choice that I suspect some PC users won't realize they're making.

Mixed Blessings and Two-Edged Swords

Technical support and the possibility of fixing things after they're sold via online software updates are certainly mixed blessings. Vendors might delay their product release dates, making time for additional testing and debugging, if premature shipment cost them more than the price of maintaining a Web page of software patches.

Most of the time, however, I believe that the two-edged sword of the fast product cycle cuts our problems down to size more often than it cuts our throats.

A Partnership for Progress

PC users constantly add—and refine—demanding software that exercises every function of hardware. This process soon exposes any weak points in either member of that software/hardware partnership.

Without the resource of round-the-clock technical support (known as "24-7" for 24-hour, 7-day availability), we'd never be able to keep this relationship together.

It's maddening to spend a morning on the phone, downloading a driver, and getting questions answered by the vendor. In most cases, though, the telephone call is toll free, and the lost morning is a small cost compared to the alternative of lost days or weeks if a PC had to go to a local repair shop.

We have to put the annoyances of technical support in the proper context, reminding ourselves that most of the alternatives are worse.

Episode 2: More Help Than You Can Imagine (But Less Than You Need)

When I wondered if my laptop's cooling fan had gone awry, I knew that I had several options. Most major PC hardware and software vendors offer several sources and varieties of information and assistance.

Support by Phone and Fax

Most vendors have, at a minimum, a toll-free telephone number. If that telephone number is not in your product documentation, you might be able to get it by calling the toll-free directory service at 800-555-1212.

We need to stop calling toll-free numbers by their generic name of "800 numbers," because there are now several area codes reserved for calls billed to the receiving party. If you get a vendor's technical support number over the phone, pay as much attention to the area code as you do to the rest of the number.

Most of the time, the initial call puts you into some kind of automated system that offers various options. These options might include a "fax-back" service, with a much shorter waiting time than talking to a real live person.

If you have a fax machine but no computer that's able to access the Internet at that moment, a fax-back service might be one of your best options. Most of these services offer some combination of voice recognition and push-button commands for choosing various categories of data. Sometimes, the first fax transmission sends you a list of codes for several dozen specialized bulletins. On your second call, you can enter a code from the list that you've received, letting you get what you need without waiting for dozens of unrelated pages to come down the line.

Support by Internet

When a PC has a narrowly focused problem but the machine is generally working all right, it's silly to leave your PC out of its own problem-solving process. A malfunctioning PC might be able to help fix itself, just as an out-of-tune car can often limp down to the shop instead of getting a tow.

Even if it's not working perfectly, your PC might still be able to help you with fast communications, graphical presentations, and accurate storage of details. All of these are useful aids to a complex servicing task.

Visiting technical support sites on the Internet might not become your hobby, but vendors do try to get you in the habit of visiting their sites before you need them. Free software updates, interesting examples of how to use a product, and other enticements can be found on elaborate Web sites such as Microsoft's at `http://www.microsoft.com` (see Figure 10.1).

A perfect example of Web-based relationship marketing is in Microsoft's free upgrade to the Paint graphical software utility that came free with Windows 95. I read—in an airline in-flight magazine of all places—that Microsoft had posted a dramatically better version of Paint as a freely available download from its Web site. I wrote the Web address in my calendar and obtained the improved Paint version as soon as I could. It was certainly worth the few minutes to do so, giving me many more options for working with different types of graphics files (and helping with several of the illustrations in this book).

Figure 10.1 highlights one of the features that makes a Web site useful: a flexible set of search commands. Rarely will you find that a vendor's information is organized just as you'd like it to be. Finding a Search command, or its equivalent, is one of your first tasks on a vendor's Web page.

I don't know if it's impressive or appalling that Microsoft's site returned 200 items when I asked for only those things that were new within the past seven days. I do know that the filtering powers of a good search facility are the only way to stay on top of such floods of potentially crucial detail.

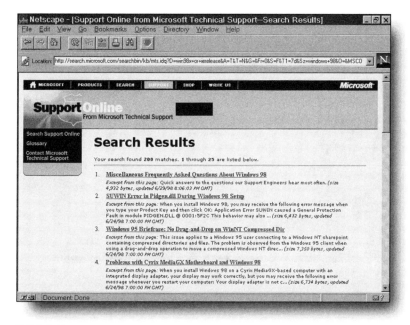

FIGURE 10.1
An extensive technical support site on the Web quickly loses its appeal unless it's equipped with search facilities that match the extent of its data. Microsoft's site, for example, returned 200 items when I asked for things that were new within the week before this query. Search tools are essential to help you zero in on what you need.

What I Found for My Fan

To resume our tale: With my laptop's suspect cooling fan on my mind, my Web destination was Dell's site at `http://www.dell.com` (see Figure 10.2). This well-organized site gives an excellent cross-section of all the types of support the Internet can offer.

Tech Notes

Product manuals often bear only a casual relationship to the product that actually ships. Printed manuals are often incomplete and rarely well-indexed. Technical notes on a vendor's site usually include a great deal of detailed information on specific versions of a product, including obscure but serious interactions between that product and other popular hardware and software.

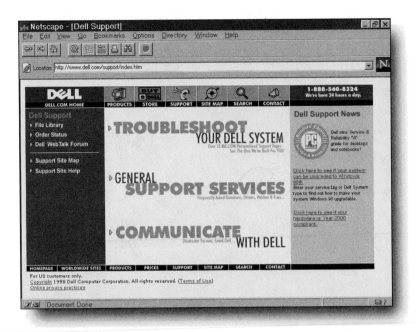

FIGURE 10.2
Every known form of online technical support appears somewhere on Dell's well-organized Web site. Technical notes, frequently asked questions (FAQs), and interactive discussions among customers and Dell representatives
are all just a few clicks away.

Finding the Good Stuff

Online technical notes, unlike printed manuals, can use the Web's distinctive *hyper-links* to call up related items of information with a click of the mouse. Some vendors use the straightforward Web convention of underlining words that act as gateways to other data; other vendors, with more artistry than good sense, use elaborate graphical effects. One typical artsy approach is a photo or drawing of a product, studded with invisible "hot spots" that can be clicked for additional information on that aspect of the pictured item.

Sometimes, you have to move your mouse around the screen, like a beachcomber with a metal detector on a quest for buried jewelry. When your mouse pointer's usual arrow turns into a pointing finger, you know something's there.

Be encouraged, however, by the likelihood that technical notes can generally be searched by keywords or by concepts. Unless you're just browsing for interesting items, use searching early and aggressively to narrow down the field.

With good search facilities, an extensive tech-notes library is a wonderful accessory to your PC—and it's an add-on that you don't usually pay for, except with your time.

Last Year's Machine?

Despite my liking for online documents, however, I have to warn you that your printed manuals for an older product might be more accurate than a vendor's online references (the ones for my laptop, for example, as excerpted in Figure 10.3). Online references might be quite irrelevant if your product has been updated since you bought your unit.

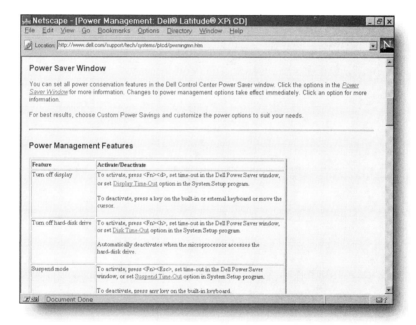

FIGURE 10.3
Online technical documentation might not include all previous versions. If you have an older version of a product, the technical notes on the vendor's Web site won't necessarily reflect your product's configuration. You might have better luck with the manuals that came with your purchase, so don't lose track of such documents, especially their all-important addenda sheets.

For example, when I went to Dell's site in search of information on my laptop's "Always run system fan" command, I found nothing on this topic. The XPi CD's Power Saver screen, as portrayed in the online notes, didn't even include this option.

Apparently, the Web site's notes on the Power Saver control panel were only correct for the current version. There was no help for the fan command on my ancient (18 months old) configuration.

Newsgroups

The weakness of technical notes is that they focus, for the most part, on foreseeable questions and concerns. I have yet to meet the vendor that didn't also receive dozens, hundreds, or even thousands of questions that the vendor's technical staff and documentation writers could never anticipate.

In many cases, we're talking about questions that relate to products or tasks that didn't even exist when the vendor's own product was released. Technical notes are constrained, moreover, by the vendor's likely reluctance to admit to errors—let alone to confess to gross misjudgment or lack of vision.

Fortunately, and courageously, many vendors provide a forum for customers to share bald facts and candid opinions. Interactive discussion areas, such as the one shown in Figure 10.4, often feature regular and prompt replies from both vendor employees and independent experts (who are sometimes compensated by the vendor, but are often volunteers).

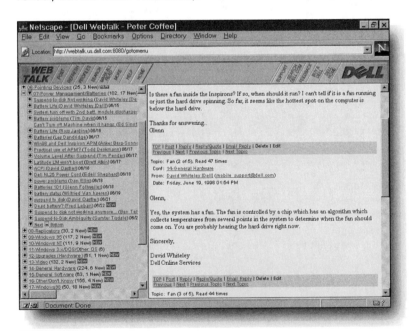

FIGURE 10.4
Interactive discussion areas keep a vendor honest by giving customers a place to share their confusion or dissatisfaction with a product. Most vendor forum areas feature regular, timely aid from the vendor's experts and from leading users whose knowledge is valued by all.

"Netiquette" and FAQs

Within the social environment of online discussion, certain conventions have grown up—as they do in any community.

For example, it's considered poor form to TYPE YOUR MESSAGE IN CAPITAL LETTERS UNLESS YOU'RE TRYING TO "SHOUT."

It's also considered rude to ask a question that has been recently asked and answered. You can avoid this social error in two ways.

Don't Repeat Recent Questions

Recent discussion topics remain online for quite some time, either weeks or months depending on the intensity of discussion and the amount of disk space a vendor chooses to provide.

Like other components of Web site content, past messages can usually be searched. Search facilities for Dell's interactive forum appear in Figure 10.5.

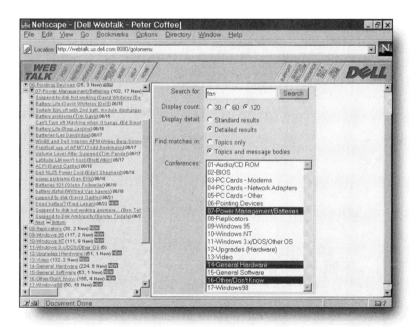

FIGURE 10.5
An interactive message forum can be a gold mine or a trash heap. Even a gold mine demands that you go through a lot of gravel to find the useful nuggets—search facilities like these on Dell's support forum help you refine the raw material.

Don't Repeat "Frequent" Questions

Some questions won't show up in a search of recent questions, precisely because these questions were once so common that they've been captured in a listing called a FAQ (rhymes with "track")—an acronym for "Frequently Asked Questions" (see Figure 10.6).

A Frequently Asked Question belies its name, because a question that's in the FAQ is a question that should never again be asked (unless you have some genuinely new variation). People are expected to have browsed the FAQs—and seen the answer to any given FAQ—before they enter the forum section to ask their "frequent" question anew.

Few things annoy forum participants more than the person who says "I suppose this is in the FAQs, but I was wondering… ": such a person is admitting he knows that the FAQs exist, but is saying (in effect) that the time of other forum participants is not worth saving by checking FAQs first. FAQ documents also tend to be more carefully written than the typical, top-of-the-head reply to a technical question, so browsing the FAQs is good sense as well as good manners.

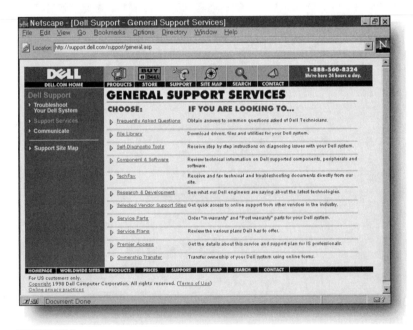

FIGURE 10.6
Interactive discussion areas should be your last resort, however tempting it might be just to ask the experts and wait for an answer. Other resources, such as those listed on this Web page, will often be a quicker and more authoritative source of needed information.

It's polite to investigate all of a Web site's resources, such as the broad array shown in Figure 10.6, before you ask others to spare you the effort of research. Doing the digging on your own can spare you the frustration

NOTE
In conversation, avoid giving or taking offense by confusing "FAQs" with "facts." You might think that someone is asking, "Is that a fact?" The actual question might have been, "Is that a FAQ?" The first might seem sarcastic or indifferent, but the second is merely a query.

(or worse) that results from following well-meant suggestions based on outdated knowledge or lacking crucial warnings.

Episode 3: Success! Then Setbacks...and Survival

Browsing my way through Dell's extensive support site, I found some useful things, but nothing that was precisely what I needed.

I found a discussion, for example, of fan arrangements on a more recent line of laptop machines than my Latitude XPi CD (refer to Figure 10.4), but nothing on my system's mysterious "Always run system fan" option.

I went to the next level, calling the company's toll-free telephone number and describing my concern to the representative. "You need to update your BIOS," was the reply. "That's a problem we sometimes see on machines with the version on your unit."

The Map Is Not the Territory

Returning to the Web site and finding my way to its file library, I located the instructions for how to download and install the latest version of the BIOS (a concept that we discussed in Chapter 5). The instructions were specific, but they were wrong.

A step-by-step description told me how to set up a floppy disk that I could use to start my machine, and how to copy the BIOS update program onto that disk. I was told to boot my machine with that disk and then to issue the update command from the DOS prompt. (If I were a Windows user without substantial DOS experience, all of this would have been terribly opaque.)

What the Web site actually sent me, though, was a program file that I could run to create a disk that would boot and install the update all in one step. The differences in the procedure were tiny, but they were crucial.

NOTE
PCs too often require a user to have faith and follow directions, because the system's underlying concepts are so abstract that they are impossible to deduce by common sense. When the directions are even slightly incorrect, your knowledge of lower-level concepts is your essential guide back to safe ground. My laptop BIOS update process demonstrates, somewhat sadly, why books like this are needed: PCs are still in their surly adolescence. A user who had never seen a DOS prompt would simply be unable to bridge the gap between the instructions and the reality. As Boy Scout leaders always say, "The map is not the territory." Computer documentation is only an effort to describe what someone thinks a PC will do. A PC makes its own rules.

First, Do No Harm

When I had the update disk all prepared, I started to perform the BIOS update procedure—the actual procedure, not the mythical version in those precise but outdated instructions.

Before things really got going, however, I stopped. I thought about how stupid I would feel if something went wrong and I wound up unable to start my machine, with the most recent files for this book locked inside a comatose box.

I sighed, got out my Zip drive, and made a fresh backup of the 90 Mbytes of files making up the first nine chapters of this book (along with their illustrations). Then I held my breath and did the deed, flashing the BIOS from its original Version 3 all the way up to Version 10…

… and I wound up with a machine that couldn't see its PCMCIA slots. I had no modem, unless I wanted to plug one into the serial port. This was a serious problem.

I found out just how serious the problem was when it took three more calls, each to a different service representative, to figure out what was wrong.

Take Out the Brain; A New One Will Grow

Remarkably, the solution was the opposite of what any sane person would think. To make my laptop see its PCMCIA slots again, I went through an elaborate process—talked through by a Dell technician—of deleting every reference to PCMCIA slots from every nook and cranny of Windows. There are a lot of nooks and crannies.

When we had finally excised all previous knowledge of slots and modems from the machine, it woke up from its coma and said—in effect—"Oh, what are these?" Telling me that it had detected new hardware, Windows offered to install the needed software to use the PCMCIA (PC card) slots, and did so.

Two hours after the process began, I had a machine with an updated BIOS *and* a working modem—but still, so far as I could tell, no functioning fan. Enabling the mysterious "Always run system fan" option still produced no telltale sound.

We might call this a limited victory, because the benefits of the new BIOS weren't at all apparent. Even so, I heaved a sigh of relief that rattled the windows. I got back to work, with quite a tale to tell.

Epilog: The Moral of the Story

At 4:39 that afternoon, when I was finally hitting my stride on this chapter, my system's fan came on. I'm not glad that my laptop was having another hot, tiring day, but I sure was relieved to know that it was still able to care for itself.

In the process of "solving" what might have been a nonexistent problem with my fan, I wound up with a highly motivated tour of a state-of-the-art technical support operation. I'm not being sarcastic in my praise for Dell's support facilities. The fact is that Dell's varied and extensive resources, including its patient and careful technicians, performed a system update that will probably make my system run better.

The process took much less time than any other means of support could have done. A visit to even a local repair shop would have taken at least as long. Furthermore, an outside repair shop would have involved the risk of having a stranger work with the personal data on my hard disk. That's a risk I'm happy to avoid.

I hope that this account will help you adjust your expectations for your own future dealings with any vendor's technical support organization. Specifically,

- People might not recognize your problem as one that they've solved before.
- People might not give you precisely accurate information.
- Web sites might not have the specific information you need.
- The first thing you try, even if you follow directions exactly, might seem to do more harm than good.

If you don't do anything rash, and you're not embarrassed to ask for further details, and you tell the person at the other end of the phone *exactly* what you've tried and *exactly* what you're seeing, you'll probably wind up with your problem solved.

If you've backed up your important work before you start changing your system's settings, the worst that can happen is that you'll have to move to another machine while the one that you "fixed" goes into the shop to get the job done over—and done right. As worst-case scenarios go, this isn't too bad.

Utility Software: Swiss Army Knives Versus Snake Oil

BIOS updates like the one I described in the first several sections of this chapter are among the most extreme examples of adding functions and prolonging your system's useful life by simply adding software. I have other examples, but also some cautionary tales I should share.

Some Stuff Just Doesn't Work

For example, PC product reviewers didn't exactly cover themselves with glory in the case of a utility software product called SoftRAM. By rearranging Windows' normal allocations of memory, SoftRAM allegedly increased the effective memory capacity of a PC.

Some publications swallowed the claims without even stopping to chew. In May 1995, for example, *Computer Retail Week* stated that "SoftRAM doubles the amount of a PC's available physical RAM." In November 1995, *Government Computer News* breathlessly reported on an updated version of the product, writing that "A rendering of analog dials and digital readouts indicates percentage of total available system resources before and after loading.... After testing SoftRAM95, I'm satisfied on all counts."

By May 1996, however, the story was unraveling. In an article by Larry Seltzer (who also served as technical editor of this book), *PC Magazine* laid out the facts: "Our testing clearly indicated that SoftRAM95 did not actually perform RAM compression. SoftRAM95 did not increase system resources... *although its system-monitoring program presented numbers that seem to indicate that it did* [emphasis added]."

By the end of 1997, my colleagues at *PC Week* Labs had written the final epitaph for this product's final version, saying, "SoftRAM 3.0 exemplifies the kind of thing that *PC Week* readers should avoid…. It is probably possible to alter the automatically optimized installation of Windows 95 enough to make SoftRAM 3.0 a helpful repair tool. That's not enough reason to buy it."

The moral of the story: If it sounds like magic, it's probably fantasy. Look for independent reviews that actually test the product, instead of believing those that merely repeat what the product says it's doing.

Some Stuff Is Worth Ten Times Its Price

Some utility software *will* dramatically improve your PC. We've already talked, for example, about PowerQuest's PartitionMagic (described at length in Chapter 2).

By breaking your hard disk into smaller sections and thereby increasing the aggregate number of allocatable units of storage, PartitionMagic can substantially increase your disk's effective capacity under all but the latest versions of Windows.

Another tool that will keep your PC running more smoothly is Quarterdeck's CleanSweep Deluxe, which applies a variety of methods to find and remove hard-disk space-wasters. Some hard-disk clutter accumulates when software doesn't uninstall itself completely when you try to take it off of your PC. Other files quietly appropriate space while you're looking around on the Internet (more details in Chapter 17). CleanSweep Deluxe is thorough, but careful, in figuring out what you don't need.

Symantec's Norton Utilities, which I mentioned in Chapter 2, provide some facilities for finding and removing many space-wasting files on your hard disk. The Norton Utilities also provide antivirus capability, detecting and defeating many types of malicious software (more details in Chapter 17's section on "cybercrime"). If you're constantly trying out software from questionable sources, you might want the more complete protection of the full-scale Norton AntiVirus package: Compared to similar products, my colleagues at *PC Magazine* find the Norton product "effective and easy to use."

My personal experience is that the Norton-brand products are especially strong in the area of automatic online updates. This is a critical feature in a volatile area such as virus recognition.

Upgrading: "There's Grandfather's Axe"

There comes a time when incremental steps, such as a BIOS update, clearly don't suffice. If you're trying to run Windows 95, for example, on a pre-Pentium processor or with only 8 Mbytes of RAM, you're not getting the kind of results that are worth the effort of learning to use a PC.

When you need to make the jump to a whole new level of performance, you're no longer talking about "technical support." You're talking about an "upgrade."

PC upgrades are like automobile upgrades: Some people love the idea of putting a new engine into their car, and other people are on a first-name basis with the leasing representative at the local auto dealer.

Another analogy that comes to mind is the story about the man who bragged that he was still using his grandfather's axe. "We had to put on a new head five years ago, and I replaced the handle last year, but that old axe is still going strong." Of course, it's in great shape—in everything but name, it's a brand new axe. Some PC upgrades also turn out that way.

The Blind Taste Test

I believe that my colleagues and I at *PC Week* Labs have done the most scientific study that's ever been made of the cost-effectiveness of various PC upgrades.

In 1992, we gave 40 users a script of tasks to perform on eight different systems. Each test machine represented a different upgrade path from the typical corporate PC of the time; that is, from a system with a 286-class processor, three generations before the Pentium, that was clearly too slow to run Windows.

The candidate systems were literally "under the table"—the systems were hidden by a concealing cabinet, so the users did not know which technology they were testing. The systems were identified by number.

Some of the systems represented only a CPU upgrade from the 286 base case; others upgraded the video card and memory; still others replaced the entire system "motherboard." Some of the candidate "upgrades" were whole new systems. All of the candidates were evaluated for their readiness to move a user up to the convenience of graphical computing with Windows 3.1.

Value Versus Cost

We asked users to assign a perceived value to each machine they tried—that is, to say what they thought they'd be willing to pay for a system with that level of performance. We calculated the average ratio of perceived value to actual cost for each of the eight alternatives.

The results could not have been more clearcut. A complete motherboard replacement, providing a whole new processor, memory subsystem, BIOS, and other system facilities was the only solution we found that yielded *more* than its cost in terms of perceived added value. A whole new machine, not top-of-the-line but on what was then the second tier of technology, finished in second place; its perceived value was almost 90% of its cost.

Piecemeal Upgrades Don't Work

Other strategies, such as adding only memory or adding a faster video card, simply didn't do the job: The resulting configurations weren't balanced. The greater performance of the added components was hamstrung by the other, outdated hardware.

The judges estimated the incremental upgrades to be worth small fractions of their actual cost, with ratios ranging from around 65% down to just over 15%.

The worst results came from a processor-only upgrade, installing a faster CPU but leaving RAM and other subsystems untouched. When asked to estimate the value of the resulting "upgraded" system, one user (who didn't know the system's configuration but only saw how well it worked) wrote "How much will you pay me to use this?"

Some Things Don't Change

Fast-forward the time machine from our test in 1992 to six years later, when my colleagues at *PC Magazine* asked a similar question about the kind of upgrade needed to move up to Windows 98.

Is there a six-year echo in here? This is what analysts Cade Metz and Robert Anthony had to say: "In a 486-class PC, you must replace your motherboard and add RAM for true performance enhancements." Their findings confirm what we determined in 1992—a system has to be balanced.

A PC has to have the memory capacity and throughput to keep a faster processor well supplied with data and "elbow room." The storage and display subsystems must be able to feed in data and reveal the results of computations at rates that can keep up with the CPU's speed. Anything else, except for specialized tasks that stress only one subsystem, is just a waste of money—and also a waste of time, because even a motherboard upgrade is hard to integrate with other components. Smaller upgrades require intimate knowledge of a system.

Some Upgrades Do Make Sense

There are two incremental upgrades that are reasonably easy to perform and that will almost certainly give you substantial benefits. These two strong options are adding memory and adding a second hard disk.

We talked about memory expansion in Chapter 5. Though details vary from one PC to another, most PCs can be expanded to 32 or even 64Mbytes of memory.

You will find that having more than 16Mbytes makes a noticeable difference in smooth operation, with much less time spent swapping material back and forth between memory and the hard disk. On typical performance tests, such as I'll discuss later, a doubling from 16 to 32Mbytes of memory should accelerate your system by almost 10%.

A new hard disk, adding to the one that came with your machine (assuming that your system has an empty "drive bay") yields the obvious benefits of capacity and safety. Your critical files can be stored on two physically separate devices, and you'll have more space for files that you don't need to store in duplicate.

I hesitate to suggest that a second hard disk solves your data backup problems, because the second hard disk will have many failure modes in common with the first one. A power surge, a fire or flood, or theft of your PC can take your second disk with it as easily as the first. Removable storage, such as a Zip drive or magnetic tape, is a safer strategy—*if you remove it* and store it elsewhere after the backups are made.

If you decide to add a second hard disk, a common mistake is failure to set up the new disk unit as a "slave." The drive that boots your machine is configured as a "master," assuming that you're using the common IDE-type drives I described in Chapter 5. The drive that you add might also come from the factory with "master" settings; these must be changed, according to the directions that come with the disk, for second-disk operation.

Upgrades Should Let You Do More

Generally, I feel that a PC upgrade should let your PC do something new instead of just doing things faster. A backup storage device lets your PC protect your data. A digital camera or scanner lets your PC work with new kinds of data. A CD-ROM, which you can add with an hour's work, gives you access to the latest software and packaged information.

If you get the urge to improve your PC, I hope that you'll consider such options after adequate memory and disk space are in hand.

Real Measures of PC Performance

Speed does matter, and there are two ways to compare your PC against the prevailing state of the art and determine how much you might gain by an upgrade or replacement.

Applications Tests

The best way, for most purposes, to measure a PC's performance is by running the actual programs that make your PC useful to you. It takes a lot of work, however, to develop test scripts that represent your activities and automate these scripts to devise a hands-off test that's consistent from one run to another.

Rather than developing your own application-based test, a far less time-consuming option is to use the Winstone benchmark suite produced by the Ziff-Davis Benchmark Operation.

The Winstone suite uses actual code from popular commercial software. As a result of this design, the suite is available only in CD-ROM form, because it's just too big to download from the Internet.

With all of its support files, Winstone 98 (the current version at the time this book was written) comprises more than a third of a gigabyte of programs and data files (see Figure 10.7). The CD-ROM package can be ordered for a $5 handling fee. Instructions are available on the Internet at `http://www.zdnet.com/zdbop/` `regfrm.html`.

FIGURE 10.7
More than a third of a billion bytes of program and data files make the Winstone benchmark suite, from Ziff-Davis Benchmark Operation, one of the most thorough tests you can perform to measure a system's useful performance. Available only on CD, Winstone is given away at PC trade shows and is available for $5 via the Internet address that appears in the text.

Like any reputable benchmark, Winstone takes pains to record every possible detail of your PC's setup at the time you run the tests (see Figure 10.8). Many conditions can change your measured values, especially the number and type of any programs you might be running at the same time that the tests are in progress.

Unless you're trying to determine the load that a program places on your system by measuring Winstone performance while that program is in use, it's best to run Winstone (or any other performance test) as your PC's only task.

A comprehensive test suite such as Winstone is extremely time-consuming, but the program allows you to focus on specific applications if you know what tasks will be most critical to you (see Figure 10.9).

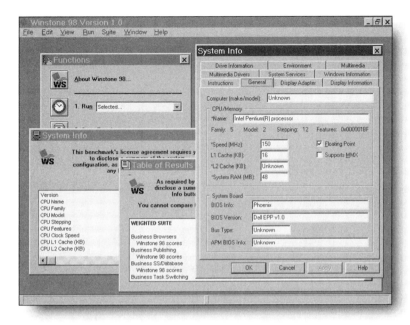

FIGURE 10.8
Performance measurements are almost worthless without a detailed description of how your system was set up and what else it was doing (the less, the better) while the tests were underway.

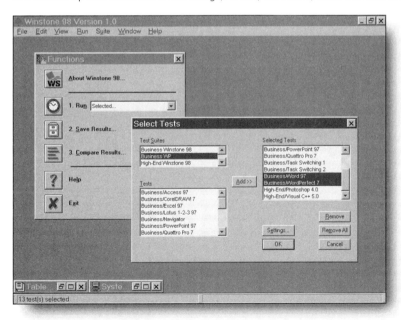

FIGURE 10.9
Choose the tests that reflect the tasks for which speed matters to you, and you can shorten measurement times while still getting the comparative figures that will help you choose an upgrade or a replacement.

Subsystem Tests

If you're comparing hardware performance at the level of specific components, such as one hard disk versus another, a useful approach is the subsystem test.

A subsystem test is a crafty piece of software that exercises one subsystem, such as the video display, doing a well-defined task, such as rendering text.

Ziff-Davis Benchmark Operation offers a subsystem test suite, WinBench, that permits fine-grained choices of what you will test (see Figure 10.10). Unlike the application tests of Winstone, which measure what typical software typically does, the subsystem tests of WinBench are severe—by design—in probing the ragged edge of a PC's capabilities (see Figure 10.11).

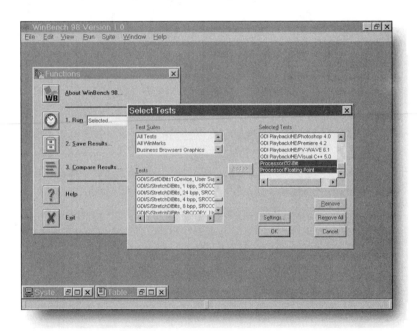

FIGURE 10.10

WinBench, unlike Winstone, uses invented tests rather than actual commercial software as the basis for its measurements. Like Winstone, though, WinBench (also from Ziff-Davis Benchmark Operation, or ZDBOp) lets you choose exactly what tests you want to make.

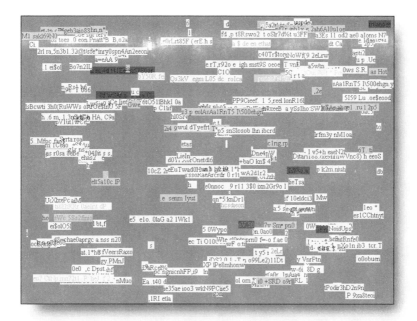

FIGURE 10.11
Narrowly focused tests, such as this text-rendering exercise, let WinBench pinpoint the areas in which a given PC system might have surprising areas of weakness.

At almost 6 Mbytes, the online subset version of WinBench will tie up your modem for quite some time, but that subset is available from `http://www.zdnet.com/zdbop/winbench.html`. This online version omits the bulky files required for testing video, CD-ROM, and graphics capabilities.

The full WinBench suite, like Winstone, can be ordered for $5 from the Web address given in the preceding section. These discs are also given away in huge numbers at many PC trade shows.

Quick Tests, Quick Comparisons

Weighing in at less than half the size of the online WinBench subset, a compact suite called SpeedRate is available on the Web at `http://wwwzdnet.com/zdhelp/tools_help/speedrate/speedrate.html`.

After you download, install, and run SpeedRate, the program automatically prepares a report that compares your test results against those achieved by a wide range of other PCs (see Figure 10.12).

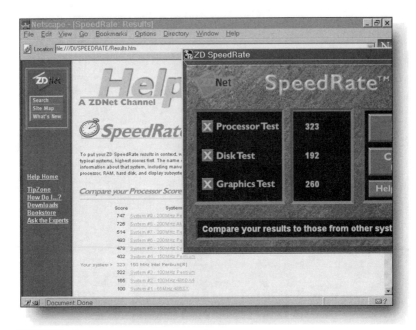

FIGURE 10.12
Smaller than the bulky WinBench and the enormous Winstone suites, SpeedRate is ZDBOp's convenient choice for quick download, measurement, and comparison against other typical PC hardware.

What About Used PCs?

Benchmark suites, such as those just described, exercise a PC's functions in such a thorough manner that these suites can be excellent tools for validating the overall condition of a used PC.

Buying a Used Machine

You'll want to look for a PC that's reasonably clean, inside and out (check for accumulations of dust in cooling fans and vents). A clean PC has probably been well treated in other respects as well. If the system also runs a comprehensive suite such as WinBench without errors and with performance in the typical range for a system in its class, a used PC might be an excellent value.

Remember, that used PC was probably a top-of-the-line system only 18 months or so before it arrived at the swap meet. Eighteen months is a short time in the life of a modern PC, except as measured by performance. I've gotten many years out of every PC I've owned, though they've moved down the ladder to less critical applications at a fairly rapid rate.

Selling or Donating a System

On the other side of the transaction, a "used PC" might be one that you already own. Perhaps you're contemplating a "new system" upgrade strategy and wondering what to do with the old machine—affectionately known as "the boat anchor" or "the doorstop" in conversations on this subject.

As I said a few paragraphs ago, that PC was probably a topnotch system when you bought it, and it would probably get a place of honor in a nearby church office or classroom.

Your personal income tax situation might make donating, rather than selling, your old PC quite attractive. Consult any reputable tax preparation manual for guidelines on how to value donated property, which generally does not require a formal appraisal if valued at less than $5,000.

Should you decide to sell your unit, a knowledgeable buyer will probably be impressed if you have all of the original packaging and manuals in good condition and accompanying the machine. Having a test suite installed and ready to run, even if it's only something as simple as SpeedRate, might also close the deal more quickly at a better price for you.

Be reasonable, however, in your expectations of how much you'll get for your used machine. PC prices plummet with age.

The local newspaper's classified ads might be a source of comparative prices that you can use as a guide to what you can ask for your PC. Ham radio swap meets are active markets for used PCs, but generally establish a price floor. Radio hams don't mind tinkering, so they won't pay the premium price that a nontechnical buyer might be willing to meet for a "cream puff" machine.

What We've Learned

PCs age gracefully if treated with care and if used for a stable set of tasks with infrequent changes to their hardware or software setups.

If you try to keep your machine up to the ever-rising state of the art, you'll spend as much (especially if you put any value on your time) as you would by buying a new machine every three years or so. Net cost of a new PC can be reduced by giving your old machine, as a tax-deductible contribution, to a deserving church or school.

Utility software ranges from superb to worse than useless. Product reviews span the same range. Read reviews with a critical eye and look for evidence of actual testing—as opposed to credulous narration of what a product claims to be doing.

Performance measurement software does a tricky job, but comprehensive suites are available free or for a minimal shipping cost. Application-based tests are bulky and time-consuming, but provide realistic measures of what a PC can do.

Subsystem-level measurements give you more insight into a particular PC's strengths and soft spots. A subsystem-level suite is a powerful tool for finding problems in a used machine, which can be an excellent value if it's "clean" in every sense of the term.

Someday, even a pampered PC will need the expert help of either a vendor representative or another experienced user. PC vendors' Web sites are the venue of choice for a huge variety of support resources. Use the search facilities and respect the social conventions that make a support center useful to you and to others.

"We've always got
customer feedback
telling us that the
machines are too
complicated and that
they're not natural
enough."

—BILL GATES, MICROSOFT
FOUNDER/CEO, MAY 1998

The State of Our Software

ITH THIS CHAPTER, we cross an important boundary. Chapters 1 through 10 have talked about things that computers do. The rest of this book will talk about things that people do, or would like to do, with computers.

Much of the time, I'm sorry to say, what people do with their computers is call them names and contemplate physical violence. People often get mad at their PCs, and most of the time the cause of that anger is software.

Good Software Is a Matter of Opinion

This book's first 10 chapters focus on hardware.

What hardware does is a fact.

How software should work is an opinion.

To a large extent, therefore, this chapter makes a transition from facts to opinions.

More Choices Than You Might Realize. . .

Your own opinion matters, perhaps more than you realize, because software has never been more "soft." The same piece of software, on two different users' PCs, often behaves in significantly different ways because of different preference settings.

For example, I can start up Microsoft Word on the machine that I'm using to write this book and get a screen arrangement like the one you see in Figure 11.1. The left margin strip shows special codes that tell me how each paragraph is styled, but the onscreen text is arranged in an outline form that shows me the organization of what I'm writing.

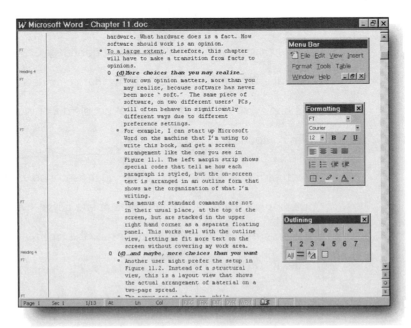

FIGURE 11.1
This arrangement of Microsoft Word doesn't look much like the standard setup. Menus and toolbars are not in their usual locations, and the text is arranged to show its structure rather than its appearance on the page.

The menus of standard commands are not in their usual place at the top of the screen, but are stacked in the upper-right corner as a separate floating panel. This works well with the outline view, letting me fit more text on the screen while keeping the menus outside of my editing area.

. . .and Maybe More Choices Than You Want

Another user might prefer the setup in Figure 11.2. Instead of a structural view, this is a layout view that shows the actual arrangement of material on a two-page spread. (You wouldn't use this view on a small display like the one on my laptop machine, but a large desktop screen with high resolution can handle this setup with ease.)

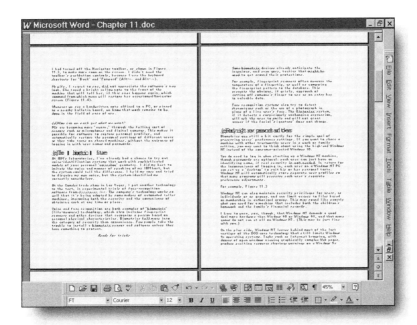

FIGURE 11.2
A layout-oriented view of Word is just as different from the normal arrangement as it is from the setup in Figure 11.1. Here, a two-page spread appears in its "as-printed" format, with a different set of controls in unconventional positions. It's hard to "talk" someone through a program, while giving assistance over the phone or in a book or article, when the program provides such flexibility.

In Figure 11.2, the menus are in their usual place at the top of the window, while formatting choices are displayed and changed by control panels down at the bottom of the screen. All of these locations—and all of the contents of each of these control panels—are subject to change by the user. This is truly "soft" ware.

The Tip of the Iceberg

The choices that you can make, such as the ones I've highlighted in Figures 11.1 and 11.2, might seem innumerable. They're just the tip of the iceberg, though, compared to the number of choices that were made beneath the surface by the designers of a program such as Word.

Teach Your Programs Well

For example, Word uses the keyboard combination Ctrl+Backspace to delete the word before your current position in a file. Repeated typing of Ctrl+Backspace moves you backward through the file, one word or one punctuation character at a time, deleting as you go.

Word was not the first program to use Ctrl+Backspace for a backward word delete; personally, I adopted this command years ago after using other software that behaved the same way. When I started using the KEDIT text editor, I decided to "teach" KEDIT to use this familiar command.

Figure 11.3 shows the method I used to add Ctrl+Backspace to KEDIT's vocabulary. The figure shows a definition that I wrote in KEDIT's internal programming language, KEXX, telling the program how to respond to a Ctrl+Backspace command in every possible situation. These instructions cover the special cases of typing Ctrl+Backspace at the beginning of a line or at the beginning of a file or in the command-line area of the screen instead of in the area used for text.

KEXX is a "high-level" language in the sense that it lets me say such things as "delete the next word" (`sos delword`) instead of breaking down that instruction into machine-level baby talk (of the kind we saw in Chapter 4). Even so, you can see that this simple behavior requires punctilious description.

Responding to "Why," and Not Just "What"

You can see impressive attention to intuitive ease of use in many PC software packages. For example, a multifunction product called Framework (from the now-defunct company Ashton-Tate) would behave in two different ways when you moved up and down through a document with the up- and down-arrow keys.

If you were moving through a Framework document, and moved to the end of a line with the End key, your up or down movements after that command would jump you to the end of each successive line. If you moved to the end of a line with right-arrow keystrokes, though, any subsequent up or down movements would keep you in the same column on the screen. Your cursor would not jump to the different columns where the different lines each ended.

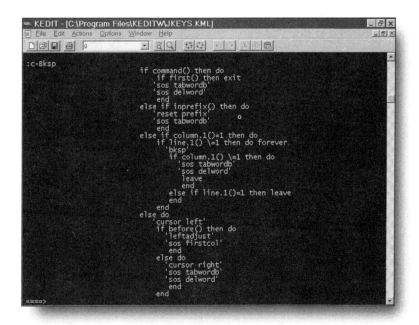

FIGURE 11.3
One simple behavior, the backward word deletion of the Ctrl+Backspace keyboard shortcut, requires this much detail to define all possible cases—even when we already have commands for pieces of the task, such as deleting a single word from a file.

Framework's behavior, though subtle, represented a nice piece of thoughtful design. If you moved to the end of the line with End, the software showed you the ends of other lines as well. If you moved to a particular column with right-arrow keystrokes, the software assumed that your target was that column of the screen and kept you there.

Complexity Does Not Excuse Poor Quality

We've looked at tiny fragments of software behavior. We can multiply their complexity by the number of different things you expect to do with a word processor, or a spreadsheet, or any other piece of nontrivial PC software. You can see why these programs are essentially impossible to write without a single quirk that someone will call an error.

In pointing out the obstacles that face a PC programmer, I don't intend to excuse a program that "crashes." (This is the term we use when a program stops accepting commands, or when a program veers off into random areas of memory and corrupts other programs' data or instructions.) There is no excuse for defects of that kind.

Crash recovery is an entire subindustry within the PC software market, and I guess that says a lot. When a piece of software crashes in Windows, the three-key combination of Ctrl+Alt+Delete brings up a control panel that might give you the chance to stop only the single program that's having a problem (the program whose name is followed by the label, "Not Responding"). Other utilities, such as Symantec's Norton CrashGuard, intercept and sometimes can correct the problems that lead to a crash.

Crash recovery in Windows 95 is better than you might expect, considering the fairly fragile foundation of "classic" DOS that's not very far below the pretty face. It's even possible to shut down Explorer (the entire user interface), which then restarts itself in a less-confused incarnation.

Individual applications sometimes provide their own crash recovery features, such as an automatic backup of work in progress at some user-defined time interval. If your software has such a feature, take the time to enable it with settings that fit your personal habits.

If You Don't Like It, Change It

In many cases, people dismiss a piece of software as "full of bugs" when they're really talking about legitimate design decisions. I'm especially distressed when people complain about a "bug" in a program, not realizing that the behavior can be changed if a user doesn't like it.

When Word Seems to Be Too Helpful

For example, suppose that I decide to change a sentence in one of the previous paragraphs. Suppose that I decide to say, "and its errors corrupt programs' data," instead of the original, "and corrupts other programs' data."

After adding the words, "its errors," I might place my mouse after the "t" in "corrupts" and begin to drag my mouse to the right so as to select the "s" and the following "other." I would then expect to delete both that letter and that word with a single tap of either the Backspace or the Delete key.

When my onscreen pointer touched the "o" in "other," I might be annoyed to see the selected area of text suddenly stretch its starting point backward toward the beginning of the document. Without any action on my part, the selected area expanded to include the entire word "corrupts," instead of just the final "s."

Fuming with annoyance, I might find by trial and error that I could separate the "s" from "corrupt" by adding a space before selecting and deleting. Alternatively, I might find that I could position the cursor before the "s" and then hold down the Shift key while tapping the right-arrow key all the way to the end of "other."

I might adopt either of these methods for selecting part of a word; I might go on for years in the belief that Word had an irritating bug that kept me from using my mouse to do this simple operation.

You Can Decide What Help You Want To Receive

Nothing would ever call my attention to the **Edit** tab in the Options window that I can summon up from the **Tools** menu. I might never find the simple checkbox next to the option description, **When selecting, automatically select entire word** (see Figure 11.4). Yet, there it is. With the box "unchecked," I need never be bothered by this behavior again.

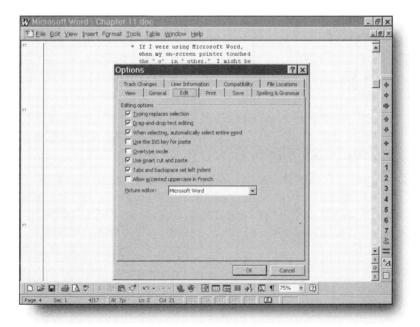

FIGURE 11.4
If a program is driving you crazy, it's possible that the behavior you don't like is a user-controllable option. Word's automatic selection of entire words is a feature to some, but annoying to others. The important thing to realize is that this behavior is yours to change.

If I ever do want to automatically select whole words with the mouse, I don't even need to go to the trouble of drilling down to the **Tools**, **Options**, **Edit** list of choices. I can just click twice in rapid succession to select the entire word around the cursor, and then hold down the button while dragging the mouse to extend the selected region word by word.

Like riding a bicycle, describing the double-click+drag maneuver is harder than doing it when you've learned the habit. It would be nice if this habit could be learned just once and used in all Windows programs, but that consistency has yet to be achieved.

Why We Call PCs "Personal"

Imagine the task of a user-support technician, or even just your PC-expert friend, trying to assist someone over the phone in performing anything more than the simplest task with software that's as "soft" as Microsoft Word." Okay, look for your Formatting tools. I don't know where they are—just look around the screen. Oh, wait a minute, pull down your **View** menu and pick the **Toolbars** item and tell me if **Formatting** is checked. Your menus? They're somewhere on the screen. . . "

On a machine that's used by only one person, the freedom to configure a single piece of software in many different ways is clearly a feature. From one day to another, or from one document to another, I frequently use the flexibility of Word and other applications to make their arrangement suit the task at hand.

Why We Don't Call PCs "Multi-Personal"

On a machine that's shared by several workers or by the members of a family, ease of changing a program's setup can become a problem. The other day, for example, my wife started up the Netscape Navigator browser on our family-room PC to send an email message to her parents. She stared at the screen and asked, "Where's the Back button?" (that is, the onscreen button for going to a previous Internet address).

I had turned off the Navigator toolbar, as shown in Figure 11.5, to make more room on the screen for Web page contents. I didn't need the toolbar's pushbutton controls, because I use the keyboard shortcuts for Back and Forward (Alt+left-arrow key and Alt+right-arrow key).

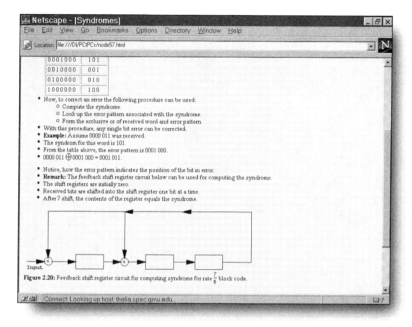

FIGURE 11.5
If you expect to see large, friendly onscreen "button" controls at the top of your Web-browser window, you might feel a little lost if your familiar browser program appears without these accustomed aids.

My wife, I regret to say, did not appreciate the software's new look. She taped a bright yellow note to the front of the machine that will tell her, if this ever happens again, which command from which menu will restore her accustomed Navigator screen (see Figure 11.6).

Whenever we see a handwritten note affixed to a PC or pinned to a nearby bulletin board, we know that work remains to be done in the field of ease of use.

Get What You Want. . . and Keep It to Yourself

If you want to share a machine with other users in a work or family setting, you might want to think about using the high-end Windows NT instead of the consumer-oriented Windows 95 or its successor, Windows 98.

You do need to log in when starting up a Windows NT machine, though passwords are optional. Each user can just have an identifying name if real security is not needed.

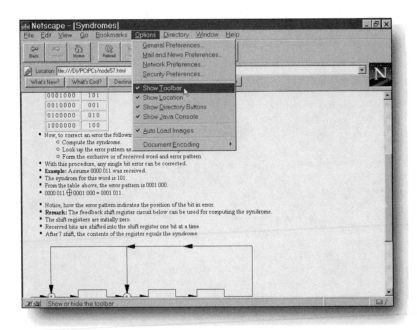

FIGURE 11.6
Making software do what you want is often just a matter of knowing how to ask. Alternatively, you can use an operating system that maintains different setups for each of several users, or wait for "biometric" systems that recognize your voice or your face and restore your software settings without being asked.

The Windows NT Option

In return for the inconvenience of logging in, each user on a Windows NT PC can set up a "desktop" to suit her personal taste. Windows NT automatically stores separate user profiles, so that many programs preserve each user's separate preference adjustments.

Windows NT can also maintain security privileges for users, as individuals or as groups, and can limit access to files based on membership in authorized groups. This might be exactly what you need for a family PC that stores both the children's homework and the family's financial records.

Windows 9x versions also have facilities for defining multiple users, each with personal preferences such as desktop arrangements, but Windows 9x systems do not protect any user's private data from anyone else.

I have to warn, you, though, that Windows NT demands a good deal more hardware than Windows 95 or Windows 98, and many PC games do not run at all on Windows NT. (This might be just fine with you.)

On the plus side, Windows NT leaves behind most of the last vestiges of the DOS core technology that still limits Windows 9x operating systems. Tasks such as Internet browsing, with dozens of open windows viewing graphically complex Web pages, produce exciting resource shortage warnings on a Windows 9x machine. Such heavy workloads are boringly routine on Windows NT.

Token Measures

I'll go into more detail on the perils of passwords in Chapter 17's section on "cyber-crime." We're talking here about convenient ways of telling a PC who you are, so I'll mention the growing use of physical tokens.

One token design is the button-shaped unit proposed by Dallas Semiconductor Corp., easily incorporated into a keychain or ring (see Figure 11.7). Unlike a simple electronic key, whose signal could be intercepted once and reused at a later time, a button of this type contains an active device that participates in a cryptographic exchange.

FIGURE 11.7
A compact, rugged identification button can contain a tiny computer that participates in a secret-code exchange, proving who you are in a way that can't be intercepted for imitation by others.

By surprisingly simple methods, which I'll describe in Chapter 17, it is possible for devices to agree on a secret key that an eavesdropper cannot determine. The key is undiscoverable even if the eavesdropper knows the method being used and is able to intercept the entire conversation between the two devices.

It is also possible to build a device that generates a changing password, depending on the date and the time of day. Unlike an ordinary password, which can be copied or intercepted and reused at any later time, these dynamic passwords require the user to have the token device in her possession at the time of seeking access. Such devices can be rugged and compact, no larger or thicker than an ordinary credit card.

The "Biometric" Future

None of us really wants to memorize passwords or worry about having our identity tokens stolen. Fortunately, PCs are becoming more "aware" through the falling cost of sensors, such as microphones and digital cameras, making it possible for software to recognize us and restore our personal settings (including our access to personal files) without the nuisance of logging in with usernames or passwords.

At IBM's laboratories, I've already had a chance to try out voice-identification systems that work with sophisticated models of your personal vocal anatomy. I did my best to imitate my IBM host's voice and manner of speaking, but the system could tell the difference. I held my nose and tried to disguise my own voice, but the system identified me correctly, nonetheless.

At the 1997 Fall Comdex trade show in Las Vegas, I put another technology to the test in experimental trials of face-recognition software from Visionics Corp. The company's technology works so well that it's being adopted by some makers of automated teller machines, augmenting traditional PIN codes to improve both the security and the convenience of obtaining cash at any time or place.

Voice and face recognition are both examples of *biometric* (literally, life-measure) technology, which also includes fingerprint scanners and other devices that recognize a person based on personal physical characteristics. Today, biometrics falls more into the category of security than convenience—few people take the trouble to install a biometric sensor and software unless they have something special to protect. The growing popularity of PC sound and video options will soon make biometrics a low-cost option.

READY FOR TRICKS

Some biometric devices already anticipate the ingenious, and even gory, tactics that might be used to get around their protections.

For example, fingerprint scanners often measure the temperature of a fingertip, as well as comparing the fingerprint pattern to the database. This prevents the obvious, if grisly, approach of cutting off someone's finger to use as an entry key to valuable data.

Face-recognition systems also try to detect shenanigans, such as the use of a photograph in place of a live user's face. If the Visionics system detects a suspiciously unchanging expression, it asks the user to smile and will not grant access if the facial "signature" does not change in response to that request.

Some Things Just Have to Be Learned

Despite the growing ease of customizing our software and preserving our personal preferences, a PC still presents a large set of conventions that must be learned.

We learn the PC's "rules of the road" for the same reason that we teach ourselves to look to the right, not to the left, when crossing the road in England. It doesn't matter whether driving on the right, U.S. style, is a better or worse way to do things. The only thing that matters is what works, which depends on where we are.

A Moving Experience

I once had to train a group of experienced secretaries to make the move from Wang word processors to the Apple Macintosh. Our first stumbling block was the Move command.

On the Wang, moving text was a "modal" operation; you entered a "moving mode," and you couldn't go back to writing or editing until you finished moving.

Being a dedicated word processor, the Wang had many keys that were specially designated for word processing operations. One such key was the Move key. If you pressed the key, the system would ask you, "Move what?"

You would mark the text you wanted to move and then press the key again. The system would ask, "Move where?" You'd move your onscreen marker to the desired new location, press the Move key one more time, and that was that.

So Many Ways to Lose

The Macintosh design avoided modes to the greatest possible extent, and this avoidance carries through to Windows today. Avoiding modes forced Macintosh programs to take a different approach from the Wang, making the simple task of moving text quite frightening to former Wang users.

The Macintosh gave many people their first exposure to the idea of the "clipboard" (since adopted by Windows and by most other graphical "shells"). We looked at the Windows Clipboard back in Chapter 1, where we noted that Windows 95's online introduction never tells you about this crucial concept.

The Clipboard transforms the "moving" of text into an operation performed by the user, not directed by the machine. If you want to move a paragraph from one place to another, you "cut" that paragraph (thus copying it to the Clipboard memory and deleting it from its original location in the document). You then "paste" the paragraph at the desired new location.

Moving via the Clipboard is non-modal. You can cut a paragraph, go to the place where you want to move it, notice that the move will make another sentence unnecessary, delete the redundant sentence, and then paste in the paragraph that explains the point more clearly.

You can follow a sequence of steps that follows your train of thought, instead of treating the moving of text as a monolithic operation. The Clipboard approach works better for people who compose a document at the keyboard, writing and rewriting to express their own ideas.

For the people whom I was training, however, the flexibility of the Macintosh was not a benefit. When they moved text, they did it because someone had marked up a written or previously printed draft of a document—because someone had circled a paragraph and drawn an arrow with a note that said, "Move this here." They did not need, or appreciate, the added flexibility of doing other things between the first and last steps in a movement operation.

Cutting, as the first step in moving, looked dangerous to these former Wang users. They were used to a "move" that made text appear in its new location immediately after it disappeared from where it had been before. The text to be moved was always present at one location or another, while Clipboard contents exist in a perilous state.

Whatever's on the Clipboard is discarded—irrevocably and without warning—if the user forgetfully cuts, or copies, something else before pasting what was to be moved.

Just What Can Be "Undone"?

Talking of irrevocable changes brings up the subject of "Undo."

An Undo feature should be part of almost every piece of PC software. Unfortunately, different programs vary greatly in what their Undos will undo.

Undo, and Undo the Undo

Many programs provide the basic feature of a single-level Undo and Redo. If I open a new file in the Windows Notepad program, for example, the **Undo** menu command (usually found in a program's **Edit** menu) is initially "grayed out," as shown in Figure 11.8. There is nothing that can be undone.

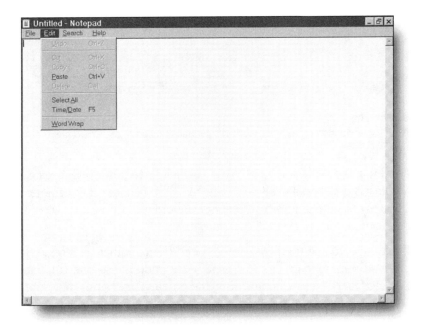

FIGURE 11.8
An empty file has no history of actions: There is nothing to undo.

If I type a word and then pull down the **Edit** menu again, I see that the **Undo** command is now available (see Figure 11.9). If I choose that **Undo** command, or type its shortcut key (usually Ctrl+Z, as indicated in the figure), my typing is undone and I'm back to an empty file.

FIGURE 11.9
After we've added text to a file, we have undoable actions—the **Undo** menu option comes alive.

I'm not in the same state that I was in when I had a new file, because my **Undo** command is still available (see Figure 11.10). If I choose that command again, I undo my "Undo" and recover my typed word (see Figure 11.11). This is a single-level Undo/Redo.

If I cut a word and then cut another word from another location in the file, the first cut word can no longer be recovered. I can undo the second cut, and redo that cut, but the first cut text is gone. This is the potential user error that rightly worried my Macintosh trainees.

Undo, and Then Undo What Came Before

An Undo capability is much more useful when it remembers, and can reverse or repeat, a series of several actions.

For example, when we can open a new document in Microsoft Word, we see that the **Undo** command is disabled as it was for a new file in Notepad (see Figure 11.12). Word takes the trouble to change the command to **Can't Undo**, as well as using the grayed-out appearance that indicates inactive menu items.

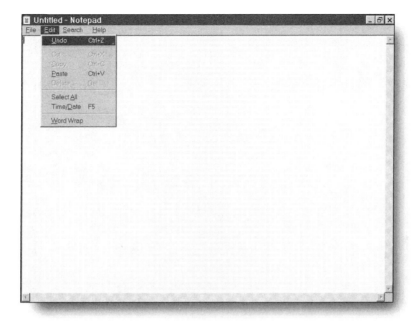

FIGURE 11.10
Going back to an empty file with **Undo** leaves the **Undo** menu option still enabled. . .

FIGURE 11.11
. . .because we can undo the "Undo" and restore the deleted content.

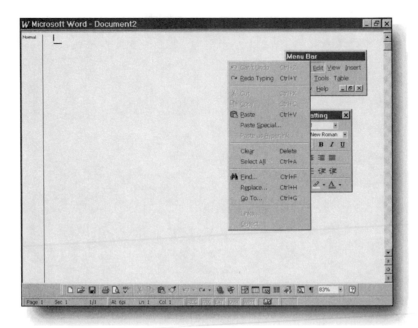

FIGURE 11.12
A more complete Undo capability uses dynamic menus to provide more information. . .

If we enter a word in the new file, creating a reversible action, the menu command changes to **Undo Typing** (see Figure 11.13). Compared to the simple Notepad, Word is a bit more communicative about exactly what it's prepared to undo.

Suppose that I now center my one-word paragraph on the page and examine my Undo options once more. Now I find the menu reading **Undo Paragraph Alignment**. If I choose this command, my text goes back to the left edge of the page, and my Undo options now read **Undo Typing** and **Redo Paragraph Alignment** (see Figure 11.14).

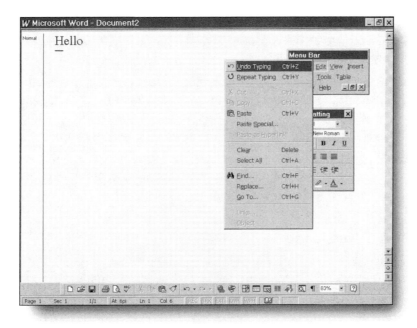

FIGURE 11.13
. . .such as exactly what the program is able to undo at any moment.

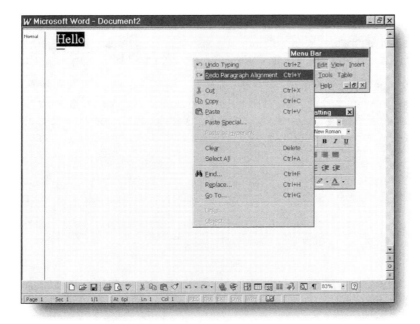

FIGURE 11.14
After undoing one action, we find the menu now offering to go in either direction through time: to undo the action that came before, or to redo the action we just reversed.

Word has maintained a history of my actions during this session. The program is prepared to go all the way back to my empty file, if I so desire—and from that empty file, to redo all the way back to my centered paragraph.

Word will not, however, maintain a multibranched tree of actions. If I undo my centering action and then change the left-adjusted text to a different color, I've chopped off the branch of my action tree that included the centering command. That centering action can no longer be redone from the **Edit** menu.

I can undo the color change and undo the typing to get back to an empty file; I can redo the typing and redo the color change to get back to where I was. All memory of the centering operation has been lost.

Not a True Undo

Because Word has a multilevel Undo, it can protect a user against the error that I discussed when talking about the hazards of "cut" commands.

If I cut some text, that text is copied to the Clipboard and deleted from my document. If I cut another piece of text, the second piece of text is also deleted from the document, and a copy of the second cut item replaces the first cut item on the Clipboard.

I might suddenly realize that I failed to complete a move operation with the first piece of text. If I choose the **Undo** command, the second cut item is restored to its original location in the document, but the Clipboard is *not* restored. I can confirm this by using the Clipboard Viewer accessory that I showed you in Chapter 1.

I might think that I would now have to reconstruct the lost text from memory, because it doesn't seem to be anywhere in the PC. With one more **Undo** command, however, my first cut item reappears in its original position, even though the Clipboard remains unaware of both my errors and my recovery actions.

Undo has not functioned at the level of the entire machine; undoing the second cut did not put me back in exactly the state that I was in before I made that cut. Undoing the first cut, however, *has* restored me to a state where I can start over.

I can cut the first text anew, placing it on the Clipboard, and this time I can paste that text to its new location before I use the Clipboard for something else.

A Link from the Middle of the Chain

Multilevel Undo can let us reverse an action that we took some time ago, without undoing every subsequent action.

If you deleted something, for example, but you've changed your mind and you want to get it back, you don't have to undo every other change you've made since that deletion. You can give **Undo** commands until the item in question reappears, and then copy the item to the Clipboard. You can then give **Redo** commands until you get back to the point where you changed your mind. None of your other actions has been lost, but the recovered item is safely stowed on the Clipboard so that you can paste it wherever you want.

One Feature Down, One Hundred to Go

We've seen that we can spend pages on our mental model of a single software feature, the **Undo** command. I chose this feature as a case study, so to speak, because almost every modern PC program has some form of this command, and yet its details can vary greatly from one piece of software to another.

Possible design decisions might include the following:

- Preserve Undo history for only a certain number of actions.

- Flush the Undo list when you save your file, on the assumption that doing a "save" means you're happy with what you have.

- Preserve a separate Undo sequence for each of several open projects (such as more than one open Word document), or provide only a single Undo sequence for an entire session across all projects.

- Save the Undo list along with a project file, so that you can resume work on a project at any future time with your last several actions still available for inspection and reversal.

- Maintain parallel Undo lists for content and appearance, so that you can undo changes such as color and alignment without affecting changes to text or computations.

Your entire approach to a task might be changed by the difference between a limited, fragile Undo capability and a comprehensive, forgiving version of the same feature. And Undo is only one of literally hundreds of features in any piece of software—or, at least, in any software that does more than the narrowest of tasks. That's why entire books get written about individual PC software products.

Uncivil War: Programmers Versus Users

Despite the astonishing capability of most of our PC software, many users think ill of programmers as a class.

Users grow especially angry regarding the subject of "bugs," as we might properly refer to the many genuine defects in PC programs. ("Misfeature" and "wart" are common terms for behaviors we don't like, but that happen by design and not by error.)

Buggy software has a simple cure: Don't buy it. Don't use it. Don't let anyone tell you that you have to use a product that doesn't work very well because "it's the industry standard."

If something is a standard, other products will offer ways to exchange data with products based on that standard. If you can deliver your work in the standard format, nothing else should matter.

It's You, Not the Software, That's Productive

You should use simple software that works, not "powerful" software that wastes your time with its defects, because what you accomplish has more to do with you than with the software that you use. This is not an opinion—it is a measured fact.

In a study at Bell Labs, researchers measured the performance of 74 people in a text-editing task. The test subjects used two different tools: a screen-based editor (similar to Windows Notepad) and a command-based line editor (similar to the crude EDLIN tool that came with early DOS PCs).

ABOUT COMMAND-BASED TOOLS

Text-editing software offers one of the best comparisons between old and new approaches to software—that is, between command-based and direct-manipulation (or screen-based) designs.

Essentially, a screen-based editor makes it easy for *you* to change your text, by marking and typing and pulling down menus in the manner of Windows or the Macintosh. A command-based editor, such as KEDIT (which I described in Chapter 2), lets you tell the *editor* how to change your text. For example, you can type a command such as change /bug/wart/ all *, changing all occurrences of "bug" to "wart" on every line in a file.

If command-based interaction sounds awkward, consider one valuable benefit: A command-based editor makes it easy to turn any operation, no matter how complex, into its own new command. Most command-based tools let you record and play back a stream of lower-level commands. You can give the commands a name, or you can attach them to a special key (like the Ctrl+Backspace script that I wrote for KEDIT, shown in earlier Figure 11.3).

Some screen-based tools also offer scripting facilities that record a series of actions for reuse. These vary in their capability to deal with any changes that you might make in the onscreen arrangement of a program's visual controls.

I might want to set up a standard document format to use for a series of reports. In a screen-oriented program, I would typically accomplish this by first going through all of the menu choices and other point-and-click operations involved in creating that format. Then I would use some feature such as a "document template" option to make a starting point for creating similar documents in the future. If I wondered exactly what I specified as that standard format, it might be a laborious process to go through all of the settings and write them down so I could describe them to some-one else.

With a command-based tool, my standard format would merely be a list of com-mands. For example, in KEDIT I can set up my format for writing a newspaper-style story (a long narrow column) with the commands in Table 11.1. The KEXX commands on the left correspond to plain-English format instructions on the right, making this script a concise description of a newspaper-style standard format that can be invoked with a chosen special key or named command.

TABLE 11.1   Newspaper Column Script

KEXX Command	Meaning
mar 1 43 +5	Set margins
wordw on	Wrap long lines
format noj extend si	Don't justify text to right margin; treat indents as new paragraphs; single-space after periods
eofout eoleof	Use end-of-line and end-of-file codes when saving files to disk
tabs 1 6 46	Set tabs
color arrow cyan on black; color cmdline cyan on black	Set screen colors to tell me what format I'm using

Notice the final commands in the table, setting screen colors to show me which for-mat I've chosen. It's been literally years since I looked at this list of commands—I just have a special key that rotates me through my predefined formats, and I stop when I see the color I want.

I don't need to remember these command codes. I just remember one key and my color codes, and let the computer do the work. I think that's how it should be.

Command-based programs can be much more productive than "easy-to-use" interac-tive programs that let you do anything easily. . . and let you do it again, and again, and again, with the program never learning to do the task itself. The capability to define and use new commands is an important part of making software usefully "soft."

In their comparison of different users employing both screen- and command-driven software, the Bell Labs researchers found a strong relationship between task performance and the age of the test subject—younger people did better. There was a strong relationship between task performance and the test subject's score on a general-purpose ability test—people with good reasoning skills and good memories did better.

Surprisingly, though, there was little relationship between task performance and the software that the subject used, even though the editing tools were substantially different in design. Knowing the subject's general ability scores, for example, was twenty times as useful in predicting task performance as knowing which editing tool the subject was given.

Even more surprising, overall, is the enormous difference between best and worst performance among different users of any kind of computer in any kind of task. In another study, the slowest of twenty users took three to six times as long as the fastest user to complete sample editing tasks. Among twenty programmers, the worst performers at various programming tasks took *fifty* times as long as the best.

It's Not What You Can Do: It's What You Can Undo

"The reasons for the discrepancy [between best and worst task performance when using computers] are quite clear," says psychology professor Thomas K. Landauer in his highly readable and fascinating book, *The Trouble with Computers* (MIT Press, 1995). Landauer's book is the source of much of the data in this chapter.

In addition to the effects of different skills in abstract thinking, Landauer asserts, "The power and complexity of computers provides greater opportunity for disastrous errors." Perhaps it's now clear why I gave so much space in this chapter to the matter of Undo commands.

Like a fish that is unaware of water, I've gone for years without really being aware of the error-recovery tactics that I use all the time. When I think about just the few hundred hours of computer time I've put into this book, I realize that there have been at least five occasions when reversing a mistake (whether made by me or by Word) has saved me from losing an hour or more of work.

Based on my own experience, even after sixteen years of using PCs, I have to agree with Landauer's view. Achieving high productivity with computers is not so much a matter of knowing how to make them do more as a matter of knowing how to make them Undo more.

Making Your PC Sing

The subject of undoing errors makes me think of the time that I was on a school field trip with one of my sons, accompanied by my wife's father. We were sitting at an outdoor table, finishing our lunch, when my father-in-law discovered that a bird on a branch overhead had decorated the shoulder of his shirt. "For some people, they sing," he muttered ruefully, as he scrubbed off the unsolicited contribution.

For some people, PCs seem to sing, while other people probably feel that they have more in common with my father-in-law when considering what PCs do to them. Really, though, PCs do it to everyone. Some people just make better use of a PC's tools for cleaning up the mess.

Bad Software Is Bad for Your Health

Even the best Undo facility often fails to contain the damage that's caused by actual defects in the software. As I said before, I urge you to shun buggy software, not only as a matter of productivity. I tell you to stay away from software that doesn't work because ill-behaved software can cause you physical harm as well as wasting your time.

How can software injure you? At the MIT Media Laboratory, test subjects were monitored with various devices that sensed and recorded physical responses to various computer-using tasks. One of the most revealing measures is the electrical signal in the masseter muscle, which shows when the jaw is clenched in anger.

Striking patterns emerged when researchers monitored students playing violent computer games. The most pronounced stress did not come when a user was "killed" in the game, but when the software did not operate correctly.

When a software defect caused unpredictable delays, the jaw muscles clenched strongly. Other indicators, such as blood flow, also showed excessive stress.

We have enough things in our lives that make us angry without subjecting ourselves to the physical damage that comes from chronic anger at software that fails or malfunctions.

We Make Life Hard for Programmers

While computer users clench their jaws and think unkind thoughts about programmers, the people who write PC software are often equally angry with their customers.

The New Hacker's Dictionary (3rd Ed.) includes the uncomplimentary entry, "**luser** /loo'zr/ *n.* A user. . . (*luser* and *loser* are pronounced identically). . . the term is often seen in program comments."

The core of the conflict lies in the fact that software *seems* easy to change. The apparent flexibility of software leads buyers to ask for what seem to be easily added features, failing to appreciate the overall impact of their requests.

Programming is a discipline that attracts people who like to make things work and who get satisfaction from solving a problem. The problem is that users continually change their definition of the problem to be solved.

One humorous essay compared the typical software buyer to a would-be home buyer who tells an architect, "Please design and build me a house. . . between 2 and 45 bedrooms. . . modern design. . . accommodate my 1952 refrigerator. . . 75-foot swimming pool. . . without impacting the final cost."

Changing a complex piece of software after a project is well underway is like getting out of a tar pit—to use an image that's often evoked in the field of software engineering. You can pull loose one foot or one arm, but in the process, you find that your other limbs are even more deeply stuck.

Let me tell you about the things that can happen inside a piece of software, and how a program's mistakes can give us insight into the choices that a programmer has to make.

When Software Trusts Its Data

I once had occasion to send a file from a PC to a Macintosh. Both machines were using Microsoft Word, which uses the same document format on either type of machine (by means that I described in Chapter 4).

When I opened the document on the Macintosh, the program tried to "paginate" the file; that is, to divide the document into separate pages for printing. The screen remained blank while the page counter started at 126 and kept on counting. It counted well into the 190s, which was odd because this was only an 8-page document. Then, the program crashed.

I never would have predicted what I found. Somehow, in the course of transferring the file, its formatting codes had become impossible to carry out. The text had a right indent of more than 17 inches, which left 10 inches *less* than a zero-length line for the text—in other words, a negative line width. Meanwhile, the spacing of the lines was almost 3 feet apart, which meant that the program could not put even a single line on an 11-inch page.

You can't create negative-length lines or 3-foot line spacings by any ordinary means. The program won't let you do this. At some level, though, the people designing the program relied on this fact and didn't bother to deal with a file that somehow might have come to contain such impossible instructions.

Sadly, "Safe" Means "Slow"

Should software always be watching its back, so to speak? Should every step that a program takes include provisions for detecting and handling worst-case scenarios?

Some programmers consider it a point of pride to write such "bullet-proof" code, while others get their satisfaction from writing the fastest possible programs (which get their speed, in large measure, by making optimistic assumptions).

Product reviews often notice marked speed differences between one product and another. Few product reviewers take the time to throw deliberately messed-up data at a program to see if it knows enough to turn down poisoned food.

Software and Random Death

In one remarkable case, a programmer got frustrated on a day when he was using a remote computer by means of a telephone-line connection. The line was noisy, and his commands were often corrupted by random characters that he had not typed. He found that in far too many cases, the "garbage" input caused the remote machine to crash.

The programmer decided to make a systematic study of this problem. The result was an article in the December 1990 issue of the professional journal, *Communications of the ACM* (Association for Computing Machinery), titled "An Empirical Study of the Reliability of UNIX Utilities."

The article's authors reported that they were able to crash roughly a third of the utility programs on a typical UNIX computer—and sometimes even crash the entire machine—by feeding in random commands. Programming shortcuts, they found, were typically the cause of this fragile behavior.

So Why Do We Trust Computers?

People's attitude toward software seems to be the opposite of their attitude toward Congressional representatives.

People often say that they don't trust Congress, but they think that their own representative is doing a good job. Conversely, people can tell you at length about the bugs in the software they personally use, but they still seem to trust computers more than they should.

From Science Fairs. . .

I was involved for several years in organizing an elementary school's science fairs. I thought it would increase students' motivation if we gave awards for art, for data collection, and for various other aspects of excellent projects as well as recognizing overall winners. I built a huge spreadsheet to process the detailed scores and generate the overall rankings.

Occasionally, science fair winners turned out to be children of some of the parents on the organizing committee. That makes sense, when you think about it. Which kids are in homes where science gets a lot of attention and where there are ideas and equipment on hand to help create an interesting project? But still, I worried that people might think the process had been rigged.

When the scores were announced, however, the principal's comments included the phrase, "The scores were all fed into a computer." I could see people nodding their heads, as if this guaranteed that the process had been fair. It was a remarkable demonstration.

Actually, using computers would have made it much easier to bias the results, but people think of computers as being somehow inherently fair. This is a misplaced trust.

. . .to "System Delusions"

I'm often quite astonished to see how people seem to suspend their normal judgment when they get a result from a computer instead of from some other source.

In his 1975 book *Systemantics* (Pocket Books), Dr. John Gall tells of a medical clinic whose computer once mailed a bill for $111.11 to every patient served by that clinic during the previous year. Someone was operating the computer on the day that it printed out those 50,000 bills; a dozen people were hired to stuff, seal, and stamp the envelopes for this unusually large number of bills that had to be mailed. No one asked if something might be wrong.

"The system had hypnotized them," theorized Gall, who later coined the Fundamental Theorem of Systemantics ("system antics"): "New systems generate new problems."

Data Matters, Too

I don't want to leave the general topic of software without a few words about data. What a computer knows is just as important as what a computer can do with that information.

For example, when my oldest son was in second grade, he had an assignment to come up with lists of words that met certain conditions. Counting each letter A as a 1, each B as a 2, and so on, he was supposed to find examples of words whose letter values added up to 50 or 100 points.

After he'd done the best he could, I decided to use this problem as an introduction to programming. I asked him to explain to me the process by which he figured out the total "points" for a word. While he talked, I typed. When he was done, I helped him read the BASIC-language program that did what he had just described.

We ran the program and found far more "special" words than he had ever imagined there would be. There were almost four hundred 50-point words, from "abalone" to "yet." There were over a thousand 100-point words, from "abatements" to "zittern."

Ah, but where did we get the list of words that we could run through that program to find the special words we were seeking? That was the other lesson that I wanted to teach my son that day.

Programs, in general, are useless without a generous supply of accurate data. No result is any better than the facts that feed the process. (I used the reference dictionary from a simple spell-check program.)

What We've Learned

"Using a PC," wrote Ted Nelson in his 1987 book, *Computer Lib* (Tempus Books), "may be compared to juggling with straight razors. Using the Macintosh is like shaving with a bowling pin."

Nelson captures the dilemma of power versus ease of use. We don't want a computer that refuses to do useful things. We don't want a computer that cheerfully agrees to do destructive things. We certainly don't want a computer that does random, unpredictable, inconsistent things.

In general, software is getting more complex at a rate that exceeds the improvement in programming tools and methods. Designers of automatic appliances, such as auto-focus cameras, sneer at what they call (in the words of a Sony engineer, quoted in *Fortune* magazine in July of 1998) the "PC attitude": "If it works, okay. If it doesn't? Reboot it!"

We vote with our pocketbooks in the ongoing popularity contest that constitutes the PC software marketplace. There are simple, reliable pieces of software, and there are sophisticated products that make things easy when they're working and waste a lot of our time with their quirks and defects.

The choice between these design approaches is made, in the long run, by buyers rather than by programmers.

"Almost nothing is easy
the way it should be;
only a few things fit
together."

—TED NELSON,
Computer Lib

The Suite Spot:
Where Software (Mostly) Works Right

FTER THE CAUTIONARY TONE of Chapter 11, this chapter begins the fun part of the book.

If this were a driving class, the first 10 chapters would have been the classes in basic mechanics. Chapter 11 would have been the movie of footage from real motor vehicle crashes, meant to give the new student driver a healthy respect for the things that go wrong out there.

This chapter is like the morning when the instructor hands you the keys and tells you to take the car out on the road. Now, we'll see what this thing can do.

Your Job Doesn't Come on a CD-ROM

Most of our packaged PC software supports a task, not a career. It's easy to find a piece of software that does "word processing." It's harder to find a piece of software that does "script writing" or "contract preparation" or "court transcription."

I'm on a not-very-quiet crusade to encourage software buyers to demand tools that truly fit their jobs. Too many people have redefined the way they work in terms of the software that they use. I want people to demand that software adapt to what the user wants to do, instead of leading users to redefine their problems in terms of the available solutions.

Software's Low-Level Mission

When you go out to buy your new PC a wardrobe of attractive software, you might think that you need to order one of everything. I remember a 1980s cartoon showing an executive speaking into his desktop intercom: "Miss Jones, my new computer does word processing, spreadsheets, and databases. Please bring in some words, some numbers, and some data."

The point of that cartoon was that the executive was letting his new tool change his definition of his job. His job remained the making of decisions, at least as much so as it had been the day before his PC arrived. He had no more need for additional low-level information than he'd had the day before.

Unfortunately, the first generation of PC software really wasn't suited to anything but working with the simplest, most low-level types of raw data. In fact, with few and slow connections to other information sources, a PC was poorly suited to anything but creating new data from scratch.

A PC made a good tool for a secretary whose work began with dictation tapes or handwritten drafts, or for an engineer whose work began with a concept and some estimated figures. An early PC was not a suitable tool for most of the tasks in the crucial class we call "decision support."

Many of the products I'll show you in the next several chapters are very much aimed at decision support tasks, but too many of these products are poorly known to most PC users.

Your High-Level Goals

A modern PC has the connections to bring in floods of information from outside sources, by every means from the Internet to the CD-ROM. The software that you buy should not just create possibilities—it should offer you information to guide you in using its power. Software should be judged for what it knows, as well as for what it can do with what you know.

A software's "knowledge" often takes the form of predefined, generic versions of common work products, such as standard layouts for various documents or types of analysis. Products compete to offer the most natural and useful automated assistance for tailoring these generic versions to your particular needs.

Most of the interesting things people do are not conveniently pigeonholed into word tasks, numbers tasks, data tasks, and so on. We need a broader view that takes in management functions, office operations functions, personal activities, and other categories.

Within various functions and activities, you will see some tasks that work with lists, others that work with numbers, and still others that produce documents and carry on communications with other people. A PC can be most useful if its software takes an eclectic approach that matches the varying demands on a busy PC user.

Software Suites Let You Define the Job

When I was setting up PCs in the mid-1980s, there was a fairly standard set of office software: WordPerfect for documents, 1-2-3 for numbers and charts, and dBASE III for working with interrelated lists and tables. All three products came from separate companies, and none of them worked the same way.

Today's PC buyer can get much more capability than that from the best separate products in the 1980s, while spending much less money and enjoying much greater ease of learning and coordinated use. Many PC buyers need nothing more—and should settle for nothing less—than the impressive capability and unsurpassed convenience of a packaged software suite such as Microsoft Works.

Figure 12.1 shows the opening screen of Works. At first, you might wonder why I'm making such a fuss about functions and activities instead of mere tasks—Works just seems to be offering the same old separate functions under a common umbrella.

FIGURE 12.1
One of Microsoft Works' opening screens takes a traditional PC orientation, offering tools, rather than listing likely tasks.

If we click on another tab of the Works Task Launcher, we get quite a different view of what this program is prepared to do for us (see Figure 12.2).

Notice the icons next to the various entries in the list of Works' TaskWizards. Each icon indicates the main Works tool that will be a foundation of this task, but we'll soon see that the separate tools can readily cooperate.

FIGURE 12.2
We can reveal a task-oriented view of Works' capabilities with just a click of the mouse.

Well-Dressed Words Get Attention

One common task for both the home and office PC is the creation of newsletters, whether for an organization within a company or for a youth soccer league. If we used a PC as nothing but an electronic typewriter, we could still make these documents come together more quickly than any other way. For example, we can dramatically reduce retyping by having contributions come in via electronic mail or on floppy disks, as PCs become more common in homes as well as in offices.

We can make newsletters more attractive—and therefore more likely to be read—with graphics elements such as illustrations and tables of contents. This isn't just self-indulgent decoration: An important announcement won't be overlooked if it jumps off the page in larger type.

Why not package the proven elements of good newsletter design and let the user "just add content"? A good packaged suite gives you a running start on using advanced document layout features with aids of the kind that you see in Figure 12.3.

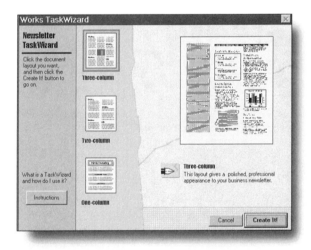

FIGURE 12.3
Alternative newsletter styles take us a quantum jump beyond "electronic typing."

Templates and Wizards

Having chosen a newsletter format, we find ourselves editing a "template" page. This uses several product features that are easy to learn by example but that we might never think to seek out in the product's manuals or online help—if only because we wouldn't know what to call them. How would *you* look up "a big, interesting-looking title that runs up the edge of the page"?

A TaskWizard, as Microsoft calls it, bridges the "what to call it" gap. Automated task aids make product features available, as in Figure 12.4, by demonstration instead of by incantation.

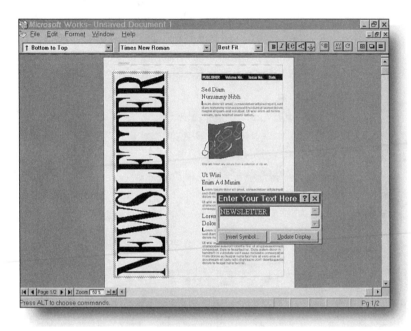

FIGURE 12.4
A working demonstration is the best reference manual for software features that are hard to name.

Originally a Microsoft trade name, *wizard* has become a generic term for a software feature that leads you through a multistep process. Wizards are a mixed blessing: It's possible, for example, to find a wizard taking far more time to be far more general than you need, when all you wanted was a guide to the basic use of a feature.

In the world of Windows software, wizards enjoy a fairly high degree of consistency, thanks to construction aids ("wizard wizards"?) that Microsoft and other toolmakers include in their programming products. In general, a wizard asks you to make choices or to enter specific information in a series of steps.

Each step typically ends with a choice. The usual options are **Next** (to provide more information) or **Finish** (if you've furnished everything the program needs and you just want the wizard to make simple assumptions about any other options that might exist).

Good software design practice always includes a **Cancel** option that returns you to your original situation.

Changing a Wizard's Work

Regrettably, wizards can become a crutch for people who design software products as well as for people who use them. It's well and good, for example, to have a wizard that helps you lay out a complex document, but it should be easy to make subsequent changes to the resulting design.

I have seen too many products in which it was easier—or seemed easier—to go through the wizard from scratch again than to make just the change I wanted to make. When getting a demonstration of a product, admire the wizards and then ask, "What if I decide to change [something] later? How do I do that?" I would say that re-running the wizard should rarely be part of the answer.

Clean Up Your Spreadsheet with Logic

A suite such as Works is just as proactive with numbers as with words. For example, an order form can be developed with a word processor, using table design features of the kind that we'll see in Chapter 14. A better use of a PC, however, is to make the form do more of the work by incorporating calculation rules (such as extending prices and adding taxes) into the form itself.

An "active form"—one that fills in its own blanks with information that depends on other filled-in items—is the perfect application for a PC *spreadsheet* program (a popular number-crunching tool that we'll look at more thoroughly in Chapter 14). Works offers an Order Form Wizard (see Figure 12.5). Now, we'll see what kind of expert knowledge the program can bring.

FIGURE 12.5
A spreadsheet can be more than rows and columns of numbers. Works offers several working examples that you can tailor.

In Figure 12.6, we see the relatively advanced spreadsheet features that Works incorporates into an order form template. This is not just a simple grid of the kind that most novice users would create. The form makes effective use of borders to make visually clear which numbers relate to each other. The form also uses clear labels to reduce input errors. For example, the % sign next to the tax field deters the common error of entering a fraction (such as 0.08 for 8%) when the spreadsheet is already dividing the entered value by 100.

Notice that the form is not cluttered by "zero" entries in places where the spreadsheet will calculate a value but where the related data has not yet been entered. The formula near the top of Figure 12.6 shows how this is done. The spreadsheet enters an empty label (denoted by " ") in the tax space, unless there are entries in both the tax rate field (Column E, Row 31) and the labor subtotal field (Column G, Row 30).

If both the tax rate and the labor subtotal entries have been made (as determined by the logical #AND# expression in the formula), the spreadsheet computes and displays the tax.

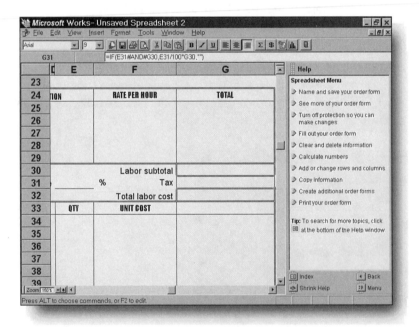

FIGURE 12.6
We can keep our spreadsheet uncluttered by spurious zeros with the formula tricks we see in Works' spreadsheet templates.

Communications: Just Another Kind of Document

I said that early PCs were too often starved for data. Communications from one PC to another can be a forbidding process, with all the jargon that we saw in Chapter 7 of protocols and communication parameters.

An integrated suite makes it easier to get online and to use the results of getting connected as raw material for new projects.

In Figure 12.7, we see how easily Works integrates outside communications into its environment of many types of documents. A communications window has menus for telephone settings and buttons along the top of the screen for such tasks as setting up a communications session.

Figure 12.7 also shows us the exposed sharp edges of data communication. Can you sense the sinking feeling of a novice PC user who has followed the instructions for "getting online" to a service such as CompuServe, who has heard the PC's modem (via its speaker) dial up and connect, and who sees that mess on the screen? What has happened?

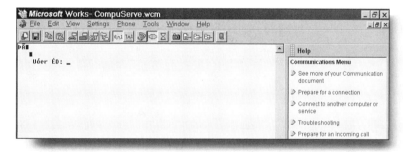

FIGURE 12.7
Garbage characters are one of the gremlins that scare many users away from data communication.

Fortunately, a useful item is right there on the always present Works **Help** menu. For communications, that menu includes the promising item, **Troubleshooting**.

If we click on the **Troubleshooting** choice, we get a list of common problems that includes this one: **You see strange characters.** Yes, that would be us.

Choosing the "strange characters" item, we're advised to click on one of the buttons marked **7,e,1** or **8,n,1**; that is, on whichever of these buttons is not already selected. Do we need to know—or even temporarily care—that these represent alternatives between 7 versus 8 data bits? If you've read Chapter 7, it might not bother you to have the matter stated this way, but who really cares?

We just want to read what we receive from the computer at the other end of the line. We click and we press the Enter key to tell the machine at the other end to try again, and this time we get an input prompt that makes sense (as shown in Figure 12.8).

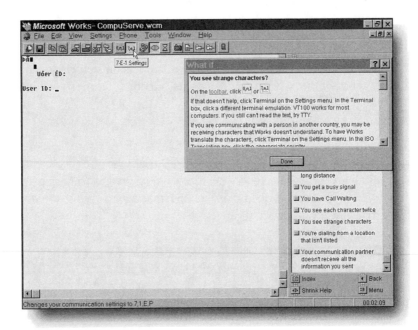

FIGURE 12.8
Plain English problem-solving, with solutions readily available on the screen, goes a long way toward streamlining PC learning.

Moving Data Across Different Tools

I don't know about you, but when I go online to a service such as CompuServe, I do it because there's information up there that I need. Usually, that means I'll be cutting and pasting and editing quotations or summaries, or possibly incorporating statistics into a document.

I would want Works, or any other software suite, to anticipate the exchange of information between different users.

With my communications session still in progress, I can summon up the Works Task Launcher and tell it that I want to open a new document with the Word Processor tool (see Figure 12.9).

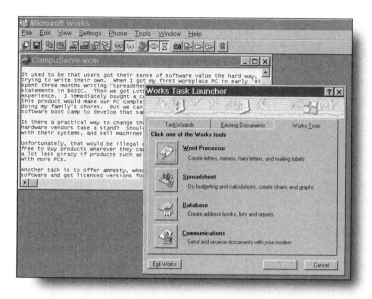

FIGURE 12.9
We can work with multiple documents, of several different types, within the Works environment.

I can use my mouse to select a particular quotation (in this case, one of my own past comments on Works) from the communications window, which is still connected to CompuServe. I have not had to go through any abstract operations, such as saving my communications session to a file and then finding and opening that file. The information is simply there on my desktop.

Holding down the button of the mouse, I click on the selected block of text. Note that Works, more usefully than most other applications, changes the mouse pointer by adding the word **DRAG** to tell me what I can now do (see Figure 12.10).

I drag the text that I selected in my communications window, moving my mouse into the empty document that appeared when I clicked the Word Processor button in Figure 12.9. The mouse pointer now carries the label **COPY**, as you can see in Figure 12.11.

Releasing the mouse, I get a document containing the selected material from my communications window (see Figure 12.12).

A more savvy Works user would not have bothered to call up the Task Launcher to open a blank document. Think about what you'd do if you were reading a physical newspaper and you saw something worth saving. Would you get out a piece of paper and a jar of rubber cement and carefully affix the clipping to the blank document? Or would you just rip out the story and put it on a stack of items to follow up or file?

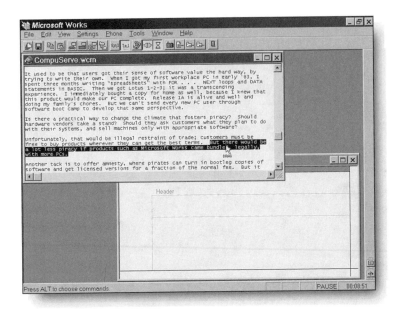

FIGURE 12.10
Works tells us, with a labeled pointer icon, that our mouse is ready to drag selected text to another location.

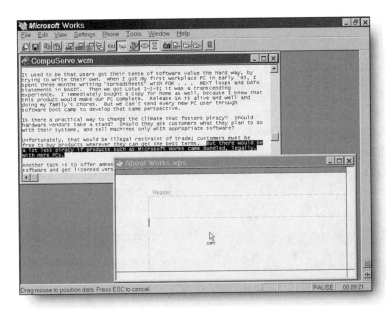

FIGURE 12.11
When we drag to another open window, the mouse understands that we want to copy information from one type of window to another.

In Figure 12.13, you see me handling an electronic "clipping" just as I would in the physical world. I'm simply dragging it to my desktop, getting the same **COPY** indication that I saw when dragging into an empty document.

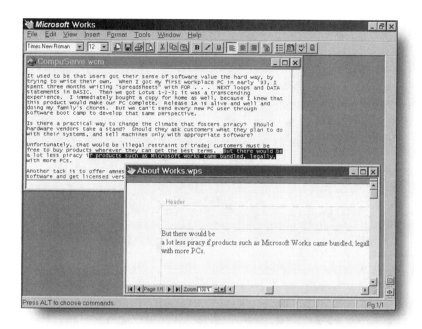

FIGURE 12.12
A word processing document now captures a fragment of our communications transcript.

When I release the mouse button, Works obligingly creates a new blank document (see Figure 12.14) to hold the dragged citation.

Lists of Data Can Look Smart, and Act Smart

When I want to work with lists of data, Works shows me the capabilities of its advanced features by example, just as it did when working with numbers in a spreadsheet. If I call up the wizard for a library database, I get much more than a bare list of empty rows and columns. I get an organized starting point that shows me some of the things I might want to be sure I capture, up front, to perform that task (see Figure 12.15).

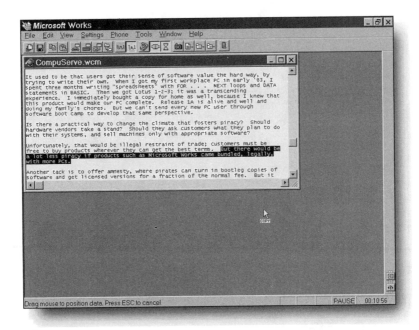

FIGURE 12.13
What does it mean to copy text to the Works desktop?

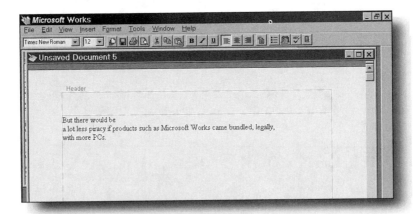

FIGURE 12.14
When we copy text to the Works desktop, Works can only assume that we want to create a new Works document—and it does so.

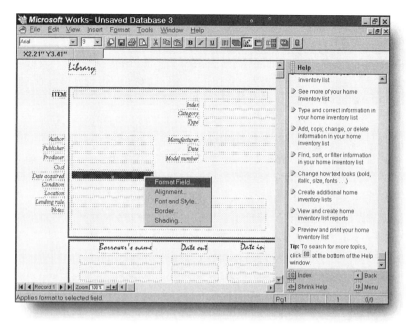

FIGURE 12.15
A database, like a spreadsheet, can be more than just rows. Works shows us how to lay out a readable form.

Works even shows me the proper way of using data field formats, such as Date (see Figure 12.16), to ensure that I will not enter the wrong kind of information in a field. Failure to use proper data can keep me from later sorting or locating items as I had planned to do.

The Document as a Container

Life gets much more interesting when we look at using more than one type of tool within a single *compound document*. Instead of writing a letter, for example, and saying "The figures are attached," wouldn't you rather just include the figures in your word processing document?

You might think that including the figures with the text would mean typing in the numbers as an ordinary table and losing the ability to have the computer use its spreadsheet capabilities to do the math for you. Modern software doesn't force such an unattractive choice. In a suite such as Works or an integrating environment such as Windows, you can quite easily use the capabilities of many separate tools in a coordinated way.

For example, Figure 12.17 shows me starting a document that clearly calls for supporting numbers. I've also opened a spreadsheet so that I'll only have to enter the numbers that are independent data, letting the computer calculate differences and add up gross and net totals.

I can drag the spreadsheet into my document in progress, just as I dragged text from a communications window into another document window. The dragged spreadsheet elements don't just appear as text, however, but as a formatted table (see Figure 12.18). This alone is not too bad a trick.

If I activate the table that seemed to be a demoted spreadsheet (in Works, with two rapid clicks of the mouse), the table remembers its origins and "grows" a spreadsheet's rows and columns around its numbers (see Figure 12.19).

Moreover, I can edit numbers and see the spreadsheet's logic update the figures that are changed by that new data (see Figure 12.20).

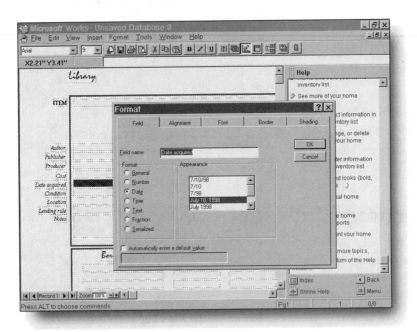

FIGURE 12.16
Using a specialized data type, such as a formatted date, makes entering irrelevant data by accident harder to do. Works shows us, by example, what works.

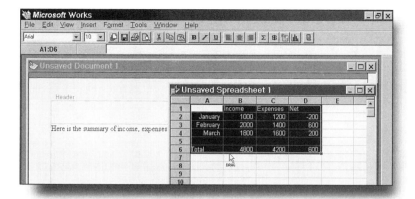

FIGURE 12.17
We can drag more complex types of data, such as a spreadsheet fragment, into a document.

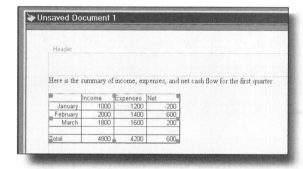

FIGURE 12.18
At first, a spreadsheet that's pasted in a document appears to have been demoted to a simple table.

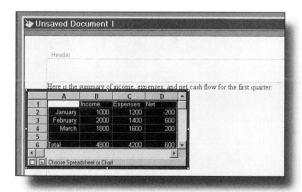

FIGURE 12.19
What looks like an ordinary table can return to spreadsheet mode.

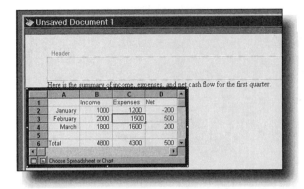

FIGURE 12.20
We can edit numbers and let a spreadsheet calculate the impact of the changes.

When my numbers go back under cover, so to speak, returning to their appearance as a mild-mannered table of text, the numbers are all consistent—but I only had to edit one value (see Figure 12.21). We say that our document is acting as a *container* for "foreign" data types such as a spreadsheet-based dynamic table. These rich data types extend the document's "native" data type, which (of course) is text.

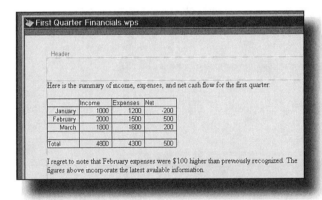

FIGURE 12.21
Back in table mode, the edited spreadsheet now gives the document the latest available calculations.

You might wonder if I needed to launch a separate spreadsheet window in the first place. The Task Launcher turned out to be the long way around the block when I was dragging text into a document. Is there a direct route for creating a table that can think like a spreadsheet while living inside a document?

There are direct routes for embedding not just spreadsheets but many types of objects in a document. In Figure 12.22, you see the menu available within a Works document for inserting objects of many types that I would otherwise create by opening a separate tool.

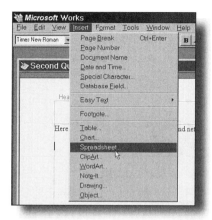

FIGURE 12.22
We don't even need to create a dynamic table in a separate spreadsheet window.

After choosing and inserting a spreadsheet object, I can go ahead and describe the calculations I want to perform in creating a table of numbers with mathematical relationships, such as gross and net subtotals and grand totals (see Figure 12.23).

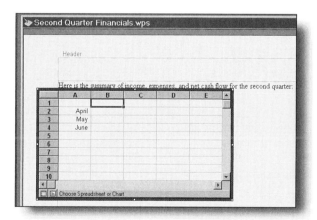

FIGURE 12.23
An inserted spreadsheet object can be developed within a document's workspace.

Creating the Data-Enriched Document

Spreadsheets and documents work together to automate repetitive calculations, and databases work with documents to eliminate other repetitive operations. Works spares me the tedious, programming-like process of learning to do a "mail merge," where a form letter plugs different words (such as a different name and address and salutation) into each of a set of otherwise identical documents.

An Insert Field window enables me to choose from available database lists (see Figure 12.24) and to select, by name, the items that should be copied from successive records in the chosen list.

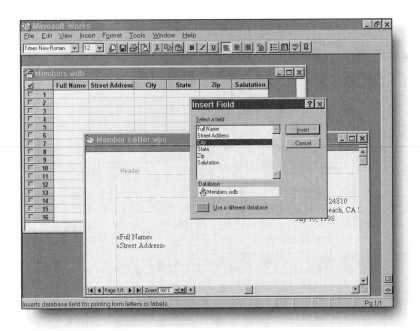

FIGURE 12.24
A document can consult a database for the names of entries in a multiple "merge" operation.

When I start to print my document, Works detects the presence of the coded *place-holders* and offers, automatically, to print multiple copies (see Figure 12.25). I get one customized document for each record in the corresponding list, which might be the current active membership of an organization.

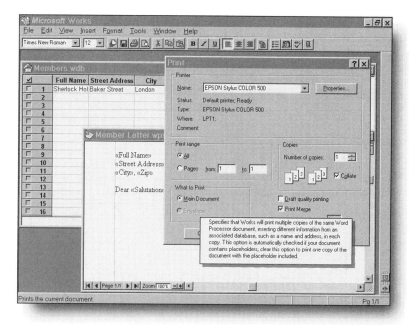

FIGURE 12.25
Works automatically offers to print a customized copy of the document that uses each set of data, as in a mass mailing.

Building an Executive Suite

For users who need full-strength software with exotic features over and above Works' generally capable tools, step-up options include both Microsoft Office and Lotus SmartSuite.

Office and SmartSuite use the main Windows desktop as their work area because they lack a self-contained desktop like the one in Works. Office puts its version of the Works Task Launcher into the Windows 95 Start menu (see Figure 12.26), and SmartSuite puts its own startup aids into other parts of the Windows desktop.

I'll show you the main components of SmartSuite in Chapters 13 through 16 when we look at the separate types of software in more detail.

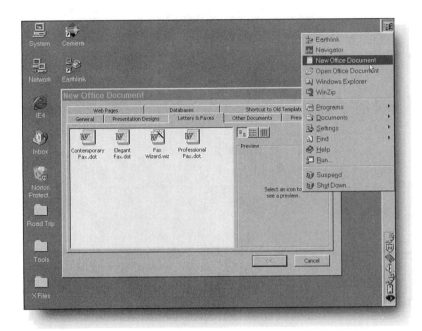

FIGURE 12.26
Microsoft Office makes all of Windows the desktop for its separate but cooperating tools.

You Can Tell They're Just Living Together

Microsoft Office has achieved impressive market share, and the product often serves as Microsoft's showcase for new Windows features. I have to warn you, though, that the integration between separately developed modules (such as those of Office or SmartSuite) might be less consistent than you see in a well-packaged product such as Works.

For example, Figure 12.27 shows the result of copying a chart from Microsoft's Excel spreadsheet into Microsoft's Paint (a graphics accessory program that's part of the basic Windows 95 package). When Paint starts up, it creates a rather small "empty canvas" for your work. The Excel chart obligingly squeezes itself into that small space, which is not at all what I wanted.

When I saw the tiny chart that Paint proposed to create for me, I was perplexed. I had not seen this happen, for example, when I copied graphics from Microsoft Word documents into the Paint editor (either for editing or for conversion to some other graphics file type).

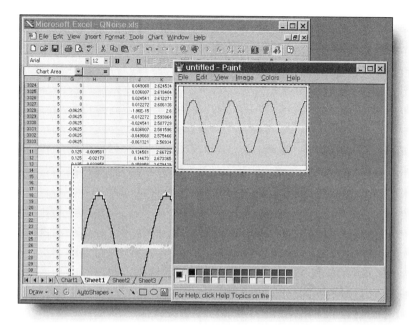

FIGURE 12.27
When is a "paste" not a "paste"? Pasting from Excel into Paint squeezes a chart into the available space. . .

Then I had the bright idea of opening an empty document in Word, copying the chart from Excel to Word, and copying from Word to Paint. The copy from Excel to Word was encouraging, giving me a chart in my document that was just as large as I had made it in Excel.

The copy from Word to Paint completed my joy. Paint asked me if I wanted to make the working area larger (see Figure 12.28).

When I accepted the offer of an enlarged graphics workspace, Paint gave me the full-size chart I wanted (see Figure 12.29).

A Matter of Learning How the Program "Thinks"

I'm not saying that there's a bug in one or more of these programs—even though copying from Excel to Word and from Word to Paint produces a different result than copying from Excel directly to Paint. Actually, I suspect that this is a designed behavior, reflecting someone's idea that spreadsheet charts don't originate in formatted documents, although Word graphics do.

One could argue that spreadsheet charts should let a receiving graphics editor determine their size, as does happen when I copy from Excel to Paint. One could also maintain that a graphics editor should take the size of a document's graphics as given. Personally, I would call this an example of thinking too hard. What does it say about me that I could even come up with this tortuous logic? Don't answer that, please.

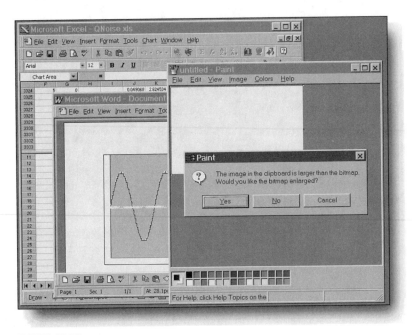

FIGURE 12.28
. . . but pasting to Word and then from Word to Paint preserves the chart's desired size.

When the Pieces Work Together

Most of the time, interaction among the elements of Microsoft Office is more predictable than the quirky graphics sizing I've just described.

I can drag a block of text and numeric *cells* from an Excel spreadsheet into a Word document just as easily as I performed the similar operation in Works. During the Excel-to-Word drag, however, I won't get helpful Works-style labels next to my mouse pointers—only a more cryptic box with an adjacent plus symbol to show me that I'm making a copy and not performing a move (see Figure 12.30).

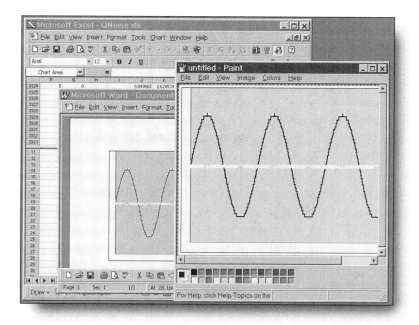

FIGURE 12.29
The chart that takes the long way there winds up with more to show for the trip.

When I drag Excel data into a Word document, that dragged data still knows where it came from, as was the case in Works. I can activate spreadsheet-style editing facilities around the resulting table. You might have to look twice to realize that the foreground spreadsheet in Figure 12.31 is inside a window titled Microsoft Word.

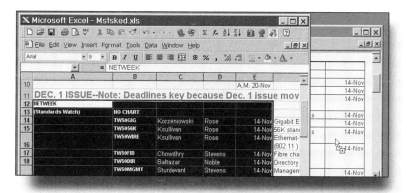

FIGURE 12.30
Dragging a block of data from Excel to Word produces a table, as in Works.

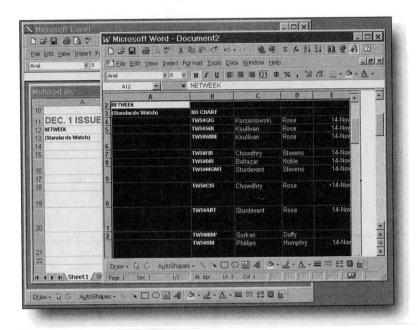

FIGURE 12.31
The pasted-in table in Word still knows that it's a spreadsheet object.

Also as in Works, I don't even need to use an outside tool such as Excel to create a spreadsheet-type object within a word processing document. I can call up a menu of available types of objects to create and insert in a document (see Figure 12.32). A Windows machine maintains a "registry" of information that includes the names and types of objects it can create with the software installed on that PC.

A Copy That Keeps on Copying

I need to warn you that the interaction between various PC applications can be almost too good. Suppose that you copy a block of numbers from a spreadsheet into a document, with the intention of preserving that set of numbers as a starting point for future comparisons against updated estimates.

Suppose that you then change some assumptions, resulting in new numbers, and paste the revised numbers into the same document—only to see that both sets of numbers in your document are identical, reflecting the changed scenario. What happened?

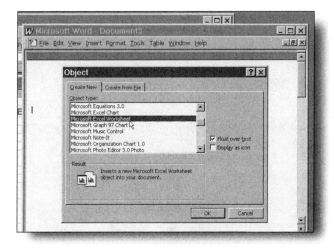

FIGURE 12.32
Word can create, in place, a wide range of objects that will be serviced by other Windows applications.

Figure 12.33 shows the likely explanation: An item can be pasted (by using the **Paste Special** command in the **Edit** menu of most programs) with the option **Paste Link** instead of the simpler, normal **Paste**.

Figure 12.34 shows an example of the continuing interaction between an original file and a pasted-link portion of that file. In the foreground, I've changed an entry in an Excel spreadsheet from "No chart" to read "Chart coming." The corresponding entry in my Word document automatically changed to match.

If I meant to use my Word document as any kind of audit trail of changes in my plans, the document will fail in that role—only the final plan will appear. I might wind up with several copies of that final plan. If the pasted copies were pasted as links to the master file, I will get a copy for each time I thought I was taking a snapshot of my changing outlook.

Let me close this discussion of software suites with a final note on Microsoft Office and its integration with the Windows desktop. I can drag items out of an Office program, such as Excel, without dragging them to any particular destination, just as I can with Works (see Figure 12.35). Understanding that such a drag is just putting a copy of something aside for later use, Windows creates an item (with the unflattering label of "scrap") on the desktop for that purpose.

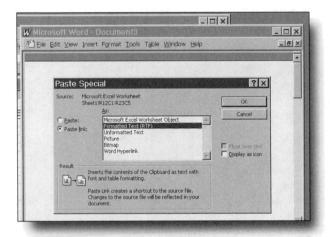

FIGURE 12.33
An object can be pasted in the form of a continuing link to the original object (which might be, for example, a spreadsheet that is referenced by many documents).

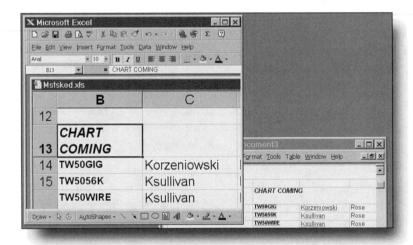

FIGURE 12.34
When the pasted object represents a link, rather than a copy, any change to the original carries through dynamically to the copy.

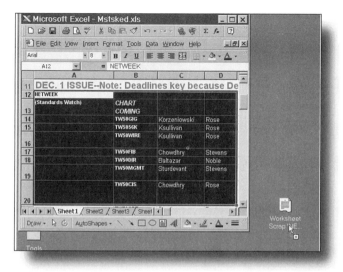

FIGURE 12.35
When we drag data from a tool to the Windows desktop, any of several tools might be the ultimate user of that data. Windows creates a "scrap" object for later use rather than assuming a
target program (as Works did).

What We've Learned

You should expect more from software than a basket of capabilities. You should
also expect working examples of practical results, presented in a form that makes
those examples readily adaptable to your work.

Software suites encourage you to choose the tool that fits the task, instead of making the task conform to the capabilities of the tool. Suites make it easy to use each
tool for what it does well and to combine the products of several tools into a single
compound document.

Integration in a suite designed and sold as one product is generally better than in
separate products. Separate software products can be designed to use common
interface mechanisms, letting them act as containers for each others' objects, but
there might be differences in how the different products respond to different
sources of even a single type of data.

Finally, for excellent reasons, a compound document sometimes contains its own
copies of data and sometimes preserves links to the source of that data for automatic updates. If you're making a historical record, don't outsmart yourself with
links that perform Orwellian automatic rewrites. Don't find yourself, as my fellow
PC columnist Stephen Manes puts it, "debugging your documents."

"**WYSIAYG**. . . Describes
a user interface under
which 'What You See Is
All You Get'. . . most
often used of editors,
word processors, and
document formatting
programs."

—ERIC S. RAYMOND (ED.),
The New Hacker's Dictionary
(3rd Ed.)

Word Processing, Plain and Fancy

ORD PROCESSING IS THE PC application that always crashes the party. No matter what you had in mind when you bought your PC, the odds are overwhelming that your machine will also wind up with the task of writing reports on your projects.

There's a great deal more to word processing than its obvious role as an electronic typewriter. Ease of correction is a benefit, to be sure; so is flexible choice of fonts and other attributes for your text. To enjoy these benefits fully, however, you have to avoid a few common errors in making the transition from typing to word processing.

We'll begin with a review of the most common mistakes that are made in using word processing's core capabilities, and then we'll look at some less well-known potentials.

Breaking Lines Is Bad to Do

Figure 13.1 shows a sample of text entered into a word processor—in this case, Microsoft Word. I entered this text exactly as I would with a typewriter: I used the Enter key at the end of each line to give me my line breaks, and I used a simple typewriter-style font called Courier New.

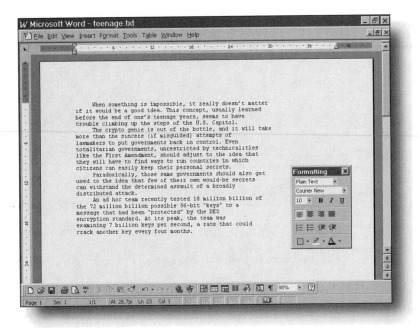

FIGURE 13.1
Although text on the screen may look just fine, it might be riddled with invisible obstacles to your later editing operations.

The Courier New font has two important characteristics. It uses the same amount of width on the typed line for every character in a given size, as a typewriter does. It is also a TrueType font, which means (as we discussed in Chapter 6) that it can readily be resized while still retaining its proper appearance.

Suppose I decide to use the resizing freedom I get from TrueType technology. I might, for example, increase the size of my text from 10 point (at 72 points to the inch) up to a more readable 14-point font in this same Courier New typeface.

Figure 13.2 shows the distressing result of enlarging my font. The *hard returns* that I placed at the ends of my lines are still there, but several of my original lines have become too wide to fit between the margins of my page. The word processor has wrapped the lines to fit, but the hard returns impose extra line breaks soon afterward, leaving me with many awkward line fragments.

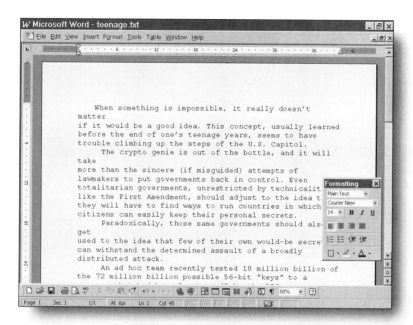

FIGURE 13.2
When text is resized, hard return line breaks are in awkward places.

Figure 13.3 shows the proper way to set up paragraphs of text with any PC word processor. Instead of putting fixed line breaks in my text as originally entered, I only press the Enter key to create a line break at the end of a paragraph. I have used the option in Word of making paragraph marks visible, as you can see in the figure.

The text of each paragraph has neatly wrapped itself to fit within the margins. I could even turn on automatic hyphenation to make the fit still better, but most readers find the "ragged right" text in Figure 13.3 easier to read unless the document is laid out in narrow columns.

If I enlarge my text when it has the proper paragraph formatting shown in Figure 13.3, I'll get the result in Figure 13.4. All of my line breaks move around as needed, with only paragraph breaks being preserved—exactly as I would want.

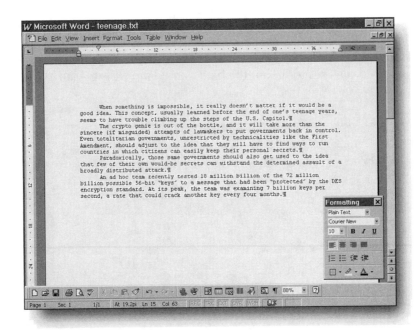

FIGURE 13.3
Visible paragraph breaks, revealed with an option available in most word processors, show the appropriate technique for entering text.

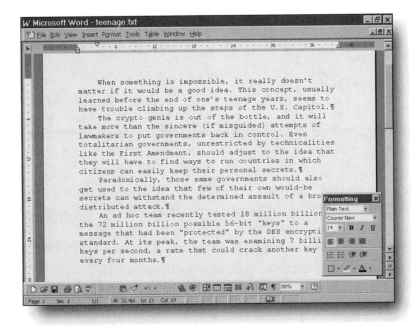

FIGURE 13.4
Properly entered text can be resized without other time-consuming adjustments.

Tables: Take Time Now to Save Time Later

The use of hard line returns is the first basic word processing error. The use of spaces to line up columns of text is the second common habit that makes life harder than it needs to be.

Figure 13.5 shows the beginning of a document that falls naturally into a format of several aligned columns. I've entered this text as if I were typing; I've used that familiar Courier New typeface, and I've simply lined up columns on successive lines by inserting spaces.

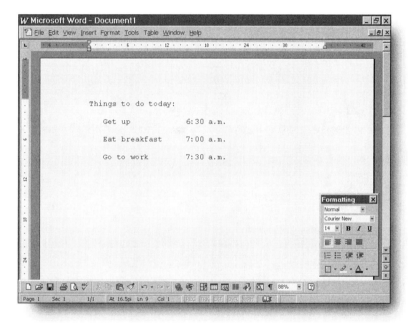

FIGURE 13.5
When typing a table, it's tempting just to line things up with spaces.

Figure 13.6 shows the first "uh-oh" that's likely to hit me when I pad my columns with spaces, typewriter style. I've just entered an item that's a good deal wider than the first three entries in the same column. Do I go back to the previous entries and add more spaces to move their second-column items farther to the right? Do I insert a line break in my long item?

Note that if I use a line break, I'll wind up with the second column's appointment time embedded in a sentence or phrase of the first column. I'll regret this if I'm ever searching for a location or a file by looking for a phrase that I remember using in a document, but that I wound up filling with a time of day mixed in, as far as a document search operation is concerned.

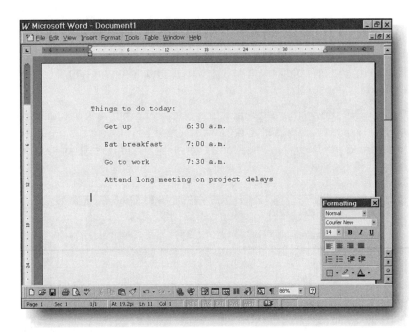

FIGURE 13.6
An extra-long item creates a dilemma: Adjust everything else or break the new item into several lines?

Figure 13.7 shows the second pitfall of using spaces for alignment. What if I change from a fixed-width ("monospace") typeface such as Courier New to more of a typeset look with a typeface such as Times New Roman? Apart from looking better, variable-width fonts (also called "proportionally spaced") fit more information onto a page at any given font size. You can see, however, that the letters' variable widths make it hard to align columns with spaces in a familiar manner.

My document layout gets somewhat better if I use tabs, rather than spaces, for column alignment. In Figure 13.8, I've used tabs and I've turned on the option of making tab characters visible. Most word processors permit this as an aid to spotting formatting problems.

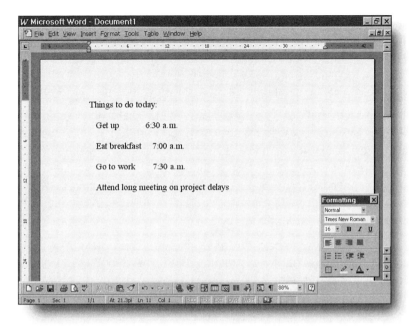

FIGURE 13.7
Proportionally spaced fonts defy simple alignment using spaces; you'll rarely make the result look right.

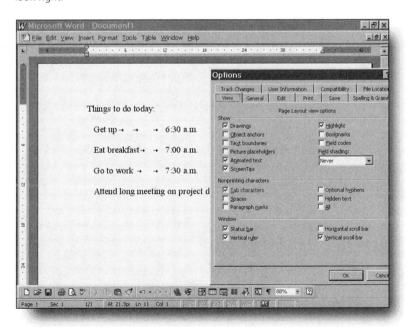

FIGURE 13.8
Tabs, rather than spaces, provide exact alignment—but still don't deal with extra-long items.

We can see that using tabs, with their default spacing, doesn't set us up to make later changes as smoothly as we'd like. If I later change the text in the first column of the first line of the table, making it longer by a word or two, I'll suddenly have extra tabs in that line. I'll have to edit these by hand, which means that I can't use a simple, automatic search-and-replace unless I follow it with a manual "layout patrol."

It might seem that I could solve my problem by changing the spacing of the tab settings for these paragraphs, arranging for them to have a single tab at the location of the second column instead of the multiple, closely spaced tabs that are the default arrangement. Don't forget, though, that I've already been surprised by one entry that needed to be longer than the others in its column. I might get an especially verbose item that's even longer than a full line. Custom tab settings won't help me deal with that situation.

Figure 13.9 shows the best way of laying out tables of text. It uses, not surprisingly, a table—a feature that far too many PC users never bother to learn, even if their word processor supports it with ease.

Word, for example, transforms text into tables, using any of several rules. In my example, I've gone back and taken out extra tabs so that there's only one tab between adjacent items, and I've checked the box that makes tabs the column separation points.

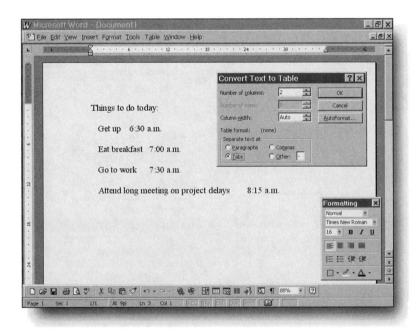

FIGURE 13.9
Converting text to a table solves several problems at once.

Figure 13.10 shows the first result of converting my multicolumn text to a table, and it's kind of ugly. This might not be the look, with those heavy dividing lines, that I really want for this situation.

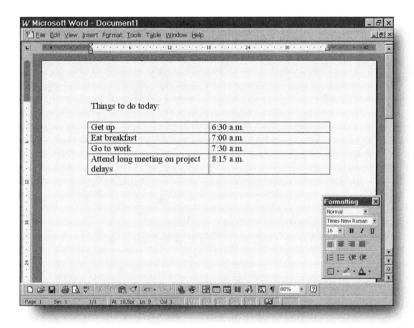

FIGURE 13.10
You might not like the default appearance of a table, with its clutter of dividing lines.

Figures 13.11 and 13.12 show Word's facility for "lightening up" my table by suppressing the borders, both within and around my text. In Figure 13.12, you can see that I've chosen to turn off all borders. I could have retained a box around the table as a whole while just getting rid of the internal dividers (horizontal, vertical, or both), or kept any other subset of my borders and dividers with any of several line styles.

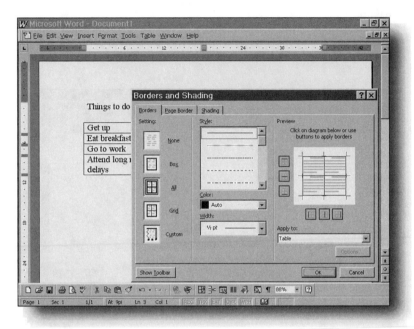

FIGURE 13.11
Most word processors with a table feature let you control both the outer borders around cells and the inner borders between cells.

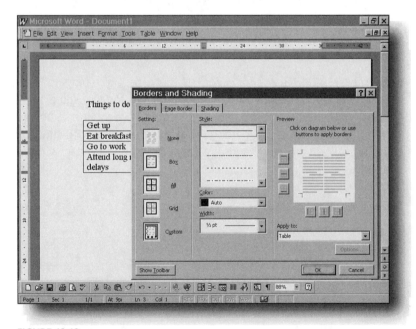

FIGURE 13.12
With a few clicks of the mouse, all borders can be removed.

Figure 13.13 shows the final result: The line breaks are where they should be, the abnormally long items wrap within the width of their columns, and everything that should be a single chunk of text (for purposes of later searching or replacing) is in its own neat package.

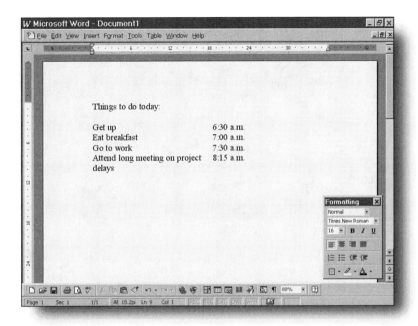

FIGURE 13.13
A borderless table handles long items, proportionally spaced fonts, and other formatting headaches.

Do You Get the Picture?

It would be overkill to dress up a simple to-do list with clip art, but let me use this opportunity to show a useful feature of Word's art library. If I wanted to add a clock to highlight the importance of time, for example, I might summon up the Microsoft Clip Gallery from Word's Insert menu. I'm talking about the same menu that we used in Chapter 12 to insert a spreadsheet-type object in a document.

Figure 13.14 shows the sinking-feeling sight of that huge clip art collection. Let's see, where would I look for clocks? Under Hardware? or Household? or where?

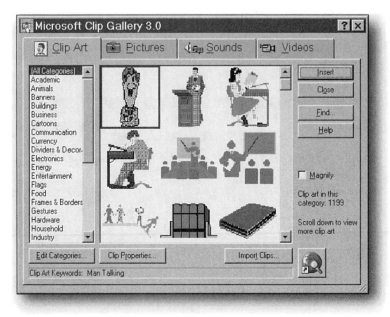

FIGURE 13.14
Clip art can be a cure that's worse than the disease if you're overwhelmed by choices and not sure where to look for what you want.

Figure 13.15 shows a better option than searching by hand through the clip art library. I've called up the library's own search utility and asked it to find all pictures that are tagged with the keyword "clock."

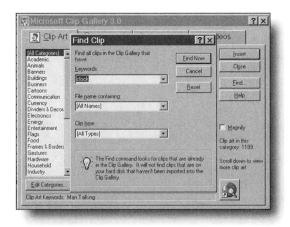

FIGURE 13.15
A searchable clip art library saves time.

Figure 13.16 shows the result of my search. The Clip Gallery packages all of its clocks in a new, temporary category containing the results from my search. This illustrates something that I can't say too often about using PCs: Their software is there to do the boring and time-consuming parts of a task.

Any time you find yourself thinking, "Gosh, this is going to take forever," the odds are good that you're overlooking a built-in tool or shortcut that's been put there to deal with that problem.

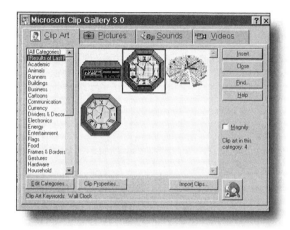

FIGURE 13.16
We get what we want by learning how to make the PC do the work.

Competition: Focus on Ease of Use

Microsoft Word, despite its widespread use, is not The Last Best Word Processor. In fact, many people loathe its complexity, which often buries a useful feature under several layers of opaquely named menus.

Microsoft puts a lot of effort into resolving usability problems; for example, they videotaped users to determine that "Options" was a much better name than "Preferences" for a menu of personal settings inside a piece of software.

Regardless of Microsoft's efforts to make Word be all things to all writers, there's plenty of room in this world for more than one word processing program. Let me show you some of the best.

Lotus Word Pro

Lotus Word Pro does a judicious job of bringing many features up from their obscure locations in Word to more accessible menus, with better onscreen support. Figure 13.17 shows Word Pro leading the user through construction of a *drop capital* to open a new paragraph.

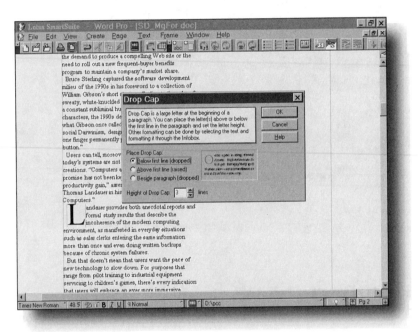

FIGURE 13.17
Lotus Word Pro makes many advanced features more accessible than they are in Microsoft Word.

When Word Pro creates a drop capital, it's actually creating a specialized frame within a document. What makes for good usability, however, is the way that Word Pro makes the feature available in terms of what it does rather than how it does it.

I don't have to figure out that frames are the way to do a drop cap and then learn the special case of using a frame for this purpose. I just go to Word Pro's top-level **Create** menu and pick **Drop Cap**.

If I later go back to make any changes, I'll see Word Pro's frame control options (see Figure 13.18). It's an axiom, though, that I can learn to use any feature—no matter how complex—if my starting point is a working example of how that feature does something useful.

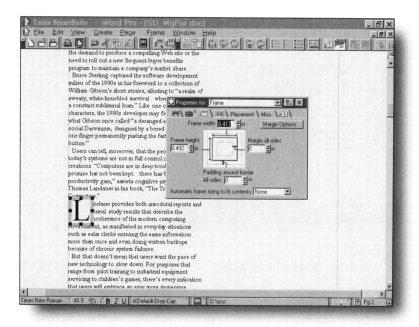

FIGURE 13.18
Word Pro makes things available based on what they *do*, but still lets me work with things based on what they *are*. It doesn't "dumb down."

Before I move on to other word processing products, let me note that Lotus has gone to great lengths to make the Internet a part of the productivity toolkit in their latest SmartSuite package (which includes Word Pro). Figure 13.19, for example, shows the integral Internet-searching that Apple Computer trumpeted as a forthcoming novelty in their next-generation Macintosh computers, months after it was already available on PCs.

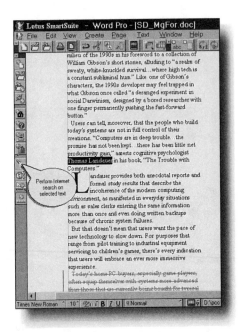

FIGURE 13.19
Internet integration highlights Lotus Development's latest versions of its SmartSuite applications.

In Chapter 11, I showed you some of the flexibility that you get from a program such as Microsoft Word in the area of viewing your work in progress. Many users might find appeal in Word Pro's more elaborate document views, which combine efficient draft-text displays with formatted views of overall document appearance, as shown in Figure 13.20.

Adobe FrameMaker

I mentioned Word Pro's use of frames to hold elements such as drop capitals within a page. Some word processing programs adopt the idea of frames to an even greater degree, making it easy to achieve such effects as precise positioning of graphics or other special elements on the page.

Page composition aids were once the domain of specialized desktop publishing products, but now find their way into most high-end word processors for the PC. Of special interest, however, is a product called FrameMaker, rare in its breadth of support for many types of computers, including the Windows PC.

My engineer wife is emphatic in declaring that FrameMaker is the best, most capable word processor there is. FrameMaker keeps my wife happy by making its advanced features easy to locate and figure out, as shown in Figure 13.21.

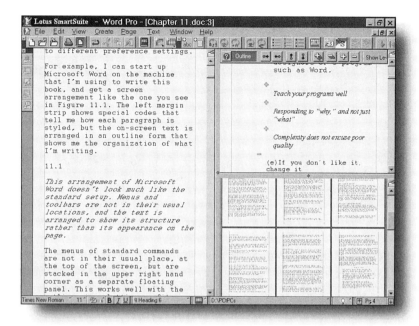

FIGURE 13.20
Task-oriented views highlight Lotus Word Pro.

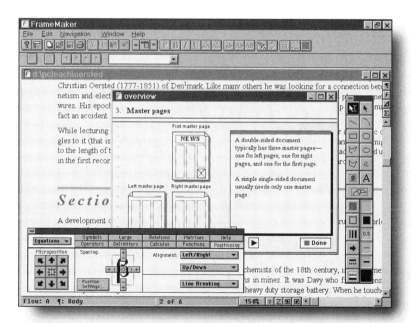

FIGURE 13.21
FrameMaker offers power, precision, and ease of use in creating complex documents on more than one type of computer.

Inspiration: A Different Way of Working with Ideas

An important word processing feature is the capability to work with outline views, which turn your work into a multilevel structure. Outline editing tools let you "promote" and "demote" material to different levels, and let you move sections or subsections to reorder your ideas.

Most word processors provide an outline view of some kind. I probably sound like a grade school teacher when I tell you that it's worth some effort to learn your word processor's particular conventions for viewing and manipulating text in outline form. I do practice what I preach, though—most of this book was written in Word's outline view.

At one time, I did almost all of my work (not just word processing) in an early PC product called Framework that put everything into an outline. Like Microsoft Works (which we examined in Chapter 12), Framework had windows for documents, spreadsheets, databases, and communications, but it had an overall organizational tool of nested frames to hold those various elements in a single outline-structured file.

I would start a new file each week, accumulating my electronic mail, my assignment memos, my draft work products, and my final output, all in one place.

Sadly, Framework never made the transition to the larger memory capacity of modern PCs, and I found it too limiting to squeeze everything into the 64KB chunks of its individual frames. The product has since been spun off to new owners, though, who might be able to bring its good ideas forward onto the modern PC platform.

In the meantime, another product does something at least as interesting with the basic idea of outlines. Figure 13.22 shows an opening screen from a project built with Inspiration, from Inspiration Software. At first, this might not seem very innovative—it looks like any other hierarchical "idea processor," as some outline-oriented tools call themselves.

Figure 13.23 shows Inspiration's more startling side—it not only views a hierarchy of ideas as a text-based outline but also as a striking diagram with a number of powerful automatic aids for turning diagrams into effective discussion-leading tools. Various levels of detail can be hidden and revealed in the diagram view, just as in the text view.

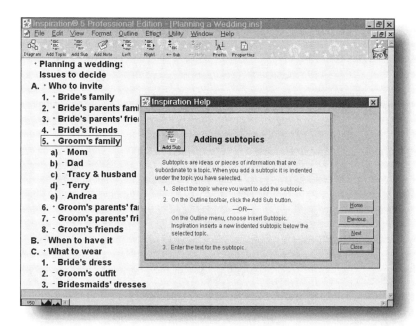

FIGURE 13.22
An outline processor emphasizes ease of looking at hierarchies of ideas.

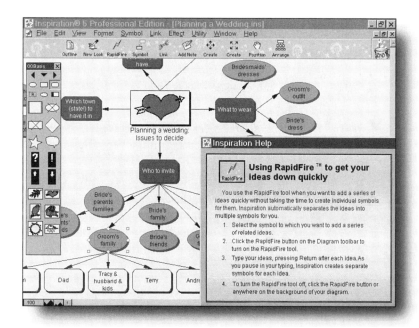

FIGURE 13.23
Inspiration goes beyond text-oriented outlines by integrating diagrams as alternate views.

Figures 13.24 through 13.26 show a major advantage of using a product such as Inspiration instead of a general-purpose diagramming tool. In Figure 13.24, a discussion has begun with the central topic of product positioning. The definition of the target customer has been raised as an element of this discussion.

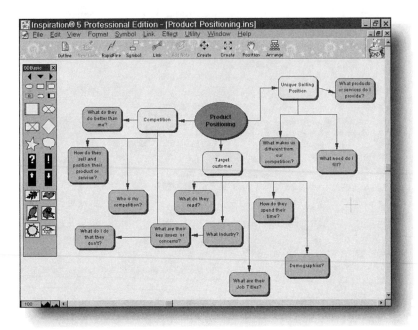

FIGURE 13.24

This formal diagram, with automatically drawn, squared-off connections, keeps those connections intact even when objects are moved to new positions.

At some point in the discussion, it's easy to imagine someone saying, "We've got this all inside out. If we define our target customer properly, we won't need to talk about product positioning. The definition of the target customer is the same thing as the positioning of the product. It's better to talk about the customer, though, because it keeps us from looking for excuses to keep making what we already know how to make."

Unlike an ordinary diagramming tool, Inspiration is designed for the ripples and dips that come up in a discussion of ideas, with a **Change Main Idea** menu command that you're not likely to find in a general-purpose diagram product. In Figure 13.25, I've selected `Target Customer` and refocused the discussion on that node in my diagram.

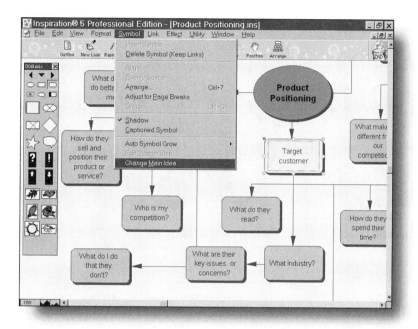

FIGURE 13.25
Unlike a general-purpose diagramming tool, Inspiration incorporates high-level operations such as changing the focus of a discussion.

In Figure 13.26, I've spent less than a minute on other adjustments to my diagram, such as reversing the direction of the arrow that links `Target Customer` to `Product Positioning`. My discussion now has a visual aid to match its new direction. You can imagine how effective this would be if a skilled user of the software is leading a group discussion with Inspiration and a video projector (of the kind we discussed in Chapter 6).

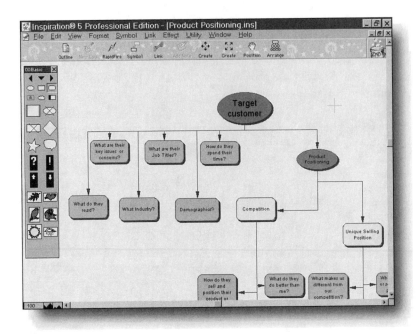

FIGURE 13.26
A menu command and a few small adjustments give a whole new view of what's going on.

Back to Embedded Codes: Living with HTML

Before we move on from words to numbers, I have to note an unfortunate backward movement in document authoring. Early word processors worked with embedded codes for their formatting instructions, such as their creation of lists or their use of embedded images.

From the early 1980s on, propelled by the example of the Macintosh, PC word processing software moved toward the goal of editing a document as it would appear to its reader. Some users, preferring the power and flexibility of command-driven products (especially for large and complex tasks), derisively called the Macintosh approach What You See Is *All* You Get (WYSIAYG). This was a counterpunch against the more common acronym, WYSIWYG (What You See Is What You Get), coined to describe the Mac-inspired wave of visually interactive software.

With the growing importance of the Internet as a channel for publication, many PC users are going back to editing document format codes; specifically, the coded "tags" of Hypertext Markup Language (HTML), which we'll discuss in Chapter 17.

It is possible to do normal, visual editing of your document in a product such as Word or Word Pro and then to save the result as HTML directly from the normal **Save As** menu option. Many people don't find the result satisfactory, because automatic HTML generation can be overly conservative and can yield HTML files that are hard to maintain with the usual tools.

If publishing to the Internet and the Web is one of your goals, you'll probably want to look at an HTML-oriented editor such as HomeSite from Allaire (see Figure 13.27).

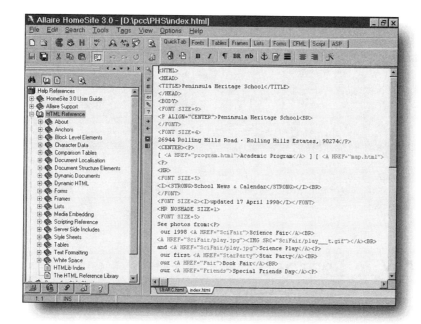

FIGURE 13.27
Allaire's HomeSite editor assists in composition of World Wide Web pages using Hypertext Markup Language (HTML).

HomeSite uses distinctive colors to highlight the elements of an HTML file, as does the Kedit editor that I've used in several chapters of this book and as do Internet-oriented design tools such as Microsoft's Visual InterDev.

HomeSite is less programmer-oriented, though, than many Web-oriented tools, providing built-in help for composing HTML and facilities for previewing the appearance of your Web page (see Figure 13.28).

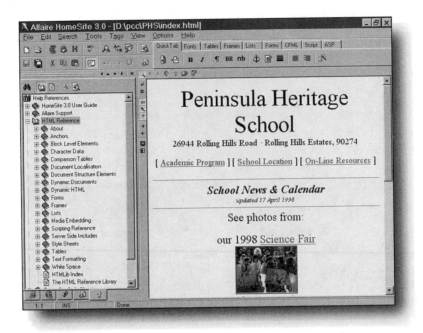

FIGURE 13.28
HomeSite's integrated HTML preview lets you "debug your document" before you release it as a Web page.

What We've Learned

People get more benefit from word processing software when they take the time up front to enter text in ways that preserve flexibility later on. Proper formatting of paragraphs makes it easier to resize fonts or to search and replace key phrases.

When you think in terms of paragraphs rather than lines, the logical structure of your text can take priority. The software can do the mere grunt work of layout.

Ease of understanding advanced word processing features makes all the difference in getting any benefit from those features. Genuine differences in the approach to product usability are reflected in competing tools such as Word, Word Pro, FrameMaker, and others.

At a time when many products are focusing on Windows, FrameMaker leaves your options open for working with other users with many different types of computers.

Your work with words might benefit from the brainstorming aids of a product such as Inspiration. You might also need to think about the special needs of publishing to the Web as opposed to targeting paper as the medium for delivering your work. A Web-oriented editor such as HomeSite might deserve a place on your list of candidates.

*"The PC soon blossomed
as the Uzi of creative
corporate accounting.
The What-If moved to
Why-Not, indicting the
spreadsheet as the chief
culprit in the 1980s
S&L scandal."*

—STAN KELLY-BOOTLE, 1995

By the Numbers:
Spreadsheets and Other Math Tools

EW THINGS ARE MORE MISUNDERSTOOD than the working relationship between computers and math. Many people know that PCs can do arithmetic, using popular tools such as spreadsheets, but they're fuzzy on the details of how to make the most of the PC's speed and consistency.

Few people realize that PCs can go beyond arithmetic to work with algebra, calculus, and other higher forms of mathematics. PC software can do operations on symbols in a very advanced form of a word processor's search-and-replace command. An answer in the form of an equation leads to much more complete understanding, more quickly, than a spreadsheet's numeric answers.

Even fewer people know that PCs can work with uncertain numbers, producing estimates of risk and giving an objective basis for best-case and worst-case projections. In addition to statistics tools, which generally require a good deal of knowledge to use, risk-analysis tools can automate repetitive sampling or provide built-in expert guidance in choosing from various forecasting techniques.

Spreadsheets: Propelling the PC Invasion

The basic idea of the computer spreadsheet propelled the desktop computer onto its first wave of corporate desktops. People bought a spreadsheet software package and something to run it. The PC was just the platform for this incredibly important planning and analysis tool.

Figure 14.1 shows the beginning of setting up a basic spreadsheet—the same one, in fact, that I used as an example in Chapter 12. We have raw data on income and expense, by month, for a quarterly period; we want to produce the corresponding subtotals and grand totals.

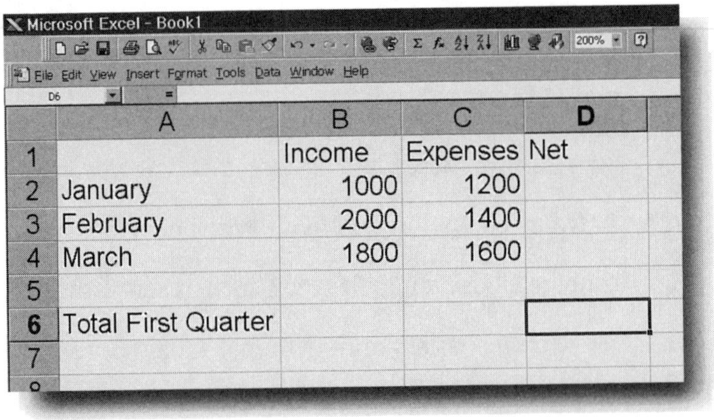

FIGURE 14.1
A spreadsheet begins with facts, or at least with estimates.

The first key idea of the spreadsheet is the notion of the formula. In Figure 14.2, I entered a formula in the cell where I want to display January's net income. I want the value in Column D, Row 2, to be calculated by subtracting the value in C2 from the value in B2.

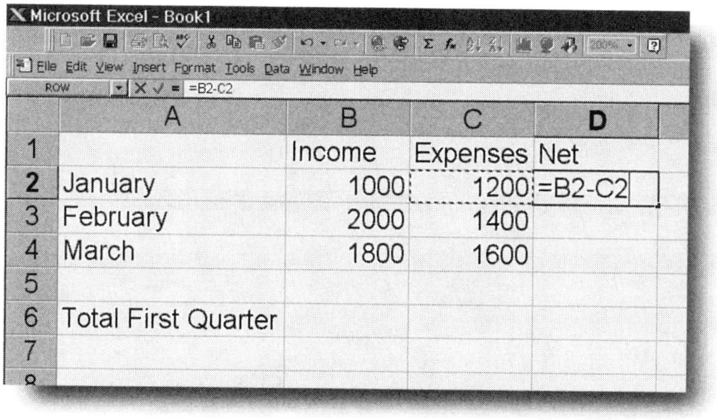

FIGURE 14.2
Formulas capture relationships between facts and conclusions.

Completing the formula with the Enter key, I now see the value rather than the formula in the D2 position. How do I know that this is a calculated result, not a fixed value entered from the keyboard? I can see the formula in the entry/editing field near the top of the screen (see Figure 14.3).

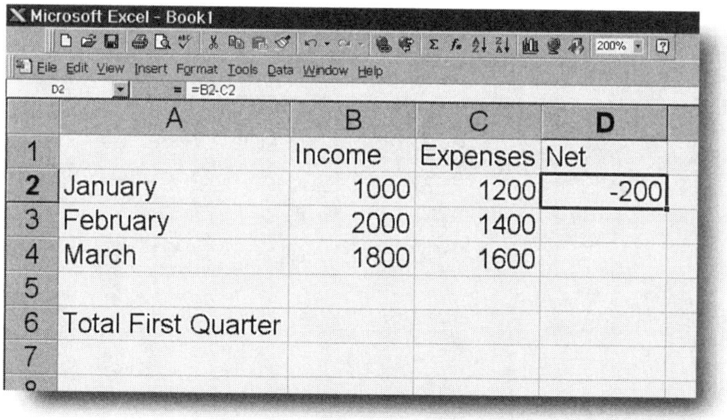

FIGURE 14.3
A formula result appears like any other number, but we can still see the formula near the top of the screen.

Do I now need to enter matching formulas in every other row of the column? That would be time-consuming and error-prone. Remember what I said in Chapter 13: Whenever you find yourself thinking that a task seems repetitive, there's probably a way to make your PC do it for you.

In Figure 14.4, I used the regular Copy command that's found in most Windows software to copy cell D2 to the Clipboard. Selecting the entire group of rows where I want my monthly net values, I paste the D2 formula to all these rows at once (see Figure 14.5).

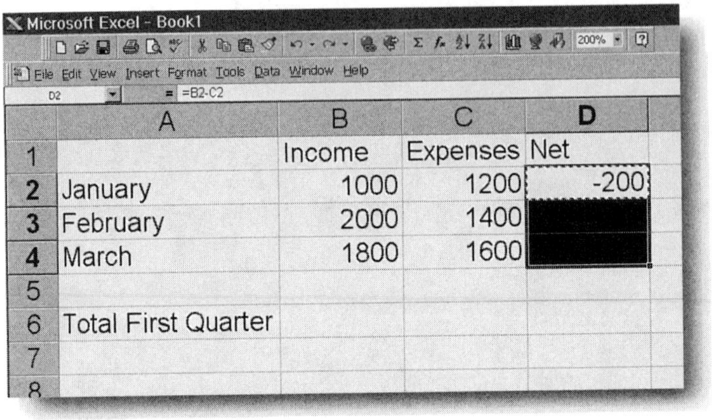

FIGURE 14.4
Copying a formula prepares us to apply the same calculation to many rows.

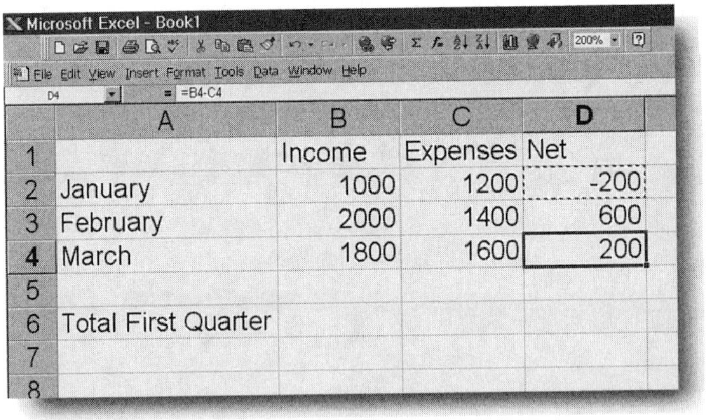

FIGURE 14.5
Relative formulas automatically adjust themselves to work with cells in the same relative position.

Note that in Row 4, for example, the copied formula automatically adjusts itself to refer to the cells from columns B and C in that row. This is called *relative* addressing of cells. When a formula is copied to another place, a spreadsheet normally assumes that any references to other cells should be copied relative to the new location. What really got copied, in this case, was the equivalent of "subtract the first leftward value from the value to the left of it."

In Figure 14.6, I've begun to add my columns to produce monthly subtotals. I could enter =B2+B3+B4, but this would be tedious if I had dozens or hundreds of rows to add up. Of course, there's an easier way: in this case, a SUM function.

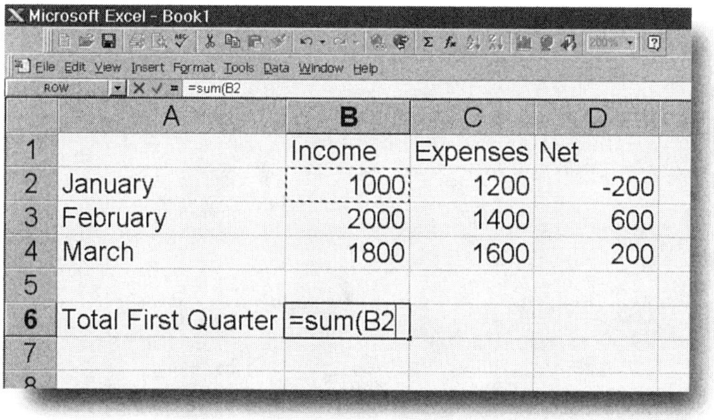

FIGURE 14.6
SUM is a built-in function, one of a huge vocabulary.

SUM is one of the huge vocabulary of built-in functions that makes a spreadsheet useful for business, engineering, science, and many other tasks.

Like many functions, SUM operates on a *range*; that is, a group of other cells—almost always a rectangular group. In Figure 14.7, I select the range of cells to be summed. You can generally choose a range by typing in the corner locations, or you can use the mouse or keyboard to select a group of cells visually.

Some spreadsheets let you give names to ranges, so that a formula reads something like =SUM(MonthlyDetails). This is much easier to read, reducing the chance of error.

In Figure 14.8, I've already copied the column-total formula to the other columns. I'm getting ready to add a row for overhead estimates, which I plan to calculate as a percentage of both my income and my expense activities. I've entered a formula in column B and a trial overhead percentage in column A. Everything looks fine.

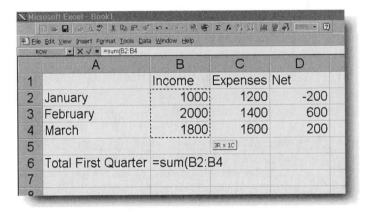

FIGURE 14.7
Visual selection of cell groups makes it easy to build spreadsheet formulas that operate on any number of data items.

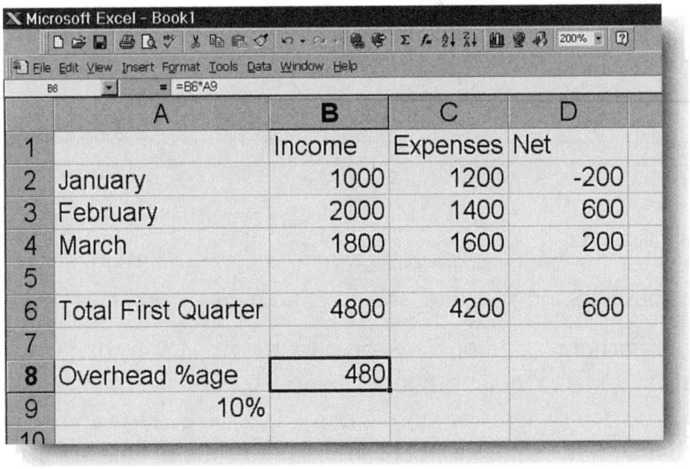

FIGURE 14.8
We're ready to apply a percentage to several adjacent entries.

In Figure 14.9, though, things are anything but fine. I've copied my formula from column B to the other two columns, but I'm not seeing my percentages across the board. Columns C and D are showing me a value of zero. What happened?

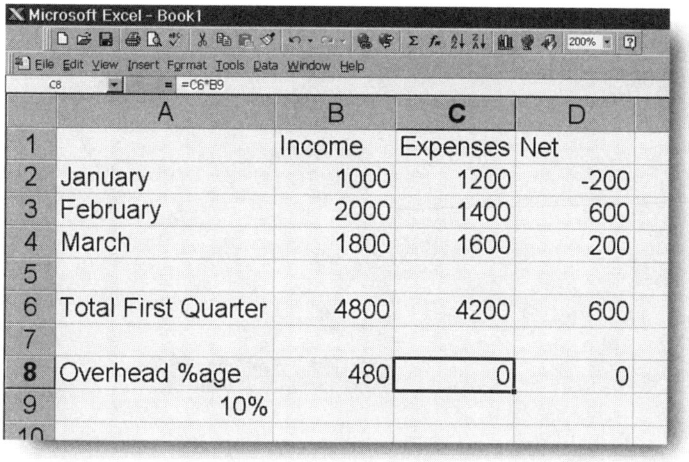

	A	B	C	D
1		Income	Expenses	Net
2	January	1000	1200	-200
3	February	2000	1400	600
4	March	1800	1600	200
5				
6	Total First Quarter	4800	4200	600
7				
8	Overhead %age	480	0	0
9	10%			

FIGURE 14.9
Relative formulas don't work correctly when several cells need to refer to a single cell rather than to a cell that's always in the same relative position.

Remember, normal formula copying is a relative operation. Columns C and D are looking in columns B and C, respectively, for their percentages. Those cells are empty and therefore act like zeros in any calculations.

What I needed to do was use a special code in my formula in column B to say that the overhead percentage would always be found in column A. I do this, as shown in Figure 14.10, by putting a $ symbol in the formula, thus: `=B6*$A9`.

The $ preceding the `A` says that the formula, when copied, should adjust the column of the first term (the base figure on which I'm calculating the overhead) but should continue to refer to column A for the overhead percentage. Figure 14.11 shows that this worked exactly as desired. I can change the overhead percentage in its one entered location and have that change reflected across all columns and in all subsequent formulas (such as the Operating Net row that I added at the bottom of the sheet).

It's hard to draw a definite line between "numbers products" and "data products," though I've tried to do that in separating Chapters 14 and 15. Spreadsheets span both worlds, with most offering simple database facilities such as sorting their rows by various combinations of columns (see Figure 14.12).

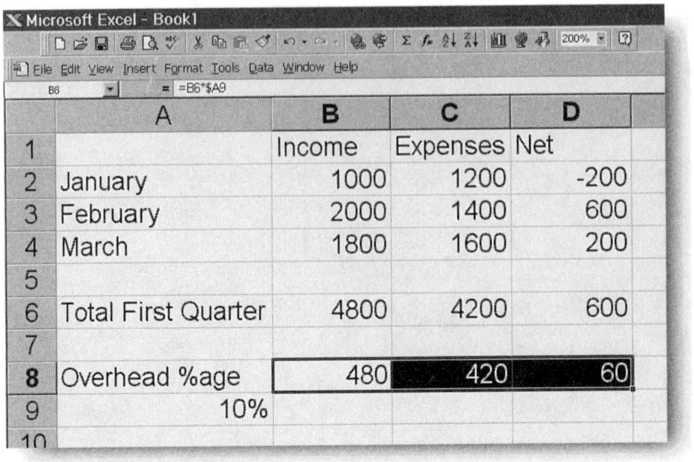

	A	B	C	D
1		Income	Expenses	Net
2	January	1000	1200	-200
3	February	2000	1400	600
4	March	1800	1600	200
5				
6	Total First Quarter	4800	4200	600
7				
8	Overhead %age	480	420	60
9	10%			

FIGURE 14.10
Overriding the normal, relative mode, we can make several cells all look at the same column so that we can now adjust a percentage in just one place.

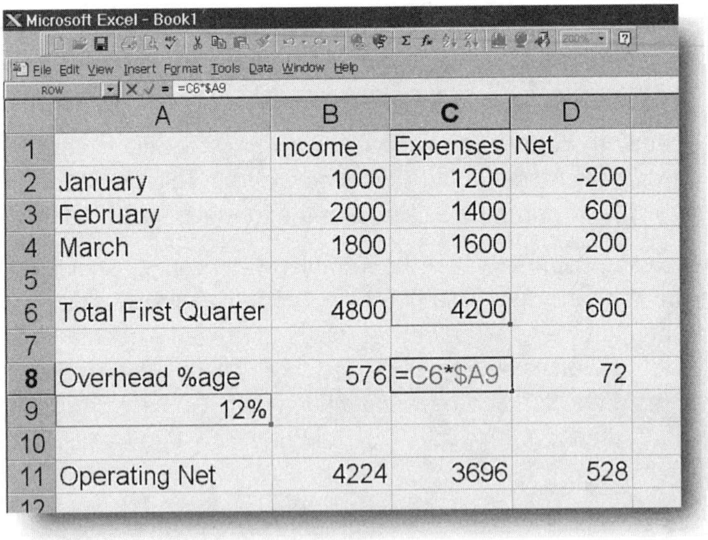

	A	B	C	D
1		Income	Expenses	Net
2	January	1000	1200	-200
3	February	2000	1400	600
4	March	1800	1600	200
5				
6	Total First Quarter	4800	4200	600
7				
8	Overhead %age	576	=C6*$A9	72
9	12%			
10				
11	Operating Net	4224	3696	528

FIGURE 14.11
With care in setting up our formulas, we've built an efficient planning and reporting tool.

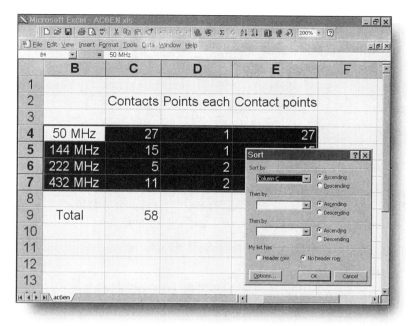

FIGURE 14.12
Able to perform simple list management operations, a spreadsheet overlaps the features of a basic database tool.

When sorting rows, it's important to avoid disturbing the logic of formulas that depend on those rows. Note that in Figure 14.13, the column totals are still correct. In a complex spreadsheet, I recommend the use of borders and other visual elements to remind you of logical groups of cells that should stay in the same location even if they're sorted into a different sequence.

In addition to having a foothold in the world of databases, spreadsheets also encroach on the turf of presentation software with their often elaborate options for creating analytic charts. In Figure 14.14, I've summoned up a pie-chart tool that's leading me through the process of choosing ranges of cells to serve as the data and the labels for my "slices."

Figure 14.15 shows the chart in place on my spreadsheet page. Note that one of my four category labels is not visible in the legend. Manual inspection and editing is a final step in preparing a spreadsheet as in releasing any other document.

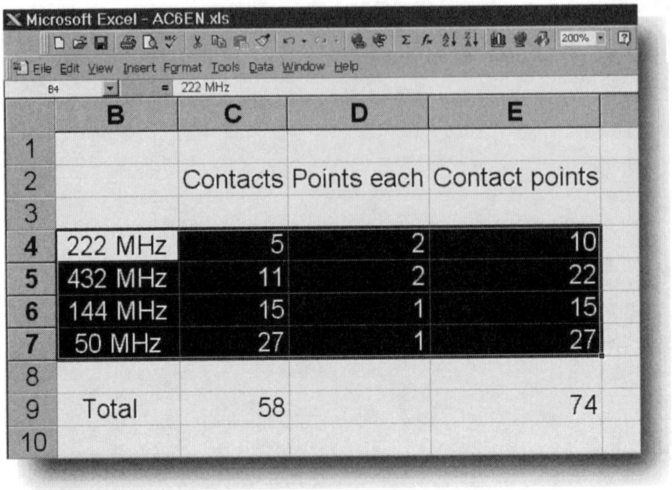

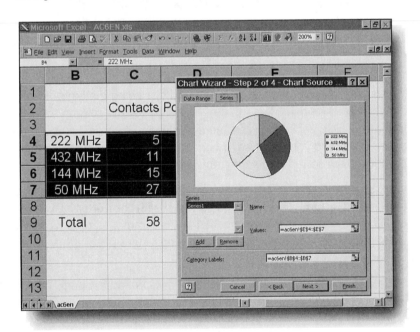

FIGURE 14.13
Careful selection of cell groups keeps formula relationships intact, even after operations such as sorting.

FIGURE 14.14
Charts add insight to numbers.

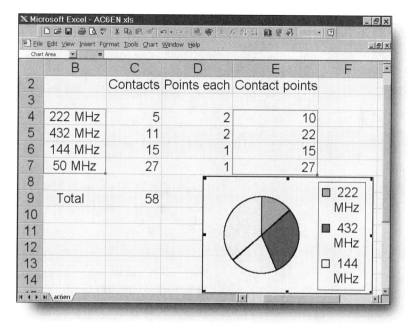

FIGURE 14.15
Compare the final chart against its preview, and adjust as needed to make all desired elements visible.

In Figure 14.16, I show an option for handling later editing of your data. Suppose I determined that a recording error had placed some events in the wrong category. I could go back and change the two values, subtracting from one and adding to another, but this loses all record of what happened. If someone later compares raw data sheets against my spreadsheet, they might think that the error was mine.

To preserve an "audit trail," I've given the error its own labeled cell. I've edited the values in C5 and C6 to make them into formulas that both refer to the single error entry.

For Figure 14.16, I've also enabled the option of viewing formulas rather than their values. You might do this as part of a final audit on this spreadsheet. The repetitive structure of most spreadsheet formulas usually makes an error jump out quickly from this view.

Note also that the pie chart has changed its appearance to reflect the changes in my numbers. This linkage of all related elements is what makes spreadsheets such popular and productive tools.

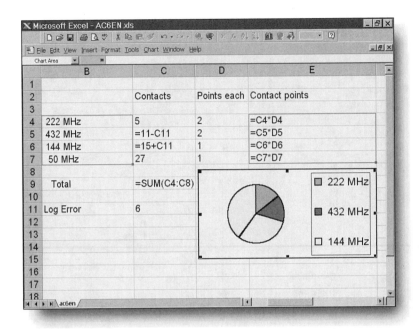

FIGURE 14.16
Use a spreadsheet to create an audit trail, recording changes as formulas with labeled entries instead of burying valuable information in uninformative summaries.

Don't Kid Yourself: You Aren't Suddenly Smarter

Before I show you some variations on the spreadsheet theme and several other kinds of "MBA-ware," I want to talk about a topic that had a lot to do with my decision to write this book.

When I was looking into the face of a twelve-week schedule to produce more than 150,000 words, I told myself that I'd better have something pretty important to tell you that you might not hear from anyone else. Then I remembered a research paper that crossed my desk several years ago. It was an academic paper, with an academic title: "Computer-Assisted Decision Making: Performance, Beliefs, and the Illusion of Control" (by Jeffrey Kottemann, Fred Davis, and William Remus).

Researchers gave the same business-planning task to 26 test subjects, all of them MBA student volunteers. The students each took part in a production-planning simulation that covered several periods of time. All the students were interacting with software to receive instructions, see simulation data, and enter their decisions. All the students believed that they were all doing the same task with the same tools.

Unknown to the students, only some of them had an extra capability on their simulation screens of entering alternative forecasts and estimating the effects of those different situations. This is often known, informally, as a "what-if" capability; it's one of the main things people do with spreadsheets.

The group that had the what-if feature did not do measurably better than the group that did not have that aid from the computer. The what-if group did spend more time, which is a concern. Even this productivity issue, though, is secondary.

Here is the most important finding of the "Illusion" paper and a major reason for my deciding to write this book. The what-if group *believed* that they were doing a better job.

The students in the group with the more elaborate software were more likely than the other group to agree with statements such as, "I find that I can predict actual demand very accurately." They were more likely than the other group to estimate their performance as being better than that of other participants, even though they believed that all participants in the study were using identical software.

I find it troubling that people would take longer to perform a task and would do it no better than they did before, while still forming a belief that they're suddenly performing better than other decision-makers. I have to wonder how many business planners are gazing into their electronic navels, so to speak, instead of using the same time to go out and talk with customers and walk their own factory floors to get a better handle on the real facts.

Before I saw the paper by Kottemann et al., I had already seen highly paid managers spending ridiculous amounts of time fiddling with spreadsheets. I had seen people investigating alternatives that were separated by tiny differences in assumptions—differences that were smaller than the errors in historical data, let alone smaller than the uncertainties of their forecasts.

I had seen far too many cases of people "backing into" a decision to do something, based on adjusting their assumptions until the outcome fell into an acceptable range. I heard people justify their actions by saying that the final numbers were within the likely range. They generally ignored the fact that all their numbers were winding up at the optimistic end of the range. People like me who raised statistical objections to this approach were dismissed as splitting hairs.

Based on what I've seen and what others have reported, I've made it one of my missions to make people aware of their own ability to fool themselves with their PCs. It's my practice to show, whenever I can, the relatively unknown types of software that actually *can* help people make better decisions by modeling real life's uncertainties.

Making Assumptions Explicit: Crystal Ball

Because many people already have spreadsheets, it's relatively easy to get them to try a spreadsheet add-on product such as Decisioneering's Crystal Ball.

Figure 14.17 shows the essential idea of Crystal Ball. Instead of treating numbers as simple values, Crystal Ball lets you treat a number as a range of values with some kind of probability distribution.

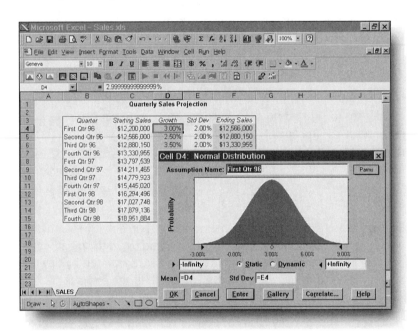

FIGURE 14.17
Spreadsheets, in many cases, work with assumptions and estimates. A product such as Decisioneering's Crystal Ball makes explicit the uncertainties of numbers.

The classic "bell curve" in Figure 14.17 is a familiar way of representing uncertainty, but many other types of distribution are a better fit with different real-world situations. For example, a tossed coin's "average" outcome might be landing on its edge, but that doesn't happen very often. Our tax planning might depend on our estimated chances of a Republican or a Democratic majority in Congress after the next election. We need to be able to model events with "lumpy" or uneven likelihoods.

Figure 14.18 shows a gallery of available probability curves that we can plug into any cell in a Crystal Ball model, including the Custom distribution (which opens up a drawing pad where we can lay out any desired probability profile).

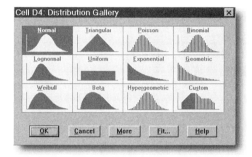

FIGURE 14.18
Different probability curves capture what we know, or suspect, about the extreme behaviors a number might show in real life.

After we've chosen our probability model, we turn it on and let it run. A simulation engine takes over, sampling values from the possible ranges based on our probabilities, and builds a distribution of outcomes as shown in Figure 14.19.

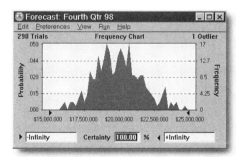

FIGURE 14.19
Initially, a simulation does not look like a classical probability prediction; there is no smooth, bell-shaped curve.

Initially, the outcomes from a simulation are somewhat "spiky," just as a tossed coin might initially come up heads several times in a row before the overall 50/50 behavior becomes apparent. Between Figure 14.19 and Figure 14.20, you can see the outcomes curve smoothing toward a final bell-like shape.

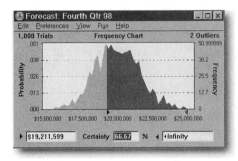

FIGURE 14.20
The final outcome is a smoother shape overall, and quite good enough to answer important planning questions such as the 2-to-1 odds point on project return.

More useful than the shape of the curve, though, is Crystal Ball's capability to answer specific planning questions. In Figure 14.20, I've typed the value **66.67**% into the window at the bottom center of the forecast view: the curve has automatically shaded itself to show me the point of 2-to-1 odds.

Armed with this forecast, I can go to my management and say, "We estimate a 2-to-1 chance of better than $19.2 million in first-year sales and less than a 1 percent chance of coming in below $15 million." Any discussion is likely to focus on areas of uncertainty, with broadening or narrowing or shifting of entire ranges of assumptions, rather than tiny fiddling adjustments that ignore the overall picture of risk and reward.

Forecasting: Beyond the Simple Trend

Crystal Ball uses probability, but there's another well-developed body of knowledge for predicting future events: *time-series forecasting*. There are proven techniques for modeling seasonal cycles, growth trends, and other behaviors that vitally affect our plans.

Many spreadsheets can perform the basic forecasting calculation called *linear regression* to determine the straight line that comes closest to fitting a collection of points on a graph. Straight-line fits, like spreadsheets, are notoriously easy to abuse (even if by accident), especially when we're working with small sets of data.

Forecasts that will influence major plans should have the benefit of a tool such as Business Forecast Systems' Forecast Pro (see Figure 14.21).

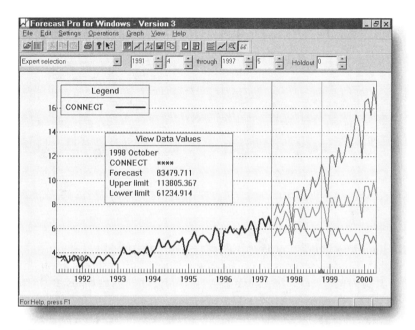

FIGURE 14.21
Forecast Pro models time-series forecasts with risk analysis, using proven methods for projecting seasonal variation and other common phenomena.

Unlike some statistics products, which require a fair amount of expertise to apply, Forecast Pro includes a built-in analyzer that looks for certain patterns in data and recommends methods based on experts' rules of thumb. The forecast algorithms can then generate likely, optimistic, and pessimistic scenarios, as in Figure 14.21.

Scheduling and Task Planning

Another area plagued by uncertainty is any kind of project schedule. Many tasks link schedules and budgets, as when assigning people to a project and estimating the cost of their time. A spreadsheet like the one in Figure 14.22 might seem a logical starting point.

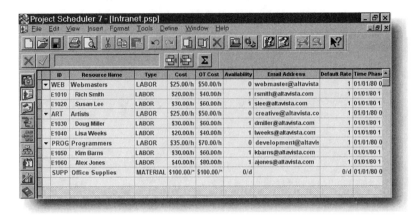

FIGURE 14.22
What looks like a spreadsheet just captures one view of a project's key characteristics—in this case, its personnel.

On the other hand, a project is also a collection of tasks to be performed, as well as a collection of resources to be assigned. Figure 14.23 shows another way of breaking down the same project, with its tasks and their schedules as the focus.

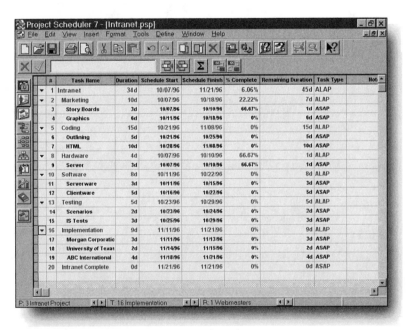

FIGURE 14.23
A project is also its list of tasks—but more than that, because some tasks depend on the completion of other tasks.

The problem with Figure 14.23 is that we can't see what depends on what else. We can't tell what has to be done before another task can begin, and we can't see which tasks have "slack" time and can be given low priority.

We might decide to use a tool such as Inspiration, which we saw in Chapter 13, to visualize relationships on a diagram. Another diagram view, this time in Project Scheduler, appears in Figure 14.24.

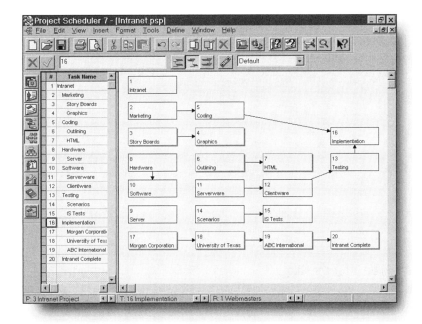

FIGURE 14.24
Links between tasks are illuminating but don't show needed information about the *time* the tasks take to complete.

What we really want, though, is one piece of software that ties together all the ideas that go into planning a project. We want to list the available resources, assign those resources to tasks, model tasks' dependencies on each other—and show how the whole thing looks in terms of time, as shown in Figure 14.25.

Figures 14.22 through 14.25 all represent different views from a single piece of software, Scitor Project Scheduler. Like Crystal Ball, Project Scheduler is one of those products that I make a point of showing to people when I want them to understand how PCs should help us work smarter.

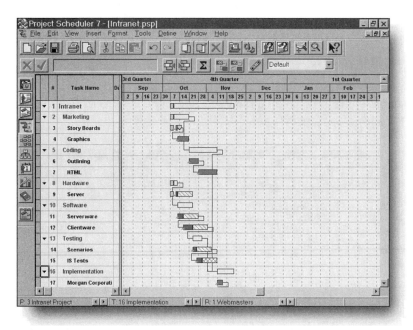

FIGURE 14.25

A project management package such as Scitor Project Scheduler pulls together many different views of a project and its development over time.

Being built for the task of modeling work across time, Project Scheduler incorporates such concepts as different work calendars—it "knows" about weekends and holidays. The option of adding overtime to a project would be a laborious exercise if you tried to do it with a general-purpose spreadsheet, but with Project Scheduler it is literally a menu choice (see Figure 14.26).

Perhaps most important of all in a project-scheduling tool is its capability to tell you when late task completion is a problem. In Figure 14.27, the task of setting up a "server" computer is scheduled to take five days. Cross-hatching at the end of the bar on the schedule, with the word **No** under that bar, shows that this not a "critical" task—there is free time for late completion without affecting other activities.

In Figure 14.28, I've stretched the completion time of this task out to 30 days— literally stretched it, in the sense of dragging the mouse across the screen. The **No** has turned into a **Yes**, showing that this task has suddenly become a factor in the overall completion date for the project. The tasks higher up on the chart, previously labeled **Yes**, now show a **No** and indicate a new "slack time" at the ends of their bars on the schedule.

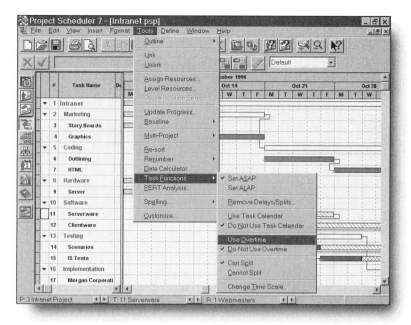

FIGURE 14.26
Knowledge, such as the nature of regular and overtime calendars, is part of the Project Scheduler toolkit.

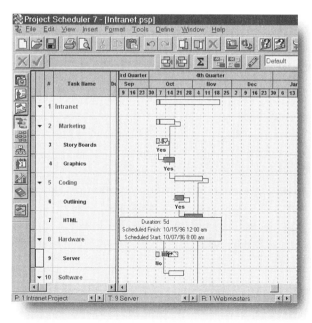

FIGURE 14.27
Project Scheduler gives vital insight into which tasks have room for delay without affecting the overall completion date.

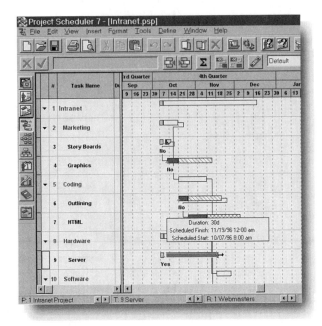

FIGURE 14.28
Interactive adjustment of task completion dates, with detection of new "critical" tasks, makes Project Scheduler a tool for determining which uncertainties can't be tolerated.

Suppose that someone asks me, "How late can I be before it becomes a problem?" I can simply grab the end of the taskbar on the screen and drag to the right until the **No** becomes a **Yes** and the bar turns red, and then read the corresponding completion date. We can then begin to talk about shifting resources, changing work schedules, and juggling all of the elements that go into getting things done. That's what PCs should do for us.

Data Visualization

In addition to visual models of risk and time, computer graphics can turn virtually any quantity into a visual model that lets our eye and brain do what they're designed for: spotting changes and recognizing patterns. In Figure 14.29, for example, I've used another spreadsheet (1-2-3, from Lotus) to visualize census data in terms of a colored map.

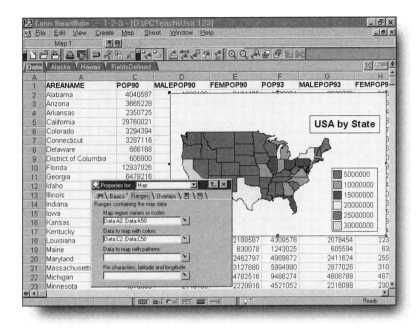

FIGURE 14.29
Spreadsheets such as Lotus 1-2-3 (shown) or Microsoft Excel can present geographic data on map displays.

Other, more demanding visualization tasks call for the graphics capabilities of something like Matlab from The MathWorks. Like several high-priced math tools, Matlab is available in a student edition that's priced and sold like a college textbook.

Matlab uses a programming language, as shown in Figure 14.30, but it is not inherently more complex than the formulas of any typical spreadsheet. Moreover, unlike some programs, a project that's written up as a Matlab program can be moved to many types of computers.

Matlab offers many options for visualizing data, whether as a landscape of peaks and valleys (see Figure 14.31) or as a contour map (see Figure 14.32). These might seem like very abstract displays, but they take on more interest if you imagine the choices you face in your own daily routine.

For example, the plot in Figure 14.32 could be showing return on investments as the bright and dark shadings, with estimated risk on the horizontal scale and minimum investment on the vertical. Suddenly, that bright spot near the upper middle of the plot takes on a personality: It's a high-return, moderate-risk investment with a fairly large minimum stake.

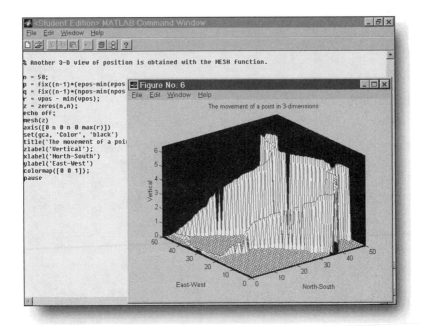

FIGURE 14.30
Portable programming language and advanced graphics displays make Matlab a vital tool for scientists, engineers, and—increasingly—Wall Street traders.

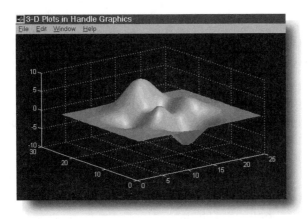

FIGURE 14.31
How do you like to look at data? As a 3D view...

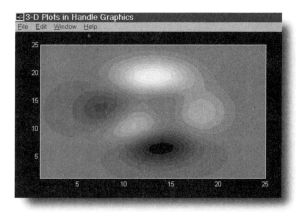

FIGURE 14.32
...or as an overhead, contour-style plot?

We can also apply the power of mathematics software to tasks as concrete as visualizing movements of a mechanism. New cars and airplanes are essentially designed with tools like Mathematica, from Wolfram Research, shown in Figure 14.33.

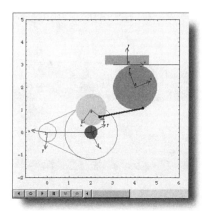

FIGURE 14.33
Mathematica lets us visualize a moving mechanism as an animation based on equations that define components' relative motions.

In earlier chapters, I've harped on the idea that you can't do a thing without adequate data. Mathematica demonstrates this with packaged libraries such as Scientific Astronomer, which combines astronomical data with raw math power to deliver products such as the eclipse map in Figure 14.34.

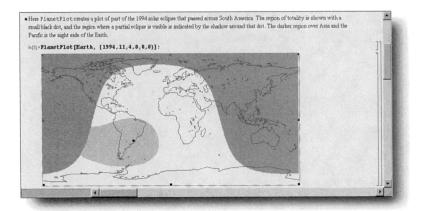

■ Here PlanetPlot creates a plot of part of the 1994 solar eclipse that passed across South America. The region of totality is shown with a small black dot, and the region where a partial eclipse is visible is indicated by the shadow around that dot. The darker region over Asia and the Pacific is the night side of the Earth.

In[3]:=PlanetPlot[Earth, {1994,11,4,0,0,0}];

FIGURE 14.34
Informed by adequate data, your PC and capable math tools can explain the past and predict the future.

Under the hood, Mathematica is doing more than just calculation. The core of the product can manipulate symbols by recognizing patterns and knowing the rules for changing one pattern into another. This is the essence of such human skills as solving equations not just for one set of values but with algebra that yields answers for any values (see Figure 14.35).

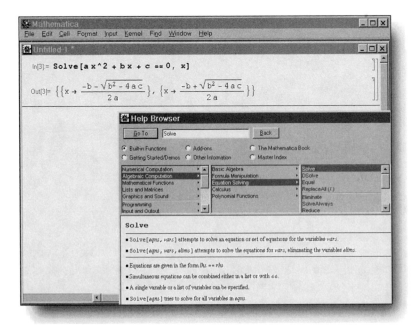

FIGURE 14.35
Perhaps you've forgotten the quadratic formula, but Mathematica can re-derive it on request.

Much less expensive than Mathematica, but sharing some of its remarkable mathematical power, is Derive from Soft Warehouse (see Figure 14.36). Derive is actually built into one high-end graphing calculator and is readily affordable by high school students—either in that built-in form or packaged to run on a Windows PC.

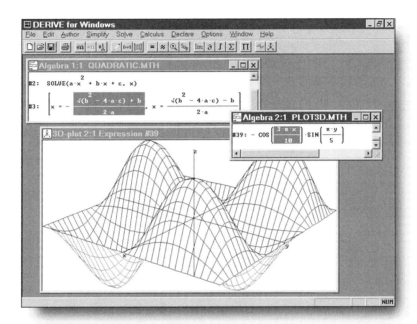

FIGURE 14.36
Derive is a more affordable graphing calculator.

What We've Learned

Spreadsheet software has made computers useful in new ways by bringing customized problem-solving to people who weren't well-served by previous tools with demanding skill requirements.

Spreadsheets are a form of programming. When writing formulas in a spreadsheet's built-in language, we have to master relative-mode and absolute-mode addressing of other cells. With these ideas learned, we can write formulas that quickly adapt themselves during a simple copy-and-paste operation.

Research shows that so-called "what-if" analysis easily turns into a tool for concocting optimistic scenarios. Objective risk analysis, with tools such as Crystal Ball or Forecast Pro, reduces the chance of fooling yourself.

Uncertainties across time are especially important, and a project management tool such as Project Scheduler helps manage them. Visualization of other numeric data can be done in a variety of ways with tools such as Matlab and Mathematica.

"As someday it may happen that a victim must be found, I've got a little list—I've got a little list."

—GILBERT AND SULLIVAN
The Mikado

Listing Heavily:
PC Database Management

*E*VEN THE SIMPLEST COMPUTERS are good at comparing one thing to another, rapidly and consistently and in quantity. This makes computers perfect for the tasks of storing, retrieving, and summarizing data.

Operations on data that involve minimal calculation but large amounts of sorting and combining and other relationship tracking are called *database management*.

The word *database* is used in many ways. It can mean:

- A simple collection of facts, such as a list of names and addresses

- A related set of several collections of facts, plus the rules for allowable operations on those facts (for example, never deleting an order from a list of pending orders if it has not been shipped)

- A piece of software that performs database operations (such as Microsoft Access or Lotus Approach)

In the third sense, that of database management software, some database products are as unlike Access or Approach as an 18-wheeler is unlike a pickup truck. Both are trucks, but they're used in different ways and require quite different skills.

We're not going to look at the 18-wheelers, such as Oracle or Microsoft SQL Server or IBM DB2, because these are products for use by professional programmers. A PC database product makes a good front-end tool, though, for pulling down small sets of data from a larger machine and for looking at that data in various ways.

In short words, a corporate database might run on an IBM database that feeds a departmental database to a PC-based database. Database is one of those words that just has to be interpreted in context.

List Management Is the Beginning

Simple operations, such as sorting and finding items in a list, are often called *list management* to distinguish them from the more complex category of database management. We can do list management with many text editors and word processors. For example, in Figure 15.1, I've selected a column of text in a simple file, using our tried and true KEDIT. The onscreen command, `sort block descending`, sorts the line of the file based on the contents of the marked block to give me the result in Figure 15.2.

Spreadsheets can also do list management, sometimes with multicolumn sorting. We saw Microsoft Excel's sorting facility in Figure 14.12 in Chapter 14, "By the Numbers: Spreadsheets and Other Math Tools."

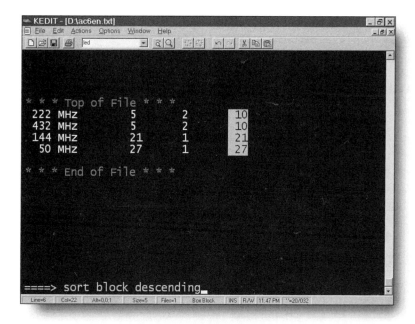

FIGURE 15.1
Even a text editor can perform some data management tasks.

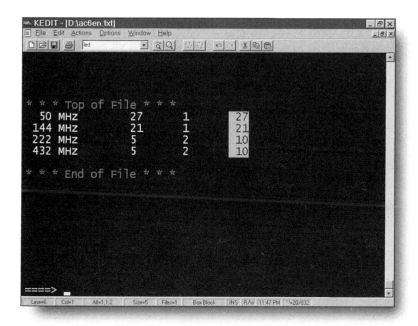

FIGURE 15.2
Simple list management is the beginning of a full-fledged database.

We can even do database-style operations, such as finding duplicates, in a spreadsheet. I can sort my lines of data and then add a blank column to the right of the column whose values I used for the sorting operation. In each cell of the new blank column, I can enter a formula that says, in effect, "If the cell to the left holds the same value as the cell below it, display the word 'Duplicate'; otherwise, display nothing." Duplicate entries will quickly jump out.

I can modify the duplicate-finding technique I just described to detect missing entries in what should be a list of consecutive numbers: "If the value to the left is greater by 1 than the value above it, display nothing; otherwise display 'Missing Value.'" I can perform many other analyses on data with a spreadsheet's powerful vocabulary of built-in functions and calculating tools.

From the List to the Database: Why and How

I can't continue to use a text editor or a spreadsheet as my list manager when I move beyond the simplest tasks. If several people are using the same collection of data, I can't let all of them load the entire collection into memory at once—how would I merge their separate changes?

If a computer crashes, I don't want to lose every change that I've made since a file was last saved. I would rather make a change to a record and then immediately write the changed record back to the storage system (which also makes the changed record visible to other users on a network).

I might want to ask a question that involves more than one set of data, such as "Sort the customers by zip code and by date of most recent order." Do I really want to keep a copy of every customer's name and address as part of my record of every order placed by every customer? Do I really want to change all of those records whenever a customer moves?

Whether it's for reasons of complexity or reliability, you might need to move beyond list management tools to a database product such as Microsoft Access or Lotus Approach. I'll use Access to demonstrate the elements of a common PC database product.

The Tables Are the Data

A database, properly speaking, is more than just a collection of facts. It begins, however, with one or more such collections, commonly called the *tables* (see Figure 15.3).

FIGURE 15.3
Tables are physical collections of records.

In Figure 15.3, I've opened up a table of orders that have been received by a mythical gourmet foods company called Northwind. A table looks like a spreadsheet, but note that the columns have names rather than the mere code letters that we've seen in spreadsheets so far.

NOTE
The Northwind database is a famous example. It ships with Microsoft Access, and parts of it have actually been found inside large commercial projects. Some people evidently start a project by opening the working Northwind example and adding on; their projects wind up with hidden tables of gourmet foods buried inside them like vestigial organs.

Every row in a table (called a *record*) has the same, repeating structure, and each column (called a *field*) means the same thing in every record. This contrasts with a spreadsheet's often irregular structure.

I might have some *computed fields* in a database: For example, I might calculate and store the sales tax on a transaction in a column of each record. I would define that field with a formula, similar to formulas I might use in a spreadsheet.

A computed field formula in a database can refer only to fields within one record. Unlike a spreadsheet formula, which can refer to any of the spreadsheet's columns and rows, a record of a database is an independent unit, so a computed field can work only within its own row.

Records don't know about one another. I can't have a record that stores average values for all of my other records; I have to make calculations like that in some other way.

There Are Relationships Between Groups of Records

In Figure 15.3, we're looking at orders—but an order typically includes several items, and a typical customer places several orders at different times.

If I'm using a simple list manager, I have a problem. Every item of every order has to be accompanied by all of the information for that order (date placed, date promised, and so on). I also have to include customer information, such as name and address, along with every item. Otherwise, how can I tell a stock clerk what to pick, when, and which order includes a given picked item?

At some point, I'll get tired of so much duplication. I'll look for a way to store customer information once and let a customer's order records look up the information in a customer directory when I print an order or view it on the screen. I'll look for a way to store order dates just once and let the items on that order look up their parent order and the order's parent customer when I view that item's information.

The notion of a relationship between different tables leads to the term *relational database*, which is what most people mean when they say "a 'real' database." List management is also called "flat-file" database management. A relational database is not flat, but is a bumpy topography of connections of the kind shown in Figure 15.4.

Notice, in Figure 15.4, the markings at the ends of the connections between my various tables. A given order detail appears in only one order, but an order can include any number of order details. We say that there is a one-to-many relationship between Orders and Order Details. A given order is placed by only one customer, but a customer might place any number of orders, so we say that there is a many-to-one relationship between Orders and Customers.

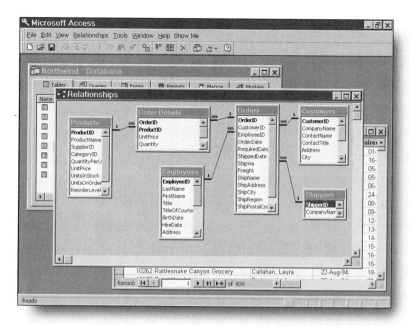

FIGURE 15.4
Connections define not just links, but meanings, such as a one-to-many relationship between a customer and a customer's orders.

Also notice that each linked pair of tables has at least one field name in common. Every Product has a Product ID, and every Order Detail makes reference to a Product ID. Every Customer has a Customer ID, and every Order makes reference to a Customer ID. These common attributes allow economy of storage and the ease we get from a relational database of changing (for example) a customer's telephone number in one and only one place.

Some Questions Get Asked Many Times

When I want to ask a question about my data, I don't really want to think about which facts are in which table. I don't want to say, "Show me the names of customers from the Customers table, sorted by zip code from the same table, and within each zip code by the date from the Orders table of the most recent order, using Customer ID as the linking attribute." That's not how PCs make us more productive.

We get more productive by asking that verbose question once and giving that question a convenient name so that we can ask it again whenever we like. That named question is called a database *query*, and a list of typical queries appears in Figure 15.5.

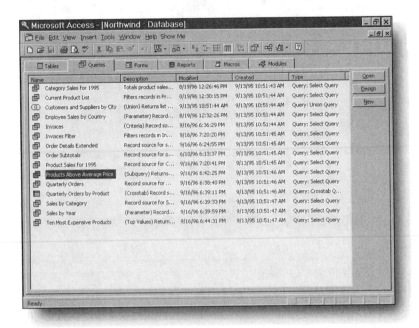

FIGURE 15.5
Queries give names to our frequently repeated questions.

Instead of stating a query in a command language, I can often define a query by filling in a table like the one in Figure 15.6. This query will show me:

- The product name (first column)

- The unit price (second column) from the Products table

- Sorted in descending order of unit price (second column, third line)

- Including only those products whose price is greater than the average of all prices in that table (second column, fifth line)

Do you remember that I said we'd find a way to ask questions involving calculations on more than one record at a time? There it is.

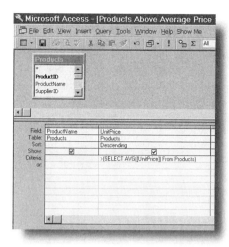

FIGURE 15.6
A tabular representation shows me the structure of a query without a programming language.

When I invoke this query, I get back what looks like a table (see Figure 15.7). Unlike a true table, however, this table exists only as needed to answer the Products Above Average Price query. No physical collection of data exists that contains only these records, but we can use this "virtual table" as if it were an actual table in carrying out other database operations.

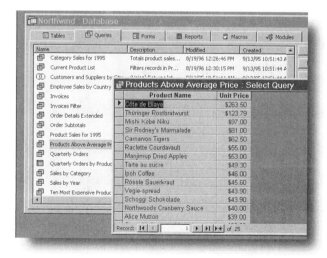

FIGURE 15.7
The result of a query looks and behaves like a physical table, although no such table actually exists.

Database Forms: For Entry and Review

When we want to add information to a collection of data, we're used to the idea of filling in a form. Forms make it easy to group related things and to fit many items into a compact layout. You wouldn't want to work your way across a row of fields if you were filling in your income tax return.

Designing a form can be an important part of making a database easy to use and can have a large impact on avoiding inaccurate or inconsistent entries that poison any database application. Figure 15.8 shows a form that might be devised for taking an order over the telephone, incorporating both the order information and a collection of details within that order.

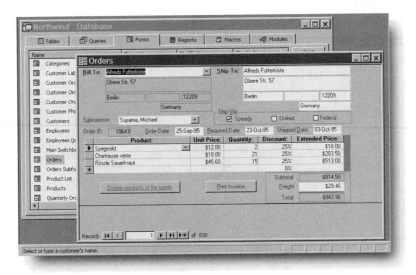

FIGURE 15.8
Forms accelerate data entry and speed data review.

Figure 15.9 shows the bones beneath the skin, so to speak, putting the form in Figure 15.8 into a design mode that reveals the large number of elements that have to be designed and placed to make that efficient-looking screen. Perhaps you're thinking, "Gosh, that looks like a lot of work." You should be thinking, "Gosh, I wonder how I get the PC to do that for me."

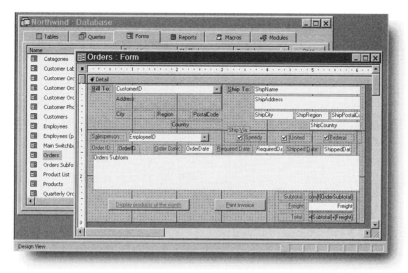

FIGURE 15.9
Form construction, by hand, is tedious.

In Figure 15.10, I'm beginning the process of requesting an automatic form design. After opening a Form Wizard, I choose the tables or queries (remember, a query can be treated as if it's a physical table) that will "feed" this form.

FIGURE 15.10
Automated aids are the best way to get started on constructing forms for a database.

In Figure 15.11, I choose a layout, and in Figure 15.12, I see the result. This is not as complete as the form in Figure 15.8, because I did not make any provision for showing order details. I'm merely illustrating the automated process that eliminates much of the tedium of choosing and placing elements on a form.

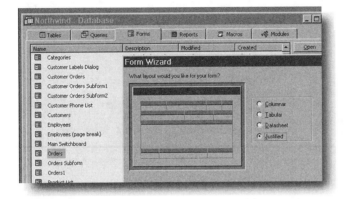

FIGURE 15.11
Choosing a layout...

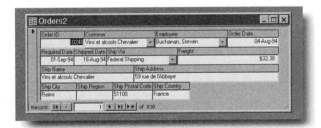

FIGURE 15.12
...leads me to my ready-to-use form...

Remember, always, that the form is not the data. I always retain the option of going from my form view to a spreadsheet-like view of my records, as shown in Figure 15.13.

FIGURE 15.13
...but a form is just another view of my data, which can still be seen "unfiltered."

Reports Adjust Themselves to Current Data

An important function for many databases is generation of formatted reports. Unlike a spreadsheet, in which the number of rows of data is part of its layout, the number of records in a database is flexible.

A database report generator works dynamically with the current size of the database. A report can be anything from a simple list to an elaborate multilevel analysis.

Far too many PC users edit spreadsheets or edit tables in a word processor, by hand, to produce their printed reports. Many tasks could be handled with far less effort if the information were in a database, where it could be summarized automatically on demand.

If it looks like work, your PC should probably be doing it for you.

Generating a report is a lot like building a form: Most database products offer automated aids for the process. In Figure 15.14, I choose a layout; in Figure 15.15, I see the result.

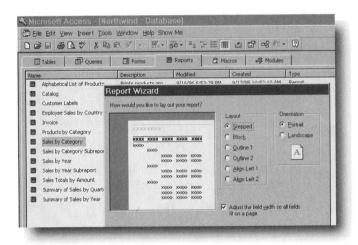

FIGURE 15.14
Choosing a layout for a printed report…

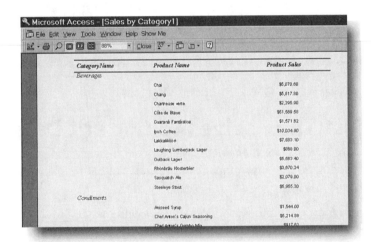

FIGURE 15.15
…leads to a dynamically generated summary with less manual editing than is needed for printing a spreadsheet that's used as a data collector.

Approach Models Common Tasks

As I commented in Chapter 12, we don't want to reinvent common business processes just because a PC makes the process somewhat automatic. If you want to do a common task, a good piece of software gives you a predefined way to do what's commonly required. Figure 15.16 shows a list of built-in database "SmartMasters" in Lotus Approach, which in many ways is even more "approach-able" than Microsoft Access.

FIGURE 15.16
Common data management tasks get off to a fast start with Lotus Approach.

If I choose a checkbook task, for example, Approach gives me a running start. The product predefines fields and visual forms that I can quickly use, both as a working example and as a foundation for adding and adjusting elements to meet my exact preferences (see Figure 15.17).

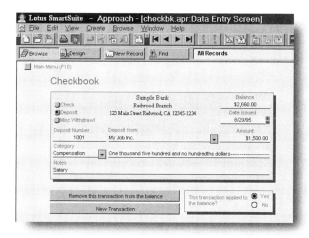

FIGURE 15.17
Approach offers predesigned, customizable forms.

Industrial-Strength Data

A serious business database also incorporates rules for maintaining its data. One data maintenance rule might be "Never delete the entry for a customer if that customer has ordered from us in the past 12 months." This type of rule would be called a "business rule."

Even more important are data integrity rules, such as "Never delete a customer's shipping address while any order from that customer is still open." Violating a business rule might be bad for business, but violating a data integrity rule means that your database no longer works.

An order that goes to look for its linked customer data will run in circles, scream, and shout if there is no record in the Customers table with the proper value for the linking attribute (such as a Customer ID number).

A large database might be the foundation of a business, and it should be designed and built as carefully as any other piece of industrial equipment.

What We've Learned

Many kinds of PC software have sprouted list management commands, which are easy to add to a tool such as a text editor or spreadsheet.

Operations that involve several connected tables, or that benefit from reliability-oriented design, call for a more capable database management tool.

Tables hold data and can give you opportunities for efficient, cross-referenced sharing of information in one-to-many or many-to-one relationships.

Queries can return what look like tables, but really represent virtual collections of data that meet various criteria in a named, repeatable search.

Forms and reports would be time-consuming to construct, but are quickly produced by automated aids.

Competing products seek to offer intuitive help with common tasks to accelerate and enhance database design.

"The entire effect of an individual on the world stems from what he can communicate to the world."

—DOUGLAS ENGELBART, 1963

Inform, Persuade, Deceive:
Graphics and Presentations

*I*F NO ONE REMEMBERS ANYTHING ELSE that I ever say or write, I hope that someone will at least remember my column in *PC Week* for May 3, 1993. Here's how it began:

"You spend an hour writing a memo on your word processor. It goes to eight people, who each spend 5 minutes reading it. They don't get the point. Total time wasted by all involved: 1 hour, 40 minutes.

"You spend an hour using your charting program to produce a report. You take half an hour to present it to the same eight people and they still don't get the point. Total time wasted: 5.5 hours.

"Now consider a presentation graphics tool. Say you spend two days creating a major presentation and an hour delivering the spiel to 100 colleagues. They don't get the point. Total time wasted: 117 hours, or almost 15 working days.

"If an ineffective memo is workplace suicide, then a bad presentation is mass murder."

In Chapter 6, I sang the praises of graphics and video hardware. This chapter, our last on software that simply runs on your standalone PC, is about the products that turn graphic potential into results that change things.

Presentations Change Minds

There must be something that you want to change—change your career, change your community, change the arrangement of furniture in your room. PC graphics and presentation tools can help you get that vision of change across to the audience that matters, whether it's your interior decorator or your annual Town Meeting or your company's annual strategy conference.

To stick with a recurring theme from these past several chapters, good software doesn't just open the door—it pulls you in. In the case of presentation tools, the current state of the art goes beyond an automated slide show to give you active support in deciding what points you need to make.

Figure 16.1 shows Microsoft PowerPoint, which (along with Lotus Freelance Graphics) dominates the market. Both products have key features in common, including an opening selection of standard presentation types.

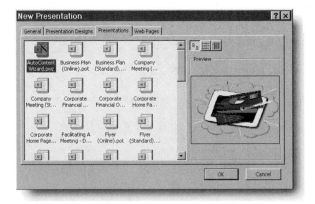

FIGURE 16.1
Standardized presentation types accelerate the process of preparing a persuasive briefing.

In Figure 16.2, I'm beginning the process of assembling a new presentation. Choosing the basic type of talk that I want to give, I answer a few simple questions and wind up with the outline in Figure 16.3.

FIGURE 16.2
Active guidance through program features highlights most presentation tools, including Microsoft PowerPoint.

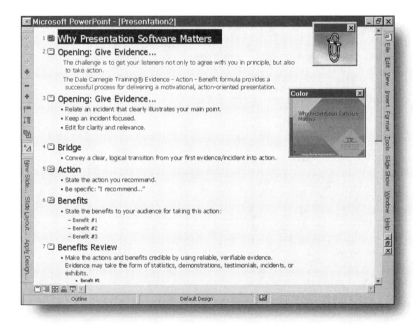

FIGURE 16.3
An overall outline view lets me think about content instead of being distracted by appearance.

Black letters on white text used to be quite enough to get your point across, and I'm tempted to try it again sometime, but people have grown used to a gentler and more colorful look. Any good presentation package gives you a library of several graphics styles, along with predefined layouts as shown in Figure 16.4.

FIGURE 16.4
Graphics themes help you tailor a presentation to an audience and a mood.

In Chapter 15, I said that the form is not the data. In this chapter, I'll echo that by saying that the theme is not the content. For example, Figure 16.5 shows a slide from my presentation on software usability at an IBM technical conference. Suppose I wanted to present the same material to a group of bankers instead of a group of engineers?

I can recall the graphics gallery that I used when I started to build my presentation (see Figure 16.6), choose another style, and apply it without changing my content. PowerPoint moves the old content to the new look (see Figure 16.7).

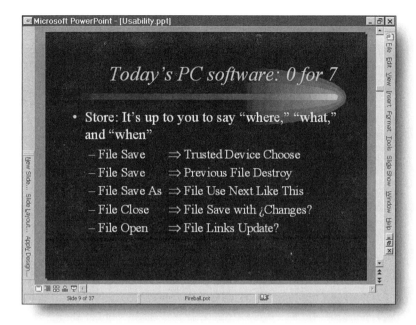

FIGURE 16.5
A chart can start with one look…

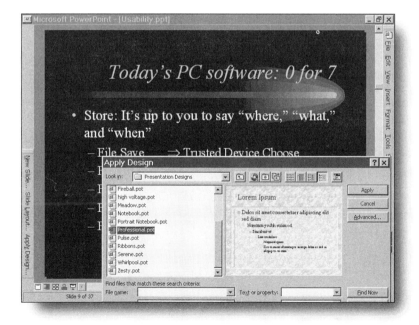

FIGURE 16.6
…and go through a change of face…

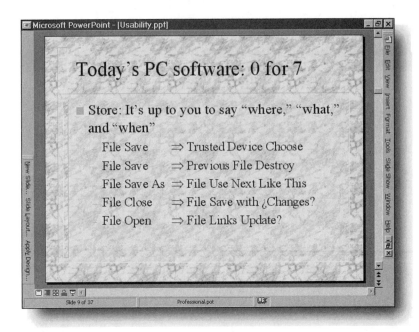

FIGURE 16.7
...to put the same content in a different package.

Personally, I always have to fight the temptation to put too much on a single chart. A presentation tool usually helps you with this by recommending font sizes for various elements of a chart. Many graphics tools can make different recommendations for, say, printed handouts versus a theater presentation.

Just as an Outline view lets you move around your paragraphs in a document, a Slide Sorter view lets you rearrange the succession of charts in a presentation. In Figure 16.8, I drag a slide to a new position, just as I might drag a paragraph of text or a range of spreadsheet cells. Figure 16.9 shows the slide in its new sequential position.

In the Slide Sorter view, you can see small pictographs at the lower left corners of each slide. These indicate that I've chosen various transition effects, such as "building" a chart one item at a time instead of revealing all of the points on a list at once.

In Figure 16.10, you see a "dissolve" effect, caught in the act of adding a final element to a chart as I reach that point in my talk.

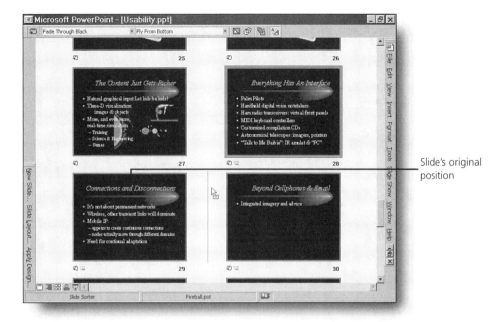

Slide's original position

FIGURE 16.8
Dragging a slide in the sorter view…

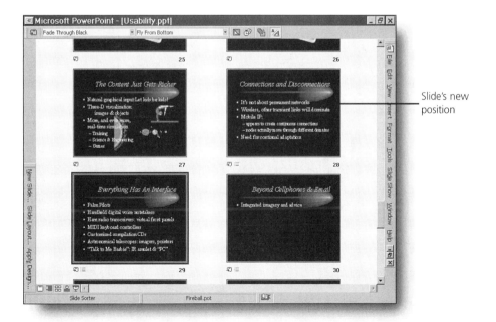

Slide's new position

FIGURE 16.9
…lets me make my points in a different order.

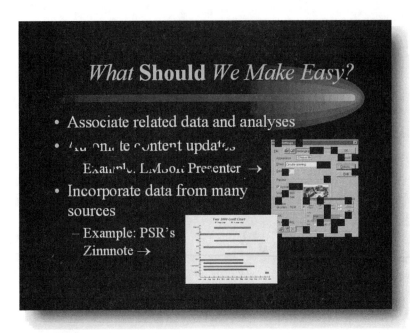

FIGURE 16.10
Dissolves and other effects can be overused but can also be effective in keeping a presentation energetic.

As with fonts in a word processor, it's easy to overuse transitions and automations. It's especially easy to overuse sound effects, which PowerPoint and other presentation tools also provide. Be restrained—pick a look that works for you and vary it only to make a point.

Prepackaged Presentation Experts

Like Lotus Approach, with its fully defined "typical" applications for database design, Lotus Freelance Graphics goes the extra mile to give the user more than just a basic framework for making presentations. The program provides a large collection of expert presentation types and graphics aids associated with well-known authorities in various areas. Figure 16.11 shows some of its gallery of presentation options.

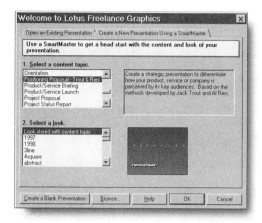

FIGURE 16.11
Lotus Freelance Graphics offers "brand name" presentations based on well-known authorities' guidelines.

Graphics that you might not take the time to prepare can do a lot to make you look more prepared (see Figure 16.12). Freelance Graphics supports you with quite a collection of elaborate chart types, based on the recommendations of well-known presenters (see Figure 16.13).

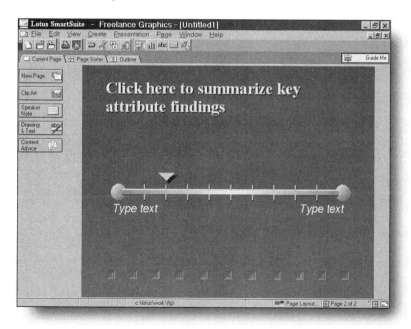

FIGURE 16.12
Specialized graphics can support particular points in a structured presentation.

FIGURE 16.13
Prepackaged presentation outlines help you cover vital elements of a persuasive talk.

It's Hard to Be Consistent

I ran across one interesting "gotcha" in Freelance Graphics that I mention here because it's a good reminder of the workarounds we sometimes need to devise. Lotus has gone to great lengths to incorporate the Internet directly into the process of using the products in its SmartSuite collection, for which Freelance Graphics plays the same position that PowerPoint plays for Microsoft Office.

Freelance Graphics offers, for example, a facility for searching the World Wide Web for selected text, streamlining the process of researching a talk.

Great, I thought, as I put together a briefing on the growing importance of hand-held devices. I inserted a "quote balloon" as a placeholder for a comment that I would obtain from a recognized authority and typed "handheld computers" as the phrase for which I would search (see Figure 16.14).

Freelance responded with a perplexing error message, "There was no text select-ed." Oh? Then what's that on the screen in Figure 16.15?

Wondering what was going on, I remembered a similar experience in PowerPoint, where text that was enclosed in a graphics element did not appear in an outline view of my presentation. I shifted to the similar view in Freelance Graphics (see Figure 16.16) and, sure enough, the text in the quote balloon is not part of the presentation's text...if you see what I mean. Or perhaps I should say, "if you don't see."

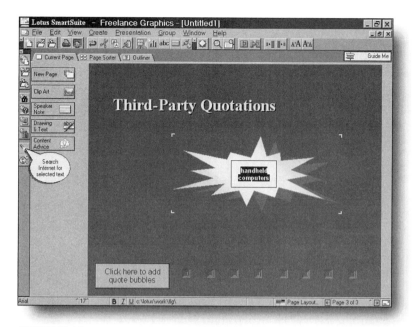

FIGURE 16.14
It looks as if I can set up a "placeholder" text and then replace it with an Internet-searched comment…

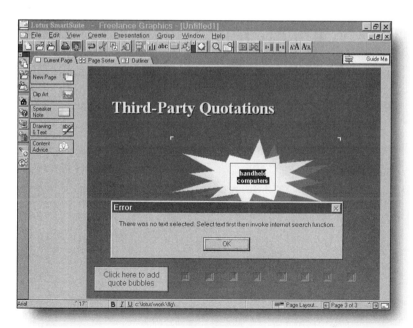

FIGURE 16.15
…but Freelance Graphics (like PowerPoint in a similar situation) sees no selected text—even though it's right there on the screen.

FIGURE 16.16
The Outline view reveals the blind spot for text that's part of art.

In the Outline view, I entered my search phrase again. In the thumbnail view of my chart, at the upper left in Figure 16.17, you can see that this corresponds to entering `Handheld computers` on my slide without an enclosing balloon. With this "real text" selected, the search consented to proceed.

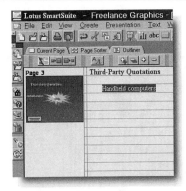

FIGURE 16.17
There's text, and then again there's text; without the enclosing art, Freelance Graphics can see and search on the desired phrase.

NOTE
It sounds like something out of *Alice in Wonderland*, but it's pointless to yell at the screen: "Stupid computer! What do you mean, no text is selected?" The program decides what counts as "text" from one moment to the next, and it's interesting that Freelance Graphics and PowerPoint have a similar blind spot in this regard.

Both Freelance Graphics and PowerPoint anticipate that you might be "presenting" to an audience on the Internet. Both programs make it easy for you to generate your presentation in the form of a prebuilt Web site, which you can deploy by methods that I'll describe in Chapter 17.

There are, however, Web site construction tools more suited to the task of creating and managing a pool of information assets that you want to link together in different ways for Internet access.

You can do a lot on the Web with minimal tools, such as an ordinary text editor and a reference book for the Hypertext Markup Language (HTML). Using special tags, HTML embeds information on linkage to other information, as I'll show in Chapter 17. If a plain text editor is too clumsy, you can move up to an HTML-oriented editor, such as Allaire's HomeSite (discussed in Chapter 13).

NetObjects Fusion is my recommendation for people who want the next step in added ease of generating links between pages and visualizing their connections (see Figure 16.18). Fusion's page-layout tools combine the best of desktop publishing with the specific facilities needed to manage Web site content (see Figure 16.19).

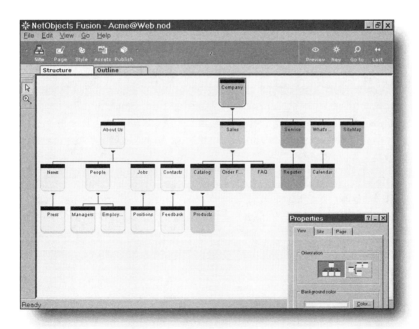

FIGURE 16.18
When "presenting" to an audience via the Web, a site construction product such as NetObjects Fusion may be the right tool for the job.

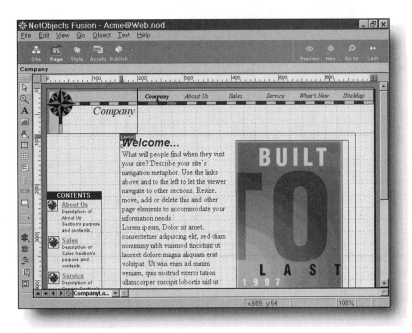

FIGURE 16.19
Web page design, as well as Web site assembly, gets a fast start from Fusion.

CAD Offers Precision at Different Scales

Sometimes your most important audience is only one person—it might be your spouse, it might be your architect. Figure 16.20 shows a tool that could help the communication between you and either of those parties: Autodesk's AutoCAD LT 97.

You'll want to understand the difference between a computer-aided drafting tool, such as AutoCAD LT 97, and an ordinary illustration tool, such as Microsoft Paint. AutoCAD maintains an internal model—a database if you will—of the objects in your drawing. It "knows" that there's a detailed drawing of the base of the basement wall, even if that drawing is much too small to be seen in the full-house view of Figure 16.20.

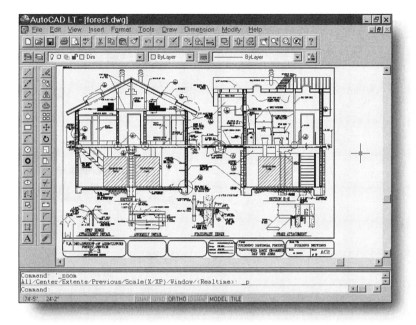

FIGURE 16.20
A computer-aided drafting (CAD) product such as AutoCAD LT 97 is a different type of tool for putting together an image that communicates.

In Figure 16.21, I zoom in on the basement wall detail. (The Aerial View window at lower right puts a box around what we're currently seeing in the main view.) We could get right down to the screw heads on that flange in the center of the drawing, if they were part of the internal model.

Compare a CAD program's freedom to adjust a drawing's scale against the limited flexibility of a paint-type program. In Figure 16.22, I show a rectangle/circle combination at lower right, and I zoom in on the place where the circle touches the corner of the rectangle. In Figure 16.23, I create a similar drawing in Paint. In Figure 16.24, I zoom in and see that we're just magnifying pixels.

When the "circle" is drawn, Paint loses all notions of its "circleness." That circle is just black pixels on a white background as far as Paint is concerned. A CAD tool knows better.

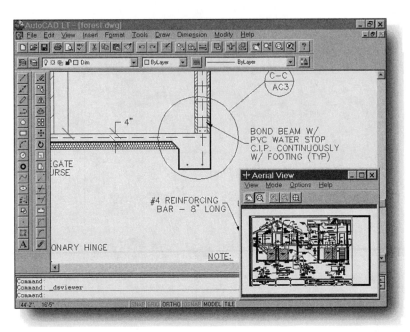

FIGURE 16.21
With floating-point math internals, AutoCAD LT 97 and other CAD products can handle the very large, and the very small, within a single drawing.

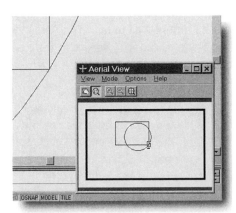

FIGURE 16.22
Zooming in on an intersection in a CAD tool reveals geometric precision.

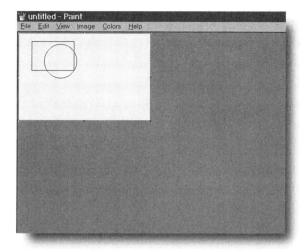

FIGURE 16.23
A paint-type program looks as if it shows the same geometry...

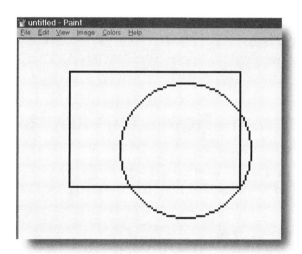

FIGURE 16.24
...but an enlarged view of the paint-type file shows pixels, not geometric objects, as the drawing's contents.

Because AutoCAD LT knows about my circle and my rectangle as objects and not just pixels, it can notice things like midpoints of sides. If I enable an automatic "snapping" behavior, AutoCAD LT prompts me when I'm close to connecting a new drawing object to a special point on another object.

In Figure 16.25, for example, a radius from the circle goes exactly to the midpoint of the topmost side of the rectangle. I don't have to measure, or carefully nudge my mouse, or type in a location—I just get a helpful "intelligent" behavior from the software.

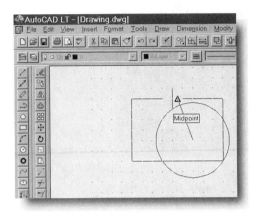

FIGURE 16.25
With internal knowledge of object geometry, AutoCAD LT 97 can offer to assist with precise placement of connections to "interesting" points such as midpoints of edges.

"Smart" Paint Programs Figure Out What They're Seeing

On the other hand, sometimes I want to deal with an image that is just a bunch of pixels. A digital camera, for example, just sends me pixels; it's up to me to decide what's there.

In Figure 16.26, I use Jasc Software's Paint Shop Pro on a digital photo to extract an object from its background. As I move my mouse in segments around the object of interest, a **Smart Edge** option looks for sharp changes in color that indicate a boundary.

With the entire perimeter defined, as in Figure 16.27, I can copy the irregular bunch of pixels into a blank new drawing, as in Figure 16.28.

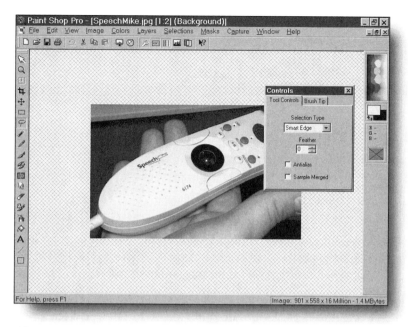

FIGURE 16.26
A paint-type program like Paint Shop Pro doesn't have definite knowledge of object boundaries...

FIGURE 16.27
...but it interprets edges as best it can from boundaries with high contrast...

FIGURE 16.28
...and lets me extract an object from its background.

The process of automatic edge detection is certainly not as good as the human eye and brain in its ability to interpret a scene. In Figure 16.29, I try to extract a picture of a Sharp multifunction unit from the cluttered counter of a trade show exhibit booth.

If you look closely at the far side of the paper feeder, you'll see an irregularity where the light-colored object behind the unit has fooled the edge-detection algorithm.

FIGURE 16.29
Similar colors fool automatic edge detection (near left side of paper feeder in photo).

In Figure 16.30, I repair the damage by using an "eyedropper" tool to copy the colors of nearby pixels and a brush with a realistically blurry edge to fill in the defects in the extracted outline.

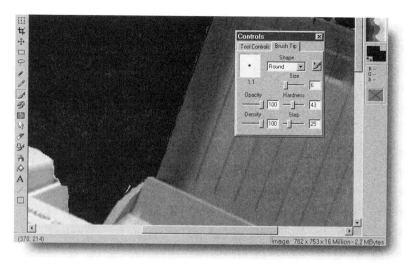

FIGURE 16.30
With digital editing tools, I can repair defects to almost undetectable degree.

With a professional's experience, such a repair could fool anyone but another expert. I could use this technique to put two people face to face who have never met, showing them in a place where neither one has ever been.

A Tool for Every Purpose

Graphics tools show the kind of specialization that's possible in PC software. CAD programs can be extended with libraries of special objects, such as mechanical or architectural components; paint programs can be extended with libraries of images or special effects.

There are even graphics editors that are constructed with a single task in mind. I show one example—a quilt-design program called Quilt-Pro, in Figure 16.31. Layout, comparison of different color combinations, printing of patterns, and so on are radically streamlined with a product like this, as compared to manual methods.

A PC to run a quilt-design tool or other specialized software doesn't need to cost any more than a medium-grade sewing machine. Something like Quilt-Pro is in the same category today that a spreadsheet was in the early years of the PC: "I need this software and something to run it."

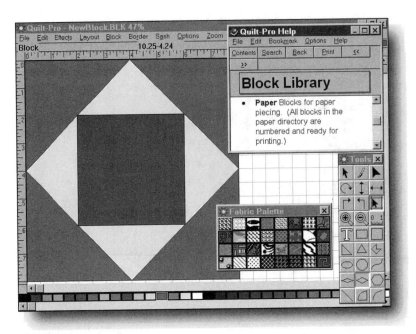

FIGURE 16.31
Specialized graphics products streamline almost any task, even hobbies such as quilt design.

What We've Learned

As with the software suites in Chapter 12, the presentation tools in this chapter gain value by automating steps and by prepackaging experts' recommendations.

These are complex products, and some of their attractive features are marred by annoying blind spots.

CAD tools and paint tools convey different kinds of images. CAD tools are ideal for images that contain details at many different scales, while paint tools offer flexibility in manipulating photographs and other unstructured content.

Whatever the task, you're likely to find specialized software that does it particularly well. Graphics are one of the best examples of this trend in PC packages.

"Computer systems have often proved to be insecure, unreliable, and unpredictable.... Society has yet to come to terms with the consequences."

—TOM FORESTER AND
PERRY MORRISON
Computer Ethics: Cautionary Tales and Ethical Dilemmas in Computing (2nd Ed.)

Roses and Thorns:
Imperfect Systems, the Internet, and Cybercrime

COMPUTERS, AND THOSE WHO BUILD and talk about computers, create high expectations.

With startling speed, the world has grown accustomed to Moore's Law rates of improvement—doubling the performance, or halving the cost, in 18 months—in a wide range of products and services.

Are We There Yet?

We've pretty much achieved the state of affairs that science fiction writer (and PC commentator) Jerry Pournelle defined as the goal of the PC revolution. Essentially, Jerry said that any known fact, or any computable result of known facts, would soon be available to anyone.

Jerry was predicting universal access to facts and calculations, as I recall, in the early 1980s. At that time, a fully equipped PC had less memory than a basic graphics card has now and had less processing power than many current children's toys. His prediction was therefore a bit more daring than it might seem today.

Access to Knowledge and Know-how

The Pournelle predictions for personal computing have turned to realities even more quickly than Jerry could have expected. We've seen the most obscure factual knowledge become widely available through the Internet; we've seen the most exotic procedural knowledge become an off-the-shelf product in the form of tools such as Mathematica.

The impact of computers, especially personal computers, goes far beyond mailing list management and numeric calculations, far beyond the tasks that used to be considered the domain of "data processing" or "management information systems."

Social goals and ideals, such as freedom of the press, have taken on new meaning now that almost anyone can afford to own and operate a personal printing press—or even, in effect, a broadcast studio. We can reach a local audience with a laser printer or a worldwide audience with a site on the World Wide Web.

There is, however, an irony in the use of personal computers as communication tools. Technology delivers the compelling truths of image and sound to any point in the world in seconds; the same technology makes it harder to tell the difference between truth and fiction, due to the effectiveness of digital editing tools such as those we saw near the end of Chapter 16.

How Do We Lock Our Doors?

Ideals such as personal privacy take on new urgency as previous limits on acceptable behavior fail to keep pace with our migration to cyberspace. People would notice if someone walked down the block, trying every front door to see if it was locked; it is much less obvious when someone does the same thing, metaphorically speaking, in our newly built neighborhoods of computer databases.

Data theft leaves the stolen property in place, turning even the detection of a crime into a far more difficult task than it is in the physical world.

We have the technical means, such as the techniques of strong encryption, to keep our personal information safe against any known technology. The use of these techniques, however, is controversial, because government agencies fear the criminal opportunities that arise when anyone can transfer impenetrable secrets—and even "electronic cash" payments—by wholly untraceable methods.

"Follow the money" used to be a guiding principle for those who would root out wrongdoing, but electronic money leaves no trail and involves no need for face-to-face meetings. How do police "stake out" the Internet or "wiretap" a wireless link that is using nearly undetectable spread-spectrum radio methods?

Corporations and governments used to have resources that were out of the reach of individuals, but today anyone can own a computer powerful enough to break many formerly adequate codes, and everyone uses public networks that make it possible to intercept sensitive communications. Large institutions still haven't figured out how to deal with this new equality.

Trusting Computers: Is There a Choice?

So far, moreover, I've only talked about the consequences of information technology that does what it's supposed to do. I have not addressed the subject of imperfect systems and the dilemma that's created by systems that are wonderful when they're working—but deadly when they go down.

When I say "deadly," I do not mean just in the sense of disabling a business. I mean that computers can kill people, if automated systems are entrusted with tasks such as monitoring patient care in hospitals or maintaining safety in airline operations.

Computers become especially unpredictable as they cease being self-contained "electronic brains" and instead become participants in a continuous exchange of information. There is particular hazard in the use of data links that are based on similar technologies but that use those technologies in uncoordinated fashion. For example, *Software Engineering Notes* reported the death of a man whose heartbeat-regulating pacemaker was inadvertently reprogrammed by a retail store's antitheft system.

Ordinary people are carrying devices that might have come from an episode of *Star Trek* (or, for that matter, from a James Bond movie)—little blinking, beeping boxes that exchange data and carry out programmed actions. In such a world, complex and catastrophic failure scenarios cease to be the domain of military strategists and NASA mission planners; they become the stuff of everyday life.

Is This Where We Wanted to Be?

Even when these systems are doing only what they're supposed to do, we should step back and look at the big picture of what it means to become more productive by means of information technology.

It's good that a parent can take time to attend a school event with a child, knowing that a wireless modem and a pocket-sized Palm III "assistant" will deliver an email memo if there's an urgent problem at work. On the other hand, we might prefer to measure productivity in terms of getting more done in an 8-hour day—not in terms of making it possible to be at work, in spirit if not in body, 16 hours a day.

Computers, as former Avis CEO Robert Townsend said, are like roads: You have to decide where you want them to take you, and build them in that direction even if it isn't the easiest route to follow. Are you merely following technology's road map, or are you drawing a map that leads to the places you want to go?

The Internet: A Road Around the World

Both the pleasures and the perils of personal computers get much of their potential from the Internet.

There are other resources with which your PC can connect, giving you access to expert advice, social contact, and up-to-date information. There are other realms in which your PC can encounter the bad bits as well as the good.

Increasingly, though, the Internet is the environment. Every other information resource has to provide some kind of Internet access, or risk becoming irrelevant.

Most PC products, whether hardware or software, now have some kind of Internet relationship. New PCs arrive in an Internet-ready configuration, and new software offers to download the latest product updates during installation and at regular intervals thereafter.

What the Internet Is Not

To understand what the Internet is today, let's look at why it was built.

I've lost track of the number of histories of the Internet that attribute its invention to the threat of nuclear war. "The original idea," reads one typical account, "was to build a network capable of carrying military and government information during a 'nuclear event.'" Even *Time* magazine says so.

The people who were present at the creation beg to differ.

Budgets, Not Bombs

In 1966, Bob Taylor was the newly appointed director of the Information Processing Techniques Office (IPTO) at the Advanced Research Projects Agency (ARPA) of the U.S. Department of Defense. Taylor paid a call on the head of the agency, Charles Herzfeld, to discuss the growing problem of demand for computer resources among the contractors (mostly academic teams at research universities) who were carrying out IPTO's studies.

Computers weren't small and they weren't cheap, Taylor observed, as narrated in *Where Wizards Stay Up Late: The Origins of The Internet* (a history compiled in 1996 by Katie Hafner and Matthew Lyon). "Why not tie them together?" Similar needs could be met by shared facilities, instead of through wasteful duplication of the second-rate systems that would result from budgets spread too thin.

The heart of the networking problem was the matter of compatibility. It was impossible for the Department of Defense, the largest buyer of computers in the world, to grant a sole-source contract to any one maker of computers. It was unlikely that different companies would soon reach agreement on technical standards at a time when technology was still developing so rapidly—as it continues doing today.

Taylor proposed to develop a networking scheme that would let different types of computers work together, regardless of their differing internal details. As a secondary benefit, a network might be devised with redundant connections that would keep the network operating even if it lost one or more of its data paths between different computing centers.

Packets, Not Circuits

At a time when computers "weren't small and weren't cheap," Taylor's team took a daring approach. During an early discussion of "the networking experiment," Wesley Clark (of Washington University in St. Louis) made the radical suggestion of treating the participating computers as clients of the network, instead of as slaves of one another's users.

Instead of burdening the connected computers with the added workload of managing their interactions, the team conceived of a network with its own distributed intelligence.

ARPA hired the firm of Bolt Beranek and Newman to design and build a set of high-speed, message-processing computers. With their own capability to find a path between any two points on the network, these Interface Message Processors (IMPs) would make any two participating computers seem to be directly connected to each other.

NOTE

The first time I heard the term "IMP," I thought it was being used as an ironic comment on mischievous little creatures—as a slang term akin to "gremlins." When my confusion showed, my then coworker Steve Crocker kindly scribbled a note explaining the meaning of the term. Ten years would pass before I learned that Steve wrote crucial parts of the first IMP's processing software and that he was in the room on the day that the first IMP passed its first test.

I tell this story as a reminder that all of this stuff is still so new. "It's like discovering that mountains, oceans, weather, fire, and gravity were each once somebody's bright idea," as Stewart Brand said after reading *When Wizards Stay Up Late*.

The ARPA experimental network did not actually create a dedicated path between any pair of machines. Instead, the messages from any machine to any other machine were broken into groups of bits called *packets*.

In addition to the bits that represented the contents of the message, a packet would be wrapped, so to speak, in additional bits that showed the packet's origin and destination.

Packets en route from any machine to any other machine might find themselves interleaved on a single connection between any two IMPs. Eventually, however, the packets for any given machine—and only those packets—would travel across the final link that connected one of the IMPs to the target computer.

Packet-based data transfer represents a form of time-division multiplexing, an idea that we mentioned briefly in Chapter 7. In principle, time-division multiplexing is no more complex than the sharing of a single TV channel between programs and commercials.

Unlike the 15-second time slots of TV commercials, however, the tempo of packet operations on ARPA's net was expected to be extremely fast. Specifications called for a remote system to respond with no more than half a second's delay.

Putting It All Together

The ARPA experiment achieved new levels of both flexibility and reliability, thanks to the properties of packet-based data communication.

Many Paths

When a message was broken up into packets, it would not matter if packets arrived in the order that they were sent. Packets would carry information on their sequence within a message, and received packets could be reordered to reconstruct the transmitted data.

With the capability to deal with out-of-order deliveries, the network could use different types of connection paths with different delivery speeds. A message in progress might be switched, for example, from a satellite link (up and back, a round trip of more than 40,000 miles) to a ground-based connection (about 3,000 miles from coast to coast). Packets that were sent later might then arrive earlier, due to the ground link's shorter travel time, until the packets in transit via the satellite were all flushed out of the pipeline.

One Protocol

To get the benefits of the network's reliability and its ease of connection to other resources, a machine only needed to know one set of conversational rules: one *protocol*, in the parlance of data communications. A participating machine only needed to interact with the IMPs.

The network could therefore accommodate new types of computers with no additional effort required by established network participants. Each new participant went through the same initiation, in a manner of speaking, by learning the common protocol—and joining the growing club.

Still Growing

From its tiny beginnings as a research project, with a budget of $1 million to build four IMPs, the ARPAnet grew into today's Internet.

When people started to view information in graphical formats instead of merely exchanging files of text and data, the more colorful name of "World Wide Web" came into use for that style of Internet access.

Today's common expression, "It's on the Web," conveys the rich and growing collection of linked information that's readily available to anyone with an Internet connection and *Web browser* software (whose workings we'll examine later).

What Makes the Internet Run

You can use the Internet for years without knowing a thing about its internal workings. If you don't care how it works but only about the things that the Internet can do for you, I suggest that you skip ahead to the section titled "Traveling the World Wide Web."

If you're still here, I assume that you'd like to look under the hood and see how the Internet finds things. How can typing "`http://www.pcweek.com`" tell a box full of chips that you want the latest and most complete news about corporate information technology (just to pick a random example, of course)?

Internet Protocol (IP)

The stuff that goes across the Internet is packets of data, as discussed previously. The essential thing that a packet needs to know is where it's supposed to be delivered. Everything else is a detail.

Errors in content, for example, can be handled by the kind of error-detection and error-correction methods that we've discussed in previous chapters. In the worst case, a recipient can ask for a packet to be sent again.

If the packet doesn't get to the right place, though, even in imperfect form, the intended recipient won't even know that someone out there has something to say. Internet Protocol (IP) gets packets to the place where they're supposed to go.

IPv4: 32 Bits Are Not Enough

IP is the core of the Internet, and an IP address is the core of IP. Without an IP address, you're nowhere—at least, as far as the Internet is concerned. IP addresses, however, are quickly becoming a scarce commodity.

At the time this book is written, the prevailing version of IP is version 4 (IPv4 for short). IPv4 uses a 32-bit address that uniquely identifies the intended delivery point.

It's awkward to speak in 32-bit strings or to remember a single decimal number that might range from 0 to just over 4 billion, so an IPv4 address is usually written as a set of four numbers separated by periods. Each of these numbers represents the value of one 8-bit group, and each number can therefore range from 0 to 255. Figure 17.1 shows a Windows 95 control panel that includes some typical IPv4 addresses.

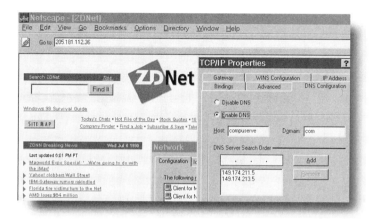

FIGURE 17.1
IP addresses (center and top) identify physical locations on the network. An IPv4 address consists of 4 bytes (32 bits) and is written as four numbers (each in the range from 0 to 255) that are separated by periods.

With 32 bits, IPv4 can represent 4.3 billion different addresses. This is a big number, but it's not big enough to give even one IP address to every living person.

In such cities as Los Angeles, telephone companies are frantically adding area codes in an effort to keep up with the number of personal "addresses" on the phone system (home phone, business phone, cellular phone, fax...). In the same way, the 32-bit IP address space will gain much-needed breathing room with the coming migration to IPv6, a 128-bit scheme.

How many addresses can you define with 128 bits? Enough to give 60,000 trillion trillion addresses to every human being who was alive in 1996. Yes, I meant to say "trillion" twice.

It's hard to imagine a shortfall in IP addresses after the IPv6 expansion, at least as long as Earth remains the only known inhabited planet. You might well have several dozen devices in your home, your car, and even on your person, each with a separate IP address and some kind of wireless link to other devices—IPv6 will make this entirely possible.

IPv6 offers more than a larger address space. The protocol update includes important improvements to Internet security. For example, under IPv6 it is harder for one location to send messages that appear to come from some other location.

Enhanced IP security amplifies the Mobile IP extensions that I mentioned in Chapter 9, which require a secure way of letting a moving user give a new forwarding location to a "home base" computer. IPv6 security will make it easier for us to stay connected at all times—assuming, as I said at the beginning of the chapter, that this is something you *want* to do.

You won't need to know, or care, when IPv6 comes into use. You don't type out 32-bit IPv4 addresses today, and you won't have to type out raw IPv6 addresses tomorrow. It might be that people will find it easier to reassign IPv4 addresses, automatically, to different devices at different times than to make the changes needed to Internet systems to enable IPv6 adoption.

I mention the IPv6 technology to demonstrate that the Internet itself, as well as the content of the Web that we access via the Internet, is very much a work in progress.

Do You Need to Know Your IP Address?

You might wonder where you get your personal IP address. In most cases, you don't need a permanent IP address; your Internet Service Provider assigns an address to you each time you log in. Your computer uses that address, automatically, for that one session only.

Your email address, like your telephone number, is yours alone. Your IP address can be different whenever you dial up, with different users using any given IP address from one moment to the next.

Permanent IP addresses might have to become more common when we're constantly connected, either by wireless means or by a device such as a "cable modem" of the kind that I described in Chapter 7. Address assignment, however, will probably remain invisible to users, in the same way that you know your own telephone number but have no idea which circuit your phone company uses for your home's connection.

While writing this chapter, I moved my office out of my home to a nearby office building; the telephone number stayed the same, even though the "network address" of my phone was changed. IP addresses are just as transparent to users.

Transmission Control Protocol (TCP)

In Figure 17.1, the central window bears the title "TCP/IP Properties." We know about IP, but what's this "TCP" thing?

TCP and IP work together like a bus driver and a tour guide in a group excursion through Europe. The driver finds the route that will get you to your next point of interest, but the guide with the clipboard and whistle makes sure that everyone is on the bus when it leaves for the next destination.

IP is the driver—admittedly, a somewhat casual driver who won't call the home office if a passenger falls out the back door during the trip. TCP (Transmission Control Protocol) is the guide, who actually takes responsibility for your safe arrival.

It's possible to communicate across the Internet with IP alone, by simply sending packets according to the User Datagram Protocol (UDP). Conveniently, those transmitted packets can be referred to as User Datagram Packets (UDPs), employing a single acronym for both what is sent and how it is sent.

Sending a UDP is like sending a fax. You send the message and forget about it—you don't hang around the mail room waiting for confirmation that the message was delivered. If the communication link is reliable, UDP communication can be faster than the time-consuming confirmation procedures used by TCP.

TCP is often worth its overhead, however, because it improves the reliability of Internet transactions. The combination of TCP and IP verifies that packets were received, without errors, at the designated IP address.

The compound name, TCP/IP, is spoken as the letters alone: "T C P I P," without saying "slash" in the middle. To a great extent, TCP/IP is the true name of the thing that we usually call "the Internet."

The Internet is not a physical thing: You can't tell whether a computer is part of the Internet by looking at it or even by checking the connections to the computer. The Internet is not something that can be owned. The Internet exists in the cooperation of its participants, with TCP/IP as the mechanism of that cooperation.

Domain Name Service (DNS)

In Figure 17.1, the **Go to** box near the top of the screen shows the IP address that I entered to view the ZDNet news site.

A moment later, those numbers were replaced on my screen by what most people find a preferable way of describing an Internet location, as shown in Figure 17.2: the label `http://www.zdnet.com/`. That label didn't come from nowhere—it is maintained, along with others like it, on one of several computers that are called Domain Name Servers.

FIGURE 17.2
URLs lead to IP addresses like the one seen in Figure 17.1, through the Domain Name Service.

Look back at Figure 17.1. The IP addresses in the middle of the screen are the ones where my computer looks for cross-reference information between cryptic 32-bit IP addresses and more easily remembered names.

If I could "crack" one or more Domain Name Servers, many people who request a common Web site name such as "www.zdnet.com" could wind up viewing my Web page instead of the one maintained by Ziff-Davis. Many Internet services control against this possibility by using various forms of verification to ensure that the site that answers a request is the one that was meant to answer.

Uniform Resource Locators (URLs)

The `http://www.zdnet.com/` label in Figure 17.2 is a Uniform Resource Locator (URL). Every URL consists of two parts: a scheme (in this case, `http:`) and a scheme-specific part.

The format of the scheme-specific part of a URL varies depending (logically enough) on the scheme. For example, if the scheme were `file:`, the scheme-specific part would have the format of a fully qualified path name to a file on my own machine (see Figure 17.3).

FIGURE 17.3
A URL can point to a local file as easily as it can to a distant Internet resource.

It's a revelation to many PC users that URLs are not just for use on the Internet. A URL can point to one of your own local files, to an interactive session with a computer on the other side of the world, or to an electronic mail link (using a `mailto:` scheme) with anyone who has an Internet mail address.

URLs are not limited to static "place names" on the Internet; a URL can contain additional information that a computer at another location can interpret as commands to be followed. The remote computer can then produce a stream of text, sent to you and to no one else, that looks like any other Web page—except that this "page" exists only for you.

You can see a command-type URL in Figure 17.4, where I've asked the HotBot Internet search facility to find Web-accessible information on the subject of "cookies." I did not have to compose that messy-looking "location" in the box at the top of the screen—the search engine built that command string from the filled-in fields of a search request form and fed the result back to me.

If I "bookmark" the page of my search results, I can capture the corresponding command and be able to regenerate this search at a later time by simply clicking on this entry in my bookmarks.

FIGURE 17.4
A URL can contain commands, as well as naming a "place" on the network.

With the growing use of dynamic data generation, we'll never be able to size up the Web in terms of the number of pages of information it offers. There are as many pages of data on the Web as there are questions that people want to ask, products that people want to buy, and tasks that people want another computer to perform.

Hypertext Transfer Protocol (HTTP)

A large, fast-growing fraction of the URLs crossing the Internet have a scheme of `http:` (meaning Hypertext Transfer Protocol). Behind the friendly point-and-click façade of a Web browser program (such as Netscape Navigator or Microsoft Internet Explorer), HTTP is making connections across the Internet, asking remote systems for information, receiving the information, and closing the connection.

When I click on an underlined item on the screen that's displaying a Web page, the browser produces a command such as `GET /pub/WWW/TheProject.html HTTP/1.0`. Aren't you glad you don't have to type little messages like these? Web browser tools, in general, do an excellent job of hiding the lengthy and boring conversations that take place between your PC and the remote computing facilities that you use.

A session on the Web involves an enormous number of separate conversations, because every HTTP interaction makes a whole new start. Your browser repeats the four-part sequence of connection, request, response, and close.

There is no continuity. Every request is a new conversation, with no way of retaining any context from what might have happened just seconds before.

May I Offer You a Cookie?

In many cases, a Web site can do useful things if it can maintain some context during a series of interactions. For example, a retail Web site has to have some way of recording what you want to buy, as you add items to your order before you go to the "checkout" phase of your session.

Many Web browser programs provide a standard way of letting a remote Web site store information (only for that site's use) on your own PC's hard disk. These stored items are commonly called *cookies*, and they're a widely misunderstood part of the Web.

When you accept cookies, it does not mean that a remote Web site is getting free rein to write all over your hard disk or that a remote computer can read whatever it likes from your computer. The remote computer asks your browser to add an item to a particular file; that is, to the browser's cookies file. The remote computer can ask the browser to retrieve that remote machine's stored items from that file.

It is the browser program on your PC, not the remote computer, that interacts with your files. This limits the potential for abuse.

Cookies Can Get Too Fresh

Entire books have been written on the subject of cookies and on the ways they can be used—and, to venture an editorial comment, misused—to add context to your interactions on the Web.

Cookies can be used, for example, by a service that sells advertising on many different Web sites to deliver advertising that is tailored to your personal patterns of activity. You might see a different advertisement at the top of a Web page than another user will see when viewing "the same" page.

If you want to limit your PC's cookie intake, you can set your browser to alert you whenever a remote site asks to "set a cookie"(see Figure 17.5). You can also choose to deny any request (see Figure 17.6). The worst that can happen is that you might get a message from a site saying that it is unable to complete some operation you've requested because your browser is not recording needed information. You can then decide if you want to repeat the process, this time accepting the cookie.

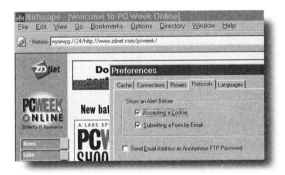

FIGURE 17.5
You can let cookies be set without your attention, or you can ask to be alerted to any cookie request.

Cookies Can Be Convenient

One useful thing about cookies is that they can hold such information as a user name and password. A cookie can let you enter a site that requires, for example, paid membership in an organization without typing your name and password every time.

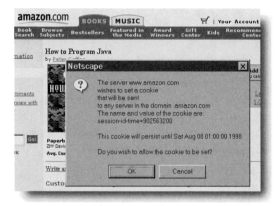

FIGURE 17.6
You can choose to deny permission to set a cookie and see if the remote computer complains that it's trying to do you a favor that requires a cookie to carry it out.

Figure 17.7 shows an online article from a site maintained by the American Association for the Advancement of Science. This site requires paid membership for full access to its articles. Note my name in the upper left corner of the screen—the site identifies me by reading an entry that's preserved, from one session to the next, in my cookies file.

FIGURE 17.7
Automatic login to limited-access Web sites is a convenient benefit of cookies—unless someone else uses your PC or copies your cookie file and gains illicit access to sensitive data.

Save Your Cookies for Yourself

Automatic logon to controlled Web sites is a mixed blessing. Your cookies file, which is just a simple text file that can be viewed in many ways, might be storing information that you would not normally disclose to a coworker (or even to some members of your family).

If you share a PC with other people, you might want to block the acceptance of cookies, even if it does mean entering passwords or credit card numbers or other data whenever a remote computer needs that information.

Computer and Internet Security

Wait a minute—did I just talk about sending credit card numbers across the Internet? Yes, I did, and this is not as dangerous or foolish as you might have heard.

If you think about the Internet's design, you'll see the potential for invasion of your privacy that arises when packets of data go running around in search of their destinations. Many computers handle a packet en route, and packets bear both their origin and their destination addresses in plain sight. Their content is likewise open to inspection.

If someone wants to know what you're saying, to whom, the information is out there. Fortunately, so are the tools for protecting your personal data.

Cryptography: It's Not Just for Spies Anymore

The message of cheap computing power pervades this book, and this chapter is no exception. One of the things that we get from cheap computers is the capability to use mathematically demanding methods of privacy protection, generically known as "strong encryption."

Figure 17.8 shows one strong cryptographic technique, called a Diffie-Hellman exchange, that has particular importance to network communications. This remarkable process lets us negotiate a secret key to be shared between two parties. We can establish this key with no previous secret contact between those parties and in full view of any eavesdroppers.

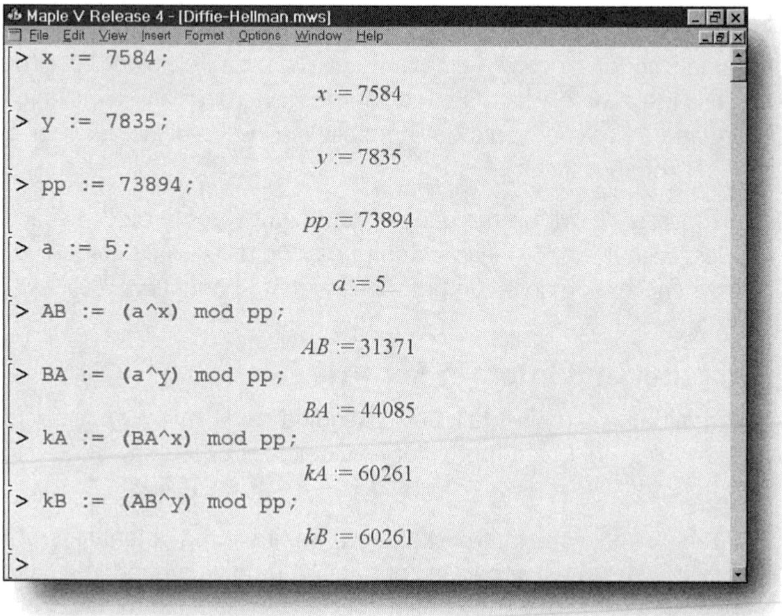

FIGURE 17.8
A Diffie-Hellman cryptographic exchange creates, and preserves, a secret encryption key—even if performed in full view of any eavesdropper.

Even with full knowledge of the process, an eavesdropper with any feasible level of computing capability will not be able to determine the key that we produce in any usefully short period of time. By "usefully short," I'm talking about sizable fractions of the age of the universe.

We can therefore use a negotiated key to encode the rest of our conversation, with high confidence in the confidentiality of our exchange (at least, in the portion of that exchange that travels on the network). Protecting your electronic mail archives or your message printouts is up to you; the network's job is done when the message is securely delivered.

In a Diffie-Hellman exchange, I pick a number: call it x. The other party picks another number: call it y. Only I know the value of x; only the other party knows the value of y.

By general agreement among a group of users, we have previously settled on two values that I will call a and pp. These values can be built in to a Web browser or other communications software. I don't need to know what these values are, as long as the other party is using the same values.

A mathematical operation of the type called a one-way or trapdoor function lets me generate another number, using my secret x along with the public a and pp. The other party performs the same operation, using y with a and pp. We exchange those generated values, which I will call AB and BA (one value is sent by party A to party B, the other value is sent by B to A).

Note that any eavesdropper can see the values of AB and BA and can be assumed to know the values of a and pp. The generating function is called one-way, however, because it is fairly easy to compute AB and BA from x, y, a, and pp, but it is effectively impossible to reverse the process and determine the values of x or y.

Now, here is the remarkable thing. I can use the value of BA in combination with my still-secret value of x to produce a final result—a secret key—that I will call kA. Party B can use the value of AB in combination with B's still-secret value of y to produce a value that I will call kB.

The values of kA and kB will be the same.

I emphasize that the values of x and y are never transmitted and cannot be determined, because of the one-way characteristic of the generating function. The now-shared secret key cannot be deduced by anyone else—even someone who's been watching the entire process.

The demonstration that I perform here uses numbers small enough to find by brute-force search. With larger numbers, however, the process is proof against any feasible attack using any known mathematical techniques.

Clocks and Codes

The key mathematical idea in many strong encryption methods is *modular arithmetic*, also called "clock arithmetic."

If I go around the clock more than once during a period of more than 12 hours, I can't tell how much time has passed. When the clock gets back to the point where I started, I can't tell how many times I've been around before.

If it's midnight now, it's easy to figure out that 100 hours from now will be four o'clock in the morning. But if it's four in the morning, I don't know if the elapsed time has been 4 hours, or 28 hours, or 52 hours, or 76 hours, or 100 hours, or any other value of the form $24 \times n + 4$.

We can say that 100 *mod* 24 is 4: It's an easy calculation, but not reversible. That's a one-way function, and the demonstration in Figure 17.8 shows a cryptographic application of the concept.

Secure Sockets Layer (SSL)

When you enter a retail Web site or a site that handles other sensitive information, your Web browser can participate in a Secure Sockets Layer (SSL) transaction. You enable this with an option setting in your browser, as shown in Figure 17.9; you can choose to be advised when a secure exchange begins, as shown in Figure 17.10.

FIGURE 17.9
You get to decide if you want to trust the protections of a Secure Sockets Layer for protecting your data en route.

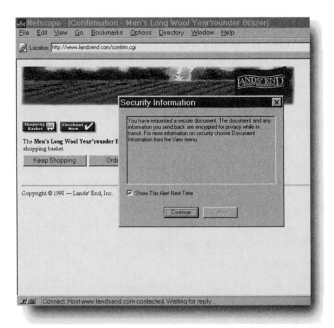

FIGURE 17.10
You can choose to be alerted when you cross the line from normal operation to confidential data exchange.

You'll see some kind of indicator, such as the unbroken key that appears at the bottom left corner in Figure 17.11, when you are in a secure mode.

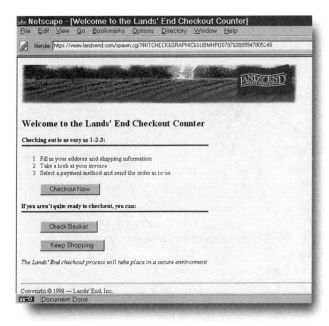

FIGURE 17.11
A distinctive icon serves as confirmation that your data exchanges are protected against any eavesdropper.

When security is enabled, your packets become sealed envelopes. People can still see where those packets are going, which is a privacy issue in itself, but the contents are unreadable by anyone but the intended recipient.

Protecting Yourself with Passwords

Encryption is only half of a privacy solution. The other half is authentication; that is, proving that you are who you say you are.

It does no good to prevent eavesdroppers from watching you check your bank balance if anyone can read your account number off of one of your checks and log in, pretending to be you.

Traditionally, we prove our identity with passwords. There are other common identity checks, such as your mother's maiden name or the month in which you were born, but such personal data is all too easy to find—on the Internet and also by other means.

Most people do a poor job of choosing passwords. In a typical audit of one computer installation, security analysts looked at more than 3,000 passwords; fewer than 500 were hard to guess. When choosing passwords, people tend to use English words, or backward spellings of words, or their own automobile license plate numbers, or other nonsecret identifiers. Passwords are often short enough to find by a brute-force search—in the study mentioned previously, more than 20% of the passwords were only five letters (all capitals or all small letters).

Cryptography experts estimate that each character of password length is the equivalent of adding about four bits to a randomly created binary key like the one produced in a Diffie-Hellman exchange. A 56-bit key, of the kind used by the

NOTE
A typical five-letter password that doesn't mix uppercase and lowercase letters can be found by trying (on average) only 11,881,376 random guesses. That's a big number to you or to me, but not to a computer.

Biometric techniques or "smart" tokens (both described in Chapter 11) help us avoid the need to choose and manage passwords.

now aging Data Encryption Standard, is therefore equivalent to about a 14-character password. Most people use shorter passwords, but even DES is considered quite inadequate for real security today.

Hypertext Markup Language (HTML)

The core Internet technologies of TCP/IP, DNS, URLs, and HTTP are just delivery tools; the security technologies of SSL and passwords and the state-saving function of cookies are just logistic details. None of these things is the Web.

The innovation that transformed the Internet from a research tool to a "civilian" information utility was the introduction of Hypertext Markup Language, or HTML, as a means of presenting Internet content and information connections in a simple visual form.

A document specialist at CERN, the European Laboratory for High Energy Physics, proposed the notion of the Web in a document that estimated the total effort as three months' work for four software engineers plus a programmer.

Writing in the spring of 1989, proposal author Tim Berners-Lee said that "Potentially, HyperText provides a single user-interface to many large classes of stored information such as reports, notes, databases, computer documentation, and on-line systems help… There is a potential large benefit from the integration of a variety of systems in a way which allows a user to follow links pointing from one piece of information to another one."

It would seem that the world agrees.

Just Beneath the Surface

You can see the HTML underpinnings of any Web page with any Web browser that has a View Source command as seen in Figure 17.12.

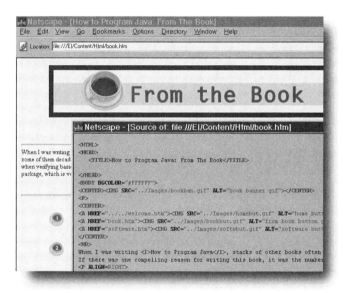

FIGURE 17.12
A View Source command shows you the mechanics of presenting attractive pages to any Web user, near or far.

HTML combines ordinary text with special *tags* that a browser interprets as instructions. An HTML page is data, but in a sense it is also a program. Different browsers can display the same page in different ways, using alternative tags that allow for trade-offs between attractive appearance and data transfer speed.

Tags can embed an image in a page or incorporate small programs called *scripts* that can make a Web page as interactive as any ordinary Windows program. By using HTML as a program's front end, a programmer makes that program usable from any computer that has an HTML browser and a connection (Internet or other) to the computer where the program is running.

The Browser: On the Surface

I'm taking for granted your ability to locate, run, and use an HTML browser on your PC. New PCs come with such software ready to use, and any startup package for a new Internet account will give you the software and plenty of help in figuring out its commands.

Three key ideas are involved in using any typical browser. I've already shown the basic mechanism of entering a URL in a location field at the top of the screen to take you to a page on the Web. That's idea #1.

A sub-idea is that of saving locations by using "bookmarks" or "favorites" or some other term that varies from one kind of browser to another. Whatever name is used, your browser builds a collection of URLs (usually accessible by the title of the page last seen at that location) for you to revisit at will.

The second key idea is that of following hyperlinks, usually appearing on your screen as underlined words or phrases or as inviting graphics. Clicking on a link results in some action, typically the display of a different page.

The third key idea is that of using the Forward and Back operations, usually accessible through obvious onscreen pushbuttons that you click with your mouse. Your browser maintains an internal list of places where it's been, working much like the simple Undo/Redo queue in a word processor or other PC software. If clicking on a hyperlink takes you to something that isn't useful, clicking on the Back button (or using an equivalent keyboard shortcut) takes you back to where you were before.

As long as you don't then start down some other path, the Forward command lets you retrace a journey through several connected pages, even if you back up by many steps.

When you go Forward, you usually see that a page becomes visible much more quickly than it did the first time you viewed it. Your browser maintains a *cache* of local copies of large elements, such as graphics, and displays them from your hard disk instead of reloading them across the communication line.

If you view Web pages with many complex graphics, your browser's cache might wind up consuming tens of megabytes of disk space. You need to make your own decisions about how much cache space you want to allocate; most browsers offer this as a convenient adjustment from an options control panel.

Most browsers let you clear the cache whenever you like if you want to eliminate all local records of having visited a particular site or if you have a temporary need for some extra disk space. Smaller caches, or frequently cleared caches, will slow your routine Web operations.

Traveling the World Wide Web

You don't need to know the workings, or even the names, of Internet core technologies to get a lot of value from the World Wide Web.

Some data suggests that the Web has become the major competitor to prime-time television shows, in terms of consuming people's scarce leisure time.

Surfing

What do people do on the Web? The common expression is "surfing"—following the connections from one site to another and enjoying the discovery of fascinating facts or interesting ideas.

I maintain a Web site, for example, on behalf of my amateur radio club. In addition to information on club activities, the club's page offers links to other useful sites, such as the U.S. Naval Observatory's time-of-day service and the current local weather (see Figure 17.13).

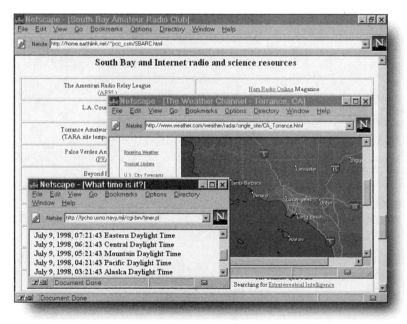

FIGURE 17.13
An interesting Web site combines unique remote resources with current data of local interest, creating a combination that appeals to many visitors.

In Figure 17.14, you can see the degree of connection that's involved in creating an engaging Web site. At upper right is a representation of my radio club site. Visualize its "home page" at the center of the wheel-like structure, with the spokes of that wheel being links to other sites.

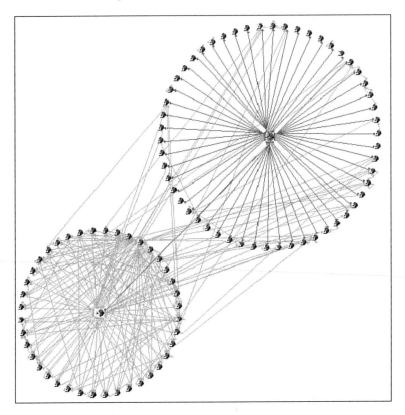

FIGURE 17.14
This structural view shows the many resources accessible from a radio club's Web site (top right) and the overlap with the connections offered by a national radio organization.

At lower left in Figure 17.14 is the "wheel" of the Web site for the national amateur radio association, the American Radio Relay League (ARRL). You can see that many of the sites to which I've linked are themselves linked to ARRL. On the other hand, you can also see that someone who comes from the ARRL site to mine will find many links that ARRL's site does not directly provide. That's surfing.

Shopping

In the earlier section on security technologies, I addressed the common concerns that make many people reluctant to try the convenience of Web-based shopping.

I should note that some Web sites that invite you to place an order by using simple form and mail technologies lack the protections of SSL or other security schemes. This is as bad an idea as placing a telephone order, giving your credit card number, while using a cellular phone or a home cordless phone. The odds are on your side, but you're making life easy for the bad guys.

There are many responsible retail sites that can save you enough on just a few purchases to pay back the cost of your Internet service for a year. Lands' End, for example, maintains an Overstocks page with dramatic discounts that you'll never see (or will probably see too late) in their printed catalogs.

Well-designed retail sites combine the timeliness of a showroom visit with the convenience of catalog shopping and the complete technical detail of a briefing at the factory. Dell, whose site plays such a prominent part in Chapter 10, makes it easy to examine and price alternative PC configurations via the Web. So does Micron, my runner-up recommendation for new PC buyers.

Sharing

Most Internet accounts include some space allowance for a personal Web site on the service provider's machines. Details vary from one provider to another.

In general, creating a personal Web page is easy with free or inexpensive tools. You can get enough instruction in HTML from online tutorials so you'll be able to set up a page like my radio club's with just a simple text editor (see Figure 17.15). Notepad, for example, should be present on any Windows PC, and HTML is just punctuated text.

When your draft page is prepared, you can preview its appearance with your browser. Remember, local files are just another kind of URL.

Then you can upload the file to your site with a utility program such as John Junod's WS_FTP32 (see Figure 17.16). This program is free to U.S. government, academic, and noncommercial individual users and can be obtained via the Internet.

It's likely that your Internet Service Provider offers WS_FTP32, or an equivalent tool, for download from the ISP's support site. The latest versions are even easier to use than the version shown here.

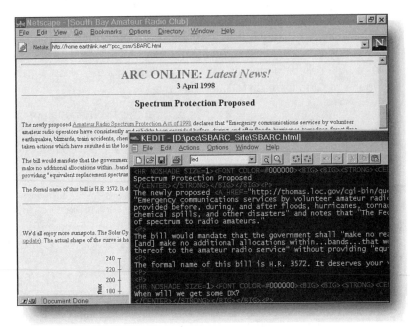

FIGURE 17.15
Simple tools, such as an ordinary text editor, are quite enough to create a good-looking Web page that's packed with resources.

After your HTML file is in place on your ISP's host machine, all that's left is to tell other people it's there. Internet index services, such as HotBot and AltaVista, often invite submittal of new URLs with category information. People who maintain related Web pages are often willing to add a link to your new page from theirs.

Most Web pages have some kind of feedback link that sends mail to the maintainer of a page, giving you a convenient way of calling your new page to the attention of someone who's likely to be interested.

FIGURE 17.16
Support tools such as WS_FTP32, available at no charge for noncommercial use, complete your toolkit for placing original material in front of a worldwide audience.

Cybercrime

Becoming a Web page publisher is a lot like becoming a homeowner. Suddenly, you find yourself thinking about property values and the quality of the neighborhood in a different way.

If your carefully polished Web page can't be viewed, for example, because some mischief-maker has saturated your ISP's server with a "ping attack," you're likely to resent it. (A "ping attack" is the electronic equivalent of a campaign of hang-up phone calls; it consumes the system's attention, preventing its normal work.)

Putting the Threats in Context

The benefits of computers are their speed, their capability (through software) to respond to different situations with different behaviors, and their capability to function without human supervision. All of these benefits are also potential threats, but other important artifacts of our time are equally able to harm as well as help.

Computer security is an issue and makes many people nervous about using credit cards across the Internet. We didn't need the Internet, however, to have widespread problems with credit card fraud. People who obtain your credit card number in the course of doing their jobs can sell an accumulated list of numbers, whether those numbers arrive by phone or fax or electronic mail or even by armored car.

Most credit card fraud involves people who won't be stopped from seeing your number by any Internet encryption scheme, because they have to see the number to complete the transaction. Security will always come down to trusting the people with whom we do business.

Anyone who accepts personal checks, or even paper money, has already decided to accept some risk of fraud in return for greater convenience. That risk of fraud might be preferable to the risk of other forms of crime, such as simple robbery.

It's not clearly better to have people carrying assets with intrinsic value and with no means of being traced to their rightful owner. We don't want to go back to the days of weighing gold dust on the counter and traveling with armed guards on top of our stagecoaches. We therefore need to accept the idea that Internet commerce is just a new variation on the age-old problem of authenticating means of payment.

Information Warfare

Some types of crime are somewhat specific to the realm of information systems. As we become dependent on the speed of computers and networks, we become hostage to their continued operation. We can be damaged by any act that slows our computers' functions, even if the data they hold stays private and unharmed. Administrative convenience features can turn into modes of attack unless the possibility of malice is recognized—and headed off—at an early stage of design.

Large computer networks need to be designed and operated with a healthy topping of constructive paranoia. Many computer products, including most PC hardware and software, originated as single-user or trusted-user designs; it is hard to add robust security to such a system after the fact. The possibility of secure operation needs to be part of the basic design.

An operating system such as UNIX or Windows NT, not Windows 95 or the Macintosh OS, is a necessary starting point if you're building an information system that has to protect valuable data against both malice and accident.

If accidents are the concern, you should devote substantial attention to physical issues such as offsite storage of backup data.

If malice is the concern, you should be focusing on matters such as audit procedures and logging of computer operations.

PC Virus Protection

One morning, I recall, my first Windows 95 machine suddenly ceased to see its CD-ROM drive. Ten minutes later, it finally occurred to me that I might have a virus problem.

Sure enough, IBM's antivirus program (one of the best, along with Symantec's Norton product) detected an infection. I won't name the virus, because I don't want to give its creator the satisfaction.

It took hours of work to wipe the hard disk clean and restore my system to a useful state. I still don't know how the PC "caught" the bug, but this was a machine that I routinely used to test software from many companies for possible review in *PC Week*. I'm glad that I was isolating product tests to a single machine at that time. I have not always followed this practice, and few of us can afford to keep a "scratch" machine for this purpose.

Types of Malicious Programs

What, exactly, is a *computer virus*? In their book on computer ethics, which I cite at the beginning of this chapter, Tom Forester and Perry Morrison offer the following list of types of malicious codes, using common names that are often used in slightly different ways:

- *Trojan horse*. A program that creates a permanent entry path, for later use, into a system whose security has been temporarily breached. A Trojan horse might grant administrative privileges to a user who would not normally have the authority, for example, to read other users' files.

- *Logic bomb*. A program that performs some destructive act after a certain time delay or after some event. Sometimes, a logic bomb is written to "detonate" if not reset within a certain period of time; it will wreak havoc at some unpredictable time, most likely in some untraceable way, if the programmer who creates it and maintains it is fired by an employer.

- *Virus*. A program that looks for opportunities to copy itself to other systems, sometimes (but not always) with other malicious side effects such as erasing files on "infected" machines (perhaps on some particular date).

● *Worm.* Like a virus, a program that seeks to spread to other systems, but generally in a manner that exploits the properties of computer networks (viruses tend to be designed for spreading via files or floppy disks or other exchangeable media).

Motives of Virus Creators

In his 1990 anthology, *Computers Under Attack: Intruders, Worms, and Viruses*, editor Peter J. Denning narrates one of his conversations about computer viruses with someone who asked, "You mean those things aren't germs? They're created intentionally by people? Why would anyone do that?" Why, indeed?

Viruses and worms are written for many reasons, ranging from destructive impulses to benign (but often irresponsible) curiosity about whether a technique will work. Some of these programs do damage by intent, others only by accident. For example, a virus might interfere with the normal operation of a carelessly written utility program that expects a region of memory to be unused and crashes if a virus conceals itself in that range of addresses.

The Internet Worm

It's impossible to make blanket statements about viruses and worms, because there are so many special cases that can be exploited by crafty programmers. One of the best-known malefactors, the Internet Worm of November 1988, would spread only to Sun 3 and VAX computers running a particular version of the UNIX operating system—but thousands of machines fit this description.

The Internet Worm did no intentional damage, but it created so many copies of itself that it paralyzed the infested systems by using all of their computational capacity. Network interactions spread the program to at least 3,000 machines (about 5% of the computers on the Internet at that time). Their paralysis affected the users of many other systems by reducing overall network performance.

Trade-offs and Preventions

There are book-length treatments of virus and worm behavior, especially in the larger context of security policy for large computer sites. In your personal computing, the virus problem is a trade-off between safety and flexibility.

If you buy a new PC, and run only the software that comes on that PC, and work only with data that you create on that PC, your likelihood of worm and virus problems is almost nil.

If you routinely download and try out programs from unknown sources, and if you open complex documents (with embedded "macro" instructions) from authors you don't know, you are likely to have virus problems within a year or two.

Antivirus software is cheap and is easy to install and use; as virus technology "improves" (if that's the right word), the better antivirus vendors (such as Symantec) offer automatic online updates (as shown in Figure 17.17).

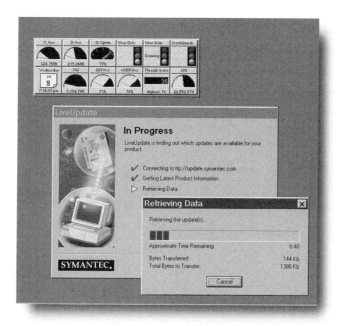

FIGURE 17.17
Your antivirus protection is never left behind by new attacks if the product you choose provides live online updates like those from Symantec Corp.

What We've Learned

In *Systemantics*, previously referenced in Chapter 11, John Gall asserts that "A complex system that works is invariably found to have evolved from a simple system that works. A complex system designed from scratch never works... you have to start with a working simple system."

The complex system of a Windows PC and the complex systems of the Internet and the Web both began with working simple systems. It is their strength, and their weakness, that both our PCs and our networks retain the core technologies that made them work in the beginning.

The DOS machine at the heart of a Windows PC is like the low-level part of a human brain that can keep you breathing when nothing else is working. When Windows gets tied up in its complexity, we can do things from a DOS window and a DEBUG "-" prompt that can get us back to work—or at least, preserve our data for another try.

That DOS core is also the point of attack, however, for virus programs and makes it hard to keep programs from interfering with one another's operations.

The simple ideas that lie at the heart of the Internet and the Web don't always scale up well to handle the challenges of worldwide communication, but they make it possible to do small things at small cost. Without that ease of entry, the Internet and the Web would never have grown so popular and wouldn't have problems of scale. There is no escape from that paradox.

When PCs were new, you had to have an engineer's inclination to understand and fix things if you wanted to do useful work. Today's Windows PC is much closer to being an "information appliance," and the Web is close to being an "information utility" that anyone can use.

I hope this book helps you fill the gaps implied by that crucial word "close."

Common PC File Types:
File Name Extensions and File Descriptions

*I*DEALLY, IT WOULD BE your PC's problem to know what kinds of files
hold what kinds of data and to know which programs you can use
to view or change the information in various kinds of files. Ideally.

Until we get to that point with PCs (which other types of computers, such as the Macintosh, are much closer to reaching), the following list might help you puzzle out many problems. These
problems won't happen every day, but they might well highlight
(if that's the word) your five or six worst computer days in any
given year.

- **386:** Virtual device driver. See **VXD**.

- **ASC:** ASCII file. See **TXT**.

- **AU:** Audio file format, common on computers running the UNIX operating system; standard audio format for Java-based programs (such as those that add active content to many Web pages).

- **AVI:** Audio Video Interleave file, a common format for video clips with sound tracks. AVI files wrap video segments around associated audio data in **WAV** format.

  There are no time stamps or frame counts in AVI files; they merely indicate the desired rate of playback for the video frames and hope for the best. AVI makes no provision for recovery of real-time synchronization if playback is interrupted or delayed.

  You'll find more than you could possibly want to know about AVI files on the World Wide Web at `http://www.rahul.net/jfm/avicont.html`.

- **BAK:** Backup file, often created automatically by a program as a safety feature in case of an error while you're saving a changed file.

  If your PC does not complete the process of saving a file, or if you try to open a file and get an error message, you might find the previously saved version of your work in a file with the same main filename but with an extension of BAK. For example, mywork.doc might be backed up as mywork.bak.

  You should determine, from user manuals or online help, the extent and enabling commands of any automatic backup options a piece of software might provide.

  Many disk management utility programs will locate and offer to eliminate any leftover BAK files on your disk to recover wasted space. This is usually a safe thing to do.

- **BAT:** Batch file, containing a series of commands of the kind that might be given from a console window's command line.

  By giving a name to a series of commands, a batch file has the effect of adding that name and that series of operations to the list of commands that are already known to the PC.

For example, two built-in DOS commands can be combined to count the files on a disk that have not been backed up since the last time they were changed. From the command line, you could type:

```
attrib /s ¦ \windows\command\find /c "A "
```

The entry above executes the standard ATTRIB command (which determines the attributes of files), using the /s option that looks in all subdirectories of a disk, and then sends the result to a FIND command that looks for lines containing (in this case) the pattern "A " (indicating an archive file; that is, one that has been changed since its last backup). The /c option tells the FIND command just to report the number of lines with that "A " pattern, rather than actually listing those lines.

It's easy to create a file, named something like BAKCOUNT.BAT, that holds the command just described. At least, it's much easier than remembering and typing that command whenever you wonder if a backup operation is overdue.

A batch file is a simple text file (see **TXT**) that is usually interpreted as if the same keystrokes were being issued as interactive commands. The exceptions, when a batch file might need some extra code characters, are only of interest to those writing fairly complex scripts in the PC's "batch language," a facility that is rarely used under Windows 95 or Windows NT.

● **BMP:** Bitmap file, a graphics file containing pixel-by-pixel representations of the colors of points on the screen, along with descriptive information on the arrangement (rows, columns, number of bits per pixel) of that data.

A monochrome bitmap stores one bit, indicating (typically) black or white, for each pixel. A "deeper" bitmap holds several bits per pixel, representing either colors or shades of gray (as discussed in Chapter 6).

● **class:** Java class file, a program that runs in a *Java virtual machine*.

On a standard PC, a Java virtual machine (JVM) is a program, not a piece of hardware. A JVM module is usually associated with a Web browser program, letting the browser execute and display Java programs ("applets") that are incorporated in Web pages.

Unlike most other PC programs, which use the native hardware instructions of the CPU, a Java class file contains instructions for the JVM. The JVM program then translates these instructions into equivalent hardware commands. A class file can therefore be interpreted to run on any computer that has its own version of the JVM software (or on a computer with a "Java chip").

Because the JVM introduces a layer of control over privileges such as which files a program can open, Applets that run in a browser are intrinsically safer than other types of programs that come from an untrusted source.

● **COM:** Rarely encountered today, a COM file is a primitive form of PC program file (see **EXE**) that can only package very simple programs (no more than 64Kbytes in total size).

In modern usage, the acronym COM almost always stands for Microsoft's Component Object Model. When used this way, COM refers to a means by which two different pieces of software can treat each other as providers and users of services, without specific coordination between the designers of the cooperating products. COM is the standard by which elements such as an Excel spreadsheet object can be embedded into documents created by other pieces of software (as demonstrated in Chapter 12). When used in this sense, a "COM file" might be almost any type of application object and might not have the extension .com at all.

● **CSV:** Comma-separated–variable file, a file containing data of columnar format, such as a table of numbers, with each line of the file representing one line of the table and with commas indicating boundaries between the columns.

If a value in a CSV file contains a comma as part of the data content, the entire data block is usually placed within quotation marks—for example:

"Coffee, Peter",PC Week,"Medford, Mass."

A blank entry in a column is indicated by two consecutive commas.

If you ever prepare or edit CSV data by hand, you might find it hard to fight the habit of placing a trailing comma inside a closing quotation mark. It is vital, however, to place commas *outside* quotation marks if the commas are to perform their data-separating function.

It's often easier to work with tab-delimited files, which use tab characters rather than commas to separate the elements of a row in a table. Tab-delimited files typically use a **TXT** extension.

- **DBF:** Database file, or "dBASE file."

  The DBF format is a common representation for simple database tables, popularized by Ashton-Tate's dBASE series of products (now owned by Inprise and sold under the Borland label) and also associated with the FoxPro database tools sold by Microsoft.

  Many programs can read—and often write—DBF-format files as a way of packaging tabular data for use by many programs. A DBF is only a single table, however, lacking any way of representing multiple tables and their relationships as can a more sophisticated format such as **MDB**.

- **DIF:** Data Interchange Format, a nonproprietary format—based (like **RTF**) on ASCII codes—that can enable transfer of data between two different pieces of software that have no other format in common.

  Generic formats such as DIF generally do not retain advanced file attributes such as elaborate formatting of data (for example, font sizes or column widths). Saving a file in such a "minimal subset" format could result in the irreversible loss of many hours of work.

  It is good practice to save a file in the "native" format of the program that creates that file before attempting to export data to some other format that might not preserve all of a file's useful content.

- **DLL:** Dynamic Link Library (see Glossary entry).

- **DOC:** Generally, a document file.

  A DOC extension might indicate a simple text file (see **TXT**) whose purpose is often to provide documentation (descriptive information) about a piece of software.

  On Windows PCs, DOC most often denotes a file intended for use with Microsoft Word. This extension is used, however, by many versions of Word that create files not usable by previous versions of the program.

  Complicating the DOC problem is the fact that early copies of Word 7.0 (Word 97) would save a file as **RTF** but with a DOC extension when told to save in the format used by Word 6.0 (Word 95). When Word 97 opened such a file, it would recognize that the file was RTF and offer to save it with an RTF extension. This behavior confused many users.

A common-subset version of DOC is the Word 2.x for Windows format. If in doubt as to which version of Word another person is using, choose the File, Save As menu command and check the format from the drop-down list labeled "Save as type."

● **DOT:** A template file, used to represent a common format or collection of named text styles to ease the creation of documents with a common appearance.

Also, the word "dot" is used when reading aloud the name of a file extension. For example, "GRAPH.BMP" would always be spoken as "graph dot bmp," never as "graph period bmp."

Extensions' names can be spoken aloud to describe an entire category of files; for example, "That program is small enough to fit in a dot-COM [.**COM**] file."

● **DRV:** Driver file containing specialized program code to let a piece of software drive a particular type of attached device without modifications to the main body of the program. Driver files are usually installed automatically by an automatic setup routine, but sometimes require user action to update, possibly to support new features or enhance performance or, more often, to fix a bug.

● **DWG, DXF:** Drawing formats supported by many drafting programs.

Popularized by AutoCAD, these labels are subject to the same problem as DOC files; that is, the same extension label has moved up the food chain with each new version of the associated program, but earlier program versions or other vendors' "compatible" products might not work with files that use the latest enhancements.

● **EXE:** Executable program, a file whose name can be treated as a command to the computer, causing the "launch" of the program whose program code makes up the body of the file.

● **GIF:** Graphics Interchange Format (see Glossary entry).

GIF files might provide 1, 4, or 8 bits per pixel, representing a trade-off between appearance and file size.

A GIF file might be *interlaced*, meaning that the image often appears first in a sketchy overall form before filling in details as the rest of the file comes across a communications link. The user can then abort the download if the image is not what's needed.

Regions of a GIF-file image, typically the background, can be defined as *transparent*. A transparent region takes on the background color of a surrounding Web page, for example, instead of displaying the image within an ugly rectangular block of some arbitrary image background color. Transparency can also be used to achieve various special effects.

● **HLP:** Help file, containing descriptive information on a program's operations, sometimes as simple text (see **TXT**) but often in a searchable format designed for use with the Windows Help command and its elaborate viewing utility.

● **HTM, HTML:** Hypertext Markup Language file. HTML files are simple **TXT**-type files but contain special markup tags that represent formatting information and linkage relationships. (See Glossary entry for **HTML**.)

● **ICO:** Icon file, a file containing a small **BMP** image typically used as a visual cue for starting a program from a graphical display such as the Windows desktop.

● **INI:** Initialization file, a file containing descriptive information, often changed by option settings while a program is running to preserve information from one session to another.

For example, many programs list recently opened files in the File menu. An INI file is often used to maintain that list of recently used files. INI files are commonly simple **TXT**-type files that can be read and altered with basic editing tools.

● **JPEG, JPG:** Joint Photographic Experts Group graphics file format. (See Glossary entry for **JPEG**).

Like **MPEG**, JPEG employs many rules of thumb, based on studies of human perception, to decide what details can be discarded in the pursuit of smaller files.

JPEG and MPEG are both easier to decode (for display) than to encode (for storage). That asymmetry is often a desirable feature in a compression scheme, because image consumers don't see the compression step but are very sensitive to download time (demanding small files) and display time (demanding rapid decompression).

● **LOG:** Log file, typically created while installing a piece of software or performing other multistep operations that might be usefully recorded for later analysis.

A log file is often a simple **TXT** file of the type that can easily be opened with Windows Notepad or any other common text editor. The entries in a log file can range from easily understood dated and time-stamped messages to cryptic notations that are only of use to a specialized reporting program.

● **MDB:** Microsoft Data Base file, often associated with Microsoft Access.

Unlike a **DBF** file, which holds a simple table, an MDB file might represent a collection of tables and their relationships along with definitions of queries, reports, and other associated information.

To the extent that a database combines data with the rules for using that data, an MDB file is a true database while a DBF file is just a piece of a database.

● **MPEG, MPG:** MPEG stands for Moving Pictures Experts Group. As a file extension, MPEG or MPG are to video files what **JPEG** or **JPG** are to still picture files. Both sets of labels denote efficient compression schemes that use a lot of computational power and a lot of knowledge of subjective human perception to produce small files at the cost of losing some fine details.

● **OCX:** OLE Custom Control file, containing a module that can be used by many different programs that are communicating via the Microsoft **COM** apparatus. A single OCX file might provide data-plotting capabilities to several Windows applications or might provide calendar-page style display or selection of dates.

Installing an updated version of an OCX file might disrupt the operations of programs that relied on some particular behavior of earlier versions. Removing a program from your PC might disrupt other programs' operations if the uninstall process fails to account for multiple programs' dependencies on one or more OCX files.

● **PCX:** PC Paintbrush graphics file format, originated by ZSoft but widely supported by other vendors' graphics viewers and editing tools.

The PCX format is suitable for images such as captured computer screens (like many of the illustrations in this book). Unlike **JPEG**, PCX compression cleanly preserves sharp-edged details such as the boundaries of drawn objects. PCX yields much larger files than JPEG, however, when compressing photographs or other finely detailed images.

- **PPT:** PowerPoint presentation file, usually associated with Microsoft's presentation graphics program of the same name (see Chapter 16).

- **PRN:** Print image file; generally, a file that captures "as it would be printed" information such as page numbers, date headers and footers, and other data not normally shown on the screen.

  A PRN file might be a generic text file (see **TXT**), or it might capture a stream of data that would normally go to a printer to create graphics or styled text. It might be possible, for example, to "print to file" and then copy the resulting file to a printer (perhaps with a simple drag-and-drop operation on the Windows desktop) at a later time (for example, when a portable machine returns to the office and has printer access).

- **RTF:** Rich Text Format; like **DIF**, RTF is a generic file format that only uses standard ASCII codes and can transfer information between programs from different software manufacturers (see Chapter 2).

- **SYLK, SLK:** Symbolic Link format; a data format that preserves relationships such as those of a spreadsheet's formulas.

- **SYS:** A driver file (see **DRV**). Typically, SYS files date back to DOS programs, and Windows programs favor the DRV extension.

- **TIF, TIFF:** Tagged Image File Format, an extremely general representation, almost a language for describing images rather than a specific file format for doing so.

  Many programs claim "TIFF support," but it is literally impossible to guarantee support for every legitimate variation on this extensible standard.

- **TMP:** Temporary file. Like **BAK** files, TMP files are often created automatically and generally ought to be deleted automatically when a user shuts down a program or a PC session. Many utilities detect and offer to remove surplus TMP files to recover wasted disk space.

- **TXT:** Text file, a file containing (usually) ASCII codes for letters, numerals, and punctuation, typically without any attempt to represent fonts, typeface styles, or other "rich" text attributes.

  The TXT file type can be used to store special data-formatting codes, producing (for example) a file of type **RTF**, **DIF**, **CSV**, or **HTML**.

Text files might use "hard returns" to break lines at a convenient length for viewing, or they might use the convention of including hard returns only at paragraph ends. The latter format relies on a file-viewing program to wrap long lines on the screen, but it simplifies importation of text into a word processor document (see Chapters 2 and 13).

● **VXD:** Virtual Device Driver, a special type of driver (see **DRV**). Virtual device drivers permit programs to use external hardware without the performance penalties and the awkward memory restrictions that are required to use old-style DOS device drivers from inside Windows.

● **WAV:** Audio file format, jointly developed by Microsoft and IBM. Standard representation for sounds on Windows PCs.

● **WKS, WK1, and so on:** Worksheet file formats popularized by Lotus 1-2-3 spreadsheet program and supported by many other programs.

● **WMF:** Windows MetaFile format, a graphical file format that can hold both vector and raster (bitmap) graphics. Used to exchange graphics among Windows applications.

● **WRI:** Write file, compatible with Microsoft Write accessory program and supported by some other word processors.

● **XLS:** Excel Spreadsheet, compatible with Microsoft Excel and with many other spreadsheet programs. See entry for **DOC** regarding cross-version compatibility issues.

● **ZIP:** Compressed file, compatible with programs such as WinZip (see Chapter 3).

Note that Zip-compressed information can be distributed as an **EXE** file, containing both the compressed content and a self-extraction program to unpack the contents (one or more separate files) into their original form.

If you receive an attachment to an email message purporting to be a self-extracting Zip file, you might be in the uncomfortable and risky position of being asked to run a program that comes from an untrusted source.

An executable attachment might be a *Trojan horse*; that is, a program that appears to do something useful while also doing something else (such as corrupting data or composing an email message that feeds your confidential information back to the sender of the original message). A Trojan horse might also make a permanent change in your setup, such as creating a privileged "trap door" for another person to use in gaining control of your computer.

If you already have a program, such as WinZip, that can unpack Zip-compressed files, you might want to ask a message sender to provide data files in the form of a Zip archive (a ZIP file) for you to unpack yourself instead of sending you a self-extracting EXE file whose true functions might not be apparent.

Products
Mentioned
in This Book

*I*T'S OFTEN EASY TO FIND a company on the World Wide Web: just put www. in front of the company's name, and .com at the end, and type the resulting expression into your Web browser's location field.

The devil is in the details. Some companies use the name of their flagship product rather than the company name. Some companies use "inc" or "corp" or "usa" in their Web site's URL, because many companies have similar names. Not all companies make it easy to drill down, as it's called, from a company's home page (with fascinating facts on their latest financial results) to the stuff you actually want (like what they make and what it can do).

The following table should ease the burden of finding more information on the products that I thought worth using as examples. I have provided specific URLs, which sometimes require a lot of typing. If you'd rather click than type, you can just use the portion of the URL up to and including the .com to see the starting point of a company's online resources. Follow your mouse pointer from there. You should also do this if the specific URL returns an error message, which might happen if a company reorganizes its site (a frequent occurrence).

Company	Product	Web Address
3Com Corp.	Palm Computing Platform connected organizers	`http://palmpilot.3com.com/home.html`
	U.S. Robotics x2 and V.90 modems	`http://www.3com.com/56k/`
A.T. Cross Co. Pen Computing Group	CrossPad digital clipboard	`http://www.cross-pcg.com/`
Adesso Inc.	Nu-Form ergonomic keyboard	`http://www.adessoinc.com/`
Adobe Systems Inc.	FrameMaker document authoring and publishing software	`http://www.adobe.com/prodindex/framemaker/main.html`
Allaire Corp.	HomeSite HyperText Markup Language (HTML) editor	`http://www.allaire.com/products/HOMESITE/`
Apple Computer Inc.	Macintosh computers	`http://www.apple.com/`
Autodesk Inc.	AutoCAD LT 97 drafting software	`http://www.autodesk.com/products/acadlt/prodinfo/`
Business Forecast Systems Inc.	Forecast Pro time-series forecast software	`http://www.forecastpro.com/products.htm`
Canon U.S.A. Inc.	Optura still/video digital camera	`http://www.canondv.com/optura/prodinfo/prodinfo.html`
CH Products	Force FX feedback game controller	`http://www.chproducts.com/`

Company	Product	Web Address
Connectix Corp.	Virtual PC Windows emulation for Macintosh	`http://www.connectix.com/html/` `connectix_virtualpc.html`
Decisioneering Inc.	Crystal Ball	`http://www.decisioneering.com/` `crystal_ball/`
Dell Computer Corp.	Laptop, desktop, workstation, and server PCs	`http://www.dell.com/`
Dragon Systems Inc.	NaturallySpeaking voice dictation software	`http://www.dragonsys.com/` `products/nat-speaking.html`
Epson America Inc.	Stylus series inkjet printers	`http://www.epson.com/printer/`
Fluke Corp.	ScopeMeter portable electronic test and measurement equipment	`http://www.fluke.com/scopemeter/`
Geosystems Global Corp.	MapQuest interactive atlas services	`http://www.mapquest.com/`
Hewlett-Packard Co.	Colorado series tape storage products	`http://www.hp.com/tape/colorado/`
Hilgraeve Inc.	HyperTerminal, HyperAccess, and DropChute series communication software	`http://www.hilgraeve.com/`
Hughes Network Systems	DirecPC high-speed satellite-based Internet connectivity service	`http://www.direcpc.com/`
IBM Corp.	Anti-virus technology and information	`http://www.av.ibm.com/current/` `FrontPage/`
	PC DOS operating system	`http://www.software.ibm.com/` `os/dos/`
	ViaVoice dictation software	`http://www.software.ibm.com/` `is/voicetype/`

continues

continued

Company	Product	Web Address
Icom America Inc.	IC-R10 wide-band handheld receiver (successor to R1 shown in book)	`http://www.icomamerica.com/` `receivers/#IC-R10`
Imation Enterprises Corp.	LS-120 "SuperDisk" high-density floppy disk technology and products	`http://www.superdisk.com/` `http://www.ls120.com/`
Inprise Corp.	Borland C++ Builder programming software	`http://www.inprise.com/` `bcppbuilder/`
Inspiration Software Inc.	Inspiration visual thinking software	`http://www.inspiration.com/`
Iomega Corp.	Buz multimedia integration hardware	`http://www.iomega.com/buz/`
	Ditto tape storage	`http://www.iomega.com/product/` `ditto/`
	Zip removable disk storage	`http://www.iomega.com/product/` `zip/`
IST Development Inc.	Century Packs Year-2000 problem analysis software	`http://www.istdevelopment` `.com/products.htm`
Jasc Software Inc.	Paint Shop Pro graphics software	`http://www.jasc.com/psp5.html`
Junod Software	WS_FTP 32 file transfer software	`http://www.gabn.net/junodj/` `ws_ftp.htm`
Lucent Technologies Inc.	K56flex and V.90 modems	`http://www.k56.com/`
Kensington Microware Ltd.	ExpertMouse and Orbit trackball pointing devices	`http://www.kensington.com/` `products/`
Kinesis Corp.	Contoured and Maxim ergonomic keyboards	`http://www.kinesis-ergo.com/`

Company	Product	Web Address
Lernout & Hauspie Speech Products N.V.	Voice Xpress natural-language command software	`http://www.kurzweil.com/dictation/consumer/`
Logitech Inc.	Marble series pointing devices	`http://www.logitech.com/marble/`
	Wingman game controllers	`http://www.logitech.com/en/game+controllers/`
Lotus Development Corp.	1-2-3 (spreadsheet), Approach (database), Freelance Graphics (presentation), SmartSuite (combined package), Word Pro (word processing) software	`http://www.lotus.com/`
Mansfield Software Group Inc.	KEDIT text editing software	`http://www.kedit.com/`
The Mathworks Inc.	Matlab mathematical and data visualization software	`http://www.mathworks.com/products/matlab/`
Micron Technology Inc.	Laptop, desktop, workstation, and server PCs	`http://www.micronpc.com/`
Microsoft Corp.	Access (database), Excel (spreadsheet), Office (combined package), PowerPoint (presentation), Word (word processing) software	`http://www.microsoft.com/office/`
	Sidewinder game controller	`http://www.microsoft.com/products/hardware/sidewinder/force-feedback/`

continues

continued

Company	Product	Web Address
	Windows 95, 98, NT operating systems	`http://www.microsoft.com/windows/`
	Works integrated productivity software	`http://www.microsoft.com/works/`
Midisoft Corp.	MK-4902 MIDI controller; music teaching and composition software	`http://www.midisoft.com/`
NetObjects Inc.	Fusion Web site authoring software	`http://www.netobjects.com/products/html/nof3.html`
Netscape Communications Corp.	Navigator Web browser	`http://home.netscape.com/browsers/`
Nico Mak Computing Inc.	WinZip file compression software	`http://www.winzip.com/`
Olympus America Inc.	D-500L digital camera	`http://www.olympusamerica.com/digital/products/500L/500L.html`
	Digital Photo Studio APS camera and scanner	`http://www.olympusamerica.com/camera/photostudio/photostudio.html`
Passport Designs Inc.	Music Time Deluxe music composition software	Company no longer operating, candidate for acquisition
Philips Electronics N.V.	SpeechMike integrated voice input hardware	`http://www.speechmike.philips.com/`
PowerQuest Corp.	PartitionMagic disk management software	`http://www.powerquest.com/product/pm/`
Quarterdeck Corp.	CleanSweep series disk management software	`http://www.qdeck.com/qdeck/products/cleansweep/`
Quilt-Pro Systems Inc.	Quilt-Pro quilt design software	`http://www.quiltpro.com/`

Company	Product	Web Address
Scitor Corp.	Project Scheduler 7 project management software	`http://www.scitor.com/ps7/`
Sharp Electronics Corp.	UX-2700CM Multifunction hardware	`http://www.sharpelectronics.com/ main.asp?sect=10&pageid=AFADAB`
Smart Cable Co.	SmartCable series automatic data connection hardware	`http://www.nrsnet.com/smartcable/`
Soft Warehouse Inc.	Derive mathematical software	`http://www.derive.com/drvset.htm`
Sony Electronics Inc.	Digital Mavica floppy-disk digital camera	`http://www.sel.sony.com/SEL/ consumer/mavica/main.html`
	Multiscan Trinitron-tube displays	`http://www.ita.sel.sony.com/ products/displays/`
Symantec Corp.	Norton AntiVirus software	`http://www.symantec.com/nav/`
	Norton Utilities software	`http://www.symantec.com/nu/`
	VisualPage Web site authoring software	`http://www.symantec.com/vpage/`
Thinkstream Inc.	Scan-O-Matic image file and data management software	`http://www.thinkstream.com/ dial_overview.html`
Tripp Lite	Tripp Lite backup power hardware	`http://www.tripplite.com/`
Wolfram Research Inc.	Mathematica mathematical software	`http://www.wolfram.com/`
Ziff-Davis Benchmark Operation (ZDBOp)	Winbench, Winstone benchmarking software	`http://www.zdnet.com/zdbop/`

Glossary

A

abort To stop a computer operation before it is complete, usually because of some unforeseen condition; for example, "I aborted that file-copy operation because the target disk was full."

To abort implies that partial results of the incomplete operation remain, rather than being reversed. *See* **cancel**, **fail**.

accelerator A subsystem, usually **hardware**, that speeds a particular task or improves overall system performance by reducing **overhead** on the **CPU**—most commonly, a portion of a sophisticated graphics **card**.

adapter   (1) A **card** that goes in one of a PC's internal **slots**; (2) A piece of **hardware** that allows one type of connector to plug in to a device that's designed for another type of connector.

ADC (**Analog/digital converter**)   A device that converts continuous signals, such as those of sound, into streams of data that can be manipulated by a computer.

The quality of a microphone or other input **transducer** does not matter if the ADC is unable to capture the waveform without excessive quantization noise (see Chapter 8). An ADC with more **bits** of **resolution** provides more accurate digitization.

address   A location in **memory**, such as the address at which a program stores the **data** values that control an adapter (for example, a sound card).

Also **address space**, the number of separate locations in memory that can be represented by a particular combination of computer and operating system; for example, "A 32-bit computer has an address space of 4 **gigabytes**, but most of that is virtual."

AGP   Accelerated Graphics Port (see Chapter 5).

Alt   A **keychord** created by pressing and holding the Alt key on the keyboard immediately before some other operation, such as typing another key or clicking a button on the mouse; for example, "Use Alt+Tab to switch to the most recently used **background** program."

analog   Continuously variable (as opposed to **digital**).

antialiasing   Smoothing of onscreen edges by addition of **pixels** of intermediate color; for example, "That **bitmap** font looks bad at large sizes because there's no antialiasing."

application   A "user program," such as a word processor or spreadsheet (as opposed to a **utility**).

ASCII   American Standard Code for Information Interchange (see Chapter 3).

B

background   Taking place on the computer without the user's interaction, often without the user's knowledge; for example, "I left that 20-page report to print from the **queue** in the background, but printing those graphics sure added a lot of **overhead**."

backslash   The \ symbol, used to separate the parts of a **path** on DOS and Windows PCs. Usually not interchangeable with the **slash** (/).

bandwidth   The total capacity of an information transfer medium, usually described as either **bits** per second for data or as **Mega**Hertz (or some other multiple of **Hertz**) for **analog** signals such as video.

baud   The number of changes per second in the state of a signal. Equivalent to **bps** (bits per second) in the special case of two possible states where each change delivers only one bit of information.

binary   Having only two possible states, usually (but arbitrarily) referred to as 1 and 0 (*see* **bit**).

BIOS   Basic Input/Output System (see Chapter 5).

bit   A **binary** digit: a unit of information that reduces by half the number of possible choices. A 1-bit system has only two possible states; knowing the value of the bit identifies the state. An n-bit system has 2^n possible states. A computer that can address n bits has an **address space** of 2^n storage locations (commonly **bytes**).

Bits' values are commonly referred to as 1 or 0, but they can just as correctly be pairs of values. It's useful to use 1 or 0, because many operations on bits can be treated as ordinary arithmetic on **binary** numbers, using **Boolean** algebra.

bitmap   (1) A type of computer graphic that stores a separate **binary** value for each **pixel** (as opposed to a **compressed** graphics file); (2) A font that stores letters' shapes as bitmaps.

BMP   A filename **extension** denoting a **bitmap** file.

BNC   A twist-on connector commonly used for Ethernet and high-quality video connections (see Figure 1).

FIGURE 1
A BNC connector.

Boolean (1) A mathematical notation for expressions involving combinations of truth and falsity, named after George Boole; (2) a **data type** permitting only two values, commonly designated True and False.

boot To restart a computer. A *warm boot* restarts without turning off the power and can be done as a software command during such operations as installing a new **driver**. A *cold boot* is a power-off/power-on restart. *See* **reset**.

bps **Bits** per second.

bug A defect in a program.

bus A shared connection feeding many devices. A *power bus* provides a common voltage to many devices; a ***data*** bus offers data to all connected devices and lets each device determine which data requires action from that device.

byte A small group of **data** values, usually 8 bits.

C

cache A special memory unit that acts as an **accelerator** for some other device. A *cache **memory*** keeps recently retrieved values available to the **CPU** without the delay of repeating their retrieval across the memory **bus**; a *disk cache* reduces time-consuming disk-read and disk-write operations by holding recent "reads" and accumulating pending "writes" for efficient grouped transfer to the disk.

cancel To stop a computer operation before it is complete, usually by user action; for example, "I *canceled* that print request because I realized the font was too small." To cancel implies that the system and the user's work are restored to the state they were in before the operation was begun. *See* **abort**, **fail**.

card (1) An **adapter** that goes in one of a PC's internal **slots**; (2) A device that goes in a PC Card (also called PCMCIA) slot; (3) A plastic card, such as a credit card, bearing data in some machine-readable form such as a magnetic stripe; (4) A punched card bearing data as a pattern of holes (obsolete).

caret (1) The ^ symbol, usually found as the shifted symbol on the 6 key; (2) a prefix indicating a **Ctrl keychord**.

CCD Charge-Coupled Device (see Chapter 8).

CD-R, CD-ROM Compact Disc–Recordable (see Chapter 5).

CDPD Cellular Digital Packet Data (see Chapter 9).

Centronics A common name for a standard **parallel** port.

Clipboard   A region of **memory** used for copying and moving data from one location to another.

clock   (1) A signal used to tell the subsystems of a computer when to change to their next state of operation, based on instructions received in the previous **cycle**; (2) A piece of **hardware** that generates such signals; (3) The act of sending such signals; for example, "We can clock that chip 10% faster than its rated speed if you put an extra cooling fan on it."

CMOS (Complementary Metal Oxide Semiconductor)   A type of material used for making transistors with very low power consumption, suitable for backup memory and entering use as a low-cost alternative to **CCD**s in digital cameras.

code   (1) A pattern of symbols with no obvious meaning to a human reader; (2) a set of information that should be interpreted as instructions; (3) a program, or a portion of a program, or the act of programming; for example, "Sure, I can code that for you by Tuesday."

compress   (1) To transform **data** so that it consumes a smaller amount of memory, typically by finding repetitions in data streams or by reducing the level of detail retained in an image; for example, "The video streams took up a lot less disk space when we used MPEG-2 compression (*see also* **zip**); (2) To transform **analog** signals so that they vary over a smaller range of amplitude; for example, "I got away with less **resolution** in the **ADC** by compressing the audio before digitization."

CON, console   The "DOS window" on a typical PC.

control   Ctrl (*See* Ctrl).

CPU   Central Processing Unit (see Chapter 4).

CPU-bound, compute-bound   Taking time to complete based on the speed of the **CPU**, rather than being limited by the speed of other subsystems such as **memory**, **storage**, or network **bandwidth** (as opposed to **I/O-bound**).

CRT   Cathode Ray Tube (see Chapter 6).

Ctrl   A **keychord** created by pressing and holding the Ctrl ("control") key on the keyboard immediately before some other operation, such as typing another key or clicking a button on the mouse; for example, "Press Ctrl+Insert to copy the selected text to the **Clipboard**."

Ctrl+Alt+Del   The three-finger **keychord** that summons up last-ditch recovery tools for preventing a crash under Windows, or that reboots a DOS PC. Also called "the three-finger salute."

Ctrl+C A standard **keychord** for copying to the **Clipboard** under Windows; a standard **keychord** for **abort**ing most DOS programs and some Windows programs. Yes, we agree that this is a dangerous coincidence. Using Ctrl+Ins to perform copy operations reduces the chance of counterproductive confusion.

Ctrl+Z (1) The standard **keychord** for indicating the end of a file when entering data from the **console**; (2) The **ASCII** code 26 (decimal) or 1A (**hexadecimal**) character that indicates the end of a file or of certain other data structures.

current drive, current directory The drive or directory that will be the **default** in any operation involving opening of files.

cycle (1) A clock cycle, the smallest unit of time in which most computers can perform any complete operation; (2) Generally, a unit of computing effort; for example, "That **background** print **queue** sure steals a lot of cycles."

D

DAC (Digital/Analog Converter) A device that converts streams of data, such as a sound file, into continuous signals such as those used by an audio amplifier.

The quality of a speaker or other output device does not matter if the DAC is unable to produce a high-fidelity waveform. A DAC with lower distortion and a higher signal-to-noise ratio provides more accurate reproduction.

DAT (Digital Audio Tape) In the context of PCs, usually mentioned as a medium for backup storage.

data Any set of symbols that is treated as information rather than executed as instructions by any part of an information processing system (hardware or software).

Data is usually contrasted with **code**, as in "The chip has separate code and data **caches**," but it's hard to draw a clear line between these two species of bits. All code is data to one or more parts of the system; for example, a program that you send to someone via electronic mail is data as far as the email message handler is concerned, even if it is treated as code when it arrives.

The instructions that a processor retrieves are data, as far as the code cache is concerned; that is, the code cache retrieves the **bytes** of the instruction codes and passes them along rather than trying to "understand" them in any way. This might seem like splitting hairs, but these distinctions matter in understanding the actual hazards posed by **viruses** or other malicious programs.

data type   A class of data values that can be represented in a common way; for example, an instance of the **integer** data type is ordinarily represented as a simple **binary** number.

An instance of the **Boolean** data type requires only a single **bit**, but an instance of the image data type might require several million bits whose organization would have to be specified as a graphics **format** (such as **bitmap** or **PCX**).

DB-9, DB-25   Common connectors for PC input/output ports (see Figure 2).

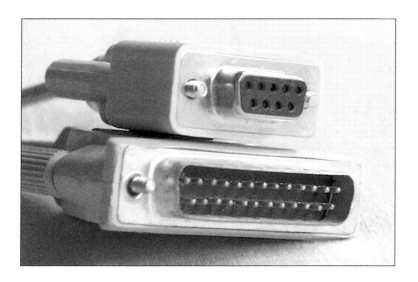

FIGURE 2
DB-9 and DB-25 connectors.

debug   To seek and correct defects in any part of an information system or electronic device; most commonly, to do this with **software**.

deep-cycle   To discharge a battery almost completely before recharging. Recommended for nickel-cadmium batteries, discouraged for most other rechargeable battery types that are commonly used with portable PCs.

default   The action that a system will take if no other action is specified; for example, "The default target for a command to erase all files is the **current directory**, not including its subdirectories."

defrag, defragment   To locate the separate regions of a **storage** device (such as a hard disk) that are storing different portions of a file and to rearrange the allocation of space on the disk so that all files occupy contiguous regions.

digital   Represented as a collection of values, often in **binary** form. The term implies some irreducible tolerance for error, due to the representation of continuous quantities by discrete, "chunky" values. Contrast with **analog**.

Ironically, "digital" is often taken to mean "better"—for example, "digital sound." This association comes from the fact that digital representations do not accumulate noise at successive stages of processing, as do all analog representations. The case remains, however, that a first-generation analog recording can be free of certain types of distortion that are inherent in digital techniques.

Essentially, digital representations start off pretty darn good and stay that way; analog representations start off better, but deteriorate quickly with handling.

digitize   To convert to digital form.

directory   (1) A list of files; (2) A group of files in a **storage** system, usually in a hierarchy of multiple levels of organization.

DLL (Dynamic Link Library)   A file containing code that more than one program may use and that needs to be loaded into memory only once to be available to all programs that need its functions.

Some DLLs are often updated, and poorly written programs might stop working when an updated DLL makes an internal change that should not affect a properly written program. Installing a new piece of software can cause other software on the same machine to function incorrectly.

DOC   A filename **extension** indicating a document file, such as a word processing project and especially a Microsoft word processing file.

DOS (Disk Operating System)   The core technology of Microsoft Windows, based on a product originally developed by another company under the name of QDOS—Quick and Dirty Operating System. Uh-huh.

double-click   To click the mouse twice, in rapid succession, without moving the pointer. Typically, this signals a default action, such as opening a file or maximizing a window.

Some people find double-clicks quite difficult to perform. Many people don't realize that every action normally performed with a double-click can also be done from a menu or by some other means in software that conforms to recommended style guides.

download   To transfer information to your system from another system.

drag   To press the button of the mouse and continue to hold it down while moving the mouse, usually for the purpose of selecting data or rearranging objects on the screen.

Variations, such as the **double-click**-and-drag, have special significance; for example, to select text word by word instead of letter by letter.

DRAM   Dynamic **RAM** (see Chapter 4).

driver   A piece of software that produces the specific, low-level instructions required by a device in response to more general requests from an **application**.

DSP (Digital Signal Processing)   The process of **digitizing** a signal, such as a sound or an image, and using mathematical techniques to perform operations such as noise reduction.

DVD   Digital Versatile Disk. Formerly Digital Video Disk (see Chapter 5).

Dvorak   The Dvorak keyboard places all five vowels on the "home row," all on the left hand, with other frequently used letters in the same row to the right. Many studies have found the result to be more productive, with less fatigue (*See also* QWERTY).

E

echo   (1) An intentional repeating of a received data stream that confirms correct receipt or that shows another observer what data is being processed; (2) An unintended, undesirable physical process on a data path that creates weak, delayed duplicates of desired signals and thereby introduces noise.

EIDE   Enhanced **IDE**.

EISA (Extended Industry Standard Architecture)   A design for internal **slots** in a PC that can hold simple **ISA cards** and can also hold more elaborate, higher-performance cards that can perform more operations on their own without creating **overhead** for the CPU.

engine   (1) A portion of a system that performs an identifiable function, such as processing graphics, often using **accelerator** technology; (2) A **hardware** module, especially one built by one company and sold to others that use it in designing other products; for example, "Most of the early desktop laser printers used a Canon print engine."

escape   (1) A special key, usually at upper left on a PC's keyboard, interpreted by many pieces of software as a **cancel** command; (2) An **ASCII** code 27, often used to signal a device that a following symbol should be interpreted as an instruction rather than as **data**; (3) Any symbol used to alter the meaning of following symbols; (4) The act of using such a symbol; for example, "You need a double **back-slash** there, because the first one just escapes the character after it."

EXE (1) A filename **extension** denoting an executable file; (2) An executable file; for example, "The EXE isn't very big, but the **run-time DLL** is enormous."

extension A portion of a filename, usually separated from the primary filename by a period, that indicates file type or other characteristics. Common extensions on PCs include **.exe** for an executable file, **.dll** for a Dynamic Link Library, **.txt** for a simple "raw text" file, **.doc** for a word processing file, **.bmp** for a bitmap graphics file, **.hlp** for a help file, and **.htm** or **.html** for a file designed to display on the World Wide Web.

Resist the temptation to use the extension as part of the meaningful name of the file. If you want someone to read a particular file on a floppy disk, for example, call the file *read_me.txt* rather than *read.me*. The former name causes the file to show up as a candidate for File Open operations in any properly designed text editor or word processor, but the latter name often makes the file invisible to such tools—the opposite of what you wanted to accomplish.

If you want to be sure that a filename will be properly understood and displayed on any kind of computer, the minimal subset of all file-naming conventions is a name of no more than eight letters, without any spaces, and an extension of no more than three letters. Assume that all filenames will be treated as all capital letters. Use underscore characters to separate "words" within a filename.

Do not use a colon, a question mark, a quotation mark, or other punctuation as part of any filename, because some of these characters have special meanings on different types of computers. For example, a Macintosh uses a colon as a path separator, in the same way that a PC uses a backslash and a UNIX system uses a slash. Many file systems treat a question mark as a "wild card" character for finding groups of filenames that fit a common pattern. Stick to letters and numeric digits, and your file can travel anywhere.

F

fail To let a multistep operation continue even though one of the steps cannot finish as expected. This is an odd usage, in that it is not the operation that fails, but the user who "fails" the operation; For example, "I told it to print 12 files, but one of them wasn't available so I failed that one and let it print the rest."

Contrast with **abort** (to stop in the middle of a step and perform no further steps) and with **cancel** (to stop in the middle of an action and try to return to the state that existed before that action began).

FAQ (Frequently Asked Questions) A collection of topics so common that they've been compiled to avoid cluttering up an interactive discussion forum (see Chapter 10). Paradoxically, a "frequently" asked question is actually one that's very poor form to ask, because you should consult the FAQ before seeking the assistance of others.

FAT, FAT32 Two methods of organizing a hard disk into files. FAT (File Allocation Table) is a 16-bit system that cannot keep track of more than 216 separate chunks of space on any disk, forcing it to waste a larger chunk of space on even a 1-byte file as a hard disk's total size gets larger.

FAT32, a 32-bit system, can track many more units of storage space and can therefore assign units of a smaller minimum size, wasting less space on collections of many small files.

On systems with the older FAT, a large disk can be divided into several partitions, each of which can then be divided into FAT's maximum number of storage units. The resulting units are smaller than the units on a single large partition, reducing wasted space.

floating-point A system of representing numbers that can range from extremely large values (typically, up to about 1.67×10^{308}) to extremely small values (typically, down to about 4.19×10^{-307}), but inherently as approximations rather than the exact values of **integers** and with much slower performance of mathematical operations.

floptical A data-storage medium that augments floppy-disk technology with optical positioning aids for more accurate placement of recording and playback hardware, thereby increasing the amount of data that can be stored on a disk. *See* **LS-120**.

focus The place on a computer screen where the user's input has an effect. On a Windows PC, usually a specific insertion point in a document or a data-entry field in a particular window of the **foreground** application.

Many applications seize the focus when they perform some action. For example, a dial-up networking monitor might seize the focus, suddenly popping up its status display on top of your work in another application, when the monitor succeeds in making a connection with another machine.

An unexpected change of focus can cause your input to have unexpected effects if you continue typing without watching the screen to see which application is processing your keystrokes.

folder A **directory**.

foreground Interacting with the user and possibly having priority in the use of system resources; for example, "I had my Web browser in the foreground, but there were five other programs running and it really slowed down my file transfers." *See* **focus**.

format (1) A visual style of text (for example, italic format); (2) A pattern followed by a set of similar data items (for example, dates in the format mm-dd-yy); (3) A manner of organizing files of data for use by applications (for example, documents in Microsoft Word 2.x format); (4) A standard physical design for storage media (for example, IBM-format 3 1/2-inch floppy disks); (5) To convert "raw text" to styled text by using margin settings, font choices, and typographic styles (for example, to format a draft document for publication); (6) To initialize a storage device or a unit of removable storage media (for example, to format a floppy disk).

Note that formatting a document (5) is a constructive operation that does not alter the essence of the data, while formatting a floppy disk (6) is a destructive operation that deletes all previously stored data.

The format of text (1) can be changed, but the format used for data (2) must often be chosen at the outset of a project in what might be an irrevocable act (as when dates are recorded with only a two-digit year).

fragmentation *See* **defragment**.

frame A single image, either a separate still image or one piece of a video stream, as in *frame buffer*, the **memory** that holds what's currently being shown on a display or *frame grabber*, a device that converts the output from an analog video source into a **digital** form.

G

G- *See* **Giga-**.

gender A class of connector. In general, a "male" connector has pins or other projections, while a "female" connector has sockets or other accommodations.

GIF (Graphics Interchange Format) An 8-bit (256-color) graphics file format that performs lossless **compression** and therefore requires larger file sizes than **JPEG**.

Giga- Billion, or 1,073,741,824 ($1,024^3$) when speaking of **digital** artifacts such as **bytes** of **storage**.

global   Affecting an entire system; for example, "Changing the system date is global to all file-storage operations."

GUI (Graphical User Interface)   A manner of interacting with a computer that's also called WIMP (windows, icons, menus, and a pointing device).

H

handshake   An exchange of signals between two devices that establishes their ability to communicate or confirms that communication has taken place.

hardware   The physical components of a system, as opposed to **software**, which consists of instructions to control the operation of those components.

Some hardware includes "hard-wired" software—for example, a ROM chip that can be replaced or (in the case of "flash" technology) rewritten to correct defects or add new functions. Such elements of a hardware device are called its *firmware*.

hex, hexadecimal   The base-16 numbering system, using digits 0–9 and A–F to represent decimal values 0 through 15 before carrying a 16 and starting over at 10. Convenient for digital work, because each hex digit corresponds to a **nybble**; a full **byte**'s value falls in the range from 00 to FF.

HSB, HSL (Hue/Saturation/Brightness, Hue/Saturation/Luminance)   Means of representing colors as sets of numbers (see Chapter 6).

HTML (Hypertext Markup Language)   A notation for representing information and connections between related information in a manner that was originally meant to be free of any assumptions about the displaying device.

Increasingly, HTML is becoming a device-specific page description language instead of a device-independent content description language (see Chapter 17).

HTTP (Hypertext Transfer Protocol)   The most common prefix to a **URL**, indicating that information can be retrieved and displayed by a browser that processes **hyperlink** connections.

hyperlink   A means of jumping from one collection of data, typically a document or a Web page, to another data source, often by clicking on an underlined or otherwise highlighted word or symbol.

Hz, Hertz   The formal name for unit of frequency, expressed as repetitions per second. Replaces "cycles per second" or "cps," though these terms persist in older documents.

I

I/O-bound Taking time to complete based on the speed of the devices attached to the computer or of the connections between those devices and the computer, and therefore not made faster by using a faster **CPU** (as opposed to **CPU-bound**).

IDE Integrated Drive Electronics (see Chapter 5).

IEEE (Institute of Electrical and Electronics Engineers) Professional association that defines many formal standards for information processing and electronic hardware (more information on the World Wide Web at http://www.ieee.org/).

integer A "counting number," often including both positive and negative values, usually represented exactly as a **binary** value whose size in **bits** determines the range of representable numbers.

IP Internet Protocol (see Chapter 17).

IR Infrared (see Chapter 5).

IRQ Interrupt Request (see Chapter 5).

ISA Industry Standard Architecture (see Chapter 5).

ISDN Integrated Services Digital Network (see Chapter 7).

ISO (International Organization for Standardization) The name is *not* an acronym but is an invented word derived from the Greek root meaning "equal" (as in an *iso*metric triangle with two sides of equal length). The short-form name was chosen to be meaningful in many languages.

Film speeds (and their digital-camera equivalents) are just one of the many ISO standards that followed the organization's inaugural release, in 1951, of the timeless classic "Standard reference temperature for industrial length measurement." More details on ISO standards and procedures are on the World Wide Web at http://www.iso.ch/.

ITU (International Telecommunications Union) A specialized agency of the United Nations, empowered to adopt international regulations and treaties that govern all ground-based and space-based use of the radio spectrum and the geostationary (**synchronous**) orbital belt and to promulgate standards for international telecommunications. More information on the World Wide Web at http://www.imf.org/external/np/sec/decdo/itu.htm.

ITU-T The Telecommunication Standardization Sector of the **ITU**, whose other sectors are designated as the Radiocommunication Sector and the Telecommunication Development Sector.

J

JPEG (1) Joint Photographic Experts Group; (2) The efficient image **compression** algorithm developed by that group, which tolerates substantial loss of detail (almost undetectable to the human eye) to achieve much smaller file sizes when storing **digital** imagery (see Chapter 8). Much, much more information on the World Wide Web at `http://www.faqs.org/faqs/jpeg-faq/`.

jumper (1) An electrical bridge, usually removable or relocatable, generally used to change the setup of a device in ways that do not require frequent adjustment— mostly supplanted by local configuration memories that enable changing of almost all setup options through software; (2) The act of installing such a bridge; for example, "You have to jumper those pins to fake out the **handshake** detection").

K

k- *See* **kilo-**.

Kermit A communication **protocol** (see Chapter 7). More information on the World Wide Web at `http://www.columbia.edu/kermit/`.

keychord A keyboard combination of two or more keys, pressed and held in sequence and released only after all have been depressed. *See* **Ctrl**, **Alt**.

kilo- Thousand, or 1,024 when speaking of **digital** artifacts such as **bytes** of **storage**.

L

LCD Liquid Crystal Display (see Chapter 6).

LED (Light Emitting Diode) A compact, rugged, energy-efficient light source.

logic Any **software** or **hardware** that examines current values of data and takes different actions depending on those values.

logical Existing only for purposes of computation; for example, "The floppy disk drive can have two different logical device names, A: or B:" (as opposed to physical).

LPT (Line Printer) Device name for **parallel port**.

LS-120 **Floptical** disk standard (see Chapter 5). More information on the World Wide Web at `http://www.ls-120.com/` and `http://www.superdisk.com/`.

M

m- *See* **milli-**.

M- *See* **Mega-**.

media   Removable storage units, such as floppy disks.

Mega-   Million, or 1,048,576 (1,024^2) when speaking of **digital** artifacts such as **bytes** of **storage**.

memory   **Hardware** holding **code** and **data** during computer operation. Generally erased when power is turned off.

micro-   Millionth.

MIDI   Musical Instrument Digital Interface (see Chapter 8). More information on the World Wide Web at `http://home.earthlink.net/~mma/` and `http://www.eeb.ele.tue.nl/midi/index.html`.

milli-   Thousandth.

MMX   Multimedia Extensions (see Chapter 4).

modal   (1) Changing behavior in different situations; for example, "Word is modal with the Tab key—in outline view, you can't put tabs in text because the Tab key demotes and promotes"; (2) Requiring a user response; for example, "That's a modal dialog box: you can't do anything else until you've clicked OK."

Moore's Law   The rule of thumb that digital technology doubles its sophistication every 18 months.

motherboard   The main circuit board of a PC, typically containing the **CPU**, **memory**, **slots**, and controllers for input and output ports.

MPEG (Moving Pictures Experts Group)   Graphics compression format similar to **JPEG**, but applies to video files.

multiplex   To send several data streams over a single channel in such a way that they can be separated by a receiver.

N

nano-   Billionth.

native   Using actual facilities available to a system, instead of imitating those facilities with general-purpose alternatives; implies a fast but inflexible approach.

netiquette   The informal social conventions governing interaction among people via electronic networks.

NMI   Nonmaskable Interrupt (see Chapter 5).

noise   Any energy on a channel that is not part of any desired signal.

nonmaskable   Not subject to being ignored.

nonmodal   *See* **modal**.

nonvolatile   Remaining intact when power is removed; for example, "Disk **storage** is nonvolatile, and memory generally is volatile."

nybble   Four bits.

O

OCR (Optical Character Recognition)   The capability to read printed matter and store it as text (suitable for searching, editing, and **reformatting**) instead of storing only an image of the page (see Chapter 8).

operator   A symbol that denotes some process or perhaps different processes in different situations; for example, + is the operator for addition with numbers, but it is also the operator for concatenation when used with filenames or character **strings**.

overhead   Burden on a machine; for example, "printing **formatted** text with **TrueType** fonts involves a lot more overhead than sending **ASCII** codes to a printer."

P

parallel port   (1) Commonly, a **Centronics**-type port of the type used by most PC printers and many other **peripherals**; (2) Generally, any port sending several **bits** at a time across parallel connections, including **SCSI** ports and as contrasted with all **serial** (sequential transfer) ports.

patch   (1) A small change to a program, supplied as a fragment of code that can be added by a user or communicated among users without support from the program's provider; (2) To install such a change.

path (1) The complete description of a file's location, beginning from the root directory of the storage device and possibly continuing down through several levels of directories; (2) A system setting that causes programs in storage locations that are listed on the path to behave as if copies of those programs were present in every directory.

PCI Peripheral Connect Interface (see Chapter 5).

PCX A filename **extension** denoting a ZSoft PC Paintbrush **format** graphics file.

peripheral Any device connected to a computer, such as a keyboard; most commonly, a major piece of equipment such as a printer.

pixel A controllable location on a display (see Chapter 6); for example, "A **VGA** screen has a **resolution** of 640×480 pixels."

platform An overall label for a combination of hardware and (optionally) systems software; for example, "The 'IBM-compatible' platform is really defined more today by Windows and Intel than by IBM, and 'Wintel' is the better name for what constitutes a 'PC' as compared to some other kind of machine."

portable (1) Easily moved from one kind of computer to another; for example, "Adobe Acrobat creates Portable Document Format files that can be viewed on almost any kind of computer"; (2) Easily relocated; for example, "Putting a handle on that 40-pound box doesn't make it portable as far as I'm concerned."

POST (Power-On Self-Test) The process by which a computer verifies its own proper functions during a cold **boot**.

POTS Plain Old Telephone Service (see Chapter 7).

prompt A symbol displayed by a device to indicate that it is ready for some user action.

protocol (1) An international, formal standard for coordinating data transfers between devices made by different manufacturers; (2) A method of packaging data for more efficient and more reliable transfer (see Chapter 7).

Q

quantize Digitize.

queue A "waiting line" for pending operations, such as printing, that enables a user to continue work while the computer manages the actions in progress.

QWERTY The common keyboard arrangement with letters QWERTY at upper left, as opposed to the Dvorak layout (*See* **Dvorak**).

R

RAM (1) **Random access** memory; (2) Commonly, rewritable random access memory, as opposed to **ROM** (which is technically non-rewritable RAM).

random access Able to access any storage location, in any sequence, in essentially the same amount of time; for example, **memory** or hard disk **storage** (as opposed to sequential storage such as that provided by magnetic tape).

raster graphics An arrangement of rows and columns of separately controllable display elements, typically dots of variable brightness; (2) A form of computer graphics based on raster display technology (as opposed to **vector** graphics).

real-time Imposing specific limits on allowable response time as part of the definition of satisfactory performance of a task.

reboot See **boot**. The "re-" variant often suggests a boot operation that is performed to clear up a problem with the machine, as opposed to the boot that is performed when turning on a PC after a period of being shut down.

reformat *See* **Format**.

refresh (1) To bring up-to-date; for example, "View Refresh makes sure that Windows Explorer is showing you the files on the floppy disk that's actually in the drive"; (2) To prevent from becoming degraded; for example, "Dynamic RAM requires regular refresh."

reset To **reboot** by means of a hardware switch, forcing a restart when a normal warm boot is prevented by system error but without the drastic step of a power-cycling cold boot.

resolution The number of pixels in a **raster** image, normally expressed as [columns]×[rows].

RGB (Red/Green/Blue) A means of representing colors as sets of numbers (see Chapter 6).

RJ-11 The standard connector for modular telephone connections (see Figure 3).

FIGURE 3
An RJ-11 connector.

ROM   Read-Only Memory; that is, non-rewritable **RAM**.

RS-232   Electronics Industries Association designation for the technical description of a standard **serial port**.

RSI   Repetitive Strain Injury (see Chapter 5).

RTF   A filename **extension** denoting a Rich Text Format file (see Chapter 2).

run-time   Occurring at, or being needed at, the time that an operation takes place; for example, "Connection speed is determined by run-time negotiation between the modems at each end of the line."

S

scratch Intended for temporary use; for example, "Identify a floppy disk holding nonessential files for scratch use during the drive test."

SCSI Small Computer System Interface (see Chapter 5).

serial port (1) Commonly, an **RS-232** port of the type used by most PC modems and many other **peripherals**; (2) Generally, any port sending **bits** in sequence on a single data path (as opposed to all types of **parallel ports**).

slash The / symbol, used to separate the parts of a **URL** on the World Wide Web and to separate portions of **console** commands on a PC. Usually not interchangeable with the **backslash** (\).

slot An internal connector for adapters (see Chapter 5), typically one of several nonproprietary types, including **ISA**, **EISA**, **PCI**, or **VESA** Local Bus (VL-Bus).

software Any instructions given to the computer in a form that can readily be changed by the user, as opposed to unalterable **hardware** and its hard-to-change built-in firmware.

SRAM Static **RAM** (see Chapter 4).

storage **Hardware** holding **code** and **data**, both during computer operation and between sessions; generally **nonvolatile**, based on magnetic **media**.

string A series of characters, usually alphabetic but sometimes including numerals, that is processed as a series of symbols instead of being interpreted as a number or an instruction code.

SVGA A display with 800×600 **resolution**.

swap To move data back and forth between **storage** and **memory**, usually to create the effect of more memory than is actually present in the computer.

synchronous Time-sensitive, requiring coordination by some common **clock** (as opposed to *asynchronous*, which implies the ability to tolerate different timing among different participants in a process).

T

T-, Tera- Trillion, or 1,099,511,627,776 (1,024^4) when speaking of **digital** artifacts such as **bytes** of **storage**.

thrash To **swap** repeatedly, usually because of insufficient **memory**.

transducer A piece of hardware that converts between two different forms of energy; for example, a microphone.

TrueType, TT A standard for representing fonts in a form that can be readily scaled to any desired size (see Chapter 6). More information on the World Wide Web at http://www.microsoft.com/typography/OTSPEC/about.htm.

TXT A filename extension that denotes a simple text file.

U

UART Universal Asynchronous Receiver/Transmitter (see Chapter 7).

Unicode A standard for representing many different types of written languages using 16-**bit codes**, including the **ASCII** codes as a subset (see Chapter 3). More information on the World Wide Web at http://www.unicode.org/.

URL Uniform Resource Locator (see Chapter 17).

USB Universal Serial Bus (see Chapter 5).

utility A piece of software that eases PC operations, such as a data-backup program. Contrast with an **application**, which does something that you'd actually purchase a PC to do.

uuencode To transform a file so that only 7 bits of each 8-bit byte are used to represent data, leaving the extra bit for use by communication **protocols** (for example, as an error-detection bit).

V

vector (1) A combination of a magnitude and a direction; (2) A form of computer graphics that stores an image as a collection of vectors (as opposed to **raster** graphics).

VESA Video Electronics Standards Association. More information on the World Wide Web at http://www.vesa.org/.

VGA   A display with 640×480 **resolution**.

virtual   Appearing to be present, but actually being imitated by some other technology; for example, "Virtual **memory** makes disk space act like an extension of the physical memory so that a processor can use more of its theoretical **address space**."

virus   A program that acts to make copies of itself that spread to other computers without the knowledge, intent, or consent of the users of any of the computers involved in the process (see Chapter 17).

volatile   Not preserved upon removal of power.

volume   (1) A **logical** drive or removable **media** unit; (2) The loudness setting of a PC's sound system.

VRAM   Video **RAM** (see Chapter 4).

W

wait state   A delay introduced in **memory** operations to accommodate slow memory chips.

wizard   An automated aid to a program operation that might otherwise seem overly complex.

X

XGA   A display with 1280×1024 **resolution**.

Xmodem   A communications **protocol** (see Chapter 7).

Y

Y2K, Year 2000   Any of the problems associated with representing dates in both the 20th and 21st centuries, especially those problems resulting from the use of only two digits to represent the year.

Ymodem   A communications **protocol** (see Chapter 7).

Z

Zip   (1) A file **compression** method; (2) The act of compressing a file by that method (see Chapter 3); (3) Iomega's removable-media **storage format** (see Chapter 5).

Zmodem   A communications **protocol** (see Chapter 7).

Index

G

G size (bytes), 30

Gall, John, 422-423

game port connections, 192

generating reports, 519-520

GIF (Graphic Interface Format) files, 126-127
extension, 584-585

gigabytes, pronunciation, 31

graphics
AutoCAD, 536-540
automatic edge detection, 542-543
digital, 305
JPEG (Joint Photographic Experts Group), 323-324
storing, 323
files, compressing, 124-127
Freelance Graphics, 530-532
Internet searches, 533
Outline view, 534-535
GIF (Graphics Interchange Format), 126-127
lenses, 307
NetObjects Fusion, 535-536
presentations, 524-525
quality of, 307-308
Quilt-Pro, 543
raster, 234, 238-239
Smart Paint programs, 540-543
transducers, 306
vector images, 234-236
building, 237-238
memory, 237-238
video adapters, 258-259

Graphics Interchange Format (GIF), 126-127

Gray color, 246

grouping bits, 99

H

half-word (chips), 100

handheld portable PCs, 356
PalmPilot, 356-358

handshaking circuits, 196

handshaking protocols, 298

handwriting pen devices, 190-192

hard disks, 217, 220
crashing, 218-219
EIDE (Enhanced Integrated Drive Electronics), 219
IDE (Integrated Drive Electronics), 219
portable PCs, 336
upgrading, 386

hard drives, 5, 30

hard returns, 457

hardware
colors, 247
Energy Star Logo rating, 253-254
Imaging, text recognition, 332-333
monitors, *see* monitors
printers, *see* printers
sound conversion, 304
video adapters, purchasing, 255, 257-259

health and safety, purchasing monitors, 255-256

heat produced, 174-175

help, 22
with communications
plain English problem solving, 434
troubleshooting, 433
Help command (Start menu), 7

hexadecimal numbering system, 99

high-density disks, 221-224

high-fidelity sound, 310-313

history of Internet, 549-551

hot swapping PC Cards, 213

HTML (Hypertext Markup Language), 56, 476-478, 566
editing, 57
file extensions, 585
tabs, representing colors, 109-110
tags, 567

HTTP (Hypertext Transfer Protocol), 558

hue (color), 246

human-readable codes, 98

hybridizing conventional and digital photographs, 330

hyperlinks, 568-570
online technical notes, 374

Hypertext Markup Language, *see* HTML

Hypertext Transfer Protocol (HTTP), 558

I

I2R formula, 342

Icon files, 585

IDE (Integrated Drive Electronics), 219

M